Richard Paul Wülker, Thomas Wright

Anglo-Saxon and Old English Vocabularies

Vol. 1

Richard Paul Wülker, Thomas Wright

Anglo-Saxon and Old English Vocabularies
Vol. 1

ISBN/EAN: 9783337075422

Printed in Europe, USA, Canada, Australia, Japan

Cover: Foto ©Paul-Georg Meister /pixelio.de

More available books at **www.hansebooks.com**

ANGLO-SAXON
AND
OLD ENGLISH VOCABULARIES

BY

THOMAS WRIGHT, Esq., M. A.,
F. S. A., HON. M. R. S. L.

SECOND EDITION.

EDITED AND COLLATED

BY

RICHARD PAUL WÜLCKER.

VOLUME I:

VOCABULARIES.

LONDON:
TRÜBNER & Co., LUDGATE HILL.
1884.

[All rights reserved.]

PREFACE TO THE PRESENT EDITION.

The Collection of Vocabularies and Glossaries which Wright in his day prepared, contained pre-eminently Latin-Anglo-Saxon and Latin-Old-English works of this kind. Wright added, however, several works in which the English stood very much in the background (as in VIII and X pp. 121—139, and 142—175 [1]), or only in entirely scattered references (as in VII pp. 96—121 [1]). Indeed in Vol. II two Old-German Vocabularies were incorporated. For the purpose of restoring a greater symmetry I have left out the five articles above-named. On the other hand, I took up anew three others; viz. 2., 7. and 15, transcripts of which were most kindly placed at my disposal. It did not fall within the plan of the book to give a complete Collection of all the Anglo-Saxon and Old-English Vocabularies and Glossaries remaining in England. The articles already incorporated by Wright have been compared anew with the MSS., as far as the MSS. were accessible.

As for lexical purposes it is most desirable to have an alphabetically arranged Index (Wright has only one arranged according to the subjects for his Vol. I [1]) such a one has been prepared by several of my pupils.

The explanatory and critical remarks of Wright I have reprinted and added my own, which I marked with "R. W." Especially in the Anglo-Saxon portion occur many references, which would have

---

[1] see original edition.

been put in the alphabetical index, if I had earlier decided to add the index.

A mistake slipped into the superscription of No. 4. It was entitled according to Wright as *Archbishop* Ælfric's Vocabulary, however, according to Dietrich's excellent investigation, the author was *Abbot* Ælfric. In the table of contents I have thus also changed it.

Only the agreeable duty remains to me to thank most heartily those who aided me in the elaboration of my work by the loan of transcripts; namely, Prof. Dr. J. Zupitza (No. 1), Miss Lucie Toulmin Smith (Nos. 2 [1] and 7), the Librarian, Dr. A. Holder (No. 9) and Dr. W. Aldis Wright (No. 15).

RICHARD PAUL WÜLCKER.

Leipsic, January 1884.

[1] As the first sheets of the text were already printed in 1877, reference in No. 2 could not be made to Zupitza's Supplement (Haupt's Zeitschrift p. 223—226).

ORIGINAL PREFACE.[1]

THE Public is indebted for the following volume to the liberality and public spirit of Mr. Joseph Mayer, whose name is now so well known to all who interest themselves in the Archæology of this country. Its design originated in a social conversation between Mr. Mayer and myself, and we have endeavoured in it to make available to labourers in the field of antiquarian research and investigation a class of documents which, though they have been hitherto almost overlooked, form a rich treasury of information on almost every subject connected with the Archæology of the Middle Ages. They have been furnished by a number of contemporary manuscripts, scattered through various libraries in this country and abroad. Of one of the most valuable of the later vocabularies here printed, the original is preserved in Mr. Mayer's own collection; and for the communication and permission to print another—the curious and interesting pictorial vocabulary which closes the series—we owe our sincere thanks to the Lord Londesborough, of whose collection the manuscript forms a part. As far as regards my own labours, I will only say, that I have endeavoured to make the texts, which are arranged in strict chronological order, as nearly as is consistent with the duty of an editor, fac-similes of those of the original manuscripts. In fact, their very errors and corruptions

[1] September 1857.

form no unimportant facts in the history of education and knowledge, and they have been carefully preserved as, under these circumstances, an integral part of the text itself. Nevertheless, whenever I have been able to meet with several copies of the same tract, I have collated them, and made use of any additional matter they furnished, without interfering with the text of that which I have chosen as the best. It will be quite evident to anybody who glances at the contents of the present volume, that it is susceptible of annotations which might be made to swell out several such volumes. I therefore beg to state that I have had no intention of loading the volume with elaborate annotations; but I have hoped that a few explanatory and illustrative notes would make the work more popular, and would render it more useful to the general reader, and their pretensions go no further.

THOMAS WRIGHT.

BROMPTON, LONDON,
September, 1857.

ORIGINAL INTRODUCTION.

The Treatises which form the present volume are interesting in several points of view. Their importance in a philological sense, as monuments of the languages which prevailed at different periods in this island, is evident at the first glance, and need not be dilated upon. They are curious records of the history of Education; and, above all, they are filled with invaluable materials for illustrating the conditions and manners of our forefathers at various periods of their history, as well as the Antiquities of the Middle Ages in general. The history of Education is a subject which is now deservedly attracting more attention than was formerly given to it. It is certainly not uninteresting to trace the various efforts which were made, at all periods of the middle ages, to simplify and render popular the forms of elementary instruction, and the several modifications which these forms underwent.

The groundwork of all school-learning was the knowledge of the Latin language; and the first tasks of the young scholar were to learn the elements of the Latin grammar, to commit to memory words and their meanings, and to practise conversation in the Latin tongue. It was this practical application of the language which contributed very largely to its corruption, for the scholar began by making himself acquainted not with the pure Latin diction of classical books, but with a nomenclature of words—many of them extremely barbarous—which it had then become customary to apply to objects of ordinary use and occurence. The lessons were given by word of mouth, as boys could not in those times be accommodated with books; but they had slates, or roughly made tablets (*tabulæ*), on which they wrote down the lesson in grammar, or the portion of vocabulary, from the lips of the master, and, after committing it to memory, erased the writing, to make place for another. The teacher had necessarily his own written exemplar of an elementary Latin grammar, as well as his own written vocabulary of words, from which he read, interpreted, and explained. The old illuminations of manuscripts give us not unfrequently pictures of the interior of the school, in which we see the scholars arranged, with their tablets, before or round the teacher, who is dictating to them. In the earlier periods of Christianity among the Anglo-Saxons, the study of the Latin language was pursued with extraordinary zeal and proportionate success, and our island was celebrated for its learned men; but as time passed on, various circumstances combined to produce a general neglect of learning, so that king Alfred complained, in the latter part of the ninth century, that very few of his subjects could translate from Latin into their mother tongue. "So clean," he said, "was teaching ruined among the English people, that there were very few even of the ecclesiastical order, southward of the Humber, who could understand their service in English, or declare forth an epistle out of Latin into English; and I think there were not many beyond Humber." It may be observed, that in the earlier period, the Northumbrian kingdom was the great seat of learning. "So few such there were," Alfred adds, "that I cannot think of a single instance to the south of the Thames when I began to reign. To God Almighty be thanks that we now have any teacher in stall."[1]

Some of the causes of this decadence in the study of Latin among the Anglo-Saxons belonged probably to a change which had taken place in the social condition of the country, and were not to be overcome. Our great-minded Anglo-Saxon king intimates that his countrymen began to prefer books translated into or compiled in their own language to Latin compositions, and his own example in labouring upon such translations, or causing others to labour upon them, contributed no doubt to give permanence to this very natural taste. Nevertheless, the study of Latin was revived in England with some success during the tenth century, and it was increased by the intercourse between the English and continental scholars. Still this study was by no means general, and at the end of this century and beginning of the next, the labours of the two Alfrics in translating and compiling in English show sufficiently the neglect of the study of Latin

---

[1] Swæ clæne hio wæs oðfeallenu on Angelcynne þæt swiðe feawa wæron behionan Humbre þe hiora þeninga cuðen understondan on Englisc, oððefurðum an ærend-gewrit of Lædene on Englisc areccean; and ic wene þætte noht monige begiondan Humbre næren. Swæ feawa hiora wæron, þæt ic furðum anne anlepne ne mæg geþencean, be suðan Temese þa þa ic to rice feng. Gode ælmihtogum sie þonc, þætte we nu ænigne on stal habbað lareowa."—*King Alfred's Preface to the Translation of Gregory's Pastorale.*

even among the English clergy, which is confirmed by the complaints of the Norman ecclesiastics after the conquest. It is to these two distinguished scholars that we owe the first elementary school-books that are known to have existed in the English language—a Latin grammar (compiled and translated from Donatus and Priscian) and Latin-English vocabularies.

It is singular how soon our forefathers began to exercise their ingenuity in arranging their elementary books—and more especially the vocabularies—in forms calculated to be most attractive to the learner, or to enable him more easily to commit them to memory. The first of the treatises printed in the present volume, which had passed successively through the hands of the two Alfrics, the archbishop and his disciple, is compiled in the form of an interesting and very amusing dialogue, so contrived as to embody a large number of the words of common occurrence in the ordinary relations of life. It is written in Latin, but accompanied with a continuous interlinear gloss in Anglo-Saxon, precisely on the plan of the modern elementary books of the Hamiltonian system of teaching, to which it has been more than once compared; but it possessed one striking difference, which must not be overlooked—that the old Anglo-Saxon treatise was glossed for the assistance of the teacher, and not, as in the modern books of this description, for the learner. In fact, it is evident that at this time the schoolmasters themselves were very imperfectly acquainted with the Latin language, and that they found it necessary to have books in which the English meaning was written above or beside the Latin word, to enable them to explain it to their scholars. It was this same ignorance which rendered it necessary to have vocabularies, or lists of Latin words, with the translation attached to them—such as those which form the bulk of the present volume. In the earlier and better period, no doubt the teacher had such lists merely in Latin, or glossed only in cases of difficulty, and he was sufficiently learned in the language to explain them himself; but now the schoolmaster required to be reminded himself of the meaning of the Latin word. Nor was this all; for, besides the very incorrect and corrupt manner in which the words are frequently written in these manuscript vocabularies, in many instances the Latin word is wrongly interpreted. Several instances of such blunders may be pointed out in Alfric's "Colloquy;"[1] and others occur frequently in the Anglo-Saxon vocabularies, some of which are indicated in the notes.

---

[1] Some of these are curious. At p. 95 l. 10 occurs the adverb *solum*, which the glossator has translated as an adjective, instead of an adverb. On p. 97, the merchant speaks of selling merchandise *carius*, dearer, than he bought it; but

These vocabularies appear to have been numerous during the later Anglo-Saxon period, and those which remain differ considerably from each other. I have included in the present volume all that are now known to exist. The last of them brings us down to at least the middle of the twelfth century, after which we lose sight of similar vocabularies, until we reach the fifteenth century.

The Anglo-Norman period presents us with a new description of vocabulary, in which the words, still kept together in their different classes, are collected into a sort of continuous discourse. Of these, the earliest, and in many respects the most curious, is that by the celebrated scholar, Alexander Neckam, in which the principal operations and professions of life are enumerated and described in a familiar style. Neckam, singularly enough for an ecclesiastic, begins with the kitchen, describes its furniture and implements and their several uses, and treats of the articles of food and of the methods of cooking them. He then turns to the possessor of the house, describes his dress and accoutrements, when remaining at home or when riding abroad, and introduces us in the sequel to his chamber and to its furniture. The chamber-maid is next introduced to us, with her household employments; and we are taken to the poultry-yard, with a chapter on the cooking of poultry and fish, and on the characteristics of good wine. We are next taught how to build a feudal castle, to fortify it, to store and to defend it; and this leads us naturally to the subject of war in general, and to arms, armour, and soldiers. From this we return to matters of a more domestic character—to the barn, the poultry-yard, and the stable, and to that important occupation of mediæval domestic life, weaving. The occupations of the country follow, and the author explains the construction of carts and waggons, the process of building an ordinary house, and its parts, the various implements and operations of farming, and the construction and use of the plough. We turn rather abruptly from agriculture to navigation, and are instructed in the different sorts of ships, and in their parts and the articles with which they were usually stored. The tools, qualifications, and duties of the mediæval scribe, the operations of the goldsmith, and a copious enumeration of ecclesiastical furniture, complete this curious treatise.

The similar treatise of John de Garlande, composed in the earlier half of the following century, differs very much from its predecessor in details

the Anglo-Saxon interpreter has translated as though it meant more beloved, evidently not understanding the phrase to which it belongs. Again, on p. 93, speaking of the fisherman's art, he evidently did not know whether the Latin *hamus* meant the hook or the bait.

and arrangement. Its author occupies himself more with the objects which meet the eye in the interior of a great city (Paris), than with feudal or agricultural life. After giving, by way of introduction, a description of the human body and its various parts and members, he proceeds with a long list of trades and manufactures, and the various articles made or sold, such as the hawker who carried shoes and other articles of leather for sale on a pole, the girdle-makers, saddlers, shield-makers, buckle-makers, dealers in needles and other such articles, makers of bridles, hucksters, frobishers (or furbishers), the shopkeepers of the Grand-Pont, glovers, hatters, bowyers, makers of brooches and clasps, bell-makers, coblers, cordwainers, furriers, street criers, menders of cups, itinerant dealers in wine, sellers of cakes, regraters, bakers, pie-makers, cooks, changers, minters, goldsmiths, clothiers, linen-drapers, apothecaries, carpenters, wheelwrights, cart-makers, millers, armourers, fullers, dyers, tanners, smiths. At this point, John de Garlande interrupts his list of trades, to describe the house of a citizen *(probus homo)* and its furniture, which is followed by the different implements necessary to a scholar, or clerk. John de Garlande then proceeds to give the learner a list of his own wardrobe. A rather quaint account of the ecclesiastical library of a priest follows, with his apparel, and the implements belonging to the service of the church. We return from the church very abruptly to the stable, and then we have a list of the various domestic implements belonging to the mistress of the house, with descriptions of the occupations and employments peculiar to women—weaving, needlework, &c. The account of a poultry-shop in the Parvis of Notre Dame furnishes an occasion for giving a list of domestic fowls; that of the fowler, for an enumeration of wild fowls; and that of the fisherman, for a list of fish. In the chapters following, John de Garlande enumerates the domestic animals he had seen in the fields, the wild ones he had met with in the king's forest, the plants and herbs which grew in his own garden, the fruits in his orchard, and the shrubs in his grove; he gives a description of his own hall, an enumeration of the ships he had seen at sea, of the various tortures of the martyrs which were suggested to his mind by the fear of shipwreck, of the jongleurs, minstrels, dancing girls, &c., who performed at the feasts of the rich, of the punishments reserved for sinners, and of the joys of the blessed.

The close of the thirteenth century introduces us to a document of a novel character, although still similar in plan. It is written in verse, no doubt that it might be more easily carried in the memory, and, instead of being intended to teach the Latin language, its purpose was to teach French to the children of the English nobility and gentry. Accordingly, the text is written in French, with an interlinear gloss in English. This "treatise," as it is called, which was written by a man evidently of aristocratic blood, named Walter de Biblesworth, marks a very important period in the history of the English language, as it shows that before the end of the thirteenth century, and perhaps subsequently to the barons' wars, that language had already become the mother tongue of the children of the Anglo-Norman nobility, and that they learnt it before they were taught French.[1]

The subjects in this treatise are arranged in an order which seems to have been considered most suitable to the class for which they were intended. Walter de Biblesworth begins with the child when new-born, tells how it is to be nursed and fed, and then proceeds to the description of the human body. In this and in other parts, the author labours to impress upon the learner the nice distinctions between words of nearly similar meaning, and the different meanings of words which are similar in sound, as well as the distinction of genders, which even then appears to

---

[1] I may perhaps be allowed to repeat here the remarks on this subject made in a paper on the History of the English Language, read before the Historic Society of Lancashire and Cheshire, and printed in their Transactions, vol. ix, p. 150, 1857. I there said, "It was not only as the language of the Normans, but as that peculiarly of the feudal aristocracy in general, that French was introduced into England under William the Conqueror; and it was in that character that it continued to be the language of the aristocracy until feudalism itself was broken down. It had ceased, however, to be exclusively their language in the thirteenth century. In the latter years of that century, a tract or treatise was written in French or Anglo-Norman verse, forming a sort of vocabulary of that language, and designed expressly for the purpose of teaching it to children. The number of copies of this tract still preserved in MS. show that it was a popular elementary book, and that it was in extensive use. The compiler was Walter de Biblesworth, a man known elsewhere as a writer of French verse, and apparently belonging himself to the aristocratic class; he was a friend of the great statesman of the reign of Edward I., Henry de Lacy, earl of Lincoln and Salisbury, and compiled the treatise we are speaking of at the request of the lady Dionysia de Monchensey. Thus all the relations of the author and of his book were of an aristocratic character. Now, Walter de Biblesworth states his object to be to instruct the rising generation in the proper use of the words of the French language, and especially in the correct application of the genders; and the French words are explained in English, implying thus that the learner was acquainted with the English language before he began to learn French. We thus ascertain the very important fact, that, before the end of the thirteenth century, the children of the aristocracy of England learnt English before they were instructed in any other language—or, in other words, that English had become their mother tongue."

have presented a difficulty to the young beginner in the French language. The description of the body itself is followed by the process of clothing it, and by an enumeration of the various articles of apparel. The author then returns again to the manners of the child, and describes its proper diet. After some rather curious instructions for the proper and distinctive use of certain classes of words, we are taken to the barn, and the teacher describes the processes of thrashing, of converting corn into meal, of baking, of the cultivation of flax, and the various stages through which it went before it is converted into linen cloth, and of brewing, as well as of the character and effects of good ale. The scholar is next taken a-fishing, and the various characteristics of the country, with the phases of the weather, and the changes of season, are pointed out to him. The fine weather offers the occasion of another rural excursion, with a description of the flowers, the fruit and other trees, the birds, and the animals which are supposed to present themselves to his view. Rural occupations are next introduced, with full descriptions of a cart and a plough. Then we witness the building of a house, and the arrangements of its different parts, the domestic processes of lighting the fire, cooking the food, and placing it on the table, and the various articles of food and their arrangement. The whole closes with the description of a great feast. The notion of composing such vocabularies in verse was applied to Latin, as well as to French, an example of which will be found also in the present volume.

During the fourteenth century, school teaching seems to have fallen greatly into neglect in this country, and we hardly find any manuscripts of these educational treatises between those of the thirteenth century and those of the fifteenth. In the latter century, however, a great movement took place,—it was the age, especially, of founding grammar-schools, so many of which were re-founded at the dissolution of papal colleges under Edward VI. A similar degradation, in fact, had taken place to that which we have remarked under the Anglo-Saxons, though the causes were not entirely the same. The influence of the great development of learning in the twelfth century, and the example of the able and elegant Latin writers whom that age had produced, extended over at least a portion of the thirteenth century; but before the end of that century, the priest was already gaining the victory over the school-master, and the power of the universities was yielding to that of the Popish church. During the two following centuries, learning was reduced almost to its lowest degree; and this became so apparent, that an effort was made to raise it by striking at what was supposed to be the root of the evil—the want or the inefficiency of the elementary schools. Those who undertook the task of reformers, however, mistook the cause of the evil, and did not understand that the Middle Ages were approaching their end, and that there was no remedy for the restoration of forms and principles which were expiring from their own exhaustion. Nevertheless, the effort seems to have been made with earnestness, and caused, in the fifteenth century, a considerable extension in the lower grades of scholastic education. The manuscripts of grammatical treatises—of school-books, in fact—now become extremely numerous. Latin-English vocabularies are also not uncommon during this period, and I have given three in the present volume—one from a manuscript in the British Museum, and the two others from private collections. The last of these, and apparently the latest in date—but it is not very easy to distinguish nicely the distinctive dates of this particular class of manuscripts during the fifteenth century—presents a new peculiarity,—it is illustrated with rude pen-and-ink drawings in the margin of many of the articles enumerated in the text of the vocabulary. These illustrations, we should imagine, were designed to assist in fixing the attention of the scholar on his task, and it thus, as the latest of these attempts at improvement, forms an appropriate conclusion to our volume. It shows us, moreover, how little of novelty there is in most of the plans for simplifying school teaching in more modern times, for in these mediæval treatises we meet with the prototypes of almost every scheme that has been proposed, from the more recent Hamiltonian system to the *Orbis Sensualium Pictus* of Comenius, which made so much noise by its novelty of plan in the earlier part of the seventeenth century.

I can hardly be doubted that the manuscripts of these vocabularies of the fifteenth century were written by schoolmasters for their own use; and we cannot help being struck by the large proportion of barbarous Latin words which are introduced into them, and by the gross blunders with which they abound, especially in their orthography. Many of the Latin words are so disguised and corrupted, that we can hardly recognise them; and in some instances, the schoolmaster has actually mistaken the genders. It is thus clear that the schoolmasters of the fifteenth century were very imperfect scholars themselves, and we can easily understand how the Latinists of the old school fell into that barbarous style of writing which drew upon them the ridicule of the classical scholars after the revival of learning, as well as their hostility to that new light which exposed their defects. These vocabularies of the fifteenth century differ so entirely from each other, both in their general arrangement and in the words introduced under each head, that there seems little room for doubt that each schoolmaster compiled his own book. This circumstance has added extremely to their philological value, as the English words in each vocabulary may be supposed to present some, at least, of the peculiarities of the dialect in which it was written. Through the preceding ages, the schoolmasters seem to have laboured under a difference of opinion as to the subject which had a claim to precedence of the others, and therefore ought to be placed at the head of the vocabulary. Archbishop Alfric gave the palm to agriculture, expressly in the Colloquy, and practically in his Vocabulary.[1] The vocabulary from the Brussels manuscript,[2] and that printed as the appendix to the present volume from the Cottonian MS,[3] begin with birds, for which it would be difficult to assign any reason. The Anglo-Saxon glossary of the other Cottonian manuscript,[4] with the semi-Saxon vocabulary abridged from it,[5] first present the more natural order of commencing with the Deity and with the human body and its parts. Alexander Neckam, as already stated, begins with the kitchen; but John de Garlande returns to the more natural order, beginning with man and the human body, which is adopted also in principle by Walter de Biblesworth. The vocabularies of the fifteenth century adopt, I think, invariably the human body as the leading subject, but they arrange the subjects which follow very diversely. Some of them, too, divide and subdivide these subjects under more numerous heads, or titles, than others.

It is this circumstance of grouping the words under different heads which gives these vocabularies their value as illustrations of the conditions and manners of society. It is evident that the compiler gave, in each case, the names of all such things as habitually presented themselves to his view, or, in other words, that he presents us with an exact list and description of all the objects which were in use at the time he wrote, and no more. We have, therefore, in each a sort of measure of the fashions, and comforts, and utilities of contemporary life, as well as in some cases of its sentiments. Thus, to begin with a man's habitation, his house—the words which describe the parts of the Anglo-Saxon house are few in number, a *heal* or hall, a *bur* or bedroom, and in some cases a *cicen* or kitchen, and the materials are chiefly beams of wood, laths, and plaister.[6] But when we come to the vocabularies of the Anglo-Norman period, we soon find traces of that ostentation in domestic buildings which William of Malmsbury assures us that the Normans introduced into this island; the house becomes more massive, and the rooms more numerous, and more diversified in their purposes. When we look at the furniture of the house, the difference is still more apparent. The description given by Alexander

[1] See pp. 90, 91, and 104 of the present volume.
[2] P. 284 of the present volume.
[3] See p. 258.
[4] P. 304.
[5] P. 536.
[6] See col. 126, 184, 185, and 326.

Neckam of the hall, the chambers, the kitchen, and the other departments of the ordinary domestic establishment in the twelfth century, and the furniture of each, almost brings them before our eyes, and nothing could be more curious than the account which the same writer gives us of the process of building and storing a castle. The bare lists of names in the vocabularies of the fifteenth century are hardly less expressive. Thus, in the earliest of these vocabularies, we have the baronial hall furnished with its board and trestles, with which the table was laid out when wanted; the table dormant, or permanent table, which was probably even then an article of rarer occurrence; benches, as the ordinary seats; a long-settle to draw up to the fire, or to place on the dais, behind the high table; a chair, for ceremonious occasions, and a stool; a cushion for the chair; bankers and dossers, or carpets to lay over the principal seats; a screen; a basin and laver, for washing the hands of the guests; andirons to support the fire, tongs to arrange it, and bellows to raise it into a flame.[1] So again, in the subject of costume, we have the names of different articles of wearing apparel in use at successive periods, from the tenth century to the end of the thirteenth, and again during the fifteenth centuries. The same thing may be said of the weapons of war. Some of these documents, and especially the *Dictionarius* of John de Garlande, throw an interesting light upon the trades and manufactures of the middle ages. Others show us the progress—or rather the want of progress—of our forefathers in the practice of agriculture. In fact, there is hardly any subject connected with mediæval life which does not receive some light from the tracts which are printed in the present volume. We here see our forefathers in all their positions of relationship, position, and occupation, from infancy to old age; we are introduced to the child in the nursery, and to the boy at his school; we see him in the clothes he wore, and with the arms that he carried to those constant wars which absorbed so much of mediæval life; we learn in minute detail how he lived, what was his food and how it was prepared, and what he drank; we see the industrious house-wife attending to her domestic cares, or busied in her usual occupations of spinning and weaving; we witness the games and amusements of the different stages of life; and we even penetrate into the retired study of the scholar.

Again, in these vocabularies the Archæologist will find the only means of identifying by their proper names a multitude of utensils, which are elsewhere named without description, or of which he is acquainted with the forms, but knows not what to call them. This is especially the case

---

[1] See col. 656, 657.

with a class of articles which have been during the last few years much more studied by antiquaries than formerly, such as mediæval pottery, and vessels for the table of glass and metal, as well as articles of jewellery and other ornaments of the person. We even gain instructive glances at notions which show us the progress of science, and at implements of various kinds which reveal to us important facts in the history of modern inventions.

None of these, perhaps, is of more importance than the curious early allusion to the use of the mariner's compass by the navigators of the western seas.[1] It is well known to all readers that this invaluable invention has been formerly supposed to have been brought from the East, and not to have been known in the West until the fourteenth century, when it was used by the Italian mariners. Allusions to it have, however, been discovered by the students of mediæval literature in works which date as far back as the thirteenth century. In the following pages, we find this invention not only alluded to in the twelfth century, but described in such a manner as to show that it was then absolutely in its infancy, and to leave little doubt of its having originated in the west. Alexander Neckam, in his treatise *de Utensilibus*, enumerates, among the ship's stores, a needle which was placed on a pivot, and when turned round and left to take its own position in repose, taught the sailors their way when the polar star was concealed from them by clouds or tempest. I have discovered a passage in another of Neckam's works, the inedited treatise *de Naturis Rerum*, which gives a more distinct account of this invention. "Mariners at sea," he says, "when through cloudy weather in the day which hides the sun, or through the darkness of the night, they lose the knowledge of the quarter of the world to which they are sailing, touch a needle with the magnet, which will turn round till, on its motion ceasing, its point will be directed towards the north." A comparison of these two passages seems to shew pretty clearly that at this time the navigators had no regular box for the compass, but that they merely carried with them a needle which had been touched with the magnet (perhaps sometimes they carried the magnet also, and touched the needle for the occasion), and that when they had to use it, they merely placed it upon some point, or pivot, on which it could turn with tolerable freedom, and then gave it a motion, and waited until it ceased moving. This mode of using the needle was, it must be confessed, rude enough. The passage in the treatise *de Utensilibus* contains one particular which is very obscure, as Neckam informs us that when the needle ceased moving it pointed towards the east *(donec cuspis acus respiciat orientem)*; and as

---

[1] In a treatise of Alexander Neckam *de Utensilibus*.

all the manuscripts agree in this reading, and it is glossed by *est*, this must be the intention of the writer. I know no way of explaining this, unless it be by the supposition that, as in the twelfth century the East was the grand object of most voyages from this part of the world, an attempt had been made to improve the magnetic needle by adding to it a limb at right angles, which should point to the east when the needle itself pointed to the north; and that this was what Neckam calls the *cuspis acus*. Between this time and the date — whatever it may be — of the poem, also quoted in my note on the passage of Neckam, which contains the first allusion to the mariner's compass in the tirteenth century, an attempt had been made to facilitate its use.[1] This was done by thrusting the needle through some substance which would not sink, and placing it upon the surface of water. Guiot de Provins, the author of the poem alluded to, calls this substance a *festu*, a stick or straw (the Latin *festuca*). The mariners, he tells us, have a contrivance depending on the qualities of the magnet, which cannot fail. The magnet, he adds, is an ugly brownish stone, to which iron is attracted. "After they have caused a needle to touch it, and placed it in a stick, they put it in the water, without anything more, and the stick keeps it on the surface. Then it turns its point towards the star with such certainty, that no man will ever have any doubt of it, nor will it ever for anything go false. When the sea is dark and hazy, that they can neither see star nor moon, they place a light by the needle, and then they have no fear of going wrong; towards the star goes the point, whereby the mariners have the knowledge to keep the right way. It is an art which cannot fail." According to another poet, the substance through which the needle was usually thrust was cork. He tells us that "the mariners who went to Friesland, or to Greece, or Acre, or Venice," were guided in their route by the polar star; but when at night, or in obscure weather, it was invisible, they discovered its position by the following contrivance: — "They thrust a needle of iron through a piece of cork, so that it is almost buried in it, and then touch it with the loadstone; then they place it in a vessel full of water, so that no one pushes it out until the water is calm, for in whatever direction the point aims, there without doubt is the polar star." The MS. in which this latter poem was found is undoubtedly of the fourteenth century; but

---

[1] In this interval, we meet with another slight but very curious allusion to the use of the magnetic needle for purposes of navigation. Jacques de Vitri, one of the historians of the crusades, who wrote about the year 1218, says, (Hist. Hier. cap. 89,) "Acus ferrea, postquam adamantem contigerit, ad stellam septentrionalem, quæ velut axis firmamenti aliis vergentibus non movetur, semper convertitur; unde valde necessarius est navigantibus in mari."

the poem itself is evidently of somewhat older date—of the beginning of that century, or not improbably of the century preceding. It is possible, therefore, that this rudely constructed mariner's compass may have continued unimproved until the fourteenth century.[1]

The philologist will appreciate the tracts printed in the following pages as a continuous series of very valuable monuments of the languages spoken in our island during the Middle Ages. It is these vocabularies alone which have preserved from oblivion a very considerable and interesting portion of the Anglo-Saxon tongue, and without their assistance our Anglo-Saxon dictionaries would be far more imperfect than they are. I have endeavoured to collect together in the present volume all the Anglo-Saxon vocabularies that are known to exist, not only on account of their diversity, but because I believe that their individual utility will be increased by thus presenting them in a collective form. They represent the Anglo-Saxon language as it existed in the tenth and eleventh centuries; and, as written no doubt in different places, they may possibly present some traces of the local dialects of that period. The curious semi-Saxon vocabulary is chiefly interesting as representing the Anglo-Saxon in its period of transition, when it was in a state of rapid decadence. The inter-

[1] This very curious poem, a sort of song, is preserved in a manuscript formerly in the collection of M. Barrois, of Paris, and now in that of Lord Ashburnham. It was first pointed out by M. Fr. Michel, who printed the portion relating to the mariner's compass in the preface to his *Lais inédits*, Paris 1836. As this is now a rare book, I have thought it desirable to give here the whole passage. It is as follows:—

La tresmontaine est de tel guise,
Qu'ele est el firmament asisse
Où ele luist et reflambie.
Li maronier qui vont en Frise,
En Gresse, en Acre, ou en Venisse,
Sevent par li toute la voie;
Pour nule riens ne so desvoie,
Tout jours se tient en une moie.
Tant est de li grans li servisse,
Se la mers est enflée ou koie
Jà ne sera c'on ne le voie,
Ne pour galerne ne pour bise.

Pour biso ne pour autre afaire
Ne laist sen dout servise à faire
La tresmontaigne clere et pure;
Les maroniers par son esclaire
Jete souvent hors de contraire,
Et de chemin les assëure.
Et quant la nuis est trop oscure,
S'est ele encor de tel nature,
C'à l'aimant fait le fer traire,
Ci que par forche et par droiture,
Et par ruille qui tous jours dure,
Sevent le liu de son repaire.

Son repaire sevent à route,
Quant li tans n'a de clarté goute,
Tout chil qui font cest maistrise,
Qui une aguille de fer boute
Si qu'ele pert presque toute
En .i. poi de liége, et l'atise
A la pierre d'aimant bise;
S'en .i. vaissel plain d' yave est mise,
Si que nus hors ne la deboute,
Si tost com l'iave s'aserise;
Car dons quel part la pointe vise,
La tresmontaigne est là sans doute.

linear gloss to Alexander Neckam, and the commentary on John de Garlande,[1] are most important monuments of the language which for a while usurped among our forefathers the place of the Anglo-Saxon, and which we know by the name of the Anglo-Norman. In the partial vocabulary of the names of plants, which follows them, we have the two languages in juxta-position, the Anglo-Saxon having then emerged from that state which has been termed semi-Saxon, and become early English. We are again introduced to the English language more generally by Walter de Biblesworth, the interlinear gloss to whose treatise represents no doubt the English of the beginning of the fourteenth century.[1] All the subsequent vocabularies given here belong, as far as the language is concerned, to the fifteenth century. As written in different parts of the country, they bear evident marks of dialect; one of them—the vocabulary in Latin verse—is a very curious relic of the dialect of the West of England at a period of which such remains are extremely rare.

[1] Omitted in the Present Edition.

CONTENTS OF VOLUME I.

	Page
Preface to the present edition	I
Original preface	III
Original introduction	V

	Column
1. Anglo-Saxon Vocabulary. 8th Century	1
2. Kentish Glosses. 9th Century	55
3. Colloquy of Ælfric	89
4. Abbot Ælfric's Vocabulary	104
5. Supplement to Ælfric's Vocabulary	168
6. Anglo-Saxon Glossary. 10th Century	192
7. Anglo-Saxon Glosses. 10th Century	248
8. Anglo-Saxon Vocabulary. 10th or 11th Century	258
9. Anglo-Saxon Vocabulary. 11th Century	284
10. Anglo-Saxon Vocabulary. 11th Century	304
11. Glosses, Latin and Anglo-Saxon. 11th Century	338
12. Miscellaneous Anglo-Saxon Glosses. 11th Century	474
13. Semi-Saxon Vocabulary. 12th Century	536
14. Vocabulary of the Names of Plants. 13th Century	554
15. Latin and English Vocabulary. 15th Century	560
16. Metrical Vocabularies. 15th Century	622
17. Names of Parts of the Human Body. 15th Century	631
18. English Vocabulary. 15th Century	633
19. Nominale. 15th Century	673
20. Pictorial Vocabulary. 15th Century	745

ERRATA.

Col. 545 *l.* 2 *for* merherbarum *read* materherbarum.

I.
ANGLO-SAXON VOCABULARY,
OF THE EIGHTH CENTURY[1].

Interpretatio nominum ebraicorum et grecorum.

Adsida, flood.
Caluariæ locus, cualmstou.
Coliferte, geþofta.
Clauis, helma.
Crepidinem, neoþouard.
Doleus, byden.
Dasile, boor.
Decurat, hornnaap.
Ferula, hreod.
Fundus, bodan.
Gemellus, getuin.
Clebulum, hrider.
Jungula, geoc-boga.
Ledo, nepflod.

Libitorium, saa.
Lignarium, uuidubinde.
Mantega, taeg.
Malina, fylled flood.
5 *Mappa,* cneoribt.
Maculosus, spec-faag.
Menta, minte.
Rastrum, raece.
Scisca, coforþrote.
10 *Sublatorium,* bloestbaelg[2].
Tantalus, aelbitu.
Ua, euwa.
Uomer, scær.

Incipit glosa secundum ordinem elimentorum alphabeti.

Abelena, haeselhnutu.
Abies, etspe.

15 *Absinthium,* wermod.
Abortus, misbyrd.

---

[1] This early and interesting monument of our language is preserved in a fine vellum manuscript in the collection of Archbishop Parker, in the Library of Corpus Christi College, Cambridge, No. XCLIV. I have no hesitation in ascribing the writing to the eighth century. It resembles rather closely that of the well-known Durham Book, its characters approaching almost to uncials. Some one has written on the first leaf, in a hand perhaps of the thirteenth century, that it belonged to the church of Canterbury — *liber Sancti Augustini Cant.* — whence it no doubt came into the possession of Archbishop Parker. It is, therefore, not improbable that this Vocabulary was originally compiled and written for the school of Canterbury. [The text of the present edition is based on a collation recently made by Prof. J. Zupitza, of Berlin. Some of the foreign terms are rendered by Latin, some by Anglo-Saxon expressions; only those rendered into Anglo-Saxon were retained, including some which were omitted by Wright. — R. W.]

[2] or *blast-baelg,* literally *a blast-bag.* The Anglo-Saxon word for bellows.

Ablata, binumine.
Abunde, genycthlice.
Abiget, wereth.
Ab euro, castansudan.
Ad euronothum, eastsuth.
Abditis, gehyddum.
Ab affrico, sudanwestan.
Ab borea, castannorþan.
Aconito, þungas.
Aceruus, muha [1].
A circio, nordanwestan.
Actionaris, folcgeroebum.
Acisculum, piic.
Aerabulus, mapuldur.
Achalantis, uel luscinia, uel roscinia, nehtegale.
Acrifolus, holegn [2].
Acega, holthona.
Accearium, steli.
Acitula, hromsa.
Acitelum, hromsan crop.
Accitulium, gæces sure.
Acinum, hindberiae.
Acris, fortis uel from [3].
Actionabatur, scirde.
Actuarius, wrace.
Accetum, gefeotodne.
Acegia, snite.
Aceti cotilla, uas, i. bolle.
Acus, netl, *uel*, gronuisc.
Accidia, tedium, uel anxietas, i. sorg.
Accinctu, denetle.
Adsutæ, gesiuwide.
Addictus, forscrifen.
Adridente, tyctende.
Aduncis, gebegdum.
Ad penses, to nyttum.
Adsensore, fultemendum.
Adclinis, to-hald, *uel incumbens*.
Atqueue, end suelce.
Ademto, gebinumini.
Adsaeclum, þegn, [*minister turpitudinis* [4]].

Adgrediuntur, geeodun.
Adlido, tonwinto.
Adnitentibus, tilgendum.
Ad libidines, wraene.
5 *Adtonitus*, blysnende.
Ad fasces, to weordmyndum.
Adfligit, gehuaeh.
Adrogantissime, wloncli.
Adplaudat, onhliorrouuit.
10 *Adcommodaturus*, uuoende.
Aduentio, sarwo.
Aduocatus, þingere.
Adhibuit, geladade, *uel aduocauit*.
Adplicuit, geþiudde.
15 *Aequatis*, efnum.
Aesculus, boece.
Aegit, wrace.
Aestuaria, fleotas.
Aere alieno, geabuli.
20 *Aegesta*, gors.
Aequipensum, ebnwege.
Afiniculum [ellende] [5], *a finibus procul*.
Afflarat, ansuaep.
25 *A fafonio*, suþanwestan.
Affricus, westsudwind.
Affectui, megsibbe, *uel dilectione*.
Agre[s]tis, wildæ.
Agastrum, aegmang.
30 *Agitatio*, unstilnis.
Agitate, onettad.
Agapem, suoesendo.
Agmen, weorod.
Alea, tebl.
35 *Aleator*, teblere.
Albulo, flio.
Alium, gaarleec.
Alba spina, heagodorn.
Alcion, isern.
40 *Alnus*, aler.
Alneum, fulaetreo.
Alietum, spaerhabuc.
Alneta, alerholt.

---

[1] This rare word also occurs in Ælfric's Heptateuch, Ex. 22,6. R. W.
[2] Cf. Leo, Angelsächsisches glossar, Halle 1872 u. 1877 pag. 125. R. W.

[3] The MS. reads *acris fortio*. R. W.
[4] These two words are added in another and later hand. R. W.
[5] Added in a later hand. R. W.

Alga, waar.
Altrinsecus, on ba halfe.
Albipedius, huitfoot.
Aluuium, meeli.
Aluiolum, aldaht.
Alga, scaldhyflas, *uel* sondhyllas.
Alternantium, staefnendra.
Alacris, snel.
Alacer, suift.
Alueus, streamraad.
Alitus, aethm.
Alumnae, fostorbearn.
Alapiciosa[1], calwa.
Aluearia, hyfi.
Altilia, foedils.
Alcido, meau.
Alcanus, þoden.
Alites, challes[2].
Alueum, eduaelle.
Alitudo, fothur.
Alligeo, recceo.
Altor, fostorfaeder.
Allox, tahae.
Allauda, lauricae.
Amisionem, forlor.
Ammentum, sceptog.
Ambrones, gredge.
Ambages, ymbsuaepe.
Ambrosea, suoetnis.
Amēns, emod.
Amites, fugultreo, *uel* reftras.
Amtes, oemsetinne wiingeardes.
Ambulas, þiustra.
Amilarius, mearh.
Ambila, laec.
Amiculo, hrægli.
Amentis, sceptloum.
Andeda, brandrod.
Aneta, enid.
Anetum, dili.
Antiae, **loccas.**
Anguens, **breer.**
Antefata, forewyrde.
Antemne, waede.

Antemna, seglgærd.
Antedoque, wyrtdrenc.
Ansatae, aetgaere.
Antena, boga.
5 *Anxius,* sorgendi.
Annua, gerlice.
Anate, clader, sticca.
Anser, goos.
Anus, ald uuif.
10 *Anguila,* el.
Anceps, tuigendi.
Antulus, caecbora.
Aporiens, anseungendi.
Aplustra, geroedro.
15 *Aper,* eobor.
Aporiamur, biað þreade.
Apiastrum, biowyrt.
Apio, merice.
Apotasia, fraetgengian.
20 *Appetitus,* gidsung.
Apparitione, getiunge.
Aparatu, aexfaru.
Applare, corscripel.
Apricitas, gethingio.
25 *Apparatum,* geþrec.
Appotheca, winfaet.
Apporeor, onsteuum, *quibus ejus uis-
    cera interno foetore coquentur,
    et inde loquendo exalauit odorem*
30 *foetorem.*
Aquilium, onga.
Aquemale, lebel.
Aquilae, segnas.
Armonia, suinsung.
35 *Ariolatus,* frihtrung.
Areoli, sceabas.
Ardia, hragra.
Argella, laam.
Argutiae, thrauuo.
40 *Arrius,* faag.
Arbutus, aespe.
Argutiae, gleaunisse.
Arx, faestin.
Archtoes, waegneþixl.

---

[1] For *alopeciosa,* a late Latin word for a state of baldness produced by a disease called in medieval Latin *alopecia,* from the Greek ἀλωπεκία.

[2] Perhaps for *callas* = men, men of war. Cf. Grein, sprachsatz II., pag. 73. R. W.

Artura, tot.
Argilla, thoae.
Arula, fyrponne.
Artemon, obersegl, *uel malus nauis.*
Armilausia, serce.
Arpago, awel, *uel* clauuo.
Arpa, earngeot.
Arnaglosa[1], wegbrade.
Arbia, ceber.
Armus, boog,
Arbatæ, sibæd.
Ars plumaria, uuyndecreft.
Archiatros, heahlecas.
Aruina, risel.
Ardebat, scaan.
Arectas, hlysnendi.
Arcessitus, feotod.
Arbitus, faestinnum.
Arcister, strelbora.
Asilo, briosa.
Asses scorteas, liþrine trymsas.
Aspaltum, spaldur.
Ascalonium, ynnelaec.
Astu, facni, *uel* fraefeli.
Ascopa, kylle.
Aspera, unsmoþi.
Asapa, earngeat.
Astur, haesualwe.
Atflarat, onsueop
Atticus, dora.
Attoniti, hlysnende, afyrhte.
Atqueue, on suilce.
Auriculum, carwicga.
Auus, aeldrafaeder.
Auriola, stigu.
Auellanus, haesl.
Aucupatione, setunge.
Ausus, gedyrstig.
Auehit, onweg aferide.
Auserunt, nomun hlodun.
Auena, atæ.

Aulea, streagl:
Auum, meli.
Auspicantur, haelsadon.
Auster, suduuind.
5 *Augur,* haelsere.
Ausurae, groeni aar [2].
Axungia, rysel.
Axredones, lynisas.
Axredo, lynis.
10 *Axis,* aex.

Bacidones, raedinne.
Bagula, bridels.
Balsis, teter.
15 *Ballista,* staeflidre.
Basterna, beer.
Batuitum, gebeaten.
Bacciuia, beger.
Ballena, horn.
20 *Barritus,* genung.
Battat, geonath.
Basterna, scrid.
Balbus, uulisp.
Balus, isernfeotor
25 *Bachantes,* uuoedende.
Baratrum, dael.
Basis, syl.
Ballationes, cnop.
Balbutus, stom, wlisp.
30 *Ban,* segn.
Rapis, treuteru [3].
Baruina, barriggae.
Balneum, stofa.
Balatus, bletid.
35 *Bariulus,* reagufinc.
Beacita, stearn.
Beta, berc, *arbor dicitur.*
Aeneficium[4], freomo.
Berrus, baar [5].
40 *Berruca,* uearte.
Bellicum, slag.

---

[1] *r* in this word is added in a later hand. R. W.

[2] Perhaps for *usurae?* R. W.

[3] Bosworth has, 'Treuteru, *a sort of standard, vexilli quoddam genus*'.

[4] Of course, this is a mere error of the scribe for *Beneficium.* R. W.

[5] *Berrus,* no doubt, here stands for *verres,* a boar.

Bena[1], higrae.
Bena, atæ.
Becta[2], stært.
Bicoca, haebreblete.
Bitumen, liim.
Bitiligo, blaecthrust, *fel*.
Bile, atr.
Bitulus, berc.
Biothanatas, seolfbonan.
Bitricius, steopfaeder.
Birbicariolus, werna.
Bitorius, erdling.
Bipertitum, herbid.
Bilance, tuiheolore.
Bibulta, billeru.
Blitum, clate.
Blessus, stom.
Bothoma[3], embrin.
Blohonicula, stoppa.
Bofellum[4], falud.
Bona, scaet.
Boreus, eastnordwind.
Bobulcus, hridhiorde.
Bouestra, radre.
Bacarius, meresuin.
Bofor, lendislieg.
Bombosa, hlaegulendi.
Botrum, clystri.
Bolides, sundgerd in scipe, *uel* metrap.
Briensis, honduyrm.
Brahiale, gyrdels.
Bratium, malt.
Bradigabo, felduop.
Broel, edisc, deortuun.
Broellarius, ediscueard.
Bruchus, cefer.
Bruncus, wrot.
Braciae, cian.
Braugina, barice.
Bulla, sigl.

Bux[5], box.
Bubo, uuf.
Buculus, rondbaeg.
Burrum, bruun.
5 *Bubalis*, weosend.
Buccula, buuc.
Bucitum, seotu.
Butio, frysca.
Bunia, byden.
10 *Bubla*, flood.
Byssum, tuin.
Byrseus, lederuyrtha.

Calculus, calc.
15 *Caccabum*, cetil.
Cados, ambras.
Cartellus, windil.
Calculus, ratio, *uel sententia*, *uel numerus*, *uel* teblstan.
20 *Cartilago*, naesgristle.
Carbunculus, spryng.
Cautere, aam.
Catapulta, flaan.
Cabillatio, glio.
25 *Camellea*[6], wulfescamb.
Canes linga[7], ribbe.
Calentes, hatende.
Caulem, steola.
Capulus, helt.
30 *Caumeuniae*, eordreste.
Catabatus, romei.
Calcar, spora.
Cauterium, merciseren.
Catasta, geloed.
35 *Cappillatur*, faexnis.
Capsis, cest.
Carcura, craet.
Caractis, uuæterþruh.
Cariscus, cuicbeam, uuice.
40 *Capitium*, hood.
Camisa, ha[a]m.

---

[1] Of course, for *verna*, a bondman. The *b* is often used for *v* in this corrupt Latin, as in the next word, which represents the Latin word *avena*. *Atæ* is an oat.
[2] For *vecta*, *vectis*.
[3] *Bothoma* or *Bothonia* perhaps for *Boedromia* which word was translated *embrin, embryne, ymbryne, anniversarius, cyclus*. R. W.
[4] *Bofellum*, for *bovillum*, a fold, Anglo-Saxon *falud, falæd*.
[5] For *buxus*.
[6] For *chamaleon*, a plant: the wolf's thistle. — [7] or *cinoglosa*. R. W.

Carix, secg.
Canalibus, wæcterdrum.
Cappa, scicging.
Castanea, cistenbeam.
Calta, reade clafre, *uel genus floris*.
Capistrum, caebestr.
Calcesta, huite clafre.
Cancer, haebrn.
Calciculium, iecsessurae[1].
Cardella, þisteltuige.
Cacomicanus, logdor.
Calomachus, haet.
Cardus, þistel.
Castorius, beber.
Caenum, wase.
Carectum, breod.
Carpella, sadulboga.
Carina, bythne.
Canti, faelge.
Cassidele, pung.
Cappa, snod.
Carpasini, græsgroeni.
Calmetum, mersc.
Caliga, scoh.
Carbo, gloed.
Carduelis, linetuige.
Caradrion, laurici.
Cantarus, wibil.
Caper, heber.
Callos, weorras, *uel* ill.
Carula, crauue.
Cartilago, grundsopa.
Capria, raha.
Cauda, steort.
Caldaria, cetil.
Cater, suearth.
Cartago, braadponne.
Caragios, lyblaccan.
Casla, heden.
Canda, boga.
Campus, brogdetende *uel* cleppetende.
Carbasus, seglbosm.
Cautionem, gewrit.
Capulum, helt.
Caumati, suole.

Cauerniculis, holum.
Capistrinum, geflit.
Cassidis, helmes.
Casus, fer.
5 *Casis*, ned.
Casso, idle.
Cassium, helm.
Cardo, heor.
Cabillatur, mandrat.
10 *Caelatum*, agraben.
Catagrinas, bleremina mecs.
Canthera, trog.
Callus, waar.
Caluarium[2], caluuerclim.
15 *Cardiolus*, uudusnite.
Callis, paat.
Capistro, caefli.
Calleo, fraefeleo.
Cauliculus, steola.
20 *Carpebat*, sclat.
Cauernus, holu.
Cartamo, lybcorn.
Carcesia, bunan.
Cessere, on wicum.
25 *Cercilus*, aesc.
Censores, geroefan.
Censeo, doema.
Cesuram, gegandende[3].
Celox, ceol.
30 *Cerus*, elh.
Cerula, heawi.
Cerasius, ciserbeam.
Cerefolium, cunelle.
Cefalus, heardhara.
35 *Cepa*, ynnilaec, cipe.
Cementum, liim, *lapidum*.
Cente, wildegoos.
Cespites, tyrb.
Cessit, geeode.
40 *Cereacus*, hornblauuere.
Cernua, hald.
Cerefolium, cerfelle.
Chaus[4], duolma, *prima confusio, omnium rerum*.
45 *Chaumos*, suol.

---

[1] Cuckoo's sour, wood sorrel. Cf. pag. 3, 22.
[2] For *caluaria*, the place of skulls.
[3] For *gegangende*?
[4] For *chaos*.

Chartamo, lybcorn.
Chorus[1], eostnordwind.
Citropodes, chroa, croha.
Cicuta, hymlice.
Cicuta, wodewistle.
Cicad, secggescere, *uel* haman.
Ciconia, store.
Cicer, bean.
Cisculus, heardheau.
Cinoglosa, ribbe.
Circinno, gabulrond.
Circius, westnordwind.
Cis, biheonan.
Cimiterium, licburg.
Circinni, windeloccas.
Circinatio, oefsung.
Cinnamomum, cymin *resina*.
Cicuanus, higrae.
Citonium, goodaepel.
Clauia, borda.
Claua, steng.
Clustella, clustorloc.
Cladica, wefl, *uel* owef.
Clinici, faertyhted.
Clauus caligaris, scohnegl.
Clasis, flota.
Clatrum, pearuc.
Clabatum, gebyrded.
Clus, teltreo.
Clima, half.
Clauicularius, caeghiorde.
Commisura, flycticlad.
Conabulum, cildatrog.
Colonus, gebuur.
Colobium, hom.
Contribulius, meig, *uel sanguine*.
Coceum bistinctum, wiolocread.
Cotizat, tebleth.
Conuexu, hualf.
Conquilium, wilocscel.
Contemtum, heuuendlice.
Conlato, oembecht.
Commeatos, sondæ.
Contubernalis, gepofta.
Coniectura, resung.
Condidit, gesette.

Conuincens, oberstaelende.
Codices, onheawas.
Consutum, gesiowed.
Corimbos, bergan.
5 *Commercium*, ceapstou, gestrion.
Corben, mand.
Conpactis, gegaedradon.
Corbus, cauuel.
Consulo, frigno.
10 *Conuicta*, oberstaeled.
Concidit, toslog.
Conparantem, gegaerwendne.
Coaluissent, suornadun.
Concedam, lytesna.
15 *Coniurati*, gemode.
Contumax, anmood.
Confusione, gemengiunge.
Concesserim, arecte.
Conpar, gehaeplice.
20 *Constipuisse*, gesuedrade.
Conuenio, ic groetu.
Contis, spreotum.
Contos, speoru.
Condicione, raedenne.
25 *Consobrinus*, gesuigran.
Cocleae, lytle sneglas.
Coffinus, mand.
Commentariensis, geroefa.
Cospis, palstr.
30 *Color*, aac.
Corylus, haesl.
Cornacula, crauue.
Cornix, crawe.
Conglutinata, gelimed.
35 *Corimbos*, leactrogas.
Colostrum, beost.
Cocleas, uuiolocas.
Conpos, faegen.
Contentus, geneord.
40 *Commentis*, seorwum.
Cors[2], *numerus militum*, tuun.
Confici, gemængan.
Competentes portiunculas, *i.* gelimplice daele.
45 *Conpagem*, gegederung.
Coituras, gegangendo.

[1] Perhaps for *Eurus*. R W
[2] For *cohors*.

Commanipularius, gescota *uel conscius, socius, collega*.
Consobrinus, sueor.
Corax, hræfn.
Commisura, cimbing.
Cox, hwetestan.
Coxa, thegh.
Conpetum, tuun, þrop.
Colicus, eoburthrote.
Colus, wulfmod.
Conca, mundleu.
Coagolum, ceselyb.
Commolitio, forgrindet.
Concisium, scelle.
Confundit, menget.
Commentum, aþoht.
Conderetur, gewarht.
Conpedium, gescroepnis.
Coleandrum, cellendre.
Colomata, **baetcolae**.
Concha, beme.
Conualuit, geuaerpte.
Consors, orsorg.
Comitauere, togelestunne.
Conclamatus, loma.
Concessit, geuuatu.
Commendabat, trymide.
Condebitores, gescolan.
Concussionibus, raednisse.
Confoti, afoedde.
Conuenientes, seruuende.
Conlisio, slaege.
Coturno, wodhae [1].
Contio, gemoot.
Costa, rib.
Contionatur, madalade, *declamat*.
Consobrinus, filius patruelis, uel moderg̅.
Confutat, oberstaelid.
Conpilat, stilith.
Cornu, ceste.
Conectit, teldat.
Concretum, gerunnen.
Conca, musclan scel.
Coccum, wioloc.

Cocilus, ampre.
Crebrat, siftið.
Crebrum, sibi.
Crucus, gelo.
5 *Cripta*, ascussum.
Crepundia, maenoe.
Cratem, flecta, uel hyrþil.
Crus, scia.
Crabro, waefs, *uel* hurnitu.
10 *Crustula, similis*, haalstaan.
Crama, flete.
Crates, hegas.
Cragacus, **styria**.
Cuniculos, smyglas.
15 *Curiositas*, feorwit, geornis.
Culcites, bed.
Cucumis, popæg.
Culmus, wyrð.
Cureulio, emil.
20 *Cupa*, byden.
Cuba, tunne.
Cummi, teoru.
Culix, mygg.
Cuculus, gaec.
25 *Cucuzata*, lepeuuince.
Culinia, cocas.
Cucuma, fyreruce.
Cuspis, palstr.
Cunae, cildcladas.
30 *Curtina*, wagryft.
Culter, saex.
Cuneus, waecg.
Cuppa, accipiendo, i. beodbollæ.
Cyprinus, forneted cli?
35
Damma, bestia, i. eola.
Defrutum, coerin.
Detulerat, brohte.
Delicatus, wrast.
40 *Destituit*, obgibeht.
Deuotaturus, wergendi.
Desis, suuær.
Desolutus, onsaelid.
Destituunt, townorpon.
45 *Destitutae*, toworpne.

[1] This interpretation of *cothurnus* is rather singular. The glossator appears to have taken *cothurnus* for *coturnix* = *woodhen*. R. W.

Decipula, bisuicfalle.
Decrepita, dobgendi.
Desidebat, unsibbade.
Defatiget, suenceth.
Delumentum, dhuehl.
Deponile, wefta.
Deconfugione, statione, hydae.
Deliberatio, ymbdriodung.
Delicatis et querulis, wrastum end seobgendum.
Defectura, aspringendi.
Decidens, gewitendi.
Debita pensio, gedaebeni geabuli.
Deditio, handgand.
Detractauit, forsooc.
Deuia callus, horweg stig.
Defferuntur, meldadun, *uel* wroegdun.
Dehiscat, tocinit.
Detriturigne, agnidine.
Dentalia, sulesrcost.
Deuinxit, geband.
Decerni, scriben.
Degloberei, flean.
Defotabat, forsuor.
Depraehendo, anfindo.
Desciuit, widstylde, *pedem retraxit.*
Defert, wroegde.
Delectum, cyri, *uel electio.*
Detestare, onseacan.
Detrimentum, wonung.
Degenerauerat, misthagch.
Desisse, tionade.
Degesto, geraedit.
Decreta, gedoht.
Deuota, cystig.
Difortium, [weggedal[1]] repudium.
Diem obiit, asualt.
Dictatorem, aldur.
Dilotis, todaeldum.
Delibutus, gesmirwid.
Dilatio, aelding.
Ditor, gefyrdro.
Dispendium, wom.
Disceptant, flitat.
Dissimulat, midid.
Disparuit, ungeseneweam.

[1] Added in another hand. R. W.

Distabuerunt, asundun.
Discensor, ungedyre.
Dilectum, [meniu] *exercitum.*
Difficile, wearnwislice.
Digitalium musculorum, fingrdoccana.
Dicam, quedol.
Dicas, quedole.
Difnis, suide micel.
Dispensatio, scir.
Dimisis, asclaecadun.
Dicimenta, tacne.
Dispectus, fraecud.
Dignitosa, meodomlice.
Disoluerat, ascaeltte.
Diuinos, uuitgan.
Distitutum, ofgefen.
Distentus, adegen.
Dolatum, gesniden.
Dodrans, egur.
Dolatura, braadlastæcus.
Dos, wituma, *uel* uuetma.
Domatis, huses.
Dolones, hunsporan.
Dromidus, afyred olbenda.
Dromidarius, sc eorodmon.
Dracontia, gimro, *dicitur.*
Dulcissapa, caerin.
Dumus, þyrne.

Eatenus, oddaet.
Ebor, elpendbaan.
Ebredio, hrisle.
Ebulum, walhwyrt.
Echo, wudumer.
Echinus, piscis, uel scel.
Edera, uuduwinde.
Eder, ifegn.
Edilitatem, hamscire.
Edissere, asaecgan.
Effosis, ahlocadum [*enebata,* asuond[2]].
Effetum, ontudri.
Eftafolium, sinfulle.
Eftafylon, gelodwyrt.
Efficaciter, [*uelociter*], fromlice.
Efficax, [*expeditus*], from.

[2] These two words are added in another hand. R. W.

Effectum, deid.
Egre, earfedlice.
Egerere, ascrepan.
Egesta, ascrepen.
Egra, slacce.
Elogio, geddi.
Eluderet, auuægde.
Electrum, elotr.
Eleborus, þung, woedeberge.
Elogia, laac.
Elegans, loquax, smicre.
Eliminat, adytid.
Elimat, gesuirbet.
Empta, geboht.
Empticius, ceapeneht.
Emolumentum, lean, fultum.
Emblema, fothr.
Emunctoria, candeltuist.
Emaones, scinneras.
Emenso, oberfoerde.
Eneruat, asuond.
Enum, cetil.
Enucleata, geondsmead.
Enixa, beorende.
Enixa est, genuit agnam, i. ceolbor lomb.
Eptasyllon[1], gelodwyrt.
Epilenticus, woda.
Eptafolium, sinfulle.
Epimenia, nest.
Ependiten, cop.
Erimio, hindberge.
Erenis [haegtis[2]], *furia.*
Erenditen, cop.
Erpica, egðe.
Erpicarius, egðere.
Erugo, rust.
Errabiles, huerbende.
Ericius, iil.
Esculus, bocce.
Euiscerata, athed.
E uestigio, [on lande], on laste.
Euidens, seotol.
Eurynis, walcyrge.
Eumenides, haehtisse.
Expeditus, abundæn.

Eximet, alieset.
Exegestus, gebero.
Expendisse, araefnde.
Exundauit, auueol.
5 *Experimentum,* andwisnis.
Exercitiis, bigangum.
Exorti, adræsti.
Exposito, geborone.
Exaltauit, stone.
10 *Expedisset,* drowode.
Expedierant, araeddun.
Exito, perditio, endistaeb.
Exoleuerunt, gesuedradun.
Ex phalange, [of dreote], of foedan.
15 *Exauctorauit,* geheende.
Expilatam, [aþryid], arytrid.
Expeditio, faerd.
Exintera, ansceat.
Explodit, excludit, atyniδ.
20 *Exagium,* andmitta.
Extale, snaedilþearm.
Exilia, gestinceum.
Expeditis, gearuum.
Exta, lesen.
25 *Exenium,* laac.
Exactor, scultheta.
Excolat, siid.
Exta, precordia, baccþearm.
Examusim, [geornlice], *absolute, certe*
30 *uel exquisite.*
Exorbitans, asuab.
Exalaparetur, suungen.
Extipices, haelsent.
Expensa, daeguuini.
35 *Exerta lingua,* naec[a]d tunge.
Excesus, egylt.
Exigebant, araefndun.
Expeditionibus, ferdun.
Examen, sue[a]rm.
40 *Extorres,* wraeccan.
Exactio, geabulesmonung.
Expediam, arecio.
Excubias, weardseld.
Expendere, to ascodenne.
45 *Exugia,* gescincio.
Expilatam, arydid.

[1] For *eptafyllon.* R. W.

[2] Added in another hand. R. W.

Expræsserunt, arehtun.
Exerceri, wesan draegtre.
Exercitatae, dare getyhtan.
Expeditio, hergiung.
Exactum, baedde.
Expeditus, *uelox*, [snel], *fortis*.

Facetia, glio.
Falc, walhhabuc.
Fasces [*libri*], goduueb.
Fagus, bocce.
Fastidium [*odium*], cymnis.
Fasianus, worhona.
Fascias, wedel.
Famfaluca, [faam], leasung.
Fasciarum, suaedila.
Falcis, wudubil, side, riftras.
Famfaluca, wapul.
Falcastrum, wudubil.
Faonius, westsudwind.
Festinatio[1], malscrung.
Falarica, ægtæro[2]
Falanx, foeda.
Farius, faag.
Facessit, suedrad.
Farsa, aerummen.
Fauo, bean.
Fasces, cynedomas.
Fastu, uulencu
Fabrile, smidlice.
Farelas, hryste.
Falerata, gehyrsti.
Feruginius, greig.
Ferox, roede, *ferae similis*.
Ferculum, disc, *uasculum*.
Ferinum, hold.
Feriatus, gerested
Fenus, spe[a]rua.
Foenus, borg.
Foederatus, getriowad.
Faecce, maere.
Fespa, waefs.
Fefellit, uuegid.
Ferula, aesedrote.
Fellus, catte.

Fenum, graes.
Ferrugine, iserngrei.
Ferruginem, *obscuritatem ferri*, i. om.
Fiber[3], bebr.
5 *Fiscilla*, taenil.
Fida, stearn
Fibra, þearm.
Filix, fearn.
Fiscillus, stictenel.
10 *Fibrae*, librlaeppan.
Fibula, hringesigl.
Fiscillis, sprinclum.
Filum, dred.
Finicia, beosu.
15 *Ficetula*, sugga.
Fibrans, risende.
Fiscalis, redagebellicum (?), wægn-
 fearu.
Fimum, goor.
20 *Fictis*, faenum.
Fistulis, þeotum.
Figite, suidigad.
Filiaster, steopsunu.
Flauum, *fuluum*, read.
25 *Flegmata*, horh.
Flabanus, suan.
Flabum, geolu.
Flagris, suiopum.
Flamma, blæd.
30 *Floccus*, loca.
Flauescit, glitinat, *albescit*.
Flagrans, stincendi.
Flebotoma, blodsaex.
Fortuna, wyrd.
35 *Forfices*, scerero.
Fouet, feormat, broedeth.
Foederatas, getreuuade.
Fornicem, bogan.
Formido, anoda.
40 *Forfex*, isern sceruru[4].
Fors wyrd.
Forceps, tong.
Fornacula, cyline heorde.
Foras, bolcan.
45 *Fortex*, edwelle.

[1] The MS. has *festinatio*. — R W.
[2] For *atgær*, a short spear or javelin, a kind of dart. Cf. p. 23, 15 *framea*.
[3] For *biber*.
[4] Cf. *forfices*. R. W.

Fornis, bogo, *supercolumnis.*
Follis, blaesbaelg.
Fornaculum, here.
Formaticus, cese, *a forma.*
Fronulus, linetuigle.
Fratuelis, geaduling.
Fratuelis, suhterga¹.
Fratuelis, broðorsunu.
Frugus, uncystig, heamul.
Frixum, afigaen.
Fraga, obet.
Fraxinus, aesc.
Fringella, finc.
Frutectum, lose, *locus ubi ponunt.*
Framea, ætgaeru.
Fons, hleor.
Fretus, bald.
Fragor, suoeg, cirm.
Fraudulenter, faeccnlice.
Frontuosus, bald.
Frutina, fultemend.
Fuscinula, awel.
Furcimen, waergrood.
Furbum, bruun.
Fundi, grundus.
Funalia, condel.
Fusum, spinel.
Fucus, faex, taelg.
Fusarius, wananbeam.
Funix², gonot, *uel* doppa, enid.
Furuncus, meard.
Fungus, suom.
Funda, lidre.
Furfures, sifiðan.
Funestauere, smiton.
Funestissima, ða deaðlicustan.
Funalia, cerei, waexcondel.
Fulgine, sooth.
Furia, haehtis.

Gargarizet, gagulsuille³.
Garrit, gionat.
Gannatura, gliu.
Galla, galluc.

Garula, crauue.
Garbas, sceabas.
Galmaria, caluuer.
Galmum, moling.
5 *Galmulum,* molegnstyeci.
Galmilla, liimcaluuer.
Gabea⁴, me[a]u.
Gabalacrum, calwer.
Gestus, gebero.
10 *Generosus,* aeðile.
Genista, brom.
Gente, wildegoos.
Genuino, tusc, *naturale.*
Genas, heagaspen.
15 *Gente,* wildegoos.
Gelum, forst.
Geumatrix, geac.
Giluus, geolu.
Gillus, grei.
20 *Gipsus,* spaeren.
Gippus, hofr.
Giluus, falu.
Gilbus, gyrno.
Gingria, spon.
25 *Glis,* egle.
Globus, leoma.
Glarea, cisilstan.
Gladiolum, saecg.
Glitilia, clife.
30 *Glomer,* clouue.
Glus, freenis.
Glaucum, heauui, grei.
Glandula, cirnel.
Glebo, unwis.
35 *Gladiatores,* cempan.
Gluten, teoru.
Gripem, gig.
Grillus, hama.
Gremen, faethm.
40 *Gramen,* quice.
Grassator, forbergend.
Grallus, brooc.
Gracilis, smæl.
Gregariorum, unaeðilsa.

¹ See Grein, sprachschatz der ags. dichter II, pag. 493. *fratuelis* for *fratruelis.* R. W.
² For *Phoenix*? R. W.
³ Cfr. *gagulsuole* meaning lascivions heat, burning; *gagolbærnes* = wantonness; and *iagul* = *gargarismus.* R. W.
⁴ For *gavia* = *larus,* gull, Germ. möve. R. W.

Gregatim, wearnmelum.
Grus, gruis, cornoch.
Grauis, cornue.
Graffium, græf.
Grunnire, grunnettan.
Graticium, wagflecta.
Gurgulio, ðrotbolla.
Gurgustium, ceosol.
Gurgustiore[1], cetan.
Gurgulio[2], emil.
Gunna, heden.

Hastilia telorum, scaeptloan.
Habitudines, geberu.
Harundo, canna, hreod.
Haustum, drync.
Habenis, gewaldleðrum.
Habile, lioðuwac.
Heus! geheresthu.
Hebitatus, astyntid.
Hebesceret, asuand.
Hebitabit, asclacade.
Heia, welga.
Herodius, walchhabuc.
Hersutum, drustum.
Helleborus, woidiberge.
Herinis[3], walerigge.
Hebetat, styntid.
Hiulca, cinendi.
Hibiscum, biscopuuyrt.
Hirundo, sualuue.
Histrix, iil.
Hinnitus, hnaeggiung.
Hyna, naectgenge.
Holor, suan.
Hora, sueg.
Horno, þysgere.
Hoctatus, gelaechtrad.
Horno, þysgere.
Holido, fule.
Honeraria, hlaestscip.
Huscide, tolice.
Humase, bimyldan.
Hyadas, raedgasram.

Hymeneos, hæmedo.
Ibices, firgengaet.
Idoneus, oxstaelde.
Igni sacrum, oman.
5 *Ignarium*, aalgewére.
Ilia, midhridir, niodanweard hype.
Illic, þanan.
Imbricibus, þaectigilum.
Inergumenos, wodan.
10 *Indruticans*, wraestendi.
Inians, grædig.
Inpetigo, teter.
Inextricabilis, untosliten.
Inluuies secundarum, hama, *in quo*
15 *fit paruulus*.
Incommodum, unbryce.
Inprouuisu, feringa.
Infestatio, unlioþuwacnis.
Infula, uueorðmynd.
20 *Inminente*, aetweosendre.
Infestus, gemenged.
Ingesta, ondoen.
Inola, eolene.
Intestinum, þearm.
25 *Interamen*, inifli[4].
Instites, suedelas.
Infima, niol.
Intexunt, wundun.
Inlex, tyctendi.
30 *Interim*, þrage.
Increpitans, hleoþrendi.
Infestus, flach.
Interceptum, arasad.
Interceptio, raepsung[5].
35 *Infandum*, manful.
Inlecebris, tychtingum.
Ingratus, lað.
Incuda, onfilti.
Inritatus, gegremid.
40 *Incitamenta*, tyhtinne.
Interasile, interana, glyffa.
Intula, uualhwyrt.
Inprobus, gemah.
Ingruerit, onhriosed.

[1] Perhaps for *gurgustia*, cf. Bosworth 22 c. R. W.
[2] For *curculio*.
[3] For *Erinnys*, the wælcyrig.

[4] Inelf or lulif means *viscera, interanea*. R. W.
[5] Perhaps ræfsung in the MS. R. W.

Inruens, þerende.
Intractabilis, unlioþuwac.
Inmunes, orceas.
In procinctu, in ðegnunge.
Intercepit, ræfsde.
Intercepit, fornoom
Interceptum est, racfsit waes.
Insimulatione, feringe.
Inpendebatur, geben waes.
Interpellare, raefsit.
Industria, geornis.
Inpendebat, salde.
In dies crudesceret, aforht.
In transmigrationem, in foernisse.
Iners, esuind [1], asolcen.
Interuentu, þingunge.
Inlectus, getyhtid.
Interlitam, bismiride.
Inpactae, onligenre.
Indigestae, unobereumenre.
Innitentes, widerhlingende.
Insolesceret, oberuuenide.
Inpulsore, baedendre.
Infractus, ungeuuemmid.
Inopimum, unasaedde.
Inditas, da gesettan.
Infici, gemengde.
Index, tacnendi, torctendi.
Inposterem [2], bisuuicend.
Inter primores, bitu [3] aeldrum.
Intercapido, firstmaere.
Insolens, foruuened.
In curia, in maedle.
Incuba, maere.
In mimo, in gliowe.
Inuisus, lath.
In estiuo cenaculi, yppe, *ubi per estatem frigus captant.*
Inuolucus, uulluc.
Inuoluco, uudubinde.
Inquilinis, geneaot [4].
Indolis, hyhtful, *uel* dieadi.
Infridat, kaelid [5]

Inruit, raesde.
Inpingit, smat, gemaercode.
Incentor, tyhtend.
Incantata, gegaelen.
5 *Incantatores,* galdriggan.
Infestationes, tionan.
Intercapidine, ginnisse.
Inundatio, gyte.
Incurrus, ongong.
10 *Inbuit,* onreod.
Infastum, sliden.
Inruptio, ongong.
Innixus, strimendi.
Incanduit, auueoll.
15 *Ineptus,* gemædid.
Intrinicio, forsliet.
Insirtim, insondgewearp.
Innitor, onhlingo [6].
Inficio, blondu.
20 *Infula,* uyrðo.
Inmoratur, wunat.
Infectum, geblonden.
Indomitus, wilde.
Instincta, onsuapen.
25 *Intransmeabili,* unoferfoer.
Inbellem, orwige.
Internicium bellum dicitur quo nullus remanet, utcualm.
Inulus, hindcaelf.
30 *In catamo,* in bæce.
Initiatum, gestoepid.
Intimandum, to cyðenne.
Iota, sochtha [7].
Jouem, þuner.
35 *Irridabant,* tyhton.
Irritum, forhogd, *inanem.*
Isic, laex.
Isca, tyndrin.
Istic, uueðer.
40 *Istuc,* hider.
Jungetum, riscðyfel.
Jurisperiti, redboran.
Jubar, earendel.

[1] For *asuind.* R. W.
[2] No doubt an error for *impostorem* R W.
[3] For *bitun, bitwin.* R. W.
[4] For *geneat colonus.* R. W.

[5] For *infrigidat.* R. W.
[6] For *onhlinie* or *onhlinio.* Cf. Beda III, 17. R. W.
[7] Perhaps an error for *iochda.* Somn.

Jugum, cnol.
Junctura, foeging.
Juuentus[1], midferh.
Juncus, risc.
Jubar, leoma.

Labrum, segn.
Larbula, egisgrima.
Lacerna, haecile, *uel* loda.
Lacessit, gremid.
*Laogoena*², crog.
Latrina, genge, groepe, *atqueductus, cloacas.*
Laudae[3], laurice.
Lacessitus, gegremid.
Læxiua, laeg.
Lacesso, suto.
Laquear, firsthrof.
Lanx, heolor.
Lanucar, flode.
Lactuca, þudistel.
Lacunar, hebenhus.
Lapatium[4], lelodrae.
Lacerta, adexe.
Larus, meau.
Lappa, clibe.
Latex, burne.
Laena, rift.
Labat, weagat.
Lana, uul.
Laquearia, firste.
Latratus, bercae.
Laudariulus, frecmase.
Ladascapiae, briensis, i. hondwyrm.
Lanterna, lehtfaet.
Lacessere, gremman.
Lepor, wood.
Lebes, huer.
Lenta, toh.
Lenocinium, tyhten.
Legit, collegit, lisit.
Lembum, listan[5].

Legula, gyrdilshringe.
Lendina, hnitu[6].
Leuir, tacur.
Lectidiclatum, geþuorneflete.
5 *Lepus, leporis,* hara.
Lentum uimen, tohgærd.
Lenticula, piose.
Lesta, borda.
Lenirent, afroebirdun[7].
10 *Ligones*, meottucas.
Liburnices, gerec.
Ligustrum, hunigsuge.
Liuida toxica, da wonnan aetrinan.
Liquentes, hlutre.
15 *Lien*, milte.
Libertabus, frioletan.
Liciatorium, hebelgerd.
Limax, snegl.
Limphaticus, woedendi.
20 *Lituus*, cryc.
Licidus, huæt.
Libertus, frioleta.
Linter, baat.
Lingula, gyrdilshringe.
25 *Limus*, laam.
Limbus, dres, liste.
Liberalitas, roopnis.
Lihargum, slaegu[8].
Linea, waebtaeg.
30 *Licium*, hebeld.
Licia, hebeld, dred.
Lima, fiil.
Lolium, ate.
Lotium, hlond.
35 *Lodix*, loda.
Locusta, lopust.
Luscus, anege.
Lucor, freceo.
Lurcones, siras.
40 *Lunulus*, mene, scillingas.
Luculentum, torhtnis.
Lumbare, gyrdilsbroec.

[1] An error for *juuencus*. R. W.
[2] For *lagena*. R. W.
[3] For *alaudae*. R. W.
[4] For *lapathum*. R. W.
[5] *list* means *a list of cloth, limbus panni.* Cf. *limbus*. R. W.

[6] *hutu* is corrected to *hnitu* in the MS. R. W.
[7] For *afroefredun*. R. W.
[8] For *letharqum*, cf. *slagu.* Bosw. 64 j. R. W.

Ludi litterari, staefplagan.
Lutraos, otr
Lucius, haecid.
Lupatis, bridelsum.
Lucanica, mærh.
Lurdus, lemphalt.
Lupus, brer [1].
Ludarius, steor.
Lumbricus, regnwyrm.
Luteum, crohha.
Lupercal, haerg.
Lumbus, side.
Luscinia, naectegale.
Luscinius, forsc.
Lupus, wulf.
Lupa, wylf.
Lupinare, uulfholu.
Lumbulos, lendebrede.
Lymphatico, woedendi.
Lymbo, dresi.

Manipulatim, þreatmelum.
Mancus, anhendi.
Maforte [2], scyfla.
Manes, dede.
Manica, glof.
Manile, lebil.
Manitergium, lin.
Margo, obr.
Malagma, salf.
Malus, apuldur.
Mandras, eouuistras.
Maceratus, þreatende.
Mastigium, suiopan.
Manubium, waelreaf.
Manticum, hondfulbeowes.
Masca, grima.
Mascus, **grima**.
Marsopicus, fina.
Marsuppia, ceodas.
Marruca, snegl.

Maiales, bearug.
Mango, mengo.
Maulistis, scyend.
Mastice, huiteudu.
5 *Malua*, hoce, cottue, *uel* gearwanleaf.
M[ar]ubium, biowyrt, *uel* hune.
Matrix, quida.
Massa, clyne.
Mapalia, byre [3].
10 *Mars, Martis*, tiig [4].
Magalia, byre.
Macilentus, gefaested.
Manere, bidan.
Madidum, obdaenit.
15 *Madefacta*, geuueted.
Machinamenta, ordone.
Mantega, taeg.
Malas, gebsias.
Mendacio conposito, geregnade.
20 *Meatim*, meomore [5].
Melarium, mirc apuldur.
Melodium, suinsung.
Melito, meditor, meadrobordan.
Mergulus, scalfur.
25 *Merx*, mertze.
Mereo, groeto.
Merula, oslæ.
Megale [6], hearma.
Medulla, merg.
30 *Mercurium*, woden.
Mentagra, bituihn.
Merga, scraeb.
Metricius, mederwyrhta.
Miluus, glioda.
35 *Milium*, miil.
Mirifillo [7], gearwe.
Minopora, deofscip [8].
Minaci, hlibendri.
Mitra, haet.
40 *Mordicos*, bibitne.
Molestissimum, earbetlicust.

---

[1] *lupus* denotes *a brier*. R. W.
[2] An error for *Mauors = instigator*.
[3] Perhaps an error for *byri* (byrig) *castella, domus*. R. W.
[4] Tiig or Tiw was the Anglo-Saxon god of war. R. W.
[5] The meaning of *meomor* is *skilful*, expert. R. W.
[6] For *megalium* a salve. *Hearma* denotes a sling for supporting a wounded arm. R. W.
[7] For *millefolio*. R. W.
[8] *deofscip* means *nauis piratica* a ship used by pirates. R. W.

Monarchia, anuualda.
Morgit[1], milcit.
Mosiclum, ragu.
Momentum, scytel.
Molibus, ormetum.
Mordacius, clouae.
Mouebor, styrid.
Moles, falthing.
Molosus, rodhund.
Morenula, eil.
Mosicum, ragu.
Mora, heorotberge.
Municeps, burgliod.
Munifica, cystigan.
Murica, gespon.
Murenula, bool.
Muluctra, ceoldre.
Munila, baeg.
Muscipula, muusfalle.
Mucro, mece.
Mugil, haeced.
Musiranus[2], screauua.
Mustela, uueosule.
Mulio, horsdegn.
Mugil, heardhara.
Mulgit, milcit.
Mus, muris, muus.
Multabitur, uuitnath.
Murilium, byrgen.
Musca[3], egesgrima.
Musica, myrgnis.
Murice, wurman.
Musca, flege.
Murus, braer.
Myrius, uuir.

Naus[a]tio, uulatunc.
Nauiter, horsclice.
Nastartium[4], tuuncressa.
Napta[5], blaecteoru.
Napta[5], tynder.
Nauus[6], *pumilio*, duerg.

Napis, naep.
Nazarei, loccas.
Nabulum, ferescaet.
Nauiter, suidfromlice.
5 *Neptam*[5], tyndre.
Netila[7], hearma.
Nepa, haebern.
Negotia, unemetta.
Nebulonis, scinlaecan.
10 *Nequiquam*, holunga.
Netum, gesiuwid.
Neruus, sionu.
Necabantur, aqualdun.
Nitorium, spinil.
15 *Nymbus*, storm.
Ninguit, sniwid[8].
Nigra spina, slaghdorn.
Nixu, werdeode.
Noctua, ulula, ule.
20 *Nomisma*, mynit.
Noctua, naehthraefn.
Naualia, faelging.
Non subsciuum, unfaecni.
Nodus, wrasan, ost.
25 *Notae*, speccan.
Notatus, oncunnen.
Nouerca, steopmoder.
Noma[9], rihtebred.
Numularius, nummorum praerogatur,
30 miyniteri.
Nurus, snoro.
Nux, hnutbeam.
Nugacitas, unnytnis.
Nucli, cirulas.
35 *Nullo negotio*, naenge earbede.
Numquid, nehuruis.

Obolitio[10], edung.
Obsides, gislas.
40 *Obrizum*, smaetegold.
Obriguit, gefreos.
Obliquum, scytehald.

[1] No doubt, an error for *molgit* or *mulget*. R. W.
[2] An error for *mus araneus*. R. W.
[3] For *masca*. R. W.
[4] For *nasturcium*. R. W.
[5] For *naphtha*. R. W.
[6] No doubt, an error for *nanus*. R. W.
[7] For *mitella*, I suppose. R. W.
[8] The MS. has: suwid. R. W.
[9] An error for *norma*. R. W.
[10] For *abolitio*. R. W.

Obnixus, strimendi.
Obreptione, criopunge.
Obestrum[1], bcost.
Optimates, gesiðas.
Obuncans, genyclede.
Obtenuit, forcuom, bigaet.
Obnixe, geornlice.
Obunca, crump.
Obuix[2], wiðerstal.
Obligamentum, lyb, lybsn[3].
Obstruit, fordytte.
Obiecte, ongensette.
Obiectus, uuitsetnis.
Obruere, oberurecan.
Obsedatus, gislhada.
Obturat, folclaemid.
Obtinuit, ofercuom.
Obiectionibus, gestalum.
Obnoxius, scyldig.
Obex, ogengel.
Obicula, geocstecca.
Occupauit, onette.
Ocreis, baangeberg.
Occa, faelging.
Occubuit, gecrong.
Occiput, hnecca.
Occabat, egide.
Ocearium, staeli.
Offendit, moette.
Offirmans[4], claemende.
Officit, werdit.
Ogastrum[5], aeggimong.
Olor, suon.
Oligia, nettae.
Olgastrum, aeggimong.
Olor, cienus, aelbitu[6].
Olim, singale.
Olastrum, staeb.
Omni modo, oeghwelce ðinga.

Omentum, maffa.
Omen, hael.
Onocratallus[7], feolufer.
Opilauit, forclæmde[8].
5 *Oppilauit clausit*, gegiscte.
Opinare[9], resigan.
Oportunitatem, gehydnis.
Opere plumario, hisiudi werci[10].
Oppilatae, bisparade.
10 *Origanum*, wurmille.
Oridanum[11], eolone.
Orcus, orc.
Oresta, ðres.
Oripilatio, celiwearte.
15 *Orcus*, ðyrs, heldiobul.
Ordinatissimam, þa gesettan.
Orbita, hueolrad.
Ortigomera, edischen.
Oratores, spelbodan.
20 *Ordinatus*, gehaeplice.
Or, onginnendi.
Orion, eburdring.
Orbia, sifan, utunda.
Orbitae, last.
25 *Oscillae*, totridan.
Oscitantes, geongendi.
Osma, suice.
Ostriger, bruunbeosu.

30 *Patrimonium*, gestrion.
Partim, sume daeli.
Palpitans, brogdetende.
Particulatim, styccimelum.
*Paludamentum, genus uestimenti bel-
35 lici*, haecile.
Patrocinium, mundbyrd.
Paraninphus, dryhtguma.
Palestra, placga.
Pastinare, settan.

---

[1] No doubt, au error for *colostrum*. R. W.

[2] For *obex*. R. W.

[3] Cf. Bosw. Dict. s. v. lib, libesne, lifesne. R. W.

[4] It seems evident from the Anglo-Saxon interpretation that this should be *affirmans*. *Offirmare* means to be stiff-necked, obstinate. R. W.

[5] Cf. *olgastrum*. R. W.

[6] Cf. Bosw. 970: ylfete, ylfetu a swan, *olor, cygnus*. R. W.

[7] *Onocrotallus* means *a pelican*. R. W.

[8] Cf. *obturat* folclæmid. R. W.

[9] For *opinari*. R. W.

[10] besiwian, bistwian means to sew together, to join; *jungere*. Bisiwed feþergeweore, Cot. 145. Cf Bosworth 161. R. W.

[11] An error for *origanum*, wild marjoram. R. W.

Palatina, raecedlic.
Panice, ruseam [1].
Parcæ, wyrde.
Parcas, burgrune.
Parabsides, gauutan.
Palearibus [2], deadraegelum.
Palas [3], scoble.
Papilio, fiffalde.
Papula, wearte.
Pampinus, crous.
Papilluus, wioluescel [4].
Palingenesean, edscaeft.
Paneta, holoponne.
Paneta, disc.
Paupilius [5], scaldhulas.
Papula, spryng.
Pandis, geapum.
Patruus, faedra.
Patruelis, faedran sunu.
Patruelis, geaduling.
Paxillum, palum, naegl.
Panpila, wibl.
Panuculum, uuefl.
Palagra, ecilma [6].
Pascsos, geroscade.
Pastinaca, wallmore.
P[a]pirum, eorisc.
Pangebant, faedun.
Palla, rift.
Parula, mase.
Papilio, buterflege.
Paliurus, sinfulle.
Pauo, pauua.
Passus, faedm, uel tuegen stridi.
Palumbes, cuscote.
Pastellus, hunigaeppel.
Pansa, scaffoot [7].
Paranymphus, dryhtguma.
Parumper, huonhlot[um].
Patera, fiola.
Papauer, popei.

Pariter, gelice.
Paruca, hicae.
Palpantum, olectendra.
Palmula, steorrodor.
5 *Parricidio*, megcualm.
Paciscitur, gedingadon.
Palagdrigus, ecilmehti.
Partigatum, uuduhona.
Palina [8], hran.
10 *Paleae*, aegnan.
Pabulatores, horshiordas.
Passim, styccimelum.
Partica, reodnaesc.
Perstrenue, fromlice.
15 *Pedisequa*, dignen.
Perpessum est, adroten is.
Perfidia, treuleasnis.
Percommoda, suacenlic, *matutinos*, morgenlic.
20 *Percrebuit*, **merewear****d**.
Perduellium, þorh gefeht.
Perseudoterum [9], ðorh ludgæt.
Percitus, hræd.
Pelices, cebise.
25 *Penduloso*, haldi.
Permixtum, gemengetlic.
Pertinaciter, annuillice.
Pessum, spilth.
Petisse, sohte.
30 *Peranticipationem*, dorh obst.
Peruispellones [10], ðorh byrgeras.
Perpendiculum, coldred.
Per hironiam [11], dorh hosp.
Perna, flicci.
35 *Pedo*, uel *paturum*, feotur.
Perpendiculum, pundur.
Pedor, reorum [12].
Penuria, wedl.
Percellitur, bid slaegen.
40 *Peruicax*, drochtig.
Pero, himming.

[1] Cf. Bosworth, pag. 295 (56⁰). R. W.
[2] For *pallaribus*. R. W.
[3] For *pala*. R. W.
[4] *wioluescel* denotes a shell-fish. R. W.
[5] = *pampinus*. R. W.
[6] Cf. *palagdrigus*. R. W.
[7] The meaning of *scaffoot* is splay- or broad- footed. R. W.

[8] For *balaena*, φάλαινα, I suppose. R.W.
[9] For *per pseudothyrum*. R. W.
[10] For *per uespillones*. R. W.
[11] For *ironiam*. R. W.
[12] For *reorung* = *mussitatio*, I suppose. R. W.

Pessum, clifhlep.
Pessul, haeca.
*Peducla*¹, luus.
Petrafocaria, flint.
Pendulus, ridusende.
Pella, sadulfelge.
Pecten, camb.
Percellitur, slaegen.
Pes, fot.
Perstant, tioludun.
Persoluio, ic drouuio.
Petulans, wraene.
Perpendit, aehtad.
Perstromata, ornamenta, steba.
Pendulus, ohældi.
Pellis, fel.
Perpes, hraed.
Petuita, sped².
Pectica, slahae.
Philosophus, uduuta.
*Phisillos*³, leceas.
Phitecus, apa.
Piraticam, wicinesccadan.
Pituita, gebrec⁴.
Pice saeuo, unamælte smeoruue.
Pingit, faehit.
*Pistrimum*⁵, cofa.
Pila, thothr.
Pittacium, osperi, clut, cleot.
Pisum, piosan.
Pistrilla, cofincel.
Pillentes, bere.
Pirus, pirge.
Pinus, furhwudu.
Pictus acu, mid nethle asiowid.
Picus, higre, fina.
Pix, picis, pic.
Pilus, her.

Piceca, neb.
Piscis, fisc.
Pistillus, gnidil.
*Plunas*⁶, plumtreu.
5 *Pliadas*, sibunsterri.
Plantago, uuegbrade.
Platisa, flooc.
Plectra, auunden.
Plataria, setin.
10 *Plus minus*, ymb dæt.
Polenta, smeodoma.
Postena, boga.
Portio, hlyte.
Populus, birce.
15 *Politis*, smoedum.
Portentum, scin.
Pilimita, hringfaag.
Porfyrio, feolufer.
Porcopiscis, styrga.
20 *Porcaster*, foor.
Porcellus, faerh.
*Pollux*⁷, duma.
*Poleo*⁸, scaebe.
Pollinis, gruiit⁹.
25 *Pollis*, grytt.
Papauer, popæg.
Posthumus, unlab.
Polentum, fahame.
Pons, bryeg.
30 *Procax*, huuæl.
Probum, seuuin.
Procuratio, sciir¹⁰.
Promulserit, lidercade.
Profusis, genythfullum.
35 *Promulgarunt*, scribun.
Prouehit, gefremid.
Procaptu, fenge.
Promaritima, saegeseotu.

---

¹ For *pediculus*. R. W.
² For *pituita* = phlegm, catarrh, rheum. R. W.
³ For *physicos*. R. W.
⁴ This explanation of *pituita* is rather singular. *Gebrec* commonly denotes a noise; here perhaps sneezing, sternutation. Cf. *reuma*. R. W.
⁵ For *pistrinum*. R. W.
⁶ For *prunus*. R. W.
⁷ An error for *pollex*. R. W.
⁸ For *polio*. R. W.
⁹ *gruiit* seems to be the same word as *grut* or *grytt*. R. W.
¹⁰ *scir* denotes as well a shire, county, province as the superintendence of a province = *praefectura*, superintendence, care, charge. R. W.

Praetextatus, gegeruuid.
Propropera[1], fraehraede.
Priuigna, nift.
Proscripsit, faerred.
Propensior, tylg.
Profligatis, forslaegenum.
Praerupta, staegilre.
Probus[2], ferht.
Proterunt, tredun.
Proterentem, naetendne.
Praefectae, frodre[3].
Profecta, gefremid·
Praecipitat, ascufid.
Praecipita, afael.
Praefaricator[4], receileas.
Praestantior, fromra.
Praesidium, spoed.
Praestante, fremmendum.
Proteri, brecan.
Praxinus, uiridus color uel æsc.
Prosapia, obcuiorisse.
Presetuas, byrga.
Pruina, hrim.
Pretersorim, **paad**.
Prifeta, driuuintra steor.
Prifignus, nefa.
Prouehitur, fremid
Prunas, gloede.
Prurigo, gycenis.
Pronus, nihold[5].
Pronuba, heordsuacpe.
Prodimur, birednæ.
Proflicta, forslægen.
Praeuentus, spoed.
Prunus, plumæ.
Progna, sualuue.
Praesorium, pund[6].

Prorostris, haehsedlum.
Praeceps, trondendi[7].
5 *Procus*, brydguma.
Prodigus, stryndere.
Praesumtio, forenyme.
Propugnaculum, briostbiorg.
Proueho, fyrdru.
10 *Proceres*, geroefan.
Propero, hraede.
Praetersorium, paad[8].
Ptysones, berecorn[9] beorende.
Putamina, hnyglan[10].
15 *Pudor*, scomo.
Pugiles, qui feriunt puncto, cosp[11].
Pulenta, briig.
Pustula, oncgseta.
Pus[12], uuorm.
Pulix, flæh.
20 *Pullentum*, fahame[13].
Puntus, brond.
Pulleium, duergedostle.
Pullus, brid.
Pulla, blaco.
25

Qualus, mand.
Quadripertitum, cocunung
Quacumque, suae suide.
Quantisper, suae suide.
30 *Quaternio*, quatern.
Quadrare, geeblicadun.
Quin etiam, aecdon.
Quisquiliæ, aegnan[14].
Quinquefolium, hraefnesfoot.
35 *Quinqueneruia*, leciwyrt[15].
Quintus, giululing.
Quocumque modo, gehwelci wega.
Quoquo modo, aengeþinga.

[1] For *propera*. The first part of the Anglo-Saxon composition is fræ = freo, meaning *celeriter*. Cf. *propero*. R. W.
[2] Perhaps an error for *phobus* = φόβος?
R W
[3] The meaning of *frod* is: wise, prudent. R. W.
[4] For *praevaricator*. R. W.
[5] The Anglo-Saxon equivalent seems to be 'igbold'. Wright reads 'nihold'. R. W.
[6] *Pund* denotes a fold, *septum*. R. W.
[7] Cf. Leo, Angelsächsisches Glossar II., 190, 25. R. W.

[8] *paad* means a smock-frock or shirt. *Tergoro* has the meaning of to cover over, to clothe. R. W.
[9] A grain of barley. R W.
[10] Cf. Bosworth 376. R. W.
[11] *Cosp* denotes a fetter. R. W.
[12] *Pus* means the matter, corruption of an ulcer. R. W.
[13] Cf. *polentum*. R. W.
[14] Cf. *paleae*. R. W.
[15] Or *læcewyrt*; cf. Leo, Gloss. 20, 9; 451, 16; 500, 12. R. W.

Raster [1], egide.
Rancidis, bitrum.
Radius, hrisl.
Rabulus [2], flitere in eobotum.
Rationato, ambaect.
Rabies, geris.
Rancor, troh.
Rastros, mettocas.
Ramnus, deofedorn.
Radio, gabulrond.
Renunculus, lundlaga.
Retentare, stouuigan.
Rema [3], stream.
Refugium, geberg.
Resina, teoru.
Reuma, gebrec.
Reses, slaec.
Respuplica, cynedoom.
Relatu, spelli.
Reciprocato, gestaefnendre.
Reclines, suaehalde.
Recessus, heolstras.
Remota, from adoenre.
Reserat, onlaec.
Remex, roedra.
Repagula, sale.
Reciprocis, wrixlindum.
Relatio, edcuide.
Retorto, gedraune [4].
Renis, hedir.
Rediua, aettaelg.
Reuerant, spunnun.
Respectus, etsith.
Reponile, gearnuuinde.
Reliunculas [5], resunge.
Rictus, grennung.
Rimosa, cionecti.
Rien [6], laendino.
Rima, getael.
Rigore, heardnisse.
Ridimiculae [7], cynewiddan.

Rigentia, forclingendu.
Ripariolus, staedsuualwe.
Roscinia, naectegale.
Rodinope, lelothrae.
5 *Rostrum*, neb, *uel* scipes caeli.
Robor, arbor, aac.
Rostratum, tindecte.
Rostris, foreuuallum, *uel* tindum.
Roscido, deawe.
10 *Rostri*, tindas.
Rotrum, nabogar [8].
Runcina, locer, sceaba.
Rumex, edric.
Rubigo, broud, oom.
15 *Ruber*, read.
Ruscus, cnioholen.
Rubisca saeltna.
Rubisca, raedda, *rabisca*.

20 *Sablo*, molde.
Salebrae, þuerhfyri [9].
Sartago, brediponne.
Sarcinatum, gesiouuid.
Sarculum, uueodhoc.
25 *Sartatecta*, gefoegnisse.
Saeuo, unslit, smeoro [10].
Salix, salh.
Sagax, gleu.
Sarmentum, spraec.
30 *Salibaribus*, midlum.
Sarcofago, licbeorg.
Sacellorum, haerga.
Sarcio, siouu.
Sarcinatum, gesiowid.
35 *Sambucus*, ellaern.
Sandalium, scete, loda.
Samburus, sueglhoru.
Salum, haeb.
Sagulum, loda.
40 *Sanguinis*, cniorisse [11].
Sardinas, heringas.

[1] Or *rastrum*. R. W.
[2] For *rabula*. The meaning of this word is a pettifogger, wrangler in actions, causes (in eobotum or eofotum). R. W.
[3] An error for rheuma, I suppose. R. W.
[4] For gedrawene. R. W.
[5] For *ratiunculas*. R. W.
[6] For *ren*. R. W.

[7] For *redimicula* a royal wreath, a diadem. R. W
[8] *nafogar* denotes an auger, a wimble. R W.
[9] The same as þurhfaru. R W
[10] Cf. *Pice saeuo* and *seuo*.
[11] The meaning of this word is a family, generation. R. W.

Saginabant, maestun.
Sandix[1], uueard.
Sardas, smeltas.
Saliunca, sure.
Salum, seeg, *uel mare*.
Salsa, sure.
Sarabare, braeccæ[2] *dicitur*.
Satiare, asoedan.
Sacra orgia, edmelu.
Scolonia[3], cipe.
Scabellum, windfona.
Scalpellum, bredisern.
Scrobibus, furum.
Scopa, besma.
Scalprum, byrs, *uel* þuarm.
Scamma[4], feld.
Saltuum, feltha.
Scylla, eduuelle[5].
Scansio, scyrft.
Sceptra, onwald.
Scena, scadu.
Scotomaticus, staerblind.
Scalpro, bore.
Scirpea, lebr, *breuis*.
Scarpinat, scripid.
Scalpellum, bor.
Scaturit, criid.
Scoria, sinder.
Scurra, scond.
Scoretus, omer.
Scrofa, sugu.
Scara, scaed.
Scniphes, mygg.
Scilla, glaedine.
Scasa, eborðrote.
Scindulis, scidum.
Scena, uuebung.
Scrobibus, groepum.

Scalmus, thol.
Sceda, taeg.
Scienices, scinneras[6].
Scirpea, eorisc leber.
5 *Scalpula*, sculdur.
Scaphum, scip.
Sciphus, bolla.
Scintella, spærca.
Scalpio, scriopu.
10 *Sceuum*, goduureci.
Scabro, unsmoedi.
Scenis, scinnum.
Semispatium, þeohsaex.
Sentina, lectha.
15 *Sentes*, dornas.
Serpillum, bradelaec.
Seditio, unsib.
Seta, byrst.
Secessus, heolstr
20 *Sella*, sadol.
Sequester, byrga.
Sclabrum, uuind.
Scalpo, clawe.
Scuporum, bliuða.
25 *Semigelato*, halfclungni.
Sero, cornisti.
Seuo, smeoru.
Serum, hwæg.
Sensim, softe.
30 *Senon*[7], cearricgge.
Senecen, gundesuilge.
Sepeliant, onsuebbað.
Sermo, spræc.
Sedulium, rægu.
35 *Senex*, ald.
Senior, aeldra.
Sibba, sigl[8]
Singultat, sicetit, *uel* gescaslaet.

---

[1] *sandix* means minium or red lead; the Anglo-Saxon equivalent: a guard or watch! R. W.

[2] The form braeceæ and bræceæ is met with as well in Latin as in Anglo-Saxon. R.W.

[3] Corrupted from *ascalonium*. R. W.

[4] *Scamma* denotes the wrestling place in the palaestra. R. W.

[5] Cf. *uertigo*. R. W.

[6] *scienices* for *scenices*. The glossator has interpreted *scena* by *scinna* (cf. *scennis*) which word denotes as well *splendour*, *beauty*, as *vision*, *representation*. Scinneras, therefore, means players, actors. R. W.

[7] *Sinon* is a sort of medicinal herb. R W.

[8] Is sibba an Latin word or perhaps the Anglo-Saxon sib, sibba? The meaning of sigl, sigel is 1. a collar, a seal; 2. a kind of grain, rye. R. W.

Sicomoros, heopan.
Situla, omber.
Sinapian, cressa.
Sicalia,[1] ryge.
Sinuosa, faedmendi.
Simpla, anfald.
Sirina, meremenin.
Singultus, gesca.
Sinnum, cirm.
Siliqua, pisanhosa.
Sisca, snidstreo.
Sinfoniaca, belone [2].
Signaum [3], segn.
Simultas, unsib.
Sinopede, redestan.
Simbulum, herebenc [4].
Sinus, byge.
Sinus, faedm.
Smus [5], wellyrgae.
Socrus, sueger.
Socer, sur [6].
Soccus, socc, slebescoh.
Solisequia, sunfolgend.
Sopio, suebbo.
Sopitis, onsuebdum.
Sollicitat, tyhted.
Sorix [7], mus.
Sortem, wyrd, *condicionem*.
Sortilegos, hlytan.
Sollicito, tyhto.
Soluat, ondest.
Sollicitare, tyhtan.
Soricarius, mushabuc.
Sopor, momna [8].
Spina, bodeg.
Spatulas rami a similitudine, spadi, dicti.
Spicas, ear.
Spatiaretur, suicade.
Spiculis, flanum.
Sponda, bencselma.

Splenis, milte.
Spina alba, haegudorn.
Spina nigra, slahdorn.
Spatula, bed.
5 *Spiramentum*, hol.
Spiato, matte.
Squalores, orfeormnisse.
Stabula, seto.
Stiba, handle.
10 *Stabulum*, stal.
Strigillum, screope.
Stragua, strel.
Stuppa, heordan.
Sternutatio, fnora.
15 *Struerer*, streide.
Sturnus, staer.
Strues, heap.
Striga, haegtis.
Stornus, dropfaag.
20 *Stipatoribus*, ymbhringendum.
Strepitu, braechtme.
Strenue, fromlice.
Strictis, getogenum.
Stiria, gecilae.
25 *Stabulum*, falaed.
Stagnum, mere.
Stilium, spinel.
Stertens, hrutende.
Stilio, braedemuus.
30 *Suppa*, ecambe.
Stangulat [9], wyrged, *uel* smorad.
Stricta macera, getogone sucorde.
Stamen, wearp.
Sternit, gehnægith.
35 *Strenas*, lybesne.
Stellatus, astaenid.
Strutio, stryta.
Stigmata, picung.
Stomachum, maga.
40 *Strigillus*, aera, aerenscrcop.
Stenax, wurpul.

---

[1] For *secalia* (*cerealia*). R. W.
[2] *belone* or *belene* denotes a kind of herb: henbane, and a sweet cake or sweet meat. R. W.
[3] So the MS. R. W.
[4] An error of the scribe for *herebecu*. Cf. *symbulum*. R. W.
[5] For *sinus*. R. W.
[6] For *swcor*, swer. R. W.
[7] *sorex* denotes a rat, a field-mouse. R. W.
[8] Perhaps an error for momra. Cf. Bosworth 44k mamrung = a sleeping. R.W.
[9] An error for *strangulat*. R. W.

Stiga, gaad.
Sturfus, fina [1].
Strabus, scelege.
Subplaudans, gelpende.
Suffundit, ablended.
Surculus, tuig, ouuaestm.
Susurio, wrohtspitel.
Surum, spearua.
Sullus, ottor.
Subarrata, geuuetfaestae.
Suspensus, ahaefd.
Sualdam, durhere.
Subfragator, mundbora.
Subsciuum, fraecni.
Successus, spoed.
Sublustris, scir.
Subulcus, snan [2].
Suesta, *suina*, sceadu.
Surgit, waexit.
Sulforia, sueflsueart.
Suspenderat, awenide.
Sucini [3], glaeres.
Subigo, wrotu.
Subcono, under haehnisse.
Sudum, lybt, *siccum*.
Sutrinator, scoere.
Subsannat, hospetæt.
Suffocacium, cecil.
Subiugatis, gededum.
Suis, suin.
Suaeder, butan todum.
Sunt, sint.
Suellium, suinin.
Subtalaris, steppescoh.
Supuratio, gelostr.
Symbulum, herebæcun.

Taxus, iuu.
Talpa, wond.
Taculus, brocc.
Talpa, wondeuueorpe.
Tabunus [4], briosa.
Tapetsa, rye.

Tabetum, bred.
Talumbus, gescadwyrt.
Taxatione, raedinne.
Tabuisset, asuond, d [5].
5 *Tantisper*, dus suide.
Taberna, winaern.
Talaria, fedrhoman.
Taurus, fear.
Taxauerat, gierende.
10 *Talus*, oneleouue.
Tabulata, dille.
Tala, webgerodes.
Tabulamen, dille.
Taenis [6], duaelum.
15 *Tegula*, tigule.
Tedis, blesum.
Teter, duerc.
Territorium, lond.
Tentigo, gesca.
20 *Tentorium*, geteld.
Tempe, sceadugeardas.
Testudo, borddeaca.
Tessera, tasul.
Tertiana, lenctinald.
25 *Terebellus*, nabogaar.
Tenticum, sprindel.
Telum, web.
Textrinum, webb.
Termofilas, faesten [7].
30 *Temonibus*, þixlum.
Teres, siunhuurful.
Temperiem, uueder.
Tehis, tegum, fodrum.
Teloniaris, uuicgeroebum.
35 *Thymus*, haet.
Tholus, hrof.
Thadalus [8], brooc.
Thessera, beeme.
Titica, uuefl.
40 *Tisifone*, uualcyrge.
Titio, brond.
Tilia, lind.
Tignarius, hrofuuyrhta.

[1] The meaning of fina is a wood pecker, *marsopicus*. R. W.
[2] No doubt an error for suan. R. W.
[3] For *succina*. R W.
[4] For *tabanus* an ox-fly. R. W.
[5] Added in the same hand. R. W.
[6] For *taeniis*. R. W.
[7] *fasten* denotes a fortress, castle, wall. R. W.
[8] An error for *caballus*, I suppose. See *taculus*, and cf. Bosw. 20p. R. W.

Tincti, sli [1].
Tilio, baest.
Tignum, tin.
Titule, gataloc.
Tibialis, baanrist.
Tipo [2], draca, *uel inflatio.*
Tigillum, first.
Tinnulus, a tinniendo dicitur, id est eran.
Tonica [3] *polimita,* hringfaag.
Torta, auunden.
Tonsa, rodr.
Tortum, coecil.
Torquet, uuraec.
Toreuma, eduuaelle.
Torax, feoluferd.
Torrentibus, streamum.
Torosa, sionuualt.
Toga, goduuebbe.
Torquent, þrungun.
Trux, unhiorde.
Trutina, heolor.
Traductus, georuuyrde.
Tragoedia, bebbi, *cantio.*
Tropea, sigebeen.
Triplia, lebl [4].
Traiectus, ðorhbrogden.
Tridens, auuel, meottoc.
Tremulus, aespe.
Trufulus, feluspreci
Transtrum, saes.
Trulla, cruce.
Turl [5], scofl.
*Triquadrum,*ðrifeodor.
Trans, bigeonan.
Tragelaphus, eleh.
Trulla, ponne.
Transfert, geuuendit.
Tribuli, braere.

Tranant, ðorhsuimmad.
Tripes, stool.
Tria, huice.
Tractibus, naescum.
5 *Trita,* ðrostle.
Truitius, draesce.
Traigis, higrae.
Tricent, ælden [6]
Tubera, clate.
10 *Tubo,* druh.
Tubolo, fala.
Turdella, ðrostle.
Turdus, serie.
Tuta, orsorg.
15 *Tuber, tumor,* asuollen.
Tudicla, thuaere.
Tutellam, scildenne.
Tuber, hofer.

20 *Ualba,* durheri.
Uatilla, gloedscofl.
Uarix, ampre.
Uangas, spadan.
Uadimonium, borggilefde.
25 *Uatilla,* isern scobl.
Uanus, gemaeded.
Uapore, aethme.
Uanna, fon.
Uacca, cuu.
30 *Uada breuia,* geuueada.
Uerbere torto, awundere suiopan [7].
Uerruca, wearte.
Uenabula, eoborspreot.
Uentriculus, ceosol [8].
35 *Uescada,* mundleu [9].
Ueror, witro.
Uexilla, seign.
Uestibulum, caebrtuun.
Uenetum, geolu.

1 For sliw? Cf. Bosw. 64t. R. W.
2 For *typhon.* R. W.
3 For *tunica.* R. W
4 ð is obliterated. R. W.
5 For *trulla,* I suppose. R. W.

6 The MS. has aeden. R. W.
7 The compiler of this glossary was evidently here taking his glosses from the Georgics of Virgil, as the reference is clearly to the third Georgic, l. 106: —
  Illi instant verbere torto.
[Other glosses seem to be taken from Virgil's Æneid. We find the glosses: *Troiae ab oris* = *a finibus Troiae,* and *Ui superum* = *uiolentia deorum,* references to the beginning of the Æneid. R. W.]
8 The MS. has ceōsol. R. W.
9 The meaning of mundleu, mundleowe is a basin. R. W.

Uertigo, eduuelle.
Uectis, seng [1].
Uespas, uuaefsas.
Uerberatorum, corthr.
Uerberatrum, flete.
Uesica, bledre.
Ueneria, smeoruwyrt.
Uespertilio, hraedemuus.
Uernaculus, frioleta.
Uecors, gemaad.
Uernacula, menen.
Uetellus, sueor.
Uertil [2], huerb.
Ueniculum [3], waegn.
Uertiginem, suinglunge.
Uesper, suansteorra.
Uetorno, faecnum.
Uermis, cordmata.
Uemiculus [4], cornuurma.
Uerbi gratia, uuordes intinga.
Uiolenter, roedelice.
Uitiginem, bleci.
Uia secta, iringes uueg [5].
Uicatum, libr.
Uittas, thuelan [6].
Uitelli, sueoras.
Uillis, uuloum.
Uitiligo, blectha.
Uitricius, steopfaeder.
Uicium, fuglesbean.
Uillosa, rye [7].
Uiscus, mistel.
Uilla, lininryee.
Uiburna, uuduuuinde.
Uirecta, quicae.
Uitiatum, awended.
Uibrat, brogdetted.
Uitiato oculo, undyhtge egan.
Uirgultum, gerd.
Uiscera tosta, gebreded flaesc.
Uibice, lelan.
Uinco, obersuido.
Uiresceret, greouue.

Uiscellum, broht.
Uiscera, tharme, thumle.
Uimen, wearp.
Uillus, uuloh.
5 *Uirgo*, unmaelo.
Uitulus, caelf.
Uitula, cucaelf.
Uistula, sugesweard.
Uibrat, borettid, *uel* diregad [8].
10 *Ultroque citroque*, hider ond hider.
Ulmus, elm.
Ulula, ulae.
Umbilicus, nabula.
Umecta, gibrec.
15 *Unibrellas*, stalu to fuglum.
Unguentum, smeoru.
Undecumque, huonan huegu [9].
Unguana, naegl.
Uoticompos, uoto ornatus, i. fægen.
20 *Uoluola*, uuduuninde.
Uorago, hool.
Uoragine, suelgendi.
Uotium, oestful.
Uoluma, gorst.
25 *Uordalium*, laesti.
Uox, stebn.
Urciolum, waetercruce.
Urna, amber.
Uris, urum.
30 *Uerticeta*, netlau.
Urguet, threatade.
Useide, tohlice.
Usurpauit, agnette.
Usia, suernit.
35 *Utensile*, geloma.
Uulgo, passim, oeghuer.
Uxorius, ceorl.

Yryseon, herescearum.
40 *Ymnus*, loob.

Zizania, laser.

[1] No doubt an error for steng. R. W.
[2] Perhaps an error for *uertigo*? R. W.
[3] For *uehiculum*. R. W.
[4] An error for *uermiculus*. R. W.
[5] Cf. W. Grimm, Deutsche heldensage 394 ff. R. W.
[6] Cf. *taenis*. R. W.
[7] Cf. *tapetsa*. R. W.
[8] Is *diregad* an Anglo-Saxon word? R. W.
[9] In the same line, after *huegu*, the scribe wrote: speru. R. W.

II.

KENTISH GLOSSES,
OF THE NINTH CENTURY [1].

1. *Glosses referring to the Proverbs of Solomon.*

I

(2ᵛ) *iacitur*, is worpen.
pennatorum, gefiðeradra.
et moliuntur fraudes, and bereafiað
sic . . . rapiunt, swa reafiað.
praedicat, bodað.
clamitat, hi clepað.
et . . . cupiunt, and gewilniað.
et . . . odibunt, and hatiað.
en proferam, efne nu ic forð brenge.
quia uocaui, forðam ic geceide
ego . . . ridebo, ic hlihe.
cum insonuerit, ðonne swæið.
ingruerit, onbricþ.
exosam, onscunede.
(3ʳ) *et detraxerunt*, and hio teldan.
et . . . perfruetur, and he breeð.
timore . . . sublato, atogenum ege

II

penes te, nih ðe.
gradientes, farende.
et omnem semitam bonam, and calne godna sidfet.

(3ᵛ) *per uias tenebrosas*, ðurh ðriostrie weogas.
qui letantur, ða geblissiað.
in rebus pessimis, on werstum ðingum.
5 *infames*, unhlisie.
que mollit, sio hnescað.
pupertatis sue, hire meiðhades.
calles, sidfatu.

III

10
non te deserant, ne forleton.
gutturi tuo, ðinre hraca.
et ne innitaris, and ne getrua ðu.
(4ʳ) *et recede*, and gewit.
15 *umbi . . lo tuo*, þinum nafelan.
et irrigatio, and leccinc.
saturitate, of gesundfulnesse.
torcularia tua, þine winwringan.
et . . . redundabunt, and genihsumiað.
20 *ne abicias*, ne awearp ðu.
nec defi . as, ne ðu ne atiara.
cum . . . coriperis, þonne þu bist ðread.
et . . . complacet, and gelicað.
25 *affluit*, swelhð.
et . . . non ualent comparari, and ne magon bion wiðmetene.
qui tenuerit, þe hefð.

---

[1] The following glosses are from a MS. of the British Museum, Cotton Vesp. D, VI. — According to the handwriting this MS. belongs to the first half of the ninth century, its dialect is that of Kent.

Zupitza lately edited these glosses in "Zeitschrift für Deutsches altertum. Neue folge, 9. bd." Our text is based on a recent collation of this reprint with the MS. in question.

Wright did not take these glosses into his collection. R. W.

stabiliuit, gestaðelade.
erumperunt, up abrycan.
rore, of deauwe.
(4ᵛ) *ne affluant*, ne aflowan.
et . . . non impinget, and ne etspernd.
ne paueas repentino terrore, ne forta ðu of ferlican ogan.
ne capiaris, det ðu ne sio gripen.
prohibere, forbiodon.
si uales et ipse benefac, gif ðu meht and ðu self tela do.
ne dicas, ne sege ðu.
cras, to morgen.
ne moliaris, ne þendu.
ne contendas, ne flit ðu.
frustra, on idel.
ne æmuleris, ne ðu ne onhere.
ne immiteris, ne ðu ne geefenlæc.
omnis inlusor, æl bismeriend.
sermocinatio eius, his wordlunc.

IV

(5ʳ) *tenellus*, myra.
et . . . adquire, and gestrion.
arripe, gegrip.
glorificaberis, ðu bist gewuldrad.
aumenta[1], eacan.
corona inclita, myrlic cynehelm.
ne delecteris, ne gelustfulla ðu.
et desere, and forlet.
dormiunt, h . . .
(5ᵛ) *et non rapitur*, and ne bið gegripen.
nisi supplantauerint, buton hi beswican.
comedunt, hi etað.
ausculta, hlest.
ne recedant, ne gewitan.
uita, lif.
quia ex ipso . . . procedit, ðara forðam forð gewit.
remoue, fram astere.
palpebre, ðinum brewum.

[1] For *augmenta*. R. W.

et . . . stabilientur, and sin gestaðelade.
nouit, wat.
peruerse, forhwerfede.
5 *faciet*, he ded.

V

ut custodias, þet ðu . . .
10 *et . . . conseruent*, and ge . . .
(6ʳ) *nitidius*, scinendre.
(*gladius*) *biceps*, twiicce.
descendunt, nider . . .
et . . . penetrant, and farað.
15 *uagi*, woriende.
et inuestigabiles[2], and unasperiendlic.
et ne recedas, and ne gewit ðu.
ne des, ne sele ðu.
et gemas, and ðu giomras.
20 *cur detestatus sum*, for hwe onscunede ic.
et . . . non adquieuit, and ne gedafede.
audiui, ic . . .
25 *docentium*, . . . ra.
magistris, . . . m.
paene, fornion.
sinagoge, werede.
de cisterna tua, of ðinum seaðe.
30 *diri . . entur*, sint gereahte.
et . . . diuide, and todel.
habeto, ðu . . .
solus, ane.
uena tua, ðin edra.
35 *et letare*, and geblissa.
adulescentiæ tuæ, ðinre giogeðe.
cerua carissima et gratissimus hinnulus, eala ðu liofeste hind and gecwemest hindcealf.
40 *inebriant*, ginddrencað.
(6ᵛ) *et . . . delectare*, and gelustfulla.
quare seduceris, for hwi eart ðu beswicen.
et foueris, and ðu bist gestrangad.
et . . . considerat, and he besceawað.
capiunt, gegripað.

[2] *ue* in *inuestigabiles* seems almost certain, but very indistinct. R. W.

et ... constingitur [1], and he bið gewriðen.
multidtudine, of ...
et ... decipietur, and he bið beswicen.

VI

si spoponderis, gif ðu behete.
defixisti, ðu afesnadest.
inlaqueatus es, ðu eart gegrinad.
et captus, and geheft.
incidisti, hrure.
discurre, irnn.
nec dormitent, ne hneppian.
cruere, si ðu ut alened [2].
dammula, hind.
aucupis, hireres [3].
ad formicam, to emet.n.
ducem, lateau.
nec praeceptorem, ne bodiend.
parat, hit gerewað.
estate, on sumere.
paululum dormitabis, gehwede hneppast.
conseres, ðu on arets [4].
(7r) quasi uiator, swa wiferend [5].
et pauperies, and ermd.
quasi uir armatus, swa gewepned wer.
impiger, nusleac [6].
homo apostata, afliged mon, .i. retrogradiens.
peruerso, ðweran.
annuit, gebeacnað [7].
terit, he treped.
iurgia, tionan.
extimplo, feringa.
et ... contereretur, and he bið forbret.
medicinam, lecedom.
et ... detestatur, and onscunoð.
sublimes, up ahafene.
machinans, saarwiende.
proferentem, forð brengende.
testem fallacem, leasa gewitnesse.
eum, ðane.

discordias, unðwernesse.
liga, gewrid.
et circumda gutturi tuo, and uton ymbsele ðinre hraca.
5 gradiantur, hi faran.
(7v) et a blanda lingua extraneæ, and fram swesere tungan uton cumenre.
concupiscat, ge ...
10 ne capiaris nutibus illius, ðe les ðu sio gegripen hiora onwaldum.
scorti, forlegese [8].
uix, uneaðe.
ut ... non ardeant, ðet ne byrnan.
15 plante eius, his fotwelme.
sic ... non erit, swa ne bið.
cum tetigerit, ðonne ethrind.
deprehensus, anfunden.
adulter, unrihthemere.
20 inopiam, ermðe.
turpitudinem, folnesse.
et ... non delebitur, and ne bið adilegad.
quia ... non parcet, forðam ne arað.
25 nec adquiescet cuiusquam precibus, ne hio ne geþafoð eniges benum.
dona plurima, manega giofa.

VII

30 et ... reconde, and behed.
quasi pupillam, swa sion.
(8r) custodiat, ða ...
dulcia, werede.
per cancellos, ðurh crepelas.
35 prospexi, ic ...
uideo, ge ...
uecordem iuuencm, gionne dysine.
transit, færd.
in obscuro, on forsworcenan.
40 aduesperescente die, geæfenedan deige.
occurrit, ongen arn.
garrula et uaga, hlud and widscridel.

45

[1] For constringitur? Z.
[2] For alesed? Z.
[3] For hiweres. Z.
[4] For asets? cf. conseres in v. XXIV. Z.
[5] Perhaps for swiferend? R. W.
[6] An error for unsleac. Z.
[7] g is rather illegible. R. W.
[8] Read forleg(t)ran or forleges(t)re. Z.

nec ualens, na megende.
consistere, wunian.
insidiatur, hio searwað.
adprehensumque deosculatur, gegripen and hio cyst.
procaci uultu, gemagnum andwlitan.
et ... blanditur, and hio swesleeð.
uictimas, onsegednesse.
debui, ic scolde.
reddidi, ic ageald.
et repperi, and ic gemete.
intexui, ic wef.
tapetibus pictis, gemetum tepedum.
aspersi, ic giondstreide.
ueni, cum.
uberibus, of udrum.
et fruamur, and wuton brucon.
cupitis amplexibus, ge ......
donec inlucescat, oððet onliohte.
(8ᵛ) *uia longissima*, ðam lengestan wig.
sacculum, sæc.
tulit, hio nam.
plene lunæ, ... les monan.
inretiuit, hio . e . te ¹.
blanditiis, swesendum.
et ... protraxit, and hio teah.
et quasi agnus lasciuiens, and swa plegende lamp.
et ignorans, and nat.
quod ... trahatur, þet togen ...
donec transfigat, oððet afestnige.
iecor eius, his lifere.
uel ut si auis festinet, oððe swa ... efst fugel.
de periculo, be freeednesse.
quia ... agitur, þet hit . s don.
ne abstrahatur, ne sio atogen.
neque decipiaris, ne þu ne sio beswicen.
fortissimi quique, gehwilce stongeste².

¹ Perhaps trepte? Z.
² For strongeste. Z
³ *done* in ondone is not clear. R. W.
⁴ These letters are very doubtful. R. W.
⁵ *ið* in betwih is obliterated. R. W.
⁶ Read upahafenesse, cf. *omnis arrogans* in v. XVI. Z.

[*ab*] *ea*, hire.
penetrantes, farende.
in interiora, on ða inran.

VIII

in ipsis foribus, on ðam forðtege.
clamito, ic ..
et ... animaduertite, and ongiotað.
de rebus magnis, be mestum ðingum.
10 (9ʳ) *aperientur*, siont ondone ³.
ut ... praedicent, ðet hio bodian.
guttur meum, min hraca.
et ... detestabuntur, and onse ... ad⁴.
neque peruersum, ne forhwerfed.
15 *cunctis opibus pretiosissimis*, eallum dior .....
omne desiderabile, all gewilnienlic.
comparari, bion widmeten.
eruditis ... cogitationibus, gelereddum
20 gedancum.
et ... intersum, and ic betw .. ⁵ eam.
arrogantiam, u ..... e . esse ⁶.
os bilingue, twispecne muð.
et ... detestor, and ic onscunige.
25 *legum conditores*, sceptteuras ⁷.
decernunt, gescadað ⁸.
imperant, bebiodað.
potentes, rica.
opes superbe, ofermode prede ⁹.
30 (9ᵛ) *et lapide presiosa*, and diorweorðum stane
et genimina mea, and mine cidas.
ut ditem, ðet ic geweolegie.
et ... repleam, and ic gefelle.
35 *possedit*, ahte.
initium ¹⁰, on fruman.
quicquam, enig ðinc.
antequam ... faceret, er don ðe he dede.
40 *eterno*, ... m.
ordinata sum, ic eam geendebyrd.

⁷ Zupitza reads: scepttenras, but *scept* in scepttenras is very doubtful. R. W.
⁸ *ge* and *ad* in gescadad are quite illegible. R. W.
⁹ ofermode seems to be an adjective. prede a substantive (for pride, pryde). R. W.
¹⁰ The Vulgate has: *in initio*. R.W.

ex antiquis, of caldum.
et ... antequam ... fieret, and er ðan de gewurde.
necdum erant abysi, ne ða get weron grundas.
concepta, geeacnad.
necdum ... erumperant, ne ða get up brecon.
graui mole, ahefegum hefe.
necdum ... constiterant, ne ða get asette weron.
ego parturiebar, is wes geeacnad.
et cardines, and hearran
quando praeparabat, ða he gegearwade.
aderam, ic etwes.
gyro, emhferte [1].
quando ... uallabat, ða he gestrangade.
aethera, roderas.
librabat, wæi.
ne transirent, þet hi ne oferferdan.
appendebat, wei.
cuncta conponens, calle geglengende.
(10ʳ) *et delectabar,* and ic wes gelusfullad [2].
ludens, plegende.
ad fores meas, et minum gatum.
et obseruat potest[3] *ostii mei,* and begemd stude [4] minre dure.
et hauriet, and he hlet.
ledet, dered.
oderunt, ... dan [5].

IX

excidit, hio forcearf.
immolauit uictimas suas, hio offrede hiore ansegednesse.
miscuit, hio gemende.
ad arcem et ad mænia, to burge and to wealle.
relinquite, forletad.

derisorem, telend.
qui arguit, se de dread.
generat, cynd.
maculam, wam.
5 (10ᵛ) *diliget,* ... d.
da, sele.
occasionem, intigan [6].
et addetur, and si geaht.
multiplicabuntur, biod ...
10 *inlusor,* bismeriend.
portabis, du byrst.
et clamosa, and hlud.
inlecebris, on forspanegum [7].
omnino, eallunga.
15 *sedet,* hio sit.
super sellam, ofer setol.
uocaret, ... ge.
et pergentes, and ferende.
itinere suo, hio [8] sidfate.
20 *uecordi,* gedwolenum.
aque furtiue, diofende weteru.
et ... suauior, and wensure [9].
et ignorauit, and hio nat.
et ... conuiuie eius, and hiora gebiorscipes.

X

non proderunt, ne fromiad.
non affliget, ne geswend.
30 (11ʳ) *et ... subuertit,* and he gehwerf.
egestatem, wedle.
operata est, worhte.
manus remissa, aslacad hand.
35 *fortium, ...* ra.
diuitias, weolan.
parat, gegearwad.
qui ... stertit, se de hret.
operit, oferwrihd.
40 *et ... putrescet,* and forrotad.
ceditur, bid swungen.
confidentur [10]*,* getrioulice.

---

[1] Read embhwerfte. Z.
[2] For gelustfullad. R. W.
[3] An error for *postes.* R. W.
[4] Zupitza reads stode. It may be either o or u. R. W.
[5] Added in a latter hand. R W.
[6] For intingan, cf. Bosw. 40ᵉ. R. W.
[7] Read forspanungum. Z.
[8] For hiore. Z.
[9] For wensumre, cf *penuriam,* v. XXVIII. Z.
[10] So the MS instead of *confidenter.* R. W.

qui ... deprauat, se ðe gesweotelað¹.
qui annuit, se ðe gebeacnað.
uerberabitur, bið swungen.
uena, edra.
et ... aperit, and ontenð.
inuenietur, bið ...
qui indiget, se ð² wedlat.
custodienti, to gehealdene.
(11ᵛ) *non deerit,* na wana bið.
egestate, of ...
nec sociabitur, ne geferleoð.
dabitur, bið sald.
acetum, eced.
non commouebitur, ne bið astered.
(12ʳ) *parturiet,* eacnað.
et ... peribit, and forweorð.

XI

*stetera*³, anmitta.
pondus, wiht.
contumelia, tiona.
diriget, gereed.
supplantatio, biswic.
uastabit, berefat.
corruit, hreosþ.
et ... capientur, and bioð gribene ⁴.
mortuo, ... dum.
sollicitorum, ymbhedigra.
simulator, lecetere.
decipit, beswied.
liberabuntur, bioðh alesede⁵ of.
(12ᵥ) *in perditione,* on forspillednesse.
tacebit, swigað.
fraudulenter, facenlice.
archana, diohla.
fidelis, getriowe.
celat, bediolað.
commissum, gelt.
affligitur, bit geswenced.
cauet, warat.
securus, orsorh.

*mulier gratioso*⁶, gefol wif.
crudelis, welhriou.
propinquos abicit, magos aweorpð.
opus instabili, unstaðolfest weore ⁷.
5 *seminanti,* sawondum.
sectatio, efterfylgnic⁸.
uoluntas, g ...
(13ʳ) *circulus aureus,* gelden trendel.
pulcra, fe ...
10 *prestolatio,* anbidine.
diuidunt, todeled.
propria, agene.
ditiores, weliogarn.
et ... fiunt, and biod.
15 *qui inebriat,* se ðe drin ...
inebriabitur, bit drucen ⁹.
frumenta, hwetes.
maledicitur, bið wereged.
uendentium, cypendra.
20 *inuestigator,* speriend.
obprimetur, bið ...
corruet, ahriosð.
uirens folium, growende leaf
possidebit, ah.
25 *uentos,* ... s.
seruiet, ðiowað.
sapienti, ... m.

XII

30 (13ᵛ) *impie,* ... ce.
non roborabitur, ne bið gestrangad.
et ... non commouebitur, and ne bið astered.
putredo, forrotadnes.
35 *res dignas,* medeme ðine.
qui ... gerit, se ðe det.
uerte, acyrað.
doctrina sua noscitur, of his lare bit ancwawen¹⁰.
40 *excors,* modleas.
patebit, openað.

---

¹ sweotelian means to testify, prove. R.W.
² So the MS. Zupitza has de, but there is no e here, nor room for one. R. W.
³ For *statera.* Z.
⁴ For *gripene.* Z.
⁵ Is perhaps to be divided: bioð halesede of? R. W.

⁶ An error for *gratiosa.* Z.
⁷ weore is very faint in the MS. R. W.
⁸ For efterylgine, see Bosw. 24ʷ. R. W.
⁹ For *druncen.* Z.
¹⁰ For ancwawen. Z.

nouit, wat.
iumentorum suorum, his netena.
qui operatur, se de werd.
munumentum[1], getremminc.
proficiet, fremet.
malo, ... m.
effugiet, forflioh.
replebitur, bid ...
(14ʳ) *et ... retribuetur*, and bid golden.
dissimulat, forberet.
callidus, leti.
nouit, wat.
mentitur, wegð.
testis ... fraudulentus, facenful gewita.
qui promittit, se behæt.
et ... pungitur[2], and bid witnod.
labium, ... ra
concinnat, geþiod.
qui ... ineunt, de onginnad.
consilia, gedeaht.
acciderit, belipmd[3].
malo, of ...
homo uersutus, leti[4] mon.
celat, bediolad.
tributis, trifetum, gafel.
et ... letificabitur, and he bid ...
iter, sidfet.
decipiet, beswicd.
fraudulentus, facenful.
lucrum, gestrion.
(14ᵛ) *deuium*, welise[5].

XIII

inconsideratus, unbesceawad.
operantium, wercendra.
detestabitur, onscunod.
et confunditur, and he bid gescend.
æst, he is.
consilio, ... s.
reguntur, biod gereahte.

[1] Read *munimentum*, Z.
[2] The glossator explained *punitur* instead of *pungitur*. Z.
[3] An error for *belimpd*. Z.
[4] Cf. p. 68, l. 11 and p 69, l. 10, 12;

substantia festinata, geonet sped.
minuetur, bid gewanad.
paulatim, litlum and litlum.
qui differtur, þe bid geeld.
5 *affligit*, geswend.
desiderium ueniens, cumede gewilung.
(15ʳ) *alicui rei*, enigum dince.
obligat, gewrid.
uersabitur, drohtnat.
10 *uorago*, swelgend.
astutus, letig.
agit, ded.
aperiet, untend.
nuntius, boda.
15 *et ignominia ei qui deserit*, and netenes dam se de forlet.
qui .. adquiescit, se de gedafed.
arguenti, ... m.
si complebitur, gif hio bid gefelled.
20 *delectat*, gelusfullad[7].
detestantur, onscuniad.
qui fugiunt, de fliod.
et ... efficietur, and he bid geworden.
25 *persequitur*, feld.
et ... retribuentur, and bid golden.
et nepotes, and neofan.
et custoditur, and bid gehealden.
in noualibus, on dengum.
30 *et ... congregabuntur*, and biod gesamnode.
qui parcit, se de ared.
instanter, anredlice.
erudit, lerd.
35 *insaturabilis*, unasedendlic.

XIV

(15ᵛ) [*domum*] ... *exstructam*, timbrunga.
40 *despicitur*, b ...
ab eo, fram dam.
infami ... uia, on unhlisum wige.
and: lytig, letig: Oros., 5, 7. Boet. 37, 4.
R. W.
[5] Perhaps for wiiese = weglease? Z. The form *wig* is met with p. 68, l. 42; p. 76, 33.
R. W.
[6] For cumende gewilnung. Z.
[7] Cf. p. 63, l. 25. R. W.

plurime segetes, manega ecyras.
dolosus testis, facynful cydere·
prudentium, . . . ra.
facilis [1], edre.
inludit, bepæcd.
morabitur, wunad.
germinabunt, growad.
extrema, endas.
replebitur, bid . . .
astutus, letig.
(16ʳ) *operabitur*, werd.
uir uersutus, letig wær.
odiosus, hatol.
diuitum, . . . n.
qui despicit, se de forsiohd.
errant, dwoliad.
praeparant, gegearwiad.
uersipellis, ficol . i . pretti.
in paucitate, on gehwednese.
gubernatur, is begemed.
(16ᵛ) *ossuum*, bana [2].
qui calumniatur, se de hespd.
exprobat, hespd.
factori eius, his wertan.
eum, hine.
eleuat, up ahefd.

XV

responsio mollis, hnesce andswore.
sermo durus, heard spec.
fatuorum, stunra.
ebullit, wapolad.
contepplantur [3], besceawiad.
inmoderata, ungemetegead.
inridet, tirhd.
astutior fiet, wærra bid.
et . . . conturbatio, and gedrefednes.
disseminabunt, tosawad.
(17ʳ) *dissimile*, ungelic.
deserenti, forletendum.
qui . . . corripit, de dread.

[1] The glossator translates *facilius*. Z.
[2] Rather doubtful. R. W.
[3] Read *contemplantur*. Z
[4] For *exilaret*, *exhilarat*. Z.
[5] *gegladad* faint, rather doubtful. R. W·
[6] See Bosw. 69ᵇ. R. W.
[7] The Vulgate has *sepes*. R. W.

nec . . . graditur, ne he ne ged.
exiraret [4], gegladad [5].
in merore animi, on gnornunga modes.
deicitur, bid aworpen.
5 *et . . . pascitur*, and bid fed.
imperitia, of ungleaunesse.
quasi iuge conuiuium, swa singal gebiorscipe.
et insatiabiles, and unasedenlic.
10 *uocari*, b . . .
ad olera, to wertum.
quam ad uitulum saginatum, donne to fettum stiorce [6].
suscitatas, awehte.
15 *sepis* [7], haga.
absque offendiculo, buto otspernince [8].
et . . . despicit, and forsiod.
dissipantur, sin tostente [9].
confirmantur, sint . . .
20 *in sententia*, on ewide.
optimus, selest.
super eruditum, ofer geleredne.
(17ᵛ) *pulcherrimus*, fegerest.
qui sectatur, se de feld.
25 *fama bona*, god blisa.
impinguat, amest.
sapientium, . . . ra.
commorabitur, wunad.
despicit, forsiod.
30 *qui . . . adquiescit*, se de gedafed.
possessor, agend.
et . . . praecedit, and ford gewit.

XVI

35 *ponderator*, punderngeo [10].
dirigentur, b . . .
omnis arrogans, elc upahafenes.
(18ʳ) *redimitur*, is alesed.
et declinatur, and he bid aheld.
40 *cum placuerint*, ponne liciad.
disponit, gedihnad.

[8] For *buton odspernince* or *etsperuince*. Z.
[9] For *tostencte*. R. W.
[10] *pundern* means *statera*. The Anglo-Saxon expression for *ponderator* is *pundere*. Perhaps is the meaning of this gloss: *ponderator* = *puudern*, *uel* (= *ge*) *pundero* (= *pundere*)? R. W.

KENTISH GLOSSES.

pondus, pund.
iudicia, ... mas.
diuinatio, wilung.
non errabit, ne dwolad.
impie, ... e.
solium, cynesetl.
dirigetur[1], bid ...
et ... placabit, and gegladad.
imber serotinus, smelt hagol.
semita, ... ta.
declinat, ... d.
humiliari, b ...
æruditus, gelered.
repperiet, gemet.
(18ʳ) *appellabitur*, bit genemned.
maiora, mare.
percipiet, onfehd.
et ... addet, and to geecd.
composita, geglengede.
ossuum, bana.
compulit, genet.
et ... ardescit, and bird[2].
peruersus, forhwerfed.
lites, saca.
uerbosus, werdi.
et ... separat, and toscered.
lactat[3], secet.
attonitis, areahtum.
mordens, slitende.
perficit, fulfremet.
dignitatis, werdnes.
repperietur, bit gemet.
animo suo, is mode.
urbium, burga.
set ... temperantur, ac hio biod gemetgode.

XVII

buccella sicca, drege bite.
uictimis, onsegednessum.
(19ʳ) *obedit*, hersumad.
et optemperat, and hersumad.

---

[1] For *diligetur*. Z.
[2] Read: birnd. Z.
[3] *lactare* means to allure, entice; the glossator makes use of 'secean, secan' = to inquire, ask for, *adire, petere*. R. W.
[4] For bedigolad or bedioglad. R. W.

exprobrat, hespd.
letatur, b ...
senum, eldra.
non decet, ne glenget.
5 *composita*, glengede.
labium mentiens, wegende welere.
gemma, gim.
gratissima, geewemest.
prestolantis, anbidineges.
10 *celat*, bediolad[4].
amicitias, freondscipas.
repetit, gehydlæct[5].
separat, toscered.
fœderatos, gesibbade.
15 *expedit*, fremet.
urse, byrene.
raptis fetibus, odbrodenum hwelpum.
confidenti, getriowende.
20 *et ... deserit*, and forlet.
(19ᵛ) *et ... comprobatur*, and bid afandan[6].
plaudet, hafet[7].
peruersi cordis, dwerre hiortan.
25 *qui uertit*, se de cyrd.
et ... incidet, and befeld.
in ignominia sua, on his netenesse.
set nec ... letabitur, ac ne blissad.
aetatem floridam, blowende elde.
30 *exsiccat*, a ...
inferre, on geledan.
nec percutere, ne slean.
qui moderatur, se de gemetegad.
doctus, gelered.
35 *pretiosi*, diores.
spiritus, gast.
(20ʳ) *reputabitur*, bid geteald.
si conpresserit, gif he gewelt.

XVIII

40 *occasiones*, intigan[8].
reprobabilis, afadodlic[9].

---

[5] For gehydlect, geedlect. Z.
[6] An error for afandad. Z.
[7] See Bosw. 34ᵏ. R. W.
[8] For intingan, cf. p. 64, l. 7. Z.
[9] Read afandodlic. Z.

dixeris[1], du . . .
que uersantur, de drohniad[2].
contempnit, forheged.
redundans, ediende[3].
fons, burne.
inmiscent, on gemengad.
rixis, of sacum.
bilinguis, twispeces.
interiora, inran.
et dissolutus, and toslacad.
dissipantis, tostencendes.
fortissima, strengest.
currit, irnd.
(20ᵛ) *ualidus*, stran[4].
et . . . dignum, and weordne.
sustentat inbecillitatem suam, uderwreodad[5] his untrumnesse.
ad irascendum, to iorsienne.
sapientium, . . . ra.
donum, gefe.
dilatat, tobræt.
spatium, fec.
accusator sui, wrehten his selfes.
uenit, . . . d.
inuestigabit, smead.
contradictiones, widercwidas.
comprimit, ofdrect.
sors, hlet.
et . . . diiudicat, and tosced.
qui adiuuatur, de is gefultumad.
uectes, scetelas.
cum obsecrationibus, mid halsungum.
(21ʳ) *ride*[6], stidlice.
uir amicabilis, lufwendlic wer.

XIX

torquens, dreagende.
festinus, hred.
contra, on.
feruæt, weld.
animo suo, his mod.

addunt, to gemend.
quos habuit, dæ habbad.
separantur, biod toscerede.
et . . . non effugiet, and ne aflid.
5 *colunt*, weordiad.
dona, of . . .
distribuentis, todelendes.
hominis pauperis, earmne monnon.
oderunt, . . . n.
10 *insuper*, der to eacan.
procul, fior.
et . . . recesserunt, and gewiton.
qui . . . sectatur, se de feld.
abebit[7], . . . d.
15 *non decent*, ne rised.
stultum, . . . ne.
deliciæ, . . . s.
dominari, wealdan.
praetergredi, forgeman . i . forbugon.
20 *fremitus*, gremetune.
(21ᵛ) *herbam*, werta.
hiraritas[8] *eius*, his glednes.
tacta[9] *. . . perstillantia*, driopende hrof.
25 *litigosa*[10] *mulier*, sacful wif.
dantur, sint sealde.
propriæ, senderlice.
uxor prudens, glea wif.
pigredo, sleuþ odde sclcacnes.
30 *soporem*, mamor[11].
dissoluta, asclaead.
et . . . esuriet, and hinrad[12].
mortificabitur, bid ewelmed.
fenerator[13], lend.
35 *domino*, . . . ne.
uicissitudinem suam, his gewricl[14].
ne desperis[15], ne georwen du.
ad interfectionem . . . eius, to his cwale.
40 *damnum*, hendo.
cum rapuerit, donne he gegrip.

---

[1] The Vulgate has *dixerit*. Z.
[2] For drohtniad. R. W.
[3] Read ediende. Z.
[4] For strang. R. W.
[5] Read underwreodad. Z.
[6] An error for *rigide*. Z.
[7] For *habebit*. R. W.
[8] Read *hilaritas*. Z.
[9] For *tecta*. Z.
[10] For *litigiosa*. Z.
[11] See l. s. v. *sopor* R. W.
[12] For hingrad. R. W.
[13] Read *feneratur*. Z.
[14] For gewricsl. Z.
[15] An error for *desperes*. Z.

et ... apponet, and to geset.
in nouissimis tuis, on ðinum endum.
homo indigens, beðearfende mon.
et ... commorabitur, and hio wunað.
absque uisitatione, buton niosunga.
pessimi [1], metestum.
nec ... applicat, ne he ne geþiod.
flagellato, geswungen.
si ... corripueris, gif ðu dreast [2].
(22ʳ) *ignominiosus*, ungewis.
et infelix, and ungeselig.
non cesses, ne ablin ðu.
deridet, teld.
et ... deuorat, and forsweld.
parata sunt, gerewe sint.
derisoribus, telerum.
iudicia, ... s.
et mallei percutientes, and sleande slice.
corporibus, ... m.

XX

tumultuosa, maðeli.
sicut ruitus [3], swa grimetung.
qui separat, so toscered.
a contentionibus, fram flitum.
miscentur, ... d.
arare, herian.
mendicabit, he wedlat.
exhauriet, a ...
uocantur, bioð ...
beatos, ... ge.
posse [4], wiðeftan.
intuitu suo [5], on his begemene.
(22ᵥ) *et saturare*, and sio ðu ...
emptor, beccen.
cum recesserit, ðonne he gewit.
et ... gloriabitur, and hit ...
et uas pretiosum, and diorrest fet.
fideiussor, borhhond [6].

exstitit, wunade.
alieni, ... s.
calculo, of griosne.
consiliis, ... m.
5 *roborantur*, and sint gestrangade
gubernaculis, ... m.
tractanda, to smyagenne.
ad quam festinatur, to ðam ðe hit efta [7] wes.
10 *carebit*, ðolað.
(23ʳ) *pondus*, hefe.
deuorare, forswelgan.
post uota, efter behate.
et curuat, and gebegð.
15 *eos*, ða.
spiraculum, orð.
inuestigat, asperet.
roboratur, bið . .
iuuenum, ... ra.
20 *senum* ... ra.
canicies, harnes.
liuor, lela.
abstergit, adreið.
in secretioribus, on ðeohlum.
25

XXI

diuisiones, todal.
inclinabit, he ...
appendit, aweget.
30 (23ᵥ) *et impingetur*, and hio odsperd [8].
detrahent, telað.
noluerunt, ... dan.
peruersa uia, ðuer wig.
miserebitur, hi ...
35 *multato pestilente*, gewitnodum ewilde.
excogitat, dend [9].
ut detrahet [10], þet he ut atio.
qui opturat, se fordett.
ad, et.
40 *et non exaudietur*, and ne bið gehered.

[1] Perhaps for *pessimis?* The Vulgate has: *pessima.* Z.
[2] dreagan or drean means *corripere, castigare, increpare.* R. W.
[3] Read *rugitus.* Z.
[4] For *post se,* see the Vulgate XX, 7. R. W.
[5] The glossator seems to have read *in tuitu suo,* not *intuitu suo.* Z.

[6] In borhhond two *b*'s are written by mistake: bbrb, and *r* is above the line. R. W.
[7] Read efst. Z.
[8] For odsperud (= *impinget*, instead of *impingetur*) Z.
[9] For dencd. R. W.
[10] Read *detrahat.* Z.

munus absconditum, behed lac.
indignationem maximam, mestan ebylhd.
iusto, ... m.
pauor, ferht.
pui errauerit, se de gedweled.
in coetu, on weorede.
commorabitur, wunad.
epulos[1], wiste.
pinguia, fetto.
non ditabitur, ne bid geweolegad.
quam com muliere rixosa, donne mid secfullan wife.
(24ʳ) *thesaurus desiderabilis*, gewilniendlic goldhord.
iusti ... s.
dissipabit, totened[2].
fortium, strangere[3].
robur, strend[4].
et arrogans, and up ahafen.
occidunt, ofslead.
et desiderat, and gegernd.
et non cessabit, and ne ablind.
que offeruntur, de biod brohte.
testis mendax, leas gewitnes.
obediens, ... sum.
uictoriam, sige.
procaciter, geaplice.
offirmat, afestnad.
corrigit, gereed.
equus paratur, hors is gegearwad.

XXII

(24ᵛ) *operator*, werhta.
callidus, letig.
et afflictus est, and is geswenced.
damno, of hende.
in uia peruersi, on dreorum[5] wige.
prouerbium, biewide.
adolescens, iunges.
cum senuerit, donne he ealdad.
imperat, bebiot.

mutuum, to borge.
fenerantis, lened[6].
uirga, of ...
et ... consummabitur, and he bid for-
5 numen.
promptus, arod.
dedit, he ...
pauperi, ... n.
eice, ut aweorpd.
10 *et exibit*, and utged.
et supplantantur, and beod beswicene.
uerba, of ...
occidendus, to ofslanne.
fouea profunda, diop sead.
15 *incidat*[7], on ahreasd.
colligata[8] *est*, is gegederad.
et ... fugabit, and bid afligd.
(25ʳ) *ut augeat*, þet he gæce.
ditiori, weolegrum.
20 *et egebit*, and he wedlad.
sapientium, ... ra.
appone, to gesete.
redundabit, hio ...
tripliciter, driofeealdlice.
25 *firmitatem*, trumnesse.
illis, dam.
uiolentiam, strende[9].
non conteras, ne forbrec du.
et configet, and ofsticod.
30 *uiro furioso*, hathort were.
ne ... discas, de les du liornie.
qui defigunt, de afestniad.
uades, borhhande.
pro debitis, for geltum.
35 *unde restituas*, hwonon agelts du.
causæ est, dinga his.
tollas[10], nime.
operimentum, oferbredels.
(25ᵛ) *ne transgrediaris terminos an-*
40 *tiquos*, ne oferstepe du ealde gemero.
posuerunt, settan.

[1] For *epulas*. Z.
[2] An error for *tostened*. R. W.
[3] For *strangera*. R. W.
[4] For *strengd*, *strened*. R. W.
[5] So the MS. for *dweorum*. R. W.
[6] Read *lenend* or *lenendes*. Z.

[7] The Vulgate reads *incidet*. R. W.
[8] The compiler of the glosses confounded *colligare* with *colligere*. Z. Cf. p. 83, l. 41. R. W.
[9] See p. 77, l. 19 R. W.
[10] The Vulgate has *tollat*. R. W.

uidisti, ð ...
ante ignobiles, beforan eðelborenum ¹.

XXIII

cultrum, scær.
ne desideres, ne gewilnadi ².
de, of.
ut diteris, þet ðu sio geweolugad.
modum, gemet.
ne erigas, ne ðu up ne arer.
opes, wærde.
facient, ... ð.
non comedas, ne et ðu.
cibos, ... s.
arioli, dreas.
coniectoris, wiccan.
quoniam ... estimat, for ðam ðe he wenð.
quod ignorat, þet hi nat.
euomes, ðu ...
pulchros sermones tuos, ðine fegeran specce.
(26ʳ) *nec adtingas*, ne ðu ne ethrin.
intro eas, in ga.
propinquus, mygð.
ingrediatur, in ga.
aures tue, ... n.
subtrahere, ation.
si ... percusseris, gif ðu slehst.
uirga ³, of ...
morietur, he ...
et ... liberabis, and ðu alest.
renes, edran.
non emuletur, ne onberie.
prestulatio tua, þin anbidinc.
uia ... e.
comesationibus, oferætum.
qui ... conferunt, þa bregað.
uacantes, ge ...
cymbala ⁴, hearpan.
qui ... consummentur, ðe bioð fornume* ⁵.

¹ The Anglo-Saxon expression answers to the Latin *nobiles*. Z.
² An error for gewilna ðu. Z.
³ See p 78, l. 3. R. W.
⁴ The Vulgate reads *symbola*. R. W
⁵ For fornumene. Z.
⁶ Perhaps an error for cend. Z.

uestietur, bið ...
(26ᵛ) *dormitatio*, rest.
eme, bege.
exultat, ... nað.
5 *genuit*, ceið ⁶.
gaudeat ... sie.
exultet ... nie.
genuit ... d.
puteus angustus, neare pyt.
10 *incautos*, unuuere.
fouea, ... s.
suffusio. agotenes.
nonne, w ...
his, ðam.
15 *calicibus epotandis*, drunendum ⁷ calice.
flauescit, glitenat.
splenduerit, scinð.
color, blio.
20 *ingreditur*, hit ...
blande, lufwedlice ⁸.
regulus, slawerm ⁹.
diffundet, togiot.
uidebunt, ... þ.
25 *loquetur*, ... þ.
(27ʳ) *sopitus*, swefed.
repperiam, ic gemete.

XXIV

30 *dispositione*, dehtnunge.
initur, bið ongunnen.
stulto, ... m.
aperiet, h ...
uocabitur bið ...
35 *detractatur* ¹⁰, is teled.
si desperaueris, gif ðu georwenst.
lapsus ¹¹, aslidenum.
imminuetur, b ...
(27ᵛ) *qui ducuntur*, þe sion ledde.
40 *qui trahuntur*, þe sin togene.
uires, megene.
non suppetunt, ne gehelpaþ.

⁷ For druncendum or druncniendum. See p. 66, l. 16. R. W.
⁸ For lufwendlice. Z.
⁹ or slaw-wyrm = slow-worm. R. W.
¹⁰ The Vulgate has *detractor*. Z.
¹¹ The Vulgate reads *lassus*. Z.

seruatorem, weard.
fallit, wegð.
fanum, ... s.
gutturi, ... r.
quam, þane.
insidieris, searw þ [1].
uastes, reafa.
displiceat, ... ge.
cum detractoribus, mid telendum.
(28ʳ) *prepara*, gegearawa.
et ... exerce, and bega.
ut ... aedifices, þet du getimbrige.
lactes, gæl.
urtice, of netelan.
parum, litel.
inquam, witodlice.
modicum, gehwæde.
(28ᵛ) *pauxillum*, lithwon.
conseres, du on asets.
quasi cursor, swa renel.
et mendacitas, and þerflicnes.

XXV

quas transtulerunt, ða rehton.
celare, bedeahlian.
inuestigare, smegan.
rubiginem, hom.
quam ut humilieris, þonne þet du sio geniðerad.
ne proferas, ne ep ðu.
emendare, gebetan.
ne ... non possis, de les du ne meige.
cum dehonestaueris [2], ðonne du gearweordas.
et ... ne reueles, and ne onwrih ðu.
et ... non cesset, and he ne ablind.
malum, æppel.
(29ʳ) *inauris aurea*, gylden earspinl.
lenietur, bid gelidgod.
iaculum, gar.
dens putridus, forrotad tod.
et amittit, and forlet.
pallium, wefels.

carmina, lioð.
pruinas, gleda.
(29ᵛ) *domatis*, huses.
quam cum muliere litigosa [3], ðanne
5 mid flitgeornan wife.
et uena corrupta, and gewemmed weteredre.
opprimitur, bid ofðreced.
urbs patens, open burh.
10 *cohibere*, geweldan.

XXVI

indecens, ungerisenu.
quo, hwider.
15 *prolatum*, ford broht.
in quaempiam, on enine.
et chamus, and bridel.
(30ʳ) *pulchras ... t[ibi]as*, fegere scacan [4].
20 *quomodo*, swa.
*nascatur, si oncenned.
temulenti, windruncynes.
terminat, endað.
silentium, swigan.
25 *qui iterat*, de gcedleeð.
leena, wildior.
sicut ... uertitur, swe forhwerfed bid.
in cardine suo, on hiore hyrran.
sub ascella sua, under his oxne.
30 *sententias*, cwidas.
(30ᵛ) *deprehensus*, anfunden.
ludens, plegende.
sussurrone subtracto, abrodenum gedwilde.
35 *et ... conquiescunt*, and gerestað.
susurronis, desiges.
ad intima, to incundum.
quomodo si ... [uelis] [5], swil gif ðu wille.
40 *uas fictile*, lemen fet.
labia tumentia, dindendende [6] weleras.
sociata, gefcrlehte.
quando summiserit, ðonne he underdiod.

---

[1] For searwa þu. Z.
[2] The Anglo-Saxon translator has mistaken the Latin *dehonestaueris*. Z.
[3] See pag. 74, 25 and pag. 83, 22. R.W.
[4] Read *scancan*. Z.
[5] *uelis* is omitted in the MS. R. W.
[6] For dindende. Z.

qui operit, se ðe werð [1].
qui uoluit, se ðe welt.
(31ʳ) [*os*] *lubricum,* twisprece.

XXVII

pariat, atewð.
laudet, heric.
saxum, stan.
honerosa, byrdenmete [2].
grauior, hefegre.
concitati, asterede.
ferre, acuman.
calcabit, tret.
uariis odoribus, misselicum sweccum.
et ... dulcoratur, and bið geweordlcht.
(31ᵛ) *sustinuere,* fordelgiad.
dispendia, leras.
qui spopondit, þe behet.
tecta perstillantia, driopende hrofas [3].
litigosa, flitgeor [4].
comparantur, sint widmetene.
uentum, wind.
quasi qui ... teneat, swa se ðe helt.
iacuitur [5], is scerped.
et ... exacuit, and scerpð.
qui seruat, se ðe helt.
quomodo ... respendent [6], swa swa scinað.
prospicientium, behealdenra.
(32ʳ) *insatiabiles,* unasedenlic.
conflatur [7], is blawen.
in conflatorio, on smiddan.
si contuderis, deh ðu þercce [8].
quasi lipsonas [9], swa berecorn.
feriente, derccedum. [10]
diligenter, georlice [11].
sed ... tribuitur, ac is seald.
prata, geheige.
collecta sunt, sint gegaderade.

[1] For wered. The glossator confounded *operari* with *operire.* Z.
[2] So read I. R. W.
[3] See pag. 74 l. 23. R. W.
[4] For flitgeorn. Z.
[5] The Vulgate has *exacuitur.* Cf. next line. R. W.
[6] For *resplendent.* Z.

XXVIII

nemine, nenegum.
persequente, ehtende.
(32ᵛ) *paratur,* is gegearwod.
5 *commessatores .i.,* wesan oþþe eteras.
coaceruat, geheapað.
et fenore liberali, and of frilicum gestrione.
(33ʳ) *fugerit,* flio.
10 *concidet,* ahriosð.
deserit, forlet.
inuidet, angað.
(33ᵛ) *iactat,* gelpð.
concitat, aweeþ.
15 *indigebit,* bedearf.
penuriam, erða [12].

XXIX

non sequetur, ne felhð.
20 *sumpserint,* nimþ.
perdet, forleose.
inuoluet, befelt.
(34ʳ) *in posterum,* forð on.
obuiauerunt, ongen coman.
25 *correptio,* ðreal [13].
refrigerabit, he arærð.
delicias, estas.
profetia, witedom.
(34ᵛ) *delicatæ,* estelice.
30 *a pueritia,* fram cnihthade.
nutrit, fet.
procliuior, fordloten.
subleuabitur, bið up ahafen.

XXX

35
morante, wuniendum.
(35ʳ) *et ... noui,* and ic eude.
si nosti, wastu ðe nasdu.
ignitus clipeus, ferentarga.
40 *ne addas,* ne geæcdu.
et arguaris, and ðu sio ðread.

[7] The Vulgate reads *probatur.* Z.
[8] For þersce. Z.
[9] A corruption of *ptisanas.* Z.
[10] For derscendum, cf. l. 35. Z.
[11] Read geornlice. Z.
[12] Read ermda. Z.
[13] Cf. Leo, Ags. glossar, p. 390 l. 47. R. W.

inueniarisque, and ðu sio gemet.
ne deneges, ne forwern ðu.
uictui meo, minre anlifene.
ne ... inliciar, ðe les ic sio forspanen.
ad negandum, to widsacenne.
et ... furer, and ic stele.
et periurem, and ic swerige.
nec accuses, ne ðu ne wrei.
(35ʳ) *molaribus suis*, of his cintoðum.
sanguissuge, lyces.
affer affer, bren bryn.
insaturabilia, unasedenlice.
sufficit, genoh is.
qui subsannat, se ðe hyspð.
et qui despicit, and se ðe forsiohð.
partum, eacnunga.
effodiant, up adelfað.
dificilia, earfoðu.
penitus, eallunga.
colubri, nedran.
in adolescentia, on giohðhade.
tergens, dregende.
(36ʳ) *odiosam*, hatol.
in matrimonium, on gesinscipe.
minima, lyssan.
sapientiora, wisran.
formicæ, emetan.
que parant, ða gearwiað.
lepusculi, haran.
inualida, unstraŋ[1].
qui collocat, se ðe gestadelað.
cubile suum, his den.
et egreditur, and ut geð.
per turmas, ðurh heapas.
stelio, hryremus.
nititur, he geð.
in ædibus, on hofum.
gradiuntur, gað.
non incedit[2], ne stepð.
aries, ram.
et qui ... aparuit, and se ðe ateaud.
postquam eleuatus est, seoððan he hup ahafen bið.

[1] For *unstrang*. R. W.
[2] The Vulgate has *quod incedit*. Z.
[3] The Vulg. reads *emungit*. Z.
[4] Read *gnoruiendum*. Z.

in sublime, up .i. heah.
ad eliciendum, ut to ationne.
expremit, ofðreeð, swetelað.
(36ᵛ) *qui ... emulget*[3], se ðe meleð.
5 *et ... elicit*, and ut atiohð.
et ... producit, and forð gelet.
discordias, twirednesse.

XXXI

dilecte mi, eala ðu min gecorena.
nullum secretum, enig deahle.
et mutent, and hio wendan.
siceram, bior.
15 *merentibus*, grnorniendum[4].
doloris, sares.
et ... non recordentur, and ne sint gemunene[5].
et causis, and ðine.
20 *qui pertranseunt*, ðe gewitað.
decerne, toscad.
(37ʳ) *lanam*, wullaı[6].
institoris, cypan.
praedam, huðe.
25 *domesticis suis*, hiore gehusan.
et cybaria, and andlifene.
et emit, and hi bohte.
ad fortia, to streuran[7].
fussum, spinle.
30 *duplicibus*, of twifealdum.
stragulam uestem, gebliod reaf.
byssum, of twine.
indumentum, reaf.
nobilis, eðelboren.
35 *sindonem*, scetan.
cingulum, gerdels.
et ridebit, and hio hlihð.
(37ᵛ) *tu supergressa est*[8], ðu oferstope.
40 2. ALCUINI EXHORTATIO AD
GUIDONEM COMITEM.

(39ʳ) *explicare*, onwrion.
(53ᵛ) *constans*, anred.

[5] For *gemunende*. Z.
[6] For *wullan*? Z.
[7] For *strengran*. R. W.
[8] Read *es*. Z.

(61ʳ) *intentione*, on ða gerad ¹.
ualet, fremeð ².
percutit, slæhð.
(61ᵛ) *appetit*, gedinð ³.
(62ʳ) *proditor*, læwend.
praedicator, bodiend.
non ... promittitur, nis behaten.
instantissime, geornlicost.
contendat, eftsf ⁴.
principalia, heafodlicf ⁵.
originalia, frfmðlice ⁶.
(62ᵛ) *pullulant*, wfacsað ⁷.
ratum, gescad.
extirpatis, arubfdxm ⁸.
praecidere, bprckpfbn ⁹.
ex contemptu, of forhpgxngb ¹⁰.
per contumaciam, þurh bþxndfnnfsf ¹¹.
praesumtio, ðrksnfs ¹².
pertinacia, bngknnb ¹³.
(63ʳ) *lasciuia*, wild.
eneruatio, awordenes.
(66ʳ) *pollicentur*, sint behat . . . . .
condonauit, forgef.
sugestiones, lare.
tollerare, forberan ¹⁴.
constat, wunað.

¹ Omitted by Zupitza. R W.
² Omitted by Zupitza. R. W.
³ For gedined or gedined. R. W.
⁴ This kind of cipher-writing by which the consonant following a certain vowel was placed for the latter, was very much in vogue in the Middle Ages. (eftsf = eftse, being an error for efste). R. W
⁵ = heafodlice. R. W.
⁶ = fremdlice. R W.
⁷ = weacsad. R. W.
⁸ = aruaedum. Perhaps miswritten for araeudum. Z.
⁹ For bckprfbn = aciorfan? Z.

in quacumque causa, on eihwilcum dinge.
(66ᵛ) *sapores*, stencas.
sonos, sweigas.
5 *transitorias*, gewitenlice.
uolatilis, fugeles.

(77ᵛ) *pater*, fe[der] ¹⁵.
mater, modo[r].
10 *frater*, brodo[r].
soror, sweosto[r].
filius, [sun]a.
filia, dohtor.
patruus, fædera.
15 *amita mea*, min fað[u].
matertera mæa, min modriæ.
auunculus meus, min eam.
uictricius, ste[op]feder.
priuignus, ste[op]sunu ¹⁶.
20 *filiaster*, steopdohter.
uir, ciorl.
uirgo, ides.
[*puella*, mei]den ¹⁷.
mamilla, tit[t].
25 *papilla*, forw[eard] tit[t].
creuerat, wfpx ¹⁸.

¹⁰ = forhogunga. R. W.
¹¹ = aþundennese. R. W
¹² = drisnes. R. W.
¹³ = anginna. R. W.
¹⁴ Omitted by Zupitza. R. W.
¹⁵ The letters enclosed in brackets are rather illegible. R. W.
¹⁶ This gloss is very doubtful. R. W.
¹⁷ All these letters are quite gone. Zupitza reads: *puella* (mei)den. R. W.
¹⁸ = weox. R. W.
Several other glosses had been inserted here but they have become entirely illegible. R. W.

III.

THE COLLOQUY OF
ARCHBISHOP ALFRIC[1]
OF THE TENTH CENTURY.

Colloquium ad pueros linguæ Latinæ locutione exercendos, ab Ælfrico primum compilatum, et deinde ab Ælfrico Bata, eius discipulo, auctum, Latine et Saxonice.

           we   cildra   biddaþ   þe eala lareow þæt þu tæce us sprecan
   D. Nos pueri rogamus te, magister, ut doceas nos loqui
         [rihte] for þam ungelærede we syndon and gewæmmodlice we sprecaþ
Latialiter recte, quia idiote sumus, et corrupte loquimur.
          hwæt wille ge sprecan
   M. Quid uultis loqui?
         hwæt   rece we   hwæt we sprecan buton hit riht spræc sy and
   D. Quid curamus quid loquamur, nisi recta locutio sit, et
behefe næs idel oþþe fracod
utilis, non anilis, aut turpis?
          wille [ge beon] beswungen on leornunge
   M. Uultis flagellari in discendo?

---

[1] Alfric of Canterbury, by whom this Colloquy was compiled, was commonly known by the title of Alfric the Grammarian, from the active part he took in the educational movement of his time. He was for a short time bishop of Wilton, and in 995 succeeded Sigeric as archbishop of Canterbury. He died on the 16th of November, 1006. The colloquy was probably composed in the earlier period of his life, when he was a monk of Winchester. It was, as stated in the Latin title, enlarged and republished by Alfric Bata, a scholar under the archbishop when he taught in the schools at Winchester, and who is supposed to have died about the middle of the eleventh century. On both these writers, see my Biographia Britannica Literaria, Anglo-Saxon period, pp. 480—500. The enlarged edition of the colloquy, by Alfric Bata, seems to have so entirely superseded the original, that it appears to be the only one now preserved. It is here printed from a manuscript in the British Museum, MS. Cotton. Tiberius A, III., fol. 58, v°, contemporary with Alfric Bata. The only other copy known is preserved in a MS. in the Library of St John's College, Oxford, in which the title, or rubric, is, *Hanc sententiam Latini sermonis olim Ælfricus abbas composuit, qui meus fuit magister, sed tamen ego Ælfric Bata multas postea huic addidi appendices.* Some additional words from the Oxford MS. are here printed within brackets. It will not escape remark, how much superior the sentiment which pervades this Anglo-Saxon tract is to that of the later mediaeval treatises of the same description. It is impossible now to say which were the additions made by Alfric Bata to the original tract, but we may reasonably consider the whole as belonging to the tenth century.

[Our text is based on a recent collation of Wright's print with the MS.—On Alfric of Canterbury, see Dietrich in Zeitschrift für histor. Theologie, 25. bd. pag. 487 et seqq., and 26. bd. pag. 163 et seqq. R W.]

     leofre ys us beon beswungen [1] for lare þænne hit ne cunnan
 D. Carius est nobis flagellari pro doctrina, quam nescire;
ac we witan þe bilewitne wesan and nellan onbelæden swincgla us buton
sed scimus te mansuetum esse, et nolle inferre plagas nobis, nisi
þu bi to-genydd fram us
 cogaris a nobis.
    ic axie þe hwæt sprycst þu hwæt hæfst þu weorkes
 M. Interrogo te quid mihi loqueris? quid habes operis?
  ic eom geanwyrde monuc and ic sincge ælce dæg seofon
 D. Professus sum monachum, et psallam omni die septem
 tida mid gebroþrum and ic eom bysgod [on rædinga] and on sange
sinaxes [2] cum fratribus, et occupatus sum lectionibus et cantu;
ac þeah hwæþere ic wolde betwenan leornian sprecan on Leden gereorde
sed tamen uellem interim discere sermocinari Latina lingua.
   hwæt cunnon þas þine geferan
 M. Quid sciunt isti tui socii?
  sume synt yrþlincgas sume scephyrdas sume oxanhyrdas sume
 D. Alii sunt aratores, alii opiliones, quidam bubulci, quidam
eac swylce huntan sume fisceras sume fugeleras sume cypmenn
etiam uenatores, alii piscatores, alii aucupes, quidam mercatores,
sume scewyrhtan sealteras bæceras.
quidam sutores, quidam salinatores, quidam pistores loci.
   hwæt sægest þu yrþlinge hu begæst þu weorc þin
 M. Quid dicis tu, arator [3], quomodo exerces opus tuum?
  eala leof hlaford þearle ic deorfe ic ga ut on dægræd þywende
 A. O mi domine, nimium laboro; exeo diluculo, minando
oxon to felda and iugie hig to syl nys hyt swa stearc
boues ad campum, et iungo eos ad aratrum; non est tam aspera
winter þæt ic durre lutian æt ham for ege hlafordes mines ac gelukodan
hiemps ut audeam latere domi, pre timore domini mei; sed iunctis
 oxan and gefæstnodon sceare and cultre mid þære syl ælce dæg ic sceal
bobus, et confirmato uomere et cultro aratro, omni die debeo
 arian fulne æcer [4] oþþe mare
arare integrum agrum, aut plus.
    hæfst þu ænigne geferan
 M. Habes aliquem socium?
   ic hæbbe sumne cnapan þywende oxan mid gadisene þe
 A. Habeo quendam puerum minantem boues cum stimulo [5], qui
eac swilce nu has ys for cylde and hreame.
etiam modo raucus est, pre frigore et clamatione.

---

[1] The MS. has: beswugen. R. W.

[2] *Septem synaxes*, the seven canonical hours, or, more literally according to the meaning of the word, the assemblies of the monks at those hours for the several services which belonged to them. It is from this practice that the old Catholic service-books are called *Hours* (*horae*, *heures*), as containing the forms of service for the canonical hours of the day. (See further on.)

[3] The Anglo-Saxon sentiment which gave the first rank in worth and utility to the practice of agriculture, is curiously illustrated by implication here, where it is taken first in order of the occupations of men, and more directly further on, where its excellence is made the subject of discussion.

[4] The MS. reads distinctly æper, which is no doubt an error for æcer. R. W.

[5] It is a curious circumstance, as showing how little the practice of agriculture had changed in this country through many centuries, that the illuminations of manuscripts, down to a late period, represent

M. Quid amplius facis in die?
<small>hwæt mare deft þu on dæg</small>
<small>gewyslice þænne mare ic do ic sceal fyllan binnan oxan mid hig</small>
A. Certe adhuc plus facio. Debeo implere presepia boum feno,
<small>and wæterian¹ hig and scearn² heora beran ut</small>
et adaquare cos, et fimum eorum portare foras.
<small>hig hig micel gedeorf ys hyt</small>
M. O, O, magnus labor est!
<small>ge leof micel gedeorf hit ys forþam ic neom freoh.</small>
A. Etiam, magnus labor est, quia non sum liber³.
<small>[hwæt segst þu] sceaphyrde hæfst þu ænig gedeorf.</small>
M. Quid dicis tu, opilio? Habes tu aliquem laborem⁴?
<small>gea leof ic hæbbe on forewerdne morgen ic drife sceap mine to heora læse</small>
O. Etiam habeo; in primo mane mino oues meas ad pascua,
<small>and stande ofer hig on hæte and on cyle mid hundum þe læs wulfas forswelgen</small>
et sto super eas, in estu⁵ et frigore, cum canibus, ne lupi⁶ deuorent
<small>hig and ic agenlæde hig to heora loca and melke hig tweowa on dæg and heora</small>
eas, et reduco eas ad caulas, et mulgeo eas bis in die, et caulas
<small>loca ic hæbbe on þærto and cyse and buteran ic do and ic eom getrywe</small>
earum moueo insuper, et caseum et butirum facio, et fidelis sum
<small>hlaforde minon</small>
domino meo⁷.
<small>eala oxanhyrde hwæt wyrst þu</small>
M. O bubulce, quid operaris tu?
<small>eala hlaford min micel ic gedeorfe þænne se yrþlinge unscenþ</small>
B. O domine mi, multum laboro. Quando arator disiungit
<small>þa oxan ic læde hig to læse and ealle niht ic stande ofer hig waciende</small>
boues, ego duco eos ad pascua, et tota nocte sto super eos uigilando
<small>for þeofan and eft on ærne mergen ic betæce hig þam yrþlincge wel gefylde</small>
propter fures⁸, et iterum primo mane adsigno eos aratori, bene pastos
<small>and gewæterode</small>
et adaquatos.
<small>ys þæs of þinum geferum</small>
M. Est iste ex tuis sociis?
<small>gea he ys</small>
D. Etiam est.

---

the oxen yoked to the plough, driven by the ploughman, with the boy who carries the *goad* [*gadiserne*], to urge them on.

[1] The MS. by an error reads wæteterian. R. W.

[2] The glossator wrote sceasn. R. W.

[3] The agricultural labourer, among the Anglo-Saxons, was a serf (a þeow), and belonged to the lord of the land as much as the land itself, to which, in fact, he was attached. This passage of Alfric's Colloquy is a curious illustration of the feeling of commiseration for the condition of the servile class, which prevailed among the Anglo-Saxon clergy, and which disappeared at the time of the Norman conquest, when feudalism, which inculcated a profound contempt for the unnoble classes of society, was introduced into our island.

[4] The MS. reads *labore*. R. W.

[5] The MS. has *esto*. R. W.

[6] Wolves appear still at this time to have been common in England.

[7] It would appear from this passage that ewes' milk was that used principally by the Anglo-Saxons; and that it was the business of the shepherd to furnish the household with milk, butter, and cheese.

[8] Cattle were the great objects of plunder in the predatory excursions of the middle ages, and the care of the cattle at night was a duty of great importance among the Anglo-Saxons; hence the herdsman was a person of more consideration than

            canst þu ænig þing
   M. Scis tu aliquid?
            anne cræft ic cann.
   V. Unam artem scio.
            hwylcne ys
   M. Quale est?
            hunta ic eom.
   V. Uenator sum.
            hwæs
   M. Cuius?
            cineges
   V. Regis.
            hu begæst þu cræft þinne
   M. Quomodo exerces artem tuam?
          ic brede me max and sette hig on stowe gehæppre and getihte hundas
   V. Plecto mihi retia, et pono ea in loco apto, et instigo canes
mine þæt wildeor hig ehton oþ þæt hig þe cuman to þam nettan
meos ut feras persequantur, usque quo perueniunt ad retia
unforsceawodlice and þæt hig swa beon begrynode[1] and ic ofslea hig on þam maxum
inprouise, et sic inretientur, et ego iugulo eos in retibus.[2]
          ne canst þu huntian buton mid nettum
   M. Nescis uenare nisi cum retibus?
           gea butan nettum huntian ic mæg
   V. Etiam, sine retibus uenare possum.
           hu
   M. Quomodo?
          mid swiftum hundum ic betæce[3] wildeor
   V. Cum uelocibus canibus insequor feras.
          hwilce wildeor swyþost gefehþ þu
   M. Quales feras maxime capis?
         ic gefeo heortas and baras and rann and rægan and hwilon
   V. Capio ceruos, et apros, et dammas, et capreos, et aliquando
haran
lepores.
          wære þu to dæg on huntnolde
   M. Fuisti hodie in uenatione?
         ic næs forþam sunnandæg ys, ac gyrstandæg ic wæs on
   V. Non fui, quia dominicus dies est, sed heri fui in
huntunge
uenatione.

the agricultural labourer. His duties, as intimated in our text, are illustrated by what Bede tells us with regard to the poet Cædmon, in the seventh century — *Quod dum tempore quodam faceret, et relicta domo conviuii, egressus est ad stabula jumentorum, quorum ei custodia nocte illa erat delegata.* Bedae Hist. Eccles. lib. iv. c. 24. In king Alfred's Anglo-Saxon version this passage is rendered: *to neata scypene, dær heorde him wæs dære nihte beboden.*

[1] The manuscript reads begrynode, which is no doubt an error of the scribe for begrynode. R. W.

[2] The hunter among the Anglo-Saxons appears to have answered nearly to our gamekeeper, and his method of taking the game militates rather against our ordinary notions of the mediaeval passion for the chase. But the Anglo-Saxons do not appear to have been, in general, great hunters, in the sense of the word as it was taken by the Anglo-Normans, for hawking appears to have been the more favourite diversion with them.

[3] An error for betæce. R. W.

COLLOQUY OF ARCHBISHOP ALFRIC.

         hwæt gelæhtest þu
M. Quid cepisti?
       twegen heortas and ænne bar
V. Duos ceruos et unum aprum.
       hu gefencge þu hig
M. Quomodo cepisti eos?
     heortas ic gefenge on nettum and bar ic ofsloh
V. Ceruos cepi in retibus, et aprum iugulaui.
      hu wære þu dyrstig ofstiklan *bar
M. Quomodo fuisti ausus iugulare aprum?
    hundas bedrifon hyne to me and ic þær togeanes standende færlice
V. Canes perduxerunt eum ad me, et ego e contra stans subito
ofstikode hyne
iugulaui eum.
      swyþe þryste þu wære þa
M. Ualde audax fuisti tunc.
    ne sceal hunta forhtfull wesan forþam mislice wildeor
V. Non debet uenator formidolosus esse, quia uarie bestie
wuniad on wudum
morantur in siluis.
     hwæt dest þu be þinre huntunge
M. Quid facis de tua uenatione?
    ic sylle cyne swa hwæt swa ic gefo forþam ic eom hunta hys
V. Ego do regi quicquid capio, quia sum uenator eius.
     hwæt sylþ he þe
M. Quid dat ipse tibi?
    he scryt me wel and fett and hwilon syþ me hors oþþe
V. Uestit me bene et pascit, aliquando dat mihi equum, aut
beah   þæt þe lustlicor cræft minne ic begancge
armillam, ut libentius artem meam exerceam.
     hwylcne cræft canst þu
M. Qualem artem scis tu?
    ic eom fiscere
P. Ego sum piscator.
     hwæt begyst þu of þinum cræfte
M. Quid adquiris de tua arte?
    bigleofan and scrud and feoh
P. Uictum et uestitum et pecuniam [1].
     hu gefehst þu fixas
M. Quomodo capis pisces?
    ic astigie min scyp and wyrpe max mine on ea and anegil, uel æs [2],
P. Ascendo nauem, et pono retia mea in amne, et hamum
ic wyrpe and spyrtan and swa hwæt swa big gehæftad ic genime
proiicio et sportas, et quicquid ceperint sumo.
     hwæt gif hit unclæne beoþ [3] fixas
M. Quid si inmundi [4] fuerint pisces?

[1] The hunter was a man in the employ of another; his occupation was an office, or service. The fisherman worked for himself.

[2] The glossator appears to have been doubtful of the meaning of *hamus*. The word *æs* means a bait; *angil*, which means a hook, is of course the origin of our term *angling*, given to the process of fishing with the line and hook.

[3] The MS has: beoþ beoþ fixas. R.W.

[4] The MS, by an error reads *inmundo*. R. W.

          ic   utwyrpe þa unclænan[1] ut and genime me   clæne to mete
P. Ego proiiciam inmundos[2] foras, et sumo mihi mundos in escam.
       hwær cypst þu fixas þine
M. Ubi uendis pisces tuos?
    on   ceastre
P. In ciuitate.
   hwa bigþ   hi
M. Quis emit illos?
  ceasterwara ic ne mæg   swa fela [gefon] swa fela swa ic mæg[3] gesyllan
P. Ciues. Non possum tot capere quot possum uendere.
     hwilce   fixas gefehst þu
M. Quales pisces capis?
      ælas   and hacodas mynas and æleputan   sceotan and lampredan
P. Anguillas, et lucios, menas, et capitones, tructos, et murenas[4],
and swa wylcc swa   on wætere swymmaþ sprote
et qualescunque in amne   natant saliu.
     for hwi ne   fixast þu on   sæ
M. Cur non piscaris in mari
      hwilon   ic do   ac   seldon forþam micel   rewyt   me ys
P. Aliquando facio, sed raro, quia magnum nauigium mihi est
to   sæ
ad mare.
     hwæt fehst þu on   sæ
M. Quid capis in mari?
    hærincgas and leaxas mereswyn and stirian ostran and crabban   muslan
P. Alleces et isicios, delfinos et sturias, ostreas et cancros, musculas,
pinewinclan sæcoccas   fage and   floc and lopystran and fela swylces
torniculi, neptigalli, platesia, et platissa, et polipodes, et similia[5].
     wilt þu fon   sumne   hwæl
M. Uis capere aliquem cetum?
    nic
P. Nolo.
  forhwi
M. Quare?
    forhwan plyhtlic þinge hit ys gefon   hwæl   gebeorhtlicre ys me faran
P. Quia periculosa res est capere cetum. Tutius est mihi ire

---

[1] The MS. has: utclænan. R. W.
[2] Here the MS. again reads *inmundo*. R. W.
[3] In the MS. we find: ic ne mæg swa fela swa ic mæg swa fela swa ic mæg. R.W.
[4] The list of river-fish is not very large; and it is not easy to explain the absence of several which must have been in common use among our Anglo-Saxon forefathers, especially if *mynas* signify minnows, as it has been interpreted. [See the Index s. v. *mynas*. R. W.] *Eel-pout* is still the name for a small kind of eel.
[5] Herrings come first in the list of sea-fish, because they were more extensively used than any other kind of fish throughout the Middle Ages. Red-herrings figure largely in the mediaeval household accounts. The Anglo-Saxon name for the salmon, called in old English *lax*, had not been quite displaced by the Anglo-Norman one in the fourteenth century. The *mereswyn* was probably the porpoise, which was supposed to answer to the Latin *delphinus*. The sturgeon *(stiria)* is now no more eaten than the porpoise; the *fage* and *floc* were probably plaice and soles; the *sæcoccas* were no doubt cockles.

COLLOQUY OF ARCHBISHOP ALFRIC.   95

to   ea   mid scype mynan þænne faran mid manegum scypum on   huntunge
ad amnem cum [naue]¹ mea, quam ire cum multis nauibus in uenationem
hranes
ballene.
       forhwi swa
   M. Cur sic?
      forþam leofre   ys   me   gefon   fisc   þæne   ic mæg ofslean   þe
   P. Quia carius est mihi capere piscem quem possum occidere, qui
na   þæt an   me   ac eac swylce mine   geferan mid anum   slege he mæg besencean
non solum me sed etiam meos socios   uno   ictu potest mergere
oþþe gecwylman
aut mortificare.
     and þeah mænige gefoþ   hwælas and æþberstaþ frecnysse and micelne
   M. Et tamen multi capiunt cetos,² et euadunt pericula, et magnum
sceat   þanon begytaþ
pretium inde adquirunt.
     soþ   þu segst ac   ic ne geþristige for   modes mines nytenysse
   P. Uerum dicis, sed ego non audeo, propter mentis meæ ignauiam.
     hwæt sægst þu   fugelere   hu   beswicst þu fugelas
   M. Quid dicis tu, auceps? quomodo decipis aues?
     on feala wisan   ic beswice fugelas   hwilon   mid neton
   A. Multis modis decipio aues; aliquando retibus, aliquando
mid grinum   mid lime   mid hwistlunge   mid hafoce
laqueis, aliquando glutino, aliquando   sibilo,   aliquando accipitre,
mid treppan
aliquando decipula.
     hæfst þu   hafoc
   M. Habes accipitrem?
     ic hæbbe
   A. Habeo.
     canst þu temian   hig
   M. Scis domitare eos?
     gea   ic cann hwæt sceoldon hig me   buton ic cuþe temian   hig
   A. Etiam scio. Quid deberent mihi, nisi scirem domitare eos?
     syle me   ænne   hafoc
   V. Da mihi unum accipitrem.
     ic sylle   lustlice gyf þu sylst   me   ænne   swyftne hund   hwylcne
   A. Dabo libenter, si dederis mihi unum uelocem canem. Qualem
hafoc   wilt þu habban   þone maran hwæþer þe þæne læssan
accipitrem uis habere, maiorem   aut   minorem?
     syle me   þæne maran
   V. Da mihi maiorem.
     hu   afest þu   hafocas   þine
   M. Quomodo pascis accipitres tuos?

---

[1] The Cotton MS. has *homo mea* (for *homo*). But the Anglo-Saxon translation answers to *naue* not to *homo*. R. W.

[2] There are many reasons for believing that the whale trade was carried on to a considerable extent by the Anglo-Saxons, as well as by the northern nations. The walrus was an object of value then, on account of its teeth, which, under the name of whales'-bone, were used in place of ivory, and form the substance of many ornamental objects in our cabinets.

          hig   fedaþ   hig sylfe and me on   wintra   and on lenegten ic læte hig
   A. Ipsi pascunt   se   et me in hieme, et in   uere dimitto eos
ætwindan to   wuda   and genyme   me   briddas on hærfæste and temige   hig
auolare ad siluam, et   capio   mihi pullos¹ in autumno, et domito   eos,
           and forhwi forlæst   þu   þa getemedon ætwindan fram þe
   M. Et cur permittis [tu]   domitos   auolare a te?
        forþam ic nelle fedan hig on sumera forþam þe hig þearle   etaþ
   A. Quia nolo pascere eos in estate, eo   quod nimium comedunt.
     and manige fedaþ þa getemodon ofer   sumor   þæt eft hig habban
   M. Et multi pascunt   domitos super estatem, ut iterum habeant
gearuwe
paratos.
         gea   swa hig doþ ac   ic   nelle o² þæt an   deorfan   ofer hig
   A. Etiam sic faciunt, sed ego nolo in tantum laborare super eos,
forþam ic cann oþre na   þæt   ænne ac eac swilce manige gefon
quia scio alios non solum unum sed etiam   plures capere³.
     hwæt sægst þu mancgere⁴
   M. Quid dicis tu, mercator?
        ic secge   þæt behefe ic eom ge cinge and ealdormannum and
   MER. Ego dico quod utilis   sum et regi et   ducibus   et
weligum and eallum follce
diuitibus et omni populo.
      and   hu
   M. Et quomodo?
         ic astige min scyp mid hlæstum   minum and rowe   ofer
   MER. Ego ascendo nauem cum mercibus meis, et nauigo ultra
sælice   dælas and cype mine þinge and bicge þincg dyrwyrde þa on þisum
marinas partes et uendo meas res, et emo res pretiosas quæ in hac
lande   ne   beoþ acennede and ic hit togrlæde eow hider mid micclan plihte
terra non   nascuntur, et   adduco   uobis huc, cum magno periculo
ofer   sæ and hwylon forlidenesse ic þolie mid   lyre ealra   þinga
super mare, et aliquando naufragium patior, cum iactura omnium rerum
minra   uneaþe cwic ætberstende
mearum, uix uiuus euadens.
     hwylce þinc gelædst þu   us
   M. Quales res adduces nobis?
        pællas and sidan   deorwyrþe gymmas and gold selcuþe
   MER. Purpurum, et sericum, pretiosas gemmas, et aurum, uarias
reaf and wyrtgemange win   and   ele ylpesban and mæstlinge   ær and
uestes, et pigmenta, uinum, et oleum, ebur, et auricalcum, æs, et
   tin   swefel and   glæs   and þylces   fela
stagnum, sulfur, et uitrum, et   his similia⁵.

---

¹ The MS. has *pullo*. R. W.

² So the MS. Not: oþ þæt, as Wright read. R. W.

³ The MS. by an error reads *cape* for *capere*. R. W.

⁴ It is a curious instance of the degradation through which words go, that what was in the Saxon period the designation for the most elevated description of merchant, *mancgere*, is now only a term for small dealers, and principally in petty wares, *monger*.

⁵ We must no doubt consider this as a list of the most valuable articles imported into this country under the Anglo-Saxons. *Purpura*, or, as it is translated in Anglo-Saxon, *pællas*, was a sort of rich stuff brought from the east, and is coupled with silk. *Pigmenta*, explained by *wyrtgemanc*, appears to have been

COLLOQUY OF ARCHBISHOP ALFRIC.

   wilt þu syllan þinge þine her eal swa þu hi gebohtest þær
M. Uis uendere res tuas hic, sicut emisti illic?

   Ic nelle hwæt þænne me fremode gedeorf min ac ic wielle[1]
MER. Nolo. Quid tunc mihi proficit labor meus? Sed uolo
heora cypen her luflicor þonne [ic] gebicge þær þæt sum gestreon me
uendere hic carius quam emi illic ut aliquod lucrum mihi
ic begyte þanon ic me afede and min wif and minne sunu
adquiram, unde me pascam et uxorem et filios.

   þu sceowyrhta hwæt wyrcst þu us nytwyrþnessæ
M. Tu, sutor, quid operaris nobis utilitatis?

   ys witodlice cræft min behefe þearle eow and neodþearf
S. Est quidem ars mea utilis ualde uobis et necessaria.

   hu
M. Quomodo?

   ic bicge hyda and fell and gearkie hig mid cræfte minon and wyrce
S. Ego emo cutes et pelles, et preparo eas arte mea, et facio
of him gescy mistlices cynnes swyftleras and sceos leþerhosa and
ex eis calciamenta diuersi generis, subtalares et ficones, coligas et
butericas bridelþwancgas and geræda flaxan *uel* pinnan[2] and higdifatu spurleþera
utres, frenos et falera, flascones et calidilia[3], calcaria
and hælftra pusan and fætelsas and nan eower nele oferwintran buton
et chamos, peras et marsupia, et nemo uestrum uult hiemare sine
minon cræfte
mea arte.

   sealtera hwæt us fremaþ cræft þin
M. O salinator, quid nobis proficit ars tua?

   þearle fremaþ cræft min eow eallum nan eower blisse bryed
S. Multum prodest ars mea omnibus, nemo uestrum gaudio fruitur
on gererdinege oþþe mete buton cræft min gistliþe him beo
in prandio aut cena nisi ars mea hospita ei fuerit[4].

   hu
M. Quomodo?

---

a general term for perfumes. Glass appears to have been little made in England during the Saxon period; and the enumeration of the metals would seem to show that the great mining operations of the Romans had ceased after the Saxon invasion.

[1] So the MS. R. W.

[2] It will be seen by this enumeration of articles, that the business of the Anglo-Saxon shoewright was much more extensive than that of the modern shoemaker; in fact, all articles made of leather came within his province. Among these were leathern flasks, and various other vessels, as well as leather bags and purses (*pusan and fætelsas*).

[3] It is doubtful, whether the MS. has *calidilia* or *casidilia*. R. W.

[4] The importance of the salter is better understood when we consider that, as the produce of the land was in the Middle Ages almost entirely consumed on the spot, and it was not easy to get supplies of provisions from a distance, immense quantities of victuals of all kinds were salted, in order that they might keep during the whole year round, and were preserved in vast larders and storehouses. This habit of eating so much salt meat, would cause meats eaten without salt to be considered insipid. In fact, the quantity of salt used in the Middle Ages must have been enormous; and to it, probably, we must ascribe the prevalence of those diseases which excited so much horror under the name of leprosy.

　　　　　hwylc　　manna　þurh werodum¹ þurhbrycþ mettum buton swæcce sealtes
　　S. Quis hominum dulcibus　　perfruitur cibis sine sapore salis?
　　hwa　gefylþ　cleafan　his oþþe　hedderna　buton cræfte² minon　efne
　　Quis repplet cellaria sua siue promptuaria sine arte　mea? Ecce
butergeþweor ælc and cysgerunn losaþ eow buton ic hyrde ætwese eow þe
　　butirum omne et caseum perit uobis, nisi ego custos adsim,　qui
　　ne furþoon an　wyrtum　eowrum butan me　brucaþ
　nec saltem　oleribus uestris sine me utimini.
　　　　　[hwæt segst þu] bæcere hwam fremaþ [cræft þin] oþþe hwæþer we butan
　　M. Quid dicis tu, pistor?³ Cui prodest ars tua, aut　　si　　sine
þe　magon　　lif　adreogan
te possimus uitam ducere?
　　　　　ge magon　　　þurh sum　　　fæc butan [minon cræfte lif adreogan
　　P. Potestis quidem per aliquod spatium sine　arte　mea uitam ducere,
ac]　　na lancge ne　to　　wel soþlice butan cræfte minon ælc　beod　æmtig
sed non diu, nec adeo bene; nam sine arte　mea omnis mensa uacua
byþ gesewen and buton hlafe　ælc　mete to wlættan byþ gehwyrfed ic heortan
uidetur esse, et sine pane omnis cibus in nausium conuertitur. Ego cor
　mannes gestrangie　ic　mægen　wera　　　and furþon litlinegas nellaþ for-
hominis confirmo, ego robur uirorum sum, et　nec paruuli uolunt præ-
bigean me
terire me.
　　　　　[hwæt secgaþ we be coce] hwæþer we beþurfon on æuigon cræfte
　　M. Quid dicimus de coco,　si　indigemus in aliquo　arte eius?
　　　　　　　gif ge me ut adrifaþ fram eowrum geferscypæ　ge etaþ
　　Dicit cocus: Si me expellitis a　uestro collegio, manducabitis
　wyrta　eowre grene and flæscmettas eowre hreawe and　　furþon fætt
holera uestra uirida, et　carnes uestras crudas, et nec saltem pingue
broþ ge magon [butan cræfte minon habban]
ius potestis sine arte mea habere.
　　　　　we ne reccaþ [be cræfte þinon] ne he us　neodþearf ys forþam we
　　M. Non curamus de arte　tua,　nec nobis neccessaria est, quia nos
sylfe　magon　seoþan　þa þinge þe　to seoþenne synd and brædan þa þinge þe
ipsi possumus coquere　　quæ　　coquenda sunt et assare　que
to brædene synd
assanda sunt.⁴
　　　　　gif ge forþy me fram adryfaþ þæt ge þus don　þonne beo ge
　　Dicit cocus: Si ideo me expellitis, ut　sic faciatis, tunc eritis
ealle　þrælas and nan　　eower ne biþ hlaford and þeahhwæþere buton [cræfte
omnes serui,⁵ et nullus uestrum erit dominus; et　　tamen sine arte
minon] ge　　ne etaþ
mea non manducatis.

---

¹ The glossator seems to have repeated the preposition "þurh" of þurhbrycþ before "werodum". R. W.
² By an error the MS. reads: buton seræfte. R. W.
³ The Cotton MS. reads pastor. R. W.
⁴ The writer of the colloquy is here expressing the feeling of the more strictly sober part of the community, against the extravagance of the table, which seems to have been increasing very much during the latter part of the Anglo-Saxon period.
⁵ The Cotton MS., by an evident error, has coci. R. W.

COLLOQUY OF ARCHBISHOP ALFRIC.   99

     eala   munuc   þe   me   tospycst   efne ic hæbbe afandod þe habban
M. O monache, qui mihi locutus es, ecce   probaui   te habere
gode   geferan and þearle   neodþearfe and ic ahsie þa
bonos socios, et ualde necessarios; qui sunt illi?
         ic hæbbe smiþas isenesmiþas goldsmiþ seoloforsmiþ   arsmiþ
D. Habeo fabros, ferrarium, aurificem, argentarium, ærarium,
treowwyrhtan and manegra oþre mistlicra cræfta biggencoras
lignarium, et multos alios uariarum artium operatores.[1]
       hæfst ænigne[2]   wisne   geþeahtan
M. Habes aliquem sapientem consiliarium?
    gewislice ic hæbbe [hu   mæg]   ure gegaderunge buton geþeahtynde
D. Certe habeo. Quomodo potest nostra congregatio sine consiliario
beon wissod
regi?
       [hwæt segst þu] wisa   hwilc cræft þe geþuht betwux þas furþra
M. Quid dicis tu, sapiens? que ars tibi uidetur inter istas prior
wesan
esse?
     [ic secge þe[me ys geþuht godes þeowdom betweoh þas cræftas ealdorscype
C. Dico tibi, mihi uidetur seruitium Dei inter istas artes primatum
healdan swa swa hit [ys] geræd on godspelle fyrmest secead   rice godes
tenere, sicut   legitur in euangelio, Primum querite regnum Dei
and rihwisnesse hys and þas þinge ealle beoþ togehyhte eow
et iustitiam eius, et   hæc omnia adiicientur uobis.
         and hwilc þe geþuht betwux cræftas woruld[3] heoldan ealdordom
M. Et quales tibi uidetur inter artes seculares retinere primatum?
    eorþtilþ   forþam se yrþling us   ealle   fett
C. Agricultura, quia arator nos omnes pascit.[4]
  se smiþ   secgd hwanon [þam yrþlinge] sylanscear oþþe culter þe na
Ferrarius dicit:[5] Unde   arator uomer aut culter, qui nec
gade haefþ buton of cræfte minon hwanon fiscere ancgel oþþe sceowyrhton
stimulum habet nisi ex arte mea? Unde piscatori hamus, aut   sutori
  æl   oþþe seamere nædl nis hit of minon geweorce
subula, siue sartori[6] acus? nonne ex meo opere?
   se geþeahtend andsweraþ soþ witodlice sægst ac   eallum   us leofre
Consiliarius respondit: Uerum quidem dicis; sed omnibus nobis carius
ys   wikian mid þe yrþlinege þonne mid þe forþam se yrþling syld us
est hospitari apud te aratorem quam apud te; quia   arator dat nobis

---

[1] *Smith* was the general term for a worker in metals, and *wright* for one who worked in wood, and other materials. Hence, in the later English period, *smith* (which, in Anglo-Saxon, when used without any characteristic addition, was understood as applying more particularly to the worker in iron,) became the particular name of a blacksmith, and *wright* of a carpenter, as it is still in Scotland. The iron-smith (isene-smid) of the Anglo-Saxons was our blacksmith and whitesmith combined.

[2] The MS. has erroneously: ænigre. R W.

[3] *Sic MS.* for cræftas worulde or woruld cræftas. R. W.

[4] This notion of the pre-eminence of agriculture above all other crafts, has been noticed before. It is no less curious to remark, at this very early period, the sort of antagonism between the agricultural and the trading and manufacturing portion of the community, which seems to have existed in all ages in modern times. The artisans who are introduced in the colloquy, rise up indignantly to protest against the superiority which the "wise man" ascribes to agriculture.

[5] The MS. omitted the *t* in *dicit*. R.W.

[6] The MS. reads *saltori*. R. W.

hlaf and drenc þu hwæt sylst us on smiþþan þinre buton isenne
panem et potum; tu quid das nobis in officina[1] tua, nisi ferreas
fyrspearcan and swegincga beatendra slecgea and blawendra byliga
scintillas et sonitus tundentium malleorum et flantium[2] follium?
se treowwyrhta segd hwile eower ne notaþ cræfte minon þonne hus
   Lignarius dicit: Quis uestrum non utitur arte mea, cum domos,
and mistlice fata and scypa eow eallum ic wyrce
et diuersa uasa, et naues, omnibus fabrico?
   se golsmiþ[3] andwyrt eala trywwyrta forhwi swa sprycst þu þonne ne furþon
   Ferrarius respondit: O lignarie, cur sic loqueris, cum nec saltem
an þyrl [buton cræfte minou] þu ne miht don
unum foramen sine arte mea   uales facere?
  se geþeahtend sægþ eala geferan and gode wyrhtan uton towurpon hwætlicor
   Consiliarius dicit: O socii et boni operarii, dissoluamus citius
þas geflitu and sy sibb and geþwærnyss betweoh us and framige
has contentiones, et sit pax et concordia inter nos, et prosit
urum gebwylcum oþron on crafte hys and gedwærian symble mid þam yrþinge
unusquisque alteri arte sua, et conueniamus semper apud aratorem,
þær we bicleofan us and foddor horsum urum habbaþ and þis geþeaht
ubi uictum nobis et pabula equis nostris habemus; et hoc consilium
ic sylle eallum wyrhtum þæt anra gehwylc cræft his georulice begange
do omnibus operariis, ut unusquisque artem suam diligenter exerceat;
forþam se þe cræft his forlæt he byþ forlæten fram þam cræfte swa hwæder
quia qui artem suam dimiserit, ipse dimittatur ab arte. Siue
þu sy swa mæsseprest swa munuc swa ceorl swa kempa bega oþþe behwyrf
sis sacerdos, siue monachus, seu laicus, seu miles, exerce
þe sylfne on þisum and beo þæt þu eart forþam micel hynd[4] and
temet ipsum in hoc; et esto quod es, quia magnum dampnum et
sceamu byt is menn nelle wesan þæt þæt he ys and þæt þe he wesan sceal
uerecundia est homini nolle[5] esse quod est et quod esse debet.
      eala cild   hu eow licaþ þeos spæc
   M. O pueri, quomodo uobis placet ista locutio?
       wel   heo licaþ us ac þearle deoplice sprycst and ofer
   D. Bene quidem placet nobis, sed ualde profunde loqueris, et ultra
mæþe ure þu forþtyht spræce ac sprec us æfter urum
etatem nostram protrahis sermonem; sed loquere nobis juxta nostrum
andgyte þæt we magon understandan þa þing þe þu specst
intellectum, ut possimus intelligere que loqueris?
         ic ahsige eow forhwi swa geornlice leornia ge
   M. Interrogo uos cur tam diligenter discitis.
       forþam we nellaþ wesan swa stunte nytenu þa nan þing witaþ buton
   D. Quia nolumus esse sicut bruta animalia, quæ nihil sciunt nisi
gærs[6] and wæter
herbam et aquam.
           and hwæt wille ge
   M. Et quid uultis uos?
        [we] wyllaþ wesan wise
   D. Uolumus esse sapientes.

---

[1] The scribe by an evident error wrote: *officia*. R. W.
[2] The MS. has: *flantiu*. R. W.
[3] So the MS. R. W
[4] *Sic MS.*; not *hynd*. R. W.
[5] The MS. reads *nelle*. R. W.
[6] The MS. reads *gard* instead of *gærs*. R. W.

M. Qua sapientia? Uultis esse uersipelles, aut milleformes, in mendaciis uafri,[1] in loquelis astuti, uersuti, bene loquentes et male cogitantes, dulcibus uerbis dediti, dolum intus alentes, sicut sepulchrum depicto mausoleo intus plenum fetore?

D. Nolumus sic esse sapientes, quia non est sapiens qui[3] simulatione semet ipsum decipit.

M. Sed quomodo uultis?

D. Uolumus esse simplices sine hipochrisi, et sapientes, ut declinemus a malo et faciamus bona; adhuc tamen profundius nobiscum disputas quam ætas nostra capere possit; sed loquere nobis nostro more, non tam profunde.

M. Et ego faciam sicut rogatis. Tu, puer, quid fecisti hodie?

D. Multas res feci. Hac nocte, quando signum audiui, surrexi de lectulo et exiui ad ecclesiam, et cantaui nocturnam cum fratribus; deinde cantauimus de omnibus sanctis et matutinales laudes; post hæc, primam, et vii. psalmos, cum letaniis, et primam missam; deinde tertiam, et fecimus missam de die; post hæc cantauimus sextam, et manducauimus, et bibimus, et dormiuimus, et iterum surreximus, et cantauimus nonam, et modo sumus hic coram te, parati audire quid nobis dixeris.

---

[1] The Cotton MS. has *astuti* for *uafri*.
[2] The scribe wrote: *fan.* R. W.
[3] The MS. has: *qua simulatione.* R.W.
[4] In *cyrcean* the writer omitted the r. R. W.
[5] So the MS. R. W.
[6] The scribe wrote: drucon. R. W.
[7] The account here given of the regular occupations of the young monk, during a part of the day, is very curious. The *uhtsang*, or *nocturn*, called at a later period *matutina*, or *matins*, began at three o'clock in the morning, at which the monk was called from his bed by the ringing of the church bell. The service of *prime* followed, at six o'clock; after which came *underntide*, or *tierce*, at about nine o'clock — and *middag*, or *sext*, at noon. It appears that the monks had no meal until after the mid-day service; and that after it they retired to sleep, from which they were roused to perform the service of *none*, about two o'clock. It appears not to have been till after this latter ser-

        hwænne wylle ge syngan   æfen   oþþe   nihtsange
  M. Quando uultis cantare uesperum aut completorium?[1]
      þonne hyt tima byþ
  D. Quando tempus erit.
      wære þu todæg beswuncgen
  M. Fuisti hodie uerberatus?
      ic næs forþam wærlice ic me heold
  D. Non fui, quia caute me tenui.
      and   hu   þine geferan
  M. Et quomodo tui socii?
      hwæt me   ahsast   be   þam   ic ne deor yppan þe digla
  D. Quid me interrogas de hoc? Non audeo pandere tibi secreta
ure   anra gehwylc wat gif he beswuncgen wæs oþþe na
nostra. Unusquisque scit si flagellatus erat an non.
      hwæt   ytst þu   on dæg
  M. Quid manducas in die?
      gyt flæscmettum ic bruce fordam cild ic eom under gyrda drohtniende
  D. Adhuc carnibus uescor,[2] quia puer sum sub uirga degens.
      hwæt mare   ytst þu
  M. Quid plus manducas?
      wyrta and ægra fisc and   cyse   buteran and beana and ealle
  D. Holera et oua, pisces et caseum, butirum et fabas, et omnia
clæne þinge ic ete   mid   micelre þancunge
munda manduco, cum gratiarum actione.
      swyþe waxgeorn eart þu þonne þu ealle þinge etst þe þe toforan
  M. Ualde edax es, cum omnia manducas que tibi appo-
[gesette synd]
nuntur.
      ic ne eom swa micel swelgere þæt ic ealle cynn   metta   on anre
  D. Non sum tam uorax ut omnia genera ciborum in una
gereordinge etan mæge
refectione edere possum.
      ac   hu
  M. Sed quomodo?
      ic bruce hwilon þisum mettum   oþrum mid syfernysse
  D. Uescor aliquando his cibis, et aliquando aliis, cum sobrietate,
swa swa dafnad munuce   næs mid oferhropse forþam ic eom nan gluto
sicut decet monachum, non cum uoracitate, quia non sum gluto.
      and hwæt drincst þu
  M. Et quid bibis?
      eala   gif ic hæbbe oþþe wæter gif ic næbbe   ealu
  D. Ceruisam, si habeo, uel aquam, si non habeo ceruisam.
      ne drincst þu   win
  M. Nonne bibis uinum?

---

vice that they were properly at liberty to attend to other business; and the boys, or younger members of the community, then went to school.

[1] The evening service, or vespers, commenced at four o'clock and *nihtsang*, or compline, at seven, which finished the canonical service of the day.

[2] There would seem to be an error here, for the child evidently means to say, not that he eat meat, but that he did not eat meat, because he was as yet too young.

COLLOQUY OF ARCHBISHOP ALFRIC.

   ic ne eom swa spedig þæt ic mæge bicgean me win and win
  D. Non sum tam diues ut possim emere mihi uinum ; et uinum
nys drenc cilda ne dysgra ac ealdra and wisra
non est potus puerorum siue stultorum, sed senum et sapientum.
   hwær slæpst
  M. Ubi dormis?
    on slæpern mid gebroþrum
  D. In dormitorio cum fratribus.
   hwa awecþ þe to uhtsancge
  M. Quis excitat te ad nocturnos?
    hwilon ic gehyre cnyll and ic erise [1] hwilon lareow min
  D. Aliquando audio signum, et surgo; aliquando magister meus
awecþ me stiþlice mid gyrde
excitat me duriter cum uirga.
    eala ge [gode] cildra and wynsume leorneras eow manaþ eower lareow
  M. O probi pueri, et uenusti mathites, uos hortatur uester eruditor
þæt ge byrsumian godcundum larum and þæt ge healdan eow sylfe ænlice
ut pareatis diuinis disciplinis, et obseruetis uosmet eleganter
on ælcere stowe   gaþ   þeawlice þonne ge gehyran cyricean
ubique locorum. Inceditis morigerate, cum auscultaueritis ecclesie
bellan and gaþ into cyrcean and abugaþ eadmodlice to halgum
campanas, et ingredimini in orationem, et inclinate suppliciter ad almas
wefodum and standaþ þeawlice and singad anmodlice and gebidiaþ
aras, et state disciplinabiliter, et concinite unanimiter et interuenite
for eowrum synnum and gaþ ut butan hygeleaste to claustre oþþe
pro uestris erratibus, et egredimini sine scirilitatem in claustrum uel
to leorninge.
in gimnasium.

    [1] So the MS. for *arise*. R. W.

IV.
ARCHBISHOP ALFRIC'S VOCABULARY,
OF THE TENTH CENTURY.[1]

DE INSTRUMENTIS AGRICOLARUM.
Uomer, uel uomis, scear.
Aratrum, sulh.[2]
Aratio, eriung.
Buris, sulhbeam.
Stercoratio, dingiung.[3]
Fimus, dinig.[3]
Dentale, cipp.
Stiba, sulhhandla.
Occatio, egegung.

Rastrum, uel rastellum, raca.
Traha, ciþe.
Runcatio, weodung.
Tragum, drægnet, *uel* drǽge.
5 *Stimulus,* ga[d].
Aculeus, sticel, *uel* gadisen.
Ueractum, lenctenerde.
Sulcus, furh.
Circus, uel circulus, widþe.
10 *Funiculus, uel funis,* rap.
Proscissio, landbrǽce.
Ouile, sceapahus.

[1] The vocabulary, or glossary, of archbishop Alfric, is printed from one of the manuscripts of Junius, in the Bodleian Library at Oxford; it usually follows Alfric's Anglo-Saxon translation from the Latin Grammar of Priscian, which was the favourite class-book of the mediaeval schools. It was transcribed, not always correctly, by or for Junius, from a MS. in the possession of Reubens the painter, which is no longer known to exist. This manuscript, from an apparent reference to king Cnut, seems to be not older than the eleventh century, when Alfric's original vocabulary was perhaps considerably modified, and this no doubt gave it the irregular character it here presents. The following lines were prefixed to it in the MS

Præsulis hic redolent Ælfrici lypsana summi,
  Qui rector patriæ perstitit Angligenæ,
Inter pontifices rutilans ceu mystica lampas,
  Defensor regni, necne salus populi.
Heu nostram fera mors extinxit nempe lucernam,
  Heu nostri cecidit fons quoque consilii,
Hunc sexta decimaque kalendas namque Decembris,
  Assumpsit Michahel, seu dedit Emanuhel.

The object of these vocabularies was chiefly twofold; first, to interpret Latin words to the Anglo-Saxon scholar, and secondly, to furnish him with the Latin words for the common objects of life. The vocabulary of Alfric would seem to have been originally arranged with a view to the latter object; but we find the plan often broken into, by the introduction of words which have nothing to do with those which they immediately follow, and which appear, in some instances, to have been taken almost at hazard from an alphabetical dictionary. In accordance with the character given to the science of agriculture, in the colloquy, it takes the precedence of all other subjects in the vocabulary.

[2] A plough is still called *a sull,* in the dialects of the West of England.

[3] So the MS. of Junius. But *dinig* is nothing but a misreading of *dung* (= Germ. dung). See the Anglo-Saxon version of the Holy Gospels, Luc. 13, 8. R. W.

Bucetum, hryðra fald.
Bouile stabulum, scepensteal, *uel* fald.
Uitularius, cealfahus.
Bobellum, fald.
Subula, æl.
Repagulum, salpanra.
Acrum, sceneen.
Scops, bisme.
Caule, sceapa locu.
Æquiale, horsern.
Uanga, spada.
Coniuncla, þristra.
Turminosus, fortogen.
Surculus, wingeardes screadungisen. 15
Terebrum, nauegar.[1]
Pastinatum, plantsticca.
Fossorium, costere, *uel* delfisen, *uel* spadu, *uel* pal.
Ligo, becca, *uel palus, uel fustis.*
Falcastrum, siþe, *uel* bill.
Serrula, saga, *uel* snide.
Ferrarius, isernwyrhte.
Plaustrum, uel carrum, wæn.
Rota, hweol.
Cantus, felga.
Modiolus, nauebe.
Radii, spacan.
Temo, uel arctoes, þisl.
Hircipes, uel tribula, egþa.
Spadatus, uel eunuchizatus, belisnod.[2]
Sarcina, seam, *uel* berðen.
Propolim, uel pertica, stod.
Scudicia, uel fossorium, spad.
Jugum, ioc.
Jugales, ioctema.
Artena, boga.
Obicula, iocsticca.
Rotabulum, myxforce, *uel* ofenraca.

Capistorium, corntroh.
Tritorium, þerscel.[3]
Cybutum, uel cistella, cest, *uel* earc.
Mozitia, uel arcula, tæg.
5 *Sitarchia,* metefætels, *uel* sceatcod.
Astraba, fotbret.
Saccus, bigerdel.
Arpax, geara feng, *uel lupus.*
Arpago, uel palum, hooc.
10 *Columbar,* sceacul, *uel* bend.
Limes, fotsidgerif.
Scrupulum, ynca.
Manuliatus, uel manicatus, geslefed.
Pigrus, uel lentus, sleac, *uel* slaw.

Epiphania, ætewung.[4]
Scenophegia, getimbra halgung, *uel* geteld wurþung.
Neomenia, niwemona.
20 *Encenia,* niwecirchalgung.
Sinagoga, gegaderung
Cerimonia, uel orgia, g.[5] gelddagas, þæt sind halige.
Heresis, kyre, *uel* gedwelo - æfter-
25 felgund.
Palla, cyrtel, *uel* oferbrædels.
Murenula, uel torques, swurboh.
Redimicula, kæuinge.
Reticulum, feaxnet.
30 *Monilia,* menas.
Inaures, earpreonas, *uel* earhringas.
Lunula, bend.
Tenia, tæppan, *uel* dolsmeltas.
Catelle, swurracenteh.
35 *Uitta,* snod.
Rigula, feaxnet.
Ricinum, winpel, *uel* orl.
Discriminalia, uplegene, *uel* feaxpreonas.

[1] *Nauegar,* an auger. (Cf. p. 44 l. 11 s. v. *rotrum*). Alfric introduces, in his enumeration, tools necessary or useful to the agriculturist, which are not absolutely agricultural instruments.

[2] This word is no doubt introduced here as applied to animals, and records one of the operations in farming.

[3] A flail, still called in Lancashire a *thresshel.*

[4] Quitting entirely the subject of agriculture, the compiler of the vocabulary introduces abruptly a number of words belonging to ecclesiastical affairs, which are oddly enough mixed with a few words of a different description.

[5] The *ḡ* stands no doubt for *Græcè,* meaning that the preceding word is Greek, and not Latin.

Orarium, uel ciclas, orl.
Calamistrum, feaxnædel.
Menstruum opus, monþes weorc.
Uomex, uel uomens, spiwere.
Stipes, stipitis, treowwessteb.
Stips, stipitis, wist, *uel* anleofa, *uel* ælmesse.
Superstitio, superfluitas, oferflowenes.
Gimnosophista, nacod plegere.
Ariolus, wigbedwiglere.
Aruspex, dægmelsceawere.[1]
Augur, uel auspex, fugelweohlere.
Astrologus, uel magus, uel mathematicus, tungelwitega, geberdwiglære.
Scinodens, twiseltode.
Puerperium, byseberðlinge.
Puerpera, cildiungwif.
Uirago, ceorlstrang fæmne.
Portentum, uel prodigium, uel ostentum, fortacen.
Satiri, uel fauni, uel sehni,[2] *uel fauni ficarii,* unfæle men, wudewasan, unfæle wihtu.
Ueredus, crætehors.
Mannus, uel brunnicus, geþracen hors.
Burdo, hors of steden, *uel* of asrenne.
Alfa, i. initium, angin.[3]
Abra, i. ancilla, þinen, wyln.
Acha, i. uirtus, strengð.

Acer, i. uehemens, strang.
Achor, i. conturbatio, drefing.
Actionator, folcgerefa.
Acisculum, pic.
Asscopa, flaxe oþþe cylle.
Agape, ælmesse.
Altanus, þoden.
Anastasis, dygelnyssum.[4]
Angiportus, i. refrigerium nauium, hyð.
Ardamo, i. gusto, ic gesmecge.
Andreporesis, i. homo utriusque generis, bæddel.
Centaurus, uel ippocentaurus, healf man and healf hors.
Onocentaurus, healf mann and healf assa.
Agrestis, wilde.
Brunda, heortes heafod.
Orbis, uel firmamentum, ymbhwerft.
Rotella, uel orbiculus, lytel ymbhweorft.

NOMINA OMNIUM HOMINUM COMMUNITER.[5]

Imperator, Cesar, uel Augustus, casere.
Basileus, kining.
Regillus, undercyning.

[1] The compiler has singularly misunderstood the Latin word *aruspex*. *Dægmal-sceawere* signifies literally one who announces or proclaims the hours of the day.

[2] Somner conjectures, perhaps rightly, that *sehni* is a corruption of *obsceni.*

[3] This, and the words which follow, were evidently taken from an alphabetical glossary. It may perhaps be well to observe, with regard to them, as well as to many Latin words in this vocabulary, that the Anglo-Saxon scholars did not take their standard of Latin from the good classical writers, but they sought their words in the *Origines* of Isidore, and in writings of that class; and they affected, especially, barbarous compounds from the Greek. The words, here given in alphabetical order, belong chiefly to these two classes. From this circumstance, also, it appears that there are Anglo-Saxon words in the vocabulary, at the meaning of which we can only guess, on account of the obscurity or corruptness of the Latin equivalents.

[4] It is evident that the compiler of this part of the vocabulary mistook entirely the meaning of the Latin word, and imagined it to be *anastrus*, or something of that kind, meaning *without stars*. It is hardly necessary to say that *dygelnyssum* means *in secrecy*, or *in darkness.*

[5] It will be seen at once that, in the list of political terms which follow, the compiler has sought to explain the words in use in the Roman empire by their nearest Anglo-Saxon equivalents, and not to give the Latin to the terms in use under the Anglo-Saxon government. Nevertheless, some of them are extremely curious as helping us to understand the real import of the Anglo-Saxon words.

Diadema, kynegerd.
Sceptrum, cynegerd.
Ducatus, ealdordom.
Consul, gerefa.
Proconsul, undergerefa.
Exconsul, hiredgerefa.
Monarces, anwalda.
Prætor, uel præfectus, uel præpositus, uel quæstor, burhgerefa.
Tribunus, manna ealdor.
Millenarius, þusendrica.
Ciliarcus, þusendes ealdor.
Præses, scirgerefa.
Centurio, hundredes ealdor.
Quinquagenarius, uel pentecontarcus, fiftiga ealdor.
Cohors, fifhund cempena ealdor.
Emeritus, alæten cempa.
Tyro, iungwiga.
Optiones, gecorene cempan.
Sinmistes, uel consecretalis, gehala, *uel* geruna.
Rebellio, widercwyda.
Excubiæ, dægwæccan.
Excubitor, uigil, dægweard.
Uigiliæ, nihtwæccan.
Ueltes, swifte ærendracan.
Turma, þrittig ridwigena.
Legio, feþu.
Acies, geræwud[1] feða.
Manipulus, twahund cempna.
Castrum, fyrd.
Castra, fyrdwic.
Exercitus, here.
Cuneus, getrymmed feþa.
Alæ, fedes.
Nodus, getrum.
Agmen, gangend feða.
Ciues, burhwara.
Oppidanus, burhseta.
Uulgus, uel plebs, heanra burhwered.

Senatus, ealdormanna duguð.
Censores, uel judices, uel arbitri, deman.
Proceres, uel primores, uel primarii,
5   yldest burhwara.
Municeps, portgerefa, *uel* burhwita.
Curiales, uel decuriales, burhgerefa.
Commentariensis, gerefa.
Exactor, hæcewol.
10 *Collegiati*, ræplingeweardes.
Mercedarii, hyregildan.
Publicanus, wicgerefa.
Uillicus, uel actor, uel curator, uel procurator, uel rector, tungerefa.
15 *Colonus*, oðres eardes landseta.[2]
Inquilinus, tungebur.
Indigena, inlenda.
Uernaculus, inbirdling.
Uernula, fostorling.
20 *Ædilis*, hofweard, *uel* byriweard, *uel* botlweard.
Libertus, freolæta.
Libertinus, freolætan sunu.
Titirus, scyphyred.
25 *Canum seruitor*, hundwæalh.
Pirata, uel piraticus, uel cilix, wicing, *uel* scegðman.
Archipiratra, yldest wicing.
Uappa, awærde.
30 *Uafer, uel fatuus, uel socors*, abroten, *uel* dwæs.
Cernuus, pronus, uel inclinatus, hnitol, *uel* eadmod.
Himeneos, hæmeda.
35 *Æquæuus, uel coetaneus*, efneald.
Cliuosus, clifig, tohyld.
Coturnus, ofermod.
Pabulator, horshyrde, *uel* fodderbrytta.
40 *Agressor*, strudere, *uel* reafere.
Sarcitector, uel tignarius, hrofwyrhta.

[1] Not *gerœrud* as Wright printed. R. W.
[2] This is one of several instances which occur in the course of the vocabulary, of the mistaking, by the Anglo-Saxon translator, of the real meaning of the Latin word: *colonus* was no doubt, from the other words in connexion with it, intended to be taken in its original sense of a husbandman, whereas the translator seems to have taken it in its secondary meaning of a colonist. A little further down, the name so familiar to the readers of Virgil, *Tityrus*, is given as a general word for a shepherd.

Carpentarius, wænwyrhta.
Lignarius, treowwyrhta.
Opifex, cræftiga.
Fullones, fulleres.
Nauicularius, scipwyrhta.
Architectus, yldestwyrhta.[1]
Cimentarius, wealwyrhta.
Latomus, stanwyrhta.
Caligarius, læstwyrhta.
Lapidicina, uel lapidicedium, stan-hywet.

Pestilentia, uel contagium, uel lues, cwealm.[2]
Carbunculus, spring, *uel* angset, *uel pustula,* cwydele, *uel pustella,* swelca.
Scotomia,[3] swinglung.
Spasmos, hramma, *uel* swiung.
Titanus, oferbæcgeteung.[4]
Telum, i. dolor lateris, sticwærc, sticadl.
Yleos, hrifwerc, *uel* hrifteung.[5]
Ydrofobam, uel limphatici, wæterfyrhtnys.
Epilepsia, uel caduca, uel laruatio, uel comitialis, bræccoþu, fylleseoc.
Reuma, bræc.
Coriza, nebgebræc.
Brancos, hræcgebræc.
Tipus, lengtenadl.
Pleuriticus, on sidan lama, *uel* sidadl.

Raucedo, hasnys.
Arteriasis, sweorcoþu.
Suspirium, hriung, *uel* siccetung.
Apostema, swyle.
5 *Enpus,* ingeswel.
Peripleumonia, blothræcung.
Emoptois, blotspiung.
Phtisis, wyrshræcing, *uel* wyrs uspiung.[6]
10 *Ypaticus,* liferadl.
Lienosus, milteseoc.
Nefresis, lendenwyrc.
Cacexia, yfeladl.
Atrophia, meteafliung.
15 *Sciascis,* hipwerc.
Uertibulum, hwyrfban.
Artericus, uel artriticus, lidadl.
Caucalus, cyselstan.
Disuria, uel stranguria, earfod læte
20 micga.
Strictura, gebynd.
Saturiasis, synwrænnys, *uel* galscipe.
Diarria, utsiht.
Dissenteria, blodig utsiht.
25 *Lienteria,* mete utsiht.
Colum, hrop.[7]
Colica, hropwyrc.
Orificium, ælces kynnes mud *uel* dyrl.
30 *Alopecia,* feaxfeallung.
Parodite, earcoþu, *ota, g.* ear.
Inpetigo, teter.

---

[1] Here, again, the translator has mistaken the meaning of his word rather singularly, for he supposed that the import of the first member of the compound word was the same in *architectus* as in *archepiscopus,* and words of that class.

[2] We now have a list of diseases, which no doubt includes all those that were known to the Saxon physicians, commencing with the most fearful of all — the plague. In *sticwærc* and *sticadl* we have a term which is still preserved in the popular word *stitch,* applied to a pain in the side (= Germ. *seitenstechen*). One of the names for the epilepsy, *fylleseoc,* was preserved in the later term: the falling sickness. *Swyle,* for an aposteme, is preserved in the provincial word *swail;* and *wild-fire* is, I think, still in some parts used for the erysipelas. [Cf. Germ. *wildes viur* = *erysipelas, sacer ignis.* R. W.] But in general the Anglo-Saxon names for diseases, which were mostly popular expressions or translations of the Latin, have been lost in the English language.

[3] An error for *scotoma* a fainting fit, swoon. R. W.

[4] Cf. Bosw. 50*l*. R. W.

[5] The meaning of hrifteung is: a pain in the bowels, *iliaca passio.* Wright misprinted: hrig-teung. R. W.

[6] Sic MS. R. W.

[7] This word still exists in the provincial name *ropes,* for bowels. *Colum* is the Greek κῶλον

Erysipila, wilde fyr.
Serpedo, pytful wyrmses.
Prurigo, emertung.
Pruritus, gicþa.
Uerruca, wearte.
Nictalmus, nihtege.
Satiriasis, weartene heap.
Elephanticus, uel hicteris, uel artuatus, sydmycleadl.
Ordeolus, stigend.
Furunculus, uel antrax, angseta.
Oscedo, mudcoþu.
Frenus, mudberstinge.
Ulcus, rotung.
Tabes, gemolsnad flæsc, *uel* forrotad.
Pharmacia, sealflæcung.
Ligatura, sarclad.
Picra, biterwyrtdrenc.
Tiriaca, drenc wid attre.
Catartica, i. purgatoria, wyrtdrenc.
Catapodia, swylgende drenc.
Diamoron, berigdrene.
Colliria, eagsealfe.
Girba, se ealra mæsta mortere.
Pilurus, uel pistor, se þe pilaþ, *uel* tribulaþ.
Tipsana, berengebered corn.
Stacten, stor þe bid ofgewringe.

Fas, Godes riht.[1]
Jus, mennisc riht.
Jus naturale, geeynde riht.
Solempnitas, þeaw, *uel* wise.
Stipendium, scipe, *uel* bigleofa.
Pragma, æbod, *uel* intinga.
Pragmatica negotia, æbodas, *uel* ceapunge.
Hereditas, yrfeweardnes.
Legatum, gewriten yrfe.
Legatum testamentum, heahgerefan gesetnysse.
Legatarius, yrfeweardwritere.
Testator, yrfewritend.
Intestata hereditas, ungewriten yrfe.
Ruptum testamentum, unewedene yrfebec.

Suppressum testamentum, forswiged yrfebec.
Cretio, yrfefyrt.
Nuncupatio, underne yrfebec.
Jus liberorum, samhiwna yrfebec.
Familiæ erciscundæ, yrfegedal.
Mandatum, haudfæstnung.
Satura lex, mænibredædom.
Rodia lex, scipmanna riht.
Cirographum, rædinggewrit, *uel* handgewrit.
Donatio, forgifung.
Dos, morgengifu.
Conditio, geewyde, *uel* gewyrd.
Stipulatio, gehat.
Sacramentum, adwed, *uel* adegehat.
Res, æht, *uel* þinc.
Jus, decretum, uel lex, andweald.
Peculium, heanra mann, *uel* ceorlic æhta.
Locatio, behyring, *uel* gehyred feoh.
Conduco, ic ahyre.
Congressio, gefeoht.
Jus publicum, caldormanna riht.
Jus quiritum, weala sunderriht.
Plebisscita, medricra gesetnyssa.
Senatus consultum, ricera gesetnes.
Constitutio, kyninga gesetnysse.
Responsa, geaxode domas.
Jurisconsultus, uel iurisperitus, rihtscrifendom.
Res credita, gelened feoh, *uel* on borh geseald.
Usura, wæmstsceat.
Commodum, læn.
Precarium, landeslæn.
Mutuum, wrixlung.
Depositum, to healdenne, *uel* ædfæst tæht, *uel* becwyddod.
Pignus, wed, *uel* alæned feoh.
Arra, gylden wedd, *uel* feoh.
Arrabona, uel arrabo, wedd, *uel* wedlac.
Fiducia, forweddad feoh.
Ypotheca, feohlænung butan borge.

[1] Here we commence another series of terms, belonging to the Roman law, which appears to be quite out of its place, and was perhaps an addition to the original vocabulary.

Parricidii actio, mægmorþres witnung.
Inficiatio, uel abiuratio, borges andsæc.
Ambitus iudicium, gebohtre scire witnung.
Maiestatis reus, wið cyning forwyrht.
Compedes, fotfetera.
Nerui boia, fotcopsa, *uel* sweorscacul.
Anguilla, uel scutica, swipa.
Scorpio, ostig gyrd, *uel* tindig.
Eculeus, unhela þrepel.
Ignominia, scande.
Infamia, unhlisa.
Exilium, wræcsið.
Postliminium, edcyr of spræcside.
Relegatus, to wite asend mid unsehte.
Patibulum, galga.[1]
Culleum, ælces cynnes witnung.
Fabæ frese, uel pilate, gepunede beane.
Facinus, scæððæd.
Uis potestatis, ricera manna need.
Calumnia, holtihte, *uel* teone.
Seditio, folcslite, *uel* æswicung, sacu, ceast.
Sacrilegium, godesfees ðeofð.
Stuprum, raptum, wifa nydnimung.
Adulterium, cwena geligr, *uel* unriht hæmed.
Balus, isern feter.
Bagula, bridel, *i. frenum*.
Momentum, to hwile læn.
Instrumentum, tool.
Instructum, gewroht.
Usus, nittung, *uel* notu, *uel* corðwæstm, cess, to æte alyfed.
Merces, cepeþinge.
Commercium, cepena ðinga gewrixle.
Bicoca, hæferblæte, *uel* pur.[2]

Bobla, flod.
Bargina, boccfel.
Bulgæ, leþercoddas.
Bacharus, mereswyn.
5 *Burdus*, seamere.
Bases, tredelas, *uel* stæpas.
Crepusculum, glomung.[3]
Conticinium, cwylttid, *uel* gebedgiht.
10 *Aupicium initium*, angin.
Uibrissæ, nosterla hær.
Zenia, gifu.
Sales, wynsum gamen.
Stiria stillicidia, ises gicel.
15 *Olympias*, fif wintra fæc.
Lustrum quinquennium, fif wintra fæc.
Bimus, uel biennis, uel bimulus, twiwinter. [winter.
20 *Trimus,[4] uel triennis, uel trimulus*, driÆuum, uel ætas perpetua*, widerfeorlic, *uel* ece.
Prestigium,[5] scinhiw.
Arpa, ærengeat.
25 *Lotium*, hlom, *uel* migca.
Submanicatus, be slyfan gebunden.
Comitia, wyrdsciras.
Draconarii, uel uexillarii, uel signiferi, segnboran, tacnboran.
30 *Purulentus*, wurmsihtig.
Uermiculus, cornwurma.
Melinum, uel croceum, geolu.
Centumpellio, feleferþ.
Lithologia, stanlesung.
35 *Lithostratos*, stanbricge.
Taberna, boccest.
Glarea, glitis, uel samia, sand.
Flebotomus, blodsex.
Flebotomarius, blodlætere.
40 *Fiscus, uel saccus publicus*, biggyrdel.
Rudera, uel ruina, geswapa, *uel* meox.

[1] *Galga*, the gallows, appears to have been the usual form of capital punishment among the Anglo-Saxons, and is represented not uncommonly in the early illuminated manuscripts.

[2] The extracts from the alphabetical glossary, now in the letter B, recommence here. Neither the Latin words, nor their Anglo-Saxon equivalents, are always intelligible.

[3] The Anglo-Saxon word for twilight is still preserved in the Scottish *gloming*. The words which follow, are of a very miscellaneous character.

[4] So the MS. R. W. [*rigium*. R. W.

[5] Junius seems to have written *pres-*

Quisquiliæ, æppelscreada, *uel* corn-
  æsceda.
Capreoli, wingeardbogas.
Quitinas, *ḡ. cadacas*,[1] milscre treowa
  blostman.
Subacta coria, *uel medicata*, *uel con-
  fecta*, getannede hyd.
Feriatus, restedæg.
Jaculum, *uel funda*, widnyt, *uel* fla.
Coragium, mædena byrgen.
Aquagium, wæterþeote.
Hostimentum, widerriht, *uel* edlean.
Idolothytum, idelgildofrung.
Galerus, *uel pilleus*, fellen hæt.
Annicto, *uel annuto*, ic wincie.
Camilema, leaces sex.
Subplaudo, ic gilpe.
Repatrio, ic hamsidie.
Obunco, ic ymbelippe.
Obrigesco, ic stifie.
Oppando, *oppansus*, ic adenige.
Infesto, ic ehtige.
Expertus, *i. multum peritus*, þurh-
  lǽred, *uel* gleaw.
Expers, *indoctus*, dælleas, *uel* cræft-
  leas.

NOMINA FERARUM.

Animal, ælc cuce þinc, *uel* nyten.[2]
Pecus, *iumentum*, ælces kynnes nyten.
Fera, wilddeor.
Bellua, rede deor.
Elephans, ylp.
Promuscida, ylpes bile, *uel* wrot.
Unicornis, *uel monoceros*, *uel rino-
  ceros*, anhyrne deor.
Griffes, eow, fiderfote fugel.
Urus, wesend.
Bubalus, wilde oxa.
Fiber, *castor*, *ponticus*, befer.
Raturus, ræt.
Lutria, otor.
Netila, hearma.
Ferunca, *uel ferunculus*, meard.

[1] So the MS. R. W. — *milisc* means
mitis. Cf. Bosw. 461. R. W.
[2] Wright misprinted *nyhten*. R. W.
[3] So the MS. R. W.

Scirra aquilinus, *sciurus*, acwern.
Taxus, *uel meles*, *cuniculus*, broc.
Bromus marinus, seolh.
Linx, lox.
Glis, sisemus.
Mustella, wesle.
Camelus, *uel dromeda*, olfend.
Simia, *uel spinx*, apa.
Talpa, *uel talpo*, wandewurpe.
Licos, wulf.
Lepus, *uel lagos*, *ḡ.*, hara.
Ceruus, *uel eripes*, heortbuc.
Cerua, hind.
Damula, *uel caprea*, *uel dorcas*, *ḡ*,
  hræge.
Capreus, rahdeor.
Hinnulus, hindcealf.
Uulpes, fox.
Purcastor,[3] foor.
Aper, wilde bar.
Uerres, tam bar.
Magalis, bearh.
Scrofa, sugu.
Sus, swyn.
Suilla, *uel sucula*, gilte.
Suilli, *uel porcelli*, *uel nefrendes*,
  fearas.
Caper, *uel hircus*, *uel tragos*, bucca.
Capra ægida, gatbuccan hyrde.
Hedus, ticcen.
Ibix, firinggat.
Sonipes, hors.[4]
Equifer, wilde cynnes hors.
Agaso, horsþen.
Jumentum, hryorif.[5]
Equa, mere.
Canterius, hengst.
Faussarius, steda.
Equartium, stood.
Poledrus, fola.
Sagma, seamsadol.
Sagmarius equus, seamhors.
Antela, fordgyrd.
Postela, æfterræpe.

[4] Cf. the *Index*. R. W.
[5] So read I. Wright printed: *hryofif*,
Bosw. *hwyorif*. R. W.

Subligar, þearmgyrd.
Scansile, stirap.
Corbus, sadulboga
Sella, sadul.
Centrum, uel filtrum, felt
Frenum, uel lupatum, midl.
Chamus, bridles midl.
Bogula, saliuare, brydel.
Ducale, latteh.
Mulus, mul.
Asinus, assa.
Onager, wilde assa.
Ursus, bera.
Ursa, byrene.
Muriceps, uel musio, murilegus, catt.
Sorex, mus.
Canis, hund.
Canicula, bicge.
Millus, uel collarium, sweorteh.
Molossus, rydda.
Inutilis canis, hrodhund.
Cinomia, hundesfleoge.
Ricinus, hundesfleoge.
Bos, oxa.
Uacca, uel buccula, cu.
Anniculus, uel trio, steoroxa.
Uitulus, cealf.
Iuuencus, uel uitula, steor.
Annicula, uel uaccula, heahfore.
Iuniculus, iung hryþer.
Iuuenca, iung cu.
Imus,[1] oxa on þam forman teame.
Binus, on þam æfteran teame.
Mutinus, gadinca, *uel* hnoc.
Altilium, fæt heahfore.
Altile, fedels.
Aries, ramm.
Triennis, þry-winter, sumer gildeto.

Ouis, uel mandritis, g. scep.
Mandra, uel ouile, locc.
Ueruex, uel manto, weþer.
Agnus, cinist[2] (*sic*) lamb.
5 *Magnicaper*, ormæte buccan.

DE NOMINIBUS INSECTORUM.

Musca, fleoge.
Chosdrus, uel castros, beomoder.
10 *Fucus*, dran.
Crabro, hyrnet.
Oestrum, beaw, *uel* hyrnette.
Blatta, nihtbuttorfleoge.
Uespa, wæps.
15 *Apis, uel melle*, beo.
Atticus, uel burdo, dora.
Scarabeus, scearnfifel.
Papilio, buttorfleoge.
Locusta, astaco, gærstapa.
20 *Bruchus*, ceafor.
Cinomya, hundesfleoge.
Bibiones, uel mustiones, muscfleotan, *uel* wurma smite.[3]
Culex, stut.[4]
25 *Cicindela*, se glisigenda wibba.[5]
Formica, æmete.
Loppe, fleonde næddre, *uel* attorcoppe.[6]
Gurgulio, cawelwurm.
30 *Scinifes, uel tado*,[7] gnæt.
Limax, snægl.
Testudo, gehused snægl.
Bombyx, sidwyrm, *uel* scolewyrm.
Eruca, mælscæafa.
35 *Termes, uel teredo*, wyrm þe borad treow.
Sanguisuga, uel hirudo, læce.
Pulex, fleo.

---

[1] Wright printed *Unus*. R. W.

[2] I do not understand this word. But I think *cinist* to be an Anglo-Saxon expression. Wright printed it in italics as belonging to *agnus*. R. W.

[3] So the MS.; not *sinite* as Wright read. R. W.

[4] A gnat is still called *a stut* in Somersetshire.

[5] The glittering worm, no doubt the glow-worm.

[6] The word *attercoppa* is generally explained as signifying a spider, and it continued to be used apparently in that sense in English until the fifteenth century; yet in some cases this meaning appears to be doubtful. In an A.-S. MS. in the Cottonian library, Vitel. C. III., we have drawings of the *attercoppa* of that period, which by no means agree with the notion of its being a spider. One of them is engraved in my Archæological Album, p. 182.

[7] So the MS.; not *tudo*. R. W.

Pediculus, uel sexpes, lus.
Lens, uel lendix, hnitu.
Cimex, maþu.
Tippula, wæter-buca, *uel* gat.
Tinea, modde.
Tamus,[1] maþa, mite.
Culex, micge.
Mordiculus, bitela.
Botrax, uel botraca, yce.
Rana, frogga.[2]
Buffo, tadige.
Lacerta, uel stilio, efete.
Emigranus, flæscmaþu.
Blatta, eorwicga.
Stellio, slawyrm.
Tauri, eordeaferas.
Spalangius, slawyrm.
Surio, uel briensis, uel sirineus, handwyrm.
Musaraneus, screawa.
Istrix, se mara igil.
Lumbricus, renwyrm, *uel* angeltwicce.
Chelio, testudo, uel marina gugalia, sæsnæl, *uel* pinewinclan.
Ricinus, hundeswyrm.
Usia, swineslus.
Buprestis, twinwyrm.

NOMINA UASORUM.[3]

Amfora, sester.
Cantarus, winsester.[4]
Crater, uel canna, canne.
Patera, mele.
Alabastrum, stænen elefæt.
Cocula, olfata.
Karchesia, melas.
Caupus, uel obba, cuppe.
Fiala, uel scala, bledu.
Cratera, eardefæt.

Ciatus, hnæp.
Anthlia, hnæp.
Dolium, cyf.
Fundum, bydenbotm.
5 *Hauritorium,* hlæden.
Patella, panne.
Colatorium, seohhe.
Cribrum, syfe.
Cupa, tunne.
10 *Tympanum,* tunnebotm.
Cistella, uel cartallum, windel.
Corbis, uel qualus, tænel.
Batus, amber.
Sartago, uel frixorium, hyrsting-
15 panne.
Canistrum, uel aluearium, hyf.
Cophinus, wilige.
Orca, orc.
Enophorum, winfæt.
20 *Quasillus,* litel tænel.
Flaxa, flaxe.
Lagena, æscen.
Anfora, crocca.
Situla, stoppa.[5]
25 *Ansa,* sal.
Ydria, uel soriscula, wæterfæt.
Mulctrale, uel sinum, uel mulctrum, meolcfæt.
Uter, byt.
30 *Scortia,* leþrenfæt.
Flasco, buterue.
Lenticula, ærenbyt.
Sciffus, læuel.
Emicadium, elefæt.
35 *Urceus, uel immansiterna,* ceac.
Acetabulum, æcedfæt.
Emistis, andrece fæt, *uel trapetum.*
Cucuma, cyperen hwer.
Lebes, hwer, *uel* cytel.

---

[1] *Sic MS.*; Wright read: *tomus.* R. W.

[2] It is curious that in the eyes of the Anglo-Saxon naturalists, the frog, the toad, the lizard or eft (*efete*), and other reptiles, were usually placed under the head of insects; and this odd classification was preserved to rather a late period. Here we have the shrew-mouse (*screawe*), and the hedgehog (*istrix, igil*), as well as the slow-worm (*slaw-wyrm*), and the periwinkle (*pinewinela,* or *sa-snæl*), placed in the same category.

[3] This chapter, and what follows, appear to have been accidentally displaced, and so interposed between the list of insects and the list of birds.

[4] Wright, by an error, has: wincester. R. W.

[5] The modern word *stoop.*

Cacabus, cytel.
Gillo, wægel.
Malluuiæ, handþweales fæt.
Pelluuiæ, fotþweales fæt.
Paropsis, uel catinus, læpeldre fæt.
Trisilis, þryfotad fæt.
Patena, huseldisc.
Cimbia, scipfæt.
Lagena, læmen fæt.
Sartago, isen panne.
Arula, uel batilla, fyrpanne.
Pixis, bixen box.

Domus, uel lar, hus.[1]
Supellex, yddisc.
Cubiculum, bedcofa, *uel* bur.
Cubicularius, burþen.
Camerarius, bedþen.
Culcites, feþerbed.
Plumacius, bedbolster.
Capitale, heafdbolster.
Ceruical, wangere.
Stragula, wæstling.
Sindo, scyte.
Puluillus, lytel pyle.
Fulcrum, eal bedreaf.
Uestis, clamis, scrud.
Sagum, hwitel.
Cunabulum, cradel.
Cune, uel crebundie, cildclades.
Planeta, cæppe.
Penula, gerenod cæppe.
Prætexta, cildes scrud.
Manualis, handlin.
Mantium, glof.
Zona, gyrdel.

Colobium, smoc, *uel* syrc.
Tubroces, uel brace, strapulas.
Perizomata, uel campestria, uel succinctoria, wædbrec.
5 *Manicæ, uel brachilia*, slyfa.
Toral, rooc.
Amphibalum, ruhhrægel.
Anabola, winpel.
Pedula, meo.
10 *Commissura*, clut.
Glomus, clypen.
Uitta, snod.
Limbus, stemning, *uel* hem.
Fascia, wyninge.
15 *Fascia*, nostle.
Uallegias, wynegas.
Instita, þræs.
Callicula, rocc.
Stigmentum, ful maal on rægel.
20 *Textrinum opus*, towlic weorc.
Colus, distæf.
Fusus, spinl.
Cernui, fotleaste læshosum.[2]
Fico, sco.
25 *Soleæ*, solen.
Subtalares, swyfteleares.
Baxeæ, wifes sceos.
Coturnus, triwen sceo.[3]
Caligarius, læstweorhta.
30 *Talares*, unhege sceos.
Ocreæ, uel tibiales, leþerhosa.
Calopodium, uel mustricula, læste.
Obstrigelli, rifelingas.[4]
Nebris, sceat, *uel* heortes hyd.
35 *Bulga*, hydig fæt.
Polymita, uel oculata, hringfagh.[5]

[1] From the list of vessels of different kinds, the vocabulary goes on to describe the house, with its parts and contents, beginning with the chamber, because probably it was the room in which, being less public, most of the articles of any value were kept, and which had most furniture. Of the names here given to the chamber, the first, *bedcofa*, means literally a bed-recess, or bed-closet; for the bed-room was probably, in earlier times and in the ordinary houses, only a recess from the room in which the family lived. *Bur* is the *bower* of a later period, when it was used as the poetical term for the lady's room. The enumeration of articles of dress is also introduced here in the sequel, as they were usually kept in the bed-chamber.

[2] Cf. Bosworth, 40w. R. W.

[3] *i. e.*, a wooden shoe — a rather curious interpretation of the Latin *cothurnus*.

[4] A rough shoe, worn by the Scots in the fourteenth century, was called a *riveling*. [Cf. f. i. Minot's poems: roughfute rivelings. R. W.]

[5] Cf. pag. 40, 17 s, v. *Pilimita*. R. W.

Orbiculata, ligrægel.
Sigillum, uel bulla, insegel.
Arcus, forbigels.
Columna, swer.
Excussorium, flor on huse.
Tectum, þecen, *uel* rof.
Ualua, hlidgata.
Patronus, stapul.
Ascensorium, stæger.
Destina, uel postis, uel fulcimen, stipere.
Secessus, digle hus.
Tignum, ræfter.
Asseres, lætta.[1]
Laquear, fyrst.
Cleta cratis, hyrdel.
Uectis, steng.
Paxillus, cyrfel, *uel* litel stigul.
Sardanium, butere.
Taxea, spic.
Palestra, gewinstow.
Arca, uel scrinium, scrin.
Conuocatio, geladung.
Altar, uel ara, weofod.
Crux, uel staurus, rod.
Lampas, blase.
Lucernarium, leohtfæt.
Emunctorium, candelsnytels.
Papirus, weoce.
Horologium, dægmæl.
Gnomon, dægmælspilu.
Salinare, uel salinum, sealtfæt.[2]
Gausape, beodrægl.
Mensorium, meose. [sacca.
Legula, uel coclea, uel code, mete-
Dapes, uel fercula, wista, *uel* sand.
Fercula, bærdisc.
Discifer, uel discoforus, discþen.
Satira, hlæddisc.

Mantile, handhrægl.
Mappula, bearmclad, *uel* rægl.
Mappa, wætersceat.
Foculare, heord.
5 *Focarius*, fyrbeta.
Carbo, coll.
Pruna, gled.
Titio, uel torris, brand.
Andena, uel tripes, brandisen.
10 *Fuscinula, uel tridens*, awul.
Ueru, spitu.
Rotabulum, ofenraca.[3]
Uerriculum, uel scopæ, bysm.
Olitor, lectunward.
15 *Comedia*, racu, tunlic spæc.
Pastillus, litel hlaf.
Assura, uel assatura, bræde.
Coctus, gesoden and gebacen.
Elixus cibus, gesoden mæt on wæ-
20 tere.
Offa, uel frustum, sticce.
Offella, uel particula, spices snæd.
Offarius, uel particularius, twickere.
Gastrimargia, gyfernys, *uel* oferfil.
25 *Isicia*, mærhgehæt.
Omenta, uel membrana, fylmena.
Formentum, ofenbacen hlaf.
Polentum, wurtmete mid meluwe.
Spumaticum, mete of meluwe and
30 of bane gesoden.
Minutal, gebeaten fisc. [flæsc.
Martisia, uel baptitura, gebeaten
Succidia, eald hryterflæsc.[4]
Obesta, beost.
35 *Colostrum*, byst.
Silotrum, pillsape.
Excoriatus, beflæ.
Culliola, hnutehula.

---

[1] This humble enumeration of the parts of a common dwelling-house, posts, rafters, laths, a roof, and a floor, (it is evidently supposed to be built of nothing but timber,) offers a strong contrast with the elaborate details in the later vocabularies, and reminds us of the remarks of William of Malmesbury, on the great development of domestic architecture after the Norman Conquest.

[2] We are now supposed to return to the hall, or eating room, and to the dinner table. The list of articles of cookery is not very numerous; nor does it bespeak a very high degree of refinement in gastronomy.

[3] So the MS. Wright read: ofer-raca. R. W.

[4] For hryderflæsc, I suppose. But the meaning of *succidia* is: a flitch of bacon. R. W.

DE GENERIBUS POTIONUM.[1]

Ceruisia, celea, eala.
Uinum, merum, win.
Acetum, eced.
Oleum, ele.
Oleaginus, elebeamen.
Olea, uel oliua, elebeam.
Medo, medu, uel medus.
Mellicratum, geswet win
Ydromellum, beor, uel ofetes wos.
Oximellum, geswet eced.
Inomellum, must mid hunig gemenged.
Mulsum, beor.
Mustum, niwe win.
Sicera, ælces kinnes gewring butan wine and wætere.
Liquor, wæta.
Sapa, perewos.
Falernum, þæt seleste win.
Infertum uinum, messewin.
Limpidum uinum, scir win.
Spurcum uinum, ful win.
Crudum uinum, weala win.
Succinacium uinum, geolu win.
Honorarium uinum, hlaforda win.
Compositum uinum, uel conditum, gewyrtod win.
Mirratum uinum, gemenged mid myrran.
Defecatum uinum, gehluttrad win.
Meracum uinum, gehlyttrod win.
Defrutum uinum, gesoden win, uel passum.
Fecula, gesoden winberigen.
Carenum, morad.
Fauus, beobread.
Liquamen, uel garum, fiscbryne.
Salsugo muria, bryne.
Serum, hwæg.
Raptura, syring.
Coagulum, rynning.
Coagulatus, gerunnen.

Oxygala, sur meolc, acidum lac.
Colustrum, bysting, dicce meolc.
Pusta, hacine.
Sapa, æftereala.
Lexinum, lehmealtwurt.
Acinum, mealtwurt.
Feces, drosna.
Issiguum, stream, uel wæto.
Caupo, tabernarius, tæppere, winbrytta.
Diuisor, dælere.
Dispensator, dihtnere.
Economus, stiward.
Ephemeris, anes dæges weorc.
Diarium, dægwine.
Bucida, qui boues mactat, hryþerheawere.

Cantor, sangere.
Trenos, sarlic sang.
Præcentor, foresingend.
Threnum, wanung.
Succentor, æftersingend.
Ymeneus, uel epithalamium, brydsang.
Concentor, midsingend.
Monodia, g, latersicinium, quasi solicinium, þæt is anes sones.
Bicinium, twegra sang.
Ymnus, lofsang.
Chorus, singende heap.
Chorea, hluddra sang.
Matutinum officium, uhtgebed, uel þenung.
Uespertinum officium, æfengebed, uel þeowdom.
Responsorium, reps.
Lectio, ræding.
Diaphonia, ungeswege sang.
Canticum, sum swegesang.
Psalmus, proprie, hearpsang.
Canticum, psalm æfter hærpansang.
Psalmus, ær hærpansang.
Armonia, geþwære sang.
Simphonia, answege sang.

[1] From the dishes we are introduced to the drinks of the Anglo-Saxons, which appear to be proportionally more numerous. They are followed by another batch of words relating to ecclesiastical matters, and others of a miscellaneous character; after which we return again to the subject of natural history, in a list of birds.

Fertum, messelac.
Offertorium, lancsang.[1]
Oblatio, ofrung.
Dano, sawlsceat, *uel* syndrig godes lac.[2]
Dedicatum, gode gesyld.
Consecratum, gode gehalgad.
Officium, þenung.
Immolatio, onsægung.
Sacrificium, offrung.
Mactatio, snidung.
Holocaustum, caloffrung.
Libatio, wintifer.
Omilia, folclic lar. [ung.[3]
Ceremoniæ ḡ. orgia, geldhaealhalg-
Mvnus, uel zenia, lac.
Eleemosyna, uel agape, ælmesse.
Donum, datum, uel donatum, gifu.
Pretium, wurd.
Depretiatus, wurdleas.
Care ualet, pretiosum est, deor hit is.
Uile ualet, undeor hit is.
Care uendidit, deore he hit bohte, *uel* sealde.
Uile uendidit, undeore he bohte.
Uilis, waclic.
Carus, leof.
Odiosus, þurhlad.
Uiuus, cuce.
Rediuiuus, geedcuced.
Mortuus, dead.
Defunctus, fordfaren.
Defungitur, fordfærd.
Longæuus, langlife.
Capillamenta, rupe odd[4] drisne.
Polio, ic smedie.
Plano, uel leuigo, ic gegnide.
Conficio, ic gemenge.

Commolio, ic grinde.
Commolitus, gegrunde.
Deuoto, ic wyrge.
Deuotatio, wergnes, *uel* gehat.
5 *Compensatio*, edleanung.

NOMINA AUIUM.

Cignus, ylfete.
Pauo, pauus, pawe.
10 *Aquila*, earn.
Beacita, uel sturnus, stearn.
Herodios, ḡ., swan.
Olor, swan.
Ardea, hragra, *diomedea*.
15 *Ficedula*, swertling.
Strix, uel cauanna, uel noctua, uel ulula, ule.
Lucinia, uel philomela, nightegale.
Mergus, scealfr.
20 *Mergulus*, fugeldoppe.
Auca, gos.
Aucarius, goshafuc.
Anser, ganra.
Anas, ened.
25 *Ciconia*, storc.
Rubisca, rudduc.[5]
Auricinctus, goldfinc.
Alauda, lauerce.
Bugium, hæfenblæte.[6]
30 *Alcedo, uel alcion*, mæw.[7]
Columba, culfer.[8]
Palumbus, wudeculfre.
Bitorius, uel pintorus, wrenna.
Cicada, uicetula, hegesugge.[9]
35 *Cicada*, hilhama.
Turdus, scric.[10]
Cornix, crawe.
Buteo, cyta.

[1] *Lænan* means *commodare, offerre*. lane- or lane-sang seems to be a literal translation of *offertorium*. R. W.

[2] Perhaps an error for *donum*. The sawlsceat was a custom different from the general church tax (cyricsceat). Cf. Leges Aedelstani: And ic wille eac ... þæt man agyfe þa cyricsceattas and þa sawlsceattas etc. R. W.

[3] Cf. pag. 107, l. 22. R. W.

[4] The writer omitted *e* in odd. R.W.

[5] *Ruddock* continued long to be the regular English name for the redbreast, or robin; and I am not sure that it has yet entirely disappeared from our local dialects.

[6] Cf. pag. 9, l. 4. R. W.

[7] See pag. 24, l. 7. R. W.

[8] The pigeon is still called *a culver* in some of our dialects.

[9] The hedge-sparrow is still called, in Gloucestershire, a *haysuck*.

[10] The shrike.

Turtur, turtle.
Coruus, remn.
Nicticorax, nihtremn.
Gracculus, uel monedula, ceo.[1]
Gaia, uel catanus, higere.
Cuculus, geac.
Stronus, stærn.
Turdus, stær.[2]
Turdella, se mare stær.
Coturnix, ærschen.
Pica, agu.
Pluuialis, hulfestre.
Bubo, uf.
Picus, fina.
Gracculus, uel garrulus, hroc.
Miluus, glida.[3]
Ibis, geolna.
Fulica, dopenid.
Uultur, earngeap.
Aceta, snite, *uel* wudecocc.
Grus, cran.
Florentius, goldfinc.
Luscinus, geolewearte.
Parrax, wrenna, *uel* hicemase.
Merula, uel plara, þrosle.
Accipiter, uel raptor, spearhafoc.
Cintus, uel frugellus, goldfinc.
Hirundo, swalewe.
Carduelis, linetwige.
Rapariolus, fiscere.
Tanticus, ærdling.
Capo, capun.
Gallus, coc.
Gallinaceus, capun.
Pullus, cicen.
Falco, uel capus, a capiendo, wealh-hafoc.
Scoricarius, bleripittel.

Bardioriolus, colmase.
Oscines aues, wigole fugules.

NOMINA HERBARUM.[4]

5 *Apiago,* beowyrt.
Lilium, lilie.
Fafida, leomuc.[5]
Colochintida, wylde cyrfet.
Rosa, rose.
10 *Brionia, uel ampelos leuce,* $\bar{g}$., hwit wilde wingeard.
Labrusca, wilde wingerd.
Brabasca, uel amplos male, blac wingeard.
15 *Botanicum, uel uiridarium,* wyrttun.
Cucumerarium, wyrttun.
Caluna, mægþa.
Feniculum, fynel.
Nepita, næpte.
20 *Adriatica, uel malum terræ,* galluc.
Costus, cost.
Trifolium, geacessure,[6] *uel* þrilefe.
Uaccinium, branwyrt.
Abrotonum, superne wude.
25 *Lubestica,* lufestice.
Uolui, sinwealte swammas.
Sinpatus, cneowhole.
Solsequium, uel heliotropium, solsece, *uel* sigelhwerfe.
30 *Astula regia,* wuderofe.
Millefolium, uel myriflon, $\bar{g}.$ *uel centefolia,* gæruwe.
Tanaceta, helde.
Samum, hylwurt.
35 *Herba,* gærs, *uel* wyrt.
Butunus, heope.
Apium, merce.
Uenenifuga, atterlaþe.

---

[1] *Ceo* is the modern word *chough.*

[2] The stare, or starling. One would suppose that in the next line *mare* is an error for *lassa.*

[3] *Glede* continued to be the usual English name for the kite till a comparatively late period, and will be found in our vocabularies of the fifteenth century.

[4] The list of plants is rather copious, and many of their Anglo-Saxon names are still preserved as the popular names of wild plants. The cause of the list being so numerous was no doubt the circumstance of their being so much used for medicinal purposes.

[5] This is the reading of the MS. R. W.

[6] *Geaces-sure* or *gœces-sure,* literally cuckoo's-sour, was the plant we now know by the name of wood-sorrel, which is still called in some parts of the country *cuckoo-sorrel.*

Febrefugia, uel febrifuga, feferfuge.
Ruta, rude.
Blitum, uel lappa, clate, *uel* clyfwyrt.[1]
Simphoniaca, hennebelle.
Gersussa, biscopwyrt.
Ramusium, ramesan.
Dilla, uel acrocorium, docce.
Anetum, dile.
Cucumer, hwerhwette.
Anadonia, feldwyrd.
Gladiolum, glædene.
Cinaglossa, uel plantago, uel lapatium, wegbræde.[2]
Artemisia, uel matrum herba, mugwyrt.
Annuosa, æscþrotu.
Amorfolia, clate.
Cepe, ennelec.
Saxifraga, sundcorn.
Philantropium, lappa, clate.
Auris leporis, halswyrt.
Ebulum, walwyrt.
Allium, garleac.
Herba munda, giþcorn.
Poletis, hwitleac.
Melletina, medewyrt.
Porrus, porleac.
Cameleon, g., wulfescamb.
Cynocephaleon, heortelæfre.
Electrum, elehtre.
Ficus, ficwyrt.
Papauer, popig.
Saliunca, wilde popig.
Apiaster, wudemerce.
Petrosilion, stanmerce.
Menta, minte.
Alumen, uel stipteria, efne.
Uiola, hofe.
Gerobotana, uel uerbena, uel sagmen, biscopwyrtil.
Calta, uel trifillon, clæfre.

Crispa, uictoriola, smeringwyrt.
Centaurea, eordgealle.
Strumus, uel uua lupina, nihtscada.
Saluia, fenfearn.
5 *Collocasia,* harewinta.
Filix, fearn.
Herba putida, mægþa.
Cresco, kerse.
Uermiculi, mæddre.
10 *Filix arboratica,* eferfearn.
Sintea, uel senecion, grundeswelge.[3]
Nap siluatica, sperewyrt, *uel* wilde næp.
Carex, uel sabium, uel lisca, secg.
15 *Rubia,* mæddre.
Juncus, risc.
Scirpus, ærisc.
Bremium, earisc.
Ulua, græde.
20 *Gramen,* cwice.
Alga, sæwaur.[4]
Consolda, dægesege.
Raphanum, uel radix, rædic.
Tursus, cimia, crop.
25 *Centaurea major,* curmelle.
Brittannica, cusloppe.
Malua, malwe, *uel* geormenletic.
Pastinaca, feldmora.
Daucus, wealmora.
30 *Napus,* næp.
Citocatia, giþcorn.
Cariota, waldmora.
Sinapis, senep.
Cucurbita, cyrfæt.
35 *Papirus,* duþhamor.
Nasturtium, tunkerse.
Rapa, næp.
Fungus, uel tuber, metteswam.
Carduus, þistel.
Coliandrum, celendre.
Cerefolium, cærfille.
Elleborum, uel ueratrum, wodeþistle.

[1] *Clyf-wyrt* is generally understood as designating the plant now called *foxglove* (the *digitalis purpurea*). The Anglo-Saxon herbal of the Cottonian MS. (Vitel. C. III.) gives three names of this plant — clyfwyrt sume man hatad foxesclife, sume eawyrt.
[2] See pag. 10, 26 and 13, 10. R. W.
[3] Now softened down into *groundsell,* the name of a well-known plant.
[4] Still called *waure* in Kent.

Cicuta, hemlic.
Aconita, þung.
Betonica, seo læsse biscop[wyrt].
Urtica, netle.
Archangelica, blinde netle.
Sisimbrium, balsminte.
Calamus, uel canna, uel harundo, reod.
Quinquefolium, pentafillon, fifleafe.
Uinca, peruincæ.
Uiscerago, mistiltan.
Marrubium, uel prassium, harhune.
Canicula, argentilla.
Fraga, streaberige.
Framen, streaberiewisan.
Nimphea, eadocca.[1]
Eruca, calfwyrt.
Caballopodia, uel ungula caballi, cologræig.[2]
Ciminum, cymen.
Agrimonia, sticwyrt.
Modera, cicenamete.
Helena, horshelene.
Diptamnus, uel bibulcos, wilde næp.
Sandix, wad.
Fucus, waad.
Tinctura, teging.
Arboracia, uel lapsana, cal.
Alfa, ædelfyrdingwyrt.
Origanum, warmelle.
Altea, uel euiscus, seomint.
Cardamon, cærse.
Pionia, pionia.
Mandragora, eordæppel.
Oxylapation, ḡ., anes cynnes clate.
Brionia, wild cyrfet, *uel* hwit wingeard.

Satirion, suðerige.
Pollegia, hylwyrt.
Hermodactyla, crawanleac.
Centaurea minor, banwyrt.
5 *Hedera nigra*, wudebinde.
Pappus, þistles blostm.
Sarrabum, wilde lactuce.
Fromos, uel lucernaris, uel insana, uel lucubros, candelwyrt.

10 NOMINA ABBORUM.

Arbor, treow.
Quercus, uel ilex, ac.
Robur, iung ac.
15 *Quernum*, acleac.
Corilus, hæsel.
Saginus, hwit hæsel.
Juglantis, uel nux, hnutu.
Fraxinus, æsc.
20 *Æsculus*, boc.
Fagus, boc.
Faginus, becen.
Suberies, mæstentriow.
Nemus, uel lucus, bearu.
25 *Saltus*, holt.
Spartus, þyfel.
Arbustum, iung treow.
Truncus, stoc.
Stipes, stofn.[3]
30 *Sirculus, uel uirgultum*, sprauta.
Daphnis, uel laurus, laurbeam.
Seno, uel tilia, lind.
Malus, apulder.[4]
Malus matranus, surmelst apulder.
35 *Malomellus*, swite apulder.
Mespila, openærs.[5]
Pirus, pirige.[6]

[1] Literally, the water-dock, the beautiful plant we now call the water-lily. One might suppose that the Anglo-Saxons named their plants with more regard to the leaves than to the flowers, to judge by this instance.

[2] An error for coltgræig. R. W.

[3] This word is still preserved in Leicestershire under the form *stovin*, signifying the stump of a tree.

[4] The Anglo-Saxon name of the apple-tree is preserved in the names of several places, such as Appledurford, or Appledurcomb, in the Isle of Wight, Appledore in Kent, and another Appledore in Devonshire, and perhaps Appledram in Sussex.

[5] It is rather singular that we should find this not very delicate name of the medlar at so early a period. It is found in MSS. of the fifteenth century, and is a word sufficiently familiar to the readers of the popular literature of the sixteenth and seventeenth centuries.

[6] In the fifteenth century the English name for the pear-tree still continued to be *piry, pire,* or *perye.*

Persicarius, persoctreow.
Cariscus, cwicbeam.
Pinus, pintreow.
Prunus, plumtreow.
Ficus, ficbeam.
Cerasus, cyrstreow.
Cornus, corntreow.
Carica, ficappel.
Morus, uel rubus, morbeam.
Palma, palmtwig, *uel* palm.
Abies, uel gallica, gyrtreow.
Ulmus, ulmtreow.
Genesta, brom.
Taxus, iw.
Acer, mapulder;[1] *acernum,* mapul- dern.
Populus, byrc.
Marica, uel brogus, hæþ.[2]
Alnus, alr.
Castanea, cystel, *uel* cystbeam.[3]
Glans, æcern.
Granum, cyrnel.
Corimbi, berigen.
Flos, blostm.
Cauliculus, stela.
Radix, wyrtruma.
Uimen, læl.
Uiticella, wiþwinde.[4]
Pirorium, læferbed.
Pirus, gladiolus, læfer.
Ramus, boga.
Olea, oliua, elebeam.
Amurca, elesdrosna.
Oleaster, unwæstmbære elebeam.
Betulus, byrc.
Betulentum, byrcholt.
Rubus, heopbrymel.
Acrifolius, holen.
Gignalia, **hagan.**

Uariculus, hwitingtreow.
Cresis, cwictreow.
Sicomorus, uel celsa, æps.
Pruniculus, plumsla.
5 *Flaui, uel mori,* blaceberian.
Ligustrum, hunisuge.
Bacido, botrus, clyster.
Accidinetum, gost.
Coquimella, uel prunus, uel nixa,
10 plumtreow.
Amigdala, uel nutida, magdalatreow.
Nux, uel nucarius, hnutbeam.
Buxus, box.
Ornus, eow.
15 *Cedrus,* cederbeam.
Cedria, hissæp.
Abellanæ, hæsl, *uel* hæselhnutu.
Sentes, þornas; *senticosus,* þorniht.
Frutex, þyfel.
20 *Ramnus,* þifeþorn.
Spina, þorn.
Tribulus, þorn.
Alba spina, hægþorn.
Spina, uel sentrix, þyfel.
25 *Uepres,* bremlas.
Mastix, uel resina, cuter.
Carpo balsami, balsames blæd.
Opobalsamum, balsames tear.
Uitis, wintreow.
30 *Salix,* wiþig.[5]
Mirica, hæþ.
Silua, wudu; *calones,* wudicras.
Lignum, abæawan treow.
Stirps, styb, *uel* spranca.[6]
35 *Glans, glandis,* picbred.
Amenus locus, luffendlic stede.
Claua, styng.[7]
Contus, spreot.

[1] *Mapulder,* the maple. It still occurs in the Anglo-Saxon form in names of places, as in Mappledurwell in Hampshire, and Mapplederham in Oxfordshire.

[2] *Marica* seems to be only an error for *myrica,* under which form it is repeated below. hæþ means *erica, thymum,* thyme.

[3] The modern word *chestnut* is merely *cystknut,* the nut of the cyst-tree.

[4] *Withwind* is still a name for the wild convolvulus; but how it came to find a place among trees, is not clear. The same may be said of the bulrush (*lafer*).

[5] *Withy* is still a common provincial name for the willow.

[6] So the MS.; Wright has: sprauta. But *sprauta* means: a sprout, *surculus,* not: a stem or trunk of a tree. — Cf. pag. 149 l. 23. R. W.

[7] The compiler of the vocabulary now

Capsella, scrin.
Cardinarius, i. primarius, se yldesta.
Causidicus, aduocatus, forespeca.
Carpentum, currus, horswæn.
Caragius, fugelhwata.
Circinum, mæltange.
Emisperia, healftryndel.
Clatrum, pearruc.
Tribus, cneores.
Cimiterium, poliandrium, halig leger-[stow].
Coccum, rubicundum, bis tinctum, weolcread.
Conquilium, weolocesscyll.
Contubernalis, geþofta.
Coclea, gewind.
Conniueo, ic wincige.
Confuto, ic oferstæle.
Conflatilis, gegoten.
Columen, i. culmen, rof.
Commentator, expositor, dihtere.
Conspiratio, gecwidrædden.
Crates, i. flecta, hyrdel.
Crisoletus, auricolor, goldbleoh.
Bida, uel basterna, uel capsus, uel currus, uel esseda, uel quadriga, uel carpentum, cræt.
Capsus, betogan cræt.
Cuba, byden.
Pilentum, uel petorritum, uel rada, crat.
Carracutium, hehhwiolad wæn
Crepido, uteweard.
Cassata, forhrered.
Clasendis, sweordes scead.
Categia, i. telum, gesceot.
Oppidum, fæsten.
Urbanus, burhsita. *uel* burhman.
Ciuis, ceasterware.
Castellum, wic, *uel* lytel port.

goes off again into a series of miscellaneous words, which are at first taken, as in several instances before, from an alphabetical dictionary of the Latin language. He first breaks into the regularity of the alphabetical words by introducing one or two on account of their similar meaning, or from contrast, and then he leaves them altogether.

Molendinarius, uel molinarius, mylenwyrd.
Molitura, grist.
Cerealis pistor, gristra.
5 *Pistor*, bæcere.
Pistrinum, bæcern.
Fornax, clibanus, ofn.
Cribrum, sife.
Cribellum, lytel sife.
10 *Uannus*, fann.
Uentilabrum, windwigsyfe.
Capisterium, hridder.
Taratantara, hridder.
Sporta, cawl.
15 *Corbes*, leap.
Tritorium, þerscel.
Pila, pilstre.
Pilum, pilstampe.
Pilunus, pilere.
20 *Apludes, uel cantalna*, hwæte gryttan.
Ergasterium, werchus.
Officina, smiððe.
Incus, anfilte.
Aries, ram to wurce.
25 *Securis, uel secespita*, æx.
Dolabrum, bradæx.
Bipennis, twibille, *uel* stanæx.
Falcastrum, bill.
Ascia, adesa.
30 *Falciola, uel falcicula*, sicol.
Falx, siðe.
Uitrum, uel hialum, glæs.
Electrum, smylting, *uel* glær.
Metallum, ælces kynnes wecg, *uel*
35 ora oððe clyna.
Massa, dað, *uel* bloma.[1]

NOMINA ARMORUM.[2]

Arma, wæpna.
40 *Armamentarium*, wæpnahus.

[1] *Bloma*, the metal taken from the ores. It is the origin of the technical term *bloomery*, for the places where one of the operations of smelting is performed. (Bosworth has: "dah" instead of dað. R.W.)

[2] In this chapter we have apparently a tolerably good account of the arms, offensive and defensive, of the Anglo-Saxon fighting men. The former are the

Galea, leþerhelm.
Cassis, irsenhelm.
Corona, diadema, cynehelm.
Lorica, uel torax, uel squama, byrne.[1]
Gladius, uel machera, uel spata, uel framea, uel pugio, sweord.
Spatarius, swyrdbora.
Armiger, wæpenbora.
Signifer, uel uexillifer, tacnbora.
Lancea, falarica, spere.
Uenabulum, barspere, *uel* huntigspere.
Sica, litel sweord.
Capulum, hilte.
Mucro, swurdes ord. [feoht.
Intestinum bellum, necheburena ge-
Ciuile bellum, burware[2] gefeoht.
Asta, quiris, sceaft.
Uagina, scead.
Manubrium, hæft and helfe.
Rasorium, scearsex.
Nouaculum, næglsex.
Faretra, coker.
Telum, sagitta, fla.[3]
Arcus, boga.
Anquina, bogenstreng.
Scutum, uel clipeus, uel parma, scyld.
Pelta, lytel scyld.
Umbo, randbeh, *uel bucula.*
Funda, lythre.
Fundiblum, stæflithere.
Classica, blædhornas.
Ensis, hiltleas sweord.
Capulus, hilte.
Mucro, ælces wæpnes ord.
Machera, anecge sweord.

sword and spear, bows and arrows for the archer, and slings; the latter are principally the shield, the helm, and the byrnie or coat of mail.

[1] The *byrnie,* or *brunie,* of early English poetry, where it seems to be used as a general term for the armour of the body—

   The knyghtis redy on justers,
   Alle yarmed swithe wel.
   Brony, and launce, and sweord of stel.
               Kyng Alisaundre, l. 1867.

[2] So the MS. R. W.

Pugio, uel clunabulum, lytel sweord, *uel* hypesex. [reaf.
Spolia, uel manubie, uel prede, here-
Preda, reaflac.
5 *Hasta,* getridwet spere.
Hastilia, gafelucas.[4]
Contus, spereleas sceaft.
Trudes, uel amites, spreotas.
Claua, uel cateia, uel teutona, anes
10 cynnes gesceot.
Pila, gesceot.
Lancea, wigar,
Amentum, wegures gewidspere.
Falarica, uel fala, wigspere.
15 *Telum, uel obeliscus,* flaa.
Sagitta, uel spiculum, gefyderad flaa.
Scorpius, gæттrad flaa.
Cuspis, sceaft.
Coriti, bogefodder.
20 *Theca,* fodder.
Dolones, stæfsweord.
Balista, gelocen boge.
Clipeus, testudo, scyld.
Ancile, sintryndel,[5] lytel scyld.
25 *Peltæ, uel parme,* þa læssan scyldas.
Apex, summitas galeæ, helmes top.
Crista, helmes camb.
Conus, helmes byge.
Speculea, seawere.
30 *Bipennis,* twybill.
Caduceatores, uel pacifici, gesibbe ærendracan.
Præfeciales, gefeohtes bodan.

35 *NOMINA XII. VENTORUM.*[6]
Subsolanus, easten wind.
Auster, uel nothus, suden wind.

[3] The word *flo,* for an arrow, was in use in the English language as late as the time of Chaucer.

[4] The *gavelok* of the English of a later period. Thus we are told in one of the metrical romances—

   Gavelokes also thikke flowe
   So gnattes, ichil avowe.
        Arthour and Merlin, p. 338.

[5] I read in the MS.: sintryndel. R. W.

[6] This list of names of the points of the winds, is substantially the same as the list of Frankish names which Eginhard

Fauonius, uel zephirus, westen wind.
Septentrio, norðan wind.
Uulturnus, eastan suðan wind.
Eurus, euroauster, norðan eastan wind.
Euroafricus, suðan easten wind.
Africus, suðan westan wind.
Corus, norðan westan ƿind.
Cireius, norðan easten wind. [wind.
Aquilo, uel boreas, norðan westan

Spiracula, unclænra gasta wunungstow.
Baratrum, uorago profunda, cwicsusl, *uel* hellelic deopnes.
Erebum, hellescead.
Stix, hellemere.
Tartara, uel gehenna, hellewite.
Infernus, helle.
Colonia, i. peregrinorum cultura, elelændra eorðbigennys.
Municipium, burhscipe.
Uicus, wic.
Castellum, port.
Castrum, heahfæsten.
Pagi, tunstede.
Conciliabula, manna gegaderung.
Compita, ceorla samnung, *uel* gemotstow.

Platea, wid stræt.
Quintane, fifte dæl þære strete.
Murus, weal.
Menia, burhweall.
Porta, portgeat.
Promurale, foreburh.
Turris, stypel.
Propugnacula, wighus.
Arx, se hihsta wighus.
Cocleæ, adulseaþe.[1] [burge.
Forus, uel prorostra, motstow on
Curia, domhus.
Theatrum, wafungstede.[2]
Amphitheatrum, syneweald wafungstede.
Farus, here-beac[n].
Coclea, windelstan.
Circuitus, ascensus, gewind.
Termas, uel gymnasium, bæþstede.
Apodyterium, baðiendra manna hus, *i. domus quo uestimenta balneantium ponuntur,* þær hi hi unscredað inne.
Tabernæ, uel gurgustia, lytle hus of bredan.
Macellum, flæcstræt, *uel* flæccyping.
Mercatum, ceping.
Teloneum,[2] scipmanne myrt se ceping.
Apoditerium, breawern.

Vulturnus, [eastan norðan wind.]
Eurus, eastan suðan wind.
Euroauster, suðan eastan wind.
Austroafricus, suðan westan wind.
Africus, westan suðan wind.
Corus, westan norðan wind.
Circius, norðan westan wind.
Aquilo, norðan eastan wind.

[1] Adul-seaþe, or adel-seaþe, is a sewer or sink. *Cocleæ* is an evident error for *cloaca.*

[2] Literally, *a place for sights,* explaining the word according to its Greek derivation. This, and the translation of the following word (*syneweald wafungstede,* a circular place for sights), show that our Anglo-Saxon forefathers were not acquainted with the uses of theatres and amphitheatres, and had no words in their language to express them.

[3] Cf. Bosw. pag. 21ᵛ *s. v.* ceapsceamul.

R. W.

imagined to have been first given to the winds by Charlemagne. Ventis vero hoc modo nomina imposuit, ut subsolanum vocaret *ostroniwint,* eurum *ostsundroni,* euroaustrum *sundostroni,* austrum *sundroni,* austroafricum *sundwestroni,* africum *westsundroni,* zephyrum *westroni,* corum *westnordroni,* circium *nordwestroni,* septentrionem *nordroni,* aquilonem *nordostroni,* vulturnum *ostnordroni. Vit. Caroli Imp., p. 92, ed Teulet.* The writer of the manuscript of our Anglo-Saxon vocabulary has evidently made some confusion in copying the list, so as to leave one wind entirely out. It probably stood originally thus, which would agree exactly with the list and description given by Isidore, lib. xiii., c. 11:

Subsolanus, eastan wind.
Auster, uel nothus, suþan wind.
Favonius, vel zephirus, westan wind.
Septentrio, norþan wind.

Librarius, uel bibliopola, uel antiquarius, uel scriba, uel fenestella, wrytere.
Festinitas, solempnitas, uel celebritas, uel ceremonia, freolsdæg.
Fasti, weoredagas.
Scena, uel tabernaculum, geteld.
Capitilauium, heafodþweal.
Manulauium, handþweal.
Pedilauium, fotþweal.
Cenum, miox.[1]
Fauilla, ysle.
Gleba, turf.
Labina, sliddor.
Uolutabrum, sol, *uel* gesyd.
Uligo, moor.
Sabulum, molde.
Argilla, laam.
Samia, clæg.
Sulphur, swefel.
Alumen, efne.
Creta, uel cimola, hwit heard stan.
Creta argentea, spærstan.
Bitumen, anes cynnes lim.
Arena, sand.
Agger, eordbyre, *uel* geworht stræt, *strata uel delapidata.*
Uallum, scidwealles eordbyri.[2]
Iter, uel itus, cadfere weg.
Itiner,[3] lang and steare weg.
Actus, anes wænes gangweg.
Uia, twegra wæna gangweg.
Publica uia, ealles hereweg.
Priuata uia, tuunweg.
Semita, manna pað.
Callis, deora pað.
Tramites, wæterweg.
Diuortia, diuerticula, mistlice woge wegas.
Compita, weggelæta.
Ambitus, twicen.

Orbita, wænes sweþ.
Limus, lutum, fenn.[4]
Rus, unered land.
Satio, seminatio, sædnað.
5 *Fundus,* þrop.
Alluuius ager, wæterig æcer.
Noualis ager, brocen land, *uel* geworht land.
Proscissio, landopenung.
10 *Squalidus ager,* forlætan æcer.
Uliginosus ager, fennig æcer.
Subcisiua, hryding.
Centuria, twahund æcera.
Area, breda þiling, *uel* flor on to
15 þerscenne.
Pratum, mæd.
Fines, gemære.
Limites, hafudland.
Decumanus, tiode hafudæcer.
20 *Pertica,* metgeard.
Porca, balc.
Miliarium, leouue, mile.
Passus, stæpe.
Stadium, furlang.
25 *Diuersorium,* tocirhus, *uel* cumenhus.
Hospitium, uel metatum, cumena wicung.
Prandium, underngereord.
Cena, æfengereord.
30 *Merenda,* nonmete.
Tabulatorium, wahdyling.
Entheca, g̃., suppellex, ineddisc, *uel* inorf.
Canalis, þeote.
35 *Tegulæ, imbrices, lateres, uel laterculi,* hroftigla.
Silex, flint.
Scopulum, torr.
Spelea, uel spelunca, scræf.
40 *Cautes, uel murices,* scearpeste stanas.
Calculus, sæcysul.

---

[1] The Anglo-Saxon *miox,* or *meox,* dung, filth, is the origin of the provincial term *mixen,* a dunghill, and of the modern muck.

[2] Literally, an embankment for a wall of palings; a curious mode of interpreting the Latin, which would seem to intimate that the *valla* which surrounded the Saxon camps or residences were always, or at least usually, crowned with palings, or timber fences.

[3] So the MS. R. W.

[4] The word *fen* preserved its original meaning of mud, in the English language, till at least the fifteenth century.

Scrupulus, lytel stan.
Cos, hwetstan.
Pumex, pumicstan.
Calcisuia, gebærdstan.[1]
Gagates, gagatstan.
Pirites, uel focaris lapis, fyrstan.
Specularis, þurhscyne stan.
Succinum, uel electrum, sap, smelting.
Flestria, gim þe bið on coches micga.[2]
Aurum obrizum, read gold.
Brattea,[3] gylden læfr.
Pecuarius, feohstrang man.
Pondus, uel pondo, gewyht, *uel* pund.
Dipondius, twegra pundra gewiht.
Trutina, wæga.
Lanx, scale.
Bilances, twa scale.
Examen, wægetunge.
Momentana, uel statam, sytlewæga.[4]
Campana, wulwæga.

NOMINA TRITICI SUNT.

Frumentum, corn.
Scandula, twisld corn.
Farrago, grene berecræs.[5]
Spica, ear.
Arista, egla.[6]
Culmus, healm.[7]
Folliculus, codd.
Stipulæ, healmes laf.
Palea, ceaf.
Migma, æsceda.
Legumen, ofet.
Uicia, musepise.

Caudex, uel codex,[8] hrind.

Liber, seo inre hrind.
Spadones, unberende telgan.
Capreoli, uel cincinni, uel uncinuli, wingearda hocas þe hi mid bindað þæt him nehst bið.
Corimbi, wingearda hringa.
Præcoquæ, rædripe winberige.
Ceraunie, reade winberige.
Aminea uitis, hwit wingeard.
Ablaqueatio, niderwart treowes delfing, bedelfing.
Putatio, screadung.
Cima, crop.
Propaginatio, wintwiga plantung.
Fossio, dicung.
Fossor, dikere.
Arbusta, iung treow, *uel* treowstede.
Frutecta, plur., þyfelas.
Capreoli, wingearda gewind. [*mora.*
Auiaria, weglæsa beara, *secreta nеRecidiua,* edgrowung.
Plantaria, gesawena plantan.
Plante, treowes sprancan.
Radix, wyrtrume.
Surculus, wæterboh.
Uirgultum, telgan.
Germen, berende boh.
Matura mors, ripe dead.
Immatura, unripe dead.
Fomes, geswælud spoon, *uel* tynder.
Præcoquus fructus, rædripe wæstm.
Ramnus, uel sentix ursina, dyfeþorn.
Herbitum, orfgebitt.
Crustumie, uel uolemis, uel insana, uel melimendrum, healfreade peran.
Digladior, pugno, ic feohte.
Derogo, ic ofteo.

---

[1] Somner conjectures that, in this article, the Latin should be *calx viva,* and the Anglo-Saxon *gebærn stan,* or *gebærned stan.*

[2] The precious stone, pretended, according to a legend of great antiquity, to be found in the maw or gizzard of a cock, is called by Pliny *alectoria* (from the Greek ἀλέκτωρ, a cock), and by Isidore *electria.* The latter word seems to have been corrupted by our compiler into *flestria.*

[3] So the MS. R. W.

[4] sytle- or sitl- (= setl-) wæga means *statera,* R. W.

[5] *Cræs* is no doubt an error for *græs.*

[6] The beards of barley are still called *ails* in Essex.

[7] The straw of corn, as well as the stalks of many other plants, are still called *haulm* in many of our provincial dialects.

[8] An error for *cortex.* R. W.

Derogatio, lehtrung.
Degenero, ic misdeo.
Deriuo, ic gelæde.
Discludo, ic todæle.
Discriminatus, geglenged.

Saltus, hlyp.[1]
Luctatio, wraxlung.
Spectacula, uel ludicra, yppe, *uel* weardsteal.
Orcestra, uel pulpitus, gligmanna yppe.
Carceres, horsa steal.
Auriga, scridwisa, *uel* wænere.
Tragedi, uel comedi, unweorde scopes.
Temelici, idel sangere.
Histriones, truþas.
Mimus, jocista, scurra, gligmon.
Pantomimus, gligman.
Saltator, tumbere.
Alea, tæfel.
Aleœ, tæfelstanas.
Aleator, tæflere.
Pirgus, cyningstan on tæfle.
Tessere, uel lepusculœ, federscite tæfel.
Tessellœ, lytle feþerscite florstanas.
Pila, uel sfera, doþer.
Rogus, aad.
Strues, wudefine.
Calones, wudigeras.
Mationes, stanwirhte.
Fistulœ, þeote.
Constructio, uel instructio, hyrdung.
Instructio, ealdere timbrunga bote.
Constructio, niwe timbrung.
Norma, wæterpund.
Circinum, mæltange.
Centrum, mæltanges prica.
Epigri, uel claui, nægles.
Perpendiculum, wealles rihtungþred.
Commissura, borda gefeg.

Sectio, cliofung.
Serra, saga.

UESTIUM NOMINA.

5 *Uestitus*, hræglung.
Habitus, scruud.
Cultus, reaf.
Tunica, tunice.
Bombicinum, seolcen.
10 *Bombix*, seolcwyrm.
Sericum, seole.
Olosericum, eal seolcen.
Tramasericum, seolcen ab.[2]
Bissum, *ḡ., papagen*, swiþe hwit
15 fleax.
Lineum, linen.
Laneum, wyllen.
Linostema, linen wearp, *uel* wyllen ab.
20 *Praesegmina, praecisiones*, screadan.
Segmentata uestis, geræwen hrægel.
Pauidensis, dicce gewefen hrægel.
Leuidensis, denne gewefen hrægel.
Clauus, uel purpura, purpuren hræ-
25 gel.
Polymita, fealahiwes hrægel.
Ralla, uel rasilis, wogum bewerod hrægel.
Interpola uestis, geedniwod eald hræ-
30 gel.
Panucla, geclutad hrægel.
Acu picta, uel frigia, gediht, *uel* gesiwed hrægel.
Trilicis, þrylen hrægel.
35 *Colobium*, slefleas scrud.
Leuitonarium, slefleas ancra scrud.
Lumbare, uel renale, lenden sidreaf.
Linna, hnysce hwitel.
Renones, stiðe and ruge breost-
40 rocces,
Birrus, unsmeðe hrægel.
Diplois, twifeld hrægel.

---

[1] After another intercalation from the alphabetical dictionary, the compiler now proceeds to give a rather brief list of games and amusements. Leaping and wrestling appear here as the principal gymnastic sports in use among the Anglo-Saxons.

[2] The yarn of a weaver's warp is, I believe, still called an *abb*.

Melotes, uel pera, gæten, *uel* broccen rooc.
Anaboladium, uel sindo, linen heafodes wrigels.
Circumtectum, tryndyled reaf.
Trabea, cynelic reaf.
Paludamentum, caseres reaf to gefeohte.
Regillum, uel peplum, uel palla, uel amiculum, riceræ wife hrægl, *uel* deorwurde wæfels.
Fimbria, fnado, *uel* læppan.
Stola, uel ricinum, orl.
Sipla, an healfhruh tæppet.
Stuppa, æcumbe.[1]
Tomentum, hnygela.
Platum, seolce hnygele.
Tinctura, deah.
Coccus, read deah.
Ferrugo, blac purpur.
Calathus, wearpfæt.
Pensum, uel diarium, dægwine.
Infula, biscopheafodlin.
Cidaris, uel mitra, hufe.
Diadema, bend agimmed and gesmided.
Nimbus, mid golde gesiwud bend.
Capitulum, uel capitularium, heafodclaþ, *uel* cappa.
Antiæ, earloccas.
Monile, uel serpentinum, myne, *uel* sweorbeh.
Antrax, uel clauus, uel strophium, angseta, *uel* gyrdel, *uel* agimmed gerdel.
Carbunculus, seo blace begne.
Fibula, preon, *uel* oferfeng, *uel* dalc.
Speculea, sceawere.
Periscelides, scangbendas.
Tinius, smede ringce.
Zona, uel zonarium, uel brachile, uel redimiculum, gyrdel.
Baltheus, swyrdes gyrdel.
Ungulus, agymmed hringe.
Samothracius, geheafdod hringce.

Subfibulum, uel subligaculum, underhwrædel.
Fasciola, nosle, *uel* sarclad.
Saccus, uel fiscus, kingesgafoles bigerdel.
Saccellus, lytel sæc.
Marsupium, uel marsippa, seod.
Mastruga, crusne.
Clamis, hacele, *uel* fotsid scicecl.[2]
Sagum, hwitel.
Toga candida, uel cretata, gehwit hrægel.
Toga, sidreaf swilce meteres wyreed on anlicnysse.
Toga palmata, uel toga picta, sigereaf.
Cinctus gabinus, twilæpped scrud on twam healfan gescredde swa meteras metad on anlicnyssan.
Anelus, lytel hring.
Inauris, earpreon, *uel* earring.
Calamanca, hæt.

Accubitus, hnylung.
Affluentia, oferflowendnys.
Opulentia, metes genihtsumnys.
Epulæ, wist.
Dapes, kininga wist, *uel* estas.
Merendo, meridiendo, to middan dæge ic ete.
Fermentacius panis, gehafen hlaf.
Azimus, deorf.
Cibarius, ceorlisc hlaf.
Acrizimus panis, gesecorid hlaf.
Siligineus, uel triticeus, hwæten hlaf.
Subcinericeus, uel focarius, heordbacen hlaf.
Clibanius, ofenbacen hlaf.
Frixus panis, gehyrst hlaf.
Amolium, dust of dæm ...
Simila, uel pollis, smedma.
Inuolucrum, gewynd.
Thorus genialis, brydbed.
Pluteus, brederes beddes inneweard.
Sponda, uthealf þæs beddes.

---

[1] What we now call *oakum, i. e.,* the hemp from old ropes.

[2] So the MS R. W.

Lectica, bedrest.
Storea, uel psiata, meatta.
Cama, sccort bed wid cordan.
Bajanula, ferbed.
Scabellum, uel subpedaneum, fotscamul.
Scansilia, stapas, *uel* stirapas.
Cilindrus, scort sinewealt stan, *uel* treow.
Pala, uel uentilabrum, windswingla.
Furcilla, litel forca.
Fisclum, cleseocche.
Mensurnum opus, mondes weorc.
Funalia, uel funes, candelweoca.
Lampas, candeles leoma.
Lucubrum, leohtes leohting.
Pira, upstandende herebeacn.
Rogus, bustum, forbærned [aad].
Farus, herebeacn.
Fictilia, uel samia, læmene fatu.[1]
Asierina, readdo læmene fatu.
Crisendeta, gyldena,*uel* gegylde fatu.
Celata, adrifene fatu.[2]

Cælum, heofen.
Angelus, uel nuntius, encgel.
Archangelus, heahencgel.
Stella, steorra.
Sidus, tungel.
Sol, sunne.
Luna, mona.
Firmamentum, roder.
Cursus, ryne.
Mundus, middaneard.
Tellus, terra, solum, uel aruum, eorða.
Humus, rus, aruum, molde, *uel* land.
Mare, uel aequor, sæ.
Sinus, sææbbung.
Oceanus, garsecg.
Mare eoum, eastsæ.
Mare arctoum, norðsæ.

Promuntorium, clif.

Patriarcha, heahfæder.
Propheta, uel uates, witega.
5 *Apostolus*, ærendraca.
Episcopus, biscop.
Archiepiscopus, arcebiscop.
Diaecesis, uel parochia, bisceopscir, *uel* biscopric.
10 *Rex*, cyncg.
Regnum, rice.
Sceptrum, cynegeard, cynedom.
Regina, cwen.
Imperator, uel Caesar, uel Augustus,
15 casere.
Imperatrix, uel Augusta, caseres wif.
Dux, heretoga, *uel* heorl.
Princeps, uel comes, ealdorman.
Fasces, ealdordomas.
20 *Primas*, heafodman, *uel* þegn.
Clito, ædeling.
Obses, gisel.
Satrapa, þegn.
Judex, uel censor, uel arbiter, dema.
25 *Monachus*, munuc.
Monacha, uel monialis, mynecenu.
Presbiter, mæssepreost.
Sacellanus, handpreost.
Sacerdos, sacerd, *uel* cyrepingere.
30 *Clericus*, preost, *uel* þingere.
Diaconus, uel leuita, diacon.
Subdiaconus, underdiacon.
Archidiaconus, arcediacon.
Eremita, westensetla.
35 *Anachoreta*, ancra.
Nonna, arwurðe wudewe, *uel* nunne.

Homo, man, *uel microcosmus*, læsse middaneard.[3]
40 *Anima*, sawl.
Animus, mod, *uel* gedanc.

---

[1] Earthen vessels, for which the Latin *Samia* is here used as a general term. In the next line, *Asierina* is no doubt an error of the scribe for *Aretina*. See the chapter *de vasis escariis* in Isidori Etymolog., lib. xx., c. 4.

[2] i. e., engraved or embossed vessels.

[3] *Microcosmus*, derived from the two Greek words μικρός and κόσμος. i. e. a little world, or the world in miniature, first applied metaphorically to the human frame by one of the Greek philosophers, was a favourite word with the mediæval writers to signify a man.

Spiritus, gast.
Sensus, gewit.
Intellectus, andgit.
Cogitatio, geþanc.
Corpus, lichama.
Caro, flæc.[1]
Uertex, hnol.[2] [panne.
Caluarium, forheafod, *uel* heafod-
Anciput, forheafod.
Occiput, uel postex, æfteweard hæfod.
Sinciput, oferhealf heafod.
Coma, uel cirrus, locc unscoren.
Cerebrum, uel cerebellum, brægen.
Cesaries, fex.
Uncinus, locc.
Crines, wifmannes loccas.
Timpus, þunwang.
Facies, anwlita, *uel* neb.
Uultus, andwlita, *uel* rudu.
Species, hiw.
Uisus, gesihð.
Tactus, repung, *uel* æthrin.
Auditus, hlyst.
Odor, odoratus, stenge.
Odor, brod.
Gustus, anbyrignys.
Sapor, swæcc.
Odor, olfactus, stenge.
Pili, hær.
Capilli, heafodhær.
Comae, loccas, *uel* unscoren hær.
Compago, gefeg.
Compages, gefeincga.
Frons, forheafod.
Oculus, eage; *oculi*, eagan.
Supercilia, oferbrua.
Cilia, brua.
Palpebrœ, breawas.
Circulus, dæs seohringe.
Pupilla, uel pupula, seo.
Yrqui, beahhyrne, *uel* agneras; *uol-*
  uos dicimus angulos oculorum.
Praefolium, fel ufan eagan.
Intercilium, betwux oferbruan and
  bræwum.

[1] *Sic MS.* R. W.
[2] We still use the word *noll*, in trivial speech, for the top of a man's head.

Corona, uel circulus, wulderbeah.
Tauco, hringban dæs eagan.
Lacryma, tear.
Luscus, scylegede.
5 *Monoftalmus*, anegede.
Caecus, blind.
Genae, hecgaswind.
Malae, hleor.
Maxilla, gewenge. [cinban.
10 *Mandibula*, ceacban, *uel* ceacan, *uel*
Pinnula, earlæppa, *uel* ufweard eare.
Pinnulæ, flæran, *uel* earlæppan.
Nasus, nosu.
Columna, eal ufweard nosu.
15 *Nares*, nosdyrla.
Internasus, uel interfinium, uel inter-
  pinnium, nosegristle, *uel* middel-
  flere.
Pirula, foreweard nosu.
20 *Pinnulae*, uteweard nosterle.
Auris, eare.
Labium, ufeweard lippa.
Labrum, nidera lippe.
Rostrum, foreweard feng þære lip-
25 pena togædere.
Lingua, uel plectrum, tunge, *uel*
  hearpnægel.
Sublinguium, huf.
Dentes, teð.
30 *Praecisores*, foreteð.
Canini, uel colomelli, mannes tuxas.
Molares, uel genuini, wangteð.
Ginginœ, toðaflæsc.
Aduersi dentes, ða eahta forworden
35 teþ betwux tuxum.
Palatum, uel uranon, goma, *uel* hrof
  dæs muðes.
Collum, sweora, *uel* swura.
Fauces, hracan.
40 *Arteriae*, windæddran.
Guttur, þrotu.
Mentum, cin.
Gurgulio, þrotbolla.
Chautrum, eal þrotbolla.
45 *Rumen*, wasend, *uel* edroc.[3]

[3] It must not be supposed that the words *wasend* and *edroc* are synonymous; but the compiler seems to have been

Ceruix, uel iugulum, hnecca.
Humerus, eaxla.
Ola, ufeweard exle ðæs æftran dæles.
Brachium, hearm.
Torus, uel musculus, uel lacertus, mus[cl] ðæs carmes.
Torosus, earmstrang.
Cuba, elboga.
Cubitum, fædm betwux elboga and handwyrste.
Palmus, span, uel handbred.
Ulna, eln, uel spanning betwux ðuman and scitefingre.
Uola, uel tenar, uel ir,[1] middeward hand.
Pugillus, se gripe ðære hand.
Palma, handbred.
Pugnus, fyst.
Artus, þa maran liða.
Ungula, hof.
Unguis, nægel; ungues, næglas.
Cartilago, gristle.
Impetigo, eagan wean, uel wearhbræde.
Albugo, eagflea.
Mentedra, uel oscedo, mudadl on goman.
Ascella, uel subhircos, oxn, uel ruhoxn.
Cada, hrisel; cadula, lytel hrisel.
Lacertus, bog.
Digiti, fingras.
Pollex, duma.
Index, uel salutaris, scytefinger.
Medius, uel impudicus, middelfinger.
Medicus, uel annularis, goldfinger.
Auricularis, læcefinger.
Praecordia, forebreost.
Pectus, breost.
Pectusculum, breostban.
Torax, foranbodig, uel breostbeden.
Mamilla, tit.
Ubera, meolcebreost.
Papilla, tittstrycel.

Truncus, heafodleas bodig.
Cutis, uel pellis, hyd.
Corium, uel tergus, hyd.
Costa, rib.
5 Aruina, uel adeps, uel axungia, uel abdomen, hrysel, uel gelend, uel swind, uel swines smere.
Pulpa, uel uiscum, lira.
Os, ban.
10 Nerui, sinu.
Latus, side.
Pori, i. spiramenta unde sudor emanat, licþeotan, uel swatþyrlu.
Uentriculus, mage.
15 Scapula, sculder.
Pale, gesculdre.
Interscapilium, middel gesculdru.
Dorsum, hricg.
Tergum, bæc.
20 Uertigo, hwerfa.
Uertibulum, uel uertebra, hwerban.
Spondilia, geloda, uel gelyndu.
Sacra spina, lendenban neoþeweard.
Renes, uel lumbi, lendenu, uel hypeban.
25
Catacrina, hypeban.
Aluus, rif, uel seo inre wamb.
Matrix, uterus, wifmannes innod, uel cildhama.
30 Folliculus, cildhama.
Secundae, cildhama.
Medulla, uel lucanica, mearh.
Omentum, fylmen.
Intestina, smælþearmas, uel inneweard.
35
Ilium, scare.
Ilia, smæleþearmas.
Tolia, uel porunula, reada.
Extales, snædel, uel bæc-þearm.[2]
40 Exta, midrif.
Umbilicus, navela.
Disseptum, midrif.
Clunes, hypas.
Nates, earslyre.

doubtful whether the Latin word meant the weasand (wasend), or whether it was identical with the rather similar Latin word derived from it, ruminatio.

[1] Ir seems to be an error for χειρ or chir. R. W.
[2] The MS. by an error reads: ba reþearm. R. W.

Anus, uel *uerpus*, earsþerl.
Crementum, weres sæd, uel cid.
Uesica, blæddre.
Meatus, fordgang.
Ueretrum, wæpengecynd.
Genitalia, gecendlimu.
Femen, inneweard ðeoh.
Coxa, þeoh.
Femur, utanweard þeoh.
Posteriora, bæce.
Cecum intestinum, æmuþa.
Suffragines, hamma.
Poples, hamm.
Renunculi, lundlagan.
Crus, scance; *crura*, sceanca.[1]
Genu, cneow.
Geniculi, cneowwyrste.
Sura, spærlira.
Tibiae, scina, *uel* scinban.
Pes, fot.
Talus, ancleow.[2]
Taxillus, lytel ancleow.
Plante, fotwelm.
Planta, foreweard fot.
Subtel, middel fot.
Calx, hohspor.
Solum, læst.
Uiscera, beflagen flæc, *uel* innoþes innewearde.
Cor, heorte.
Bucleamen, heorthama.
Jecor, lifre.
Pulmo, uel *fecatum*, uel *pleumon*, uel *epar*, lungen.
Splen, milte.
Rien, crop.
Lien, lundlaga.
Pulsus, clæppetung.
Fibrae, lifrelæppan, *uel* þearmas.
Fel, *uel bilis*, gealla.

Obligia, nytte.
Stomachus, maga.
Colus, roop.
Uenter, sco utre wamb.
5 *Cauliculus*, fearhhama.
Matrix, cwið, *uel* cildhama.
Mentagra, tan.
Allox, micele tan.
Botrax, yce.
10 *Mentera*, bædþearm.[3]
Hermafroditus, wæpenwifestre, *uel* scritta,[4] *uel* bæddel.
Hirniosus, healede.
Scamma in homine, se rude on þam
15 men.
Glippus, ḡ-, grymede.
Uariæ, cwydele, *uel* hwylca.
Cronculus, angseta.
Capitosus, mycelheafdode.
20 *Petilus*, litelfota.
Frontalis, *uel calidus*, steornede.
Uentriculosus, wæmbede.
Tergosus, earsode.
Genosus, cneowede.
25 *Talaricus*, cleonede.
Calcaneus, honede.
Surosus, spærlirede.
Mentagricus, tanede.
Mancus, wohhandede.
30 *Peduncus*, wohfotede.
Podagricus, deagwyrmede, *uel* deag-gede.
Flegmaticus, mældropiende.
Reumaticus, saftriende, *uel* drefliende.
35 *Molaricus*, swediende.
Plegus, earming.
Balbus, stamer.
Catax, heolt.
Blesus, plips.[5]
40 *Surdus*, *uel surdaster*, deaf.

[1] The shank. When his subjects and contemporaries gave our first Edward the title of *Long-shanks*, they meant literally long-legged, without supposing they were using any trivial or derogatory term.

[2] The ankle is still called *ankley* in Sussex; and the word *anclow* continued in use in the English language till the fifteenth century.

[3] *Mentera*, should perhaps be *entera*, or *inentera*; and *bad* appears to be a mere error of the copyist for *bac*. The process of forming *t*, *c*, and *d*, was so similar, that they are often confounded.

[4] The old English word *scrat*, which meant similarly a hermaphrodite.

[5] So the MS., not *wlips*. R. W.

Debilis, uel eneruatus, lame.
Strabus, scyleagede.
Lippus, sureagede.
Unimanus, anhende.
Æger, uel aegrotus, adlig.
Morbus, adl.
Paraclitus, bedrida.
Clinicus, hofrede.
Ulcerosus, hreofla.
Leprosus, licþrowere.
Lunaticus, monaþseoc.
Demoniacus, deofelseoc.
Energumenus, gewitseoc.
Elisa mens, uel deiecta, forscrenct.
Demens, gemendleas.
Rabidus, uel insanus, wod.
Rabies, wodnys.
Freneticus, se þe for sleape awed.
Lethargus, ungelimplice slapfulnis.
Uigil, uel uigilans, wacul.
Peruigil, durhwacul.
Uigilia, wecen.
Incolumis, gesund.
Eneruis, mægenleas.
Lotium, hweal.[1]
Urina, micga.
Minctio, miggung.
Exugium, micgern.
Callus, ile.
Uiscum, gerunnen blod.
Menstrua, monaðblod.
Fantasma, uel fantasia, gedwimor.
Pituita, i. minuta saliua, horas, *uel* hræcunda, *uel* spatlung.
Pitisso, ic spatlige.
Euomitio, spiwinge.
Oscitatio, ganung.
Singultus, siccitung.
Sternutatio, uel sternutamentum, snytinge, *uel* fneosung.
Spiratio, eðung.
Pedatio, feorting.
Fesiculatio, fisting.
Sibilatio, hwistlung.
Pluuicinatio, stanc.
Pluuicino, ic stancrige.

NOMINA COLORUM.

Color, bleoh.
Albus, hwit.
5 *Amineus, uel albus*, hwit.
Candidus, þurhhwit.
Subalbus, healfhwit.
Niger, blac.
Ater, teter, sweart.
10 *Unicolor*, anes bleos.
Bicolor, twihiwe.
Discolor, mislic bleo.
Uarius, uel discolor, fah.
Uiridis, grene.
15 *Busius*, fealu.
Dosinus, uel cinereus, assedun.
Bruntus, wann.[2]
Balidinus, bryte.
Auidius, grinu.
20 *Natius*, dun.
Giluus, geoluhwit.
Ceruinus, dunfalu.
Myrteus, bleoreod.
Glaucus, græg.
25 *Elbus*, deorcegræg.
Guttatus, cylu.
Roseus, uel rubeus, uel pheniceus, read.
Perseus, blæwen.
30 *Succinaceus, uel croceus, uel flauus*, geolu.
Ceruleus, sweart.
Limpidus, scir.

35 *Doctor, uel imbutor, uel eruditor*, lareow.
Discipulus, uel mathites, leorningcniht.
Disciplina, lar, *uel* steor.
40 *Doctrina*, lar.
Dogmatista, lareow.
Paedagogus, cildahyrde, *uel* lareow.
Documentum, uel specimen, larbysn.
Scolasticus, uel cliens, scolman.
45 *Caraxatio*, gewrit.
Epistola, uel pitacium, ærendgewrit.

[1] Not "þweal" as Wright printed. R.W. [2] Here Junius added *Lege Brunius*. R.W.

Quaternio, cine.
Planca, spelt.
Diploma, bod on cine.
Membrana, bocfel.
Scedula, ymle.
Sceda, screade.
Graphium, *uel scriptorium*, græf.
Pictor, metere.
Pictura, metinge.
Minium, read teafor.[1]
Gluten, lim to fugele.[2]
Glara, æglim.
Incaustum, *uel atramentum*, blæc.
Sculptor, *uel celator*, græfere.
Sculptura, **græft**.
Agalma, *uel iconisma*, *uel idea*, anlicnes.
Scalprum, *uel scalpellum*, *uel coelum*, græfsex.
Ingenium, orðanc.
Artifex, cræftica.
Opifex, wyrhta.
Architectus, yldest wyrhta.
Aurifex, goldsmið.
Argentarius, seolfersmið.
Ærarius, mæstlincsmið.
Nummularius, mynetere.
Palatium, kynelic botl.
Thesaurus, goldhord.
Gazophilacium, madmhus.
Ædificium, getimbrung.
Basis, post.
Postis, *uel fulcimentum*, sylle.
Forus, *uel prorostra*, motstow.
Logotheta, gemotman.
Negotium, intinga.
Negotiatio, cypineg.
Sacramentum, *uel mysterium*, geryna, *uel* digla.
Testimonium, gewitnes, *uel* gecyðnes.
Recompensatio, edlean.

Dispendium, *uel damnum*, *uel detrimentum*, hynd, *uel* lyre, *uel* hearm.
Commodum, *questus*, hyð, *uel* freme.
Commutatio, gehwearf.
5 *Nihil*, nanwiht.
Nihili, naht.
Fronimus, wis.
Prudens, snotor.
Sagax, *uel gnarus*, *uel astutus*, *uel*
10 *callidus*, petig, *uel* abered.
Frugi, *uel parcus*, uncystig.
Largus, *uel dapsilis*, cystig.
Famosus, *uel opinosus*, hlisful.
Sophus, *uel sophista*, wis.
15 *Sophista*, **wite**.
Insipidus, angeræd.[3]
Stultus, stunt.
Stultomalus, yfeldysig.
Impudens, scamleas.
20 *Tenax*, fæsthafel. [sagul.
Falcidicus, *uel falsiloquus*, unsoð-
Auarus, *uel cupidus*, gitsere.
Raptor, *uel praedo*, *uel spoliator*, reafere.
25 *Fallax*, *uel mendax*, swicol.
Planus, *uel seductor*, swica.
Elogium, *uel dictio*, saga.
Empiria, manegra embesmeagunga.
Emunctoria, candeltwist. [gerim.
30 *Ephemerides*, *numerus cotidianus*,
Emeritus, *prouectus*, geþungen.
Epithalamium, *carmen nubentium*, giftleoð.

35 *NOMINA NAUIUM.*

Nauis, *uel faselus*, scip.
Rates, scipu.
Nauiscella, *uel cimba*, *uel campolus*, *uel musculus*, sccort scip.
40 *Scapha*, *uel trieris*, litel scip, *uel* seeigð.

---

[1] This word is still preserved among the peasantry in various parts of England in the form *tiver*, applied to a composition of tar and red ochre, which is used to mark sheep, or to colour wood, and protect it against the effects of exposure to weather.

[Cf. **Grein**, sprachschatz; Vol. II pag. 526 R. W.]

[2] The compiler of the vocabulary has mistaken the Latin word *gluten* to signify here *bird-lime*, instead of *glue*.

[3] So the MS. Wright printed: *ungerad*.
R. W.

Linter, bat.
Pontonium, punt.[1]
Carabus, scipincel.
Littoraria, trohscip.
Carina, scipes botm.
Nauclerus, scipes hlaford.
Proreta, ancorman.
Gubernator, steorman.
Gubernio, steora.
Nauta, roþer.
Remex, redra.
Puppis, steorsetl.
Remus, steorroder.
Prora, ancersetl, *uel* forscip.
Trudes, sprcotas.[2]
Transtra, scipsetl.
Transtra, uel iuga, þofta.

Palmula, roðres blæd.
Antenna, segelgyrd.[3]
Cornua, segelgyrde endas.
Malus, uel artemo, mæst.
5 *Portisculus, uel hortator remigum*, sciphamor.
Anchora, uel saburra, ancra.
Uelum, segel.
Dalum lytel segel.
10 *Rudentes*, sciprapas.
Propes, fotrap.
Plagae, netrapas.
Uerriculum, drægnet.[4]
Nassa, bogenet, *uel* leap.
15 *Cassis*, deornet.
Conopeum, flcohnet.

[1] It is hardly necessary to say that the word *punt*, as a name for a sort of boat, is as well known among us in the present day, as it was among the Anglo-Saxons in the tenth century. It will be remarked how many of the Anglo-Saxon words, connected with shipping, have been preserved in our navy.

[2] Sprits — preserved especially in the term bow-sprit.
[3] The yards.
[4] As the ordinary ships were used especially for fishing, the compiler goes on naturally enough to speak of nets, (see pag. 181 l. 9—14. R. W.) with which he concludes rather abruptly.

V.

SUPPLEMENT TO ALFRIC'S VOCABULARY,[1]

OF THE TENTH OR ELEVENTH CENTURY.

Reus, scyldig.
Damnatus, fordemed.
Hosticus, uel hostilis, feondlic.
Osor, feond.
Facinus, maan.
Peiero, ic forswerige.
Gibborosus, uel strumosus, hoferede.
Profanus, manful.
Exosus, perosus, ansæte.
Callidus, geap.
Uersutus, hindergeap.
Simulator, hiwere.
Fictor, uel hipocrita, liccetere.
Adulator, uel fauisor, liffetere.
Adulatio, liffetung.
Deceptor, bepæcend.
Seductor, læfend.
Proditor, læwend.
Delator, wrohtbora.
Patricida, fæderslaga.
Parricida, mægslaga.
Cicatrix, dolhswad.
5 *Soma*, lichama.
Truncus, heafodleas bodig.
Funus, lic, *uel* hreaw.
Feretrum, bære.[2]
Mausoleum, uel bustum, kyninga
10 byrgen.
Sarcofagum, þruh.[3]
Unguina, uel unguenta, smyrels, *uel*
   scalf.
Reses, uel deses, uel piger, slaw.
15 *Infidus*, ungetreowe.
Iniuriosus, teonful.
Contentiosus, geflitful.
Impiger, uel praepes, unslæw.

[1] This Vocabulary is said to have been found, as a sort of Supplement to the former, following it in the same manuscript, but with some intervening matter of another description. It seems, indeed, to have been the design of the compiler to give at more length some classes of words which are given less numerously in the vocabulary of Alfric, such as those belonging to the family and domestic relations, some classes of natural phenomena, naval terms, the names of various classes of buildings in use among the Romans, and a few words connected with the ancient religious belief. Many words found in Alfric's vocabulary are repeated, but sometimes with variations in the interpretation, which are not without interest.

[2] A bier.

[3] This word, which is of common use in Anglo-Saxon, and is evidently connected with the modern *trough*, was preserved in the old English words *throh*, *thrugh*, and *thurwe*, signifying a coffin. A flat gravestone is still called a *through* in the dialects of the north of England.

Lentus, uel piger, sleac.
Conciliabulum, gemotstow.
Consulo tibi, ic ræde ðe.
Consulo te, ic frine ðe.
Conciliatio, gesibsumung.
Consiliator, rædgifa.
Concilio, ic gesibbige.
Concionor, uel meditor, uel precor, ic smeage.
Judex, uel consul, ealdorman.
Censor, uel arbiter, dema.
Mas, hys cild.
Sexus, werhad, *uel* wifhad.[1]
Coniunx, gemæcga.[2]
Coniuges, uel coniugales, gesinhiwan.
Coniugium, uel matrimonium, gesinscipe.
Complex, uel consentiens, gegada.
Complices, conspirantes, gegadan, *uel* geþwærniende.
Incestus, uel impurus, unclæne.
Ancilla, serua, abra, uel dula, ḡ., wyln.
Seruus, dulus, ḡ., þeowa.
Emptitius, geboht þeowa.
Uerna, uel uernaculus, imberdling, *uel* fostorling.
Alumnus, fosterfæder.
Praepositus, foreset, *uel* gerefa.
Fatigatus, atered.
Exercitatus, acostnod.
Populus, folc, *uel* byretreow.
Exercitus, here.
Procinctus, fyrdinge.
Edictum, geban.
Apparatus, gearcung.
Uulgus, uel plebs, ceorlisc folc.
Heros, hlaford.
Congregatio, concio, gegaderung.
Conuentus, conuentio, gesamnung.

Arrabo, wedlac.
Cliens, uel clientulus, cniht.
Ephebus, uel buteo, beardleas.
Galos, glos, weres swuster.
5 *Sponsalia,* brytofta, *uel* brydgifa.
Procus, wogere.
Sponsus, brydiguma.
Pronuba, hadswape.[3]
Sponsa, bryd.
10 *Paranymphus,* hadswape.
Infans, uel alogos, ḡ., unsprecende cild.[4]
Paranymphus, dryhtguma,[5] *uel* dryhtealdor.
15 *Unicuba,* anlegere wifman.
Uxoratus, þe wif hæfd.
Nimpha, bryt.
Derelicta, laf, *uel* forlæten wif.
Priuignus, steopcild.
20 *Anula, uel uetula,* eald wif.
Adolescens, uel inuestis, uel inuesticeps, geong man.
Pubetenus, frumbyrdling.
Pecuniosus, feohstrang.
25 *Locuples,* landspedig.
Gamos, bryd.
Egenus, wædla.
Leno, wemere, *uel* tihtere.
Telonearius, tolnere, *uel* tollere.
30 *Profugus,* flyma.
Exul, utlaga.
Hebes, dwæs, *uel* sott.
Hebetudo, dwæsnys, *uel* sotscipe.
Edax, uel glutto, frettol.
35 *Uorator,* grædig.
Ambro, gifere, *uel* free.
Procax, uel peruicax, gemah.
Procacitas, uel peruicacia, gemahnys.
Cachinnatio, ceahhetung, *uel* cincung.
40 *Hilaris,* glædman.

---

[1] It is curious that the Anglo-Saxon language seems to have had no abstract term for *sex*, which was expressed only severally as manhood or womanhood.
[2] The old English word *make,* applied either to husband or wife.
[3] Cf. pag. 174 l. 35. R. W.
[4] The compiler of the vocabulary has translated the Greek word *alogos*, rather than the Latin *infans*. The latter, however, is explained by Isidore, lib. xi., c. 2, thus — Infans dicitur homo primæ ætatis, dictus autem infans, quia adhuc fari nescit, id est, loqui non potest; nondum enim bene ordinatis dentibus, minor est sermonis expressio.
[5] Sic MS., not *brydguma*. R. W.

Tristis, unrot, *uel* gealh.
Mestus, uel merens, dreorig.
Fames, uel popina, hunger.
Derisio, tælhlehter.
Tripudium, gefea.
Rancor, anda.
Abstinentia, syfernys.
Abstinens, syfer.
Cura, cara.
Obesus, oferfæt.
Pinguedo, smyltnys.
Crassitudo, fætnys.
Corpulentus, diccul.
Grossus, græat.
Macer, hlæne.
Macilentus, dynnul.
Macies, uel tabitudo, hlænnes.
Gracilis, uel exilis, uel subtilis, smæl.
Exiguus, gepwæde.[1]
Irsutus, uel ispidus, ruh.
Ualidus, uel uegetus, trum.
Inualidus, unstrang.
Inbecillis, wanhal.
Sollicitus, ymbhedig.
Curiosus, carful.
Securitas, karleasnes.
Studium, bigegnes, *uel* smeagung.
Causa, uel negotium, intinga.
Obstinatus, pertinax, anwilla.
Obstinatio, pertinacia, anwilnes.
Uerecundus, uel pudens, scamfæst.
Pudicus, sideful.
Impudicus, unsideful.
Castus, clwne.
Incestus, unclæne.
Exilium, wræcsid.
Peregrinatio, ældeodignes.
Prohemium, durhlocung.
Praefatio, forespæc.
Reconciliatio, edþingung.
Pacificatio, gesibsumung.
Relegatus, wide asent.
Religatus, uel uinculatus, gewriþen.
Deportatus, to wite asent butan his gode.
Exterminator, utdræfere.

Exterminatus, ut adryfen.
Expers, dælleas.
Exsors, orhlyta.
Pater, fæder.
5 *Mater*, moder.
Auus, ealdefæder.
Patruus, fædera.
Matertera, moddrige.
Auia, ealdemoder.
10 *Proauus*, þridde fæder.
Proauuia, þridde moder.
Abauus, feowerþe fæder.
Abauia, feowerþe moder.
Tritauus, fifte fæder.
15 *Tritauuia*, fifte moder.
Familia, hyred.
Propago, cynren.
Generatio, cneores.
Soboles, uel proles, bearn, *uel* cnosl,
20 *uel* tudder.
Filius, suna.
Filia, dochtor, dohter.
Liberi, freobearn, *uel* ædelborene cild.
25 *Soror*, suster.
Filiaster, steopdohter.
Frater, broder.
Nepos, suna sune, *uel* broder sune, *uel* suster sune, þæt is nefa.
30 *Neptis*, broder dochter, *uel* suster dohter, nefene, þridde dohter.
Abnepos, feowerþe sune.
Abneptis, feowerþe dohter.
Adnepos, fifte sune.
35 *Adneptis*, fifte dohter.
Trinepos, sixte sune.
Trineptis, sixte dohter.
Agnati, fædern magas.
Cognati, meddern magas.
40 *Propinquus*, mæg, *uel* gesibling.
Patrueles, fæderan sunan.
Matrueles, moddrian sunan.
Fratres, gebrodru, *uel* gelodan, *uel* siblingas.
45 *Fratres patrueles*, fæderon sunan.
Consobrini, gesustrenu.

---

[1] Wright reads: *ychwæde*. R. W.

Sobrini, geswusterenu bearn.
Socer, sweor.
Socrus, sweger.
Gener, aþum.
Nurus, snora.
Uitricus, *uel patraster*, steopfæder.
Priuignus, steopsunu.
Patruus meus, min fædera.
Patruus meus magnus, mines fæderan fæder.
Propatruus meus, mines fæderan eldrefæder.
Abpatruus meus, mines fæderan þridde fæder.
Amita mea, min faþu.
Amita mea magna, minre faþa moder.
Proamita mea, minre faþan yldremoder.
Abamita mea, minre faþan þridde moder.
Auunculus meus, min eam.
Auunculus meus magnus, mines eames fæder.
Proauunculus meus, mines eames yldrefæder.
Abauunculus meus, mines eames þridde fæder.
Matertera mea, min moddrige.
Matertera mea magna, minre moddrige moder.
Promatertera mea, minre moddrian eldremoder.
Abmatertera mea, minre moddrian þridde moder.
Pronuba, hadswæpa; *ipsa est et paranimpha*.
Fratissa[1], broðor wif.
Leuir, tacor, *i. frater mariti*.
Janitrices, gebroþre wif.
Coniuges, gemæccan.
Nupta, beweddod.
Innuba, unbeweddod.
Coniugium, uel connubium, gesynscipe.
Contubernium, gegadorwist.

Annus, gear.

[1] So the MS. R. W.

Tempus, tid.
Cursus, ryne.
Arcus, bigels.
Iris, renboga.
5 *Pluuia*, ren.
Ninguidus, besniwod.
Tonitruum, uel tonitrus, þunor.
Fulgor, uel fulmen, ligit.
Nix, snaw.
10 *Niueus*, snawhwit.
Niualis, snawlic.
Grando, hagol.
Gelu, forst.
Pruina, hrim.
15 *Glacies*, is.
Glacialis, forstlic.
Aer, lyft.
Æther, hroder.
Uentus, wind.
20 *Nubes*, wolc.
Aura, hwiða, *uel* weder.[2]
Nimbus, scur.
Nebula, mist, *uel* genip.
Procella, storm.
25 *Imber*, færlic ren.
Ros, deaw.
Lux, leoht.
Tenebrae, uel furfuraculum, dystru.
Seculum, woruld.
30 *Æuum*, yld.
Dies, dæg.
Caligo, dimnes.
Mane, ærmyrgen.
Crepusculum, tweoneleoht, *uel* deorcung.
35 *Conticinium, uel gallicinium*, hancred.
Intempestum, uel intempesta nox, midniht.
Maligna lux, uel dubia, tweonulleoht.
40 *Matutinum*, uhtentid.
Diluculum, dægred.
Aurora, dægrima.
Prima, prim.
Tertia, undern.
45 *Sexta*, middæg.
Nona, non.
Suprema, ofernon, oððe geloten dæg.

[2] Wright printed: *reder*. R. W.

Uesperum, æfen.
Serum, bedtid.
Hora, tid.
Horoscopus, tidsceawere.
Ebdomada, uel septimana, wucu.
Mensis, monad.
Uer, lencten.[1]
Æstas, sumor.
Autumnus, hærfest.
Hyems, winter.
Uernalis dies, lengtenlic dæg.
Uer nouum, foreweard lencten, *uel* middewærd lencten.
Uer adultum, æfterwærd lencten. *Eodem modo et aestas et autumnus uocantur*, on þa ylcan wisan sumor and hærfest bioð gecigede.
Æstiuus dies, sumorlic dæg.
Autumnalis dies, hærfestlic dæg.
Hiemalis dies, winterlic dæg, *uel nox*, odde niht.
Pridie, uel esternum, ærendæg.
Postpridie, todæg.
Postperendie, oferdrige [dæg].
Centurias, getalu, *uel* heapas, *uel* hundredu.
Kalendæ, gehealddagas, *uel* halige dagas.
Nonae, ceapdagas. [*cuntur*.
Idus, swæsingdagas, *ab edendo di-*
Æquinoctium, emniht.
Frigus, cyle.
Calor, hæte.
Æstus, uel cauma, swoloþ.[2]
Feruor, hæte micel.
Siccitas, uel ariditas, drugaþe.
Humor, uel mador, wæte.
Sterilitas, uel infaecunditas, unwestmbærnys.
Fertilitas, westmbærnys.
Ubertas, genyhtsumnys.

Campus, feld.
5 *Planities*, smeþnys.
Æquor, brym, sæ.
Pascua, læs.
Pratum, mæd.
Ager, æcer.
10 *Compascuus ager*, gemæne læs.
Seges, gesawen æcer, *uel* land.
Uia, weg.
Biuia uel biuium, twiweg.
Triuium, wegelæton.
15 *Iter*, sidfæt.
Inuium, compitum, weggedal.
Inuium, ungefere, *uel* wegleas pæð.
Desertum, uel heremus, westen.
Patria, eard.[3]
20 *Pagus*, tun.
Prouincia, scir.
Mons, munt.
Tumulus, beorh.
Collis, hyll.
25 *Monticellus*, beorh ufeweard.
Uallis, dene.
Diluuium, flod.
Uadum, ford.
Pons, bricg.
30 *Aqua*, wæter.
Limpha, hluttor wæter.
Gutta, uel stilla, dropa.
Stagnum, mere.
Amnis, ea mid treowum ymbset.
35 *Flumen*, flod, *uel* yrnende ea.
Fluuius, singalflowende ea.
Ripa, stæþ.[4]
Riuus, rið.
Latex, burna.

---

[1] *Lenten*, or *Lent*, remained long in the English language in its original signification of *Spring*. Thus, in a lyric composition of the thirteenth century, (printed in Wright's *Lyric Poetry of the Thirteenth Century*, p. 43,) the approach of Spring is described as follows:
    Lenten ys come with love to toune,
    With blosmen ant with briddes roune,
    That al this blysse bryngeth.

[2] Hence our modern word *swelter*.

[3] In the Latin writers of the close of the Roman empire of the West, the word *patria* had come into use in the mere meaning of a land or province, as it is explained here.

[4] The more modern *stade*, or *staith*, which is still used in some parts of the country in the signification of a bank of a river, or, in some places, of a wharf or quay.

Torrens, broc.
Unda, eð.
Litus, strand.
Crepido, brerd, *uel* ofer.
Alueus, stream, *uel* streamracu.
Riuulus, lytel rið.
Fluctus, wealcynde ea.
Fons, well.
Latex, welspreng.
Lacus, uel lacuna, seað.
Harena, sandcesel.
Spuma, fam.
Gurges, wæl.
Abyssus, deopnys.
Uortex, edwinde.
Uorago, swelgend.
Uiuarium, fiscpol.
Euripus, uel piscina, fiscpol.
Una serta, an gerif fisca.
Tormentum, tintregung, *uel* wite.
Saltus, holt.
Solum, uel tellus, uel terra, uel aruum, land.

Aporiamur, we synd bereafod.
Bonis nostris, urum godum.
Pessime, luþerlice.
Reprehensibiliter, tallice.
Non mihi est cordi, nis me on gedance, *uel* on mode.
Non animaduerto, ic ne understande.
Non mihi occurrit, ne com hit me ongean.
Persuadeo, ic lære.
Collatio, wordmittung, *uel* wordsomnung. [beode.
Imperito, ic wealdige, *uel* oferbe-
Pecuniosus, welig.
Colorare, hiwian.
Affabre, cræftlice, *uel* smicere.
De popularibus, of beorhleodum.
Uenusto, ic cyrtenlæce.
Orno, ic smicere geglengce.
Obumbro, ic ofersceadewige.
Habilis coniunctio, gedafenlic þeodnys.
Praerogatiua, frumgifu, *uel* synder wurðmynt.

Ruminatio, ciwung, *uel* edroc, *uel* aceocung.
Ruma, uel paleare, frætlæppa.
Singultus, geocsung.
5 *Sarpta uinea*, gescreaded wingeard.
Scorteus, ledern.
Porus, uel spiramentum, orðung.
Usus, nyttung, *uel* þearf, *uel* gewuna.
Delinimentum, stracung, *uel* olæcung.
10 *Lepida, uel facunda*, getingce.
Splendida, uel ornata, beorht.
Exagonum, sixecge.
Sexangulatum, sixhernede.
Insusurrare, i. occulte detrahere, dig-
15 lice tælan.
Diuerticulum, wegtwiflung.
Compitum, wega gemittung.
Ancillantur, hyrsumiað.
Formulantur, þeowiað.
20 *Sinuatio*, besining.
Anfractus, abrocen land, *uel* hilces.
Inprouida, uel inconsiderata, unbesceawode.   [aceortlice.
Summatim, breuiter, uel commatice,
25 *Obsurduit*, adeafede.
Uolubile scema, sinewealt gesceap.
Globositas, sinewealtnes.
Semirotundum, healf-sinewealt.
Faenerata domino, gode on borh
30 geseald.
Scema locutionis, sprecewise.
Fabulositas, spellung.
Anilis fabula, ealdra cwena spell.
Sermo commentitius, gesmead spræc.
35 *Aquarum alluuio*, wætera gewæse.
Defecatio, uel purgatio, hlyttrung.
Omne genus holitorum, i. holerum, æghwylc wyrtcyn.
Omne genus arbustorum, æghwilc
40 treowcyn.
Omne genus seminarum, æghwilc sædcyn.
Zizania, laser.
Lolium, boþen; *et cetera adulterina*
45 *genera*, and odre lydre cynn
Cophinus, wilige, *uel* leap.
Conuersantur, uel commorantur, samod wuniað.

In procinctu, to gefeohte.
Promptus, gearu.
Specula, uel conspicilium, weardsteal.
Praeruptum, hengeclif.
Spectaculum, wæfd, uel wæfersyn, *uel* wafung.
Idioma, proprietas linguae, agen *uel* gecynde spræc.
Idiota, ungelæred.
Imperitus, ungleaw.
Inportunus, gemah.
Petitiosus, bedul.
Eculeus, uel catasta, wæarhrod, *uel* þrypeluf.
Distractio, ceap.
Uenditio, sala.
Contractio, uel contractus, næmingce.

NOMINA PISCIUM.

Balena, uel cete, uel cetus, uel pistrix, hwæl.
Cetarius, hwælhunta.
Delphin, uel bocharius, uel simones, mereswin.
Rombus, styria.
Lupus, uel scardo, bærs.
Gobio, blæge.[1]
Murena, uel murina, uel lampreda, merenæddra.
Murenula, tigle.
Mutus, uel mugilis, heardra.
Platesia, facg.
Esocius, uel salmo, lex.
Sparus, dunorbodu.
Lucius, hacod.
Tinca, sliw.
Tructa, truht.
Capito, myne, *uel* ælepute.
Turnus, forn.
Rocea, scylga.
Cancer, crabba.
Foca, seol.

Musculus, hran.
Polypus, loppestre.
Allec, uel iairus, uel taricius, uel sardina, hæring.
5 *Pansor*, floc.
Fannus, reohhe.
Sepia, cudele, *uel* wasescite.
Conche, uel cochlee, scille, *uel* sæsnæglas.[2]
10 *Murice, uel conchylium*, weluc.[3]
Nassa, æwul, *uel* boganet.

NOMINA NAUIUM, ET INSTRUMENTA EARUM.

15 *Linter*, bat.
Ratis, scip.
Nauicula, scippincel.
Trieris, sceiþ.
Ypogauus, horsascip.
20 *Nauta*, gereðru.
Nauclerus, sciphlaford.
Gubernator, steora.
Gubernio, steorman.
Aplustre, gereðru, *uel* scipgetawu.
25 *Archiromacus*, swiftscip.
Myoparo, hidscip.
Barca, flotscip.
Liburna, hule.[4]
Dromo, æsc, *uel* barð.
30 *Pontonium*, flyte.
Caudex, punt.
Paro, sceaþena scip.
Trabaria, anbyme scip.
Littoraria, uel tonsilla, trohscip.
35 *Cumba, uel caupolus*, þurruc.[5]
Scalpus, scip, *uel* seigl.
Cimba, uel carina, scipesbotm.
Musculos,[6] sceort scip.
Celox, flotscip.
40 *Parunculus*, plegscip.
Fori, scipesflor.
Struppus, strop, *uel* arwidde.

---

[1] The modern *bleak*, called in some parts a *blay*.
[2] *Sæ-snægl*, sea-snail, appears to have been the common name for shell-fish. I believe the term is still in use among our American brethren.
[3] *Weluc*, the modern word *whelk*.
[4] Our modern name *hulk*, for the body of the ship.
[5] Sic MS. R. W.
[6] So the MS. R. W.

Palmula, arblæd.
Antenna, uel temo, segelgyrd.
Cornua, þa twegen endas þære seglgyrde.
Transtra, þoftan.
Clauus, helma.
Artemon, uel malus, mæst.
Parastates, mæsttwist.
Prorcta, ancerman.
Gubernaculum, steorsceofl.[1]
Ponsis, sciphlædder.
Uelum, segl.
Naulum, sciptol.
Cauernamen, pranga.
Acateon, se mæsta segl.[2]
Epidromo, se medemesta segl.
Dalum, se lesta segl.
Puluini, slidor.
Puppis, steorsetl.
Anguina, cops.
Prora, ancersetl.
Funes, uel restes, rapas.
Porticulus, hamor.
Spirae, linan.
Sipara, anes fotes segl.
Propes, sceacline.
Safon, stæþ.
Rudentes, sciprapas.
Opisfera, sedingline.
Pronesium, mærelsrap.
Tonsilla, scipmærls.
Remulcus, tohline.
Strupiar, midla.
Bolidis, sundgyrd.
Cataprorates, sundline.
Æstuaria, fleotes tonette.   [yst.
Æstus, recessus et accessus maris,
Ledona, nepflod, *uel* ebba.
Malina, heahflod.

[1] Literally, the ship-shovel, the rudder.
[2] Perhaps we may conclude from this, and the two following words, that the ordinary Anglo-Saxon ships had only three sails, as here named — the large sail, the middle sail, and the small sail; but these names may be only an attempt to explain the Latin words, by describing what they meant in the want of equivalent terms.

Remex, reþra.
Peeris, gearafeng.
Uncini, bocas.
Trudes, spreotas.
5 *Accessus*, flod.
Recessus, ebbe.
Syrtes, sandrid.
Reuma, ebbe, *uel* gytestream.
Plagae, netrapas.
10 *Tragum, uel uerriculum*, drægc.
Nassa, bogenet.
Cassis, deornett.
Conopeum, fleohnet, *uel* micgnet.
Labrum, margo, uel crepido, stæþ,
15   *uel* brerd.
Loramentum, uel tormentum, widde.

Lasciua, gagol.
Allugo, fyne.
20 *Alluginatus*, fynig.[3]
Numisma, scylling.
Mensularius, pennighwyrfere.
Collybista, pennigmangere.
Trapezita, uel monetarius, mynetere.
25 *Paracaraximus*, fals pening.[4]
Folles, dyneras.
Procuratio, scir.
Procurator, scirman.
Proconsul, hehgerefa.
30 *Curator*, gerefa.
Augur, uel ariolus, wicca.
Sortilegus, tanhlytere.
Aduocatus, patronus, uel interpellator,
   forspeca, *uel* mundbora.
35 *Apologia*, ladung.
Apologeticus, beladung.

Domus, hus, hywræden.[5]
Proaula, i. domus coram aula, selde.

[3] The Latin of these two words should no doubt be *uligo* and *uliginosus*.
[4] So the MS. not *flaspenig* as Wright wrote. R. W.
[5] The words which follow are very curious. The compiler is endeavouring to explain, in Anglo-Saxon, the various descriptions of Roman buildings, and parts of a Roman house; and the way in which he does this not only shows that the

Zetas aestiuales, sumerselde.
Zetas hyemales, winterselde.
Salutatorium, gretinghus.
Consistorium, þæt hus þær man dwead heora handa.
Tricorum, uel triclinium, gereord-hus.
Epicausterium, domhus, *uel* mothus.
Thermas, bædhus, *uel* bædstow.
Gymnasium, leorninghus.
Coquina, uel culina, cicen.
Colimbus, i. aquaeductus, wæterscipes hus.
Ypodromum, goldhordhus,[1] *uel spondoromum*, digle gangern.
Ecclesia, circe.
Ædes, hofa.
Ædicula, lytel hof.
Templum, templ.
Basilica, cinges hof, *uel* cyrce.
Porticus, portic.
Peribolum, acire.
Aula, heall.
Triclinium, bur þrybeddod.[2]
Camera, bur.
Caminatum, fyrhus.
Cubiculum, bedcofa.
Refectorium, beodern.
Dormitorium, slæpern.
Auditorium, spræchus.
Capitolium, domhus.
Curia, uel senatus, upwitena spræchus.
Cella, cete.
Cellarium, hordern.
Lardarium, spichus.
Carnale, flæschus.
Apotheca, winhus.
Ærarium, feohhus.
Piscinale, fischus.
Popina, snædinghus.
Lautorium, wæscern.
Officina, smidþe, *uel* weorchus.
Equiale, horsern.
5 *Bostar, uel bouiale*, scipen.
Ouile, i. sepimenta, uel caulae, sceapahus.
Caprile, gatahus.
Casa, uel casula, insæte hus, *uel* lytel hus.
Gurgustulum, uel gurgustium, neara scræf.
Tugurium, hulc.
Magalia, uel mappalia, uel capanna,
15 byre, *uel* sceapheorden.
Carcer, uel ergastulum, uel lautumia, ewærtern.
Latrina, uel secessus, gang.
Absida, sinewealt cleofa, *uel* portic.
20 *Asseres*, latta, *uel* reafteres.
Abaso, infirmatorium, seocra manna hus.
Cancelli, lytle porticas.
Brationarium, mealthus.
25 *Pistrina*, bæcern.
Pistrilla, lytel bæcern.
Farinale, mealehus.
Granarium, cornhus.
Horreum, bern.
30 *Siccatorium*, cyln, *uel* ast.
Tornatorium, þrylhus.
Uestiarium, hrægelhus.
Bibliotheca, uel armarium, uel archiuum, boochord.
35 *Librarium*, bochus.
Salinarium, sealthus.
Caenaculum, gemæne metern.
Zenodochium, gisthus ældeodigra manna.
40 *Nosocomium*, seocra manna hus.

---

greater part of them were unknown to the Anglo-Saxons, but he gives us the Anglo-Saxon names for such buildings, and parts of buildings, as were known to our remote forefathers, and helps us to comprehend their meaning.

[1] This word is very curious as a name for a privy, in connection with the words *gold-finder*, and *gold-farmer*, which were used in the sixteenth and seventeenth centuries for a cleaner-out of privies. The durability of such popular phrases is extraordinary.

[2] A very singular translation of *triclinium*, as if it meant a three-bedded room.

Lupanar, uel circus, uel theatrum, myltestrehus.[1]
Balnearium, uel thermarium, bædhus.
Pomarium, uel cucumerarium, æppelhus.
Claustrum, fæsten, *uel* clauster.
Spelunca, uel specus, uel antrum, scræf.
Scriptorium, pisleferhus.
Aumatium, uel armarium, ælces cynnes cæpehus.
Faenile, highus.
Atrium, mycel and rum heall, *uel* cafertun.
Gazophylacium, madmhus.
Thesaurarium, goldhold.[2]
Oratorium, uel oraculum, gebedhus.
Propitiatorium, uel sanctum sanctorum, uel secretarium, uel pastoforum, gesceot bæftan þæm heahweofode.
Asylum, fridhus, *uel* generstede.
Sutrina domus, sutera hus.
Potionarium, ælces cinnes drenchus.
Caenobium, feala muneca wunung.
Ergasterium, uel operatorium, weorchus.
Genitium, towhus of wulle [3]
Parietinae, rofleasc and monleasc calde weallas.
Ypogaeum, uel subterraneum, corðbus.

Lustra, wilddeora holl and denn.
Lucus, uel nemus, beora.
Papilio, ganggeteld.
Tenda, tyldsyle.
5 *Clauus tentorii,* fitersticca.
Circumlutus locus, mid wæter ymbtyrnd stede.
Alluuium, wætergewæsc.
Netorium, inspinn.
10 *Pectica,* fleþecamb.
Liciatorium, lorh, *uel* webbeam.
Tela, langweb.
Licium, hefeld.
Lacerna, hacele geflenod, *uel* gecorded.
15
Uertigo, hwyorfa.
Suppar, interula, syrc.
Radiolum, hrisl.
Alibrum, hreol.
20 *Tramarium,* medema persa.[4]
Ragana, underhwitel.
Mataxa, uel corductum, uel stramentum, stræl, *uel* bedding.
Peblum, web.
25 *Lectisternia,* bedreaf.
Stamen, wearp.
Fulcra, eal bedreaf.
Lodix, wæstling.
Globus, clywe.
30 *Glomus,* unwunden gearn.
Glomer, globellum, cleowen.
Deponile, wefta, *uel* weft. [stæf.
Panuli, planus, uel panus, colus, dis-

---

[1] It is rather curious that the Anglo-Saxon scholar should confound a theatre with a brothel; but the mistake arose probably from his forming his judgment of the character of the Roman stage only from the ecclesiastical writers, who decried both the theatrical performances, which had become degraded enough, and the drama in general.

[2] Wright by an error printed: *goldhord.* R W.

[3] *Genitium* is apparently a corruption of *ginecœum* (*gynecæum*), the apartment of the women. Under the Franks on the Continent, and the Saxons in Britain, the term *gynecæum* was preserved in the mansions of the great, and was applied to the room in which the maidens attached to the noble lady's household were assembled, in the various employments peculiar to them, such as the various branches of spinning, weaving, sewing, embroidering, &c., of which the lord made a profit. It is probably with this idea that the Anglo-Saxon compiler of the glossary interprets *gynecæum* as "a towhouse of wool." The different words belonging to weaving, and women's domestic employments, follow immediately after.

[4] I read *persa,* not *wersa* as Wright does. R W.

Ciclas, uel oraria, orlas.
Apidiscus, webhoc.
Ordior, ic hefaldige.
Insubula,[1] webbeamas.
Percussorium, slege.
Tara, webgereþru.
Pecten, bannuccamb.
Texo, ic wefe.
Texta, gewefen.
Textor, webba.
Textrix, webbestre.
Trama, uel subtemen, oweb, *uel* ob.
Polymita, uel orbiculata, wingfah.
Ependeton, cop, *uel* hoppada, *uel* ufrescrud.   [wurdscipas.
Fasces, ealdordomas, *uel* þa hehstan
Flamininus honor, biscoplic wurdscipe.
Flammeolum, uel flammeum, biscopes huf.
Flamen, biscop.
Mancipatio, þeowdom.
Manumissor, freotgifa.
Manumissio, freotgife.
Emancipatio, freodom.
Manus impositio, handgang.
Manumissus, gefreod.
Liricus, scop.
Poema, leod.
Poesis, leodweorc.
Poeta, uel uates, leodwyrhta.
Tragicus, uel comicus, unwurd scop.
Pythonissa, hellerune, *uel* hægtesse.
Horoscopus, dægmelsccawere.[2]

Mathematicus, tungelwitega, *uel* gebyrdwitega.
Sortilegus, tanhlyta.
Oreades, muntælfen.
5 *Dryades,* wuduelfen.
Moides, feldelfen.
Hamadryades, wylde elfen.
Naiades, sæelfen.
Castalides, dunelfen.
10 *Penates,* cofgodas.
Tisiphona, wælcyrre.[3]
Parcae, hægtesse.
Satyri, uel fauni, unfæle men.
Ficarii, uel inuii, wudewasan.[4]
15 *Abatis,* fœtfellere.
Lictor, uel uirgifer, hyldere.
Lanio, uel lanista, uel carnifex, uel macellarius, hyldere, *uel* cwellere, *uel* flæctawere.
20 *Quaestionarius,* dema.
Creditor, lænere.
Ariolus, wicca.
Commentariensis, gerefa.
A secretis, uel principis consiliarius,
25 geruna.
A responsis, i. magister responsorum, yldest ærendraca.
A caliculis, magister calicum, yldest byrla.
30 *Assecla,* folgere.
Teloneum, tolsetl.
Pincerna, byrle.
Plagiarius, nytena deof.
Questor, dema.

[1] An error of the scribe for *insubulæ*.   R. W.

[2] The compiler has again followed the derivation of the word, instead of the meaning of the word itself; and, instead of interpreting *horoscopus* as one who tells people's fortunes by calculating their nativities, he took it to mean one who announces the hours of the day. The words which follow are curious illustrations of the fairy mythology of our forefathers.

[3] The Anglo-Saxon of this and the following word appear to be transposed. *Hægtesse* means properly a fury, or, in its modern representative, a hag, and would apply singly to Tysiphone, while *wæl-cyrian* was the name of the three fates of the Anglo-Saxon mythology. (*sic!* R W.)

[The MS. by an error has: wælcyrte. R. W.]

[4] The Anglo-Saxon of this and the preceding word seem to have been similarly transposed. It furnishes us with a very curious and instructive example of the long preservation of words connected with popular superstitions; for, in Withal's *Dictionarie,* ed. 1608, p. 62, we have, in the list of four-footed beasts, "a woodwose, *satyrus.*"

Transilio, ic oferhleape.
Transilitor, oferhleapend.
Questus, uel lucrum, gestreon.
Altilis, fedels.
Citharedus, hearpere.
Citharistria,[1] hearpestre.
Auledus, reodpipere.[2]
Salpista, aule, bymere.
Salpica, bymesangere.
Salpizo, uel buccino, ic byme.[3]
Sponsor, uel praes, uel fideiussor,vel uas, uel uadator, borhhand.
Æmulus, gesaca, *uel* gewinna.
Accidiosus, uel tediosus, asolcen.
Petitor, uel petax, biddere.
Pygmaeus, uel nanus, uel pumilio, dweorg.
Paponius, druncen.
Cancellarius, uel scriniarius, burþen.
Sacri scriniarius, cyrcweard.
Antigrafus, writere.
Æstimator, æhtere.
Æstimatio, æhtunge.
Lana sucida, uel sucilenta, una- wæscen wull. [fen.
Sideratus, uel ictuatus, færunge astor-
Dextrochirium, brad earmbeah.
Dissologia, twigspræc.
Acetabulum, uel garale, ecedfæt.
Exentera, unsceot, *uel* geopena.
Decorticatum, æfelle, *uel* rindleas.
Struma, halsgang.
Neuum, werhbræde.
Eucharis, swæs, *uel* wynsum.
Facetus, swæswyrde.

Facetiae, wynsum gliw.
Delumentum,[4] þweal.
Commonitorium, uel pictacium, ærend- gewrit.
5 *Canalis, uel colimbus, uel aquaeduc- tus*, wæterþeote.
Cataclysmus, brymflod.
Ductilis, astrengd.
Prouentus, sped.
10 *Argutiae*, gleawnys.
Academice, snotorlice.
Affectuose, uel deuote, holdlice.
Euax, wilcume.
Eatenus, uel eotenus, oð þæt.
15 *Gratiosus*, ðoneful.
Officiosus, estful, *uel* gehyrsum.
Inofficiosus, ingratus, unestful.
Uotiuus, estful.
Lentus, waac.
20 *Familiaris*, hiwcuð.
Affabilis, wordwynsum.
Inaptus,[b] ungefege.
Incongruus, ungepæslic.
Familiaritas, hiwcuðrædnys.
25 *Contubernalis, uel socius*, gefera.
Contubernium, gadorwist.
Terribilis, ahwilc, *uel egeslic, uel* dryslic.
Siliquastrum, uel cathedra quadrata,
30   fiþerscyte setel.
Corollarium, i. merces, med.
Peripetasma, limbstefning.
Cementum, grundstanas.
Basis, syll.
35 *Fultura*, fotstan.

---

[1] So the MS. R. W.
[2] The compiler perhaps thought the pipe of the Roman minstrel was a pipe of reeds. Somner supposes that *aule*, in the next line, should be *auletes*, or *auledus*.
[3] *Beme* was the common word in old English for a trumpet, and *bemere* for a trumpeter.
[4] No doubt an error for *delutamentum*.
[5] So the MS. R. W.

VI.

ANGLO-SAXON GLOSSARY,

OF THE TENTH CENTURY.[1]

Argumentum, wærgeapnis.

Bainus, þerscel.
Baista, g., glasin.
Balidus, dun.
Balus, isern feotor.
Balatus, hlowung.
Balatio, crop. |*i.* searu.
Ballista, catapulta, uel machina belli,
Balbus, qui uult loqui et non potest,
 wlips,[2] *uel* swetwyrda.
Balbutus, stomer.
Balsis, teter.
Ballum, þoþer.
Baltheum, cingulum, uel belt.
Balla loca prasinum,[3] brunbasu.
Bapis, i. hortus, uel teru.
Barritus, geonung, *uel dissimilis*,
 geþota, rarung.

Bardus, stultus, ineptus, uel babiger.
Barbarus, i. truculentus, gentilis seruus, uel ungereord.
Barius, uarius, fah.
5 *Baratrum, i. terre hiatus*, dæl, *uel* færseaþ.[4]
Baratorium, byre.
Bathma, i. femora, þeoh.
Baxus, sicol.
10 *Beabis, beatum facis*, þu geadgast.
Beneficium, i. donum, freme, gife.
Benetum, uel scirbasu.
Beneficus, benefactor, fremful.
Beneplacita, geeweme.
15 *Bena*,[5] ate.
Benignitas, fremsumnes. [bora.
Belliger, i. miles, bellator, wæpen-
Bellicosus, pugnandi cupidus, wigbære.

---

[1] This alphabetical glossary, valuable in several points of view, is taken from a manuscript of the tenth century in the library of the British Museum, MS. Harl. No. 3376. It is, in the original, a glossary of difficult and uncommon Latin words, explained in Latin; but to the Latin explanations the compiler, or others who possessed the manuscript after him, have added a considerable number of interpretations in English of the time, or as it is now called technically by philologists, Anglo-Saxon. These I have collected from it in the following pages. It is, as will be seen, truncated.

[2] Here the scribe wrote *wlips*, not *plips*. Cf. pag. 161 l. 39. R. W.

[3] *Prasinum* means: green as leek. Is *balla loca* perhaps an error for: παλλευκος? R. W.

[4] Wright printed: seaþ = sheath, *vagina*. But I read: seaþ = pit, lake, gulph. Cf. Bosw. pag. 61t. R. W.

[5] The writer means *uena* (= *bena*) or *auena*. Cf. *barius* = *uarius*, *benetum* = *uenetum*, *berruca* = *uerruca* etc. R. W.

Belliter, cene.
Bellator, fihtling.
Bellona, i. furia, dea belli, mater Martis, wylfen.
Bellica, wiglic.
Beluae, bestiae maris, wylfene.
Belsarum, þyfela, *uel* boxa.
Betica, wicþegn.
Berrus, bera, *uel* bar.
Berruca, wearte.
Berbex, rom.
Bibliotheca, i. librorum repositio, bochord, *uel* fodder.[1]
Bibulis buccis, hleostrum.
Bibultum, bilhergas.
Bilina, i. temen.
Bicoca, hæferblæta.
Bictonatus, selfbona.
Biennis, twiwintre.
Biformia, twihiwe.
Bifori, twidæledre.
Bifarius, i. bilinguis, uel piscina,[2] fiscwelle.
Bifida, bis diuisa, twidæledu.
Biga, ubi ii⁰ equi currui iunguntur, horscræt.
Bigener, aworden, *uel* doc.
Bilance, twiwæge, *uel* heolore.
Bile, felle, attre.
Bilustris, twi-ferum, *uel* hiwum.
Binius, i. biennius, twiwintre.
Binas, butu.
Binas quinquies, tnwa fife.
Bino munere, twifealdre gife.
Bipennis securis, twilafte æx, *uel* twibile.
Bistinctus coccus, twegra bleo.
Bistincto cocco, of twibleoum derodine, *uel* of twitælgedun.
Bissina, candida, hwit.
Bissemis, twiga healfum.
Bisso retorto, hwite twine geþrawne.
Bis terque, VI, twiga þriga.

[1] I read *fodder*, Wright printed *rodder*
R. W.
[2] Are the first two Latin words in any connexion with the Anglo-Saxon gloss?
R. W.

Bitumen, scipter, *uel* lim.
Bitorius, wrenna, *bitriscus*.
Biuligo, niger uelamen, rift.
Bizus, **tysca**.
Bobella, swearte.
Bofor, læmbis lieg.
Boia, arcus, uel geoc.
Boias, catenas, sweorcopsas, *uel* handcopsas.
Boi, scættas.
Bolidis, sundgyrd on scipe, *uel* netrap.
Bombus, hlowung, *uox inepta, sonitus, tumultus, uel sorbellus, clamor tubis*, cyrm.
Bombicinum, seolcen gegerla.
Bombosa, hlowende, þutende.
Boreus, eastnordwind.
Borbus, cena, slim.
Bothonia, æmbern.
Botholicula, **stoppa**.
Botrus,[3] clystra.
Botrax, yce.
Bouellum, fald.
Bouile, scipen.
Bubalus, wesend.
Buban,[4] raredumle.
Bubimus, wæser.
Bucula, iuuenca, uitula, stirc.
Buccula, bue.
Buculus, uel bucularis, randbeag.
Buccis, buccellis, welrum.
Buclamen, heorthama.
Buccetum, ripfald.
Buccilla, geofola.
Bulla, gemma, uel sigl.
Bullifer, bulberende.
Bulbile, bucce. [gyrdn.
Bullas, ornamenta cinguli, forþge-
Bunia, byden.
Busius, fealu.
Burrus, rufus, niger, burlis, brun.
Burro, panno, hacole.

[3] Cf. *butros*. *Botrus* answers to Greek βοτρυς. R. W.
[4] An error for *bubo* or *bubonem*.
R. W.

Burris, curuamentum aratri, sulh-
  beam.
Butium, cyta, frisca.
Butiuncula, tunyncel.
Butros, clystra.
Buturnus, heope.
*Blandus, suauis, lenis, placidus, io-
  cundus,* liþe.
Blanda, liþe, swæs, *jocunda,* oliccung.
*Blandis sermonibus, lenis uerbis,
  liþum, uel* swet-wyrdum.
Blandide, geswæse.
Blanditur, geswæslæcþ, *adolatur,*
  oleccaþ, liþercaþ.
Blandiens, oliccende.[1]
Blasphemia, uituperatio, tæl.
Blatis, bitelum.
Blatea,[2] *lucifuga,* wicga.
Blauum, color est uestis, bleo.
Blurus, caluus, blere.
Bracile, slyfan.
Bratium, mealt.
Bradigatio, ploratio campi, feldwop.
Brateolis, laminis, platungum.
Bratea fila, torta aurea fila, þa
  aþrawenan goldþrædas.
Bresion, bulut.
Brigacus, scearbeam.
Broel,[3] *hortus ceruorum,* deortun,
Broellarius, ediscweard.
Brogus, hæþ.
Brumela, bellicum, uel sla.
Bruncus, wrot.
Bruntus, won.
Brugma, barice.
Bruuinus, lytel wicga.
Byrsarius, uel byrseus, leþerwyrhta.
Byligon, clade.
Byrrum, casul.

Cachinnus, ceahhetung.
Cacomicanus,[4] logþor.
Caducus, demoniacus, bræcseoca, *uel
  inanis.*
5 *Cadurcus,*[5] cip.
Cades, oppidum, uel wæstm.
Calcaneus, exterior pars pedis, hela.
Calcanosus, healede.
Calcatrix, tredend.
10 *Calcaria, dicta quia in calce homi-
  nis ligantur,* spuran.
Calces, ilas, wearras.
Calceos, gescy.
Calcis, finis, lim, tahspura.
15 *Calcibus,* fyrsnum, houm.
Calcis uiua, gebærnd lim.
Callidissime bestiole, prættigustan
  deore.
Caldaria, cetel.
20 *Callosa,* wearihte.
Callositas, wearihtnes, *uel* unsmeþnes.
Calmetum, merse.
Calmidus, curtina, godweb.
Callus, ile.
25 *Callis, iter pecudum,* pæþ.
Callide, ingeniose, geaplice.
Caluarium, strictura, uel calwer-
  clympe.
Calleo, decipio, ic frefelic, *callem in-
30 uestigo.*
Calecantum, uitrolum, attrum.
Caligans, obumbrans, dymmede.
Caligarius, læstwyrhta.
Caliga, scoh.   [bant.
35 *Caliginabant,* aþeostredan, *obumbra-
  baibrum,* cyllebrond.[6]
Calsus, meon.[7]
Calabit, brycgaþ.
Calatus, leap.
40 *Calamuca,* hacule.

---

[1] In the MS, the *i* is placed over an *e*.
   R. W.
[2] The MS. has: blatta. R. W.
[3] Bosw. 209 thinks *broel* an Anglo-Saxon word corrupted from Latin *brolium* or *briolium.* But the scribe, no doubt, used *broel* as an Latin expression. R. W.
[4] The scribe means κακομηχανος. R.W.
[5] *Cadurcus,* used by Iuuenal 7, 221, denotes as well *a linen blanket* only as *a bed, marriage-bed* in general. The meaning of *cip* is: *tent, booth.* Cf. *Catercus.* R. W.
[6] *Cylle* means *a censer.* Cf. *storcylle* Aelfr. Hom. II, 294. R. W.
[7] *Meo* denotes *a kind of shoe, pedule.* Cf. Bosw. 45m. R. W.

Calamistrum, walcspinl.
Calumpnia, accusatio falsa, hosp, hearmspræc, holtihte.
Camera, arcus, fornax, bigels, boga, incleofa.
Camerarius, burþen.
Camematus, gescend.
Campana, cimbala, belle.
Caninus, tux.
Candelle, burne.
Canna, eb',[1] harundo, calamus, uel bune.
Cannabum, hænep, uel pis.
Cannalis, þryng.
Cannabin, ḡ. hænep.
Cancer, crabba, forceps, hæferbite.
Cancella, gesceot, gradus ligneus.
Cantabiles, wynsume.
Cantarus, ubi aqua mittitur, uel ydria, tunne, uel animal, wifel.
Cantilena, a canendo, modulatio, uel sarlic blis.
Cantionum, uel galdra.
Canti, felga.
Canalis, þruh, uel mylentroh.
Cana[2] uellus, wulflys.
Canistrum, uas uinetum, uel tænel.
Caniglata, mælsceafa.
Canile, domus canis, hundahus.
Canini, tuxas.
Canities, grauitas, senectus, harwengnes.
Canis, uel canicula, stella quae Sirius uocatur, se hara-steorra.
Canonica, tidsangas.
Canor, modulatio, weorþung, uel cantus.
Capax, qui multum capit, andgetul, gripul, numul.
Captura, detentio, captio, hæft, uel wer.

Captiose, hedendlice.
Captiuus, hæftling.
Capsa, uel snod.
Caper, hæfergat.
5 Capella, tuba, scofle, spadu.
Capilli, heafodhær.
Capillatura, locgewind, uel fexnes.
Capillamenta, rawe, drisne.
Capitulatio, mearcung.
10 Capitula, uel heafodbolstor, origo angin.
Capital, lex, heafod.[3]
Capitale, heafodclaþ, uel wangere.
Capistrum, hælfter, uel cælfster.
15 Capitoli, hearges.
Capia,[4] raa.
Capiat, gegripe, retineat.
Capitium, hod.
Capiclum, clufu.
20 Capulus, manubrium gladii uel uniuscuiusque rei, mid hilte.
Carbasus, tumor ueli, seglbosm.
Carbasa, uela nauium, seglbosmas.
Carbasini, gærsgrene.
25 Carbunculi, bylas.
Carcesia, summitas mali, et genus poculorum, uel buna.
Carceria sunt in cacumine arboris trocliae, quasi flicteria, per quas funes trahuntur, mæstlon.[5]
30 Carcer, dictus a coarcendo, witern.
Cardis, þistlum.
Cardiacus, dicitur qui patitur laborem cordis, uel morbus cordis, heort-coþa, uel ece, modseocnes, uel unmiht.
Carpentarius, wænwyrhta.
Carpere, arripere, twiccian.
Carperabat, genicelde.
40 Carpella, sadolboga.
Carpobalsamum, balsames blæd.

---

[1] eb' seems to mean ebraice; but canna (κavva) is met with as well in Latin as in Greek. R. W.
[2] An error of the glossator for lana. R. W.
[3] Wright printed capital lex-heafod as if lex-heafod were an Anglo-Saxon word. I suppose lex to be a Latin word and heafod a literal translation of capital. R. W.
[4] An error for caprea. R. W.
[5] Bosw. 44t printed: mæstlor, but the MS. has: mæstlon. R. W.

Carnali commercio, flæsclicum gemange.
Carnifex, interfector, feorhbona.
Carpsit, discerpsit, trahit, euellit, uel tæst.
Carpunt, uellint, plucciaþ.
Cartallus, fiscella, windel.
Cartilago, grundsopa.
Coriza, sternutatio, fnora.
Carracutium, uehiculum, scrid, quasi *carrum acutum*.
Caradrum, dolor ossium, banwærc.
Caracalla, cappa.
Caractis, wæterþruh.
Caracter, ḡ., stilus, figura, ferrum coloratum, quo note pecudibus inuruntur, mearcisern.
Carismata dona, gastgifu, *uel* haligu.
Cariar, bædling.[1]
Cariscus, modica musca, wic, *uel* cwicbeam.
Carix, secg.
Caries, putredo lignorum, uel ferri, sindor, *uel uestutas*.
Carios, lybbestran.
Carecta, loca caricis plena, spinacurium, secgihtig, *uel* hreodihtig.
Carectum, hreod.
Care uendidit, deore bebohte.
Carolios, atrox, inobediens, unhere.
Cassabundus, uacillans, titubans, hreosende.
Cassaretur, aidlad.[2]
Cassatum, hid.
Cassata, forhrered.
Casses, retia, uel cassan.
Cassium, conum, helm.
Cassidis, helmes.
Cassidile, wung.
Cassibus, calamitatibus, uel ferum, uel helme.
Cassus, inanis, scelus, malum, uacuus, uel fær.

Casla,[3] spring.
Castalidas nymphas, þa manfullan gydena, *uel* dunelfa.
Castor, befer.
Castra, oppida, loca altissima sita, dicta quasi casa alta, herewic, *uel* gefylco.
Cataplasma, medicamentum, cliþa.
Catacrinas, hypban.
Catalecticus, ubi in pede uersus una sillaba deest, þy metercund.
Cataclismus, diluuium, brym, *uel* holm.
Catarticum potus, lybcorn.[4]
Catasta, genus supplicii eculeo simile, uel woepe, *nomen ludi, uel* geled, *quadrupalium*.
Catenatis lacertis, geracod teagodum earmum.
Catercus, cip.
Cateruatim, gregatim, multipliciter, heapmælum.
Catus, doctus, ingeniosus, sacer, uel bolla.
Catholicus, geleafful, *rectus*.
Catholice fidei, þæs geleaflican geleafan.
Capriolus, raa.
Capriole, ræge.
Caprioli, dicti quod capiant arbores, wingeardhocgas.
Cauantur, euacuantur, þyrliaþ.
Caua, splendida, hol.
Cauea, domus in theatro, deorfald.
Cauernamen, wrong.
Cauernas, holu, speluncas, scræfu, *concauas petras*.
Cauillum, cauillatio, conuitium, bismrung, geflit.
Cauta, wærlic, sollicita.
Cauculus, dolor renum, uel lapis in uesice, blædre, *i. urina in lapidem uertitur*.

---

[1] *bædling* denotes a carrier of letters. Cf. Bosw. pag. 124. R. W.
[2] So read I. Wright has: *asolad*. R. W.
[3] An error for *Castalia*, I suppose. R. W.
[4] *lybcorn* means: wild saffron, *carthamus*. R. W.

Caucale, ease, *uel* nœster.
Cauda, steort.
Cauterium, mearcisern, *uel* tynder.[1]
Cautela, i. astutia, wærscipe.
Cautere, i. aam.[2]
Cautes, i. aspera saxa in mari, uel torres, uel cludas, *uel rupes.*
Caulas, g., locu, *i. munimenta ouium, uel sepimenta ouilium.*
Caulus, cawel.
Cauliculus, steola, *ramunculus,* twigu.
Caulon, crop.
Caupus, i. tabernarius qui uinum uendit, tæppere.
Cautus, i. sagax, prouidens, acutus, wær.
Confirmatio, fæstnung.
Caumene, hlywþa, *uel* cordreste.
Caumatio, swolig. [syfað.
Causatur, i. querelatur, causam dicit,
Causauit, seofade.
Caustica, nocens, unhere, sceþdende.
Causas, res, incan, *uel* þing.
Causidicus, i. legator, disertus, facundus, spelboda.
Cerimoniae, i. hostiae, ritus sacrificandi, religiones, sacrificia, geld.
Cereus, wexcandel.
Cerealis pistor, i. gristra.
Cerethei, rædchere.
Cereuma, uel celeuma, idem et toma, i. leta cantatio, lewisplega.
Cerebrum, brægen, *uel* exe.
Ceratos agros, gedyngde æceras.
Cerastus, tapor.
Ceruinus, dunfealu.
Ceruix, sweora.
Ceruical, i. capitale, bolster, *uel* wongere.
Certaui, contendi, ic flat, *pvgnaui,* ic wan, *conaui, dimicaui.*
Cercinum, risn.
Ceruellum, i. ceutrum, brægen.
Cerula, uel nox, uel celina, i. nigra, obscura unda, uel laguflod.

Ceruleus, i. glaucus, grenehæwen, fah, deorc. *Color est inter album et nigrum, subniger.*
Cerulei profundi, deorcre dypan.
Ceruleis turbinibus, lageflodum þodenum.
Cerimingius, hearpanstapas.
Cerotum, unguentum de cera, wexsealf.
Centuclum, felt.
Centumcilio, i. pellis, feleferð, *uel centumpellis.*
Centipillium, i. omentum, film.
Celeum, ceruise, ealu.
Celestis bibliothece, bocgesamnunge.
Celibatus, i. sine uxore uir, uel uiduatus, uel abstinentia uirginitatis, clængeorn.
Celibes, i. casti, steriles, celestem uitam ducentes, clængeorne.
Celibea Tempe, heofenlicre ræminge.
Celsa agreste, sicomorus, heortberge.
Cellarium, incleofa, *sic dictum quia in ea colligantur ministeria mensarum uel quae necessaria uictui supersunt.*
Celatum, i. pictum, agrafen, astemped.
Celatura, i. sculptura, græft.
Celon, stempingisern.
Celox, uel cilion, i. species nauis, i. ceol, *uel* stempingisern.
Cementum, i. cesura lapidis, uel lim, *uel mendacium cogitatum.*
Cementa, i. petre, grundstanas, *uel funes.*
Ceminigi, hearpanstala.
Cenosas, þa fennigan meras, *i. paludes paludosas, uel* adelihtan, fulan, *lutosas, fetidas, immundas.*
Ceno, i. luto, mixe, horwe.
Cenobium, i. congregatio, mynsterlif.
Cenantibus, i. uescentibus, reordendum.
Cenum, i. luti uorago, uel lutum sub aquis fetidum, i. wase, *uel* fæn.

---

[1] Cf. *caracter* pag. 200 l. 15. R. W.

[2] καυτήριον denotes *a marking-iron.* R. W.

Cenulenti, i. lutosi, olidi, fule.
Ceniluti, swina hlose.
Congium reddit, tala, *uel* mycel gropa.
Cetus, i. congregatio, conuentus, werud, multitudo.
Ceca formidine, blindre fyrhto.
Cephalus, ō., heafodpanne.
Cephalia, i. dolor capitis, uel cephalargia, heafod-wærc, *uel* ece.
Ceutrum, þrotbolla.
Cesa, i. abscisa, occisa, aheawen.
Cesaream tributum, i. regalis, gafol.
Cessam, i. desistam, cessauero, ic gestille, *uel* ablinne.
Cessio, i. typ.
Cesura, toheawenne.
Chronographus, tidscriptor.
Cinnamomum, resina, suderne rind.
Cinthium, mitra, snod.
Cinum, hagan.
Cicinnus, i. uinnus, loc.
Cicindilibus, weocum.
Cinereus, deterrimus color, æscfealu, *uel* æscgræg.
Cittis, fylmenum. [fatum.
Ciatis, i. calathis, uasis, uel beod-
Cistula, sporta, uel cyst.
Cistella, capsilla, cartellum, tænel.
Cisalpina, quasi circa[1] *Alpes, ex ista parte,* beheonan.
Circillus, nauicula, uel heardheawa.
Cirrus, crinus, loc.
Circinnus, gafelrod.
Circumspectio, circuitus, embeþonc, *uel* sceawung, *cautio.*
Cirta, aedrenc, *uel nomen loci.*
Circopythicos, sprinca.
Circumuenientium, embdrydiendra.
Circentium, ringsittendra.[2]
Ciromitus, dun.
Circulus decennouenalis, se niganteoþa[3] getælcircul.
Cicur, i. mansuetus, placidus, manþwære.

Ciclamina, slite.
Cicla, orel, ryft.
Cicer, beancyn.
Cicidemon, nædderbita.
Cione, stapole.
Ciula, ceol.
Cimosis, fleo on eagum.
Cimex, summitas arboris, uel maþa.
Cimentum, stanlim.
Cidaricus, handswyle.
Ciprum, cipersealf.
Cipus, croplec.
Clangenti sistro, sonanti tube, blawendre.
Clangor, tubarum sonus, uel uox tubae, dyne, geþun, cyrm.
Claua, fuste, steng, *uel* borda.
Clauus calicularis, scohnægl.
Claumentia, claua, steng.
Claus, lignum tentorii, uel telde.
Clauatum, sutum, uel gebyrd.
Clauato, signato, getacnod.
Cadicla, wefl, *uel* oweb.
Clades, pestes, cwyld.
Clamosa, oferhlud.
Classica, sciphere, *uel* swegas.
Classicis, flotlicum, sciplicum.
Clasmatorius, efractor, husbrycel.
Clarus, insignis, nobilis, perspicuus, mære.
Clatrum, i. pearroc, hegstæf.
Clatica, wefta.
Cliuosum, i. inclinatum, clifæhtig.
Cliens, i. socius, þegn, gesiþa.
Clinice, i. lectus, tetrus, fortihtend.
Cliuium, i. discensum, helde, burhsteal.
Clima, i. plaga, ascensio, epl.
Cluit, pollet, uiget, nobilitat, þihþ, *uel defendit.*
Clunis, renibus, coxe, gupan.
Clustella, clusterloc.
Conici, conari, ræswian.
Commodus, i. honestus, congruus,

---

[1] There can be no doubt that this is an error for *citra Alpes.*
[2] The MS. has embringsittendra. R.W.
[3] The scribe corrected niganteoþa from neoganteoþa. R. W.

utilis, aptus, gehyþlic, þæslic, *uel*
 gescræpe.
Commodum, lucrum, utile, læn, ge-
 scræpe.
Commodius, congruentius, gehyþlicor.
Commoditas, i. utilitas, behefnes,
 nytweorþnes.
Commolitis, forgrundenum.
Comosus, sceagode.
Comotio, gewrixl.
*Commisura, s. dicitur tabularum con-
 iunctio,* gefeg, cimbing, clut, *uel*
 flihteclaþ.
Comis, uel ramis, i. bogum.
*Cominiscitur, recordatur, commen-
 tatur, fingitur,* he sarwaþ.
Comicus, s. est qui comedia[1] *scribit,
 cantator, uel artifex canticorum
 seculorum, idem satyricus, i.* scop,
 ioculator, poeta.
Comitatus, consecutus, uel gesiþ-
 ræden.
Comite uita, sospite uitae,[2] gelæsten-
 dum life.
Commisio, conflictus, gefeoht.
Commilitonibus, sociis, uel campge-
 ferum, *uel* gerefum.
*Comitiales, i. garritores, uel dies
 mensi, uel* ylfie, *uel* monaþseoce,
 uel dagas.
Comitiorum dies, honorum dies, ar-
 dagas, *uel* weordungdagas.
Commissoria, tabularum coniunctio,
 treowfeging.
Comitata, i. sociata, gemidsiþegad,
 uel geferlæht.
Comitarisne tu? hu ne midsiþgadest
 þu?
Commissus, preceptum, beboden.
Committat, tradat, uel gefremeþ.
Comitatur, sequitur, midsiþige.
*Commenta, i. tractationes, machina-
 menta, excogitata, adiumenta, astutia, argumenta, machinationes, ficta,
 fraudes,* onþanc, *dicta, mendacia,*
 sarwa.

Commentarius, stærtractere, *uel* hal-
 sere.
Commeatos, sande. [dan.
Comeant, simul pergebant, midfer-
Comeans, socius, gesiþa.
Commanipularius, collega, miles, in-
 cempa, *uel* gescota.
Commanipulares, commilitones, socii,
 gefylce.
Competa clausa, betyndan wega ge-
 lætan.
Competis, terminis, wega gelætum.
Competum, uel compitum, i. uilla,
 uel þingstow, *uel* þrop.
*Competitor, amicus, uel rogator bap-
 tismi,* fulwihtbena.
Compendiose, breuiter, gægne.
Compendiosius, ametendlicor.
Comperhennis, ece efenlic.
*Comperit, i. intellexit, cognouit, in-
 uenit, didicit,* onfunde.
*Competentes partiunculas, conueni-
 entes,* gelimplice dæle.
Competentibus horis, on þæslicum
 timan.
*Compagines, i. coniunctiones, iunc-
 turae,* gefeg.
Compagem, iuncturam, uel gegade-
 rung.
Compaginum, coniunctionum, gefo-
 gum.
Compar germane, similis fratri, ge-
 mæc.
Comparatus, i. assimilatus, geefen-
 licad, *inuentus,* wiþmeten.
Comparare, i. emere, uel ceapigan.
Comparatio, wiþmetenes.
Copla, poples, hom.
*Compos ... potens, facetus, potens,
 prudens, uel* getælwis.
Comptus, i. ornatus, geglengad.
Communi diuidendo actio, gemanan
 gedal.
Completorium, gefyllingtid.[3]
Complodere, uel concutere, conlidere,
 cnyllan.

---
[1] Read *comedias.* R. W.
[2] An error for *uita.* R. W.

[3] *Completorium* was the last of the

Conpluta, bolster.
Complanans, geemnettende.
Conprehensus, oferfangen.
Copsus, syl, securis.
Conprobat, geseþ.
Coaptat, i. coniungat, geþæslæcþ.
Coagulum, ceslyb.
Coagitatum, geheapod.
Coagolatio, gemang.
Coax i. cra, uox ranarum uel cor-
Coangustant, arctant, genyrwiaþ.
Conflagrat, i. conburet, he ameraþ,
  concremat. [blawen.
Conflatum, incensum, onæled, ge-
Confragosum, cyrmende.
Confectos, i. compositos, mixtos, uel
  bewelde.
Conflixit, i. certauit, gewon.
Confricatus, i. limatus, exprimatus,
  tocwysed, uel gebeowed.
Confrixa, gecocsade.
Confirmatio, assertio, trymnes.
Confirmo, i. astruo, ic geseþe, uel
  afæstnie.
Conficiam, i. confundam, ic genæto.
Conficiebantur, efenstaledan.
Cognata, i. coniuncta, propinqua,
  gesib, uel cuþ.
Cognate propinquitatis, mægcuþre
  sibbe.
Conglutinata, commixta, gelimed.
Congelauerat, tosomne geræt.
Congrua, i. conuenientia, þa gelimp-
  lican, þæslic.
Congruunt, geþæslæcaþ, uel þæslæcan.
Congressibus, i. pugnis, of anwigum,
  uel gewinnum.
Congrediens certando, winnende.
Confutat, i. confundit, conuincit, ofer-
  stælþ, gescent.
Confusum, i. permixtum, inconditum,
  obscurum, inordinatum, impolitum,
  uel forscamed.

Confudisti, conturbasti, uel gedrefdest,
  diuidisti, þu gescendest.
Confugium, i. statium, portus, hyþ.
Coniectura, i. opinatio, estimatio, in-
  terpretatio, uel ræswung, uel rædels,
  consimilia.
Consero, i. interpono, coniecto, con-
  iungo, ic embsette.
Consessum, gemot.
Consenior, efenealda. [getred.
Constipatio, i. conuentio hominum,
Constipata, i. consita, repleta, cir-
  cumdata, embþrungen, uel hringed.[1]
Constipuit, i. defecit, gesweþrade, uel
  congregauit.
Consternat, i. perterritat, contristat,
  conuincat, indomitat, fyrhtaþ, ge-
  bregþ, geacolmodaþ, deicit, uel
  ofercymþ, confudit.
Constans, stabilis, gestæþþig, anræde.
Consistorium, stalern.
Consideratus, cordatus, wel bescea-
  wod.
Consideratio, foresceawung.
Consuluit, i. ammonuit, interrogauit,
  befran.
Consulens, i. consilium tenens, proui-
  dens, uel rædende.
Consulo, i. requiro, uel inquiro, ic
  frine, uel ic ræde.
Consultas, consilia, rædas.
Consumptor, i. deuorator, gifre,
  grædig, gluto.
Consumptum, i. deuoratum, degluti-
  tum, ofertogen, finitum.
Consuetam opem, gewunelic weorc.
Consuetudinariis, gewunelican.
Consummabilis aeui, gefyllendlicre
  eldo, impleto aeuo.
Conspicatio, i. conspirago, facen-
  gecwys.
Conspirauerant, geanlæhtan, uel ge-
  anwyrdan.

canonical hours, which completed the religious service of the day. It is here
rather literally translated by the Anglo-
Saxon word.

[1] Cf. circentium, pag. 204 l. 39. R. W.
[2] In Andreas l. 377 we meet with
acolmod in the meaning of: timid, of a
fearful mind. R. W.

Conspiret, i. consentiet, geþwærie, *uel* samod orþie.[1]
Conspicue, i. preclare, healice, beorhtlice.
Consobrini, i. ex sorore et fratre, uel ex duabus sororibus, geswegran, gesweosternu, *uel* gesweoras.
Consobrinus, filius patruelis, sweor.
Consocierunt, coniunxerunt, geferlæhton.
Consona, geswege.
Colonus, i. incola, cultor, inquilinus, bigenga, tilia, inbuend.
Colono fine, gebyrdum gemære.
Coloni nimbi, i. manna, pluuiae famulantes, geþensume scuras.
Colostrum, i. lac nouum, beost, *uel* obestum.
Colomata, hacole.
Collocatio, i. extremitas, gestaþelung.
Colos, i. color conciliatus, copor.
Colosus, i. infirmus, hreof.
Colomacus, genesta, hæþ.
Colobium, dictum quia longum est, et sine manicis, loþa, hom, *uel* smoc, mentel.
Conlatum, i. simbolum, confessio, congregatum, datum, simul comportatum, tributum, uel þurhtogen.
Conlatio, i. conductio, comparatio, consiliatio, i. datio, contentio, geþeahtung, gescead, *uel* racu.[2]
Colapsus, i. colafus, pugnus, fyst, *uel tarastrus.*
Conlationes, raca.
Collarium, sweorclaþ, *uel* teg, *uel* sal.
Collatum, i. uas in quo deportatur uinum, uel crogcyn.
Collegiati, ræpingweardas.
Colera, uentris inflatio, uel solutio, wyrms.
Colerata, fucata, getælged.

Colestrum, beost.[3]
Colum, cum quo colat uinum, uel instrumentum rusticum, uel intestinum cratis, uel roscidum, uel wulmod, *uel carbo,* rop.
Columbarium, mæst
Coniuctantia, depugnantia, þa samwinnendan.
Conlidit, i. allidit, ætspearn, *offendit.*
Conliserint, tosomne cnyllaþ.
Colibates,[4] hegsteald men.
Colica, colum, ropwære.
Colimbus, i. concrematus, uel wætergelæt.
Colit, i. uenerat, begæþ.
Collidium, unmyrge plega.
Contabescunt, i. exsiccant, hy aswindaþ, *uel* heo beoþ unbliþe.
Contribulus, i. ciues, consanguineus, mæg, gelanda, *parens,* gesib, *propinquus, uel simul tribulatus.*
Contritio, geþræstednes, *uel* gebrysednes, forgnidennes.
Contriuit, geþræste, *minuit,* fortræd.
Contemptus, i. contemptio, forhogung.
Contemplatio, foresceawung.
Contemplantibus, intuentibus, sceawiendum.
Contentus, i. sufficiens, eþhelde, *uel* geþæf, fulhealden.
Contenta, sinu concluso, belocenum fenge.
Conterat, genæt, geyrmþ, forbryt, tobrecþ.
Contegit, i. consuit, beþeacþ.
Contecta, beþeaht.
Contingat, i. fiat, eueniat, pertinet, attingat, tangat, petat, ætrinþ, getilþ.
Contigit, i. accidit, euenit, gelamp,[5] getilde.
Conticinium, cwyldtid, swignes.
Conticiscent, silebant, uel siccitan.

---

[1] Wright by a misprint has: samodonþle. Orþion means *spirare,* samod orþie is therefore a literal translation of: *conspirare.* Cf. Bosw. pag. 52ᵇ. R. W.
[2] The MS. has: *of racu.* R. W.
[3] Cf. *colostrum* pag 210, l. 17. R. W.
[4] So the MS. R. W.
[5] *gelimp* is corrected to *gelamp* in the MS. R. W.

Continet, i. habet, tenet, embhæfþ.
Continuanda, to anlætenne.
Contubernia, societas, gemana.
Contubernalis, i. domesticus, comes, conuiua, assecla, geþofta.
Contubernali sodalitate, geþeodlicre geferrædenne.
Contumax, i. superbus, anmoda, *contemptor.*
Contudit, i. domauit, forstynt, *fregit, compressit.*
Cotula, uel catus, bolla.
Contractauit, i. palpauit, gegrapade.
Contra mille nocendi artes, ongæn þusendfealde deriende cræftas.
Contionator, i. locutor, motere, *uel* maþelere.
Contionatur, i. conclamat, loquitur, contestatur in populo, maþelaþ.
Contrecta, i. palpa, handla.
Cotizat, tæflaþ.
Coticulus, uel coticula, lytel hwetstan.
Cotilla, bolle.[1]
Cocula, aalfatu, crusne, *uel* heden.[2] *Omnia uasa coquendi sic dicuntur.*
Coculus, frence.
Cocologus,[3] wordsomnere.
Coccum bistinctum, weolocread, *uel* twihiwe godweb.
Cocleae, lytle snæglas, *uel* weolocas.
Conuenticula, conuentus, gemetinega.
Conuenientes nuptae, gedafenlice forgifene.
Conuersor, i. locumuto, utor, habito, ic drohtige, *maneo.*
Conualuit, i. confortauit, gewyrpte.
Conuolatus, alatus, flihtas.
Conuoluit, i. cingit, embhrincþ.
Conuical, nehgebur.
Condit, i. abscondit, reseruat, uel selt, *uel* gehyt.
Condicta, i. decreta, uel ewidas.
Condiuit, saliuit, gendstredde.
Condictiorius, esnecund.

Codices, onheawas. *uel* rinda.
Conditio, i. status, iudicio, procreatio, natura, sors, regula, lex, rectitudo, gescæp, gewyrd, gescæft, gebyrd.
Condensa, i. spissa, secreta, þicce, *uel* oferþeaht.
Condescendo, niþer astigende.
Condolomata, articula, leoþu-sar, *uel* geþind.
Conductor, mercennarius, hyra.
Conductum, gearnwinde.
Conductio, gebyrung, *uel* behyred feoh.
Conuiator, gegenga.
Conuictor, conuiua, gebeor.
Corimbi, i. uiti racemi, uel botriones, uel circuli, wingeard-hringas, *uel* bergan, *uel* croppas, *bacce.*
Corimbus, cacumen nauis, leahtroh.
Coriza, i. sternutatio, cartilagines, nebgebræc, *uel* fnora.
Cornipedum, hornfotedne.
Cordias, bytteblid.
Correctio, þreal.
Corrector, styrend, *increpator.*
Corporalis inlecebre, lichamlicre unalefednesse.
Cohors, d.[4] *milites, uel* þreat.
Coruscatio, i. fulgor, splendor, ligræsc, *uel* æling.
Corupeta, gnohioc.[5]
Coragium, i. uirginale funus, uel wop.
Coortat, i. monet, uel corrigit, uel hyrt, *docet.*
Concentus, i. adunationes multarum uocum, efenhleoþrung, *uel* dream.
Concessit, i. permisit, concedit, alyfde, *dedit.*
Concessio, typ.
Conceptos dolores, þa angunnenan sar.
Conceptacula, andfenge-stowe.
Conche, et cocleae, sæsnæglas.

[1] Cf. *cotula,* l. 12. R. W.
[2] Cf. pag. 214, l. 36. R. W.
[3] The scribe means *catalogus.* R. W.
[4] *d* means: *dicit, dicitur* or *dicuntur.* R. W.
[5] I doubt whether the MS. has *gnohioc* or *guohioc.* R. W.

Conca, i. coclea, mundleow.
Concidit, i. cecidit, uel tosloh, forheow.
Conciliabulum, locus sinodali,[1] sinaþstow.
Concinnatas, congregatas, geheapod.
Concisium, scelle.
Concipit, i. accipit, intelligit, embrehþ, onfeng, geeacnaþ.
Concreta, i. commixta, coniuncta, coadunata, gerunnen.
Concretio, i. coagolatio, cennung, gemang, gescæp.
Conclamatus, i. commotus, conuocatus, desperatus, uel loma.
Conclusum, finitum, embfangen.
Coniuratus, i. concordatus, consentiens, gemoda.
Coniugalis, gemæclic.
Coniunctim, gædertangne.
Coniuncta, þistra.
Coniurante polo, mid þwæriendum heofene.
Coniuncto actu, geþeodre dæde.
Conquirens, i. causans, meditans, uel begetend.
Coeternus, efenece.
Coheres, efn yrfeweard.
Coituras pergente, gegangende.
Connuntiator, i. adsertor, geseþend.
Concaluit, ahatode, exardescit.
Conauerit, geteohhade.
Conabuli, geþeode.
Concutit, i. turbat, terreat, toseæcþ, of þryscep, percutit.
Cocula, crusne, uel heden.
Coxe, þeoh.
Cratem, i. flecta, hyrdel, hege, flehtran.
Craticula, hyrste, bæcering.
Cratus, bolla.
Cratium, waga.
Crapulatus, i. subito inebriatus, oferfylled, geilleroccad.[2]

[1] Read: sinodalis.
R. W.
[2] Cf. Spelm. Psalterium, 77, 71: tan-

Cracinus, worhen.
Crama, fleote.
Crabro, hyrnetu.
Crebrat, i. frangit, sift.
5 Crebrum, cribellum, sife.
Crepaculum, sonum, dyne, uel geþun.
Crepat, i. sonat, cracaþ, brastlaþ.
Crementum, i. augmentum, wæstm, ciþ.
10 Cremium, i. frixorium, hyrstepanne.
Crepundium, i. monile gutturis, myne.
Crepundia, i. insignia, indicia, cunabula, frætwunga.
Crepuit, i. sonuit, brastlade.
15 Crepitat, i. resonat, scylþ, cyrmþ, ræscetteþ.
Crepitus, i. sonitus, fragor, sonus, conflictus, cyrm, flamen, fragor, sweg.
20 Crepitantia lora, brastliende bendas, strengas, uel bendas.
Creta, i. nata, currus, þoe, uel cræt.
Cretabulus, beaw.
Crebris, i. spissis, gelomlicum.
25 Crebro, i. celebro, frequenter, manifesto, oft, rædlice.
Creporibus, byrstum.
Crepo, ui, tum, sono, uel ic smuge.
Cresis, ewietreow.   [mandæd.
30 Crimen, i. peccatum, scyld, lehter,
Crinis, -nalis, loc.
Crysolachan, i. aureum olus, uel atriplex, i. tunmelde.
Cristas, i. comas, uel combas on
35 fugele, uel loccas.
Crocus, i. lutei coloris, geolu.
Croceus, i. rubicundus, rubeus, geolu, uel græg.
Croceata cacumina, þa ageolewedan
40 yplenu.[3]
Crouitorium, gærstun.
Cronculus, onesæta.
Crudescit, i. seuit, inualescit, reawde, uel blodgade.

quam potens crapulatus a vino = swa swa geillorocad (sic!) fram wine. R. W.
[3] I read yplenu or ypleno. Wright has yplenei. R. W.

Cruentata, i. sanguinolenta, sanguinata, geblodgad, uel sanguinea.
Cruscula, scinu.
Crus, sceanca.
Crustula, helsta, uel rinde.
Crucicola, rodbigenga.
Crustus, cyrten.
Cunabula, i. crepundia, initia, rudimenta, uel panni infantiae, cildclaþas, uel cradelas, uel primordia.
Cuneus, i. densus populus, turba, þreat, uel getrymedfeþa, uel wecg.
Cuneata, gefered, sociata.
Cuniullus, lytel wære.
Cuniculum, i. foramen, canalis, puteum, monumentum, uel greop.
Cuniculus, snægl, smygels.
Cunctatur, i. dubitat, moratur, hesitat, þrydaþ, trepidat, interrogat, tardat.
Cupide, i. auare, syfiende.
Cubicularius, custos cubili, bedþegn.
Cubitum, elnboga, uel fæþm.
Cubile, burcot.
Cuba, i. ulna, elnboga, uel hondwyrst.
Cumulus, i. tumulus, apex, aceruus, coaceruatio, beorg.
Cum infami eulogio, mid þy unæþelan gydde, uel unweorþlican.
Cummi, teru.
Cultrix, i. inseruiens, bigengestre.
Culmus, i. stramen spicarum, exercitus, healm, uel stela.
Culocrisolus, erþling.
Curia, i. domus consilii, conuentus, gemothus, uel stow, congregatio.
Curuanas, scethas.
Cursat, currit, þocarad, cursitat.
Curuatura, biging.
Curiosus, fyrwetgeorn.
Curiositas, ferwetnes.
Curiose, fyrewyttre.
Cura (s. dicitur quod cor agitat, i. conturbat), i. sollicitudo, cogitatio, studium, uel medicina, curatio, uel lacnung, uel gymen, uel hogu.
Cucurrit, þurharn.

Cupidineo, on grædigum.
Cupa, uel cupo, byden.
Cupide, i. auare, syfiende.
Cuiuis, cuilibet, ænigum.
5 Cudo, i. percutio, cedo, uel onfilte.
Cyrographum, i. conscriptio hominis, uel man, manualis scriptio, gewrit ræden, uel agnung.
Cyprum, coper.
10 Cyprinus, cypren.
Cyclis, rynum.
Cyanea lapis, hæwenstan.
Cycropide, cicropisces.

15 Decrepita, i. uetula,[1] forweren, ualde senex.
Decretum, i. institutum, positum, consilium, placitum, geþoht, statutum, laga, diffinitum, gesetnes, iudicium.
20 Decipulosa, i. inlecebrosa, leahterfulle, uel forspenninga.
Decanus, i. princeps militibus, uel tyna aldor.
Decaluatum, decollatum, besceoren.
25 De cortice cornu, of corntreowes rindum.
De concordi, be geþwærlicre.
De consanguineo, of gesibbum, uel of freondhealdlicum.
30 Decliui, i. proni, inclinati, humiliati, uel aheldre.
Deceptrix, fallax, seductrix, biswica.
Deceptio, i. fraus, lotwrænc, biswicung.
35 Deeruente, ofblodene.
Defigitet,[2] i. defatiget, lassat, swenceþ, flagellat.
Defectura, aspringende.
Defectus, i. terminus, asprungen, defectio.
40 Defectio, geteorung.
Defecatum, i. liquidum, purum, ahluttrad.
Defrutum, i. uinum, medo, geswet, 45 uel weall.
Defricatum, abeowed.

---

[1] Forwetet in the margin
[2] Sic MS. R. W.

Defuit, i. absens fuit, ateorada, *i. absens fuit.*
Deglobere, spoliare, uel beflean.
Degener, i. ignobilis, æcnosle, *dissimilis parentibus.*
Degeneri languore, æcnoslum adle, *uel* unæþelre.
Degesta, i. disposita, clarificata, serena, praeclara, uel gescerede.
Degenerat, misþihþ.
Degestio, i. egestio, driting.
Degenerante, geæcnosliendum.
Delicatus, i. tenerus, querulus, amoenus, unbrocheard, *uel* sefta, *pomposus, dilectus,* mearuwe.
Deliciosa, i. amabilior, leta, eþgeorn, *uel* estful.
Delicius, i. in deliciis amatus, estgeorn, estful.
Delibratio, ymbþrydung.
Delitescit, i. moram facit, latet, occultat, abscondit, betinþ, *uel* dyrnþ, *tardat,* lataþ.
Delinuit, olehte, *i.* geloccade.
Delibor, i. immolor, uel ic beo onlesed.
Delumentum, i. lauatio, þweal.
Deludis, i decipis, bepæhst[1], *uel* wægest.
De latebrosis recessibus, of dymmum diglum, *uel* of dyrnum.
Delatera, unlybbe.
Delectatio, lustbærnes, *uel* lufsumnes.
Delento fruto, of þiccum felde, *de denso campo.*
Delenifica, bliþe word.
Delebra, tang.
Demolitur, bid forsworfen, *i. exterminatur, uel* forgniden.
Demoniaticus, insanus, amens, uel woda.
Demonico globo, deofelicum geferscipe.
Deminute, gewanude, *uel* gelytlade.

Demulceat, blanditur, olecce.
Demptus, abscissus, genumen.
Dentile, toþsticca.
Dentale, s. est aratri pars prima in qua uomer inducitur quasi dens, sule-reost, *uel* þroc.
Densescit, spissat,[2] þiccaþ.
Deneger,[3] *i. ignobilis,* æcnosle, mægþleas.
Depeculatus, i. uastatus, depraedatus, depopulatus, bescyred.
Dependo, i. reddo, persoluam, dabo, satisfacio, sustento, mensuro, ic agylde.
Deprauat, i. maculat, confundit, uel geweþ, *flectat.*
De post fetantes, æfter þon tuddorfostre, *uel* of þam siþborenum.
Depo,[4] wefta.
Deponile, weftan.
Depositum, i commendatum, læn.
Depromo, i. ostendo, profero, protulero, exposuero, geyppe.
Deprono saltu, of þy mere.
De recessibus, i. de occultis, uel de secretis interioribus, of heolhstrum, of diglum.
Deruta, i. euersa, ahwerfde.
Derare, gewidagur gedon.
Destinatus, i. missus, ordinatus, deputatus, uel foreteohþad.
Destitutae, i. derelictae, desertae, uel toworpne.
Desertor, i. interfector, seductor, æswica,[5] *uastator.*
Deserta, s. uocata quae non seruntur, destituta, alætan.
Desequuntur, i. accusabant, uel meldadan.
Desteruit, somniauit, reat.
Desiderabilis, wilsumlic.
Desidet, i. discordat, uel desistit, distat, defert, unsibbaþ.
Desicit, tetreþ.

---

[1] Cf. Bosw. pag 159; Leo, pag. 210, R.W.
[2] The MS reads: *spissas*. R. W.
[3] *Sic MS*. R. W.

[4] An error for *deponile*, see the next word. R. W.
[5] The glossator means: *æscwiga*. R W.

Desiduus, i. desidiosus, ignauus, diuturnus, disiduo i. diuturne, simle.
Desile, bor.
Desiderantissimus, i. qui desideratur, gelustfullesta.
Desiccet, adrugie.
De sanguinibus, of blodgemongum.
Desolutus, i. liberatus, onlesed, unsæled.
Desolatum, i. orbatum, toslopen, *dissipatum.*
Desoluit, arafaþ. [lysend.
Desolator, uastator, westend, to-
Desudans, i. laborans, winnende, *uel* swætende.
Deteriorauerunt, wyrsadon.
Deteriora, þa sæmran.
Deterius, wyrs.
Detrudere, sy þu onbesceofen.
Detrusis, i. expulsis, uel exclusis, praecipitatis, onbesceofenum, *perturbatis.*
Detractatio, uituperatio, tæl.
Detritu rugine, agnidene.
Deturpans, i. dissipans, maculans, atoliende.
Deuotus, i. largus, honorabilis, eystig, *uoluntarius.*
Deuotio, i. obsequio, bonitas, honor, estfulnes.
Deuenustat, deformat, geatolhiwaþ.
Deuium, sloh.
Deuia, s. loca secreta et abdita, quasi extra uia, uel inuia, sine uia, orwegnes.
Deuia callus, orweg stig.
Deuiat, i. errat, declinat, onwoh cerþ.
Deuulgatissimum, i. opinatissimum, þone hlisfullestan.
Deifice contemplationis, þære godlican, *uel* godeundre besceawunga.
Dehinc, i. deinde, abhinc, rursum, . . . dein, uel þonane, *uel* forþan.
De ingenito fomite, of geeyndelicre tyndran.

Deditio, i. traditio, handgang.
Dedignor, ic forhogige.
Dedalei tecti, of daliscre þecene.
Debita, i. obnoxia, merita, iura, nead.
Debita pensio, i. digna tributa, gedafene gaful.
Debitis, gedefum, *congruis.*
Debitus usus, i. congruus, neadgewuna, *uel* geneadod bryce.
Debitor, i. obnoxius, reus, uel neadgylda.
Deordinauit, i. exauctorauit, gehende.
Dehiscens, i. absorbens, subsidens, aperiens, inhians, patefaciens, scindens, uel einende.
Dealibus. i. deificis, godlicum.
Deambulacrum, circuitus, embgong.
Dealbabor, ic beo gehwitad, *uel* ablicen.
Dextrocerium, i. brachiale, armillum, uel torium, earmbeag.
Dextralis, i. dextre abilis, handæx.
Dextro cornu, fram swiþre healfe.
Deiector, aworpenra, *i. humilior.*
Dictator, i. dictor, relator, praeceptor, imperator, dihtnere, *ordinator, prescriptor.*
Dictu, i. dicione, sagu, *uel oratione.*
Dicio, uel arbitrio, iudicio, uel ratione, lege, uel dihte.
Dicax, i. facundus, qui uerbis iocatur in quamlibet rem, uel ewedel.
Differt, i. moratur, prolongat, sustinet, distat, diuidit, tardat, eleaþ, *uel* tostænt.[1]
Differentius, i. eminentius, todæledlicor, *uel* rum.
Diffusa, i. sparsa, dispersa, tobrædde.
Diffidentia, disperantia,[2] ortreownes.
Difficiliore, i. grauiore, earfeþran.
Digesti, i. sereni, leui, uel praedicti, gelihte.
Digesta, i. ordinata, composita, uel exposita, enarata, geendebyrde.

[1] See Leo. ags. gloss. pag. 476, 33 and Bosw. pag. 77ᵘ. R. W.

[2] So the MS. R. W.

Dignitas, i. honestas, excellentia, fastigium, weorþscipe, *uel* geþungenes.
Digniosa, i. mediocriter, medomlice.
Dignissimus, se weorþesta.
Digamma, uel uau, uel f.
Dinexa, i. uetusta, þa ealdan.
Dinosci, intellegi, tocnawen.
Dimissa, i. humilia, abogene, toslopene.
Dilatio, i. mora, elding.
Dilatum, i. adductum, amplificatum, proditum, prolongatum, geyld.
Dilatant, tobrædaþ.
Dilatauerunt, i. aperuerunt, hi geopenadon.
Dilitum, gegniden.
Dilitiscendo, miþende.
Dilituisse, i. celasse, gedyrnan.
Diligenter, willendlice.
Dilectaque rura, and þa lufwende eardas, *uel* leofe.
Diriuatiuum, deductum, scyriendlic.
Diriguit, i. obstipuit, horruit, induruit, ablycde.
Diripio, i. rapio, abstraho, aufero, eripio, ic ætbrede, *uel* ic forgripe.
Dirigit, i. regit, gereceþ, *extendit.*
Dirigebar, ic wæs gereht.
Directanei, fordrihte.
Dire parce, i. contrarii doctores, uel reþre wylfenne.[1]
Diremptam, uastatam, uel genumenan.
Directi callis, rihtes siþfætes.
Diro, grimre.
Dirutus, i. erutus, ahryred.
Disceptant, lacerant, i. contendunt, flitaþ, *disputant.*
Discerpit, lacerat, toslit, *i. deuorat, carpit,* ploccaþ, *discernit.*
Discerne, i. diiudica, toscead.
Dispectior, forsewenlicra.
Dispensatio, dihtnung, brytnung, scir, gedal, *uel* diht.
Dispendium, i. damnum, impedimentum, defectio, periculum, detrimentum, æfwendla, wonung, wom, wana, *uel* henþa.
Dispersae, i. distribute, date, þa gestrodnan, *uel* tostencte.
Disperatio,[2] ormodnes.
Dispertiens, brytniende.
Discoforus, discifer, uel stiweard.
Discolus, i. difficilis, contrarius, wiþercora.
Discordator, discors, ungeþwæra.
Discoriat, hyldeþ.
Discolor, i. dissimilis, ungebleoh, *sine colore.*
Discrimen, i. periculum, damnum, orleahter.
Discriminale, uplegen, *uel* cæfing.
Discriminare, tosceadan, *i. diuidere.*
Disenteria, blodig utsiht.
Dissentio, discordia, uel geter.
Dissertitudo, astutia, gleawnes.
Dissides, i. tardi, læte.
Dissiluit, descendit, gelihte, *uel dissilit.*
Dissiliunt, toscutan.
Discidium, i. separatio, diuisio, ruma.
Discipulatus, lareowdom, *uel* leornung.
Discretum, detractum, uel gesceadwislic.
Discretor, i. diuisor, tosceadend.
Discrepent, distant, tosceadaþ.
Discretio, i. diuisio, gesceadwisnes.
Discretus, i. modestus, gesceadwis.
Disparuit, i. euanuit, gedwan.
*Dispari murice, ungemæcere wurman.
Dispartire, tostene.
Distenta, i. extenta, aþened, tobræd.
Distentat, tobræde.
Distent, i. separent, tostandaþ.
Discrepat, discordat, interest, tostent.
Distantes uires, i. discordes, tostandendum mægna.
Distabuit, aswand.
Disputat, i. tractat, estimat, contendit, uel flit.

[1] Cf. pag. 194 l, 3, 6. R. W.

[2] Sic MS. R. W.

Disputatio, i. deceptio, seductio, contentio, beswicung, *meditatio.*
Distitutum, i. donatum, agifen.
Distinat, i. disponit, contendit, mittit, teohhaþ, asent.
Dissona, i. discordantia, incongrua, ungeswega, *uel* gehleoþre, *uel* ungerade.
Dissociabile, i. separabile, insociabile, ungeferlices.
Dissolutio, towesnes, *uel* tolesednes, *dispersio.*
Discutiens, i. iudicans, querens, uel sweagende.
Dispono, ic geendebyrde, *uel* gefadige, *uel* todæle.
Distulit, i. moram fecit, tardauit, prolongauit, abduxit, ylde, elcode.
Districtio, rigor, stræc.[1]
Districtior, i. rigidior, stiþlicor.
Distortum, misbroden.
Diuexum, i. inclinatum, pronum, stæþhlepe.
Diuortium, i. discidium, diuisio coniugiorum, hiwgedal. [ung.
Diuinatio, prophetia, diuinitas, hals-
Diuinos, ariolos, witgan.
Diua, welig.
Diurnum, i. unius diei, dægrynum, *uel* dæglicum.
Diurne psalmodie, þæs dæglican sealmsanges.
Diurnae asce, dæghryne mettas.
Dolatum, i. incisum, planum, hywyt.
Dolatura, i. lata securis, brad æx.
Dolosus, i. insidiosus, fraudulentus, callidus, inwitful, *uel* racenful.
Dolua, toroc.
Docta uitrix, gelæred ofer swiþestre.
Docta fastigia, gelærede æþrotu.
Domestica scissura, hiwcudlic geter.
Dote, gife.
Donat, gewelegade, forgæf.
Domat, superat, gewylt, temaþ.

Domuit, i. uicit, mitigauit, wylde.
Domui, hiwhrædenne.
Dormitatio, hnappung.
Donatio, landbec.[2]
Donaria sancta, i. sacrificia, halige gife.
Dos, -tis, dotalis, i. wed, gifu, *uel* fædren feoh.
Dosmui,[3] thorie.
Doto, -as, dono, uel gifu.
Dodrans, i. malina, egur.
Dodrante, dreariende.
Draconarius, i. uexillarius, signifer, segnbora.
Dulcis sapor,[4] *i. dulcis odor,* swete smæc.
Dulcisone, i. blanda, weredre, *uel* wynsumre.
Dulcifauo, weredum beobreade, *uel* swæsum.
Dulcedo, werednes.
Ductili, i. leui, fusili, uel astrenged.
Dumus, i. spina, spineta, þyrne.
Dumas, spinas, uel græfe.
Duodeno solio, twelffealdum setle.
Duodenus apex, twelffeald geþungennes.
Dure, i. pertinaciter, pessime, heardlice.
Duxit, i. adduxit, brohte, *uel estimauit.*
Durus, crudelis, asper, stiþ, reþe.

Ea intentione, on þa gerad.
Earundem, þara sylfra.
Ebur, i. os elefantis, a barro dictum, i. ab elefanto, elpenban.
Eclipsis, i. solis uel lune defectio, onsprungennes.
Echinus, i. piscis, cancer, uel scel.
Eculeus, stimulus, uel þrypel, *genus tormenti.*
Ecclesiasticis dogmatis, ciriclicre, doctrinis.

---

[1] Wright by an error printed: *strat*. R. W.
[2] A charter, or deed of land.
[3] Read: *domui*. R. W.
[4] The MS. reads: *sapa*. R. W.

Edax i. uorax, uorator, etol, gifre.
Ederetur, nasceretur, i. manducetur, proferetur, wæs geypt.
Edes, i. templum, hofa.
Edendis dapibus, ætlicum estum.
Edita, i. alta, creata, formata, scripta, facta, instituta, nata, locuta, adnuntiata, roborata, uel gehigde.
Edite, i. renate, renouate, reparate, constitute, uel gesettaþ.   10
Edilitas, ætnes.
Edisserit, i. explanat, enarrat, exponit, scripsit, refert, uel arecþ.
Edomitus, untemed, wilde.
Effatum, dæd.
Effarier, dicere, asæcgan.   15
Efferus, i. seuerus, ferox, immansuetus, reþa.
Effeto, i. sine foetu, ebetato, debilitato, euacuato, exinanito, ortydre[1].   20
Effeta, i. sine foetu, debilia, priuata, sine fructu, uel gelde, *uacuata, ineruata, sterilis, stulta.*
Effecit, i. perfecit, fecit, geworhte, *uel* dampnauit.   25
Effectus, i. factus, operatio, portatus, peritia, fered, *uel* geworden.
Effectibus, i. operibus, monitionibus, uel dædum.
Efficax, hwæt, *i. citus, expeditus,*   30
astutus, acutus, sollers, peritus, arud.
Efficaciter, i. uelociter, caflice, scearplice.
Efficit, i. perficit, facit, he gefremeþ,   35
uel gewyrcþ.
Effrenus, unmidled, *uel* unsæled.
Effrenate, amidludes.
Effossis, i. euulsis, ut aneddum, *subuersis.*
Effoth, bat.
Effunde, i. sperne, sparge, trahe, ateoh, *interfice.*
Effugentur, syn afligde.
Effusione, on todale.   45

Egerere, ascrepan.
Egentum, þyrfendra.
Egestus, gebæro.
Egre, i. grauiter, dolenter, earfoþlice.
Egella, gorst.[2]
Egit, i. ducit, compulit, wræc.
Egra, adlig.
Elanguet, ablacode.
Electrum, i. sucus arboris, ewicscolfer, *uel* mæstling.
Elegans, i. speciosus, gratus, pulcher, wynsum, wlitig, *praecipuus, magnus.*
Elefans, ylpend.
Elefantinosa, i. maxime, þære unsmeþan.
Elinat, i. mundat, expulit, excludit, forsweorfed.
Eliminate, adrifene.
Eliquat, i. exprimit . . . mutilat, minuit, depremit, uel grint.
Elimino, i. distruo limitem, foras eicio, mortifico, expello, ic ut anyde, *uel* drife, *uel* adyde.
Elideret, i. offenderet, ascrencte.
Elisi, i. expressi, percussi, expulsi, afflicti, cesi, flagellati, ut aþyde[3], *uel* ascrencte.
Elucubratum, i. meditatum, lucidum, euigilatum, accensum, purum, hluttor.
Elumbem, i. eneruem, aswunden.
Eludit, i. decipit, beswicþ, awægþ.
Elogium, i. fama, testamentum, uerbum, carmen, fanum, uel gyd.
Elogia, i. munus, lac.
Elbus, i. medius color, dyrcegræg, *s. inter nigrum et album.*
Elongo, prolongo, ic ylde.
Eloquentia, peritia, getingnes.
Eloquenter, getynglice.
Emarcuit, elanguit, ablacode.
Emature, geþungenlice.
Emergat, i. exsurgit, eleuat, exit, uenit, up amylþ.

---

[1] So read I. Wright has: *ontydre.* R.W
[2] *Gorst* denotes a furze, *erica, rubus.*
       R. W

[3] See Bosw. 4). R. W.

Emeritus, i. ueteranus miles, geþungen, *prefectus.*
Emellus, unmeagol.
Eminentia, i. sublimitas, excellentia, celsitudo, oferhlifung.
Emigraneus, i. uermis capitis, emigraneum, i. dolor timporum, þunwonga sar.
Emigrabit, ut asceadeþ.
Empticius, i. emptor, uenditor, cepemon.
Emptorium, i. mercatus, ceapstow.
Emolumentum, i. lucrum, auxilium, questum, uel lean, *meritum laboris.*
Emulari, i. imitari, uel ellenwodian.
Emulus, i. contrarius, gewinna, wiþerwinna, æfstig, wiþerhycgende, *eminens.*
Emulatio, i. dissensio, anhering.
Emunctoria, candeltwist.[1]
Eneruat, i. marcescet, aswand.
Eneruus, i. sine uirtute, aswunden, *emortuus.*
Eneruata, asleacod, asionad.
Eneruatius, i. debilius, sleaclice. þweorlice.
Eneruiter, waclice, *turpiter.*
Enistius, erþling.
Eoi magi, easterne tungelwitegan.
Eotenus, i. eo decreto, ordine, huc usque, uel forþy.
Equanimiter, emlice, *simili modo.*
Epulemur, utan wistfullian, *uel* simblian.
Eques, i. homo equo portatus, sessor, ridda.
Equester, qui equitat, ræde-wiga, *uel* -cempa.
Eque sonore, mid gedremum swege.
Equiparat, i. coequat, i. imitatur, assimilat, uel wiþermet.
Equipensium, efenwæge.

Equitatus, ferdwerod[2], *uel* eoredgerid, *i. equitatio.*
Equo,[3] *maria,* sæyþa, *uel* holmas.
Erepta, uel abrepta,[4] *i. sublata,* gened, þa genumenan.
Erassis, leohtum.
Erimius, hindbrer.
Erugo, i. uitium frumenti, uel ferri, rust, om, *uel tinea.*
Erugine, i. rubigine, of ruste, *uel* ome.
Erue, i. defende, gener, *uel* arede.
Erumpunt, procedunt, up abrecaþ, fordbringaþ, toberstaþ.
Erumpens, i. exoriens, uphleapende.
Eruta, i. distructa, up alocene, *uel* ahrerede.
Eructuat, i. a corde emittit, bylcetteþ, rocceteþ.
Erubescant, ignescant, asceamen.
Erpica, g., egþe.
Erpicarius, egþere.
Errabilis, uertibilis, hwerfende.
Erratibus, erroribus, gedwyldum.
Eradicat, extirpat, up aluсþ.
Essentia, i. aeternitas, natura, wunung.
Estus, i. fluctus, accessus maris, unda, inquietudo, uel recessus, uel cibus, uel geter.
Estuaria, fleotas.
Ethereus, se roderlica.
Euaginat, uttihþ.
Euanesco, i. euaneo, ic fordwine.
Euertere, ahwerfdon, *uel* gehwurfan towurpan.
Euernenent,[5] streawiaþ.
Euellet, i. eruet, alyft.
Euellit, i. eradicat, exstirpat, ut aluсþ
E uestigio, statim, uel of laste.
Euidens, i. manifestus, patens, perspicuus, certum, sweotul, gewis.

[1] The Anglo-Saxon name for a pair of snuffers.
[2] Wright printed: *ferd gerod.* R. W.
[3] An error for *equor.* R. W.
[4] In the original over the *E* of *Erepta* is written *uel ab,* which means *erepta, uel abrepta.* R. W.
[5] Perhaps an error of the scribe for: *sternerent?* R. W.

E uirgine, fram wæpenleasre.
Inermi, femnan.
Euomatio, speowung.
Exhalet, i. redolet, spiret, reddit, aþyft, *fetet, uel* stemþ.
Examen . . . uel iudicium, rectitudo, discussio, uel swearm.
Examina, i. iudica, uel proba, uel amere.[1]
Exauctorauit, deordinauit, gehende.
Exagium, onmitta.
Exagonum, sixfeald.   [cræfte.
Exametro heroico, sixfealdum leoþ-
Ex aditis, i. ex ingressibus, of inferum.
Exhaustum, i. consumptum, siccatum, up abroden, *pigrum*.
Euacuatum, aslacod.
Exacerbatio, irritatio, abolgennes.
Exactor, i. postulator, scyldlæta, *i. monitor censum*.
Exacerbauit, i. prouocauit, adflixit, he tyride,[2] abealg, *uel* onscunede.
Examinasti, probasti, asude.
Exaticum,[3] sixecge-bere.
Exasperat, i. seuit, prouocat, uel abiterie.
Exercitiis, i. laboribus, studiis, bigongum.
Exercet, i. parat, adiuuat, begæþ, *fatigat*, gearwaþ.
Exercendo, to beganne.
Exercitio, i. meditatio, gymen.
Exercebor, i. laboraui, ic dearf.
Exercitate, þære getihtan.
Exercebat, fremede, beeode.
Exertum, i. sollicitum, edoctum, apertum, nacod, *nudatum*, æwæde,[4] *exporrectum, expeditum*, benæced.
Exheredet, i. exalienat de hereditate, be yrfe weardige.
Exerere, i. euaginare, proferre, exercere, uel abredan.

[1] Cf. Bosw. pag. 7b. R. W.
[2] Wright has: *lietyride*.   R. W.
[3] The glossator means: *hexastichum* (sc. *hordeum*). R. W.

Exesum, uel comessum, aholad, þurh etan fornumen.
Exequiis pluribus, mænigfealdum þenungum.
Exiliata, i. consumpta, wræcsiþe.
Exigit, myngaþ, *i. desiderat, requirit, cupit, cogit, intellegit*, aræfnaþ.
Exitus, finis, effectus, terminus, egressus, utgong, endestæf.
Exitium, i. periculum, forþsiþ, utsiþ, *mors, perdictio*.
Exhibeo, i. porrigo, prebeo, tribuo, ic bryttie, *dono, ostendo*, ic bringe.
Exhilaror, ic beo gegladad.
Ex integro, of anginne.
Eximia, nobilia, insignia, healicu.
Exhilitas,[5] hlænnes.
Exhibita, praeparata, gegearcod.
Excidium, i. euersio, expugnatio, casus, ruina, uel hereteam.
Excidit, cecidit, uel gewat.
Excipiatur, i. segregatur, sy fram asceaden.   [*uel* arydred.
Expilatam, i. conquassatam, aþryd,
Explicuit, i. formauit, uel ut alædde.
Exquisitiores, smealicran.
Extirpat, i. exterminat, eradicat, astifecað.
Extipices, i. auruspices,[6] halseras.
Extinctus, i. peremptus, occisus, mortuus, adwæsced, forþfaren, acweald.
Extrinsecus, i. separatim, utene.
Extricabile, unforfeored.
Exsicat, agat.   [scrydde.
Exfibulat, i. exsoluit, unspeon, un-
Ex passo, i. ex caleficato uino, of geweldum wine.
Exta, i. intestina, fibras pectorum, hostiare, gesen.
Extale, rop, snædelþearm, *uel* smeruþearm, *uel* bæcþearm.
Extra, i. ultra, aliena, alia, plus, praeter, uel fremde.

[4] After *æwæde* the writer added: þæs nacodan. R. W.
[5] The glossator altered *exigitas* to *exhilitas*. R. W.
[6] *Sic MS.* R. W.

Expedire, i. narrare, insinuare, explanare, soluere, gereccan.
Explicitus, liber, efficatus, from, snel.
Expeditus, i. generosus, hilaris, fortis, alacer, swift, *promptus, paratus.*
Expedierunt, aræfdon, *uel* ræddon.
Expedita, gefremed, *i. intellecta, prompta, proferta.*
Expediet, gerecce.
Expeditio, i. praeparatio exercitus, hergung, ferd.
Expeditionibus, exercitibus, fyrdum.
Expensa, i. substantia, census, dægwine.
Expenso, i. finito, gedale.
Expertus, cognitus, i. probatus, inuentus, ongeten, onfunden.
Experimentum, i. testamentum, uel onfundennes.
Expers, i. ignarus, alienus, sine parte, imperitus, inscius, priuatus, ordæla. [nod.
Experiri, i. inueniri, cognosci, acun-
Experientia, onfundennes.
Exspectabiles senatores, þa medumestan ealdras.
Expresserant, i. assimilabant, uel arehton.
Expressit, i. manifestauit, ostendit, ut aþyde,[1] *uel* awrang.
Extentio, i. tenacitas uentris, tentigo, gebind.
Exter, alienus, fremde.
Exterorum, i. peregrinorum, utancumenra. [end.
Exterminator, uastator, westend, yt-
Ex centro, i. ex medio, of midlene.
Excessus, i. culpa, delicta, ægylt, mislimp, *uel* tyddernes, *circuitus,* bigas.
Excesserit, i. culpauerit, fregerit, uel forgemeleasaþ.
Excedit, i. superat, geþihþ, oferstihþ.
Excedat, oferstige.
Exortatus, geypped.

Exortatoria, memoriter, gemyndelice.
Exordia, i. principia, frymþu.
Exortatio, i. monitio, doctrina, uel trymnes.
Exordinationes, misfadunga.
Exorbitantes, i. circuientes, declinantes, aswifende.
Exoliuerunt, i. tabuerunt, eruperunt, corripuerunt, uel geswepredon.
Excolit, colit, begæþ.
Expositio, i. tractatio, traht.
Explorat, i. inquirit ... praedat ... uastat, hergaþ.
Explodit, atyneþ.
Explodiatur, i. expellatur, sy ut aned, *uel* awrecen sy.
Extorres, i. exules, peregrini, utlendan, *extranei,* wreccean.
Extorti, aþræste.
Exprobatio, i. improperatio, obiurgatio, edwit.
Excusorium, pauimentum, flor.
Excusetur, sy beladod.
Excusso, i. emuncto, excitato, uel ascunad.
Excussor, accusator, wrohtberend.
Excussatio, lad, ladung, *uel* wroht.
Excubitores, heafodweardas.
Excussit, i. deiecit, fram aswengde, *uel* todraf.
Excussabile, ladiendlice.
Excutere, asceacan.
Excussam, expulsam, asceacene.
Excluditur, i. eiicitur, extra ponitur, biþ ut alocan.
Exulat, i. captiuatur, perigrinatur, eicitur, alienatur, fugatur, expellitur, wræclastaþ.
Exul, i. peregrinus, alienus, utlenda.
Exultat, i. gaudet, laetatur, gehiht, *gloriatur*
Exultatio, letitia, hihting.
Exugia, i. minctura, micgerne.
Exuuiae, spolie, reaf, *i. uestes mortuorum, uel pelles ferarum, uel* reaflac.

[1] Cf. *elisi* pag. 227 l. 26. R. W.

Exustus, i. spoliatus, forswæld, forhæþed.
Exundauit, i. inundauit, aweol.
Exsumptuauit, pauperauit, geyrmde.
Expulit, awearp, *eiecit.*
Extremus, ytemeste.

Fastus, ... elatio, ... uel geþungennes, *uel* gelp, *uel arrogantia.*
Fasti flatibus, i. superbie flatibus, blædum.
Fastidium, i. altitudo, odium longum, contemptum, uel nausia, uel æþrot, unmægnes, æmelnes, ælengnes, *uel* cisnes.
Fastidia, i. arrogantia, superbia, æþrotu.
Fasces, i. honores, dignitates, plagas, triumphos, cynedomas, *uel* aldor, *uel* gegerla, *uel* godweb.
Fasce, i. onere, uel hefe.
Fascellas, weoningas.
Fasellus, i. genus holeris, uel geneat.
Faseacus, nomen auis, reodmuþa.
Fabrefactum, i. ornate compositum, uel ornamentum, uel gesmidodum.
Fabrile, smiþlice.
Fabre, i. perfecte, arteficiose, ingeniose, cræftig.
Faba fresa, gegrunden bean, *s dicta quia molata est.*
Fabula, i. -bella,[1] spel, *uel* unnyt spræc.
Factio, i. coniuratio, conuuentus, ius, factiuncula, narratio, uel hosp.
Factiosa, falsa, wrohtbora.
Facinia, hortan.
Faccus, exercitus, here.
Falerato, i. ornato, uel fictitio, gerædod, gehyrste.
Fallentis fortunae, wægendre gesælignesse, *uel* bepæcendre.
Faltum, embheped.
Falx, falcis, wingeardseax, rifter, *uel* sicul.

Falcicula, bocisern.
Falcarius, i. falciferens, uel falcifera, siþberend, *uel* mæþre.
Falcastrum, i. ferramentum curuum, a similitudine falcis uocatum, wudubil, *uel* foddur.
Falsa imagine, leasæ gehiwunga.
Falsi nebulo, þæs leasan scinlæcan.
Falconus, hafocere.
Faleras, i. iactabas, uel gehyrste.
Falanx, i. exercitus, multitudo militum, cohors, þreat, herig, feþa.
Falarica, i. theca gladii, tele genus uel aste[2] *grandis, uel lancea magna,* ætgar.
Fausta adclamantes, i. alto canendo, uel herigend sang, *uel* lofsang.
Fauor, i. fama, honor, testimonium laudis, laus, laetitia, wyrþmynd, *uel* hliwing.
Fauorabilis, laudabilis, famosus, hlisful.
Fauus, i. fabe, uel beobread.
Fafamentio,[3] eþungum.
Fauet, i. adulatur, oleceþ, *adiuuat, opitulatur, assentit,* hyrt, *uel consentit, placat.*
Fauillantium, yslendra.
Fauus, þu hliwsast.
Fatidictu,[4] of sage.
Fatiscit, uel fatescit, i. euanescit, dissoluitur, desinit, discedit, lacessit, fordwinþ, mylt, sweþrede, aswand, ateorade, *dissipat, deficit.*
Fatis, gewyrdum.
Fatigat, gewæce, *uel* drecce.
Fata, i. fortuna, euentus, uel dicta; locuta, gewyrda.
Famosum tropheum, hlisfulne sigor.
Familia, hiwræden, *uel familiaritas,* cneoris.
Familiarissimum, þone hiwcuþestan.
Familice frugalitatis, hungerlicre gneþelicnesse.
Famulatus, þeowdom.

[1] The glossator means to say: *fabella.* R. W.
[2] = *hastae.* R. W.
[3] *Fauamentio* is altered to *fafamentio* in the MS. R W.
[4] Wright reads: *fatidicum.* R. W.

Fanaticia, godwrecnes.
Fanatice, i. profani, hearhlicre, þæs hæþenan, *uel* templicre.
Fanaticus, i. minister templi, futura praecinens, uel ylfig.
Fantasia, i. imaginatio, admiratio, delusio mentis, reuelatio, multitudo, fantasma, scinlac, *uel* hiw.
Farius, uel fah, *i. loquax*.
Farcire, i. fulcire, acrammian.
Farra, i. triticum, frumentum, uel bleodu.
Farsa, i. impleta, acrummen.
Faratorium, byres.
Feralia, i. lugubria, mortifera, mortalia, tristia, noxia, luctuosa, uel deriendlican, replican.
Feraces glebas, þa wæstmbære tyrf.
Ferratas acies, þa isnodan truman.
Ferale monstrum, replic scinhiw.
Feralis bestia, reþe nyten.
Ferres, i. sustinebas, þu þoladest, contuleras.
Fere, i. admodum, prope, aliquoties, pene, forte, uel reþa.
Fereatis, i. quietis, restendum, securis.
Ferunt, i. portant, fatentur, sustinent, dicunt, uel forþyldiaþ, urgatur, prebent, bringaþ.
Ferrugo, uel ferrugineus, i. color purpurae subnigrae, isengræg.
Ferruginem, i. rasura ferri, gesweorf.
Ferrugineo flore, omigum blostme, *uel* isengrægum blostme, *uel purpureo*.
Ferus, i. crudelis, immitis, durus, reþe.
Ferula, i. harundo, uirgula, uel nomen holeris, æscþrote.
Fermun, hald.
Fermentum, hæf, *uel* beorma.
Fertur, i. dicitur, ostenditur, uel wæs fered.

Ferna, slypræsn.
Fertum, mæsselac, *uel* gehladen.
Fertilitas, i. habundantia, wæstmbærnes.
Ferreus umbo, isen randbeag.
Feruentibus, i. festinantibus, onettendum cretum.
Feruor, i. calor, wylm.
Fercula, cibaria, swæsendo.
Feruidus, weallende.
Feritas, i. crudelitas, ferocitas, inclementia, duritia, reþnes.
Feriatus, pausatus, quietus, gerestad.
Feria, weorcdæg, *i. fando dicta, quasi faria*.
Feriati dies, restedagas.
Feribus, snasum.[1]
Ferinum, i. superbum, deorenum.
Ferinis jubis, deorenum fihtum.
Ferri fodina, in quo loco ferrum foditur, isern ore.
Ferocitas,[2] *uel crudelitas*, rednes.
Ferocia, i. crudelitates, reþnessa.
Festis choreis, mundis, þreatum, *uel sanctis*.
Fesso stamine, i. lassato pondere, wihte.
Fesiculatio, fisting.
Fespa, wæsp.[3]
Femur, þeoh, *uel* hype.
Femininum sexus, wifhad.
Femineis, wiflices.
Feniceum, i. coccineum, rubrum, uel basu.
Fenisece, mæþeras.
Fenile, heghus.
Fenus, i. lucrum, usura, uel borg, *uel* læn.
Fenerator, uel commodator, uel creditor, redditor, lænend, *uel* strude.
Fefellit, i. delusit, wægde, *uel* bepæhte.
Fellitat, i. decipit, suggit, beswicþ.
Felici reditu, gesæligum edhwyrftum.

---

[1] *Snas* denotes: a spit, dart used in war, *ueru*.
R. W.

[2] The MS. has: *ferocitas i. ferocitas*.
R. W.

[3] So the MS., for *uespa*.

Fellita, i. decepta, beswicenre.
Feletki, feþehere.
Fetose, tudderfulle, teamfulle, *uel* tuddre.
Foetus, i. fructus, partus, filius, tudder, soboles.
Foeta, i. fecunda, plena, grauida, eacenu.
Federatus, i. coniunctus, gewæred, *uel pacificatus, amicus.*
Foedera, i. pacta amicitiae, wæra, *certa amicitia.*
Fedus, deformis, turpis, uel ful, *uel* pudor.
Foedatus, fedus redditus, deturpatus, uel geunwlitegad.
Foedus, i. pactum, iuratio, coniunctio, wære.
Feda, i. turpia, uel polluta, ful.
Feculentus, i. fece plenus, dræstig.
Fecundus, i. copiosus, fructuosus, uel habundans, uel tydriend.
Fecundare, i. multiplicare, gewæstm bærian.
Fex, i. uirus, uel drosna.
Febris, bryneadl.
Filatum, gearn.
Filiscetum, gearnbed.
Fistulas, i. arterias, earþyrel.
Fibra, i. uena, iecoris intestina, lifer-læppa, þearm.
Fibrans, hrysiende.
Fibula, s. dicta quod ligat, cnæp, sigl, spennels.
Finicium, i. coccinum luteris, beasu.
Finistris, þyrlum. [gedal.
Finium regum, dorum actio, gemæra
Findit, i. rupit, toclyfþ.
Finxit, i. figurabat, biwade.
Firmator, i. adsertor, geseþend.
Firmaretur, i. consolidat, wæs getrymed, *uel* gestaþolad, *uel* gefæstnad.
Firmo fulcimento, trumre underwreþinege.

Fidibus, i. fidis cithare, strengum.
Fidi prepositi, getrywes ingehides.
Fida comes, i. fidelis, getreow gesiþa.
Fiducia, i. confidentia, byldu.
Fiducialius, baldlicor.
Fidei commissum, on treowe gelæton.
Figmenta, i. plasmatio, mendacia, hiwunga, lignes, *uaria figura, compositio.*
Figulum, tigele.
Fit, i. contingit, euenit, uel sit, fuit, uel erit, biþ.
Fither, snædelþearm.
Fixi, i. solidaui, firmaui, constitui, ic afæstnode.
Fialas, steapas.
Flammaticus, ligen.
Flammeolum, i. umbra solis, sunsceadu.
Flammeum, uel ligen.
Flaminea, i. episcopali gradus, bisceophadas, *uel* sacerd.
Flammiger, ligberend.
Flammicomos ortus, ligliccede [1] upspringas.
Flammicomis, ligloccum.
Flammigeris quadrigis, ligbærum scridum, *uel* cræstum.
Flauum, i. fuluum, rubeum, geoleread, *uel* geolecrog.
Flauescit, i. maturescit, glitenaþ, *uel* geolwaþ, *splendescit.*
Flaua cesaries, geola feax.
Flaua specie, of glæteriendum, *uel* scylfrum hiwe, *uel* doxum.
Flaccentia,[2] *contracta,* aclungre.
Flactris, i. pontibus, uel fleoþomum.
Flabra, i. flatus uentorum, blædas, *uel fabula.*
Flagitiosus, i. corruptor, criminosus, manful.
Flagitia, i. uitia, i. spurcitia, fyrendæda, mandæda, *scelera.*
Flagrorum, i. flagellorum, swipena.[3]

---

[1] An error for *ligloccede upspringas,* see the next word. R. W.
[2] So the MS. R. W.
[3] Wright has: *swipera.* R. W.

Flatus, i. uentus, s. aura, spiritus, procella, oroþ, *uel* eþung.
Flasca, g. flascumna, uel flasce, trywen byt *dicte, pro uehendis ac recendendis.*
Flagrantis furie, byrnendes galscipes, *uel* reþnesse.
Flegma, i. saliua, flegmon, g., horh, *uel* mældropa.
Fleumon, uel dicitur inflammans, i. infirmitas stomachi, magan untrumnes.
Flemen, -nis, flentium humor, tear.
Fleba, flyne.
Flebiles, werendlice.
Flebo, flebilis, werendlic.
Flebotomum, blodsex.
Flecta, hyrdel.
Flectit, curuat, inclinat, gebigþ.
Flexo tramite, inclinato, gebigdre stige.
Flores, blostma, *s. nominati quod cito defluant de arboribus.*
Florescit, i. floret, blewþ, *crescit,* grewþ.
Florent, blowaþ.
Florei cespitis, blowendre tyrf.
Floralia, þa blowendlican.
Floruit, grytte.
Floriferum, i. blostmbære.
Florigeri, blostmbæres.
Floribus, uel ornamentis, blostmum.
Florida tellus, i. florulenta terra, blowende eorþe.
Floccio, unriht.
Flosculus, blostm.
Fluctuat, i. uacillat, dubitat, anxiatur, cogitat, estuat, woraþ.
Fluctiuagi ponti, þæs yþiendan sæs.
Fluentis, i. lasciue, i. galre.[1]
Fluido, i. fluenti, flowendum.
Fluitent, flowen.
Fluuiali, flodenum.
Fluminei lauacri, flodenes þweales.
Flustra, i. unda, yþ, ædwella.
Fluens, stream.

Fluxum, i. superfluitas, oferflownes.
Fluxit, decurrit, manauit, fleow.
Fluctiuagam praedam, þay þworigendan huþa.
Foramina, þyrel.
Foratorium, heardheawe, *uel* nafogar.
Foro, i. loco iudicario, uel ceapstræte.
Fota, i. confortata, uel sealf.
Fotus, i. nutritus, refectus, recreatus, calefactus, uel gelacnod.
Fontona, þa wyllican, *uel* welle.
Focarius, fyrbeta.
Focca, scolh.
Focilat, i. reficit, gehyrt, *uel* gehlywþ.
Foculare, heorth.
Furnus, tynder.
Fodina, gylden wecg.[2]
Fordalium, gesoden wyrtmete.
Fomes, i. incendium, astula minuta, tynder.
Fomentat, lexnode.
Fomenta, i. adiumenta, adiutoria, medicamenta, nutrimenta, uel sententia, uel swæsunga.
Fomet, feormeþ.
Fouet, i. nutrit, pascit, uel gehlywþ.
Foueae, seaþes.
Fouere, i. alere, auxiliari, gehliwan.
Fouerat, i. educauerat, gehyrte.
Folle bubulum, i. uas piceum, uel hwite cylle.
Folliginis, belgum.
Follis, blædbylig, *linus, mantica fabrilis.*
Forcipes, tangan.
Forcelle, gæfle, *dictae quod frumenta celluntur, i. commouentur, unde et oscilla.*
Fordalium, wyrta.
Forfices, ræglsceara.
Forpices, fexsceara.
Forsitan, i. forsan, fortasse, wenunga, wenis, *uel utique.*
Fouessoria, dicta quod foueam faciat, quasi fouessoria, mattoc, *uel* handspitel.

---

[1] So the MS, not *gabre*. R W.

[2] A gold mine.

Fragor, i. strepitus tonitruum, fremitus, cyrm, *uel* sweg, *sonitus.*
Fraga, uel ofet, *s. est terra fortis et inculta.*
Fracium, i. pumorum, streabergan, *uel* corþbergan.[1]
Fragmine, i. particulis, gebryeum.
Fraglat, i. odorat, odorem dat, stemþ, stincþ.
Fraglantes, i. olentes, odorantes, stemende.
Frangenda, þa tobrytendlican.
Fragiles honores, tyddre weorþmyntas.
Fragili bello, uel inbecilli, tyddrum gefeohte.
Fratoribus, gestunum.
Fratricidi, broþorsleges.
Fraus, s. dicitur quasi fracta fides, facn, *mendacium, deceptio.*
Fraudulenter, i. astute, facenlice.
Fraudauerat, uastauerat, bescyrede, *uel* bedælde.
Fraudulentas, þa fæcnan.
Fraudulenta, i. subdola, facenful.
Frenarier, beon gemidlad.
Freneticus, i. demoniaticus, amens, insanus, gewitleasa.
Frendens, hnægende, fnæsettende,[2] *uel* grymettende, *irascens.*
Frendit, i. stridet dentibus, irascitur, rugiet, grymetteþ.
Frenus, muþberstung.
Frenit, i. perstrepit, furit, rugit, seuit, irascitur, indignabitur, gristbataþ, *ardet, flat, gemit, clamat,* grymetteþ.
Fremitus, i. mugitus, uel rugitus, grymettung, *uel* bremung.
Frequentat, uusitat, i. iterat, repetit, gelomlæcþ.
Frequentissimus, i. celeberrimus, brymest.

Frequens, celer, assidua, gelomlie.
Frequentes, gelomlican, *densos, multos.*
Fressa, i. molita, fracta, diuisa, gegrunden.
Fretus, i. fiduciam habens, gebyld, getruwad.
Frigesco, i. frigeo, algeo, ic cealdige.
Frigens, frigidus, i. deficiens, gelidus, uel brytende.
Frico, abstraho, uello, gebrytte.
Frigida pestis, colewyld.
Frigi, bærned, *uel* gehyrsted.
Frigula, i. uasa fictilia, inutilia, falsa dicta, ficta, inania machina, uel unsoþe saga.
Frigor, i. timor, gelu, pruina, rigor, bruma, hiemps, uel cele.
Friuolus, i. mendax, fictus, ineptus, inutilis, leuis, bismerlic.
Frixura, wylm, *uel* hyrsting.
Frixa, bræde.
Frixorium, i. sartago, cremium, hyrstepanne, *uel* spæc, cocorpanne.
Frixiri, i. coqui, brædan.
Frons, hleor, *uel* wlita.
Frontes, qualitates, uel wlitan.
Frondes, s. dicuntur quod ferant uirgultas uel umbras, geleafris, *uel* bogas.
Frondea, þa geþufan.
Frondente, blowendum, *splendente.*[3]
Frondescere, growen.
Frondea robora, geþufe beamas, *uel* helmas.
Frondet, comat, gewlitegaþ.
Frondea ficus, i. frondosa, geþuf ficbeam, *uel* helm, *uel* rug.
Frondiferi nemoris, helmbæres bearuwæs.
Frondigeris coronis, helmberendum wuldorbeagum.
Frondosis dumis, ramosis, geþufum græfum.

---

[1] In German the strawberry is called: *erdbeere.* R. W.

[2] In Old-English *fnasten* is met with in the meaning of: *spirare, flare.* Cf. Havel. 548, Gaw. 1702. R. W.

[3] I read: *spelndente*, which is but an error of the scribe for *splendente*. Wright printed: spelndene, and mistook it for an Anglo-Saxon word. R. W.

Fronduerat, greow.
Frondus, bog.
Frontialis, steorrede. [bald.
Frontuosus, i. curiosus, gemah, *uel*
Frugalitas, i. temperantia, parcitas,
spærnes, gneþelicnes.
Frugalis, largus, gifend.
Fruges, frumenta, ofet, wæstm.
Frugi, parcus uti, gemetfæst.
Frugifer, ubertas, wæstmbærne.
Frunculas, wearte, byle.
Frustrum, i. incassum, on idel.
Frustrari, aidlian.
Frustratim, i. particulatim, minutatim, sticmælum, dælmælum.
Frustris, i. partibus, sticcum.
Frustum, bita, *dictum quod capiatur a fragmine*.[1]
Frutectum, i. arborum densitas, uel ramus, þyfel.
Frutices, ramos, þyrne.
Frutex, frutecta, þyfel.
Fuga, i. fugatio, fleam.
Fugax, i. fugitiua, fugiens, flygul.[2]
Fugaces turmas, þa eargan mengo, *uel ueloces*.
Fugat, flicþ, *aufert*, flymþ.
Fugitiuus, i. interdum qui fugit, flugul.
Fucus, deag, *uel* telg.
Fugo, ic aflige.
Fugus,[3] bece.
Fuligo, sot.
Fumus, rec, lig.
Fumigabunt, smeocaþ.
Fumarat, reohte, reac.
Funalia cerei, i. candela de cere, wexcandel, *uel lucernarum stuppe*.
Funalis, gemetlic.
Funeratus, sepultus, humatus, uel ræw.
Funebrem, luctuosum, heofendlice.
Funestauere, maculauere, smittodan.
Funestissima, mortalia, þa deadlicostan.
Funesta, i. scelesta, criminosa, unhyre.
Funestus, crudelis, perniciosus, wælgrim, unhere.
Funeste, wedende.
Funiculus, modicum funus, rap, *uel* strene.
Furor enim animi cito finitur, uel grauius est quam ira, reþnes, woden, dream.
Furuerunt, insanierunt, reþegadan.
Furia, insania, amentia, wodscipe, reþnes.
Furunculus, mearþ, *uel* ongscta, wearte, *uel* byl.
Furie, burhrunan, reþe.
Furias, iras, reþscipas, *uel* hatheortnessa.
Furit, irascitur, wet.
Fusarius, trabs uinee, winbeam.[4]
Fusus, uel spinl.
Fusile, nitorium, leui ductili, gegoten.
Fusi, uel spinle, *prostrati*, gescende.
Futile, i. inane, inutile, leue, labile, instabilis, infirmus, hwiper.
Fulcior, sustentor, ic eom embtrymed.
Fulcimentum, i. adminiculum, wraþe.
Fulcris, thoris, lectis, uel wræþstuþum, *uel* heofodbolstrum, *uel* bedreafum.
Fulgura, ligræse, uel ligas.
Fulmine ictus, percussus, ligbæres.
Fullo, webwyrhta.
Fuluum, flauum, splendidum, nigrum, geolu, *rubeum, rubicundum*, fealu.
Fuluis metallis, geolewum andweorcum.
Furca, furcula (*diminutiue*), gæfle.
Furca, wearhrod.
Furcifer, wearh.
Furua, fusca, nigra, deorc.
Furtiua, clandestina, secreta, furtune latentia, stulur.
Furtunum, fatum, gewif, wyrd.

---

[1] A bit; a small piece bitten off.
[2] Here I read *flygul*, but *s. v. fugitiuus* the scribe wrote *flugul*. R. W.
[3] An error for *fagus*. R. W.
[4] Here Wright passed over two pages: fol. 92v and 93r. R. W.

Furfures, purgamentum farinae, æsceadan.
Fuscus, i. niger uel tenebrosus, deorc, dungræg.
Fuscatus, i. denigratus, obnubilatus, asweartad, forsworcen, forþysmed.
Fusa,[1] spinl.
Fusi, i. dispersi, confusi, uel gendgotene.
Fustrum, sæmotu.
Fusu, dictum quod per ipsum fundatur quod netum est, spinl.
Fundat, edificat, consolidat, construat, gestaþelaþ.

Fundamentum, uel fundamen, s. dictum quod fundus sit domui, staþol.
Fundamen, staþol.
Fundali stridore, liþerlicum swege.
5 *Fundatum, consolidatum,* gestaþelad.
Fundos, bocland, uel landrice.
Functus, usus, genotad.
Fungus, spongus, dicta ab uligine, swom.[2]
10 *Fungor, utor, perago,* ic nyttige.
Fungalis, luscinia, nihtegale.
Future mercis, toweardes gestreones.[3]

[1] An error for *fusus,* see also *fusu.* R. W.

[2] Wright printed "iwom?" But there is no reason to do so, the word "swom" is quite legible. R. W.

[3] Here the MS. breaks off. R. W.

VII.

ANGLO-SAXON GLOSSES,

OF THE TENTH CENTURY.[1]

[*Quod etiam iusti uenia indigeant.*]
quaedam, sume.
patitur, þolaþ.
mala, yfela.
pugnam, gewinn.
internis, þan incundum.
exteriora, þa yttran.
mouent, styriaþ.
numquam ita, na swa.
perfecto, on full fremedum.[2]
capitur, biþ onfangen.
uictoria, sige.
bello, gecampe.
securus, orsorh.
fruatur, bruce.
inter, betwyhs.
discordes, ungetwære.
contagia, besmitenessa.
serpunt, smugaþ.
ipsaque, þa sylfan.

gaudia, gefean.
uulnus, wunde.
longa, langsum.
experientia, afangdung.
5 *notum,* cuþ.
hoc plenam,[3] on þysse fulle.
tempore, tyde.
iustitiam, rihtwisnesse.
nisi, nimþe.
10 *miserendo,* miltiende.
lauet, aþwea.
dans, syllende.
uirtutum, mægna.
munera, lac.
15 *det,* sylle.
ueniam, forgyfenesse.
[*De incognoscibilibus epigramma.*]
diuinorum operum, godcundra wurca.
secretas, digle.
20 *noscere,* onenawan.

[1] These glosses which refer to Prosper's epigrammata are taken from two leaves of a miscellaneous codex of the British Museum, Cotton. Tib. A, VII. According to the handwriting these glosses were written as early as the tenth century. Thomas Wright edited them in the Reliquiæ Antiquæ, Vol. I; but did not take them into his collection of Vocabularies. Our text is based on a recent collation of this print with the MS.
The first leaf (fol. 166r) begins with Epigramma LXXXVI, line 3 (Moguntiae 1494), then follows 166v, 165v, 165r. R.W.

[2] There appears to be an *i* before the *d* in *fremedum.* R. W.

[3] The Latin text runs thus: *Non esse hoc plenam tempore justitiam.* R. W.

causas, intingan.
humanis, menniscum.
non est, nis.
possibile, aræfniendlic.
ingeniis, orþancum.
ullo, i. aliquo, mid sumre.
intuitu, sceawunge.
speculatur, sceawaþ.
operta, oferwrigene.
qui multa, se fala.
ut lateant, þæt dlutian.[1]
scit, wat.
placuisse, gelician.
mens, mod.
imbuta, þæt getydde.
simul, samod,
omnia, ealle þing.
discit, leornaþ.
per, þurh.
operum, wurca.
speciem, hyw.
artificem, cræftean.
immensis, ongemetum.
numeris, on getelum.
ponderibus, hefum.
que suis, and his.
scrutari, smeagan.
ne cura, þæt na caru.
procax, dyrstig.
abstrusa, forditt.
laboret, swince.
nosse, cunnan.
et habere, and habban.
datur, his geseald.
[*De peccatoribus non desperandis.*]
desperandum, to ortruwienne.
sed, ac.
fiant, hi beon.
studiosius, gecnyrdlicost.[2]
supplicandum, to biddene.[2]
quia, þi þe.
numerus, getel.
sanctorum, haligra.

de numero, of getele.
auctus, geiht.[3]
impiorum, ærleasra.
morbo, mid adle.
5 *obsessis*, ofsettum.
praestanda est, to tiþienne is.
cura, caru.
medendi, lacniendes.
donec i. dum, þa hwile. [haman.
10 *in egroto corpore*, on adligum lic-
uita, life.
manet, wunaþ.
sic prauis, swa dweorum.
et uitiorum, and hleahtra.
15 *mole*, hefe.
grauatis, gehefedum.
sanctarum, haligra.
pietas est, ærfastness is.
adhibenda, to gearcygenne.
20 *precum*, gebeda.
dum, þa hwile.
possibile, aræfinendlic[4]
mutari, beon awende.
horrescat, geandracige.
25 *noctis*, nihte.
deuia, of wege.
lucis, leohtes.
amor, lufu.
conuersisque, gecyrredun.
30 *nouam*, niwe.
mentem, mod.
det, sylle.
gratia, gyfu.
qua, þære.
35 *iustificante*, gerihtwisiendre.
[*De prouidentia pacis.*]
conprehendendu, to getriwenne.
doctrina, lar.
inter, betwyh.
40 *tribulationum*, gedrefednesse.
turbines, dreohnessum.
difficulter, earfoþlice.
agnoscitur, biþ onenawen.

---

[1] *lutian* means *celare, latere*. "d" does not belong to the following word. Is it an abbreviation of "þæt"? R. W.
[2] These four words are very faint in the MS. R. W.
[3] Here begins fol. 166v. R. W
[4] Wright by an error printed: *arfaniendlic*. R W.

nec, nena.
facile, eaþelice.
inueniuntur, beoþ gemette.
in aduersitate, on wiþerwerdnesse.
praesidia, helpas.
dum non perturbant, þa whyle þe na gedrefaþ.
discrimina, horhleahtras.
pacis, sibbe.
praelia, gewinn.
nulla, na.
premunt, ofþricccaþ.[1]
exercere, bogan.
diuinis, mid codcundlicum.
conuenit, gedafnaþ.
armis, wæpnum.
consilio, mid geþehte.
omnes, ealle.
minas, þeowwracan.
tranquillam, gedefe.
et curis, and carum.
uacuam, æmtig.
mentem, mod.
inbuit, lærd.
et placidi pectoris, and gegladodes breostes.
hospes, cuma.
corde, heortan.
quieto, on gedefre.
adquiri, beon begyten.
in seuo, on reþre.
turbine, þreohnesse.
[*Quod uerum bonum nemo perdit inuitus.*]
inuitus, genedod.
amittere, forlætan.
temporalia, hwilwendlice.
[*De quaerenda perseuerantia.*]
crescere, wehsan.[2]
non cupiens, na gew...[3]
[*Expliciunt Epigrammata Prosperi.*]
[*Uersus Prosperi ad coniugem suam.*]
age iam, nu la.
precor, ic bydde.

mearum, minra.
comes, gesid.
inremota, s. inseparata, unascyrod.
rerum, þinga.
5 *trepidam*, forht.
breuem, sceort.
uitam, lif.
domino, drihtenum.
deo, gode.
10 *dicemus, uel consecremus*, utan halgian.
celeri, swyftre.
uides, þu gesyhst.
rotatu, turnunge.
15 *rapidos*, swyfte.
dies, dagas.
meare, uel pergere i. transire, faran.
fragilis, tyddres.
membra, lima.
20 *mundi*, middaneardes.
minui, wanian.
perire, losian.
labi, beon ashliden.[4]
fugit, flyhþ.
25 *omne*, eall.
quod tenemus, þæt we healdaþ.
neque..habent, ne..nabbaþ.
cupidas, grædige.
uana, idelnessa.
30 *mentes*, mod.
specie, hiwe.
trahunt, teaþ.
inani, idelum.
ubi nunc, la whær nu þa.
35 *imago*, anlicnes.
rerum est, þinga is.
ubi sunt, la whær sind.
opes, speda.
potentum, ricera.
40 *quibus*, þam.
occupare, gebysgian.
captas, gehæfte.
animas fuit, sawla wæs.
uoluptas, willa.

[1] So the MS. R. W.
[2] folio 165v begins with the last line of the epigram: *de querenda perseuerantia*. R. W.
[3] The rest of this word is cut off. R. W.
[4] So the MS. for *asliden*. R. W.

[*Prosper de fide et moribus christi-
anorum et martirum.*]
qui centum, se þe hund tweontigum.[1]
quondam, geo gefyrn.
uertebat, wende.
aratris, sulum.
ut geminos, þæt getwinne.
possit habbere,[2] mage habban.
boues, oxan.
uectus, geferod.
magnificas, mærlice.
carpentis, i. curribus, on crætum.
per urbes, gynd byrig
rus, land.
uacuum, æmtig.
fessis, gewehtum.
aeger, adlig.
adit, gefærd.
ille decem, se tyn.
celsis, healicum.
sulcans, to cleofende.
maria, sæs.
carinis, scypum.
nunc, nuna.
lembum, nauiculam i. ratem, bat.
exiguum, gehwædne.
scandit, astihþ.
ipse, sylf.
regit, styrþ.
idem, se ilca.
status, stede.
agris, æcerum.
non urbibus, ne burgum.
ullis, ænigum.
omnia que in fine, ealle and on ende.
praecipitata, besceowene.
ruunt, hreosaþ.
ferro, ysene.
peste, cwylde.
fame, hungre.
uinclis, bendum.
algore, cyle.
calore, hætan.
mille modis, mid þusend gemetum.
miseros, þa earman.

mors, deaþ
rapit, gegripþ.
una, an.
homines, menn.
5 *undique*, æghwanan.
bella, gefeoht.
fremunt, grimettaþ.
omnis, ealle.
furor, hatheortnes.
10 *excitat*, awehþ.
incumbunt, onnhigaþ.
reges, cyningas.
regibus, cyningum.
innumeris, ungerimum.
15 *impia*, arleas.
saeuit, wett.
discordia, ungedwærnes.
si concluso, gyf beclysedre.[3]
superessent, to lafe weron.
20 *tempore*, tyda.
secla, worulde.
posset, gyf mihte.
habbere, habban.
tamen, þehwheþera.
25 *occasum i. obitum nostrum*, fordsiþ
urne.
deceret, gedafnode.
finem, geendunge.
uitae, lifes.
30 *quemque*, gewhylene.
uidere, behealdan.
(*na*)*m*, (wit)odlice.
mihi, me.
quid prodest, whæt framaþ.
35 *quod longo*, þæt langum.
flumina, flod.
cursu, ryne.
semper, symle.
inexaustis, unforhladenum.
40 *prona*, forþ.
feruntur i. portantur, healdum.
aquis, wæterum.
(*m*)*ulta quod*, . . la þæt.
uicerunt, oferswiddan.
45 *saecula*, woruld.

---

[1] An error for *teontigum*. R. W.
[2] Sic MS. Cf. pag. 253 l. 24. R. W.

[3] Here begins fol. 165ʳ. R. W.

suis locis, on hira stowum.
durant, þurhwunedan.
florea rura, blosmige land.
manent, wuniaþ.
nostri, ure.
sed non mansere, ac na þurhwunedun.
parentes, fæderas.
uitam, lif.
corporis, uel temporis, tide.
hospes, cuma.
ago, ic droge
nom, na.
ergo, eornestlice.
necquicquam, on ydel.
in saecula, on worulde.
nati, acynnedde.
pereunt, losiaþ.
nobis et quibus, us and mid þam.
occidimus i. deficimus, we gewitaþ.
uitam aeternam, lif ece.
uita, life.
ut mereamur, þæt we geearnian.
in ista, on þyssum.
subeat, uel inueniat, becume.
requies, rest.
longa, langsum.
labore breui, on sceortum gedeorfe.
tamen, þehwheþera.
iste sit, i. est, þis is.
forte, wenunga.
rebellibus, wiþercorum.
asper, sticol odde teart.
rigidas i. duras, hearde.
leges, laga.
corda, heortan.

putent, wenaþ.
autem, soþlice.
grauis, swært.
mansueto, mandwæran.
5 *sarcina,* byrþen.
dorso, rhigge.[1]
ledit, deraþ.
blandum, geswæse.
mitia, þa liþan.
10 *colla,* sweoran.
iugum, nio.[2]
(to)ta mente, mid eallum mode.
deus, god.
tota ui, mid ealre strengþe.
15 *amari,* beon gelufad.
praecipitur, is beboden.
uigeat, þeo.
cura, caru.
secunda, oþer.
20 *hominis,* mannes.
sibi quisque, him ænig.
nolit, nele.
fieri, beon.
non inferat, ne onbelæde.
25 *ulli,* ænigum.
(uin)dictam, wræce.
lessus, gederod.
nesciat, na cunne.
exigere, ofgan.
30 *(co)ntentus,* (g)edæf.
modicis, on gewhædum.
uitae, forbuge.
sublimis, healic.[3]
haberi, beon gehæfd.
35

[1] So the MS. R. W.
[2] Wright printed *nio.* But this word seems to be *ioc* or *iue.* R. W.

[3] Our MS. ends with the line: *Contentus modicis uitet sublimis haberi.* R W.

VIII.

ANGLO-SAXON VOCABULARY,[1]

(OF THE TENTH OR ELEVENTH CENTURY.)

DE AUIBUS.

Aquila, earn.
Arpa, eargeat.[2]
Acega, wuducoc.
Strutio, struta.
Griphus, giw.
Ossifragus, herefong.
Anatis, ened.
Aneta, ened.
Larax,[3] ened.
Ciciris,[4] . .
Mergulus, sceálfor.
Mergus, dopfugel.
Fulix, ganot.
Anser, hwite gos.
Canta,[5] græg gos.
Olor, swon.
5 Porphyrio, fealuor.
Alacid,[6] . . . .
Accipiter, goshafuc.
Herodius, wealhhafuc.
Alietum, spearhafuc.
10 Suricaricis,[7] mushafuc.
Miluus, glida.
Butzus, tysca.[8]
Ciconia, storc.
Grus, cran.

---

[1] This Vocabulary is taken from a manuscript in the British Museum (MS. Cotton., Cleopat. A. III, fol. 76, r°), in a writing which may be of the latter part of the tenth, or of the earlier part of the eleventh century. It is preceded by a rather copious alphabetical dictionary, Latin and Anglo-Saxon, which breaks off abruptly by a mutilation of the manuscript with the letter P (No. XI in our volume); and it is followed by Anglo-Saxon glosses on Latin lives of saints (No. XII). The vocabulary itself, which presents some points of resemblance in its construction with that which is given in this volume as the Vocabulary of Archbishop Ælfric, seems to end confusedly in a gloss of this description. It contains several curious and not very common words.

[2] The meaning of this word is: a young eagle, a hen-driver, cf. Leo pag. 352, 43. Bosw. translates it: a brazen gate (!). R.W.

[3] The glossator meant to say, I suppose: Aneta ened, uel (= l) anax (for anas) ened. Cf. the next vocabulary. R. W.

[4] No Anglo-Saxon equivalent is given. R. W.

[5] Read: Ganta. R. W.

[6] Without an Anglo-Saxon equivalent. R. W.

[7] Cf. Siricaricis in the next vocabulary. R. W.

[8] tysca denotes: buteo a buzzard. R.W.

Onocratarum,[1] raredumle.
Cucu,[2] hleapewince.
Bicoca, hæferblæte.
Fusianus,[3] worhana.
Rusunia,[4] nihtegale.
Columba, culfre.
Pudumba,[5] cusceote.
Coruus, hrefn.
Cornix, crawe.
Grallus, hroc.
Cornicula, cio.
Beacita,[6] stearn.
Mursopicus,[7] fina.
Picus, higere.
Noctua, ule.
Ulula, ule.
Rubesca, seltra.[8]
Sigitula, frecmase.
Parra, cummase.
Parula, colmase.
Litorius, wærna.[9]
Tilaris, lauwerce.
Cucuzata, irþling.
Scutacus,[10] ragofinc.
Turdella, þrostle.
Merula, osle.
Scorellus, amore.
Cardella, þisteltwige.
Turdus, seric.
Trutius, þrisce.
Birbicariolus, irþling.
Ciaus, edischenn.
Pullus, cicen.
Sturnus, stær.
Florulus, goldfinc.
Passer, spearwa.
Gallus, hana.
Gallina, henn.
Hirunda,[11] swealwe.

Cuculus, geac.
Tabunus, briosa.
Musca, fleoge.
Uespertilia,[12] hreaþemus.
5 *Scnifes,* gnæt.
Culix, myge.
Uespis, wæsp.
Adticus,[13] feldbeo.
Apis, beo.
10 *Pampilio,*[14] fiffealde.
Crabro, hyrnetu.
Nocticorax,[15] nihthrefn.
Scarebius,[16] wifel.
Blata, hræþbita.
15 *Bruchus,* ceafor.
Locusta, gærshoppe.
Curculio, emel.
Cicada, hama.

20 *INCIPIT DE PISCIBUS.*
Platissa, floc.
Coclea, weoloc.
Lucius, hacod.
Tinctus, sliw.
25 *Coetus,* hwæl.
Piscis, fisc.
Ballena, uel pilina, hron.
Delfin, mereswin.
Bacharus, mereswin.
30 *Focus,* seolh.
Porcopiscis, styriga.
Isic,[17] leax.
Ostrea, ostre.
Geniscula, muxle.
35 *Cancer,* hæfern.
Sardina, hæring.
Lupus, bærs.
Murenula, æl.
Castorius, befer.

[1] For *onocrotalus.* R. W.
[2] Cf. *Cucurata* in the next vocabulary. R. W.
[3] Read *fasianus* or *phasianus.* R. W.
[4] Read *ruscinia* for *luscinia.* R. W.
[5] For *palumba.* R. W.
[6] Cf. *Beatica* in the next vocab. R. W.
[7] For *marsopicus.* R. W.
[8] a bunting, *emberiza, rubetra avis.* R. W.

[9] or *wrana.* Cf. *Bitorius* in the next vocab. R. W.
[10] Cf. *Scutatis* in the next vocab. R. W.
[11] So the MS. R. W.
[12] So the MS. R. W.
[13] Read *atticus.* R. W.
[14] For *papilio.* R. W.
[15] Read: *nycticorax.* R. W.
[16] The glossator means *scarabaeus.* R. W.
[17] Cf. *Ysox* in the next vocab. R. W.

Ludtrus, hotor.
Anguilla, smæl æl.
Ceffalus, heardra.
Sardina, smelt.

INCIPIT DE TEXTRINALIBUS.

Textrina, telum, web.
Liciatorium, webbeam.
Fussum, spinl.
Radium,[1] hrisl.
Clodica, wefl.
Deponile, wefta.
Nitorium,[2] ...
Uertelum,[3] hweorfa.
Colus, wulmod.
Glomer,[4] cliwen.
Conductum, gernwinde.
Plumaria, byrdicge.
Stamen, wearp.
Subtimen,[5] aweb.
Petica,[6] slæ.
Apidiscus, webhoc.
Scafus,[7] uma.
Tala,[8] webgereþro.
Claus,[9] teltre.
Fila, þræd.
Lana, wull.
Uellus, flis.
Leno, wifþegn.
Pedisseyua, þinen.
Alibrum, reol.
Calatum, toweht.
Insabula,[10] meodoma.

INCIPIT DE HOMINE ET DE PARTIBUS EIUS.

Homo, mann.
Antropus, mann.
Chomos,[11] middangeard.
Michrochosmos, se læssa middangeard.
Anima, saul.
Corpus, lichoma.
Caro, flæsc.
Crementum, sæd.
5 *Sensus*, sefa.
Uisus, gesihþ.
Gustus, birgnes.
Auditus, gehirnes.
Odoratus, swæc.
10 *Tactus*, hrine.
Caput, heafod.
Uertex, hnol.
Pilus, hær.
Coma, feax.
15 *Facies*, hleor.
Capillis,[12] locc.
Cerebrum, brægen.
Caluaria, heafodpanne.
Occipitium, hnecca.
20 *Capitium*, forewerd swira.
Cessaries, læ, wiffex.
Tympora,[13] þunwonge.
Uultus, anwlita.
Frons, hnifol.
25 *Supercilium*, oferbruwa.
Intercilium, betub bruwum.
Cilium, bruwa.
Palpebrae, bræwas.
Oculus, eage.
30 *Pupilla*, seo.
Papula, seo.
Corona, beag.
Lacrime, tearas.
Genae, heagoswind.
35 *Barba*, beard.
Mala,[14] ceacan.
Maxilla, ceacan.
Mentem,[15] cin.
Auris, eare.
40 *Pinnula*, ufeweard eare.

[1] For *radius*. R. W.
[2] No Anglo-Saxon equivalent given. Cf. next vocab.: *nctorium*, inspin. R. W.
[3] Read *uerticillum*. R. W.
[4] Or *glomus*. R. W.
[5] Read *subtegmen*. R. W.
[6] Cf. *Pestica* in the next vocab. R. W.
[7] For *scapus*. R. W.
[8] Cf. *Tara* in the next vocab. R. W.
[9] Read *clauus*. R. W.
[10] For *insubula*. R. W.
[11] The glossator means *cosmos*. R. W.
[12] Cf. *Capilli*, loccas, in the next vocab. R. W.
[13] For *tempora*. R. W.
[14] Read *malae* and *maxillae*. R. W.
[15] For *mentum*. R. W.

Naris, nasu.
Columpna, eall seo nasu.
Pirula, forewerd nasu.
Pennula, næsþyrel.
Flegma, horg.
Os, muþ.
Labium, welor.
Dens, toþ.
Abum,[1] neoþera welor.
Gingifa,[2] toþriman.
Precissor, foreceorfend.
Canini, hundlice.
Molares, cweornteþ.
Lingua, tunge.
Palatum, goma.
Faus,[3] hyge.
Sublinguae, undertungan.
Toles, cyrnla.[4]
Rumen, wasend.
Gurgilio, þrotbolla.
Anteriae,[5] ædre.
Collum, swira.
Ceruex, swira.
Gula, hrace.
Humeri, caxla.
Scapulus, sculdor.
Brachium, earm.
Subbrachia, underearme.
Ascilla,[6] oxtan.
Ulna, eln.
Cubitus, fæþm.
Manus, hand.
Pugnus, fæþm.
Palma, bradhand.
Uola, handbred.[7]
Artus, liþ.
Articulus, liþincel, lytel liþ.
Digiti, fingras.
Pollex, þuma.
Index, becnend. [finger.
Salutarius, halettend midemesta
Inpudicus, æwisceberend midmesta finger.
Anularis, hringfinger.

Auricularis, earclæsnend.
Ungula, nægl.
Truncus, bodig.
Torax, breost.
5 *Pectus*, breost.
Mammille, tittas.
Ubera, spana.
Lac, meolc.
Cutis, sweard.
10 *Pellis*, fel.
Pulpa, lira.
Uiscus, herþbelig.
Aruina, gelynde.
Nerui, senwe.
15 *Uertibula*, hweorban.
Gartilago, gristle.
Costa, rib.
Latus, side.
Oss, ban.
20 *Dorsum*, bryg.
Terga, bæc.
Palae, hrycriple.
Spina, hrygmergliþ.
Radiolus, ribbspacan.
25 *Medulla*, mearg.
Spondilia, hrycrib.
Sacra spina, se halga stert.
Renes, ædran.
Lumbia, lendena.
30 *Genitalia*, þa cennendlican.
Uirilia, þa werlican.
Ueretrum, teors.
Calamus, teors, þæt wæpen, *uel* lim.
Testiculi, beallucas.
35 *Uiscera*, inilve.
Meatis,[8] utgang.
Anus, bæcþearm.
Nates, earsenda.
Ydropicus, healede.
40 *Femor*, þeoh.
Femina, innewerd þeoh.
Coxa, þeohscanca.
Subfragines, hamma.
Puples, hamma.

[1] Read *album*. An error for *labrum*; cf. p. 157 l. 23. R. W.
[2] Read *gingivae*. R.W.— [3] For *faux*. R.W.
[4] Cf. *Toles* in the next vocab. R. W.
[5] Read *Arteriae*. R. W.
[6] For *asella*. R. W.
[7] See *Palma* next vocab. R. W.
[8] Read *meatus*. R. W.

Genua, cneowa.
Crura, sceancan.
Tibiae, scancan.
Surra, scanclira.
Talus, ancleow.
Planta, niþeweard fot.
Pedes, fot.
Calx, hela, hoh niþeweard.
Uiscera, inneþas.
Cor, heorte.
Sanguis, blod.
Cruor, dead blod.
Iecor, liuer.
Pulmon, lungen.
Splen, milte.
Fel, gealla.
Stomachus, maga.
Intestinum, inilue.
Onentem,[1] midhryþre.
Disceptum, neta.
Cecum, blindþearm.
Ruina, lynde.
Ansa, hringe
Cingulum, gyrdel.
Zona, gyrdel.
Ardeda, brandrida.[2]

INCIPIT DE IGNE.

Ignis, fyr.
Flamma, leg.
Flamina, blæd.
Scintilla, spearca.
Scindula, scid.
Cinis, asce.
Fauilla, ysle.
Fumus, rec.
Torris, brand.
Fax, þæcile, blysige.
Isica, tyndre.
Ignarium, algewcorc.
Lux, leoht.
Silex, flint.
Lucerna, blæccrn.

Cicindilia,[3] weocan.
Seuo, smero.

INCIPIT DE ALEA.

5 *Alea*, tæfl.
Calculus, tæflstan.
Aleator, tæflere.
Cotizo, ic tæfle, *tesseris*, tæflum.
Cerea, weax.
10 *Lampas*, leohtfæt.
Candela, candel.
Papirus, taper.
Agapis, dægmete.
Attomos, mot.
15 *Agonteta*, ellenlæce.
Agen,[4] beogang.
Aluearia, hyf.
Mel, hunig.
Apiastrum, beowyrt.

20
INCIPIT DE PLAUSTRIS ET DE PARTIBUS EIUS.

Plaustrum, wæn.
Carpentarius, wængerefa.
25 *Rota*, hweol.
Themon, þisl.
Radii, spacan.
Canti, felg.
Axedo, lynis.
30 *Iugula*, iucboga.
Axis, eax.
Altitudo, foþer.
Tabula plaustri, wængehrado.
Iugum, iuc.
35 *Modialis*, nafu.

INCIPIT DE LECTULO.

Stratum, bed.
Lectum, bed.
40 *Sindo*, scyte.
Ceruical, heafodbolster.
Puluillus, pyle.
Armilausia, serc.

---

[1] For *omentum*. R. W.
[2] brandrida seems to be the same as brandreda: *a fire-grate*. It belongs to the next section. R. W.
[3] For *cicindela*. R. W.
[4] An error for *agmen = examen*, a swarm of bees. R. W.

Tonica, tunece.
Sagum, hwitel oþþe ryft.
Cappa, sciccing.
Capsula, hacele.
Ependiten,[1] cop.
Mafors, scyfele.[2]
Sanctimonialis, nunne.
Apiarius, beocere.
Fauum, beobread.
Gratis, brod.
Altor, festerfæder.
Altrix, festermodor.
Alumnus, fosterbroþor.
Vitricius, steopfæder.
Nouerca, steopmoder.
Pupillis,[3] steopcild.
Albuga, flig.
Anguis, wæternædre.
Antidotum, drenc.
Auena, wistle.
Aruo, ierþland.
Agella, lam.
Agapa, ciepeman.
Albium, mele.
Anagrippa, anlicnes.
Apotassia, fretgenga.
Alga, **war**.
Antulum, ceac.
Antheuilus, ceacbora.
Aucupis, fuglere.
Rete, net.
Amitis, lorg.
Rudens, rap.
Aucupium, fuglung.

INCIPIT DE LIGNIS.

Fagus, bece.
Populus, birce.
Æsculus, boc.[4]
Abellanus, uel colurnus, hæsl.
Auilina, hnutu.
Nuclium,[5] cyrnel.

[1] Read *ependites.* R. W.
[2] See pag. 31 l. 24. R. W.
[3] An error for *pupillus.* R. W.
[4] Here the translator is not quite right, for *æsculus* denotes not a *beech-tree* but the *common oak-tree.* R. W.
[5] Read *nucleus.* R. W.

Butrus, hos.
Robor, ac.
Glandix,[6] æceren.
Alba spina, hægþorn.
5 *Quisquilia,* hagan.
Nigra spina, slagþorn.
Moros, slan.
Fraxinus, æsc.
Acerabulos, mabuldor.
10 *Tremulos,* æspe.
Acriuolus,[7] holen.
Beta, birce.
Alnus, alr.
Abies, sæppe, gyr.
15 *Ulnetum,*[8] alorholt.
Uirecta, wice.
Uacedo, redisn.
Cerasius, cirisbeam.
Cariscus, wice.
20 *Castaneus,* cistenbeam.
Ramnus, coltetræppe, þefandorn.
Ruscus, cneoholen, fyres.
Taxus, iw.
Torriculum, hyrwe.
25 *Myrtus,* wir.
Malus, apuldor.
Malum, æppel.
Melarium, milisc apuldor.
Metianum, milisc æppel.
30 *Plumnus,* plumtreow.
Prunum, plyme.
Pirus, pirige.
Pirum, pere.
Pinus, pintreow.
35 *Amera,* sealh.
Salix, welig.
Rubus, þyr.[9]
Tribulus, bræmbelbræer.
Acinum, hindberge.
40 *Bacce,* bergan.
Sambucus, ellen.
Timus,[10] hæþ.

[6] Read *glandis* or *glandes.* R. W.
[7] An error for *acrifolium.* R. W.
[8] Read *alnetum.* R. W.
[9] The MS. has 'þyr' or 'þyu' instead of 'þyrn'. R. W.
[10] For *thymus.* R. W.

Genista, brom.
Oliua, elebeam.
Uinea, wingeard.
Uua, winberge.
Butros,[1] geclystre.
Oleaster, windeltreow.
Ortus pomorum, apeldertun.
Ortus olerem,[2] leahtum.[3]
Folium, leaf.
Cortix, rind.
Radix, wyrtruma.
Ramus, twig.
Framen, spæc.
Roboretum, æcen.
Apeletum, spracen.
Uiuorna,[4] wuduwinde.
Eder,[5] ifig.
Fursarius, wanabeam.[6]
Fraga, streowberge.

DE HERBIS TERRÆ.

Apio,[7] merce.
Alium, garleac.
Serpulum, cropleac.
Ascolonium,[8] cipa.
Ungio,[9] yneleac.
Alba,[10] cipa, wite tun.[11]
Duricorium, holleac.
Porrum, por.
Cerefolium, ceruille.
Nasturcium, leaccersan, tuncers.[12]
Ibiscum, biscepwyrt.[13]

Coliandrum,[14] celendre.
Mento,[15] minte.
Cartamo, lybcorn.
Acitula, hramse.
5 *Acitelum*, hramsancrop.
Accitulium, iacessure.[16]
Arniglosa, wegbræde.
Cinoglosa, ribbe.
Ambila,[17] leac.
10 *Horidanum*, elone.[18]
Napis, næp.
Pastinaca, wealmore.
Seu britia, willecærse.[19]
Bibulta, billere.
15 *Eptafolium*, sinfulle.
Malna,[20] hocleaf.
Marubium, hune.
Mastica,[21] hwit cudu.
Ostrum, wyrma.[22]
20 *Omagnum*,[23] wyrmella.
Papilluum, eolxsege.[24]
Parulus, sinfulle.
Scilla, glædene.[25]
Quinqueneruia, læcewyrt.
25 *Quinqueuolium*, fifleafe.

INCIPIT DE SUIBUS.

Uistrina, stigo.
Aper, etfor.[26]
30 *Sus*, swin.
Uerrus,[27] bar.
Maialis, bearg.
Scrofa, sugu.

---

1 Read *botrus* = *botrys*. R. W
2 An error for *olerum*. R. W
3 So the MS. for *leahtun*. R. W
4 The glossator means to say: *uiburnum*. R. W.
5 Read *edera* or *hedera*. R. W.
6 The spindle-tree, *fusanum arbor*. R.W
7 For *apium*. R. W.
8 For *ascalonium*. R. W.
9 *Ungio* for *unio*. R. W.
10 *Alba* sc. *unio*. R. W.
11 *Wite* is an error for *hwite* or *white*. Half of the *n* in *tun* is cut off. The scribe wrote *tuneers*, I suppose. Cf. *Nasturcium*. R. W.
12 The MS. has *tunē*. R. W.

13 Cf. Cockayne, Leechdoms etc. Vol. II. pag. 572 s. v. *bisceopwyrt*. R. W
14 *Coliandrum* or *coriandrum*. R. W.
15 An error for *menta*. R. W.
16 Cf. pag. 11, l. 9. and pag. 3, l. 22. R W.
17 Perhaps an error for *allium*? R. W
18 Cf. Cockayne, Leechd. III. pag. 325.
19 Cf. Cock. II. p. 410. R. W.
20 Read *malua*. R. W.
21 See *Mastix* in the next vocab. R.W.
22 See Cock. II. pag. 410. R. W.
23 Read *origanum*. R. W.
24 Cf. Cock. III. pag. 324. R. W.
25 Cf. Cock. II. pag. 388. R. W.
26 Read *eofor*. R. W.
27 = *uerres*. R. W.

Porcus, ferh.
Porscaster, for.[1]
Forda, gefearh sugu.
Ausungia, rysle.
Perna, flicce.
Larda, spic.
Lucanica, mearg.
Bruncus,[2] wrot.
Ius, rop.
Suesta, swina swaþu.
Seta, byrst.
Bubullus, swan.
Extale, snædel.
Interamen, inelue.
Iulium,[3] smæreþerm.

INCIPIT DE METALLIS.

Obrizum, smæte gold.
Aurum, gold.
Aurifex, goldsmiþ.
Argentum, seolfer.
Auricalcos, grene ar, mæstline.
Aes, ar.
Succinum, glær.
Ferrum, isen.
Plumbum, lead.
Stagnum, tin.
Aurifodina, gyldingwecg.[4]
Metallum, clympre.
Faber, smiþ.
Officina, smiþþe.
Follis, blæstbelg.
Cudo,[5] anfilte.
Forceps, tang.
Carbo, col.
Malleus, hamer.

Lima, mylenstan, feol.
Cultellus, seax.
Hasta, spere.
Sicca, cultur.[6]
5 Uomer, scer.
Uatilla,[7] ferrece.
Boratorium, byres.[8]
Rotum, uel taratrum, timbor.
Desile, bor.
10 Olatrum, scafa.
Runcina, locor.
Terebellus,[9] ...
Lynibor,[9] ...
Pila, þoþor.
15
INCIPIT DE FRUGIBUS.

Ordeum, bere.[10]
Triticum, hwæte.
Singula,[11] ryge.
20 Faar, spelt.
Spica, ear.
Aresta,[12] egle.
Calmum, windelstreow.
Parirus,[13] fleawyrt.
25 Ululatus, wulfageþot.
Grues, gryt.
Iuuencibus,[14] riscþyfel.
Imbilium, leohtleap.
Botre, æþro.
30 Peana, lecþ.[15]
Coluber, snaca.
Stiba, handle.
Axima, stoc.
Mosiclum, ragu.
35 Subsiciua,[16] æscapo.
Exigia,[17] gesanco.

[1] for, fearh denotes a little pig, a farrow. Germ. ferkel. R. W.
[2] An error for trunceus = proboscis. R.W.
[3] Read ilium or illa. R. W.
[4] Cf pag. 241 l. 17. R. W.
[5] Cudo means to beat, to coin, stamp. R. W.
[6] Taken from Lat. culter = sica. R.W
[7] For uatillum or batillum. R. W.
[8] byres denotes: a burin, an engraver's tool. R. W.
[9] The Anglo-Saxon equivalent is wanting. R. W.

[10] The scribe by an error wrote twice: ordeum, bere. R. W.
[11] The writer means to say: secale. R.W.
[12] For arista. R. W.
[13] An error for papirus, I suppose. fleawyrt is called in Latin: psyllium R W.
[14] An error for iuncis. R. W.
[15] Perhaps an error for paeonia (?). 'lecþ' I do not understand. R. W.
[16] Read subseciua. R. W.
[17] Read ezupia or exrugia. R. W.

Grabra,[1] gat.
Uordalium, læste.
Gergenna, sticca.
Cornas,[2] geap.
Misarius, steda.[3]
Equa, mire.
Equus, hors.
Cabullus,[4] hengest.
Burdus,[5] seamere.
Peducla, lus.
Ascarida, hnitu.
Ladasca, pie.
Ursie,[6] sweorhnitu.
Mulus, mul.
Asina, eosol.
Camellus, oluend.
Arimentarius,[7] hierde.
Arimentum, hiord.
Boua, oxa.
Antile, heahfru.
Uacca, cu.
Foetus, melc.
Uitulus, cealf.
Taurus, fearr.
Uecta, enwintre.
Laudaris, steor.
Uolio,[8] fald.
Aubobulcus, oxnahyrde
Priueta, þriwintre steor.

INCIPIT NOMINA SECUNDUM
ORDINEM LITTERARUM.

Acris, from.
Alacris, snel, blide.
Anxius, sorgiende.
Appetitus, gitsung.

[1] An error for *capra*. R. W
[2] Read *coruus* = *curuus*. R. W.
[3] *misarius* = *emissarius* (*equus*) R.W.
[4] So the MS. R. W.
[5] Read *burdo*. R. W.
[6] See *Urcius* pag. 275 l. 15. R. W.
[7] or *armentarius*. R. W.
[8] An error for *ouile*. R. W.
[9] An error for *alliciens*, I suppose. R.W.
[10] = *auehit*. R. W.
[11] Here the glossator gives no Anglo-Saxon equivalents. R. W.
[12] The scribe seems to mean: *bucco*.
R. W.

Astu, fæcne.
Adridens,[9] tyhtende.
Alitus, æþm.
Aueit,[10] aweg fereþ.
5 *Aquile*, segnas.
Adclinas, toheald.
Adrogans, . . .[11]
Agem, . . .[11]
Adsciti, gegaderade.
10 *Augustum*, brad.
Buccum,[12] dysig.
Balus, embrin.[13]
Bona, stoppa.[14]
Bodonicula, amber.[15]
15 *Urcius*, handwyrm.
Briensis,[16] teter.
Balsis, isenfeter.[17]
Bulla, sigil.
Balsus,[18] wlips.
20 *Blessus*, stamor.
Batuitum, gebeaten.
Broel, ense.[19]
Broelarius, ediscweard.
Buculus, randbeah.
25 *Byrseus*, lypenwyrhta.
Caprea, ra.
Capre,[4] gat.
Caper, hæfer.
Edum,[20] ticcen.
30 *Hircus*, bucca.
Titula, gataloc.[21]
Titurus, gatahierde.
Calcar, spura.
Cuspis, gad.
35 *Catesta*,[22] gæleþ.
Uenator, hunta.

[13] See pag. 9 l. 18 and pag. 192 l. 14.
R. W.
[14] Cf. pag. 9 l. 19 and pag. 195 l. 21.
R. W.
[15] Cf. pag. 195 l. 20. R. W.
[16] See pag. 9 l. 31. R. W.
[17] Cf. pag. 8 l. 14 and 24; pag. 192 l. 13. R. W.
[18] An error for: *balbus*. R. W.
[19] Cf. pag. 9 l. 35: *broel* edisc and pag. 196 l. 29. R, W.
[20] Read *edus* = *hoedus*. R. W.
[21] Cf. pag. 61 l. 4. R, W.
[22] Cf. pag. 10 l. 34. R. W.

Uenabula, ...[1]
Molosus, roþhund.
Unfer, grighund.
Bruccus, ræcc.
Celox, ceol.
Capsis, cist.
Colonus, gebur.
Cistula, spirte.
Colobium, hom.
Cacabum,[2] citel.
Lenes,[3] hwer.
Lancona, cille.
Sartago, bredingpanne.
Olla, greoua.
Patella, **patella**.
Camos,[4] swol.
Scalpellum, brædisen.
Capitium, heafodsmæl.
Condicio, redin.
Clauicularius, cægbora.
Cicur, manþwære.
Crocus, gæle, geolo.
Camisa,[5] ham.
Calta, rædeclæfer.
Sarcio, ic supe.
Sarcidis, geseped is.
Oscida,[6] totrida.
Omelias,[7] spræce.
Ortodoxos, wuldorlic.
Onix, **blere**.
Caluus, calo.
Recalbus,[8] upfeax.
Procuratio, scir.
Patrocinium, mundbyrd.
Parsus, geroscod.
Plumacium, langbolster.
Pistrinum, cofa.

Pistrilla, lytel cofa.
Pristris,[9] dæge.
Panis, hlaf.
Paxmatium, bradhlaf.
5 *Sparsum*, daag.
Sparsio, dages hlæfþe.
Tinipa, gebyrgen.
Palagra, æcilma.
Pironis,[1] ...
10 *Pastula*,[10] ongseta.
Papula, wearte.
Punctus, brord.
Pugillaris, gyrdelbred.
Plutecus, apa.[11]
15 *Pendera*, fugelint.[12]
Pansa, scaffot.[13]
Paranimphus, dryhtmon.
Pronuba, hadswæpe.
Sponsus, brydguma.
20 *Sponsa*, bryd.
Thalamus, brydbur.
Nuptiae, iemung.
Sibba, feresoca.
Sarcum, weodhoclu.
25 *Scalprum*, bor.
Sternutatio fnora.
Tussis, hwosta.
Serina,[14] meremen.
Soccus, slypescos.
30 *Subtalaris*, stæppescos.
Sandix, wyrt.[15]
Stirillum, buccanbeard.
Stabula, siota.
Saginatum, iemæsted.
35 *Tinctorium*, telgung.
Tyro, cempa.
Tibialis, banrift.

---

[1] The writer omitted the Anglo-Saxon translation. R. W.
[2] Read *cacabus*. R. W.
[3] An error for *lebes*. R. W.
[4] The glossator means to say: *cauma* or *caumos*. Cf. *chaumos* pag. 12 l. 45. R. W.
[5] = *camisia*. R. W.
[6] Read *oscilla*. R. W.
[7] Or *homilias*. R. W.
[8] = *recaluus*. R. W.

[9] Sic MS. R. W.
[10] Read *pustula*. R. W.
[11] Read *phitecus* (an error for *pithecus*). Cf. pag. 39 l. 22. R. W.
[12] I doubt whether the MS. has *fugelint* or *fugelim*. R. W.
[13] Cf. pag. 37 l. 37. R. W.
[14] Read *Sirenes*. R. W.
[15] Cf. pag. 281 l. 29. R. W.

Tricilo, scora.[1]
Torax, feolufor.[2]
Tenticum, spindel.
Trulla, scofl.
Soporatus,[3] gewyrsmed.
Titillatio, kitelung.
Scabellum, windfona.
Sella, sotol.
Subsellium. scamol.
Stomachus, . . .[4]
Sambucus, saltere.
Stronius,[5] dropfag.
Balidus, dunn.[6]
Salamandra, wæternædre.
Scutum, sceld.
Scutarius, sceldwyrhta.
Sandix, wad.
Stiria, gecele.
Sinus, wellere.
Singultum,[7] gescea.
Sceda, teah.
Salum, sege.[8]
Simfoniaca, belune.[9]
Senecen, . . .[10]
Talumbus, gescaldwyrt.[11]
Uarix, ompre.
Millefolium, gearwe.
Urtica, netele.
Scirpia,[12] læfer.
Foenum, heg.
Stipula, healm.
Tentorium, ieteld.
Taber, syl.
Tegorium, lytel cyte.
Tapeta, reowu.

Tabetum, cecin.[13]
Toxi,[14] pang.
Triligium, þrielig hrægil.
Tus, inbærnis.
5 *Tibicen,* pipere.
Tubicen, bemere.
Tillinguae, tuddor.
Tertiana, lencteladl.[15]
Tridens, mettac.
10 *Tubulo,* fealo.[16]
Talpa, wund.[17]
Tolia,[18] cyrnel.
Uoluula, hymele.
Ulmus, helm.
15 *Uincus,*[19] mistellam.
Uadimonium, borgwed.
Uotibus, esteful.
Ultro citro, hider and þider.
Uestiarius, hræglweard.
20 *Exnado hior,*[20] collecti.
Exenodochia, susceptio peregrinorum.
Ymnum, lof.
Ypoteseo bassio, scirnis.
Nicalalbum, milisc æppel.[21]
25 *Passtellus,*[22] hunigæppel.
Aratrum, sulh.
Arua, yrþland.
Iuger, ioc.
Seges, æcer.
30 *Sulcus,* furh.

INCIPIT DE DOMIBUS.

Domus, hus.
Aulea, heall.
35 *Uestibulum,* cauertun.

---

[1] Cf. Bosw. 60¹. R. W.
[2] Cf. pag. 51 l. 16. R. W.
[3] An error for *suppuratus.* R. W.
[4] The scribe omitted the Anglo-Saxon equivalent. R. W.
[5] Read *sturnus.* Cf pag. 48 l. 19. R.W.
[6] Cf. pag. 192 l. 5. R. W.
[7] Read *singultus.* R. W.
[8] Cf. pag. 45 l. 5. R. W.
[9] Cf. pag. 47 l 12. R. W.
[10] No Anglo-Saxon translation given. R. W.
[11] Cf. pag. 50 l. 2. R. W.
[12] Read *scirpea.* R. W.
[13] Cf. pag. 50 l. 1. R. W.
[14] Read *toxicum.* R. W.
[15] So the MS., instead of *lenctenadl* R. W.
[16] Cf pag 52 l. 11. R. W.
[17] I read *wund* not *pund* as Wright printed. Cf. pag. 49 l. 39. R. W.
[18] Read *toles.* R. W.
[19] Read *uiscum. Mistellam* means: birdslime made of the mistletoe. R. W.
[20] Read *Exenadochior, collecti* (sic!) *e Xenodochia* etc. R. W.
[21] Cf. Bosw. 46¹. R. W.
[22] Read *pastillus.* R. W.

Camara, hrof.
Paratica, first.
Partica,[1] winbeam.
Tignus,[2] ræfter.
Trabs, beam.
Paries, wah.
Laquear, ræsn.
Tignaris, hrofwyrhta.
Pauimentum, flor.
Obstupum,[3] feorstuþu.
Ualua, duru.
Sponda, hobanca.
Spondeus, benc.
Postes, durstodl.
Limen, þerscwald.
Superliminare, oferdyre.
Spatula, bed.

INCIPIT DE MENSA.

Mensa, beod.
Discus, disc.
Catinus, scutel.
Parabsidis,[4] gabote.
Uarsalis,[5] sealtfæt.
Uas buteri, buterstoppa.
Butirum, butere.
Lac, meolc.
Uerberatum, fliete.
Lac tudiclum, geþrofen fliete.
Lac coagolatum, molcen.
Uerberaturium,[6] þwiril.
Sinum, cyrin.
Caseum, cyse.
Calmaria,[7] cealfre.
Calmum,[8] molegn.
Calmilla,[9] lim.

Serum, hwæg.
Caluiale, calwerbriw.[10]
Pultum, briw.
Coclear, cucere.[11]
5 *Clerius cibus*, wyrtmete.[12]
Quadripertitum, cocormete.[13]
Uiuertitum, ponmete.[14]
Calipeatum, hæting.
Obestrum, beost.
10 *Iuta*, awilled meolc.
Ocastrum, gemenced æg.
Offa, sticce.
Cachar,[15] lira.
Seruiunculos, forglendred.
15 *Reunculos*,[16] lundlaga.
Pincerna, byrele.
Taberna, winærn.
Uinum, win.
Mustum, neowe win.
20 *Merum*, hluttor win.
Dulcisapa, awilled win.
Uinum conditum, gewyrtod win.
Defrucatum,[17] gesweted win.
Defecatum, ahlutrod win.
25 *Mulsum*, medo.
Celia, ealo.
Ceruisa,[18] swatan.
Pollis, grut.
Sandix, wyrt.[19]
30 *Prandium*, undermete.
Cena, æfenmete.
Uiciolum,[20] cruce.
Uescada, mundlan.[21]
Manile, læuil.
35 *Alueolum*, treg.
Maniteorium,[22] handlind.

[1] Read *portica* or *porticus*. R. W.
[2] Read *tignum*. R. W.
[3] For *obstipum*. R. W.
[4] The glossator means *paropsis*. R. W.
[5] Read *uas salis*. R. W.
[6] Read *uerberatorium*. R. W.
[7] The writer means to say: *caluaria cealfre* (= *calver*). R. W.
[8] An error for *galbanum*. R. W.
[9] Or *calamilla*. R. W.
[10] Cf. Bosw. 21ᵘ. R. W.
[11] Or *cucelere*. Cf. Bosw. 22ᵗ. R. W.
[12] Cf. Bosw. pag 96ᵇ. R. W.
[13] Cf. pag. 42 l. 27. R. W.
[14] Wright printed: *ronmete*. R. W.
[15] An error for *caro*, I suppose, which was originally written *charo*. R. W.
[16] Read *renunculus*. R. W.
[17] Read *defrutatum*. R. W.
[18] = *ceruisia*. R. W.
[19] Cf. pag. 277 l. 31. R. W.
[20] The scribe seems to mean *uictilum* = *fictilum* or *fictile*. R. W.
[21] Cf. pag. 52 l. 35. R. W.
[22] Read *manutergium* handlin. R. W.

Matile,[1] sceat.
Tabulamen, þille.
Patera, hnæpp.
Cucumus,[2] popei.
Pecten, camb.
Melle dulci, leoht beor.
Ciatum,[3] steap.
Fiola, bledu.
Ciatus, bolla.
Delumentum,[4] þweal.
Poculum, wegi.
Antulum, ceac.[5]
Annona,[6] nonmete.
Origia,[7] suntreow.
Cacista, hwite clæfr.[8]
Cuba,[9] tunne.
Doleum,[10] byden.
Colicus, eoforþrote.[11]
Callus, war.
Clamidis, godweb.
Frigus, cæle.
Calor, hæto.

Choors, tun.[12]
Corus, þreat.
Sella, sylla.
Pella, radolfelt.
5 *Carpella,* sadolboga.
Cicer, bean.
Coreum,[13] hyd.
Cassidile, pung.
Coruis,[14] mand.
10 *Cornicen,* hornbora.
Culinia,[15] coc.
Coquina, cycene.
Cacobatus, hrum.
Comicus, scop.
15 *Melopius,* leohtwyrhta.
Conquilium,[16] weoloc.
Celeps, hægsteald man.
Calcarium, scoh.
Cancer, stalla.
20 *Concern,*[17] hafern.
Cartilago, leoces heafod.
Cliens, geþofta.[18]

1 Read *mantile.* R. W.
2 For *cucumis.* R. W.
3 Read *ciatus* or *cyathus.* R. W.
4 Sic MS ; not *delamentum.* R. W.
5 See pag. 6 l. 12. R. W.
6 *Annona* denotes: income, revenue. Is *Annona* an error for *Coena?*
R. W
7 Wright printed *ozigia.* R. W
8 See pag. 11 l. 7. R. W.
9 Read *cupa.* R. W.

10 = *dolium.* R. W.
11 Euforþrote is called in Latin *carlina acaulis.* R. W.
12 Cf. pag. 14 l. 41. R. W.
13 = *corium.* R. W.
14 Read *corbis.* R. W.
15 Read *culina.* R. W.
16 Read *conchilium.* R W.
17 An error for *cancer.* R. W.
18 For the remainder of this MS. see No. XII. R. W.

IX.

ANGLO-SAXON VOCABULARY,

OF THE ELEVENTH CENTURY.[1]

NOMINA UOLUCRUM.

Aquila, earn.
Arpa, earngeat.[2]
Griphus, giow.
Ossigra, gos.[3]
Cignus, elfetu.[4]
Mergulus, dopfugel.[5]
Fulix, ganot.[6]
Aneta, æned.
Uel anax,[7] æned.
Anser, uel ganra,[8] hwit gos.
Ganta, uel auca,[9] græg gos.
Olor, swann.

Alacid, mæw, *uel alcedo.*[10]
Accipiter, goshafoc, *uel aucarius.*
Herodius, wealh hafoc, *uel falco, uel capus.*
5 *Iletum,* spearhafoc.
Siricaricis, mushafoc.[11]
Miluus, uel garrulus,[10] glida.
Ciconia, store.
Grus, cran.
10 *Onagratulus,* raradumbla, þæt his pur.
Cucurata, hleapewince.
Acegia, snite.[12]
Fursianus,[13] worhana.
Luscinia, nihtegala, *uel achalantida.*

---

[1] This vocabulary is taken from a manuscript in the Royal Library at Brussels No. 539 (now No. 1829). It contains fewer classes of words than the other vocabularies, and those words are chiefly on Natural History and Anatomy; but as far as it goes, it is more copious. (Our text is based on a recent collation made by Dr. A. Holder, of Carlsruhe.) R.W.

[2] Wright printed *earngeap.* Cf. pag. 258 l. 4. R. W

[3] Cf. pag. 258 l. 8 *ossifragus* and 259 l. 7 *accipiter.* The glossator meant to say, *ossifragus,* goshafoc. R. W.

[4] Cf. pag. 35 l. 36. R. W.

[5] Literally, a dipping fowl — the moor-hen; still called in Dutch; *doopvogel.*

[6] The word is interpreted as meaning specially the pen-duck, but it seems to have been used as a general term for a sea-fowl. Ganotes bæd = the ganot's bath, was a common poetical term for the sea.

[7] Wright has *uelanax,* æned. For *anax* read *anas.* R. W.

[8] The words *uel ganra* are added in another hand. A. H

[9] The second *g* in *grag* corrected from *c. auca* is added in another hand. A. H.

[10] These two words are added in another hand. A. H.

[11] Cf. pag. 259 l. 10. R. W.

[12] Cf. *acega* pag. 258 l. 5. R W.

[13] An error for *fasianus.* Cf. pag. 260 l. 4. R. W.

ANGLO-SAXON VOCABULARY.

Columba, culfre.
Palumba, cuscote,[1] uel wuduculfre.[2]
Coruus, hræfn, uel corax.
Cornix, crawe.
Cornicula, cyo, uel graula.[3]
Gralus,[4] hroc.
Beatica, tearn.5
Marsopicus, fina, uel ficus.
Picus, higera, uel gagia.
Noctua, ule, uel strix, uel cauanna.
Rubisca, salthaga, uel rudduc.[6]
Fringilla, fine.
Sigatula, fræcmase.
Parra, colmase.
Parrula, spicmase.[7]
Bitorius,[8] wrænna, uel pintorus.
Tilaris, lawerce, uel alauda.
Ficitula, sugga.
Scutatis, ragofinc.
Merula, þrostle.
Cardella,[9] linece.
Turdus, scric.
Strutio, þryssce.[10]
Cuculus, geac, uel ciculus, tucos.
Birbicaliolus, eordling,[11] uel tanticus.
Pullus, (cy)cen.[12]
Ornithia, fugelas, uel orneas.
Stirnus, stær, uel fulix.
Passer, spearewa.
Gallus, coc.
Gallinaceus, i.[13] capun, capo.[14]
Gallina, hæn.
Ornitha, gr. hænn.

Hirundo, swealewe.
Nocticorax, nihthræfn.[15]
Ardea, hragra.
Diomedia, gr. uel herodios,[14] swan.
5 Turdella, scealfor.
Mergula, scealfor.[16]
Butio, cyta.[17]
Soricarius, bleria pyttel.[18]
Bubo, huf.
10 Pellicanus, stangella and wanfota.
Ortigometra, segescara.[19]
Coturnix, erschæn.
Philomella,[20] nihtegale.
Ciupella, hulfestran.[21]
15 Ismarus alietum, spearhafoc.
Uiperina, nædderwinde.
Scorellus, clodhamer and feldeware,
 uel bugium.

20 [DE NAUE ET PARTIBUS
 EJUS.][22]

Gubernio, i. steora.[23]
Gubernator, steorman.[23]
25 Nauta, reþra.
Nauis, scip.
Archiromacus, swift scip.
Scapha, ærendscip.
Barca, flotscip.
30 Liburna, hulc.
Dromo, æsc.[24]
Pontonium, flyte.
Trabaria, i. caudex, punt, i. ponto-
 nium.

---

[1] Still called, in different parts of the country, cushots or cowshots.
[2] The MS. has culfr. R. W.
[3] Read gracula or graculus. R. W.
[4] gralus, altered from grallus (for graclus = graculus) in MS. A. H.
[5] So the MS. A. H — Cf. pag. 260 l. 12 stearn. R. W.
[6] Cf. pag. 260 l. 17. R. W.
[7] Wright read swicmase. R. W.
[8] Cf. pag. 260 l. 21 s. v. litorius. R. W.
[9] Cf. pag. 260 l. 28. R. W.
[10] Cf. pag. 260 l. 30. R. W.
[11] Cf. pag. 260 l. 31. R. W.
[12] cy in cycen added in another hand. A. H.
[13] i means id est. R. W.
[14] Added in another hand. A. H.

[15] n in hrafn corrected from m. A. H.
[16] Cf. pag. 258 l. 13. R. W.
[17] See pag. 259 l. 12. R. W.
[18] Cf. pag. 259 l. 10 and pag. 285 l. 6. R. W.
[19] The Greek word proves that the meaning of segescara is not cicada (cf. Bosw. 61ᵂ) but coturnix (cf. Leo pag. 145, 39). R. W.
[20] The first l struck out by another hand. A. H.
[21] A r after p in ciupella struck out. A. H. Wright has hulfstan. R. W.
[22] Cf. pag. 165 ff. and 181 ff. R. W.
[23] These five words were omitted by Wright. R. W.
[24] Cf. pag. 181 l. 29. R. W.

Puppis, se æftera stemn.[1]
Cumba, þurruc.[2]
Carina, bytme.
Fori, i. tabulata nauium, scipes flor.
Columbaria, arlocu.
Remi, ara.
Trastra,[3] þoftan.
Palmula, arbled.
Antemna, seglgyrd.
Cornua, þa ytemystan endas þære seglgyrde.
Malus, mæst.
Modius, mæstcyst.[4]
Carceria, hunþyrlu.
Parastates, mæstwist.
Clauus, helma.
Gubernaculum, steorroþur.
Pons,[5] sciphlædder.[6]
Uela, seglu.
Prora, frumstemn.[7]
Funes, restes, rapas.
Spire, linan.
Propes, sceatline.[8]
Pes ueli, sceata.
Safo, stæg.[9]
Opisfera, stedingline.[10]
Prosnesium,[11] marels.
Anguina, racca.
Remulcum, tohline.
Strupiar, midln.
Cataporates,[12] sundline.
Bolidis, sundgerd.[13]
Aplustra, geredru.
Estuaria, fleotas.
Glarea, ceoselstan.

Honeraria, sciplæst.
Sirtim, sandgewurp.[14]
Jungetum, risedyfel.[15]
Ledo, nepflod.
5 *Proceris*, gearufang.
Arula, heord.
Remex, redra.
Reuma, gytestream.
Scalmus, doll.
10 *Tabule*, bord.
Uncinos, hocas.
Rostrata nauis, i. barda.
Trieris, scægd.[16]
Linter, bat.
15 *Musculus, i.* sceortscip.
Carabus, scipincel.
Littoraria, trochscip.
Puppis, steorsetl.
Prora, ancersetl.
20 *Trudes*, spreotas.
Transtra, scipsetl and þoftan.
Una serta, i. an gerif fissca, odde an snæs fissca, odde odra þinga.

25 DE MEMBRIS HOMINUM.
Anima, sawl.
Homo, man.
Antropus, man.
Microcosmus, læssa middaneard.[17]
30 *Corpus*, lichama.
Caro, flæsc.
Crementum, cid.
Sensus, sefa.
Uisus, gesyhþ.
35 *Auditus*, gehyrnes.
Odoratus, swæc.

---

[1] Wright printed *aften-stemn*. R.W
[2] Cf. pag. 181 l. 35. R. W
[3] *Sic MS.* A. H.
[4] Rasure after *mast* in *mastcyst*. A. H.
[5] Cf. pag. 182. l. 11. R. W.
[6] One *d* added above the line in the same hand. A. H.
[7] Cf. pag. 182 l. 21. R. W.
[8] Pag. 182 l. 26 we find *sceacline*. R.W.
[9] Cf. pag. 182 l. 27: *Safon* stæþ. R.W.
[10] Cf. pag. 182 l. 29. R.W. — *g* written over the line by the same hand. A. H.
[11] Read *pronesium*. Cf. pag. 182 l. 30. R. W.
[12] An error for *cataprorates*. R. W.
[13] The MS. has: sundgẏrd. A. H.
[14] Cf. pag. 183 l. 7. R. W. — *d* over the line. A. H.
[15] *s* over the line in the same hand. A. H.
[16] Cf. pag. 165 l. 41 and pag. 181 l. 18. R. W.
[17] *r* above the line by the same hand. A. H.

ANGLO-SAXON VOCABULARY.

Gustus, byrignes.
Tactus, æthrine.
Capud, heafod
Uertex, hnol.
Caluaria, heafodpanne.
Cerebrum, bɪægn.
Obcapud, foreweard eafod, *postex.*
Capilli, loccas.
Tautones,[1] bruwa.
Coma, feax.
Cesaries, pilos,[2] hær.
Crines, loccas.
Timpor, đunwange.   [oferbruwa.
Uultus, facies, uel frons, supercilium,
Intercilium, betweoh bruwum.
Cilium, bruwa.
Palpebre, bræwas.
Oculus, eage.
Lacrima, tear.
Corona, helm.
Pupilla, seo.
Gene, hagoswind.[3]
Barba, beard.
Mentum, cin.
Male, ceocan.
Maxille, cinban.
Mandibule, ceacan.
Auris, eare.
Nasus, nosu.
Cartilago, nosugrisle.
Internasum, neb.
Flegma, hrog.
Os, muđ.
Labrum, wæler.
Dens, tođ.
Ingua,[4] tođreoma.
Lingua, tunge.
Faus, weo.[5]

Palatum, mudes hrof.
Sublingua, uf.[6]
Toles, grynlas.[7]
Rumas, wasend.
5 *Gurgulium*, drotbolla.
Anteria,[8] æddre.
Gula, hracu.
Collum, swyra.
Ceruix,[9] hnoll.
10 *Humera*, eaxla.
Scapulus, sculdur.
Brachium, earm.
Ascella,[10] oxn.
Ulna, eln.
15 *Cubitus*, fæþm.
Manus, hand, duma.
Pugna, fysđ.
Pugilla,[11] gripe.
Palma, handbred, *uel salair.*
20 *Artus*, liþu.
Articuli minores, digiti, fingras.
Pollex, þuma.
Index, bycniend.
Salutaris, hæletend.
25 *Ipudicus*,[12] unewise.
Anularis, fingerlic.
Auricularis, earscrypel.
Ungula, nægel.
Truncus, bodig.
30 *Torax*, breost.
Mamille, tittas.
Pupille, seon.
Lac, meoluc.
Cutis, hid.
35 *Pellis*, fel.
Pulpa,[13] lira.
Uiscus, herđbylig.
Aruina, gelynd.[14]

---

[1] So the MS. Cf. pag. 157 l. 2. R. W.
[2] So the MS. A. H.
[3] Cf. pag. 157 l. 7. R. W. — *n* in *swind* added over the line. A. H.
[4] Read *gingiuae*. R. W.
[5] Cf. Bosw. pag. 89r. R. W. — The second stroke of *u* in *faus* is effaced. A. H.
[6] Cf. pag. 157 l. 28. R. W.
[7] *a* in *grynlas* above the line. In the line *grynlɑs*. A. H.

[8] So the MS. Originally *arteria*. A. H.
[9] *r* above the line. A. H.
[10] Cf. pag. 158 l. 28. R. W.
[11] Altered from *pugillas* in MS. A. H.
[12] Originally *Ipudicus*. A. H. — Wright printed *Pudicus*. R. W.
[13] Cf. p. 159 l. 8. R. W.
[14] *ge* and *y* above the line by another hand. In the line *lind*. A. H. — Cf. p. 159 l. 5. R. W.

Nerui, sina.[1]
Uertuba,[2] hweorfa.
Costa, ribb.
Dorsum, ricig.
Terga, bæc.
Pale, ricgrble.
Spina, hricgmeard.
Radiolus, spacau.
Spondila,[1] hricgrib.
Medulla, mearh.
Sacra spina, se haliga.[3]
Renes, æddran.
Lumbos, lændenu.
Genitalia, þa cennedan.[4]
Uirilia, d(a) wærlican.[5]
Uirilius, pintel.[6]
Calamus, teors.
Testiculi, herþan.
Uiscera, inelfe.
Meatus, utgong.
F . . em,[7] gor.
Anus, bæcdearm.
Nattes,[8] earsendu.
Femor, deoh.
Femina, inneweard deoh.
Coxa, þeohscanca.
Suffragines, hamma.
Genua, cnyowu.
Crura, sconcan.
Tibia, scina.
Surra, sperlira.
Talos, ancleo.
Pedes, fet.
Planta, fotwelma.
Calx,[9] ile.
Cor, heorte.
Sanguis, blod, *cruor mortuorum.*
Jecor, lifer.
Pulmon, lungen.

Splena, milte.
Fel, gealla.
Stomagus,[1] maga.
Intestinum,[10] inelfe.
5 *Omentum,* midhridre.
Disceptum i. reticulum, nette.
Uitalia, uiscera, renuncule, i. lundlagan.[11]

10   *NOMINA PISCIUM.*
Coetus, hwæl.
Piscis, fisc.
Pina, delfin, *uel*
Bacharus, mereswin.
15 *Ballena,* hran.
Porcopiscis, stiriga.
Usocus,[12] seolh.
Cancer, crabba.
Ysox, leax.
20 *Ostrea,* ostre.
Geniscula, muexle.
Sardina, hæring.
Platissa, floc.
Item et bubla.[13]
25 *Coclea,* weoluc.
Lucius, hacud.
Mugil, idem.
Tinctus, sliu.[14]
Lypus, bærs.
30 *Castorius,* befor.
Chephalus, heardra.
Murenula, æl
Anguilla, smæl æl.
Sartate, smylt.[15]
35 *Bisarius,* fiscwelle.

[*DE ARTE TEXTORIA.*][16]
Textrina, web, *uel telum.*
Liciatorium, webscealt.

---

[1] So the MS. R. W.
[2] Cf. p. 159 l. 20. R. W.
[3] Cf. p. 159 l. 23. R. W.
[4] Wright printed *cennendan.* R. W.
[5] *a* in *da* omitted in MS. A. H.
[6] Wright has: *uirilitas.* R. W.
[7] Two or three letters *effaced.* I think, the scribe wrote *fimum.* A. H.
[8] Wright: *nates.* R. W.
[9] An *i* blotted out before *x.* A. H.

[10] *num* in *intestinum* over an erasure. A.H.
[11] Added in another hand. A. H.
[12] The scribe means to say: *focus* or *phocus.* R. W.
[13] The reading of this line appears to be doubtful. Wright printed *Id,* etbubla. R. W.
[14] *l* over erasure. A. H.
[15] Cf. pag. 262 l. 4: *sardina,* smelt. R.W.
[16] Omitted in MS., but cf. p. 262. l. 6. R.W.

Fusum, splin.[1]
Radium, hrefl.
Cladia, wefl.
Deponile, wefta.
Nitorium, inspin.
Uertellum, hwcorfa.
Colus, wulmod.
Glomer, cliwen.
Conductum, gearnwinde.
Plumaria, byrdinge.[2]
Stamen, wearp.
Subtimen, awebb.
Pectica, flæþecomb.
Apidiscus, webhoc.
Scaphus, uma.
Tala, webgcreþru.
Claus, tæbere.[3]
Fila, dred.
Lana, wul.
Uellus, flis.

Leno, wifþegn.
Pedisequa, abra.[4]
Alibrum, riul.
Insubula, meoduma.
Ansa, hringe.[5]
Cingulum, gyrdels.
Andeda, brondreda.
Arula, fyrpanne
Sica,[6] tindre.
Scintilla, spearca.
Titium, brand.
Scindula, scid.
Lignarium,[7] algeweorc.
Finis, ærce.[8]

Fauilla, ysle.
Fumus, rec.
Accendilia, weocan.[9]

5   [*DE ALEA.*][10]
Alea, tæfel.
Calculus,[11] tæfelstan.
Aleator,[11] tæflere.

10   [*DE PLAUSTRIS.*][10]
Carpentarius, wænwyrhta.[12]
Plaustrum, wæn.
Rota, hweol.
Themon, þisle.
15 *Radii*, spacan
Canti, felgan.
Naualium, dinege.

   NOMINA HERBARUM, GRECE
20   *ET LATINE.*[13]
Scolonia,[14] ynneleac.
Anbila,[15] leac.
Acimus, hyndberige.[16]
Ambrosia, hyndhælepe.
25 *Artemesia*, mugwyrt.
Apollinaris, glofwyrt.
Cinoglossa, ribbe.
Septefllos, hymelic.[17]

30 *Astula regia*,[18] baso, popig.
Cardus, smæl þistel.
Cliton, clate.[19]
Cardamon, cærse.
Apium, merce.
35 *Botracion*, clufdung.[20]

[1] A metathese of *spinl*. R. W.
[2] Cf. p. 262 l. 18. R. W.
[3] Cf. p. 262 l. 25: *claus*, teltre. R.W
[4] Cf. p. 108 l. 28. R. W.
[5] Cf. p. 266 l. 23 ff. R. W.
[6] Cf. *isica* p. 266 l. 39. R. W.
[7] See pag. 266 l. 40. R. W.
[8] An error for *cinis*, æsce, I suppose. Cf. p. 266 l. 34. R. W.
[9] Cf. *cicindilia* p. 267 l. 1. R. W.
[10] Omitted in the MS. A. H. But cf. p. 267. R. W.
[11] Over erasure. A. H.
[12] *wæn* over erasure. A. H.
[13] *i. e.*: both Latin and Greek names of plants are here given with the Anglo-Saxon equivalents. This explains why there are so many repetitions of the same plant.
[14] Read *ascalonia*. Cf. p. 270 l. 24. R. W.
[15] Cf. p. 271 l. 9. R. W.
[16] *i* in *acimus* is written over in the same hand. A. H. The raspberry is still called a *hindberry* in the North of England.
[17] Cf. p. 136 l. 1 and Bosw. pag. 39g. R. W.
[18] Cf. p. 133 l. 30 R. W.
[19] Cf. p. 134 l. 3 and p. 9 l. 16. R.W.
[20] See Bosw. pag. 22b. R. W.

Anetum, dile.
Bobonica, hratele.
Acetula, ramese.[1]
Carix, segg.
Brassica, wuducerfille.
Acantan, beowirt.[2]
Camedus, heortclæffre.[3]
Ascolonia, cipe.
Catharticum,[4] libbcorn.
Camellea,[5] wulfescamb.
Arnaglosse, wegbrade.[6]
Cucumeris, hwærhwætte.[7]
Camesete, ellenwyrt.
Agrimonia, garclife.
Centauria, eordgealla.[8]
Coxa, þung.
Aconita, þung.
Aristologia, smerewyrt.[9]
Calitrice,[10] wæterwyrt.
Artemessia, tagantes helde.
Arthea, merscmealewe.[11]
Coantrum,[12] cellendre.
Brittanice, hæwenydele.[13]
Absinthium, weremod.
Buglosse, foxesglofa.[14]
Bacinia, berige.
Camemelon alba, se brada wulfescamb.[15] [lon.
Beneolentem, magade,[16] *uel camemel-*
Canis lingua, hundestunge.[17]
Batracion, clufwyrt.[18]

Cicuta, hymelic.[19]
Anteleuce, smæl þistel.[20]
Bucstalmum, hwit mægede.
Apasina, clife.
5 *Cerofolium*, enneleac.
Ahillea, colloncroh.
Culmus, healm.
Cicuta, wodewistle.[21]
Anchorum, mædere.[22]
10 *Apis siluatica*, wudumerce.
Conize, *lubestica*.[23]
Iris Illirica, hwatend.
Calcesta, hwite clæfre.
Fynuclum,[24] finol.
15 *Innulor*, eolone.[25]
Felicem, fearn.
Calcilum, iacessure.[26]
Lactuca, leahtric.
Cinnamomum, cymen.
20 *Furfures*, sifeða.
Leontopedium, leonfot.[27]
Felix minuta, eoforfearn.
Laterculum, beolone.
Ciclamina, slite.
25 *Lappatium*, docce, *i.* gledene, *i. carix*.
Gladiolum, secgg.
Malba, mealewe.
Gramina, cwice.
Genista, brom.
30 *Merculialis*,[27] cedele, cyrlic.
Millefolium, gearewe.

---

[1] Cf. p. 3. l. 20. R. W.
[2] Cf. p. 133 l. 5. R. W.
[3] Cf. p. 134 l. 30. R. W.
[4] Read *earthamus*. R. W.
[5] Read *chamaeleon*. R. W.
[6] *n* in *arna* corrected from *m*. A. H. — See p. 134 l. 13. R. W.
[7] Cf. p. 134 l. 10. R. W.
[8] *h* blotted out before *eord*. A. H.
[9] The first *r* over erasure. A. H.
[10] An error for *callitrichon*. R. W.
  uel al c
[11] The MS. has *Arthea*, *Mers* mealewe. A. H.
[12] Read *coriandrum*. Cf. p. 125 l. 40. R.W.
[13] Cf. p. 135 l. 26. R. W. — *h* before *y* blotted out. *l* after *y* struck out by the first scribe. H. A.
[14] Cf. Note 1 on p. 135. R. W.

[15] Cf. p 296 l. 10. R. W.
[16] Cf. p. 135 l. 7. R. W. — The second *a* in *magade* corrected from *e*. A. H.
[17] *n* in *hundes* inserted over the line. A. H.
[18] Cf. p. 295 l. 35. R. W.
[19] Cf. p. 295 l. 28. R. W.
[20] Cf. p. 295 l. 31. R. W.
[21] So the MS., not 'pistle'. Cf. Leo Gloss. p. 13 l. 36. A. H.
[22] Cf. p. 299 l. 29. R. W.
[23] Cf. Bosw. p. 43c and p. 301 l. 35. R W — *z* in *conize* corrected from *x*. An *e* is blotted out after *l* in *lubestica*. A H
[24] *y* corrected from *u* in MS. A. H.
[25] Cf. Bosw. pag. 25b. R. W.
[26] Cf. Note 6 on pag. 133. R. W.
[27] *Sic* MS. R. W.

Galla, galloc.
Erimigio, hyndberige.[1]
Mosilicum,[2] ragu.
Ebolum,[3] ellenwyrt.
Menta, minte.
Marubium,[4] harehune.
Beribalbum, greate wyrt.
Maliterre, elehtre.
Betonica, byscopwyrt.
Nasturcium,[5] tuncærse.
Fraca,[6] streawberige.
Calta, reade clefre.
Lattyride, libcorn.[7]
Fungus, swamm.
Lappa, clate.
Fenegrecio, wyllecerse.
Lagena, crog.
Lolium, ate.
Colocus, eofordrote.
Ferula, æscdrote.
Felicina, eoforfearn.[8]
Corimbus, ifigcrop.
Lugustrum,[9] hunisuce.
Delfinion, fugeleswyse.[10]
Gallitricium, wæterwyrt.
Eliotropus, sigelhweorfa.[11]
Malagma, sealf.
Gentiana, feldwyrt.
Mastix, hwit cwuda.
Heraclea, calcatrippe.
Eptafilon, gelodwyrt.

Hedera nigra, eordifig.
Erifeon, lidwyrt, *idem est ostriago.*
Herba iras, gorst.[12]
Swige, banwyrt.[13]
5 *Gallitrici,* stælwyrt [14]
Eicios,[15] haranspeccel.
Innule campane, sperewyrt.
Intula, walwyrt.[16]
Napis, næp.
10 *Pastinace,* wuducerfille.[17]
Nimphea, colloncroh.[18]
Oriathamum, colone.[19]
Rolon, carbe.[20]
Quinquenerbia,[21] ribbe.
15 *Tenedissa,* helde.[22]
Urtica, netle.
Toxa, þung.[23]
Quinquefila, hræfnesfot.
Origanum, ælere.[24]
20 *Sinfitum,* gallac.
Radiolum, eoforfearn.[25]
Prosopes, bete.
Prassion, hune.[26]
Titemallos, singrene.
25 *Ramnus,* þefedorn.
Juncus, risce.[27]
Sigsonte, stanmerce.[28]
Ocimum, mistel.
Ueneria, mædere.[29]
30 *Nereta,* sæminte.
Plantago, wegbrade.

---

[1] Cf. p. 295 l. 23. R. W.
[2] Read *mosiclum*. R. W.
[3] An *o* blotted out before *b*. A. H.
[4] *a* over erasure. A. H.
[5] *c* corrected above *t* by a later hand. A. H.
[6] Sic MS. R. W.
[7] *tt* corrected from *cc* in MS. A. H.
[8] Cf. p. 135 l. 10. R. W.
[9] So the Ms Wright printed *ligustrum*. R. W.
[10] Cf. the explanation of this word Bosw. 278. R W.
[11] Cf. p. 301 l. 10 and p. 133 l. 28. R.W.
[12] *Gorst* means: a bramble *erica, rubus*. Cf p. 300 l. 9. R. W.
[13] Cf p. 300 l. 1. R. W.
[14] Cf. p. 296 l. 19. R. W.
[15] Read *echion* or *cchium*. R. W.

[16] The scribe wrote: *walwr*. Cf p. 301 l. 3 and p. 301 l. 17. A. H.
[17] Cf. p 296 l. 5. R. W.
[18] Cf. p. 297 l. 6. R. W.
[19] Cf. p. 297 l. 15. R. W.
[20] *Rolon* seems to be an error for *robon* or *robos* = *orobos*. Cf. Cock. L. II. p. 380. R. W.
[21] The second *n* corrected from *u* in MS. A. H.
[22] The reading of the MS. seems to be an error for *tanaceta* or *tanacetum*. R.W.
[23] Cf. *Coxa* p. 296 l. 16. R. W.
[24] Wright printed *alepe*. R. W.
[25] Cf. p. 297 l. 22. R. W.
[26] Cf. p. 271 l. 17. R. W.
[27] Cf. p. 135 l. 16. R. W.
[28] Cf. p. 134 l. 36 and Bosw. p. 678. R.W.
[29] Cf. p. 300 l. 10 and p. 135 l. 15. R.W.

Uiola aurosa et uiola purpurea, banwyrt.[1]
Senecio, grundeswylige.[2]
Simphonica, beolone.[3]
Pissli, reosan.
Uiumum, fugelesleac.
Speragus, wuducærfille.
Sarpulum, brade leac.
Tribulus, gorst.[4]
Rosmarinum, feldmædere.
Obtalmon, magede.[5]
Ruscus, cneowholen.[6]
Raphanus, ancre, þæt is rædic.[7]
Thiaspis, lambescerse.
Rodinaps, ompre, docce.
Salsa, sure.
Tytymalosca, libcorn.[8]
Papauer, popig.
Umbilicum, berwinde.
Scilla, glædene.
Uictoriale, cneowholen.[9]
Perdicalis, homorwyrt.
Uiperina, nædderwyrt.
Pollegia, broðerwyrt, hælwyrt, dweorges dwostle.
Unnio, ynneleac.
Peucedanum, cammoce.
Semperuiuum, sinfulle.
Uermenaca, rædic.[10]
Pilogonus et sanguinaria, þæt is unfortredde.[11]
Uiola, simeringwyrt.
Stena, hæpcole.
Pentafilon, fifleafe.
Sandix, wad.[12]

Sinapdones, cærsan.
Sicalia, lyge.
Hierobotanum, hrætelwyrt.[13]
Brassica siluatica, wuducerefille.[14]
5 *Gramis birecta*, cwice.[15]
Solsequia, golde.
Rosmarina, sundeaw.
Gagantes, mugwyrt.[16]
Athee, sæminte.[17]
10 *Eliotropus*, sigelhweorfa.
Ruta, rude.
Iua, iue.
Sisimbrium, brocminte.[18]
Colatidis, singrene.
15 *Scilla et gladiola*, glædene.[19]
Scolonia, cipe.
Samsuhchon, cyningeswyrt.[20]
Uulnetrum, moldcorn.
Scippio, læfer.
20 *Uiticella*, weodubinde.
Poloten, crawanleac.
Scolimbos, se umbrada pistel.
Simphonia, beolone.
Senitio, syr, grundeswylige.
25 *Pastinace*, moran.
Lapadium, lelopre.
Malue herratice, geormenleaf.[21]
Canafel[22] *siluatica*, hænep.
Ebuli, ellenwyrt.
30 *Mentarium*, feldminte.
Cerefolium, cerfelle.
Sinapis, senap.
Abrotomum, sædrenewuda.
Peonia, peonia.
35 *Lubestica*, lufestice[23]

[1] See p. 137 l. 4. R. W.
[2] Cf. Cock. Leechd. III. p. 329. R. W.
[3] Cf. p. 134 l. 5. R. W.
[4] Cf. p. 299 l. 3. R. W.
[5] Cf. p. 296 l. 29. R. W.
[6] Cf. p. 133 l. 27. The plant still called *knee-holly* in the South of England.
[7] Cf. p. 135 l. 24. R. W.
[8] Cf. p. 298 l. 13. R. W.
[9] Cf. Note 6. R. W.
[10] Cf. p. 300 l. 13. R. W.
[11] The second *d* above the line. R. W.
[12] Cf. p. 136 l. 25. R. W.
[13] The scribe wrote *hratelwr̄*. Cf. p. 299. Note 16. A. H.

[14] Cf. p. 296 l. 5. R. W.
[15] Cf p. 297 l. 28. R. W.
[16] Cf p 295 l. 25. R. W.
[17] Cf. p. 299 l. 30. R. W.
[18] Cf. Cock. III p. 316. R. W.
[19] Cf. Cock. III p 328. R. W.
[20] Read *sampsychon*. R. W. — The second *n* in *cyninges* above the line in the same hand. The MS. has only *wr* instead of *wyrt*. A. H.
[21] Cf. Cock. III. p. 328. R. W. — *r* in *geormen* above the line. A. H.
[22] An error for *cannabis*. R. W.
[23] Cf. p. 297 l. 11. R. W.

Rosa, rosa.
Spimon, i. teuerion, brunwyrt.[1]
Ostriago, liþwyrt.
Muronis, cicenamete.[2]
Humblonis,[3] hegehymele.

Hulsida, camedris.[4]
Arciotidas,[5] fyrses berian.
Actis,[6] *i. sambucus,* ellen.
Elimos, i. lini semen, linsæd.

[1] Cf. Cock. III p. 316. R. W.
[2] Cf. Cock. III p. 318. R. W.
[3] Cf. Cock. III p. 331. R. W.

[4] Is *camedris* an Anglo-Saxon word?? R. W.
[5] Read *Arceuthides.* R. W.
[6] Read *Acte.* R. W.

X.

ANGLO-SAXON VOCABULARY,[1]

OF THE ELEVENTH CENTURY.

Deus omnipotens, þæt is god ælmihtig, se wæs æfre unbegunnen and æfre byd ungeendod.
Celum, heofen.
Angelus, engel.
5 Archangelus, heahengel.
Stella, steorra.
Sol, sunna.
Luna, mona.
Firmamentum, roder.
Cursus, ryne.
Mundus, uel cosmus, middaneard.
Tellus, uel terra, eorþe.
Humus, molde.
Mare, uel equor, sæ.
Pelagus, wid sæ.
Oceanum, garsege.
Homo, man.
Mas, uel masculus, werhades man.
Femina, wifhades man.
Sexus, werhad odde wifhad.

Membrum, an lim.
Membra, ma lima.
Capud, heafod.
Copita,[2] ma.
5 Uertex, hnol.
Cerebrum, bragen.
Ceruix, hnecca.
Collum, swyre.
Frons, forewearde heafod.
10 Nasus, uel naris, nosu.
Capillus, hær.
Capilli, ma.
Cesaries, fex.
Coma, loc.
15 Auris, eare.
Aures, ma.
Timpus, þunwenege.
Timpora, ma.
Maxilla, hleor.
20 Facies, ansyn.
Supercilium, oferbruwa.
Palpebre, bræwas.

[1] Although there seems to be little room for doubt that the fourth of the Vocabularies printed in the present volume is rightly ascribed to Alfric, yet in the known MSS. Alfric's Grammar is followed by a vocabulary which is differently arranged, and more condensed. This vocabulary is here printed from a copy in MS. Cotton, Julius A. II., in the British Museum. Another occurs in the MS in St. John's College, Oxford, already alluded to

[2] Read capita. Ma means ma heafdu or heafod in the plural number. R.W.

ANGLO-SAXON VOCABULARY.

Oculus, eaga.
Oculi, ma.
Pupilla, seo.
Os, muð.
Os, ban.
Medulla, mærh.
Labium, weler.
Labia, ma.
Dens, toð.
Dentes, ma.
Lingua, tunge.
Palatum, goma.
Guttur, þrota.
Mentum, cin.
Barba, beard.
Pectus, breost.
Cor, heorte.
Pulmones, lungena.
Jecur, lifer.
Fel, gealla.
Stomachus, maga.
Splen, milte.
Adeps, rysel.
Aruina, ungel.
Uiscus, innoð.
Uiscera, ma.
Ixta,[1] dearmas.
Sanguis, blod.
Caro, flæsc.
Cutis, hyd.
Pellis, fell.
Scapula, sculdra.
Dorsum, hryc.
Uenter, wamb.
Brachium, earm.
Brachia, ma.
Ulna, eleboga.
Manus, hand.
Digitus, finger.
Digiti, ma.
Unguis, nægl.
Ungues, ma.
Pollex, þuma.
Index, scytelfinger.

Medius, middelfinger.
Medicus, læcefinger.
Auricularius, earefinger.
Palma, handbred.
5 *Artus*, lið.
Latus, side.
Latera, ma.
Costa, rib.
Coste, uel costas, ma.
10 *Renes*, lendena.
Neruus, sinu.
Nerui, ma.
Uena, æddre.
Uene, ma.
15 *Femur*, þeoh.
Femora, ma.
Coxa, þeoh.
Clunis, hype.
Poples, ham.
20 *Poplites*, ma.
Genu, cneow.
Genua, ma.
Pulpa, lira.
Sura, spærlira.
25 *Crus*, sceanca.
Crura, ma.
Tibia, scyne, oððe scinban.
Talus, angcleow.[3]
Pes, fot.
30 *Pedes*, ma.
Planta, fotwylm.
Plante, uel plantas, ma.
Allox,[3] ta.
Alloces, ma.
35 *Ungula*, hof, oððe clawu.
Patriarcha, heahfæder.
Propheta, witega.
Apostolus, apostol.
Archiepiscopus, ercebisceop.
40 *Episcopus*, leodbisceop.
Diocessis,[4] *uel parochia*, bisceoprice.
Regnum, rice.
Abbas, abbod, oððe fæder.
Presbiter, mæssepreost.

---

[1] Read *exta*. R. W.
[2] e added above the line. R. W.

[3] Cf. p. 5 l. 23 and 161 l. 8. R. W.
[4] Sic MS. R. W

ANGLO-SAXON VOCABULARY.

Sacerdos, sacerd.
Clericus, preost, odde cleric.
Diaconus, uel leuita, diacon.
Subdiaconus, underdiacon.
Archidiaconus, ercediacon.
Monachus, munuc, odde an standende.
Monacha, uel monialis, mycenu.[1]
Anachorita, ancra.
Eremita, westensetla.
Nonna, arwurþe wydewe, odde nunne.
Cantor, sangere.
Cantrix, sangystre.
Lector, rædere.
Lectrix, rædistre.
Laicus, læwede man.
Coniunx, gemecca.
Coniuges, uel conjugales, gesinhiwan.
Coniungium,[2] uel matrimonium, sinscipe.
Castus, clæne.
Incestus, unclæne.
Pulcher homo, fæger man.
Formosus, wel gewlitegod.
Deformis, hiwleas.
Speciosus, uel decorus, wlitig.
Pater, fæder.
Mater, moder.
Auus, ealda fæder.
Abauus, þridde fæder.
Proauus, feorþa fæder.
Atauus, fifta fæder.
Filius, sunu.
Filia, dohter.
Soboles, bearn.
Liberi, ma bearn.
Familia, hiwræden, odde hired.
Frater, broder.
Soror, swuster.
Uitricus, steopfæder.
Nouerca, steopmoder.
Priuignus, steopsunu.
Filiaster, steopdohter.
Nepos, neua.
Neptis, bewimmen.

Altor, uel nutritor, fosterfæder.
Altrix, uel nutrix, fostermoder.
Alumpnus, fostercild.
Patruus, fædera.
5 *Matertera*, moddrige.
Auunculus, eam.
Amita, faþu.
Osculum, cos.
Propinquus, mæg.
10 *Affinis, uel consanguineos,[2]* sibling.
Amicus, freond.
Progenies, uel tribus, mægþ.
Generatio, cynren.
Gener, adum.
15 *Socer*, sweor.
Socrus, sweger.
Nurus, snoru.
Rex, cyning.
Sceptrum, cynegyrd.
20 *Regina*, cwen.
Imperator, uel cesar, uel augustus, casere.
Imperatrix, uel augusta, þes caseres cwen.
25 *Princeps*, ealdorman.
Dux, heoratoga,[3] odde lateow.
Comes, ealdorman, odde gerefa.
Clito, æþelinge.
Obses, gysel.
30 *Primas*, heafodman.
Satrapa, þegn.
Judex, dema.
Prepositus, gerefa, odde prafost.
Miles, uel adleta,[3] cempa.
35 *Exercitus*, here.
Populus, folc.
Procinctus,[4] fyrdinge.
Edictum, geban.
Uulgus, ceorlfolc.
40 *Congregatio, uel contio*, gegaderung.
Conuentus, uel conuentio, gemetinge.
Sinodus, sinod.
Dominus, uel herus, hlaford.
Matrona, fordwif.

---

[1] No doubt an error of the scribe for *mynecenu*. Cf. pag. 165. l. 26. R. W.
[2] So has the MS. R. W.
[3] Read *athleta* R. W.
[4] *Procinctus* means: (an army) prepared for battle. R. W.

Domina, hlæfdige.
Cliens, uel clientulus, incniht.
Empticius, geboht þeowa.
Uernaculus, inbyrdlinge.
Seruus, þeowa.
Ancilla, uel serua, uel abra, **wyln**.[1]
Custos, uel pastor, hyrde.
Puer, **cnapa**.
Puella, mæden, odde geong wifman.
Uirgo, mædenman.
Procus, wogere.
Sponsus, brydguma.
Sponsa, bryd.
Infans, unsprecende cild.
Uir, wer, odde wæpman.
Mulier, wif.
Maritus, ceorl þe wif hæfd.
Uxor, wif þe wer hæfd.
Uidua, widewe.
Senex, eald man.
Anus, eald wif.
Adolescens, iung man.
Iuuenis, iunglinge.
Paterfamilias, hyredes hlaford.
Materfamilias, hiredes moder odde hlæfdige.
Consiliarius, rædbora.
Consilium, ræd.
Contionator, gemotman.
Operarius, wyrhta.
Faber, uel cudó, smið.
Officina, smidde.
Ferrarius, isenwyrhta.
Lignarius, treowwyrhta.
Aurifex, goldsmið.
Argentarius, seolforsmið.
Erarius, mæslingesmið.[2]
Rusticus, æcerceorl.
Arator, yrðlinge.
Ars, cræf.[2]
Artifex, cræftca.
Opus, weorc.
Opifex, cræftca.
Architectus, yldest wyrhta.[3]

Piscator, **fiscere**.
Rete, nyt.
Amus, angel.
Uenator, hunta.
5 *Uenabulum*, barspere.
Auceps, fugelere.
Laqueus, gryn.
Trapezeta,[4] *uel nummularius*, mynetere.
10 *Nummisma*, mynet.
Sollers, mænigtiwe.
Iners, cræftleas.
Potens, mihtig.
Gigas, ent.
15 *Nanus*, dweorh.
Fidis,[5] streng.
Citharista, hearpere.
Cithara, hearpe.
Tubicen, bymere.
20 *Tuba*, byma.
Tibicen, pipere.
Musa, pipe, odde hwistle.
Fidicen, fidelere.
Fidicina, fiþelestre.
25 *Cornicen*, hornblawere.
Cornu, horn.
Fistula, hwistle.
Liticen, truð.
Lituus, truðhorn, odde sarga.
30 *Poeta*, sceop, odde leoðwyrhta.
Mimus, uel scurra, gligman.
Saltator, hleapere.
Saltatrix, hleapestre.
Mercator, uel negatiator,[6] mangere.
35 *Merx*, waru.
Pirata, wicing, odde flotman.
Classis, sciphere.
Nauis, scip.
Remus, roðer.
40 *Remex, uel nauta*, reðra.
Gubernator, uel nauclerus, steorman.
Proreta, ancerman.
Prora, þær se ancerman sit.
Puppis, steorsetl.

---

[1] Cf. p. 108 l. 28. R. W.
[2] So the MS. Read: cræft. R. W.
[3] Cf. p. 112, Note 1. R. W.

[4] Read *trapezita*. R. W.
[5] An error for *fides*. R. W.
[6] Sic MS. R. W.

ANGLO-SAXON VOCABULARY.

Anchoro,[1] ancer.
Antempna, segelgyrd.
Uelum, segl, odde wahreft.[2]
Clauus, steorsceofol, odþe nægl.
Medicus, læce.
Medicina, læcedom.
Arsura, uel ustulatio, bærnet.[3]
Potio, drenc.
Unguentum, smyrels, odde sealfe.
Malagma, clida.[4]
Salinator, sealtere.
Sutor, sutere.
Sartor, seamere.
Sartrix, seamestre.
Dispensator, dihtnere.
Diuisor, dælere.
Pincerna, byrle.
Caupo, tæppere.
Diues, welig.
Locuples, landspedig.
Inops, hafenleas.
Pauper, dearfa.
Egenus, wædla.
Fur, þeof.
Latro, seaþa.[5]
Profugus, flyma.
Exul, utlaga.
Fidelis, getreowe, odde geleafful.
Infidelis, ungetreowe.
Felix, gesælig.
Infelix, ungesælig.
Contentiosus, geflitful.
Iniuriosus, teonful.
Piger, sleac.
Inpiger, unsleaw.
Hebes, dwæs.
Parasitus, leas olecere.
Augur, wiglere.

Incantator, galere.
Ueneficus, unlybwyrhta.
Maleficus, yfeldæda.
Magus, dry.
5 *Phytonyssa*,[6] wycce.
Centurio, hundredes ealdor.
Persecutor, ehtere.
Theolenarius,[7] tollere.
Bonus homo, god man.
10 *Malus*, yfel.
Bonum, god.
Malum, yfel.
Dispendium, uel dampnum, hynd.
Iactura, lyre.
15 *Commodum*, hyd.
Res, þinge.
Anulus, hringe.
Armilla, beah.
Diadema, cynehealm.
20 *Capitium*, hæt.
Monile, myne, odde swurbeah.
Spinther, dole, odde preon.
Fibula, oferfenge.
Uitta, snod.
25 *Inauris*, earpreon.
Indigena, uel incola,[8] inlendisc.
Aduena, utan cuman.
Peregrinus, ælþeodig.
Colonus, tilia.[9]
30 *Agricola*, æcerman.
Messor, riptere.
Messis, gerip.
Aceruus, hreac, odde hype.[10]
Aratrum, sulh.
35 *Uomer*, scear.
Cultor, culter.
Jugum, geoc.
Stimulus, gad.

---

1 Read *anchora*. R. W.
2 *Wah-reft*, or *wah-rift*, means properly tapestry, or hangings for walls.
3 Burning, or cauterising, was one of the great processes of the healing art in the middle ages; and full directions for it are given in the old treatises on leechcraft.
4 Cf. Aelfr. Hom. I, 476. R. W.
5 Read *sceaþa* or *seaþa*. R. W.
6 An error for *pytonyssa*. R. W.
7 Read *telonarius*. R. W.
8 Read *incola*. R. W.
9 The compiler of this vocabulary has given a correct interpretation of the word *colonus*, as signifying a husbandman. See before, p. 111 Note 2.
10 These two Anglo-Saxon words are the originals of our modern words rick (applied to hay, &c.) and heap.

Aculeus, sticels.
Circus, uel circulus, widde.[1]
Funis, uel funiculus, rap.
Doctor, lareow.
Magister, mægister.
Scriptor, writere.
Scriptura, gewrit.
Euuangelium, id est, bonum nuntium, godspel.
Quaternio, cine.[2]
Planta, spelt.
Diploma, boga.
Enula,[3] pærl.
Pergamentum, uel membranum, bocfel.
Sceda, uel scedula, ymele.
Penna, feþer.
Graffium, græf.[4]
Pictor, metere.
Pictura, metinge.
Minium, teafor.
Gluten, lim.
Cementum, lim to wealle.
Sculptor, grafere.
Sculpture, græft.
Imaga,[5] *uel agalma*, anlycnyss.
Scalprum, uel scalpellum, græfsex.
Scola, scol.
Scolasticus,[6] scolman.
Pedagogas,[6] cildrehyrda.
Discipulus, leorningeniht.
Disciplina, lar, odde steor.
Doctrina, lar.
Miser, earminge.
Caecus, blind.
Claudus, healt.
Mutus, dumb.
Balbus, stamur.
Blessus, wlips.[7]
Surdus, deaf.
Debilis, lama.
Luscus, uel monoptalmus, anegede.

Strabo, scelgegede.
Lippus, suregede.
Mancus, anhende.
Infirmus, untrum.
5 *Eger, uel egrotdus*,[5] adlig.
Paraclytus, frofergast.
Paracliticus,[5] beddreda, odde se þe hæfd paralisin.
Leprosus, hreoflig, odde liedrowere.
10 *Lunaticus*, monadseoc.
Demoniacus, deofolseoc.
Energuminus, gewitseoc.
Morbus, adl.
Pestis, cwild.
15 *Amens, uel demens*, gemyndleas.
Rabidus, uel insanus, wod.
Sanus, hal.
Rabies, wodnys.
Incolomis,[5] gesund.
20 *Freneticus*, se þe þurh sleapleaste awet.
Frencsis, seo untrumnys.
Lethargus, uel letargicus, ungelimplice slapol.
25 *Lethargia*, ungelimplic slapolnys.
Uigil, wacol.
Uigila, wæcce.
Peruigil, þurhwacol.
Pius, arfæst.
30 *Impius*, arleas.
Justus, rihtwis.
Iniustus, unrihtwis.
Famosus, hlisful.
Fama, hlisa.
35 *Infamis*, unhlisful.
Infamia, unhlisa.
Largus, cystig.
Tenax, fæsthafod, odde uncystig.
Frugi, uel parcus, spærhende.
40 *Auarus*, gytsere.
Raptor, reafere.
Sagax, uel gnarus, gleaw.

[1] Cf. Bosw. 93r. R. W.
[2] Cf. p. 164 l. 1. R. W.
[3] An error for *gemmula*? R. W.
[4] The *graf* was the instrument used for writing on the table-book, answering to the Roman *stylus*.

[5] Sic MS. R. W.
[6] Read *pedagogus*. R. W.
[7] Cf. p. 8 l. 23 and p. 161 l. 39. R.W.

Sapiens, wis.
Insipiens, unwis.
Prudens, snoter.
Inprudens, unsnoter.
Astutus, pætig.
Stultus, stunt.
Sottus, sot.
Uerax, soðfæst.
Ueridicus, soðsagol.
Fallax, uel mendax, leas.
Falsidicus, unsoðsagol.
Testis, gewita.
Testimonium, gewitnys, oððe gecyðnys.
Sermo, uel locutio, spræc.
Cursor, rynel.
Superbus, modig.
Superbia, modignys.
Humilis, eadmod.
Humilitus,[1] eadmodnys
Uita, lif.
Anima, sawul.
Spiritus, gast.
Mors, dead.
Yris, uel arcus, renboga.
Tonitruum, þunor.
Fulgor, leget.
Pluuia, ren.
Nix, snaw.
Grando, hagol.
Gelu, forst.
Glacies, is.
Aer, lyft.
Uentus, wind.
Aura, hwida, oððe weder.
Nimbus, scur.
Procella, storm.
Nubes, wolcn.
Lux, leoht.
Tenebre, þeostru.
Flamma, lig.
Seculum, weorld.
Dies, dæg.
Nox, niht.
Mane, merien.

Uesperum, æfen.
Hora, tid.
Ebdomada, wucu.
Mensis, monað.
5 *Uer*, lengcten.
Estas, sumor.
Autumnus, herfest.
Hyemps, winter.
Uernum tempus, lenctentid.
10 *Uernalis dies*, lenctenlic dæg.
Hiemalis nox, winterlic niht.
Annus, gear.
Tempus, tima.
Hodie, to dæg.
15 *Cras*, to merigen.
Heri, gyrstan dæg.
Nunc, uel modo, nu.
Sursum, up.
Deorsum, nyðer.
20 *Calor*, hæte.
Frigus, cyle.
Ferfor,[2] mycel hæte.
Cauma, swaloð.
Siccitas, drugað, oððe hæd.
25 *Humor*, wæta.
Sterelitas, unwæstmbærnis.
Fertilitas, wæstbernys.[2]
Color, bleoh.
Albus, hwit.
30 *Niger*, blac.
Rubor, read.[2]
Fuluus, uel flauus, geolu.
Uiridis, grene.
Uarius, fah.
35 *Unius coloris*, anes bleos.
Discolor, mislices bleos.
Forma, hiw.
Fantasma, gedwimor.
Umbra, sceadu.
40 *Creator*, scyppend.
Creatura, gesceaft.[3]

Auis, uel uolatilis, fugel.
Aquila, earn.
45 *Coruus*, hræm.[4]

[1] Read *humilitas*. R. W
[2] *Sic MS.* R. W.
[3] An error for *gesceaft*. R. W.

[4] Cf. p. 322 l. 10 hremmesfot instead of hrefuesfot. R. W.

Miluus, glida.
Accipiter, heafuc.
Grus, cran.
Ardea, hragra.
Ciconia, storc.
Merula, þrostle.
Columbe,[1] culfre.
Palumba, wuduculfre.
Aneta, ened.
Alcedo, mæw.
Pauo, pawa
Olor, uel cingnus,[2] ylfette.
Rostrum, bile.
Mergus, uel mergulus, scealfra.[3]
Hyrundo, swalewe.
Passer, spearwa, oððe lytel fugel.
Turduh,[4] stær.
Ficus,[5] fina.
Auca,[6] gos.
Anser, ganra.[2]
Gallus, coc.
Gallina, hen.
Conturnix,[7] erschen.
Pullus, cicen, oððe brid, oððe fola.
Ouum, æg.
Nidus, nest.
Uespertilio, hreremus.[8]
Noctua, uel strinx,[9] ule.
Fulco, uel capum, hwealhafoc.[10]
Turtur, turtle.
Graculus, hroc.
Alauda, lauerce.
Parrax, wrenne.
Apis, beo.
Fucus, dræn.
Uespa, weaps.
Bruchus, ceafor.

Scabro,[11] hyrnete.
Scarabeus, scærnwibba.
Musca, fleoge.
Cinomia, hundes lus.
5 *Culex,* stut.
Scinifes,[12] gnæt.

Piscis, fisc.
Cetus, hwæl.
10 *Delfinus,* mereswin.
Ysicius,[13] *uel salmo,* lex.
Mugilis, uel mugil, mæcefisc.
Taricus, uel allec, hærinc.
Mullus, heardra.
15 *Tructa,* truht.
Anguilla, æl.
Fannus, reohche.
Rocea, scealga.
Canger,[14] crabba.
20 *Polipos,* loppestre.
Ostrea, uel ostreum, ostre.
Muscula, muxle.
Murena, uel murenula, myrenæddra.
Luceus, hacod.
25 *Belua,* egeslic nyten on sæ, oððe on lande.
Conchra,[15] scyl.

Fera, wildeor.
30 *Lupus,* wulf.
Leo, leo.[16]
Linx, gemencged hund and wulf.
Unicornis, anhyrned deor; þæt deor hæfþ ænne horn bufan þam twam
35 eagum, swa strangne and swa scearpne þæt he fiht wið þone myclan ylp, and hine oft ge-

---

[1] Read *columba.* R. W.
[2] So the MS. R. W.
[3] Cf. p. 258 l. 13 and p. 287 l. 5. R. W.
[4] Read *turdus.* R. W.
[5] Cf. p. 286 l. 8. R. W.
[6] The scribe means to say: *auica.* Cf. *aucarius* gosbafoc, p. 285 l. 2. R. W.
[7] So the MS. R. W.
[8] *Rere-mouse,* or *rear-mouse,* was the common name in English for a bat till a late period; and I believe it is still in use in some parts of the country.
[9] Sic MS. R. W
[10] Read *falco* and *wealhhafoc* instead of *fulco* and *hwealhafoc.* Cf. p. 132 l. 36. R. W.
[11] Read *crabro.* R. W.
[12] Cf. p. 261 l. 5 and p. 121 l. 30. R. W.
[13] Cf. p. 261 l. 32 and p. 293 l. 19. R.W.
[14] Sic MS. R. W.
[15] Read *concha.* R. W.

wundað on ðære wambe of deað.
He hatte eac *rinoceron* and
monoceron.
Griffus, fiðerfote fugel, leone gelic
on wæstme, and earne gelic on
heafde and on fiþerum; se is swa
mycel þæt he gewylt hors and
men.
Uulpis,[4] fox.
Taxo, uel melus,[1] broc.
Equus, hors.
Equa, myre.
Asinus, uel asina, assa.
Camelus, olfend.
Onager, wilde assa.
Mulus, mul.
Elefans,[4] ylp.
Ursus, bera.
Ursa, heo.[2]
Simia, apa.
Lutrius,[3] oter.
Fiber,[4] beofer.
Feruncus, mærð.
Mustela, wesle.
Talpa, wandewurpe.
Catlus, uel murilegutus, aut muriceps, cat.[5]
Yricius,[6] *uel erinacius*, il.
Glis, sisemus.
Mus, uel sorex, **mus**.
Uermis, wyrm.
Lubricus,[7] angeltwicca.
Ceruus, heort.
Cerua, hynd
Damma, uel dammula, da.
Hinnulus, hindcealf.
Capreolus, rahdeor.
Caprea, ræge.
Caper, uel hircus, bucca.
Capra, uel capella, gat.
Hedus, ticcen.
Lepus, hara.

[1] Read *meles*. R. W.
[2] *Heo*, she, i. e., the female of the bear.
[3] Read *lutra*. R. W.
[4] Sic MS. R. W.
[5] Read *murilegulus*. Cf. p. 120 l. 15. R. W.
[6] An error for *ericius*. R. W.

Porcus, uel sus, swin.
Scroffa, suga.
Aper, uel uerres, bar.
Magalis,[8] bearh.
5 *Porcellus*, fearh.
Bos, oxa.
Uacca, uel bucula, cu.
Uitulus, cealf.
Juuencus, styrc.
10 *Ouis*, sceap.
Aries, ram.
Ueruex, weþer.
Agnus, lamb.
Pecus, uel iumentum, nyten.
15 *Animal*, ælc þinge þe cucu byð.
Canis, hund.
Molosus, rydða.
Catulus, hwylp.
Dracus,[9] draca.
20 *Uipera, uel serpens, uel anguis*, næddre.
Coluber, snaca.
Rubeta, tadie.
Rana, frogga.
25 *Lacerta*, efeta.
Stellio, slawyrm.
Locusta, gærsstapa.
Sanguissuga, uel hyrundo,[7] læce.
Limax, snegel.
30 *Testudo*, se þe hæfð hus.
Formica, æmette.
Eruca, mælsceafa.
Peduculus, lus.
Pulex, flea.
35 *Cimex*, maðu.
Tinea, modðe.

Herba, gærs, oðde wyrt.
Allium, leac.
40 *Dilla*, docca.
Libestica, lufestice.[10]
Febrefugia, feferfugia.[11]

[7] Read *lumbricus*. R. W.
[8] Read *maialis*. R. W.
[9] An error for *hirudo*. R. W.
[10] Cf. p. 133 l. 25. R. W.
[11] Cf. p. 134 l. 1. R. W.

Simphoniaca, hennebelle.
Auadonia, feltwyrt.[1]
Aprotanum,[2] suðerne wudu.
Sinitia,[3] grundeswelige.
Feniculum, fenol.[4]
Anetum, dyle.
Electrum, electre.[5]
Malfa, hocleaf.
Malua crispa, symeringewyrt.
Polipedium, hremmesfot.[6]
Consolda, dægescage.
Solsequium, solsæce.
Sclaregia,[7] slarege.
Adriaca,[8] galluc.
Ruta, rude.
Betonica, seo læsse bisceopwyrt.
Petrocilium, petersilium.
Costa, cost.[9]
Epicurium, halswyrt.[10]
Millefolium, gearwe.
Tanicetum,[11] helde.
Saxifraga, sundcorn.
Citsana, fana.[12]
Calamus, uel canna, uel arundo, hreod.
Papauer, popig.
Absintium, wermod.
Urtica, netel.
Archangelica, blindnetel.
Plantago, wegbræde.
Quinquefolium, fifleafe.
Uinca, peruince.

Marubium, harhune.
Camiculo,[13] argentille.
Fraga, streawberian wisan.[14]
Ciminum, cimen.
5 *Modera*, cicenamete.[15]
Appium, merce.
Lappa, clate, odde clyfwyrt.
Helena, horselene.[16]
Sandix, wad.[17]
10 *Caula, uel magudaris*, caul.[18]
Cresco, cærse.[19]
Menta, minte.
Serpillum, fille.
Artemessia, mugwyrt.
15 *Saluia*, saluige.
Felterre, uel centauria, eordgealle.[20]
Ambrosia, hindheolað.[21]
Pionia,[22] ...
Mandragora, agene nama.[23]
20 *Pollegia*, hylwyrt,[24] odde dwyrge dwysle.
Organe, agene naman.[25]
Cardus, dystel.
Hermodoctula, uel tidolosa, crawan-
25 leac.[25]
Pastinaca, wealmora.[16]
Lilium, lilige.
Rosa, rose.
Uiola, clæfre.
30 *Agrimonia*, carclife.
Rafanu,[27] rædic.
Filex, fearn.

[1] Cf. p. 134 l. 11. R. W.
[2] Cf. Cock. Leechd. III p. 299. Read *abrotanum*. R. W.
[3] An error for *senecio*. R. W.
[4] Cf. p. 133 l. 18. R. W.
[5] Cf. Cock. Leechd. III p. 324. R. W.
[6] See p. 299 l. 18. R. W.
[7] The glossator means to say: *sclarea*. Cf. Cock. III p. 345. R. W.
[8] Cf. pag. 133 l. 20. R. W.
[9] *Costa* or *costus* denotes: the costmary *tanacetum balsamita*. R. W.
[10] *Epicurium* or *narcissus* a daffodil. Cf. p. 134 l. 22. R. W.
[11] Read *tanacetum*. R. W.
[12] Cf. p. 54 l. 42. R. W.
[13] Read *camicula* (Cock. Leechd. III p. 300) or *canicula*. Cf. p. 136 l. 13. R.W.

[14] Cf. p. 136 l. 15. R. W.
[15] Cf. p. 136 l. 22. R. W.
[16] See p. 136 l. 23. R. W.
[17] Cf. p. 136 l. 25 and 26. R. W.
[18] Cf. Cock. Leechd. III p. 317. R. W.
[19] Cf. p. 135 l. 8. R. W.
[20] See p. 135 l. 2. R. W.
[21] Cf. Cock. III p. 331. R. W.
[22] The Anglo-Saxon equivalent is omitted in the manuscript.
[23] 'Its own name,' *i. e.*, it has no Anglo-Saxon equivalent.
[24] Cf. p. 137 l. 2. R. W.
[25] Cf. *hermodactyla* p. 137 l. 3. R.W.
[26] Cf. p. 135 l. 28 and 29. R. W.
[27] Read *rafanum*. Cf. Cock. III p. 304. R. W.

Carex, sege.
Juncus, uel scyrpus, resce.[1]

Arbor, treow.
Cortex, rinde.
Flos, blosan.
Folium, leaf.
Buxus, box.
Fraxinus, æsc.
Quercus, uel ilex, ac.
Taxus, iw.
Corilus, hæsel.
Fagus, boctreow.
Alnus, alr.
Laurus, lauwerbeam.
Malus, æpeltre.
Pinus, pintreow.
Fructus, wæstm.
Baculus, stæf.
Uirga, gyrd.
Uirgultum, telgra.
Ramus, boh.
Glans, æcern.
Granum, cyrnel.
Radix, wyrtruma.
Pirus, pirige.
Prunus, plumtreow.
Ficus, fictreow.
Ulcia,[2] holen.
Populus, byrc.
Palma, twaltiga.[3]
Sabina, sauine.
Genesta, brom.
Cedrus, cederbeam.
Cypressus, næfd nænne Englisce[4] naman.
Sentes, þornas.
Frutex, dyfel.
Ramnus, fyrs.
Spina, þorn.
Uepres, bremelas.
Abies, æps.[5]

Olea, uel oliua, elebeam.
Murus,[6] morbeam.
Uitis, wintreow.
Salix, widig.
5 Silua, wudu.
Lignum, aheawen treow.
Ligna, drige wudu.
Truncus, stoc.
Styrps, styb.
10 Nemus, uel saltus, holt.
Desertum, uel heremus, westen.
Uia, weg.
Semita, pæð.
Inuium, butan wege.
15 Iter, sidfæt.
Patria, æþel.
Prouincia, uel pagus, scir.
Mons, dun.
Collis, hyl, odde beorh.
20 Uallis, dene.
Foenum, hig, odde gærs.
Ager, æcer.
Seges, asawen æcer.
Campus, feld.
25 Pascua, læswe.[7]
Pons, brygc.
Uadum, ford.
Pratum, mæd.
Aqua, wæter.
30 Gutta, uel stilla, dropa.
Stagnum, mere.
Amnis, ea.
Flumen, uel fluuius, flod.
Ripa, stæd.
35 Litus, sæstrand.
Alueus, stream.
Torrens, burna.
Riuus, rið.
Fons, wyl.
40 Arena, sandceosel
Gurgens, wæl.[8]
Uiuarium, fiscpol.

---

[1] Cf. Cock. III p. 342. R. W.
[2] Cf. Cock. Leechd. III p. 332. R. W.
[3] An error for: palmtwiga. Cf. Cock. III p 346. R. W.
[4] So the MS.
[5] Cf. Cock. III p. 311. R. W.

[6] Read morus R. W.
[7] This is the modern leasow — a word still in use, in some parts of England, in the signification of a pasture land.
[8] Read gurges. A whirlpool, called in Lancashire a weele.

Puteus, pyt.
Lacus, sead.
Latex, burna, odde broc.

Domus, hus.
Templum, tempel.
Aecclesia, cyrce, odde geleafful gaderung.
Angulus, hyrne, odde heal.
Altera,[1] weofod.
Liber, uel codex, uel uolumen, boc.
Littera, stæf.
Folium, leaf.
Pagina, tramet.
Arca, scrin.
Loculus, cyst, odde mederce.
Calix, calic.
Patina, huseldisc.
Crux, uel staurus, rod.
Candelabrum, candelstæf.
Cathedra, bisceopstæf.
Fundamentum, grundweal.[2]
Pauimentum, uel solum, flor.
Paries, wah.[4]
Tectum, þæcen, odde rof.
Fenestra, ehdyrl.[3]
Hostium,[5] duru.
Hostiarius, dureweard.
Janua, uel ualua, geat.
Arcus, uel fornix, bigels.
Columpna, swer.
Januarius, geatweard.
Clausura, loc.
Clauis, cæg.
Clauus, nægel.
Sera, hæpse.
Chorus, chor.
Gradus, stæpe.

Indicatorium, æstel.
Scabellum, sceamul.
Thus, stor.
Odor, bræþ.
5 *Turibulum*, storcyl.
Legula, sticca.
Regola, reogolsticca.
Lampas, uel lucerna, uel laterna, leohtfæt.
10 *Lichinus*,[7] blacern.
Cereus, tapor.
Cera, weax.
Candela, candel.
Munctorium, isentanga.
15 *Clocca*, belle.
Cloccarium, uel lucar, belhus.
Tintinnabulum, litel belle.
Compana,[8] mycel belle.
Uestis, uel uestimentum, uel indumentum, reaf.
20 *Alba*, albe.
Casula, mæssehacele.
Stola, stole.
Superhumerale, sculdorhrægl.
25 *Planeta*, cæppe.[9]
Manualis, handlin, odde handboc.
Cingulum, uel zona, uel cinctorium, gyrdel.
Caliga, uel ocrea, hosa.
30 *Fico*, sceo.[10]
Calciamentum, gescy.
Suptalaris,[11] swyftlere.
Tractorium, tigl.
Flagrum, uel flagellum, seypu.[12]
35 *Uirga*, gyrd.
Dormitorium, slæpern.
Lectum, uel lectulum, bed.
Stramentum, beddinge.

[1] An error for *altare*. R. W.
[2] So the MS. Read *bisceopsetl*.
[3] Literally, the ground wall. The Anglo-Saxons perhaps understood by a foundation the low wall of stone on which the wooden walls of the house were raised.
[4] *Wah*, or *wag*, was applied especially to the walls of a house, and was preserved in the later English *wawe*, or *waghe*.
[5] Ehþyrl, or eagþyrl, means literally an eye hole. A window was also called in Anglo-Saxon *eag-duru*, an eye-door.
[6] Read *ostium*.
[7] The glossator meant to say, I suppose: *licinium* = wick, or wick-yarn. R. W.
[8] Read *campana*. R. W.
[9] Cf. pag. 124 l. 31 and p. 328 l. 10. R.W.
[10] Cf. pag. 125 l. 24. R. W.
[11] Read *subtalaris*. R. W.
[12] A miswriting for *swipu*, or *swipe*. R. W.

Stragula, wæstlinge.
Sagum, hwytel.
Puluinar, pyle.
Syndo, scyte.
Fulcra, eal bedreaf.
Femoralia, bræc.
Perizomata, uel campestria, wædbrec.
Filum, þræd.
Fimbrium, fnæd.
Cappa, cæppe.
Pellicie,[1] pylece.
Colobium, uel interula, syric.
Manica, slyf.
Cuculla, cugle.
Pedulos, meon.
Commissura, clut.
Toral, roc.   [roc.
Mastruga, crusene, odde deorfellen
Tela, uel peplum, web.
Linum, fleax.
Lana, wul.
Glomus, cliwen.
Colus, distæf.
Fusus, spinl.
Textrinum opus, towlic weorc.
Latrina, gang.
Trabes, beam.
Tignum, ræfter.
Laquear, fyrst.
Cleata, hyrdel.[2]
Cymbalum, cimbal.   [ung-hus.
Refectorium, beoddern, odde gereord-
Tapeta, setrægl.
Matta, meatte.
Mensa, beod, odde myse.
Discus, disc.
Discifer, discþegn.
Minister, þen.

Lardum, spic.
Caseus, cyse.
Butyrum, butere.
Ouum, æg.
5 *Sal*, sealt.
Panis, hlaf.
Olera, wyrta.
Ceruisa, uel celea,[3] cale.
Medo, meodu.
10 *Ydromellum, uel mulsum*,[4] beor.
Lac, meolc.
Mustum, must.
Sicera, ælces cynnes gewringe buton
   wine anum.
15 *Manuterium, uel mantele*, sceat.
Cultellus, sex.
Artauus, cnif.
Uas, fæt.
Poculum, drenccuppe.
20 *Anaphus*, hnæp.[5]
Patera, bledu.
Cibus, uel esca, mete.
Potus, drenc.
Liquor, wæta.[6]
25 *Claustrum*, clauster.
Coquina, cycene.
Cocus, coc.
Ignis, uel focus, fyr.
Flamma, lig.
30 *Pruna*, gled.
An[dena],[7] brandisen.
Litio,[8] brand.
Olla, crocca.
Caccabus, cytel.
35 *Lebes*, hwyr.
Caro, flæsc.
Jus, brod.
Jutilis[9] *canis*, brodhund.

---

[1] Read *pellicia* R. W.
[2] The meaning of *hyrdel* is a hurdle, *crates*. R. W.
[3] Read *celia* R. W.
[4] Read *mulseum*. R. W.
[5] It is hardly necessary to remark that this word, which has occurred before, (see p. 123 l. 1. 2.) was the original of the later mediæval word *hanap*, also applied to a cup for the table.

[6] This is probably the origin of the modern use of the word *wet*, in such phrases as *heavy wet*, i e, strong liquor or drink, in tavern language.
[7] The scribe wrote *An, brandisen*. R W.
[8] Read *titio* R. W.
[9] The MS. has *Iutilis*, or *futilis* R.W.

Fascinula, awel.
Comedia, racu.
Daps,[1] sand.
Ferculum, bærdisc.
Uaeru,[2] spitu.
Assura, bræde.
Sartano,[3] isenpanna.
Frixorium, hyrstynge.
Coctio, gesod.
Coctus, gesoden, oððe gebacen.
Frustrum,[4] stycce.
Offa, snæd.
Mica, cruma.
Uestiarium, rægelhus.
Testamentum, cwyde.
Sigillum, insegl.
Cellarium, hyddern.
Cellerarius, hordere.
Molendenum,[5] myln.
Mola, cwyrnstan.[6]
Mel, hunig.
Uictus, bigleofa.
Pecunia, uel nummus, feoh.
Marsupium, seod.[7]
Pistrinum, bæcern.
Fornax, uel clibanus, ofen.
Pistor, bæcestre.
Granum, corn.
Farina, melu.
Bratium, mealt.
Acus, sifeþa.
Cribra,[8] *uel cribellum*, sife.
Furfures, gretta.
Fex drosna.
Anfora, sester.
Languena,[9] buc.[10]
Dolium, cyfe.

Cupa, tunne.
Utensilia, andluman.
Supplex, yddisce.
Aula, heal.
5 *Triclinium*, bur.
Solarium, upflor.
Turris, stypel.
Cardo, hearre.
Strigil, uel strigilis, horscamb.
10 *Risus*, hleahter.
Letus, bliþe.
Tristis, unrot.
Mestus, dreorig.
Famis,[2] hunger.
15 *Abundantia, uel copia*, genihtsumnys.
Letitia, blys.
Tristitia, unrotnys.
Jeiunium, fæsten.
Jeiunius,[11] fæstende.
20 *Pinguis*, fæt.
Pinguedo, fætnys.
Corpulentus, þiccol.
Macer, uel macilentus, hlæne.
Macies, lænnys.
25 *Grossus*, great.
Gracilis, smæl.
Longus, lang.
Breuis, sceort.
Magnus, mycel.
30 *Paruus*, lytel.
Fortis, strang.
Inualidus, unstrang.
Sollitus,[12] carful.
Securus, orsorh.
35 *Cura*, caru.
Securitas, orsorhnys.
Causa, intinga.

---

[1] Read *dapes*. Cf. pag. 126 l. 36. R. W.
[2] So the MS. R. W.
[3] Read *sartago*. R. W.
[4] Read *frustum*. R. W.
[5] Read *molendinum*. R. W.
[6] The *quern*, or stones turned with the hand to grind corn (the domestic mill), appears to have remained in constant use since the time of the Romans, and has fallen into disuse only very recently in some parts of the country.
[7] The bag, or purse, carried at the girdle, called at a later period of the middle ages a *gypsere* (in French *gibbecière*). The remains of this article are found not uncommonly in the Anglo-Saxon graves of the Pagan period.
[8] An error for *cribrum*. Cf. pag. 123 l. 8. R. W.
[9] Miswritten for *lagena*. R. W.
[10] What we now call a *bucket*. A pail is still called a *bouk* in Cheshire.
[11] Read *Ieiunus*. R. W.
[12] Miswritten for *sollicitus*. R. W.

Accusator, wregere.
Excusator, beladigend.
Accusatio, wregine.
Excusatio, beladung.[1]
Magnum, uel multum, mycel.
Nichil,[2] naht.
Aliquid, sum þinge.
Sella, sadol, odde setl.
Mento, felt.
Ulcea, garan.[3]
Scansile, stigrap.[4]
Corrigia, dwange.
Calcar, spura.
Antela, fordgyrd.
Postela, æfterrap.
Falere, geræðu.
Frenum, bridel.
Capistrum, hælftre.
Arma, wæpna.
Galea, helm.
Lorica, byrne.
Gladius, uel machera, uel spata, uel framea, ...[5]
Spatarius, swurdbora.
Armiger, wæpnbora.
Bellum, uel pugna, gefeoht.
Signifer, tacnbora.
Lancea, uel falarica, spere.
Uictor, sigefæst.
Uictoria, sige.
Acies, ege.
Capulum, hiltan.
Mucro, swurdes ord, odde odres wæpnes.
Sica, lytel swurd, odde handsex.
Asta,[6] *uel quiris*, sceaft.
Uagina, scead.
Manubrium, hæft.
Sagitta, uel telum, fla.
Fustis, sagol.

Uectis, stenge.
Arcus, boga.
Faretra, cocer.
Scutum, uel clipeus, scyld.
5 *Umbro*,[7] randbeah.
Funda, lipere.
Atrium, cauertun, odde inburh.
Fundibalum,[2] stæflidere.
Ciuitas, ceaster.
10 *Porta*, portgeat.
Ciuis, ceastergewara, odde portman.
Preco, bydel.
Oppidum, fæsten.
Castellum, wic, odde lytel port.
15 *Urbs*, burh.
Urbanus, burhwita.
Suburbanus, se þe sit buton dære berig.
Carcer, cweartrn.[8]
20 *Oppidanus*, se þe on fæstene sit.
Uilla, tun.
Uillanus, tunman.
Uillicus, tungerefa.
Ortus, orcyrd.[9]
25 *Ortulanus*, orcerdweard.
Pomerium, æppeltun.
Uiridiarium, wyrtun.
Horreum, bærn.
Sepes, hege.
30 *Fossa*, dic.
Puteus, pyt.
Fredium, worþig.[10]
Ferramentum, tol.
Securis, ex.
35 *Ascia*, adesa.
Terebrum, nauegar.
Terebro, ic borige.
Foramen, dyrl.
Uanga, uel fossorium, spædu.
Ligo, becca.

[1] Cf. Bosw. D. 40p. R. W.
[2] Sic **MS**. R. W.
[3] Cf. Bosw. D. 27r. R. W.
[4] The origin of our word *stirrup*. It might be supposed, from the form of the Anglo-Saxon word, that the Teutons originally used ropes for stirrups.
[5] No Anglo-Saxon equivalent is given. R. W.
[6] Read *hasta*. R. W.
[7] An error for *umbo*. R. W.
[8] Read *cweartern*. R. W.
[9] Read *hortus*. R. W.
[10] The origin of so many names of localities in England ending in -*worth* or *worthy*, as Wandsworth, Rickmansworth, Holdsworthy, &c.

Bipennis, stanex.[1]
Palus, pal.
Serra, snid.
Falx, sicol.
Falcastrum, siþe.
Acus, nædl.
Subula, æl.
Aurum, **gold**.
Argentum, seolfer.
Auricalcum, goldmæsline.[4]
Es,[4] bræs.
Stagnum, tin.
Plumbum, lead.
Uitrum, glæs.
Ferrum, isen.
Electrum, smyltinc.
Metallum, ælces cynnes wege.
Massa, bloma, odde dah.
Lapis, uel petra, stan.
Rima, uel fissura, cinu.
Marmor, marmstan.
Saxum, weorestan.
Silex, flint.
Gipsum, spærstan.
Gemma, gimstan.
Margarita, meregrota.
Calx, cealcstan.
Aries, ram.
Cimentum,[2] andweorc to wealle.
Cimentarius, wealwyrhta.
Rogus, ad.
Jocus, plega.
Locus, stow.
Omnis, ælc.
Omne, æl.
Totum, eal.
Prophanus, manful.
Exosus, uel perosus, andsæte.
Callidus, geap.
Simulator, hiwere.
Ypochrita, licectere.
Adulator, lyffetere.

Adulatio, lyffetung.
Deceptor, uel seductor, bepæcend.
Proditor, uel traditor, læwa.
Homicida, manslaga.
5 *Patricida,* fæderslaga.
Matricida, moderslaga.
Fratricida, broðorslaga.
Parricida, mægslaga.
Uulnus, wund.
10 *Cicatrix,* dolhswaþu.
Corpus, lic ægþer ge cuces ge deades.[4]
Truncus, heafodleas bodig.
Funus, lic, odde hreaw.
15 *Cadauer,* lic, odde hold.[3]
Feretrum, bær.
Uiuus, cucu.
Mortuus, dead.
Defunctus, fordfaren.
20 *Longeuus,* langlif.
Nobilis, æþelboren.
Presiosius,[4] deorwurþe.
Uilis, waclic.
Carus, leof.
25 *Odiosus,* lað.
Limen, oferslæge, odde þrexwold.
Sciffus, læfel.
Usceus,[5] ceac.
Peluis, wætermæle.
30 *Plaustrum, uel carrum,* wæn.
Rota, hweol.
Currus, uel basterna, uel hesseda, cræt.
Stabulum, fald, odde hus be wege.
35 *Caula,* loc.
Tugurium, hule.
Cella, cyte.
Mausaleum,[4] druh, odde ofergeweorc.
Monumentum, uel sepulchrum, byrigen.
40 *Sarcofagum,* durh.[6]
Elemosina, ælmesse.

[1] A stone-axe. The use of this expression, in the explanation of the Latin *bipennis,* is curious, as shewing, apparently, either that the Anglo-Saxons did use axes made of stone, or that they believed that the axes of stone, so often found in different parts of England, and usually ascribed to the Celtic population of the island, were really the Roman weapon designated by that name.
[2] Read *cementum.* R. W.
[3] Cf. Bosw. D. 37j. R. W.
[4] *Sic MS.* R. W.
[5] Read *urceus.* R. W.
[6] durh or druh cf. l. 38. R. W.

Donum, uel datum, gyfu.
Munus, lac.
Uter, byt.
Flasco, butruc.
Tentorium, uel tabernaculum, geteld.
Pretium, wurđ.
Corbis, uel cofinus, wylige, odđe meoxbearwe.[1]
Sportella, trænel.
Cartallum, windel.
Calathus, wearpfæt.
Pila, pilstoc, odđe pođer.
Loquela, spræc.
Uox, stemn.
Sonus, swæg.
Uerbum, word.
Pecten, camb.
Sopo,[2] sape.
Perna, flicce.
Sagene, sænet.
Follis, bylig.
Malleus, slege.
Lima, feole.
Scorium, synder.
Forceps, tange.
Carbo, col.
Forfex, sceara.
Nouacula, næglsex.
Cos, hwetstan.
Apricus locus, hleowstede.
Apricitas, hleowđ.
Edificium, getimbrung.
Palatium, cynebotl.
Basis, syl.
Postis, post.
Catena, racenteah.[3]
Compes, uel cippus, fotcops.
Bogia, iuc, odđe swurcops.
Manice, handcops.
Complex, gegada.
Poena, uel supplicium, wite.
Uincula, uel ligamen, bend.

Pellis, fel.
Cutis, uel corium, hyd.
Nebris, næse, odđe heorþa.[4]
Mercennarius, hyrman.
5 *Horologium,* dægmæl.
Gnomon, dægmæles pil.
Hospes, cuma.
Hospitium, gæsthus.
Hostis, uel osor, feond.
10 *Mansio,* wunung.
Thesaurus, hord.
Gazophilacium, madmhus.
Edax, uel glutto, ofereotol.
Ambro, free.[3]
15 *Gulosus,* gifre.
Procax, gemah.
Procacitas, gemahnes.
Obstinatus, anwille.
Abstinantia,[6] anwilnys.
20 *Uerecundus,* sceamfæst.
Impudens, unsceamfæst.
Pudicus, sydeful.
Inpudicus, unsydeful.
Interpres, wealhstod.
25 *Reus,* scyldig.
Damnatus, uel condempnatus, fordemed.
Peccator, synful.
Peccatum, syn.
30 *Sceleratus, uel facinorosus,* forscyldegod.
Scelus, scyld.
Facinus, uel culpa, gylt.
Adulter, forligr.
35 *Periurus,* forsworen.
Gybberosus, uel strumosus, hoferede.
Gibbus, uel struma, hofer.
Meretrix, uel scorta, myltestre.
Pelex, cyfes.
40 We ne magon swa þeah ealle naman awritan ne furþor geþencan.

---

[1] Cf. Bosw. D. 45n. R. W.
[2] Read sapo = σαπον. R. W.
[3] Cf. Bosw. D. 53x. R. W.
[4] Cf. pag. 125 l. 34. *næse* means 'tender, soft'. heorþa = heorta (hyd); cf. pag.

125 l. 34. Or = hearde *linum, stuppa?* R. W
[5] Cf. pag. 3.9 *Ambronibus* and note. R. W.
[6] So the MS. Read *obstinantia.* R.W.

XI.

GLOSSES, LATIN AND ANGLO-SAXON,

(FROM A MANUSCRIPT OF THE ELEVENTH CENTURY.[1])

Anhelantium, eþgiendra.
Agonista, oretmæcga.
Agens, wreccnde, drifende.
Auida, da gifran.
Aduehunt, ham wegad.
Amœna, da wynsuman.
Adstipulationibus, trymnessum.
Altrinsecus, on twa healfa.
Allegoriam, gebecnendlicum.[2]
Anagogen, gastlecum andgite.[3]
Autumo, estimo.
Affectum, hyldo.

Ammodum, ualde.
Argenti, seolfres.
Ac forficis, and sceara.
Aqueductum, wætergelada.
5 Aut flaua, dæs fealwan.
Antecessor, fore-iernend.
Austeritate, rednesse.
Austerius, rede.
Arroganter, gilplice.
10 Atrox, seo grimme.
Ambronibus, frecum gifrum.[4]
Apparatu, geþrece, s. adiutorio.

[1] It was a common practice with the Anglo-Saxon teacher to add in the Latin book he read in the schools an interlinear gloss, explaining the more difficult words, the meanings of which he was perhaps afraid of forgetting himself. Some one of them, in the glossary here printed, has taken evidently from several of these glossed manuscripts, the glosses, and placed them in alphabetical order, for greater facility of reference. It is preserved in a manuscript apparently of the eleventh century, MS. Cotton., Cleopatra A. III. It is especially valuable for the number of words it contains which are not found elsewhere.

[2] From becnian, beacnian to point out, show.

[3] Literally: intellectual understanding, knowledge. R. W.

[4] The word Ambro, in this sense, is not used by any pure Latin writer, but appears to have arisen originally as a sort of popular, we might say slang, word. The grammarian Pompeius Festus (lib i. p. 69, Valpy's ed.), says that the Ambrones were a people of Gaul who lost their territory by a sudden inundation of the sea, and afterwards lived by robbery and plunder, until they were crushed by Marius; hence it came into practice to call men who lived disgracefully Ambrones — "Ambrones fuerunt gens quædam Gallica qui, subita inundatione maris cum amisissent sedes suas, rapinis et prædationibus se suosque alere cœperunt;

Ad inportunum, to ðæm gemalecan.[1]
Ambronis, gifrum.
A predito, gewelegodum.[2]
Antidota, wyrtdrencas.
Accumulare, heapian.
Amminiculo, adiutorio.
Auri obriza lammina, da smæte gyldenan cladas.[3]
Arrogantiæ, gilpes.
Argumento, gleawnesse.
Argumento, orðonce, gleawnesse.
Ab inlecebrarum, from unalifendlecum.
Ambitiuntur, ymbhwyrfte, ymbhammene.[4]
Ad tantum, to swa micelre.
Adstipulatur, is sedende and cwedende.
Acies, scearpnes.
Anfractus, ðweorhfyro.
Alitis, auis.
Agapem, swæsendo.
Aporians, onscuniende.
Asperrima, ðære stræcan.
Affatim, genihtsum.
Abdicare, denegare.
Alpium, munt geofa.[5]
Ad sedandam, to gestillende.
Aduersione, drean.
A funesto, fram ðæm deadberendum.

Assertionibus, gesægenum.
Absurdum, dyslic.
Anicula, eald cwene.
Ambrosia, elesealfe,[6] *diuino odore*, þære swotstencan.
Abigerentur, pellerentur.
Aufugiunt, beflugan.
Atrocitas, grimnes.
Auerna, ancilla, mennen.
10 *A cimentario*,[7] from ðæm stanwyrhtum.
Alloquntur, tospræcon.
Animaduerti, to angitanne and to onenawenne.
15 *Apologitico*, aladiendre.
Ad liquidum, ad walan.
Attonitis, tohircniendum oðde hlosnendum.
A tortoribus, from ðæm tintergendum.
Agonizans, campiende.
A primæuo, from ðære frumildo.
Armenta, hryðera heorde.
Anachoreseos, on anacorsetle.[8]
25 *Adire*, gesecan.
Aliter, on ænige oðre wisan.
Autentica ueterum, mid ealdletre.
Adquisita, gestrined
Ad prelum, to winwringum.
30 *Astrusam*, secretam.

eos, et Cimbros, Teutonosque, C. Marius delevit; ex quo tractum est, ut turpis vitæ homines Ambrones dicerentur." At the beginning of the seventh century, Isidore gives the word in his Glosses with the somewhat more definite meaning of a waster, a consumer of patrimonies, a spendthrift, a rioter, a prodigal—"*Ambro, devorator, consumptor patrimoniorum, decoctor, luxuriosus, profusus.*" It was in this signification that it came into medieval Latin, where it was synonymous with *leccator*. Since Ducange quotes as his authority for it Gildas, Aldhelm, Boniface, and Geoffrey of Monmouth, it seems to have been a favourite word among the Anglo-Saxon Latinists. Cf. pag. 340 l. 2.
[1] Cf. Bosw. D. 294. R. W.
[2] *gewelgian* means: to make wealthy, to wax rich. R. W.
[3] *Obrizus* is a word belonging to medieval, not to pure, Latinity, and appears to mean simply, made of pure gold. The compiler of these glosses seems to have been rather imperfectly acquainted with the meaning when he added the word *auri*. The Anglo-Saxon gloss is not quite clear—perhaps it refers to the ornamentation of the dresses of people of high rank by thin plates of gold attached to them, as we know to have been the case among the Franks. (Cf. Bosw. D. 64v. R W.)
[4] Cf. *hammen* Leo Gloss. 113. R. W.
[5] This name for Alps appears to be a mere corruption of *mons Jovis*.
[6] This word, meaning literally oil-salve, seems rather a curious interpretation or explanation of the Latin word.
[7] Read *cementario*. R. W.
[8] Literally, on anachorite's seat, i. e., the position of being an anachorite, or hermit.

Aruina, rysle.
A triplicis, dæs þricfealdan.
Altor, fosterfæder.
Alexandriæ, ciuitatis.
Apologitica, fulfremedlicre.
Arcebat, bewerede.
Ad palatinas, to dæm palentlicum.
Ad tortas, to dæm won.
Archiatros, heahlæcas odde cræf-
 gan.[1]
Albo, nombee.[2]
Apostatare, æswician.
Anthletæ,[1] oretmæcgan.
Ad ultimum, da odnihstan.
Agonizarunt, ellencampedon odde
 þrowedon.
Arithmetica, rimcræft.
Adfinium, neahmaga.
Animaduerteret, da he ongitende wæs.
Ad suos libitos, to hira willum.
A fanatica, of dære godwræcan.
Astringentes, gebindende.
Amphitheatri,[1] plegstowe.
Ad argumentum, to gleawnesse.
Atrocisque, and grimmum.
Ad excubias, æt þæm weardsetlum.
Adglomerantur, togedeoddan.
Attonitis, stupefactis.
Adnecterent, gewræstan, geenyttan.
Abscedunt, hie ham ferdan.
Adultam, gewexen.
Abeuntem, on weg farendan.
Archimandrita, heahleareow.
Alimonia, edulia, alimenta, uictualia.
Aliorsum, elles hwider.
Affatim, genihtsumliee.
Ac maturescere, and ripian.
Adstipulabimur, we trymmad.[3]
Armonia, dream, swinsunge.
Aruspicum, galdorcræfta, odde hæl-
 sera.
Adibitis, gegearwedum.
Adibis, du gesecst.

Ab ingruenti, from þære onfeallendan.
Adgregatur, wæs togerimed.
Arbitraretur, wende.
A pithonibus, fram helrunum.[4]
Applaudunt, gulpan.
Agitabant, onstyredan, drifan.
Adgrederetur, he togeeode.
Adtori ...[5]
Adolesceret, wlancode.
Applicauit, tobefeold.
A circio, nordanwestan.
Abeo apud, to dan swide.
Adstridulæ, dære hristendan toswege.
Ac lictoribus, tinterdegnum.
15 *Aludentis*, dæm ton.
Amicula, das wæpelsan.[6]
Artubus, limum.
Ad prediolum, to hira sundorlande.
Arceretur, adrifen, bewered wære.
20 *Arida*, weosniendre.
Adacto, awrecenum, togedyddum.
Actionabatur, scirde.
Apice, hrofe.
Absit, wana sie.
25 *Ad inuentionum*,[1] to aneuawnessum.
Abhominentur, onscuniad.
Ac cauillantes, and tælende.
A puplicis, openlecum.
Assertionibus, sægenum.
30 *Adstipulationibus*, larum and trym-
 nessum, cydnessum.
Affectu, for hylde and lufe.
Antiæ frontis, loccas odde feaxeacan.
Assute, gesiwede.
35 *Ansatas*,[7] spreotas, ætgaras.
Aurea, da gegyldnan.
Atram, da sweartan.
Adultus, lung.[8]
Aries, wændoll.
40 *Apum, genitiuus pluralis*.
Almus, sanctus.
Auxilium, miniculum.
Accola, landleod, bugend.

[1] So the MS. R. W.
[2] i. e., name-book, an album.
[3] Cf. pag. 338 l. 7 and 343 l. 30.
[4] This Anglo-Saxon word is found elsewhere in the sense of a sorcerer.

[5] The writing is here obliterated by a stain.
[6] So the MS. Read das wæfelsan. R. W.
[7] *Hastas* is omitted. R. W.
[8] The MS. has *lung* or *lung* (?). R. W.

Adserto, defensor.
Arceri, uocari, gefetadne.
Admouit, facere jussit.
Adthletam, et amicum.
Ad fundum, grund.
Alcides, columnas.
Affectuose, holdlice.
Acriter, duriter.
Altum, magnum.
Atrox, horrens.
Abilina, hnutu.
Abies, æspe.
Absintium, wermod.
Ancilla, þinen.
Abortus, misbyrd.
Abunde, gerihtlice.
Ab Affrica, sudanwestan.
Ab borea, eastannordan.
Abditis, gehyddum.
Ab euro, eastansudan.
Ad euronothum, eastsud.
Aconita, dungas.
Accersiuit, ladode.
Ac dignariis, folegerefum.
Acisculum, pic.[1]
Achalantis, uel luscina, uel roscinia, nihtegale.
Accrabulus, joclis,[2] mapuldor.
Acrifolus, holen.
Acega, holthana.
Accearium, style.[3]
Acitula, hromsa.[4]
Acitelum, hransan crop.[4]
Accitulium, geacassure.[5]
Abilina, nomen regionis, uel hnutu.[6]
Actuarius, wræc.
Accitum, gefetodne.
Acegia, snite.
Acus, nædl, odde gronwise.

[1] A pick, for digging. *Aciculus*, or *acisculus*, is a medieval word.
[2] Cf. Cock. III pag. 337. R. W.
[3] Steel. *Accearium*, also, or more correctly *acciarium*, is not a word belonging to pure Latinity, as is the case with many which follow.
[4] Cf. Cock. III pag. 333. R. W.
[5] Cuckoo's-sorrel. It is remarkable how long plants have borne names connected with the cuckoo.

Ad caulas, to ewestrum.[6]
Adridente, tyhtende.
Ad pensas, to nyttum.
Adclinis, toheald.
5 *Adqueue*, and swilce.
Adseculam, þegn.
Adgrediuntur, geeodon.
Adtonitis, hlysnendum, tohirenien-dum.[7]
10 *Ad fasces*, to weordmyndum.
Aduocatus, dingere.
Adhibuit, geladode.
Adplicuit, gedidde.
Addicit, fordemet.
15 *Abellana*, haslhnutu.
Adfinitate, gesibnesse.
Applicabo, ic tolide, ic lide.
Anagliua, agrafene, odde aholede.
Aure tenuis,[8] smylte wedere.
20 *Auriga*, wænere.
Abenas, salas.[9]
Alueum, streamrace.
Agrestes, wudulice, odde wilde.
Anthletarum,[8] cempena.
25 *Agonis*, gewinnes.
Algosis, þæm warihtum.
Aluearii,[10] hyfe.
Ad incolatum, to eldeodignesse.
Ardui, þæs heanhades.
30 *Arcuum*, bigelsa.
Autumo, ic wene.
Ambronibus, dæm freeum.[11]
Aparatio, geþingio.
Auita, yldra fæder.
35 *Atauus*, fifta fæder.
Abnepos, feorþa sunu.
Aporians, onscuniende.[12]
Anatholi, dæs anatholes.
Actutum, sona.

[6] Cf. l. 11. R. W.
[7] Cf. pag. 341 l. 17. R. W.
[8] So the MS. R. W.
[9] Of course the Latin to this article is a vulgarism for *habenas*, reins.
[10] For *alveare*.
[11] Cf. pag. 340 l. 2. R. W.
[12] Cf. pag. 340 l. 23. R. W.

Acathemice,[1] dær cudwitlican.
Astromonia,[1] tungelcræftwisan.
Aductabant, ham feredan.
Afflatus, eacen, odde gelicnes.
Abolere, aieþan.[2]
Assantibus, brædendum.
A triplici cerebre, from þæm driefealdan brægene.
Affabiliter, luflice.
Attrite, gegnidenan.
Artus, lið.
Arcersiuit,[3] ladode.
Apertis, tobræddum.
Ariolorum, þa þæt womferht reniað, galdorgalera.
Alloces, da miclan tan.
Abegerunt, from adreofan.
Amiculis, gegerelan.
Amiculo, hrægle.
Aguste, dære ruman.
Augustum, brad.
Adtonito, dæm toduniendan.
Acri, grimme.
Atrocius, grimlicor.
Adsciti, gegaderade
Archipiratta,[3] heah sædeof.
Apicibus, stafum.
Adcisceretur, togeladede.
Atramentum, sweartnesse.
Ademptam, genumene.
Adplaudunt, gulpan.[4]
Antiquitus, gefyrn.
Agapem, ælmessum, swæscudo.[5]
Argutis, þæm swogendum, hleodregendum.
Arpagine,[6] slitunge.
Assentatrix, sio geþafigende.
Antiquariis, writerum.[7]

Antennarum, segelgyrda.
Antefatis, wærwordum.
Aurorescere, lihte.
Ansatas, speru.[8]
5 *Alumne*, fosterbearn.
Argutus, se gleawa
Anthlia, hlædhweogl.
Alis, fiderum.
Annuatim, gearlice.
10 *Actus*, gebæded.
Adultus, geweaxen.[9]
Anteritus, æreldo.
Aliger, fiderberende.
Arbina,[10] swind.
15 *Annua uota*, þa gearlican gehat.
Absidam, cleofan.
Arta, mid þa nearwan.
Alcidis, helcol.[11]
Amens, gemæd.
20 *Aprum*, eofor.
Altercaretur, cidde.
Astus, bred.
Astula, spon.
Auceps, fugelere.
25 *Argolicas*, da creaciscan.[12]
Acerra, fæte odde gledfæte.
Artis, nearewum.
Achile, scyld.
Aristis, eglum, odde earum.
30 *Arcibus*, hrofum, odde bigelsum burgum.
Allecto, wæleyrige.
Accidia, sleenes.
Acereatur, asurige.
35 *Acredinis*, surnesse.
Agiographa, *sancta scriptura*, halig gewrit.
Apocrifa, dyrngewrita.

---

[1] So the MS. R. W.
[2] aieþan or aiþan means: to cast out, to demolish. R. W.
[3] So the MS. R. W.
[4] Cf. pag. 343 l. 5. R. W.
[5] Cf. pag. 340 l. 22. R. W.
[6] For *Harpagine*.
[7] The word *antiquarius*, in the sense of a writer of books, a scribe, is found in Isidore, Orig., vi, 14. It seems at first to have been used especially for a copier of old books. See Du Cange.
[8] Cf. pag. 343 l. 35. R. W.
[9] Cf. pag. 342 l. 31. R. W.
[10] Read *arvina*.
[11] This seems to be a corruption of Hercules, *i. e.*, Alcides. Taken literally it would mean hell-coal.
[12] Greek; Greekish, in old English.

Ante postes, beforan hlidgeate.[1]
Apotheca, winfæt, winhorn.[2]
Armentorum, heorda.
Azimum, þeorf.
Adgrediar eum, ic hinc anginne.
Aceruum, muwan.
Attriuit, gebræste.
Audita, gefræge.
Anaglifa, heahgræfte.
Amulas, amelas.[3]
Argillosa, ðoihte.
Argilla, ðo.
Armamentarium, wæpenhus.
Aratiuncula, sulincela.
Aratrum, sul.
Aure tenuis,[4] smylte wedere.
Adpendes, ðu amst.
Abenas,[5] salas.
Adnitentibus, tillgendum.
Auruspices, galdorgaleras.
A cibis luculentioribus, fram swettrum mettum.
Abortiuos, beordorewelmas.
Auguria, hælsunga.
Adulta, geweaxen.[6]
Adtrectauerit, grapode.
Ad conficiendos, to gewyrcenne.
Azimos, ðeorflingas.[7]
Ac micare, and scinefrian.
Ansa, nostle.
Arula, fyrpanne[8]
Amita, fade.
Albugo, eagfleá.
Adacinum, ðagrenan.
Auricomus, gyldenfeaxa.

Affricus, westsudwind.
Agreste, wilde.
Agmen, werod.
Alba spina, hægdorn.
5 *Alcion*, isen.[9]
Alneta, alorholt.
Alga, war.
Alneum, fuletreow.
Albipedius, hwitfot.
10 *Alternantium*, stefnendra.
Alacris, snel.
Alucer,[10] swift.
Alitus, æþm.
Alium, leac.
15 *Alapiciosa*,[11] calwa.
Aluor,[12] swon, odde ilfatu.
Aura, hwioðan, odde oreþe.
Amens, æmod.
Amites, fugeltrio, ræftras.
20 *Amilarius*, mearh.[13]
Amiculo, hrægle.
Anos, hringas.
Andena, brandred.[14]
Aneta, ened, *a natanda*.
25 *Anetum*, dile.
Antena, boga.
Anxius, sorgende.
Annua, gerlice.[15]
Anaglifa, aholad.[16]
30 *Anser*, gos.
Antidotum, drenc, wyrtdrenc.
Anguila, æl.
Anceps, tweogende.
Antulus, ceacbora.
35 *Armilausia*, serce.[17]

---

[1] *i. e.*, before the back door: rather a curious and ignorant translation of *ante-postis*. ho
[2] The MS. has: win ærn. R. W.
[3] The *ama*, or its diminutive *amula*, was the sacred vessel used in the church to hold the consecrated wine, or anything else which had been consecrated.
[4] Cf. pag. 345 l. 19. R. W.
[5] Of course for *habenas*.
[6] Cf. pag. 347 l. 11. R. W.
[7] Cf. pag 348 l. 4. R. W.
[8] The fire-pan appears to have been used especially for warming the rooms occupied by the ladies. The Latin word is found in the Glossæ of Isidore.
[9] Cf. pag. 350 l. 7. R. W.
[10] So the MS. R. W.
[11] For *alopecia*, a disease which causes baldness.
[12] For *olor*. *Il-fetu* is given in Somner as an A.S. name for a swan.
[13] Cf. Bosw. D. 44z. R. W.
[14] Cf. pag. 329 l. 31. R. W.
[15] Cf. pag. 347 l. 9. R. W.
[16] Cf. pag. 345 l. 18. R. W.
[17] The sagum, or military frock, open at the sides, but covering the back and breast.

Aplustra, geredro.
Aporiamur, biod þreade.
Apiaster, swines mearce.
Apotasia, frætgengan.
Æsculos, bece.
Apricitas, hiw.
Alchior, isen.[1]
Aquilium, onga.
Arpago, awel, odde clawu.
Aquemanile, læuel.
Aciem, fedan.
Areoli, sceafas.
Armum, bog.
Asses corteas, liþerene tryinsas.
Apogium, eorþern.
Anguens, bremel.
Arrius, fag.
Ægit, fræc.
Archtoes, wænes disl.
Artemon, segl.
Arida, drignes.
Archiatros, heahlæcas.
Arcem, cnol.
A commentariis, fram trehterum.[2]
Ardebat, scan.
Ad expensas, to nyttum.
Arcersitus, fetod.[3]
Arcister, strælbora and scytta.
Aspera, unsmode.
Adsessore, fultemendum.
Atflarat, ansucop.
Aestuaria, fleotas.
Adfero, ic tobere.
Atqueue, ond swylce.[4]
Attacus, dora.
Auriculum, earwicga, odde dros.
Auster, sudwind.
Abellanus, hæsl.
Aucupatione, sætunge.
Ausus, gedyrstig.

Auehit, aweg aferede.
Auricularius, eargespeca.
Auspicentur, hælsadon.
Ausuræ, brucende.
5 *Aurocalcum*, grene ar.
Aucupium, yltwist.
Axredones, lynisas.[5]
Axredo, lynis.[6]
Adrogantissime, wlanclice.
10 *Axis*, eax.
Arcister, strælbora.
Aquila, earn.
Abdicatione, bescyrednesse.
Arpa, eargeat.[6]
15 *Abdictis*, serscrifenum.
Anser, hwite gos.
Atrium, cafertun.
Alacid, mæw.[7]
Apoplexia, færdeaþ.
20 *Accipiter*, goshafuc.[8]
Alietum, spearhafuc.[9]
Adticus, feldbeo, dora.[10]
Apis, beo.
Apostoma,[11] swyle.
25 *Ardea*, hragra.[12]
Apidiscus, webhoe.
Alibrum, reol.
Arteriaca, gebreedrenc.
Antropus, man.
30 *Amaracium*, sealscyn.
Anima, saul.
Adulterium, geligere.
Auditus, gehirnes.
Auris, eare.
35 *Album*, neodera welor.
Anterie, ædre.
Antheris, ædran.
Aruo, ierdland.
Articulus, lidincel, lytel lid.
40 *Anus*, bæcþearm.

[1] Cf. pag. 349 l. 5 and pag. 4 l. 39. R. W.
[2] *trehtere* or *trahtere* denotes: an interpretor, commentator. R. W.
[3] Cf. pag. 346 l. 12. R. W.
[4] Cf. pag. 345 l. 5 and pag. 7 l. 32. R. W.
[5] Read axedo, axedones. Cf. pag. 8 l. 9. R. W.

[6] Cf. pag. 258 l. 4. R. W.
[7] Cf. pag. 259 l. 6 and pag. 5 l. 16. R. W.
[8] Cf. pag. 259 l. 7. R. W.
[9] Cf. pag. 259 l. 9. R. W.
[10] Read *Atticus* or *Attica* (i. e., *apis*). Cf. pag. 261 l. 8. R. W.
[11] Read *apostema*. R. W.
[12] Cf. pag. 6 l. 37. R. W.

Ansa, hringe.
Apiastrum, beowyrt.
Alea, tæfl.
Aleator, tæflere.
Agapis, dægmete.
Attomos, mot.
Agontea, ellenlæca.[1]
Agen, beogang.
Altitudo, foder
Amadriades,[2] feldælbinne odde el-
  fenne.
Armilausia, serc.[3]
Apiarius, beocere.
Aggusti, þa yldestan caseras.[4]
Altrix, festermodor.[5]
Alumnus, fosterbroðor.
Anguis, wæternædre.
Abnepos, feorþa sunu.
Adnepos, fifta sunu.
Apatruus meus, mines fæderan þrid-
  da fæder.
Auena, wistle.
Albium, mele.
Agapa, ciepeman.
Anteriæ,[6] geotend, sinewind.
Anagrippa, anlicnes.
Acerua mors, ungeweaxenra deaþ.
Apotassia, fretgenga.[7]
Aquor,[8] geseunes.
Antulum, ceac.[9]
Aucupis, fuglere.[10]
Artemesia, mucgwyrt.
Arnaglosa, wegbræde.
Amitis, lorg.
Aucupium, fuglung.

Alnus, alr.
Amera, seal.[11]
Acinum, hindberige.
Apeletum, spracen.[12]
5 *Apio,* merce.[13]
Alium, gearleac.
Ascolonium, cipa
Alba cipa, hwite leac.
Arnaglosa, wegbræde.[14]
10 *Ambila,* leac.
Aurum, gold.
Aurifex, goldsmið.
Argentum, seolfor.
Æs, ar.
15 *Argentum uiuum,* ewicseolfor.
Aurifodina, gyldingwege.
Ascarida, hnitu.
Antile, heahfru.
Acris, from.
20 *Auriculum,* dros.
Anxie, geornlice.
Appetitus, gistung.
Astu, facne.
Aquile, segnas.[15]
25 *Adsciti,* gegaderade.
Arua, yrðland.
Aulœa, heal.
Annona, nonmete.
Apex, acumen.
30 *Angarizauerit,* ...[16]
Ad stauram, to wermete.
Accussor, wregend.[17]
Ascinaria, esulcweorn.[18]
Altilia, fuglas, odde amæste fugelas.
35 *Ad exitus,* to gelætum.

[1] Cf. Bosw. D. 25b R. W.
[2] Read *hamadryades.* R. W.
[3] Cf. pag. 349 l. 35. R. W.
[4] "Of Augustus, the oldest or earliest Cæsar."
[5] So the MS. R. W.
[6] Read *arteriæ.* R. W.
[7] Cf. pag. 350 l. 4. R. W.
[8] For *aquor,* no doubt.
[9] Cf. pag. 349 l. 34. R. W.
[10] Cf. pag. 347 l. 24. R. W
[11] The willow, still called the *sally* on the border of Wales and in the West of England.
[12] Cf. Cock. III pag. 345. R. W.

[13] Read *apium* Cf. Cock. III pag. 338. R. W.
[14] Cf. pag. 352 l. 33. R. W.
[15] In the book here glossed, the *aquila* were no doubt the Roman eagles, which the glossator explained as meaning an ensign or banner, *segn.*
[16] The Anglo-Saxon gloss has been erased, as though the compiler had found, after it was written, that it was erroneous.
[17] Cf. pag. 332 l. 1. R. W.
[18] *Cweorn* meant a mill, the stone of which is still called a *quern. Esul* meant an ass, and the *esul-cweorn* was merely a large quern stone turned by an ass.

Amphoram, amber.
Auulsus, aweg abroden.
Azyma, andbita, beorma.¹
Allegoriam, dæm gehiowendlican.²
Anagogen, dæm godcundan heahstan.
Adsuetæ, gewunade.
Ammodum, swiđe.
Ac priuata, and dære synderlic.
Arte plumaria, bleocræfte.
Argumento, mid ordonce.
Achademice, dære udwiottelican.
Accepto ferre, onfon.
Ariolandi, on wigbede to halsienne.
Antes, leaf.
Acutum, đa sona and hræde.
Ademptam, odbrogen.³
Ad infame, to dæm unhlisbærum.
A merulento, from dæm hlutrum.
Antes, owæstmas.
Actus, geneded.
Aprico, wearman.
Astu, facne.
Arceri, aweg adrifan.
Artius, fæstlicor.
Astu, gleawnisse and sceare
Arcebant, ut adriofan.
Abyssum, deagelnesse.
Adsciscier, to geladian and gecigean.
Arratam, beweddad.
Ausis, gedyrstignessum.
Astus, gebrægdnes, wærlotes.
Acta, genende.⁴
Anxia, geenegdu.
Acerra, rycelsbuce.
Anchile,⁵ scelde
Allectio, tyhtend.

¹ *Azyma* means *the feast of unleavened bread*. R. W.
² *gehiowian* means: simulare. R. W.
³ Cf. pag. 346 l. 30. R. W.
⁴ Cf. l. 20. R. W.
⁵ Read: ancile. R. W.
⁶ See before note 5 on p. 341. It is not clear, however, where the Anglo-Saxon writers found this name, as I am not aware that the Alps are called Mons Jovis by any ancient writer.
⁷ So the MS. R. W.
⁸ Cf. pag. 12 l. 28. R. W.

Adstipulans, fylstende and geecende and gewemende.
Alpes, munt iofes clifu.⁶
Aggerens,⁷ hlawum.
Ara, wiggebed.
Allusiones, plegan.
Abscidam, wort ic.
Articulata, rihtlidlicu.
Anhela, sworetendleca.
Achiuum, grece.
Ad instar, on gelicnesse.
Arbiter, doema.
Arsantes, đa gegendan.⁸
Adhesit, ætfealh and oncleofode.
Anfractibus, ymbgongum, bogetungum, hilcum.
Aceruos, muwan, hreacas.
Alterna, wrixliende.
Amplam, brade.
Actos, đa todrifenan.
Arcitenens, heofenhæbbend.⁹
Adunci, gebegdes.
Ambit, ymbgyrded.
Atomo,⁷ mote
Ambo, begen, butu.
Arguto, scearpe.
Arta, gefeged.
Auidæ, đære gifran.
Ad superos, to upwarum.
Adfinis, nehgebur.
Adictus, forslægen.
Aidoneæ, hearpen.¹⁰
Arcis, fæstennes.
A lanionibus, from hylderum.
Arrectas, upp arehte.
Æquis, gelicum.

⁹ This is another example of the singular blunders made by these Anglo-Saxon glossators, and of the state of learning exhibited in the ordinary schools. *Arcitenens*, the archer, was most probably, in the book from which this word was taken, used as an epithet of Apollo, but the writer of the gloss supposed it to be formed from *arx*, instead of *arcus*.
¹⁰ The Latin word is here probably a corruption of the Greek ἀηδόνες, nightingales.

Ascella, ohsta.[1]
Abortus, samboren.
Achariter,[2] baldlice.
Apporia,[3] inca.
Accedia, biternes.
Asserum, twiga.
Acinos, bergan.
Aplestia, oferfyl.
Aplesta, steorra.
Amarcas, lytle leas.
Agaso, horsdegn.
Alleh, grindle.
Appetitorum, andfang.
Armille, midlhringas.
Antela, fordgyrde.
Ascia, adesa.
Asula, iren hiord.
Auris, inneweard eare.
Auricula, utweard eare.
Articulus, handwyrst.
Auricularis, earfinger.
Aluus, mannes scaru.
Adeps, gelynd.
Albus, hwit.
Auidius, grionu.
Aureus, giolu.
Alcido, mæw.
Alauda, lawerce.
Auricinctus, goldfinc.
Ardea, hragra.[4]
Aranea, gongelwafre.[5]
Accipiter, pipat.
Acinum, maltwyrt.
Alucurus, uel thimus, hæd.[6]
Acidinetum, gorst.[7]
Alans, riscleac.[8]
Anniculus, steor.
Aries, weder.

Agnus, lamb.
Acrum, scencel.
Asellus, weorf.
Asinus, assa.
5 *Artocobus,*[9] smæl hlaf.
Aurippus, cwecesond.
Afficiar, genirwed and geenged.
Amaro, þa biteran.
Aruum, wonge.
10 *Ad oras,* to dæm gemærum.
Agitabat, styrede.
Acimum, maltwyrt.[10]
Ahiolatus,[11] frihtrung.
Anses, ræstras.
15 *Aplustra,* gerepro.[12]

Balus, isenfetor.
Bacidones, rædenne.
Bagula, bridels.
20 *Balsis,* teter.
Ballista, stæflidere, odde scaru, *i. machina bella.*
Barsterna, beer.
Baccinia, begir.
25 *Bacce,* bergan.
Ballena, hran, odde hwæl.
Barritus, ginung, odde raringe.
Battat,[13] ginad.
Basterna, cræt.
30 *Balbus,* wlisp.
Blessus, scomm.
Ballationes, cnop.
Basis, syl.
Balbutus, scom, wlisp.
35 *Bapys,* treuteru, bansegn.
Baruhina, bericge.
Balatus, blæted.
Barrulus, ragufinc.

[1] *Ohsta* means: the armpit, asella. R. W.
[2] Read: acriter. R. W.
[3] Read: aporia. R. W.
[4] Cf. pag. 6 l. 37. R. W.
[5] Cf. Bosw. D. 27r *gang-wæfre* and Leo Gl. p. 77, 55; p. 424, 16. *gange-vyfre.* R. W.
[6] Cf. Cock. Leechd. III pag. 329. R. W.
[7] Cf. Cock. III pag. 328. R. W.
[8] *Riscleac* means: allium. R. W.
[9] ἀρτόκοπος means: a baker. R. W.
[10] Cf. pag. 356 l. 33. R. W.
[11] A corruption of *Hariolatio.* The Anglo-Saxon teacher evidently, from his interpretation of *Ariolandi* in the preceding page, supposed the Latin word to be derived from *ara*, an altar.
[12] Cf. pag. 6 l. 14. R. W.
[13] Sic MS. R. W.

Beacita, stearn.
Berrus, bar.
Benigniter, medomlice.
Berruca,[1] wearte.
Berna,[1] higre.
Bettonica, aterlade.
Bicoca, hæferblæte.
Bitumen, lim.
Bile, ater.
Bitricius, steopfæder.
Birbicariolus, yrdling.[2]
Bitorius, wærna.
Blitum, clate.
Byssum, twin.[3]
Bratheas, goldfel.
Batilla, fyrscofl.
Bolidis, sundgyrd in scipe, odde rap,
  i. metrap.
Bothoma, embren.[4]
Bothonicla, stoppa.
Bobellum, falod.
Bona, scet.
Bon, scettas.
Boreus, eastnord wind.
Bobulcus, hridhierde.
Bouestra, radre.
Bocharius, mereswin.
Bofor, læmbis lieg.
Bombosa, hleglende.
Botrum, clystre.
Butros, geclystre.
Briensis, handwyrm.
Bux, borg.
Bulla, sigel.
Butio, cyta.
Bubo, uuf.
Buculus, rondbeag.
Burrum, bruun.
Badius, brun.
Bubalis, wesend.
Buccula, bucc.
Bunia, byden.
Bubla, flod.
Bratium, mealt.

Bradigabo, feldwuop.
Brucus, ceafer.
Bruncus, wrot.[5]
Bracie, cian.
5 *Byrseus,* lederwyrhta, odde lypen-
  wyrhta.
Balteum, gyrdel, odde belt.
Bata, mittan.
Blata, hrædbita.
10 *Barba,* beard.
Brachium, earm.
Butrus, hos.
Beta, birce.
Bibulta, billere.
15 *Bubullus,* swan.
Boratorium, byres.
Burdus, seamere.
Boua, oxa.
Batuitum, gebeaten.
20 *Broelarius,* edisewcard.
Butirum, butere.
Bajulat, bierd.
Bombicinum, sioleen.
Baratrum, pytte.
25 *Biothanatas,*[4] selfbonan.
Bisso retorto, hwite twine gedrawen.
Bombose, dære þutendan.
Baptisterio, fulwiht stowe.
Bucellam, cicel.
30 *Boias,* beagas.
Byrse, hyde.
Bis quingentenum, tuwa fiftig.
Bituminis, sciptaran.
Baiolabantur, borene weron.
35 *Bis senis,* tuwa healfum.
Basterne, scrides.
Bilance, twyfealdre heolra.
Basilisci, dære nædran.
Bratea fila, se gyldna dræd.
40 *Bullis,* bulum.
Bigis, cratum.
Bustis, byrgelsum.
Bucula, cealf.
Bombis, hlowengum, odde swoegum.

---

[1] Of course, an error for *verruca* and *verna*.
[2] The Saxon word is understood to signify a farmer, but whence the Latin word was obtained it is hard to say. (Cf.

pag. 9 l. 11 and 12. R. W.)
[3] The MS. has *twin* not *tyin*. R. W.
[4] So the MS. R. W.
[5] *Bruncus* seems here to be an error for *truncus.*

Bis terna, sex.
Buculam, stire.
Bellona, wælcyrge.
Bargina, ða elþeodigan oððe of elþeodisore.
Bariona, culfran sunu.
Buccis, mudum.
Bernis,[1] þeowenna.
Butra, dysige.
Barca, scip.
Brattea, se gyldna.
Buxeus, sio bixne.
Bombix, siolucwyrm, oððe sidwyrm, oððe loppe.
Bernam, þeowne.
Bachus, win.
Bellonia, wilde deor.
Bulga, bælge oððe bylge.
Barbita, beme.
Biblis, bocum.
Biblum, boc.
Biformis, twihiowe, swa swa bid healf mon and healf fear.
Batutas, þa gebeatenan.
Bulla, bula.
Bina, twegen.
Bachi, wines.
Bassia, cossas.
Biblos, bec.
Bis binis de fontibus, of feower stri- 30 colum.
Brumalia, þa winterlican.
Bratea, gylden þel arlægen.[2]
Brume, wintres.
Blandior, ic cweme.
Bellipotens, wiga oððe wigstrang.

Boreali, þære nordlican.
Borith erba fullonum, leaðorwyrt.[3]
Batis, stapul.
Bassis, stepe.
5 *Bagulum*, biotul.[4]
Bipinnis, twibill.
Baxus, sicel.
Buris, sulhbeam.
Boie, bogan.
10 *Blurus*, blere.
Busius, fealo.
Bruntus, wonn.
Balidus, hrut.
Berbigarulus, uel tanticus, yrðling.[5]
15 *Bardioriolus*, colmase.
Biturius, wrænna.
Bugium, hæferblæte.
Baptua, syring.
Betulus, byrce.[6]
20 *Betuleum*, byrcholt.
Bremium, earisc.
Beta, bete.
Brittanica, cuslyppe.[7]
Bimus, on ðæm æftran teame.
25 *Berbex*, rom.
Bouile, scypen.
Bamus, derscel.[8]
Bidubium, i. marra, bill.
Barbarus, walch, *siue* ungerad.
30 *Barbarismus*, misceweden word.
Brancos, hræcgebræc.[9]
Botrax, yce.
Bibliotheca, bochord.
Bicinium, twega sang.
35 *Bigamus, i. uir unius mulieris*.[10]

[1] For *vernis*, as below *bernam* for *vernam*.
[2] Cf. l. 11. R. W.
[3] Cf. Vulgata Jerem. 2, 22 and Malach. 3, 2. R. W.
[4] *Bagula* is found in the medieval Latin writers in the sense of a bridle. The Anglo-Saxon word *byotal*, more usually written *bytt*, is represented in our modern English by *beetle*, a wooden hammer used for beating clothes.
[5] Cf. p. 358 l. 11. R. W.
[6] Cf. p. 359 l. 13. R. W.
[7] Cf. Cock. III p. 323. R. W.

[8] A flail, or implement for *thrashing*, still called in some of our local dialects a *thrashle*.
[9] It appears that this strange Latin, and its Anglo-Saxon interpretation, mean simply a sore throat, or bronchitis. A Latin saint's life, quoted in Ducange, speaking of catching a fish and drawing it ashore, has the elegant Latin phrase, *Apprehende branciam ejus et trahe in siccum*.
[10] Nobody but the writer of an Anglo-Saxon gloss would imagine that *bigamy* meant having only one wife.

Calculus, ceale, numestan.
Cacabum, citel.
Cados, ambras.
Cartellus, windel.
Cartilago, næsgristle.
Carbunculus, spryng.
Camellea, wulfescamb.
Canis lingua, ribbe, hundestunge.
Caulem, stela.
Cataracte, þeotan, wæterþruh.
Caumeunie, eordreste.[1]
Caccabatus, hrumig.
Cauterium, mearcisen.
Capsis, cyst.
Carruca, cræt.
Cariscus, cwicbeam, wice.
Capitium, hod.
Camisa, ham, cemes.
Cappa, sciccing.
Castanea, cistenbeam.
Calta, reade clæfre.
Capisternum, cæfester.
Carix, secg.
Calcesta, hwite clæfre.
Cancer, hæfern.
Calciculium, iacessure.
Cacomicanus,[2] logþer.
Calomacus, hæd.
Castorius, befer.
Cænum, wase.
Carina, bytne.
Carectum, hreod.
Canti, felga.
Cassidele, pung.
Carrassinum, grene gærs.
Cappa, snod.
Calmetum, mersc.
Caliga, scoh.

Carbo, gled.
Carduelis, linetwige.
Caradrion, læwerce.
Cantarus, wifel.
5 *Callos*, wearras, ilas.
Carula, crawe.
Cartilago, grundsopa.
Caper, hæfer.
Catrum, sweard.
10 *Caldaria*, citel.
Cartago, brædepanne.[3]
Caragios, lyblæcan.[4]
Casla, heden
Carbasus, seglbosm.
15 *Cautionem*, gewrit.
Cauerniculis, holum.
Capestrinum, geflit.
Cassidis, helmes.
Cassida, helmas.
20 *Cassus*, fær.
Cassis, ned.
Casso, **idle.**
Cassium, helm.
Cœlutum, agræfen.
25 *Canthera*, trog.
Canda, boga.
Cardiolus, wudusnite.
Callis, pað.
Capistro, cæfli.
30 *Callus*, wear.
Calleo, fræfele.
Cartomo, lybcorn.
Carceria, bunan.
Cercylus, æsc.
35 *Censores*, gerefan.
Cesuram, gegangende.
Celox, ceol.
Cefalus, heardra.

---

[1] *Caumeunia* represents a medieval Greek word, χαμευνίαι, meaning a bed laid on the ground. It is found in the lives of saints. (Cf. pag. 10 l. 30. R. W.)

[2] Another medieval Greek word, κακομήχανος, i. e. *mala machinans*. The Anglo-Saxons had rather a leaning to Greek words, which perhaps originated with Theodore of Canterbury in the seventh century. (Cf. pag. 11 l. 11. R. W.)

[3] *Brœding-panne* is interpreted in the dictionaries a frying-pan; but in medieval Latin we find the word *cartagium* used for a measure of corn or bread, *un quartier*, which is probably the meaning of the word here.

[4] *Caragius* is found in the theological writings of Bede and in other medieval writers in the sense of a sorcerer.

Cente,[1] wilde gos.
Celatum, abracod, ut aþrungen.
Cessere, onwican.
Ceriacus, hornblawere.
Chori, eastannordan windas.
Circius, westnord wind.
Circinni, windeloccas.
Cirros, loccas.
Circinnatio, efesung.
Cicuanus, higere.
Cis, beheonan.
Cicuta, hymlic.
Ciconia, storc.
Ciscillus, heardheaw.
Cinoglosa, ribbe.
Citonium, godæppel.
Cicer, bean, pisan.
Corrumpitur, is gewemmed.
Clibosum, clifihte.
Clauia, borda.
Claua, steng.
Clustella, clusterloc.
Cladica, wefl, odde owef, odde claudica.
Clasis, flota, sciphere.
Classes, scipu.
Conpescens, gestillende.
Contribuli, gesibbe.
Confectum, geblanden.
Confectus, gewæged.
Colocinthidæ, hundesewelcan.
Commissum, gefremed.
Conticiscent, swigiad.
Consuluerunt, frunian.
Conpulsus, gebæded.
Colliridam, healstan.
Coccum, weolcread.
Conlato, ambehte.
Commeatos, sande.
Conuincens, oferstælende.
Codices, onheawas.
Corimbos, berian.
Consulo, ic frine.
Coaluissent, swornodon.
Concedam, lytisna.

Coniurati, gemode.
Contumax, anmode.
Confusione, gemengunge.
Concesserim, arecte.
5 *Conpar*, gehæplice.
Constipuisse, geswidrade.
Contos, speru, odde spreotas.
Consobrinus, geswiria, odde swustur sunu.
10 *Color*, ac.
Colyrus,[2] hæsl.
Cornua, crawe.
Corimbos, leactrogas.[3]
Colostrum, beost.
15 *Cassan*, beost.
Coclyas, wilocas.
Commentis, ordoncum, searwum.
Confici, gemenge.
Consobrinus, swor.
20 *Corax*, hrefn.
Cox,[4] hwetstan.
Cotem, hwetestan.
Coxa, þeoh.
Conpetum, tun, þrop.
25 *Colicus*, efordrote.
Coruus, cawel.
Conpagem, gegæderong.
Coituras, gegangendo.
Coaceruassent, geheapodan.
30 *Coagulum*, cyslyb.
Commolitis, þu forgrindesþ.[4]
Concisium, scelle.
Commentum, adoht.
Conderetur, geworht.
35 *Concis*, scellum.
Coleandrum, cellendre.
Colomate, hædcole.
Contagione, besmitenesse.
Conualuit, gewyrpte.
40 *Consors*, orsorg.
Comitauere, togelæstenne.
Commendabat, trymede.
Concussionibus, rædnessum.
Confoti, afedde.
45 *Conuenientes*, syrwende.

[1] So the MS. Wright printed: cante. Cf. pag. 12 l. 37. R. W.
[2] Of course, this is a corruption of *corylus*.
[3] Cf. pag. 364 l. 42. R. W.
[4] So the MS. R. W.

Conlisio, slege.
Coturno, wodhæn.[1]
Confutat, oferstæled, odde widflited.
Conpilat, stiled.
Cornu, cyste.
Concretum, gerunnen.
Conca, musclan scil.
Conectit, teldat.
Cocilus, ompre.
Conputatio, getæl.
Catalagus,[2] getæl.
Coniectorem, swefnreccere.
Commentarii, treahteras.
Conspersam, gecneden.
Conpingite, gefegad.
Crebrat, syfted.
Crepido, rima.
Crama, flete.
Crates, hegas.
Cragacus, styria.
Cuneus, wered, wecg.
Creditor, byrga.
Cuniculos, smygelas.
Culcites, bed.
Culcitatum, bed.
Cucumis, popig.
Culix, mycg.
Culini, cocas.
Curtina, wagryft.
Culter, seax, odde scyrseax.
Chameleon, æmete.
Cythropodes, þriefete, ricelsfæt.
Compendiis, gestreonum.
Contemtibiliora, þa hirwendlican.
Contra latrantes, wid þa beorcendan.
Crebrius, gelome.
Conuenire, gerisnian.
Calce, fyrsne, stige.
Cedes, wælfill.
Coluber cerastis, gerumpenu nædre.[3]
Conpulsus, gebæded.
Cognatio, mægburg.
Cibaria, mettas.
Cum recisset, mid type geascode.

Cingebant, ymbhæfdan.
Caricarum, ciscræpla.
Conualescas, þu getrumast.
Cerethi, eoredmen, rædehere.
5 *Carpenta,* isenum græftum.
Cemedes, ealdorman.
Cognomine, freonaman.
Concusa, onscacene.
Cerimonias, onsægdnessa.
10 *Chori,* mittan.
Cimentarii, weallwyrhtan.
Capitella, heafedstol.
Canti, felga.
Coluber cerastis, nædre gehyrnedu.[3]
15 *Conmute,* onwende.
Conparuit, ætiewde.
Creuere, gesion.
Contentus, danful.
Conderunt, gesettan.
20 *Commodarent,* borgedan.
Conpingite, gefegad.
Coarim,[4] handseax.
Condies, geswet.
Crepuerit, bærstlad.
25 *Conpescens,* gestillende.
Conplosis, flocende.
Ciciris, ilnetu.
Cautibus, cliofum.
Cucu, hleapewince.
30 *Columba,* culfre.
Cornix, crawe.
Cornicula, cio.
Cucuzata, irdling.
Ciaus, edischen.
35 *Cuculus,* geac.
Cuneus, heap.
Crabro, hyrnetu.
Curculio, emel.
Cicada, hama.
40 *Coetus,* hwæl.
Coclea, weoloc.
Cancer, hæfern.
Cladica, wefl.
Colus, wulmod.

[1] The MS. has hæ. R. W.
[2] Sic MS. R. W.
[3] Cf. the Anglo-Saxon Version of 'Epistola Alexandri' (ed. by Cockayne) fol. 121 l. 15. R. W.

[4] One may doubt whether the MS. has *coarim* or perhaps *coltrim* (= coltrum or cultrum?). R. W.

Conductum, gernwinde.
Claus, teltre.
Calatum, toweht.
Chomos, middangeard.
Corpus, lichama.
Caro, flæsc.
Crementum, sæd.
Caput, heafod.
Cephal, heafud.
Coma, feax.
Capilli, loccas.
Cerebrum, brægen.
Capitium, foreweard sweora heafod.
Cessaries, læ, wiffex.
Cilium, bruwa.
Corona, beag.
Columna, eal nosu.
Canini, hundlice odde tuxas.
Collum, sweora.
Ceruex, sweora.
Cubitus, fæþm.[1]
Cutis, sweard.
Costa, rib.
Cor, heorte.
Cruor, dead blod.
Calamus, þæt wæpenlice lim.
Cecum, blindþearm.
Cingulum, gyrdel.
Cinis, acse.
Cicindilio, sc . . . .[2]
Cotizo, ic tæfle.
Carea,[7] weax.
Candela, candel.
Carpentarius, wængerefa.
Ceruical, heafedbolster.
Capsula, hacele.
Castaneus, cistenbeam.
Cortix, rind.

Cerefolium, ceruille.
Cudo, anfilte.
Carbo, col.
Calmum, windelstreow.
5 *Coluber*, snaca, odde nædre.
Cornas, geap.
Caballus, hengest.
Camellum, oluend.
Caprea, ra.
10 *Capreola*, rage.
Capra, gat.
Capri, hæferes.
Calcar, spura.
Cuspis, gad.
15 *Catesta*, gæled.
Colonus, gebyr.[3]
Cistula, spirte.
Camos,[4] swol.
Capitium, heafodsmæl.
20 *Condicio*, redin.
Clauicularius, cægbora.
Cicur,[5] mandwære.
Crocus, geolu.
Crocea, gioluwre.
25 *Calbuus*,[6] calo.
Camara, hrof.
Catinus, scutel.
Caseum, cyse.
Calmaria, cealre.
30 *Calmum*, molegn.
Caluiale, cealerbriw.
Coclear, cucelere.
Clerius[7] *cibus*, wyrtmete.
Cœlia, ealo.
35 *Ceruisa*,[7] swatan.
Cœna, æfenmete.
Cucumus, popi.
Ciatum, steap.

---

[1] The glossator has here apparently mistaken the Latin word, and supposed it referred to a measure, instead of a limb.
[2] Defaced in the MS. Cf. pag. 121 l. 25: *Cicindela se glisigenda wibba*.
R. W.
[3] The origin of the modern word *boor*, a countryman.
[4] Cf. pag. 11 l. 45 and pag. 12 l. 45.
R. W.

[5] *Cicurius* is given in Ducange as a medieval Latin word bearing the meaning of prudent, gentle, placid, mild, etc.
[6] For *calvus*. These clerical errors in this document are too numerous to mention; we have, below, *cacobatus* for *cacabatus* (blackened with soot), *celeps* for *calebs*, etc.
[7] So the MS. R. W.

Cuba, tunne.
Calamidis, godweb.
Calor, hæte.
Choors, tun.
Chorus, þreat.
Carpella, sadelboga.
Cornicem, hornbora.
Coquina, cycene.
Cacobatus, hrum.[1]
Comicus, scop.
Celeps, hægsteald man.
Cartilago, leaces heafod.
Cliens, geþofta.
Congeries, heap.
Crura, scancan.
Commissuram, gefog.
Concilio, gemote.
Comminatus, beotiende.
Coffinos, manda.
Commutatio, gewrixle.
Conducere, aheran.
Conuentione, gemote.
Comminatus, beotode.
Conquirerunt, ætsamne sohtan.
Ceruical, wangere, heafod p̄.[2]
Contubernium, gadorwiste.
Cautionem, gewrit.
Cahus,[3] dwolma.
Cribraret, syfte.
Conuiciebant, leoncwidedon.
Confertam, getrummen.
Coagitatum, gehrysed.
Cum emulo, mid widerweardum.
Calcaribus, spurum.
Calcar, spura.
Circentium, hringseta.
Carene, cerenes, oððe hunigteares.
Coxarum, bana.
Catalectico, dy metercundum.
Cronographorum, tidwritera.

Cittis, uilmenum, æpelscealum ymb da cyrnlu.
Contecta, bedeat.
Cercilo, scipe.[4]
5 *Calones,* wuderas.
Clientes, ðegnhyssas.
Clientele, þegnscole.
Cum lixarum, mid wæterbererum.
Collationes, ymbeahtas.
10 *Conflictu,* gefeohte.
Collegio, winescipe.
Curtinarum, wagryfta.
Comminiscimur, resiad, oððe somud mengad we.[5]
15 *Crepitantes,* ræscettende.
Crepitarent, ræscettan.
Concessum ...
Congeries, gesamnung.
Confectio, geregnong.
20 *Cauterio,* hoce.
Cernua, da niowelan.
Cautibus, stanum, oððe snyringum.
Cautes, clifstanas.
Collario, sale.
25 *Contionatorum,* gemotmanna.
Consulatus, gerefscipe.
Corbibus, caulum.
Cauponibus, winbryttum.
Commendenda, to bebeodenne.
30 *Crates,* hyrdlas.
Cuniculum, grep.
Carismatum, gifena.
Conspicatur, sceawode.
Conflictibus, geflitum.
35 *Cleri,* biscophyrede.[6]
Cassibus, wyrdum.
Cataplasma, læcedomnessa, oððe sealfe.
Cibbo, copse.
40 *Chaldeorum,* tungeleræftum.[7]

---

[1] Cf. Bosw. D. 38c. R. W.
[2] Cf. pag. 368 l. 35. R. W.
[3] i. e. chaus or chaos. Cf. pag. 12 l. 43. R. W.
[4] Cf. pag. 12 l. 25 and pag. 363 l. 34. R. W.
[5] Two words which follow this are unreadable through a damage of the vellum.
[6] The bishop's flock, or family, a rather picturesque expression for the clergy.
[7] Of course the writer from whom this gloss was taken used the word Chaldæi in the sense of enchanters.

Cloacarum, flodena.
Cuparum, tunnena.
Callositas, unsmednes, odde wearrihtnes.
Commercia,[1] ceapunge.
Ceni,[1] wasan.
Conibentia,[2] hæbbenga.
Consummatim, scyndendlice.
Cernuas, niole, odde hnifolcrumbe.[3]
Cleratis, clerochade.
Curbo, gebegde.
Condito, gerecanade.
Culine, cylene.
Circumquaque, ymb dæt.
Calcatur, teled is.
Calamitosa, dy hearmlican.
Crustulis, healstanum.
Crustis, herstinghlafum.
Crasso, dy fættan.
Corbos, caulas.
Catecizatus,[4] gecristnad.
Caccabatum, berumad.[5]
Casus, gelimp.
Clanculis, dæm diglum.
Catapultas, speru, boltas.
Cœlibes, hægsteald men.[6]
Cymiterio, byrgenstowe.
Caraxabimus,[7] writad.
Clatros, pearrocum.
Clatrorum, pearroca.
Castarum, wita cyn.
Cauillatione, geslitgliwe.[8]
Caracteribus, angelicnessum, odde stæfwriterum.

Citra pontum, ofer sæ.
Carybdibus, swelgendnessum.
Cirris, loceum.
Consparsione, gecynde.
5 *Competali*, æt þæm wega gelætum wæran
Calamitosam, þæt earme.
Comitiales, gebræcsioce.[9]
Cantando, galdor galende.
10 *Capulo tenus*, od hielt.
Conspiratio, facengecwis,[10] odde andwyrding.
Crista, cambihte, camb on hætte odde on helme.
15 *Congrediens*, feohtende.
Cum fratrueli, mid brodorsuna.
Colerata, getelged, odde gedeagod.
Conquilii, telges.
Cum infami eulogio, mid þy unæ-
20 þelan gidde.
Conopio, nette, fleogryfte.
Cedunt, rumad, steppad.
Cauannarum,[11] ulena.
Confer, forgeaf.
25 *Castalidas nymphas*, dunælfa.[12]
Carpere, telan.
Cultum, gyld.
Conpellens, gretende.
Consanguine, þære gesibban.
30 *Confertur*, widmeten is.
Censebat, scop.
Cartis,[13] bocum.
Certantes, flitende.
Certamine, on geflite.

---

[1] So has the MS. R. W.
[2] Read: *cohibentia*. R. W.
[3] Cf. Bosw. D. 37d. R. W.
[4] Christened, because catechising was a principal part of the ceremony.
[5] Cf. pag. 370 l. 9. R. W.
[6] Cf. pag. 370 l. 11. R. W.
[7] *Charaxare*, from the Greek, was used by the medieval Latin writers in the sense of to write. It occurs in Prudentius.
[8] Cf. pag. 10 l. 24. R. W
[9] The Anglo-Saxon word denotes: a frantic man, phreneticus. R. W.
[10] The words which follow are in a rather later hand.

[11] *Cavanna*, or *cavannus*, in the sense of an owl, is a word belonging to medieval Latin, and is found in the Anglo-Saxon writers, such as Aldhelm. It is represented in old French by the word *chouan*.
[12] Such glosses as this furnish curious illustrations of the Anglo-Saxon notions of elves or fairies; but it implies some confusion of ideas to call the Castalides mountain elves. (Cf. pag. 189 l. 9. R. W.)
[13] *Chartis*; the Anglo-Saxons called everything written in a separate form, a book. A written leaf was a book.

Consternati, ofercymene.
Clades, adla.
Conglobatur, somnode.
Cnues, eldo.
Cuderet, smiðode, oððe gescop.
Cararit, ielde.
Capisterium, hridder.
Chaliben, isern.
Chalibis, irenum.
Concinnant, heapedan.
Crudescentes, þæt þa swidfeormende.
Contrita, ofermened.
Cartula, boc.
Curam, læcedom.
Cipporum, cospa.
Coenobium, mynsterlif.
Centauri, þæs centaures.
Clancula, þa diglan.
Clanculis, mid diglum.
Catax, sio healte, oððe healt.
Calcis, limes.
Callosi, hreofe, oððe wearrihte.
Consulta, rædas.
Conpeta clausa, þa belocenan wega gelæta.
Classica, swege, oððe þa herelican.
Commentis, trahte oððe trahtaðum.
Carolios, unhiere.
Cluris,[1] æþelum.
Curis, sorgum.
Cura, sorg.
Casibus, gegongum.
Conpellere, þæt heo gebædde.
Cursant, þocerodan.
Compturum, gefrætwadne.
Conpressit, dyde.
Carperra, geniclede.
Commate, gewrite.
Certa, gewis.
Caccabis, hwerum.
Ciclades, gegirelan.
Chao,[2] dimnesse gastas.

Callosa, þa wearrihtan.
Consulis, gearcyninges.[3]
Consul, gercyning, oððe heretoga.
Cursum, hrædlice.
5 Castra, herewic, fyrdwic.
Contundunt, forstyntað.
Capessit, nam, hæfde.
Cetra, scyld.
Cenidos, atole.
10 Cient, hrepað.
Causam, þinge.
Credita, ða bebodenan.
Conpilat, strad.
Contos, spreotas, speru.
15 Cenosis, þæm adelihtum.
Capulus, holt.
Contribulibus, mægsiblicum.
Croeata, þa giolureadan.
Contente, geeweme.
20 Commanipulares, efenheapas.
Conspirati, onan gesworene.
Cæliter, heofonlice.
Cola, lim.
Commota, limes dæl.
25 Concinnabant, seredon.
Connanipularibus, efenheapum.
Caldeorum, tungelcræftig.
Conticio, swigunge.
Conticinio, swigan.
30 Contexta, awundne.
Contunsionibus, slegum.
Cyclade, hwiolfage.
Catastarum, wita.[4]
Constantina, demera.[5]
35 Citra, ofer.
Cassaretur, wæs aidlað.
Capitolii, ðæs heafodlican hearges.
Comitiales, þa symbel monaðlican adla.
Concertatio, compung and geflit.
40 Conquilini, wioletælges.
Clauatæ, bebyrde, oððe bestefnde.
Cincinni, windeloccas.

[1] Perhaps a corruption of clutis (= κλυτοῖς)? Cf. pag. 379 l. 25. R. W.
[2] Read: chaos. R. W.
[3] i. e. a king whose authority lasted a year. It was the Anglo-Saxon notion of a Roman consul.

[4] An instrument of torture, explained in some of the medieval glosses by equuleus. (Cf. pag. 372 l. 31. R. W.)
[5] demera seems to be no Anglo-Saxon word. R. W.

Conuiciorum, tioncwida.
Conlisiones, gecnosu, oððe gescæned.
Conuolatus, breahtmung.[1]
Comere, frætwian.
Conlata, forgifen.
Castalidas, þa dunlican.
Cithara, hearpan.
Corni, corntreowes.
Corbes, leapas.
Chaus, diopnis.[2]
Creuisti, þu gesege.
Creuit, geseah.
Caries, þreahs.
Chalibem, bill.
Capital, heafudslæge
Conuexa, ða hwalfan.
Cardo, staðul.
Crustis, stansticcum.
Caci, þyrses.[3]
Cluua, steng oððe wæpen.
Cyclus, ryne.
Cyclis, rynum.
Cerula, ða wonhæwan, oððe ða swearthæwenan, oððe yða.
Constellatio, leases spelles talu.
Compos, wilhremig.[1]
Cedebat, beag
Colludia, plegan.
Crete, acende.
Cruste, hlafes.
Clasma,[4] clam, oððe wed, oððe wæra.
Consulunt, ræd sohtan.
Carinæ, scipes.
Cataclismum, brimflode.
Coenidos, fule.
Coeni, fennes.
Conpillat, forstæl.
Cetra, scylde.[5]

Coenodoxia, idelgilp.[6]
Cristata, gehelmad.
Clamat, þotrað.
Caupo, winbyrele, oððe on tunnum.
5 *Condentem,* me wyreende.[7]
Cartu, wæpne.[8]
Curuis, geapum.
Crepitabant, dynedan and þunedan.
Contortis, aþrawenum ðrædum.
10 *Capitellis,* heafudlicum.
Calce, helan.
Celidrum, nædran.
Carinam, scip.
Cretus, acenned.
15 *Cuspide,* nægle, oððe spere.
Crepitum, þununge.
Cum pelago, mid sæ.
Conuoluens, wendende.
Coors, gerefa.
20 *Crepitant,* hleoðrien.
Cretus, gesceapen.
Clamidem, hacelan, oððe lachen, oððe loðan.
Cessit, beag.
25 *Constat,* cuðlice is.
Censura, dom.
Crepacula, clatrunge.
Colubros, snacan.
Crepitare, hleoðrian.
30 *Condo,* ic wyrtige.
Carpor, ic beo sliten.
Curam, ic hæle and hleonie.
Contrahat, gewyrce and togetio.
Contulerunt, brohton oððe forgeafan.
35 *Crepitat,* wreotað.
Conpertum, cuð.
Curfa, geap.
Capax, fæsthaful.

---

[1] So has the MS. R. W.
[2] Cf. pag. 374 l. 42. R. W.
[3] *Thyrs,* the giant or spectre. This was the light in which the Anglo-Saxon scholars looked upon many of the persons of classic fable, and we shall find other traces of it in these glosses. Of course, Cacus, the threeheaded son of Vulcan, is the individual here alluded to. (Cf. pag. 379 l. 22. R. W.)

[4] This barbarous word is the origin of our modern word *claim,* and meant, in medieval Latin, an action at law, for a bond or other obligation.
[5] Cf. pag. 375 l. 8. R. W.
[6] *Cænodoxia* (Greek κενοδοξία) was a word in use in medieval Latin in the sense of vain-glory.
[7] So has the MS. R. W.
[8] The MS. has *cartu* or *castu.* R. W.

Conplector, ic beclyppe.
Contagia, besmitenessa.
Ciebant, hleodriende andbetniad.
Cursat, iornd.
Ciebo, ic acliopie.
Choortes, heredreatas.
Cicada, hyllehama oðde gærstapa.
Circius et boreus, twegen nordwindas.
Conteriti, sionewaltum.
Contis, swiorum.
Cuspite, palstre.
Copus, þæt snid.
Cauo, holum.
Carica, ficæppel.
Crapula, illeracu.
Chaos, gedwolman.[1]
Cauernas, screafu.
Cruda, þa blodgan.
Casus, gegong.
Corimbos, croppas.
Coci, coces.
Cornipedum, horsa.
Columpnis, wradum.
Conexa, gebeoded.
Cyclopum, dyrsa.[2]
Calamistratis, gecrymptum.
Cohercens, gehæbbende.
Caucumine,[3] heannesse.
Comitum, gerefena.
Codea, snegl.
Cæca, blind is.
Cereri, of hwæte.
Committo, ic befæste.
Cruentos, blodge.
Cruentis, þæm blodigum.
Casum, gegong.[4]
Clauus, nægl, odde sprota.
Cauernis, holum.
Clepsydra, wæterwrite.
Concordi, somod dyrlice.
Comitentur, siþien aud færen.
Conpressa, befongen.

[1] Cf. pag. 370 l. 28. R. W.
[2] See, before, note 3 on pag. 376. A Cyclops was, in Anglo-Saxon feelings, a giant or spectre.
[3] Read: cacumine. R. W.
[4] Cf. pag. 372 l. 23. R. W.

Contingere, gehrinan.
Certare, widfeohtan.
Copia, genihtsum þæs yfeles.
Cyllineæ, cillinescum.
5 *Cati, ingeniosi.*
Caumate, swole.[5]
Carpebantur, wæran slitene.
Catasta, werod.
Celeumatis,[6] sæleoþes.
10 *Colludio,* besmitenesse.
Conpediuntur, beoþ gecyspte.
Caprarius, gathiorde.
Contestabor, ic cyþe.
Concisius, hludur.
15 *Conpluitur,* bid gerined.
Cimbula, lytlum scipe.
Conpilabat, stæl and copade.
Commonitorium, ærendgewrit.
Caraba, scip.
20 *Commissura,* flyhteclad.
Colobysta, peningmongere.
Cyclopes, anige þyrsas.[7]
Ceruleas, da hæwen grenan, odde þa grenhæwenan.
25 *Clyton,* æþeling.
Coma, blæd.
Calathus, cysefæt.
Carduus orrens, se onscunienda þystel
Ciatos, melas.[8]
30 *Colophium,* undersyre.
Corbus, sadelboga.
Corrigie, olþwongas.
Cobsus, sylætx.[9]
Cultrum, culter.
35 *Circinnum,* gafolrand.
Capitale, heafodpanne.
Cacumen capitalis, heannes þære heafodpannan.
Cerebrum, seam þære heafodpannan.
40 *Ceruellum,* brægen.
Coma, feax, sceacga.
Cesaries, dæs wonges locfeax.

[5] Cf. pag. 369 l. 18. R. W.
[6] κέλευμα, or κέλευσμα, the song sung by the sailors in rowing, to keep stroke.
[7] Cf. pag. 376 note 3. R. W.
[8] Cf. pag. 122 l. 36. R. W.
[9] So the MS. R. W.

Cartilago, se reoma þæs brægenes.
Chautrum, al se þrotbolla.
Cuba, elnboga.
Cubitus, se earm betweonan elnbogan and handwyrste.
Catacrinis, hupban.
Centumpellis, feleferð.
Calx, hela.
Conpluuium, flod.
Conpluuiosus, flode.
Cronculus,[1] ongseta.
Capitosus, micelheafdede.
Canus, fulhar.
Comosus, sceacgede.
Ceruinus, dunfealu.
Calcanosus, helade.
Cintus, fine.
Cracinus, worhen.[2]
Coturnix, edischen.
Cretabulus, beaw.
Cinomia, hundesbeo.
Ceruus, . . .[3]
Cibus, mete.
Caupo, wætan.
Capo, cucelere.
Carenum, æþele alu.
Cardus, þistel.
Cataplasma, flaeg.
Cipus, cipeleac.
Cirta, aedrene.
Corbis, leap.
Canis, hund.
Canicula, bicce.
Ceruus, heorot.
Cerua, hind.
Caule, sceapa locu.
Caprile, gata hus.
Canile, hunda hus.
Clamet, cancer.[4]
Cibborium, þæs heahalteres ofergeweorc.
Confici, bið geworht.
Cespites, tyrf.
Concretione, brode, somodwellunge.

Consuta, gesiwid.
Constipari, ymbhiwan.
Crudeli, wælhreowe.
Conuenientur, ungerisenlice.
5 Carmine rithmico, smicere leoðe.
Charismate, healicre gife.
Congerie, gerecenesse.
Commoditas, sio getæsnes.
Confecta, geworht.
10 Crepundia, glenga.
Continentia, forhæfdnes.
Consortio, gemanan.
Cum tuta, mid gesunde.
Capessunt, nimað.
15 Crebra, mid gelomlice
Conmanipulares, efenwerod.
Conuersationis, drohtunge.
Commissa, þa gefremedan.
Conflictu, gefeohte.
20 Comitata, mid siþudu.
Conpensationis, edleanunge.
Conprobatur, bið acunnod.
Comitem, gefere.
Comi, beon hyrst oððe frætwian.
25 Conposita, geglengedu.
Confutans, oferstælende.
Cernua, hnifolerump.[5]
Curuaque, gebiged.
Carmentriumphale, þæt sigorlice leoð.
30 Conici, beon ongiten.
Cimento,[4] wrade.
Climatis, hwealfe.
Climatibus, hwealfum.
Ceremonias, gescrifu, domas.
35 Copulæ, gesomnunge.
Confingat, hiwað.
Clangor, geþun.
Constantia, bielde.
Copulas, gegaderunga.
40 Coercuit, bewerede.
Crypte, einan.
Confluentibus, toflowendum.
Crepundiorum, frætwednessa, oððe þununga.

---

[1] It is a corruption of furunculus. R. W.
[2] Cf. pag. 260 l. 4. R. W.
[3] Cf. l. 34. R. W.
[4] So has the MS. R. W.
[5] Cf. pag. 372 l. 9. R. W.

Ceremoniis, godgildum.
Curuatura, crymbing, hylding.
Coniectionis, bodunge.
Collega, gefera.
Coniecturam, anspell.
Contionantur, tospræcan.
Crebruit, mærsud.
Cupidinis, lustbærnnesse.
Capidine, fyrstmearce.
Cælebri, mid mærhlisan.
Cataclismi, widsæs.
Committenda, to befæstenne.
Cum quispiam, þonne hwylc.
Conicidatur, beon onenawen.
Consulebant, geræddan.
Concinnati, þæs geregnedan.
Caracteres, mearce.[1]
Charismatum, healicra gifena.[2]
Caruerit, þolade.
Cateruas, heapum.
Comminiscuntur, ræswodan, spæcan, wæran gemunende.
Cedens, wæs forbugende.
Cisternæ, seades.
Censura, dome.
Commertio,[3] gemanan.
Contulerunt, hie forgeafan.
Concordantes, somod geþwærende.
Carnificum, þara flæscwellera.
Capax, giffæst.[3]
Consummatis, gefyldum.
Cathegorias, gehiwunge odde gebeacnunge.
Comperit, onfunde.
Cycladibus, hwegl godwebbum.[4]
Cachinnos, cancetunge.
Copulam, to þæm gemanan.
Concertatio, somodgeflit.
Canonicis, þæm regolecum.
Crudis, hreawum.
Conieciunt,[3] bewurpan.

Contubernia, gemanan.
Conpendio, getæsnes.
Certuri, æfter onfond.
Circiter, hu hugu.[5]
5 *Contulit*, forgeaf.
Conexum, gebunden.
Celibres,[3] mære.
Consulentes, rædfindende.
Cum de stuppe, of heordan.
10 *Conticinio*, þære swigunge.
Consortium, gemanan.[6]
Confusam, þa gescendan.
Cruente, þæs unhieran.
Conrosus, gnægen.
15 *Contendamus*, higien we.
Congruentia, gerisnessa.
Conclusus, betiened.
Concentus, song.
Contextas, awundene.
20 *Crematuros*, forbernende.
Confosa, þurhstungen.
Contunsionibus, slægum.[7]
Clientele, þegnrædenne, odde hiwrædenne.
25 *Consulta*, geræding.
Congruentes, gerisniende.
Coacta, genidedu.
Calumniæ, teonan.
Commenta, trahtunga.
30 *Commentariola*, trahtas.
Citra Pontum, begeondan Wendelsæ.[8]
Calcem, ende.
Clangorem, geþrete.
Charybdibus, hwyrfepolum.
35 *Conamine*, mægene.
Cerula, þære wannan.[9]
Crypta, scræfe.
Calamitatum, hearma.
Censuram, þæt gescrif.
40 *Cestarum*, dirnhæmendra.
Commodum, nyt, and getæse, and bryce

[1] The MS. has mearē.
[2] Cf. pag. 381 l. 6. R. W.
[3] So the MS. R. W.
[4] Cf. pag. 374 l. 41. R. W.
[5] Cf. the Anglo-Saxon version of Bede III, 27. R. W.
[6] Cf. l. 1. R. W.
[7] Cf. pag. 375 l. 31. R. W.

[8] The Wendel-sea of the Anglo-Saxons is generally understood to be the Mediterranean, which the Anglo-Saxons considered to be the Sea of the Vandals, or, as they called them, Wendels. The Romans understood by Pontus the Euxine.
[9] Cf. pag. 376 l. 23 and pag. 379 l. 23. R. W.

Conderet, geworhte.
Contentus, þancfull.
Cenaculi, uphuses.
Circumuenire, beswican.
Caparetur, wæs gefangen.
Conpetenti, mid gedæfenlice.
Continetur, bið hæfd.
Contionator, maþelere.
Capidinem, firstmearc.[1]
Conlisiones, gescæningnessa.
Comere, frætwum.
Cooperante, somodwyrcendum.
Conabor, ic onginne.
Classis, þreates.
Comit, gehyrsteþ.
Culmina, heahdo.
Clarus, mære.
Conamina, angin.
Cederet, cearf.
Culmina, heahþo.
Curiositas, firwetgeornes.
Crustu, i. ornatu, frætwunge.
Colum, wulmod.

Defrutum, coerin.[2]
Detulerat, brohte.
Deses, swær.
Destituunt, towurpon.
Destitute, toworpne.
Decipula, biswic.
Desidebat, unsibbade.
Defatiget, swenced.
Delumentum, þweal.
Depoline,[3] wefta.
Deliberatio, ymbþriodung.
Decidens, gewitende.
Debita pensione, gedefum gafule.
Deditio, handgong.
Detractavit, forsoc.
Devia callus, horweg stig.
Defferuntur, meldedon odde wregdan.
Dehiscat, tocineþ.
Dentalia, sules reost.

Devincxit,[4] geband.
Deglobere, flean.
Descurris, hofdelum.
Deprehendo, ic anfinde.
5 *Deprenderint,* onfundan.
Dedala, ingeniosa.
Defert, wregde.
Degeneraverat, misþah.
Desisse, teorode.
10 *Degesto,* geræded.
Decreta, geþoht.
Deviavit, onwoh cierde.
Demolitus, aiþende.
Diuinos, witgan.
15 *Dustria,* gleawnes.[5]
Desistens, ablinnende.
Desistit, ablon.
Decretum, bebod.
Decorticauit, berinde, beflog.
20 *Diem obiit,* aswealt.
Dilotis, todældum.
Ditor, gefyrdro.
Dissimilat, mideþ.
Distabuerunt, aswundon.
25 *Difficile,* wearnwislice.
Difinis, swide micel.
Dispensatio, scir.
Dimisis, aslæcadum.
Dicimenta, tacne.
30 *Dissoluerat,* aslæcte.
Distitutum, ofgifene.
Discrepantes, todælende.
Disputauit, smeade.
Diuersorium, gestærn.
35 *Discrepatio,* þridung.
Dolatum, gesniden.
Domatis, huses.
Dolones, hunspuran.
Dromidus, ofyrit olfenda.
40 *Dracantia,* gimrodor.
Dulcisapa, cyren, odde awylled win.
Dumus, þorn odde þyrne.
Deseuiet, grimsaþ.

[1] Cf. pag. 382 l. 9. R. W.
[2] Mulled, or boiled wine. The Latin is a medieval word, or rather a word used in a medieval sense; but the derivation of the Anglo-Saxon is not so evident.

See in the next column the word *dulcisapa*, and it occurs again.
[3] *Deponile*, in the supplement to Alfric s Glossary.
[4] *Sic MS.* R. W. — [5] Read: *industria*.

Despondi, gesceatwyrpe.
Discooperiens, onwreonde.
Dilatione, ildenne.
Distentus, aþegin.
Disseruit, sæde.
Deuotatio, gehat, **odde wirgnes**.
Depreuatum, **beþwyrad**.
Delegauit, **getealde**.
Detestabile, ladlic.
Desierant, ablunnan.
Differtur, bidilded.
Detestantur, laþetted.
Dextralia, earm odde earmgegirelan.
De stipite, of beame.
De sartagine, of bradre pannan.
Defricabitur, sie agniden.
Dirute, oferhryred.
Decapoleas,[1] tienceastro.
Delfin, mereswin.
Dens, tod.
Digiti, fingras.
Dorsum, hryc.
Disceptum, nette.
Duricorium, holleac.
Domus, hus.
Desile, bor.
Defecatum, ahlutrod win.
Doleum, byden.
Dedrans,[2] egor.
Decrepito, tobigende.
Dilibatus,[3] gesmyred.
Diocessin, biscopscir.
Delusus, afered, wæged.
De pilis, of hærum.
Donec transeat, od þæt þe gewiteþ.
Diffamauerunt, gewidmærsan.
Diriet, gegriped.
Dissire, gerece.
Dispertitus est, todæled is.
Decimatis, teoþingsceat.
Dissertitudinem, gleawnesse.
De obstrusis,[3] of dæm diglum.
De conca, of muscellan.

[1] Read *decapolis*. R. W.
[2] For *dodrans*.
[3] So has the MS. R. W.
[4] Dalmatia was, of course, a country, not a town; but we have many such proofs of the ignorance of the writer of some of these glosses.

Dehonestare, unweordian.
Duodecies quinquagies millia, twelfsiþum fiftig þusenda.
Disceptare, flitan.
5 *Delicate*, þære wrastlican.
Decretalibus, þæm rædendlicum.
Dalmatiæ, þære burge.[4]
Delitiscere, bemidan.
Deuotabant, wyrgdan, ad sweredan.
10 *Domatis*, huses.
Delatum, geferedne, odde aledne.
De recessibus, of heolstrum.
De clatris, of pearrocum.
De congestu, be gesomnungum.
15 *Damnatorum*, ræplinga.
De torrente, of dæm byrnendum.
Deturpans, onretteþ.
Direpta, þa genumenan.
Depeculata, þa ofdrifenan, odde þa
20 forstolenan.
Discifer, disceberend.
Dilituisse, gediernan.
De stuppe stamineo, **be** cemdan wearpe.
25 *Dactulus*, ficæppel odde palmæppel.
Distinatus, onsended.
Distratio, bibycgong.
Disparuit, forswealt, ætiewde.
De sceuo, of þæm sceolan.
30 *Dileberaret*,[3] geþohte.
Dissona, ungerade.
Dedecus, unwlites.
Donatur, geweordad.
Duxi, tealde.
35 *Deprauandam*, to mishworfenum.
Debachatus, wedende.
Decriminalia, heafodfrætennesse.
Diane, ricenne.[5]
Discrepent, scadad.
40 *Deuote*, holdlice.
Delo, swa hatte **þæt ealand**.
Deuotaturus, wyrgende.
Depromsit, ypte.

[5] This word given here as representing Diana is not, I believe, found elsewhere than in this vocabulary (ricenne seems to be a translation of ἀρτεμίς: the pure, sound, swift goddess. R. W.).

De cortice corni, of corntreowes rinde.
Dignissimus, se weorþeste.
Dignius, þa weordelicor.
Deformem, atole.
Ductum, gedon.
Digessit, awrat, oððe gerehte.
Diuexa, þa healdan.
Demebat, nom.
Donatus, forgifen.
Dehiscit, tocined.
Dialectica, wordlocum.
Diui, godes.
Dote, weotoma, oððe midwedde.
Direxit, onsende.
Discriminet, scadeþ.
Dagon, swa hatte se god.
Demptis, genumenum.
Dilubra, gield.
Ditis, helgodes.
Dramate, þy brydelican gewrite.[1]
Deluditur, wæged wæs.
Depopulis, idende.[2]
Duelli, gefeohtes.
Deuotaret, wyrgde.
Defruti, cærenes.
Dapsilis, rumheort.
Defruti, wines.
Discessurus, from gewitende.
Disparuit, gedwan.
Dedecus, unwlite, oððe sconde.
Dissimulato, bemidenum.
Dissimulare, bemiþan, oððe yldan.
Dissimulari, leasliccettan.
Dicione, on walde.
Dedat, sylle.
Delo, on dæm eglonde.[3]
Dedere, syllat.
Dumos, þyrnan.
Dumis, þyrnum.
Diuexi, þæs hwalfan.
Dites, diuites, welige.
Degebat, lifde, oððe drohtode.
Diremptas, todælende.

Defensante, gescyldendum.
Digerit, writeþ.
Discludere, aweg alucan, oððe asceadan.
5 *De uite,* of wingearde.
Dempsit, gewonede.
Dempta, gewanedum.
Dudum, ær, oððe nu.
Dogma, lare.
10 *Dogmatum,* haligra lara.
De puppe, of scipe.
Defatu, bewyrded, oþþe geionge.
Discrimina, wrætenessa.
Discriminalia, gegirelan.
15 *Discrimine,* todælednesse.
Dira, ic grimheard.
De stipite, of triowe.
Dempto, onweg adonum.
Decernere, rædan.
20 *Depellar,* ic adrife.
Directo, rihtre.
Decernere, gestihtigan.
Draconum, nædrena.
Dire, heardre.[4]
25 *Decies senos,* tan and fingras.
De uertice, of ufeweardum bergum.
Dicione, mæhe.
Dirior, bittera.
Dapes, mettas.
30 *Dicto citius,* hradur þonne ic mæge an word gecweþan.
Diues, welig.
Deliro, ic dwolie.
Deliras, þu dwolast.
35 *Dandi,* sealdnesse.
Depascor, ic ete.
Descendens, gryndende.
De fraude, of facne.
Dispendium, wom.
40 *Desidiosorum,* slawera.
Delatoribus, wregendum.
Diuortio, hiwgedale, geflite.[5]
Destinatur, wæs onsended.

---

[1] The modern dictionaries interpret this as meaning a play. Perhaps, however, the Latin *drama* is here merely a corruption of *dragma*.

[2] hydian, hidian means *vastare, depopulari.* R. W.

[3] Cf. pag. 387 l. 41. R. W.

[4] The Diræ were, of course, the Furies, but the Anglo-Saxon word here given as equivalent appears not to be found elsewhere.

[5] This word appears to be added by a rather later hand.

Destinare, to ansendan.
De curricis,[1] of crætum.
Demetarum, ametenra.
Deciduam, gewitendlic.
Disceptauimus, we flitan.
Diffitemur, we wiðsacað.
Dexterior, gesundra.
Desiuimus, we geblunnon.
Dissertas, getinge.
Deuirginauit, mægðhade benom.
Diuortium, geflit and gecid asyndrung, hiwgedal.[2]
Dolatura, bradæx.
Dapis, swete mete.
Damulus, don.
Digesta, awritene.
Diremptas, todælende.
Discretas, todælede.
Dulcedinis, swetnesse.
Dulcauit, geswette.
Debitis, gedafenum.
Dispendio, wanunge.
De latebrosis, of þæm heolstriccum.
Desistunt, ablinnað, ateoriaþ.
Disrupta, tobrocene.
Dispari, ungelice.
Differentia, toberennes.
Defectu, wanunge.
Dediti, sealde.
Degens, drohtiende.[3]
Deteramenta,[4] dofunge, dwolunge.
Dictu, gesægene.
Deputatam,[4] getealdne.
Disputationis, spræce.
Dogmatista, lareow.
De recessibus, of degolnessum.
Dirimentes, todælende.
Dirimuntur, sient todælede.
Desertissimi, swa swa þa gleawestan.
Deturpans, gescendende.
Delaturos, bringende.
Detulerit, brohte.

[1] Read *curris*. R. W.
[2] Cf. pag. 389 l. 42. R. W.
[3] Cf. pag. 388 l. 42. R. W.
[4] So has the MS. R. W.
[5] No doubt intended for *indigena*, but how it should have found a place in this truncated form under the letter D is difficult to conjecture. (Cf. pag. 385 l. 15. R. W.)

Duruerunt, þurhwunedan.
Digena,[5] landleod.
De utrarumque, bo hiera begra.
Disserentis, secgende.
5 *Deformatio*, sio unwlitegung.
Detracta, fram atoge.[4]
Dignitosam, medomlican.
Definitionem, getimbrunge.
Dicturi, we sind anspecende.
10 *Dilationis*, yldinge.
Deformes, unwlitig.
Delicias, wista.
Discutit, towearp.
Dissentit, geunþwærað.
15
Eatenus, oþþæt.
Ebor,[4] elpanban, oððe elpend.
Ebredio, hristle.
Ebulum, wealwyrt.
20 *Echo*, wudumær.[6]
Edera, wuduwinde.
Eder, ifig.
Edilitatem, hamscir.
Edulium, æt.
25 *Edissere, i. exponere*, asecgan.
Effeminati, molles, oððe bædlingas.
Eneruata, þa aswundenan.
Eneruat, aswond.
Epithalamium, brydsang.
30 *Eptafylon*, gelodwyrt.
Efficaciter, fromlice.
Efficax, from.
Effectum, dæd.
Egre, earfoðlice.
35 *Egerere*, ascrepan.
Egesta, ascrepen.
Egra, slæce.
Eluderet, awægde.
Eulogio,[7] gidde.
40 *Elleborus*, wedeberge, þung.
Elegans, smicre.
Eliminat, aideþ.

[6] A wood-mare. In the Anglo-Saxon superstitions, the Echo was supposed to be a spirit which dwelt in the wilds and mocked people who passed there, as the night-mare tormented people in bed.
[7] *u* appears to be added by a later hand. R. W.

Elogia, lac.
Elimat, geswyrfeþ.
Elimauit, gerihte.
Empta, geboht.
Emticius, ceapeniht.
Emolomentum,[1] fultum, oððe lean.
Emblemma, foþer.
Emunctoria, candeltwist.
Eneruiter, waclice.
Emonso,[1] oferferde.
Emenso, aurnenum.
Enum, citel.
Enixe, geondsmead, oððe geornlice.
Enixe, berende.
Enixa est, cilforlamb, oððe acen-
  nende wæs.
Erimo, hindberige.
Erenis,[2] hægtes.
Eumenides, hægtesse.
Erenditen, cop.
Erpica, egeþe.
Erpicarius, egeþere.
Erugo, rust.
Errabiles, hwyrfende.
Ericius, il.
Esculus, bece.
Euiscerata, æthyd.
Euidens, sweotol.
E uestigio, an laste, oððe on luste.
Expeditus, abunden.
Exegestus, gebæro.
Expendisse, aræfnde.
Exundauit, aweol.
Experimentum, andwisnes.
Exèrcitus, bigangum.
Exercitationis, raedan biionges.
Extorti, aþræste.
Exposito, geborene.
Exalauit, stane.
Expendisset, þrowode.
Expedierant, aræerdan.

Exito, endestæf.
Ex falange, of fcþan, of þreate.
Exactorauit, gehiende.
Expilatam, ahrydred, aþrid.
5 *Expeditio,* fird, herenitig.
Expeditionum, fyrda.
Exentera, ansceot.
Explodit, excludit, atyned, oððe
  asceaf on weg.
10 *Extale,* snædel, þearm.
Exta, isen.
Exilia, gestincum.
Expeditis, gearwum.
Extipices,[1] *aruspices,* hælsendas.
15 *Expensa,* dægwine, oððe andliofen.
Examusim, geornlice.
Excesus, ægylt.
Expeditionibus, firdum.
Extori, expulsi, wræccan.
20 *Exactio,* gafules manung.
Excubias, weardsetl, oððe wæccan.
Excubiis, weardum.
Exugia, gihsinga, oððe miegern.
Expresserunt, arehtun.
25 *Exercitate,* þara getyhtan.
Exactum, bædde.
Expeditus, uelox, fortis, snel.
Ex Ormista,[3] middangeardes metend.
Expressum, aþryd.
30 *Emulus,* gehata.
Et tortam panis, and hylstene hlafas.
Exagitabat, rærde.
Erumperant, fordblæstan.
Exequias, deaþþenunga.
35 *Exosas,* lade.
Eleganti forma, smicerre ansine.
Eleganti, gecorenlice.
Egregius, æmirce.
Epistilia, headfodlic, ufeweard swer.
40 *Elides,* þu cnysest.
Efferri, beran.

[1] Sic MS. R. W.
[2] For *Erynnis. Hates,* or *hægtes,* means in Anglo-Saxon a bag or fury, and it is here given as the interpretation both of the Erinnys and of the Eumenides of the ancient mythology.
[3] The title commonly given in the Middle Ages to the Historia of Paulus Orosius was *Hormesta,* or *Hormesta Mundi,* of the latter of which the Anglo-Saxon here was evidently intended to be a translation. It is very commonly written *Ormesta* in the manuscripts. The book was no doubt quoted in the gloss from which this gloss was taken, and the glossator has intended to translate the title.

Expendatur, sie awegen, oððe ahangen.
Empticius, hæftincel.[1]
Edulio, mete.
Emarcuit, forwisnode.
Emergebant, up astigan.
Emergeret, arise.
Experge, **forht.**
Euentus, gegang, oððe **gelimp.**
Excederet, ofereode.
Erarium, maþmhus.
Exactoribus, bydelum.
Extærnorum, fremdra.
Expergefactus, i. suscitatus, aweht.
Explanare, areccan.
Epar, iecur.
Esox, leax.
Exagium, onmitta.
Eptafolium, sinfulle.
Exigia, gescineo.
Equa, myre.
Equiale, horsern.
Equs, hors.
Emisarius, steda.
Edum,[2] ticcen.
Effeta, berende bið, oððe gelde, oððe afyldum.
Eucharistia, husl.
Ergastulum, hengen.
Ex mineoo,[3] of bocreade.
Euanuerit, agæþ.
Elioquin,[4] elcor.
Exterminant, unrotlice doþ.
Eructuabo, areceo.
Equor, sæ.
Edem, hus.
Expetit, gesohte, gewilne.
Enucleata, ascyled.
Enucleare, ascilian.
Euentus, wyrd.
Elimatus, adrifen.
Eliminate, adrifene.
Epicedion, licleod.

[1] Cf. pag. 392 l. 5. R. W.
[2] So has the MS. R. W.
[3] So the MS. Read: *ex minio*. R. W.
[4] This is in the manuscript corrected by an early hand to *Alloquin*.

Epitaphion, byrgenleod.
Electri, eolhsandes.
Extirpatus, aswefecad.
Extirpans, awyrtwalad.
5 *E frondosis*, of þæm helmihtum.
Eleuantuosa,[5] þære unsmeþan.
Exprimendos, to awringenne.
Epidaurum, þære mægþe.[6]
Exorcizans, halgiende.
10 *Exorcismi*, halgunge.
Expertus sit, oncunnende wæs.
Exulat, wracode.
Exulans, wraciende.
Efferra, sio reþe, oððe sio steorlease.
15 *Elosericis*, ealgodwebbum.
Effebo, ungebierde.
Exorbitans, aswifende.
Ex terite glomere,[5] of sinuwealtum cliwene.
20 *Exibuit*, gebryttade.
Equiperat, wiþmeteþ.
Expiauit, gefelsode, oððe adilegode.
Edicta, gebodo.
Expedire, reccan.
25 *Exterminans*, aieþende.
Emulatores, onhyrgend.
Eliciens, abeodende.
Edidit, awrat, oððe asægde.
Exorbitantes, aswisende.
30 *Et suoue taurili*, oðða[2] þa þe æt þæm geldum þær wæs swin and sceap and fear.
Emersisse, þæt hie up astigen.
Emersit, aras.
35 *Elis*, afliden.
Exosa, feounga.
Elucubrate, þa ahlutredan.
Equitatum, eorodum.
Elisisse, ascrenean.
40 *Experiamur*, onfinden.
Exacerbauit, gremede.
E merulento, a, from þæm hlutrum.
Extemplo, sona.

[5] The meaning of this barbarous Latin word is evidently *uneven*.
[6] The glossator appears to have taken Epidaurus for a people, instead of a town.

Elicona, swa hatte sio dun.
Ex centro, of midle.
Expers, ordæle.
Equat, hine widmete.
Exertis, on bundonne.
Extat, wæs.
Eximia, fræmere.
Edaces, þa eotendan.
Effebi, geongan, beardleases.
Excussit, fram swengde.
Exuuias, reaf.
Elicuit, geræhte, odde ut ateah, and asmeade and awrat.
Enumerans, arimende. *Idem de inlustribus uiris*.[1]
Effarier, asecgan.
Expertur, onfindende.
Euo, yldo.
Ex scola, of scole.
. . . .[2]
Eximiam, þæt fræmere.
Extis, iesende, odde innelfe.
Ex herebro, of helle.
Expolietur, sio areaht.
Extaseos, gastlicre uphefnesse.
Eleganter, gecorenlice, odde æþelice.
Euentuum, gelimpa.
Eoae, eastdaelas.
Elogio, gidde.[3]
Eeois, eastfolcum.
Eculei, on galgan geworhtre.[4]
Expletis, forslægenum.
Exalaparetur, wæs fystslægenu.
Epicurii, up on þæm rodore þara steorsceawera.[5]
Ederet, ypte, and cidde.
Et morosam, and þone softe langan.
Experiar, ic onfinde.
Eliseum, sunfeld, þæt. is neor (xna) wong.[6]
Egessit, ut aþyde.

Extalibus, roppum.
Emula, þa feondlic.
Exempta, ut atogene.
Explosis, ut adrifenum.
5 *Explosa*, adrifenre.
Effebum,[7] beardleasne.
Examen, swearm.
Exilium, wræcsiþ.
Edomiti, þæs atemedan.
10 *Eructant*, forþblawaþ.
E geminis, of getwinnum.
Experto, cuþum.
Exilis, lytel.
Elimentum, stæfrof.
15 *Eleotropam, Grece; Latine solsequium idem* sigelhweorfe.
Erro, Ic weorpe.
Et salis, and sæ.
Equore, on sæ.
20 *Eliforus*,[8] wedeberge, odde coasteræsc.
Exuuias, deaþ reaf, *idem* nelle ic him þæt lif ongeniman.
Exto, ic eam.
25 *Excepit*, ut afeng, odde ut adyde.
Exedi, ic et.
Eburneus dens, elpend toþ.
Eget, beþearf.
Exsangues, orblede.
30 *Excidium*, hryre.
Epimoenia, fostraþas.
Expedius, alifedlicur.
Editiorem, hearran.
Eheu, wa la wa.
35 *Exactores*, gerefan.
Exalabat, reac.
Extorsit, awræste.
Exactio, gaful.
Ependiten, hacele.[9]
40 *Exolescunt*, aidliaþ.
Exterum, endestæf.

[1] Apparently the title of one of the books from which these glosses are taken.
[2] A word and its gloss are here unreadable, from a stain in the vellum.
[3] Cf. pag. 391 l. 39 and pag. 392 l. 1. R. W.
[4] Cf. pag. 375 note 4. R. W.
[5] The glossator seems to have supposed that an Epicurean was an astronomer.
[6] xna is unreadable from a stain in the vellum. R. W.
[7] So has the MS. R. W.
[8] A corruption of *helleborus*. The hellebore was believed to be a remedy against madness.
[9] A priest's vest. The Latin word is given *Epidecen* and *Ependicen* in Ducange.

Eucharis, wynsum.
Exenia,[1] lac.
Enigmata, geddunga.
Et mentum, and cin.
Elbus, deorce græg.
Euomatio, spiwing.
Euomuit, ut aspau.
Excusorium, flor on huse.
Enixius, geornlicor.
Enucleata, ascealode.
Erga, ymb.
Existentibus, wesendum, beondum.
Extorrem, wræccan.
Et spontaneum, and þone wilsuman.
Et mulsæ, and þære miliscan.
Extaseos, færenga.
Experiri, acunnian.
Exorsum, onginnende.
Emulumenta,[2] gestreon.
Explodatur, is aweg adrifen, is adwæsced.
Emeritos, þa æþelan, þa gecorenan.
Euellantur, ut alocene.
Eramentum, argeweorc.
Euectus, upwegen.
Edita, seo acennede.
Editus, acenned.
Erogante, þære gedæledan.
Exitio, cwale.
Execranda, þa onscuniendlecan.
Elephantinosa, sio hreoflice.
Extricabili, ungebrocenre.
Expertem, wanhlytne.
Elideret, gebræce.
Emulabantur, wæran sacende.
Effigiæ, on hiwe.
Edictis, gebennum, odde gescrifum.
E quibus, of þæm.
Exorruit, onscunode.
Eidem, þære ilcan.
Eruta, toworpenum.
Exortatorium, trymendlic.
Exutas, ongirede.
Exibentes, gegearwiende.

Execrandum, onscuniendlic.
Excusari, beladian.
Eliganti, gerædre.
Epigrammatibus, ofergewritum.
5 Ergastula, nirwþa.
Euulsam, afyrredne.
Examine, þreate.
Exul, wræcca.
Exsangue, orsaule.
10
Facessante, sweþriendum.
Facessit, discedit, swedraþ.
Fretus, brucende, odde geweorþad.
Flustra, flod, odde hærn.
15 Flustris, sigendum.
Fouere, wirman.
Forcipis, tange.
Forceps, tang.
Forficis, sceara.
20 Furuauoracis, deorc.[2]
Flaua, þæs fealewan.
Fulua, sio fealwe.
Falerata, þa geglengedan.
Feruore, wilme, and bryne.
25 Fenerator, gafolgilda.
Fraudis, manes.
Felethi, feþemen, feþehere.
Felethei, foreirnerum.
Freti, gefyrþrede.
30 Falarica, fyrdwerod, feohtgegyrelan, ætgar, uel genus teli.
Frugalitatis, mid gneþnesse.
Futuræ, þære toweardan.
Flagitiosum, þone manfullan.
35 Facula, fecele, blysige.
Fax, fecele, blysige.
Feriatus, i. sanctus uel requies, gefreod, geresteþ.[3]
Formosa, wlitig.
40 Fucate, getelgode.
Fucatum, getelgod.
Fronde, telgan.
Fomitibus, tyndrum.
Fastu, ofermetto.

---

[1] For xenia. The E is marked with dots in the manuscript as being superfluous.
[2] Cf. pag. 401 l. 14. R. W.
[3] So has the MS. R. W.

Factiosam, þone facenfullan.
Factiones, facn.
Fati, wyrde, odde gegonges.
Fidenter, getreowlice.
Fidere, getrywan.
Fabrefactam, smicere geworhte, asmidode.
Fastigium, heannesse.
Flaminia, healdnessa.
Flebotomo, blodseaxe.[1]
Fletoma, blodseax.
Falcastrum, siþe.
Fanatice, þære deofel[gylde].
Fausta, þæs æþelan, odde rume.
Fortunæ, wyrde.
Fortuna, wyrd.
Fragore, gebrece, swoege.[2]
Fraudulenta, sio facenfulle.
Factio, searu.
Fantasma, scinhiw.
Fantasmate, scinhiwe.
Fruniscantur, brucad.
Famulatibus, þeowdomum.
Fiscillis, tænelum.
Fortuitu, wyrdgesceapum.
Fauorabile, hergendlice.
Florigera, þa blostmberendan.
Frondescit, blowed.
Factionibus, searwum.
Ferinam, þa wildeorlican.
Ferocitatem, reþnesse.
Funesti, þæs reþan and þæs deadberendan.
Funesto, þæm hatheortan.
Foetosis, tudorfæstum.
Facundia, getingnesse.
Ferebatur, wæs sæd.
Frequentantem, oft secende.
Facultas, eþelicnes.
Feralibus, mid reþlicum.
Fasciarum, sweþelum, wræda.
Fascia, wræd.
Flagitante, wilnigendum.
Farciuntur, wæran acrummene.
Frustrari, gewægnian.

[1] Cf. pag. 22 l. 33. R. W.
[2] Cf. pag. 23 l. 18. R. W.
[3] Sic MS. R. W.

Fefellisset, þa þa he leag.
Famelicum, þane hingriendan.
Familice, þa hungerlican.
Fusoque, spinle.
5 *Fusum*, spinl.
Frugalis, wæstmbære.
Frusta,[3] in sticco.
Frustatim,[3] in sticce.
Focularibus, fyrgearwungum.
10 *Fortuitu*, mid weas, gelimpe.
Fautor, gefultumiend.
Farris, hwætes, speltes.
Faar, spelt.
Furuæ, þære sweartan.
15 *Furuo*, þy sweartan.
Fuliginis, fylnesse.
Fuligine, hrume.
Figmenta, hiwung, odde leasspel.
Frontosa, mid heafod baldre.
20 *Furibundæ*, þære hatheortan.[4]
Fotam, gewyrmede, odde geholpene.
Fluminauit,[5] scan.
Fatebatur, heo andette.
Fundo, grunde.
25 *Fundi*, grundas, odde boclandes.
Fimi, gores.
Fulta, gefyrþredo.
Formidolosis, forhtigendum.
Facinus, man.
30 *Friuola*, leasunga.
Falsato, þy leasan.
Fratruele, his broþorsuna.
Formosa, mid ænlicre.
Formosior, wlitigre.
35 *Fuscinula*, awelas.
Fore, wesan, and beon.
Fàscis, sceafes.
Fasculo, sceafe.
Fuluis, geolwum, odde deorcum.
40 *Fantasmate*, þære glyderinge.
Fertur, is sæd.
Falerata, becefed.
Fulcire, wreþian.
Fulmina, ligita.
45 *Facitiæ*,[3] gleo.

[4] Cf. pag. 400 l. 34. R. W.
[5] Read: *fulminauit*. R. W.

Fagus, bece.
Fagis, becum.
Fasianus, worhana.
Fascia, sweþil, wræd.
Famfaluca,[1] leasung, odde fam.
Fasciarum, sweþila.
Falcis, wudubil, siþe, rifter.
Fasces, godweb, odde ealdordomas.
Facundia, i. eloquentia, woþ.
Famfaluca, wapul.[2]
Falcastrum, wudubil, odde siþe.[3]
Fauonius, westsudwind.
Fascinatus, i. laudatis stultæ, malscrung.[4]
Farius, fag.
Farsa, acrummen.
Fasces, cynedomas.
Fastu, wlenceo.
Falla,[5] bean.
Fabrile, smiþlice.
Fabri, cræftiglice.
Ferruginius,[6] græg.
Ferox, reþig, odde berend.
Ferculi, discas.
Fercula, swæsende.
Ferinum, hold.
Feriæs, i. quietis, uel securis, restendum.
Fenus, spearwa.
Foenus, borh.
Fenore, borge.
Foederatus, getreowed, getreude.
Fecce, mere.
Fepa,[6] wæps.
Fefellit, i. eludit, wægeþ.
Furula, æscþrote.
Femum, græs, odde hig.
Ferrugine, i. ferreo colore, isengræg, gesweorf.
Fiber, befer.
Ferrugine, græghæwe isene oþþe sinderome.

Fiscilla, tænel.
Fiscilus, stictænel.
Fida, stern, odde getrywe.
Fibra, þearm.
Fibrarum, þearma.
Fibre, þearmas.
Fibula, sigel, odde hringe, fifele.
Fiscilis, sprinclum.
Filum, þræd.
Filatum, gearn.
Fenicia, baso.
Figmenta, i. plasmatio hominum, geweorc.
Filix, fearn.
Filiscetum, fearnbed.
Felicem, fearn.
Fibras, spenas.
Ficetula, sucga.
Fibrans, hrissende.
Finiculis,[6] finul.
Fiscalis, rædegafellicum, wænfare.
Fimum, gor.
Fictis, facnum.
Fistulis, þeotum.
Figite, swiþiad.
Filiaster, steopsunu.
Flustra, i. undæ, sigend.
Flauum, i. fuluum, read.
Flegmata, horh.
Flegma, horh.
Flabanus,[6] swan.
Flabum,[7] geolu.
Flamina, biscophadas, odde blæd.
Flaminium, biscophade.
Flagris, swipum.
Floccus, loca.
Flauescit, albescit, glitenaþ.
Flagrans, stincende.
Fouit, bredeþ, feormaþ.
Formido, onoþa.
Forfix, isernfetor.

[1] This medieval Latin word seems to be entirely unknown to the lexicographers, and the Anglo-Saxon glossator himself does not appear to have been quite satisfied of its meaning; for it is explained no more than five lines below by an Anglo-Saxon word the meaning of which appears not to be known.

[2] Cf. Leo's Gloss. pag. 8 l. 13. R. W.
[3] The two last words added in a different hand-writing.
[4] Cf. Bosw. D. 44ᵏ. R. W.
[5] Of course for *faba*. R. W.
[6] So the MS. R. W.
[7] Of course for *flavum*.

Fornaculæ, cylene, heorþe.
Foros, bolca.
Fortex,[1] edwielle.
Follis, blastbelg.
Folliginis, bylgum.
Fornaculum, here.
Fronulus, linetwige.
Fratuelis,[2] *i. filius fratris,* suchtyrga.
Frugus, uncystig, odde heamol, fercuþ.
Frixum, afigen.
Fraxinus, æsc.
Fraga, ofet.
Fringella, finc.
Framea, sweord, odde ætgare.
Fretus, confidens, presumptus, bald.
Fragor, cirm, sweg, gebrec.[3]
Fraudulenter, facenlice.
Frutina, fultumend.
Fuscinula, awel.
Furuum, i. nigrum, brun.
Funalia, candela, odde candelweocan.
Fulix, ganot, odde dopened.
Furuncus, mearþ.
Fungus, swamm, odde feldswam.
Funda, liþere.
Fundibulæ, liþeran.
Funestissima, þa deadlicostan.
Funalia cerei, weaxcandel.
Funalia, i. lucernarum, stuppæ.[4]
Fuligine, soote.
Furia, hægtesse.
Furiarum, hægtessa, odde wedenheotra synna.[5]
Fœtas, melce and tydrende.
Fœtus, melc.
Fœtu, tudre, odde midbeorþre.
Fictilia, læmena.[2]
Fulchra,[2] rædescamelas.
Furibundus, weallende.

Flagrantia, blatesnung.
Furua, swearte.
Folliculum, gehopp.
Far serotina, spelt samgrene.
5 *Frigetur,* sie gehyrsted.
Fluctris, biflitum.
Facies, hleor.
Frons, hnifol, odde foreweard heafod.[6]
10 *Faus,*[7] hyge.
Femor, þeoh.
Femina, inneweard þeoh.
Fel, gealla.
Felle, geallan.
15 *Flamma,* leg.
Flammiger, legberende.
Fauilla, ysle.
Fumus, rec.
Florulus, goldfinc.
20 *Folium,* leaf.
Framen, spæc.
Fussarius, wanabeam.[5]
Fraga,[2] streowberge.
Forda,[2] gefearh, sugu.
25 *Ferrum,* isen.
Faber, smiþ.
Fiola, bledu.
Frigus, ciele.
Forfex, seer.
30 *Fucus,* telg, deag.
Fucorum, telga.
Furca, wearhrod.
Fistucam,[2] strewu, eglan.
Febricitantem, feferscocne.
35 *Fretum,* deop.
Filacteria, lyfesra.[9]
Falerato, gehyrste.
Falerarum, hyrsta.
Fornicibus, bogum.
40 *Fornicem,* bogan.
Farus, beacenstan.

---

[1] For *Vortex.*
[2] So the MS. R. W.
[3] The **last** word added in another hand and different ink.
[4] A blank is left for the gloss, as though the glossator could not find an equivalent in Anglo-Saxon. (Cf. l. **22.** R. W.)
[5] These latter words are added in a different ink.
[6] The last words in another hand.
[7] Apparently a corruption of *fauces.*
[8] Cf. pag. 270 l. 18. R. W.
[9] Cf. Beda 4, 27. R. W.

Funebre, heofendlice, hrawlic.
Fortunatum, þone gewilsæligan.[1]
Furtunatus,[2] gewifsæli.
Fato, gewife.
Fortune, gewife.
Fato, wintergegonge.
Fortuito, semnendlice.
Flamen, **biscop**,[3] odde oroþ, **odde** gast.
Farciuntur, acrummene wæran.
Fors, wyrd.
Flauescentibus, falewende.
Fotam, sealfode.
Fomentat, lacnode.
Fulminauit, lixte.
Forti, fæstes.
Fumigabundis,[4] þæs stincendan.
Flara, blædas.
Fidibus, strengum.
Falconum, wealhhafeca.
Fabrefactis, gesmicerade.
Fati, gewrites.
Fistula, wistle.
Ferit, sloh.
Faminem, spræce.
Fatescunt,[5] sweþeredan.
Fontona,[2] þa wyllican.
Fautam famam, þone cadegan hlisan.
Findit, toslaf, tocleaf.
Findere, todælan.
Facessit, fremede.
Facessunt, fremmad.
Frondosis dumis, þæm gehilmdum græfum.
Friens, brytende.
Fricabat, gebrytte.
Foeta, eacene.

[1] I read here: gewilsæligan, not gewifsæligan, but cf. the next line. R. W.
[2] So the MS. R. W.
[3] The two Anglo-Saxon words which follow are in another ink, by a glossator who seems to have understood the Latin word differently.
[4] *Fumigabundus* is given in Ducange in the sense of *fumans*.
[5] *Fatescere*, as we learn from Ducange, is another form, or rather a corruption of, *falescere*, which in medieval Latin had the meanings of *carere*, *cessare*, *finire*.

Fasce, gegirlan.
Fasciæ, breostlines.
Fantasma, scin, i. et *nebulum*.
Falancx,[2] feþa.
5 *Farcire*, acrymman.
Farsit, fylde.
Farsis, gefyldum.
Filicumque, and fearnes, odda fearna.[6]
Fucare, reode gnidan.[7]
10 *Furiis*, wedenheortnessum.
Furuiores, sweartran.
Floralia, blostmgeld.[8]
Fauorem, fultum.
Fatis, wyrdum.
15 *Flaminibus*, biscopum.
Fotu, beþinge.
Fomentat, beþede.
Fraudabere, þu bist bescered.
Functus, brucende.
20 *Fisci*, cynedomes.
Faltum, gehladen.
Faui, beobread.
Fauste, gesælge.
Flari, sweopan.
25 *Factitat*, deþ, andwyrceþ.
Furcifer, wearg.
Furcifera, þa weargberendan.
Friabant,[2] bræcan.
Fullones, wealceres.[9]
30 *Fatali*, gelimplice.
Fibras, þearmas.
Fatu, spræce.
Faciam, ic do.
Faxo, ic do.
35 *Flatu*, oreþe.
Fricans, filiende.
Fouebo, ic lufige.

In fact it represented the French *faillir*.
[6] This word is added in another ink, as a correction; for the Latin word is in the genitive case plural.
[7] Literally to paint with red, referring to the painting of the face. We should say in English, *to rouge*.
[8] The glossator seems to have supposed that the name of the *Floralia* was derived, not from Flora, but from *flos*.
[9] A fuller is still called in Lancashire a *walker*.

Fouet, fedeþ.
Frutescit, þufaþ, and wridaþ.
Frondosis, þufugum.
Furibus, mus, þeofum.[1]
Frutecta, ...
Fatescit, adeadaþ.
Fraudor, ic com bescyred.
Fingunt, gehiowiaþ.
Funestam, þa wælhreowan, odde þone hragifran.
Fecunda, wæstmbæru.
Friuola, leasunge.
Fraudaret, bescyrede.
Frutecta, gewrid, odde þuftas.[2]
Fessum, meþne
Fusco, sweartum.
Fulcit, wreþeþ.
Flagrantior, swiþstincendre.
Furtiua, stulur.
Furtum, stala.
Ferarum, wilddeora.
Fatum, gegon.
Fata, deaþwyrde.
Fabrica, weorce.
Funambulus, rapgon.
Fingo, ic hiwige.
Fasci,[3] swearte.
Fuge, fleamas.
Fugitiuus, frætum.
Fatuiter, dyslice.
Fugacia, þa fleondan.
Fullonum, leaþorwyrt.
Ferrugineas, þa isengrægan.
Foeneratur, stryneþ.
Fascinatio, gebeotung.
Fetta, clæfra.[4]
Focus, seol.
Fusorium, delfisen.
Foratorium, uel terebellum, nafogar.

Falx, siþe.
Fauces, goman.
Faucibus, geaflum.
Fiber, snædel, þearm.
5 *Frontialis*, steorrede.
Fordalium,[5] gesoden wyrtmete.
Formaticum, uel formellum, cyse.
Folialis, crompeht.
Ferculum, ælces cynnes panmete.
10 *Formentum*, ofenbacen hlaf.
Ficus, ficbeam.
Flaga, hindberian.[6]
Fragos, heorotberge.
Flauia, uel mori, blace berian.
15 *Fascinium*, streuberie.
Fraga, streuberian.[7]
Fenuculum, finul.
Febrifuga, feferfuge.
Frumentum, hwæte.
20 *Farina*, melu.
Fas, riht, odde godes riht.
Fastidia, aþrotenes.
Fessa, geswenced.
Furias, wuhunga.
25 *Furfures*, syfeþa.
Filix minuta, eoforfearn.
Fenegrecio, wyllecærse.[8]
Ferula, æscþrote.
Filicina, eoforfearn.
30 *Filia aurisa*, banwyrt.[9]
Fuscus, tægl, odde feax.
Finicia,[10] baso.
Fusarius, wananbeam.[11]
Foederatas, getrewde.
35 *Faonius*, westsuþwind.
Febris a feruore nominatur, id est, bryneadl.
Frenesis, weding *Græci mentem frenas dicunt, hinc et freneticus*.
40 *Fleumon*, magan untrymnes *dictum*

---

[1] Cf. pag. 411 l. 1. R. W.
[2] These two words are written in another hand.
[3] Read *fusci*, cf. l. 16. R. W.
[4] Cf. pag. 134 l. 42. R. W.
[5] So the MS. R. W.
[6] Cf. pag. 269 l. 39, **pag. 295** l. 23, pag. 298 l. 2. R. W.
[7] Cf. pag. 136 l. 14 and pag. 270 l. 19. R. W.
[8] Read: *foeno graeco*. Cf. pag. 298 l. 16. R. W.
[9] Read: *viola aurosa*. Cf. pag. 300 l. 1. R. W.
[10] For *Phænicia*, of purple colour.
[11] Cf. pag. 405 l. 22. R. W.

apoplegi, quod interpretatur inflammans.
Frunculus, quasi ferunculus, id est ongseta, *Græce antrax, ab igne.*
Frenus, muþbersting.
Farmacida, in Latinum medicamina sonat, **id est** scalflǽcnung, *id est formantur nomina farmaceaticus et farmaceatica* **et** *farmaceaticum.*
Flebotomum, blodseax, odder ædderseax. *Græce namque fleps, uena, tomum uero incisio nominatur.*
Foedus fecerunt, wǽre genoman.
Familia erciscundæ, yrfegedal, *quia erciscunda enim apud ueteres diuisio nuncupabatur.*
Finium regundorum actio ordo, gemǽra gedal.
Fructus, æfsweore, *siue læneslandes* bryce.
Facinus, sceþdǽd.
Flagitium, legerteam, odde tiht.
Filix, fearn, *cuius radix utilis est ad soluendam difficultatem pariendi.*
Fundum, fǽtes botm.
Foculare, heort.
Fastorum libri, cyninga bec, *siue* consula bec.
Fertum, mǽsselac.
Furiæ, burgrunan.
Functi, gerefan.
Familia, cneoris. *Hæc autem in patre terminatur.*
Fratres, gebroþor, *et aliquando gemǽgas, aliquando* gelondan, *quas Latini paternitates interpretantur.*
Fratres patrueles, suctyrian, *sic dictus est ad patres eorum, si fratres inter se fuerunt.*
Fratrueles autem matertæræ[1] filii, hoc est modrigan sunu.
Fratrissa, fratris uxor, hoc est broþorwif.
Fauces, hracan, *quod per eas famur uoces.*

[1] Sic MS. R. W.
[2] Cf. pag. 404 l. 25. R. W.
[3] Cf. pag. 405 l. 41. R. W.

Furo, mearþ,[2] *idem deminutiue furunculus, a furuo dictus, unde et fur.*
Frutices, scoomhylti.
Farus, Grecum est nomen, nam fos, lux, oros autem uisio, aput[1] eos nominatur, hinc compositum nomen est fari, id est fyrtor.[3]
Fornum, hlafofn, *a farre dictum.*
Forus, ubi uua calcatur, hoc est wingetred.
Faba pressa, gegrunden bean.
Frondes, geleafhris.
Fomes, spoon. *Idem astula.*
Fructus, in eo malum cidonium, siue malum cotonium, id est codæppel.
Feniculum, finol, *Græce matron.*
Fascia, seaxclað, odde wrǽdwridels.
Fasciola, sarclaþ.
Far, grut.
Farcimen, gehǽcca, odde mearhǽccel.
Flasce, trinnubyttæ,[4] *eadem et flascones.*
Fiscus, kyninga **scod.**
Farcille, berigeblæ.
Folles, þa mǽstan dignoras.
Fafida, hleomoc.[5]
Fercula, cyninggereordo.
Fornicibus, holum stanum.
Freneticus, brǽcseoc.
Fomentam, tyndre.
Furus, styccu.
Fumigabundus, stynicndum.[6]
Falanges, hereþrym.
Frico, ic gnide.
Ferunca, merð.
ALLE PATER.
LU FILIUS.
IA SPIRITUS SANCTUS.

Gastrimargia, gifernes.
Gregatim, heapmǽlum, odde wrǽdmǽlum.
Gestiant, girnað.
Gymnasio, on plegestowum.

[4] Is *trinnubyttæ* an Anglo-Saxon word? R. W.
[5] Cf. Cock. Leechd. III, pag. 332. R. W.
[6] Cf. pag. 406 l. 17. R. W.

Gramina, grædas.
Granigera, þa cornberendan.
Glumula,[1] gewrid, egenu, oððe scealu.
Garrulitas, geonung.
Gluten, lim, oððe tero.
Glutinatum, tosomne gelimed.
Gestus,[2] gebærum.
Gestu, gebæro.
Gulosa, mid giferre.
Gentilitatis, hædennesse.
Gnarus, se wisa.
Generositas, æþelborennes.
Gerosam,[3] þæt æþele.
Grauitate, lare.
Grassatoribus, þeofum.
Glebulis, turfum.
Glebe, tyrf.
Grassator, hergiend and ahiðend.
Glareis, ceoslum.
Gymnosophistis, heahlareowum.
Geometrica, eorþgemet.
Gazarum, þara gestreona.
Gestibus, gebærum.
Genuinis,[4] tuxum.
Gurguliones, þrotbollan.
Gula, hrace.
Gradatim, fægre, oððe fotmælum.
Gloriatur, gilpað.
Genuini, ewiþenliere.
Gratatur, blissaþ.
Gannature, cancettende.
Glomerantibus, ymbheapiendum.
Geneliatici,[5] hæþene.
Gurgurizat,[6] iagulswyled.
Garret, geonaþ.
Garrula, sio hlydende.
Galla, galluc.
Garula, crawe.
Grauculus,[7] hroc.

Garbas, sceafas.
Galmaria,[8] calwere.
Gabalacrum, calwer.
Galmum, molegn.[9]
5 *Galmilla*, lim, molegen.
Gente,[10] wilde gos.
Geumatrex, geac.
Gipsus, spæren.
Gigrars, cora.
10 *Glarea*, cisilstan.[11]
Gladiolum, secg.
Glis, fonfyr, oððe egle.
Glomer, cleowen.
Glacum,[12] hæwen, oððe græg.
15 *Glus*,[13] freenes, oððe lim.
Glitilia, clife.
Globus, leoma.
Globis, leomum.
Glandula, cyrnel.
20 *Gladiatores*, cempan.
Gripem, giu.[14]
Griphus, giu.[14]
Gratia, œst, gifu.
Grillus, hama.
25 *Gregariorum*, unæþelra.
Gurgustium, cesol.
Galeatum, gehylmed.
Grandeuus, frod.
Germanus, æwenbroþor.
30 *Gibbus*, hoferede.
Gausape, sceat.
Grus, cran.
Grallus, hroc.
Gallus, hana.
35 *Gallicinium*, honcred-tid.
Gallina, henn.
Geniscula, muexle.
Gustus, birgnes.
Gena, heagospind.
40 *Gingifa*, toþrima.

[1] For *glomulus*, in the sense, apparently, of a little heap.
[2] So the MS. R. W.
[3] Sic, for *ynerosam*.
[4] Cf. pag. 157 l. 39. R. W.
[5] Sic, for *gentilici*. R. W.
[6] Sic, for *gargarizat*.
[7] Sic, for *graculus*. R. W.
[8] For *calvaria*. R. W.
[9] Cf. Bosw. D. 460. R. W.
[10] Sic, for *gante*. R. W.
[11] Cf. pag. 412 l. 20. R. W.
[12] For *glaucum*.
[13] For *glis*, apparently.
[14] Cf. pag. 258 l. 7. R. W.

Gartilago,[1] gristle.
Genitalia, þa cennendlican.
Genua, cneowa.
Gratis, brod.
Glandix, æceren.
Genista, brom.
Genescletum, bromfæsten.
Grues, gryt.
Grabra, gat.[2]
Gergenna,[3] sticca.
Grammaticorum, stæfwriterum.
Glaucoma, eagseoung.
Genesi, fatu.
Gesticulatio, plega.
Gradatim, softe.
Gerula, berend.
Gymnica, þa uþwitlican.
Gener, aþum.
Gypsan, dracan.
Germanas, getwisan.
Gemellos, getwisan.
Gorgoneis, þæm hellicum.
Gurgustia, hus.
Geruli, berend.[4]
Grammate, gewrite.
Glomerauit, ymbhringde.
Grassantibus, hiđendum.
Gliribus, eglum.[5]
Geseos,[6] cneoris boca.
Gloriosas, saltim, huhugu.
Gallicula, scos.
Gracili, þære lytlan.
Gipsa, nædre.[7]
Gorgoneo, aterlicum, odde biter.[8]
Glescit,[9] weaxeþ.
Geminum, twifalde.
Gestat, bireþ.
Glesco,[9] ic weaxe.
Gnostica, þa Greciscan.

Garrio, ic hlyde.
Gramine, græse.
Gramen, cwice.
Gremium, bearm.
5 *Gyrens*, ymbfonde.
Grosse, greatre.
Grossas et graciles, great and smæl.
Gracilis, lytel.
Grandem, micel.
10 *Genitrix*, flind.
Gentis, mines cynnes.
Germine, mid minre grownesse.
Grauis, sio þicce ærlyft, odde gestæþþig.
15 *Gradu lento*, listnie and lategange.
Geminus, twyfeald.
Granata, æpeltreowu.
Gillone,[10] stænan.
Gotium, feld.
20 *Gotia*, feldas.
Graticula,[11] bæcering.
Glebenus, eaghyll from þæm ongnoran.
Gigra,[12] se flæsc toþ wiþæftan þone
25 tux.
Gemitus, geomrung.
Galbus, þynne monn.
Giluus, gioluhwit.
Guttatus, cylew.
30 *Genosus*, cneowade.
Gans, grege gos.
Gignalia, hagan.
Gnesis, cwietreow.[13]
Gesce, eall hwite wysan.
35 *Gracilis*, smæl.
Genas, hleor.
Gelu, forst.
Girba, se **calra** mæsta mortere.
Geomantia, þurh eorþan witgung.

---
[1] Of course for *cartilago*.
[2] Read: *capra*. R. W.
[3] *Gergenna* is a medieval Latin word for what we call in modern English a cowlstaff; we can easily understand why it was called in Anglo-Saxon a *stik*.
[4] Cf. l. 16. R. W.
[5] Cf. pag. 413 l. 12. R. W.
[6] Sic, for *genesros*.
[7] Cf. l. 19. R. W.

[8] Cf. l. 22. R. W.
[9] Apparently for *crescit* and *cresco*.
[10] *Gillo* was a medieval Latin word for an amphora or wine vessel, and is preserved in German under the form of *geltz*, a pail.
[11] Sic, for *craticula*.
[12] The MS. has *gigra* or *gigna*. Cf. pag. 157 l. 33 and pag. 264 l. 10. R. W.
[13] Cf. pag. 139 l. 2. R. W.

Glaucus, glæseneage.
Gagates, sæcol.
Gerabotane, biscopwyrt.[1]
Gleba silicis, stanes floh.
Geneales, brydræst.
Gigrillus,[2] wince.
Gladiolum, glædene.
Grissa garina, wordcærsa.[3]
Gotuna, cammuc.[4]
Germanitatis, brodorsibbe.
Gimnicis artibus, uþwitlicum.
Gramina, ciþas.
Grunnire, grennigan.
Gazas, feohgestreon.
Gallitricum, wæterwyrt.[5]
Gentiana, feldwyrt.
Gagantes, mucgwyrt.[6]
Grandisona tuba, hludstefne byme.
Grandescit, crescit, micelaþ.

Horrendus, þæt egesfulle.
Hiulca, cinende.
Historiographus, stæfwritere.[7]
Heresceret, tocleofode,[8] and oþfcalh.
Hortantur, lærdan.
Hortamini, lærad.
Hiulcas, þa giniendan, oððe tara.
Hortamentis, lare.
Hortus, wyrtun.
Holitor,[9] leacweard.
Hironiam, þurh smicernesse, and hiwunge.
Heroicis, mid eorllicum.
Historia, racu
Habitudo, gebæro.

Habitudine, onsiene.
Haustum, drync.
Habenis, salum, oððe geweald-leþerum.
5 *Habile*, liþowac.
Heus, gehyrs þu?
Hebitatus,[10] astynt.
Hebeti, dysige.
Hebesceret, aswand.
10 *Herodius*, wealhhafuc.[11]
Hauritoria,[12] hlædhwiogl.
Herinis,[13] wælcyrge.
Hibiscum,[14]biscopwyrt,merscmealwe.
Hirundo, swealwe.
15 *Hyna*,[15] nihtgenge.
Holor, swan.
Hora, sweg.
Hoctatus, geleahtrod.
Honeraria, scyphlæst.
20 *Holido*, fule.
Humare, bemyldan.
Hymeneos, wifþing, gifta, hæmed.
Histriatarum, waledra.
Hispidus, ruh.
25 *Hirsutus*, ruh.
Homo, mann.
Horidanum, elene.[16]
Hasta, spere.
Hostimen, leasung, oððe wundor.
30 *Hidropicos*,[17] wæterfull.
Hesitantes, tweogende.
Hesperiæ, Eotoles.
Herculus, hearge.
Hierophantorum, scincræfta.[18]
35 *Hircitallo*, hyse, wise.

[1] Cf. pag. 134 l. 40. R. W.
[2] Sic, for *gyrgillus*.
[3] So the MS. R. W.
[4] Cf. Cock. Leechd. III, pag. 316. R. W.
[5] Cf. pag. 296 l. 19. R. W.
[6] Cf. pag. 301 l. 8. R. W.
[7] The Anglo-Saxon word means properly a grammarian, and not a historiographer.
[8] The meaning of *tocleofian* is: adhærescere. R. W.
[9] Of course, for *olitor*, and the next word for *ironiam*, but the first meaning given to the latter is not a proof of the scholarship of the glossator.
[10] Sic MS. R. W.

[11] i. e. the Welsh-hawk, the falcon. In the Anglo-Saxon period the favourite hawk for falconry was obtained from Wales. (Cf. pag. 259 l. 8. R. W.)
[12] Cf. Bosw. Dict. 36p. R. W.
[13] A corruption for *Erinnys*, one of the Furies.
[14] Cf. pag. 270 l. 33. R. W.
[15] Read *hyena* (= the nightwanderer). R. W.
[16] Cf. pag. 271 l. 10. R. W.
[17] Originally written *hidripicus*, but corrected in a different ink, as given in the text.
[18] i. e. conjurers, magicians.

Hymenis, peninge.
Humectans, wætende.
Herebi,[1] helle.
Horrisonis, gryrelicum.
Honera,[1] ic bere.
Horrendum, gryrum.
Horrida, ic eom gryrelic.
Hausi, ic gehierde.
Horno,[2] **gierstandæge**.
Hamus, hoc.
Hospes, gast.
Hilidros, i. *celidros*, nædran.
Hesperius, swana steorra.[3]
Humerus, excl.
Hinulus, hindcealf.
Hircus, bucca.
Horrcum, beren.
Hordeum, bere.
Hebitauit, aslacude.
Hrodia[1] *lex*, cipemonna riht.
Hereditas, ierfe.
Hostia proprie, fyrdtimber.
Hincneomon,[4] næderbita.
Herba proprie, gærs.
Hedera nigra, wudubind, corþifig.[5]
Hierobotanim, rædic.[6]
Herba iras, gorst.[7]
Hinnulicapini, eldne.

Insitum, gecynde.
Imis, of neoþeweardum.
Iubare, leoman.
In imo, inoþan.
Ita prorsus, eallenga.
Infulas, weorþmynd.
In catalogo, on getæle.
Infectis, geætredum, bewyledum, befyledum.
Inconuenienter, ungerisenlice.
In oromate, on gastlicre gesihþe.
Instrumentis, andgeloman.
Iacturam, æfwyrdlan.

Inmunes, clæclease, laþlease.
Inextricabilem, þa unabrecendlican.
Indæptæ, þære begitenan.
Inportunus, se gema.
5 *Internicionis*, ewilde, forwyrde.
Ingruere, ongehreosan.
Inhianter, grædelice.
Inhians, grædig.
Ilibus, smælþearmum.[8]
10 *Intestinum*, þearm.
Incompta, ungefrætwodu.
Inguina, smælþearmas.
Insolescat, wlancaþ.
Insolentiam, wlence.
15 *Intercapidinis*, firstmearces.[9]
Indruticans,[10] wræstende, odde wlancende.
Indagantes, aspyrigende, odde asmeagende.
20 *Instanter*, baldlice.
Inlecebrarum, unalifendlecum.
Increpuerit, þunode, odde hleoþrede.
In simulacra, on anlicnesse.
Inlibatæ, þære ungederedan.
25 *In clandistino*, on þæm diglan.
Introrsum, inn.
In cunis, in cildcradelum.
Ingerebat, ongebrohte.
In gemino, on twyfealdre.
30 *Ingeminent*, getwyfylden.
Ignaris, unwisum.
Integritatis, onwealhnesse.
Integer, onwalh.
Idoneam, þanefulle.
35 *Ingluuiæ*, frecnesse.[11]
Inexperto, unafundenum.
In remoto, asyndedre.
Incommoditate, ungetæsnesse.
Inuisendum, to secanne.
40 *Intulerit*, ongebrohte.
Inter, betwux.
Instinctu, onbryrdinge.

[1] Sic MS. R. W.
[2] Read: *hesterno*. R. W.
[3] i. e. the shepherds' star.
[4] For *Ichneumon*.
[5] Cf. pag. 299 l. 1. R. W.
[6] Cf. pag. 135 l. 23. R. W.

[7] Cf. pag. 299 l. 3. R. W.
[8] Cf. pag. 159 l. 37. R. W.
[9] Cf. pag. 27 l. 31 and pag. 384 l. 9. R. W.
[10] So the MS. R. W.
[11] Read: *fretnesse*. R. W.

Instincta, inswapen.
Inuisum, þone laþan.
Inuisa, þa laþan.
Inpudens, scomleas.
Inuisorum, laþra.
Inuestes cateruas, þa ænlecan heapas and þa ungebyrdan heapas.
Imperii, rices.
Imperitat, wealdeþ.
Incestium, hæmed.
Incestus, forhealden.
In arida, on drigum.
Incestatur, hæmend.
Infamiam, to unhlisan.
Infamis, þæs unhliseadgan, orret- scipe.
Inedia, wædlnes.
Ingesserunt, inræcan.
Ingruens, onfillende, odde hreosende.
Inluuiem, widl and ful.
Illinc, donan.
Istinc, heonan.
In tantum, swa swiþe.
In conum, on heannesse.
Ilico, raþe.
Inultus, geþreatod and genided.
Inuitant, geniddan.
Interualla, hwilsticcu.
Incentor, wrehtend, tyhtend.
Intra, binnan.
Iubelemus, þæt freolsger.[1]
Impendebatur, wæs brytnod.
Infra, æfter.
Inquiens, cweþende.
Indicia, tacn.
Indigena, landleod.
Interpellata, hio wæs beden.
Inproperio,[2] hospe.
Inpingere, onspurnan, odde æfæstan.
Insimulare, gewregan.
Insimulatio, wrohte.
Inlustris, þære æþelican.
Incommodum, unbriece, ungescræpe, inutile.

In consortio, on þæm gemanum.
Inconsulte, unrædlice.
Indolem, gebierdne, þone æþelan geongan.
5 *Instigauit,* onbryrde.
Insigniter, æþelice.
Inrumpere, inræsan.
Inruptiones, onræsan.
Inceptis, onginne.
10 *In pulpito,* on rædescamole.[3]
In tribulano territorio, on þæm suador gereflande.
Interimitur, wearþ ofslægen.
Inerguminum, þære gewitseocan.
15 *Inerguminos,* wodan.
Inpensa, gebryttodre.
Ianitor, duruweard.
Insignis, mære.
Insignia, mærnesse.
20 *Insignem,* mærne.
Inpudicarum, unclænra.
Inlicias, ongespanest.
Inprobus, unsæle, gemah.
Infectum, ungeworht, geblanden.
25 *Iuris,* æwe.
Innupti, unforgifenum.
In rapinam, on reaflac.
Iecor, lifer.
In clero, on preostheape.
30 *Inflexibili,* unabegendlicre.
Indulcauit, geswette.
Intemerata, ungearwyrd.
Infesta, þa reþan.
Infestationes, teonan.
35 *Ineunte,* ongangendre.
Imbricibus, hroftigelum.
Ingluuiem, in þane wasend.[4]
Iamque, somod.
Inertes, ungleawe.
40 *Idem,* hoc.
Igni sacrum, oman.[5]
Ignarium,[6] algeweorc.
Intertiare, geborhfæstan.
Inima,[7] untosliten.

[1] The meaning of *freols* is: a time of freedom, holy day, feast; freolsger denotes: a feast-year, jubilee. R. W.
[2] Read: inprobrio (or opprobrio). R. W.
[3] Cf. pag. 404 l. 40. R. W.

[4] Cf. pag. 419 l. 35. R. W.
[5] Read: ignis sacer or ignem sacrum. Cf. pag. 26 l. 4. R. W.
[6] Sic, for *igniarium*. R. W.
[7] So has the MS. R. W.

Inpetigo, teter.
Impetigo, eagan wenn, odde weargebræde.
Inprouisu, færinga, hrædlice.
Infestatio, unleoþowacnes.
Infestatione, sorheriunge.
Inminente, ætwesendre.
Ingesta, ondoen.
Infestus, ungetæse.
Inola, colone.[1]
Instites, sweþelas.
Intexunt, awunden.
Iners, æswind, asoleen.
Interlitam, besmyred.
Indigeste, unofercumene.
Infici, gemengde.
Inpastorem,[2] biswicend.
Inter primores, between ieldrum.
Inuolucus, weoluc.
Inquilinis,[3] geneat.
Indolis, hyhtful, þionde, þone gleawan.
Inpingit, gemearcode, *uel signat*.
Incantata, gegælen.
Incantatores, galdrigean.
Intentatis, biotiaþ.
Inundatio, gyte.
Incursus, ongon.
Intrinicio,[4] forsliet.
In sirtim, on sandgeweorp.
Inmoratur, wunaþ.
Intransmeabili, unoferfere.
Inbellem, orwige.
Initiatum, gesteped, gehalgodne.
In catamo, in bæce.
Iota, sohetha.[5]
Irridabant, tyhton.
Isca, tyndre.[6]
Iuncus, rise.[7]
Iungetum,[8] riseþyfel.

Iuuencibus, riseþyfel.
In capsella, on ciste.
In sitharciis,[9] in fætelsum.
In triclinio, on þreofealdum huse.[10]
5 *Incursere*, onslogan.
Industria, gleaunes.
Inperauit, wilt.
In antris, on holum.
Iugeri, æceras.
10 *In nemore*, on bearwe.
Ibices, fyrengatum.[11]
In singultum, in sicettunge and geoxunge.
Inclyti, mære.
15 *Inclitum*, mærne.
In competis, on wega gemotum.
Ignaui, earge.
In conclaui, on cofan.
In iubilo, on drime.
20 *In clangore*, on hwelunge.
In fastigio, in heannesse.
Indictio, gecwed.
Iuniperum, quicbeam.
Instaura, geedniwa.
25 *In tritura*, in trifelunge.
Insontam, unsynnige.
Inibis, ongang.
Interrasilem, inheald.
Imperitia, unglædnes.
30 *In pelicatu*,[8] on cifeshade.
Inpetigine, on tetere.[12]
Inpulerit, bædt.
In prouectione, on wegfore.
Irqui, ongneras.
35 *Interceptus est*, aranad wæs.
Isic, leax.
Insabula, meodoma.
Intercilium, betwuh bruwum.
Index, becnend, scytefinger.
40 *Iugula*, iucboga.

[1] Cf. Cock. Leechd. III pag. 325. R. W.
[2] Read: *impostorem*. R. W.
[3] So has the MS. R. W.
[4] An error for *internecio*. R. W.
[5] Cf. pag. 28 l. 33. R. W.
[6] Cf. pag. 28 l. 38. R. W.
[7] Cf. pag. 135 l. 16 and pag. 299 l. 26. R. W.
[8] Read: *juncetum*. R. W.
[9] Sic, for *sitarchiis*. R. W.
[10] The glossator has singularly mistranslated this word, through bungling at the derivation.
[11] Cf. pag. 26 l. 2. R. W.
[12] It seems evident, from the Anglo-Saxon interpretation, that the author of this gloss took the Latin for two words,

Iugum, iuc.
Iuger, iuc.
Ibiscum, biscopwyrt.[1]
Imbilium, leohtleap.
Iurisperiti, rædboran.
Inimum,[2] gliw.
Inruunt, onhreosaþ.
Impetu, þære ...
In zonis, in gyrdelsum.
Inter natos, betwuh bearnum.
In biuio, in twega wega gelæte.
In agonia,[3] in elne.
Inualescebant, strangedon, swiþedon.
In natataria, on sundmere.
Institis, in swaþum.
In preterium,[4] in mæþelern.
In cateno, in tisege.
Inproba, gemah.
Inprouitatem, gemangnesse.
In gimnasio, on leorninghuse.
In propatulo, on æwiscnesse.
In gastrimargiæ,[3] in gifernesse.
Inmunitas, orceasnes.
In atomo, in breahtme.
Inter biothanatas, betweonan self-myrþras.
Instinctu, tihtnesse.
In genitali, in þære gecyndelcum.
Inprecatatur, bæd.
Inauditum, ungefræge.
Inletus, getyhted.
Insectiones, ehtnesse.
Infiscaretur, gegafelod, bestroden wære.
Inrosatum, or rosena.
Interpellans, gretende.
In focularibus, on heordum.
Intempestiue, in swigean midre nihte.
Indulte, þæs alefdan.

Inexpertus, unandwis.
In tribuli, in þæm gesibbum.
Ineluctuabilis,[5] þa unoferwinnene.
Indegitamenta,[6] þara boca.
5 *Interpres,* wealhstod.
In luxum, in lust.
Incanduisset, onhatode.
In tribulanam, in þa burh.
In basileon, on cyninga bocum.
10 *Inlicias,* spones.
Insectatum, ehtende.[7]
Improperasse, þæt hie ætwite.
Indisciplinatorum, unþeawfulra.
Inter Scyllam, betwuh þa frecnesse
15 stowe.
Indisruptis, untoslitenum.
Iconisma, gelicnes.
Imbribus, scurum.
In Tempis, on scenfeldum.[8]
20 *Ignicomis,* se fyrfeaxna.
Incestans, gewemde.
Ingurgitat, wæteþ.
In extasi, in modes heannesse, on gastlicre gesihde.
25 *Infindens,* gerawende, slitende, and ceorfende.
In ueribus, in fnasum.
Infidus, ungetreowe.
Infamare, georrettan.
30 *Inflictis,* onslægum.
Inuestis, ungebyrd.
Iaculatas, þa flanihtan.
Inpiger, unsleac.
Inspirans, onswætende.
35 *In diuos,* in god.
Ioppiter, þunor, odde dur.[9]
In Latio, in Eatole.
Infecit, geblende.
Illexit, beswac, getihte.[10]

---

[1] Cf. pag. 270 l. 33. R. W.
[2] *Inimum* is an evident and gross blunder of the Anglo-Saxon glossator, who, in arranging the Latin words in alphabetical order, misread *in* for *m*. It should be *Mimus.*
[3] So the MS. R. W.
[4] For *pratorium.*
[5] Read: *ineluctabilis.* R. W.

[6] Sic, for *indigitamenta.* R. W.
[7] Cf. pag. 424 l. 32. R. W.
[8] „In the bright-fields." The Anglo-Saxon interpretation of the classical Tempe.
[9] In this rather curious gloss, the two names of the northern god are introduced to explain the classical Jupiter.
[10] This word is in another hand, but nearly contemporary.

In thermas, on bæþe.
Incultis, unbeganum.
Irritat, gremede.
In spira,[1] in hringe.
Instantia, inwunenesse.
In carruca, on scride, oþþe on **cræte**.
In preceps, **on** scyteræs, oþþe **on** færfyll, unforesceawadlic.
Ingenitam, æþelborene.
In conticinio,[2] in swigunge.
Intentabat, beotade.
Intentarentur, waran beotende.
Inficere, gehiwian, geregnian.
Itidentidem, eft gelice.
Impetrare, begitan.
Inpolito, reþum.
In quis, on þæm.
Ictibus, slægum.
Infandum, þæt manwræce, manful.
Infausti, þæs ungesæligan.
Iuuencum, steor.
Iuniculus, iung hryþer.
Infestos, þa unhioran.
Infecta, gewemde.
In spera,[1] on hringgewindlan.
In cupis, on bydenum.
In giro, on ymbhwyrfte.
In occa, on fyrh.
Ius, **æriht.**
Ius, brod.
Incus, onfilte.
In margine, on ofre.
Infandas, þa manfullan.
Infecta, gewæcte.
In saltibus, on wuduwaldum.
Itidem, þæt ilce.
Iuuenta, iuguþhad.
Index, tæcned.
Insanum, þone weddendan.
Iuuabat, lysted.
In palato, in goman, þær mon þone smæc todæleþ.
In gracilem, on smælne.

[1] For *in sphera*.
[2] *Conticinium* was the medieval Latin word for midnight.
[3] For *infrigat*, of course.
[4] Cf. pag. 426 l. 19. R. W.

Insulsior, unsaltera.
Inficians, lehtriende.
Inpedit, agæleþ.
In frigore, on cele.
5 *Infridat*,[3] cælþ.
Iam, geara, oþþe geogara.
Incolomi, gesundum.
Inermis, ungewæpnad.
Inter saxa, betweonan stanas.
10 *Inheret*, oncliofad.
In cespites, on tyrf.
Incerta, ungewis.
Iuga, duna swioran.
Infandum, sio godwræce.[4]
15 *Insomnes*, unslæpige.
Inplumen, ungefeþerednc.
Insertum, ingeseted.
In olitorum, in geweaxenra.
In cucumerario, on wyrttune.
20 *Inmane*, ungemetlic.
Inauris, earhring.
Indruto, sæflode.[5]
Institor, cipemann.
Ierarchon, heah **landrica.**
25 *Ipotamus*, **sæhengest.**
Internasus, nosgrisele.
Inens,[6] cinn.
Ilium, rysle.
Ibin, rindeclifre.[7]
30 *Isica*, mearhgehæc.[8]
Imus, oxa on frumteame.
Ippus, indrihtenwieg.
Interdum, oft.
Internicies, ferhqualu.[6]
35 *Iusta lance*, mid þa efnan helurblede.
In glanigeris, in þæm stanberendum.
In exercitatione, on behogadnesse.
Inaniter, unnytlice.
Iactatis, gelegdum.
40 *Imperalis*[6] *hypodromi*, þæs caserlican huses.
In sabanis, on scetum.
Incentor, tyhtere.

[5] *sæflod* means: sea-flood, tide, inundation. R. W.
[6] So the MS. R. W.
[7] Cf. Bosw. D. 55y. R. W.
[8] Cf. pag. 127 l. 25. R. W.

Inrumpere, onblæstan.
Ingenuis, mid tuxum.[1]
Infatigabiliter, ungedrehtlice.
Ineluctabilis, unafohtendlic.
Inepta, þa ungelimplican.
In frixorio, on bræde pannan.
Idus, swæsenddagas.
Intende, beheald.
Inperbitas,[2] gemah.
In orbem, on þysne mislecan ymbhwyft[3] and bleofagan.
Interna, þa inlecan.
Inditur, is ingelæded.
Inditus, bediped.
Intento, higiendre.
Iure, anwalde.
Inrita, se unnytta and forhogoda.
Increpitans, hleþrende.
Inlecebris, tihtennum.
Ingratus, lad.
Inuisus, lad.
Incitamenta, tyhtenne.
Intula, wealewyrt.
Intractabilis, inliþewac.[4]
Industria, geornesse.
Inpendebat, sealde.
In dies crudesceret, aford.[5]
Interuentu, þingunge.
In pacte, an slægenre.
Innitentes, wiþerhlyniende.
Inpulsore, bædendre.
Infractus, gewemmed.
Inopinum, unasedde.
Inditas, þa gesettan.
Inter primores, betweoh yldrum.
Inuoluco, wiþewinde.[6]
Ibices, firgengæt.[7]
Inconstans, unfæstræd.
Ius, mennisc riht.
Ius naturale, gecynde riht.
Ius ciuile, anre burge riht.

Ius gentium, calra þeoda riht.
Ius militare, cempena riht.
Ius puplicum,[3] ealdormanna riht.
Ius Quiritum, Romwara sundorriht.
5 *Iurisconsultus, iurisperitus, id est*, rihtscrifend, *siue* domsettend.
Ius liberarum, somhiwena yrfebec.
Inritum testamentum, awægune yrfebec.
Inofficiosum testamentum, unarlice yrfebec.
Ius, anwald, *a iure possidendo*.
Intestata hereditas, ungewriten yrfe, *eadem et caduca*.
15 *Instrumentum*, tohl.[8]
Instructum, geworht weorc.
Integri restitutione, ofstondene beod, *siue* ofstouden feoh.
Iniuria, unriht.
20 *Infictiatio*, borges andsaca, *idem et abiuratio*.
Incerta iudicium, geligra witnung.
Ignominium, seondehlewung, *siue* fraceþu, *idem et infamium*.
25 *Intempestum*, midniht.
In centurias seniorum et iuniorum diuisus; centurias getalu *siue* heapas *dictæ*.
Insipidum, quod saporem non habet,
30 *hoc est* unmeagle *siue* æmelle.
Inuitat me, he me lathath.
Inuitat se, he him thinget.[9]
Infurcarunt, ahengon.
Infurcatus, ahongen.
35 *Inculcare, sepe repetere, et aliquando inculcare est* inbecwedan; *est enim metaforicos ab eo quod est calcara*.[8]
Immolatio, onsægegiung.
Inquilinus, tungebur.[10]
40 *Indigine*,[a] inlenda.
Interpinnium, mildelflera.[11]

[1] Cf. pag. 412 l. 25. R. W.
[2] For *improbitas*.
[3] So the MS. R. W.
[4] So the MS. Cf. pag. 27 l. 2. R. W.
[5] aford is the translation of *in dies*, not of *crudesceret*. Cf. pag. 27 l. 13. R. W.
[6] The wild convolvulus, or bindweed.
[7] Cf. pag. 423 l. 11. R. W.
[8] Sic MS.

[9] In the manuscript, here and in the line preceding, the *th* is used instead of the Anglo-Saxon letter. This occurs again a little further on, but very rarely. (Cf. Nr. l. R. W.)
[10] Cf. pag. 27 l. 41 and pag. 422 l. 20. R. W.
[11] Read: *middelflera*. Cf. pag. 157 l. 17. R. W.

Interscapulum, mildelgescyldru.[1]
Intestina, þearmas.
Ieiuna, smælþearmas.
Iricius, se læssa il.
Istrix, se mara il.[2]
Ilex, accyn.[3]
Indicum, basu hæwen.
Insubuli, webbeamas.[4]
Idromelum, æppelwin, beor.
Iris illirica, hwatend.
Inelaborate, ungeswuncenre.
Inminutus, onboren.

Lupatis, bridlum, *frœnis*.
Lento, þæm ton, lihte, odde late.[5]
Lapa, clife.[6]
Lenta, toh.
Luxus, wynne.
Lego, ic lese.
Luxoria, wynn.
Lenocinia, leastihtinge, leasoleeung.
Lamentabile, heafsang.
Lasciuia, gagolbærnesse.
Lunulis, mynum.[7]
Lunules, mynescillingas.[7]
Liburnas, flotscipu.
Labara,[8] segnes, gudfana.
Lima, feol, odde mylenstan.
Laturus, adreogende.
Laturæ, adreag.
Lustramenta, deofolgild.
Liniamento, hlodan, gegirelan.
Liniamentis, hræglgewædum.
Latuerunt, bemidon.
Ludificare, gebysmerian.
Liquentis, (þære) flitan gesceafte.
Liminium (f)irste.
Liquidas, þa hlutran and þa sciran.
Lymphas, wæter.

[1] Read: *middelgescyldru*.
[2] The greater *it* was the porcupine, the lesser the hedgehog. (Cf. pag. 122 l. 21. R. W.)
[3] Cf. Bosw. D. 1ᵗ. R. W.
[4] Cf. pag. 423 l. 37. R. W.
[5] Cf. l. 17 and pag. 29 l. 39. R. W.
[6] Cf. pag. 29 l. 26. R. W.
[7] Cf. pag. 30 l 40. R. W.
[8] Read: *labra*. R. W.

Liuoris, æfestes.
Lacertum, earm.
Lenocinia, tyhtenne.
Lenocinantibus, leastyhtendum.
5 *Liuoris*, lædde andan.
Liuor, wam.
Latebra, heolstre.
Litterature, namrædenne.
Largiriæ,[9] gifernesse.
10 *Liberalitate*, freodome, odde cystignesse.
Lectitando, eft rædende.
Lentesceret, oncleofode.
Ludorum, plegena.
15 *Lustratur*, geclænsod.
Lustris, facum, odde fifgearum.
Lis, gecid.
Laterculis, getalum.
Leuirum, tacor.[10]
20 *Longiusculæ*, feor, odde wide.
Liuidas, da wanihtan.
Libida,[9] þa wannan.
Limpidis, scinendum.
Ludibrio, bysmer.
25 *Luctatorum*, wræstliendra.
Luctatur,[11] wræstlere.
Letamen, gor, scear.
Longius, wide.
Lupercatibus, godgildum.
30 *Libescant*,[9] æfestian, lælian.
Lustro, ryne.
Lepida, mid wlæcre, þær egetyngan, wod.[12]
Leporis, wlætnesse.
35 *Larbula*,[13] egesegrima.
Lagena, croh.
Legythum, croh.
Laude,[14] lawerce.
Lexiua, leah.[15]

[9] Sic MS.
[10] Cf. pag. 30 l. 3. R. W.
[11] Read: *luctator*. R. W.
[12] Cf. pag. 29 l. 37. R. W.
[13] For *laruula*, the diminutive of *larua*, a hag or witch. (Cf. pag. 29 l. 8. R. W.)
[14] Of course for *alauda*, a lark. Another instance of our glossator's ignorance.
[15] Cf. pag. 29 l. 16. R. W.

Lacessitus, gegremed.
Latrariis, bordþacan.[1]
Laquear, fierst.[2]
Laquearea, fierste.[3]
Lacunar, flode, hrof.[4]
Lacessiens, gremmende.
Lactuca, þudistel, leahtric.[5]
Lacunar, hushefen, odde heofenhrof.
Larus, meu.
Lebetes, hweras.
Laena, rift.
Labat,[6] wagaþ, aslad, and gefioll.
Latratur, byree.[7]
Lardariulus, freemase.[8]
Lebes, hwer.[9]
Lingula, gyrdelhringe.[10]
Legula, gyrdelhringe.[10]
Lembum, liste, odde þræs.[11]
Limbus, listum odde þræsum.
Lendina, hnitu.[12]
Lepidum, lista . . þ . . .[11]
Lectidiclatum, geþroren flyte.[13]
Lepus, hara.
Lentum uimen, tohgerd.[14]
Lenticula, pise, ærenu, elebyt.[15]
Lesta, borda.
Ligones, mettocas.[16]
Libramentum, lifer.
Liburnices, geree.
Liuida toxica, þa wonnan ætrenan.
Libertabus, friglætan.
Libertus, friglæta.
Liciatorium, hefeldgyrd.

Limax, snægl.
Ligustrum, hunigsuge.
Liliagrum, slægn.[17]
Licidus, hwet.
5 *Liquidus*, hwet.
Liscisque, mid læfrum.
Liberalitas, ropnes.
Linea, webtawa.
Licia, hefeldþræde.
10 *Licium*, hefeld.
Lucor, freeed.[18]
Lumbare, gyrdel odde brec.
Luculentum, torhtnes.
Ludi litterare,[19] stæfplegan.
15 *Lutrus*, otor.
Lucius, hacod.
Lurdus, lemphealt.
Lupus, bears.
Ludares, steor.[20]
20 *Lumbricus*, renwyrm.
Luteum, crocea.
Lupercal, hearh.[21]
Lucum, hearga.
Luscinia, nihtegale.
25 *Luscinius*, froex.[22]
Lupa,[23] wulf.
Lupinare, wulfholu.
Lumbulos, lendebræde.
Lactans, sucende.
30 *Luxus*,[24] heof.
Luxerunt, weopan.
Ligonem, mattue.[25]
Lagones, mattucas.[25]

---

[1] Cf. Bosw. D. 19u. R. W.
[2] Cf. pag. 29 l. 18. R. W.
[3] Cf. pag. 29 l. 31. R. W.
[4] Cf. pag. 29 l. 22 and l. 8. R. W
[5] Cf. pag. 29 l. 21. R. W.
[6] Cf. pag. 29 l. 29. R. W.
[7] Cf. pag. 29 l. 32. R. W.
[8] Cf. pag. 29 l. 33. R. W.
[9] Cf. pag. 29 l. 38. R. W.
[10] Cf. pag. 30 l. 1 and 24. R. W.
[11] Cf. pag. 29 l. 42. R. W.
[12] Cf. pag. 30 l. 2. R. W.
[13] Cf. pag. 30 l. 4. R. W.
[14] Cf. pag. 30 l. 6. R. W.
[15] Cf. pag. 30 l. 7. R. W.
[16] Cf. pag. 30 l. 10. R. W.
[17] Cf. pag. 30 l. 28. R. W.
[18] Cf. pag. 30 l. 38. R. W
[19] So has the MS. R. W.
[20] Cf. pag. 31 l. 8. R. W.
[21] *Hearh* means a temple, or holy place, as in the next line, where *lucus* is intended no doubt for a holy grove. The glossator appears to have been ill acquainted with the meaning of the word *lupercal*.
[22] Cf. pag. 31 l. 14. R. W.
[23] Cf. pag 31 l. 15 and 16. R. W.
[24] Read: *luctus*. R. W.
[25] Cf. pag. 432 l 27. R. W.

Lorica anata,[1] hringedu byrne.
Limpidissimos, þa hlutresdan.[2]
Lustrata, geondhworfen.
Lora, rapas.
Luteres,[3] tigelan.
Leunculi, leonhwelpas.
Lecitho,[4] elehorn.
Linxerunt, liccedon.
Linxere, liccigan.
Linies, þu smyrest.
Liniuit, smyrede.
Lenis, smede.
Lita, gesmyrede and gehyrde.
Lentis, pysan.[5]
Lacinia, lappan.
Lacos, laca.
Linum, fleax.
Labrum, brerd.
Lucanica, mearh.[6]
Luciuida, leohtsceawigend.
Lygistra,[7] hopu.
Larax, ened.[8]
Litorius, wærna.[9]
Locusta, gærshoppe.
Lana, wull.
Luporum, wull.[10]
Leno, wifþegn.
Lanugine, flyse.
Lacrime, tearas.
Lanugo, wullknoppa.[11]
Labium, welor.
Labellis, welerum.
Lingua, tunge.
Lac, meolc.
Lectantium, meolocsucendra.
Latus, side.

Lumbia,[12] lendena.
Lucerna, blæcern.
Lichinis,[13] blæcernum.
Lux, leoht.
5 *Lampas*, leohtfæt.
Lectum, bed.
Larda, spic.
Lanterne, leohtfætes.
Lancona, cylle.
10 *Laquear*, ræsn.
Limen, þereswold, odde duru.
Lactudiclum, geþroren flyte.[14]
Lac coagolatum, molcen.
Larbanum, segl.[15]
15 *Labara*, gegyrele.
Luxcus, (a)nige.[16]
Lintre, bate.
Lintrum, lytle bate.
Lixa, leah.[17]
20 *Legumen*, bean.
Latrena, genge.[18]
Latex, burna.
Laticum, wætera.
Lacertus, efete.
25 *Limphale*, wæter.
Locuste, stapan.
Lunaticos, bræcseoce.
Loculos, seodas.
Loculum, seodcyst.
30 *Lintrem*, bat.
Liquido, andgitlice.
Lurcones, sliteras.
Lacertosis, dæm earmswiþum.
Luxoriante, fæste gebuf.
35 *Librantis*, heolorende.
Librate, ahiolorod.

---

[1] For *hamata*, ringed mail.
[2] Read: hlutrestan.
[3] Sic, for *lateres*. R. W.
[4] Read: *lecythos*. R. W.
[5] Cf. pag. 30 l. 7 and 432 l. 25. R. W.
[6] *Lucanica* denotes a *sausage* (= mearh-gehæc). R. W.
[7] Read: *ligustra*. R. W.
[8] Cf. pag. 258 l. 11. R. W.
[9] Cf. pag. 260 l. 21 and pag. 286 l. 16. R. W.
[10] *wull* is an error for *wulf*, or *wulfa*. R. W.
[11] Bosw. printed *wullknoppa* (36 f). R. W
[12] So has the MS. R. W.
[13] *Lichinis*, an error for *lychnuchis*? R. W.
[14] Cf. pag. 30 l. 4 and 432 l. 22. R. W.
[15] Read: *labanum*. R. W.
[16] Read: *luscus*, *anige*. Cf. pag. 30 l. 37. R. W.
[17] Cf. pag. 431 l. 39. R. W.
[18] Cf. pag. 29 l. 12. R. W.

Liniamento, limgelecg.
Liberalitatis, rumheortnesse.
Liminio,[1] wræcsiþe.
Libitos, licongum.
Lurca, fretan.[2]
Lurcatur, freted.
Loeto tenus, od dead.
Loetaliter, deadlice.
Latrinarum, gengena.[3]
Lupercalibus, þæm gildendum.[4]
Lictorum, þegna.[5]
Lenonum, sponera, wægnera.[6]
Liture, liming.
Lepida, getinge.
Labescit, aglad.
Laturi, þrowgende.[7]
Larbatos,[8] hreofe.
Luto, wurmaman.[9]
Laudacismi, þære uncysest.[7]
Læti, wyrþenna.
Lauta munia,[7] þa clænan þenunga.
Lances, beodas.
Libelli, pundes.
Lacessant, sliten odde gremeden.
Lippos oculos, da surigan eagan.
Lautos, clæne.
Lentescunt, toadan, tedan.
Lodix, loda.
Lictor, þegn, witnere.
Lautea, dæm giolwum.
Libosas, da giolwan.
Lenticule, croges odde ampellan.
Labe, womme.
Ludrica, plegan, luftas.[10]
Luendi, þrowgende.[11]
Lectissima, þæt gecoreneste.

Larbata, se unf . . .[12]
Latrat, beorceþ.[13]
Lita, attre gemæled.
Lento defruto, geswettum.[14]
5 *Lurconibus,* slitendlicum.
Lurcare, forgle(ndrian).[15]
Lixarum, wæterberere, odde nedlungum.
Lautumiæ, carcernes.
10 *Legithum,*[16] ampellan, odde elefæt.
Lictorum, witniendra þiowa, odde flæsewellera.
Libidus,[17] da wonnan.
Lupercalia, gelegergield.
15 *Luem,* adle and wole.
Latona, þures modur.[18]
Ligustra, blostman.
Lauta, þa clænan odde *munda.*
Lances, wægscala.
20 *Lutea,* þæt giolureade.
Lent.., druncen, drynewirig.
Liram, hearpan.
Lauri, laurbeames.
Laribus, fyrum.
25 *Larem,* fyr.
Lurida, da sweartan.
Luridus, wan and blæc.
Lutex,[19] sæ.
Libros, rinde.
30 *Luebant,* þoledan, and þrowedan.
Lethea, þæm helwenlican.
Lustra, færeltu.
Liquitur, formelteþ.
Laterculus, talu.[20]
35 *Lampas Titanea,* þæt sunlice leohtfæt.

---

[1] For *e limine? eliminatio?* R. W.
[2] Read: *lurcare* or *lurcari.* R. W.
[3] Cf. pag. 435 l. 21. R. W.
[4] Cf. pag. 437 l. 14. R. W.
[5] Cf. l. 29 and pag. 437 l. 11. R. W.
[6] Cf. pag. 171 l. 28. R. W.
[7] So has the MS. R. W.
[8] Apparently for *larvatos.* (Cf. pag. 431 l. 35. R. W.)
[9] Cf. Cock. III, pag. 349. R. W.
[10] Read: *ludicra,* and *lustas.* R. W.
[11] Cf. l. 16. R. W.
[12] *unfægra,* I suppose. R. W.

[13] Cf. pag. 432 l. 13. R. W.
[14] Cf. pag. 128 l. 34 and pag. 281 l. 23. R. W.
[15] The glossator seems to have translated: *forglendrian.* Cf. Leo Gl. 359 l. 52. R. W.
[16] For *lecythum.*
[17] For *lividos.*
[18] Thor's mother, a curious illustration of the northern mythology.
[19] Read: *latex.* R. W.
[20] The meaning of *laterculum* is a catalogue of employments. R. W.

Lumina, mine eagan.
Luminibus, eagum.
Lusit, plegode.
Ludo, ic plege.
Ligor, ic beo bunden.
Lesis, dæm gederedum.
Lacerata, tocorfen.
Libat, byrgeþ.
Legit, ceoseþ.
Luxerat, heofde.[1]
Lanio, slaga.
Laguoenas, ambras.[2]
Lanio, flæscmangere.
Lorumentum,[3] widde.
Lappis, clatum.
Limpus, honsteore.[4]
Lemprida,[5] lempedu.
Lapidaria, cweornbill.
Lacontrapis, angeltwecca.[6]
Lisca, secg.
Lilium, lilie.
Leo, lio.
Leontopedium, lionfot.
Leena, lio.
Lugubriter, hefelice.
Lurconibus, grædgum.
Longanimem, langsume.
Lustrans, fælsende.
Lustraturus, geondferende.
Liberalitatis,[7] stæflecum.
Limphaticum, wodan.[8]
Litaturus, onsacende.
Leuius, ædre.
Longe lateque, side and wide.
Litrat, onblæwþ.[9]
Lusit, beswac.
Libet, racsode.
Lustrat, clænsade.

Lapsa, brohte.
Lacerna, hacele, oððe lotha.
Lymphatico, wedende.[10]
Lien, milte.
5 *Lucunar*, flode.[11]
Locium, ate.
Limu,[12] reowe.
Lena, reowe.
Lena linea, linen reowe.
10 *Lithargiam*, gimynde biniming.[13]
Lienosis, milteodu.[14]
Lienteria, mete utsihd.[15]
Ligamentum, onwritung.[16]
Ligatura, sarclad.
15 *Libri iuris*, æbec.
Lex, folcrædenne, *siue* calles folces gesetnes.
Legatum, gewriten yrfe.
Legaturius, gewriten yrfeweard.
20 *Locatio*, behyrung *siue* behyred feoh.
Lamentum, sape.
Lotium, hlond.
Lana sucida, unawaxen wul.
Lectio, bocræding.
25 *Lectores*, bocræderas.
Lyrici, scopas.
Liberi, suna.
Lumbi, hupbanan.
Lacus ubi frugum liquor decurrit, id
30 *est* winmere *siue* wincole.
Limus, slim.
Lolium, lasur.
Linea, rihtebred.
Leuidensis, thynwefen hrægl.[17]
35 *Lebes*, lytel cytel.
Licinius, weoce.[18]
Leptefilos, hymlie.[19]
Laterculum, belene.

[1] Cf. pag. 433 l. 30. R. W.
[2] Cf. pag. 431 l. 36. R. W.
[3] Read: *loramentum*. R. W.
[4] Cf. Bosw. D. 371. R. W.
[5] Sic MS.
[6] Cf. pag. 122 l. 22. R. W.
[7] The meaning of *staflec* is: belonging to letters, literary. R. W.
[8] Cf. pag. 30 l. 19. R. W.
[9] Read: *lituat*? R. W.
[10] Cf. pag. 438 l. 31. R. W.

[11] Read: *lacunar*. R. W.
[12] Read: *lana* or *lena*. Cf. next line. R. W.
[13] Read: *lithargiam*. R. W.
[14] Cf. pag. 113 l. 11. R. W.
[15] Cf. pag. 113 l. 25. R. W.
[16] Read: onwridung. R. W.
[17] Cf. pag. 151 l. 23. R. W.
[18] Read: *licinium*. R. W.
[19] Read: *septefilos*. Cf. pag. 295 l. 28. R. W.

Lappatium, docce.
Lattyride, lybcorn.
Lapadiun, lelodre.[1]
Lassar uel æsdre, gyþrife.[2]
Ludiuaga, wandriendu.
Latibulum, syretum.

Machinam, searocræft.
Molimen, searo.
Moliuntur, syrwad.
Memoriale, eowres gemyndelican.
Mentis, modes, gleawnes.
Mucrone, sweorde.
Mucronibus, sweordum.
Mulsæ, þære milisean.
Macheram, sweord.
Munificentiam, festnunge.
Malagma, læcedome, clame.
Meri, þæs clænan wines.
Mala, æppel.
Malus, apuldor.
Mestam, þa unrotan.
Mala granata, æppelcyrnlu.[5]
Malifer, æpelbere.
Monarchiam, anwald.
Molaribus, grindetoþum, tuxum.
Macheram, mece.[4]
Mucrone, mece.[5]
Municipes, burhware.
Manipulatim, heapmælum.
Maniplis, heapum.
Mulionis, horsþegnes.
Manipulo, heape.
Mentam . ., gema . . .
Minutatim, styccemælum.
Membratim, limmælum.
Malleoli, þara spaca speldra.[6]

Morarum, ieldinga.
Morosa, eldendlice.
Manubias, herereaf.
Macilento, gehlænedum.
5 *Moenia,* weallas.
Moema,[7] stangetimbru.
Magnificum, micellic.
Matrone, þære hlafdian.
Municipum,[13] burhscipe.
10 *Municipatu,* burhræddenne.
Municipium, þære burge.
Mandibularum, geagla.
Minaretur, beotode.
Mactus, se myrwa, eced.
15 *Musitantes,* þa runiendan.
Mancum, anhende.
Mandras, locu.[8]
. . . . .[9]
. . , .
20 *Mastigiis,* leadesclynum, leadstafum.
Minacem, þa ormætan.
Merita, geearnunga.
Macta, þa magecetan.[10]
Matrimonia, hæmedgemanan.
25 *Muliercule,* earmum wife.
Marginem, ofor.
Marginibus, ofrum.
Mitescere, growan, milescian.
Marsupia, seodas.
30 *Mediocri,* gneþre.
Marsum, wyrmgalere.[11]
Mecharum,[12] dyrnlicendra.
Mecham, forlegisse.
Martyrizauit, þrowode.
35 *Maris,* wyrmhælseras.
Munuscula, lac.
Magestratibus,[13] ealdormanna.

---

[1] So the MS. Cf. pag. 298 l. 13. R. W.
[2] Read: *laser. l.* is used as well in Anglo-Saxon as in Latin. Cf. pag. 54 l. 42 and pag. 439 l. 32. R. W.
[3] This is probably one of the glossator's errors. *Æppelcyrnlu* would mean an applekernel or pippin. He was unacquainted with pomegranates.
[4] Cf. l. 16. R. W.
[5] Cf l. 13 and 14. R. W.
[6] Cf. Bosw. D. 66º. R. W.

[7] This word is clearly written with *m* in the MS.
[8] *Mandra* denotes a team, set of horses, of mules etc. The meaning of loc is a fold. R. W.
[9] The next words have become entirely illegible. R. W.
[10] Cf. Bosw. D. 44j. R. W.
[11] Cf. l. 35. R. W.
[12] Read: *mæcharum.* Cf. next line. R. W.
[13] So has the MS. R. W.

Militiæ, wigropes dugude.[1]
Matronalis, þære hiwlican.
Muricibus, wurmum.
Mitre, eowre hættas.
Meticulosis, þæm forhtiendlicum.
Manice, slyfan.
Maturius, tidlicor, hrædlicor.
Mastigias, ða læla.[2]
Mastigium, swipan.
Magnopere, naht swide.
Metricam,[3] eorþgemet.
Musicam, swinsungeræft.
Mechanicam, læcecræft.[4]
Matertere, modrigan.
Matertera mea materna, minre modrigan moder.
Memorant, gemunad.
Marcescunt, forwærniad.
Marcida, þa forwisnedan.
Mauors, wig, odde gefeoht.
Maforte, scyfla.[5]
Mafortibus, scyfelum.
Manica, glof.
Manicula, glof.
Manitegrum, lim.[6]
Maceratus, þreatende.
Manubium, wælreaf.
Manticum, handfulbeowæs.[7]
Mascus,[8] grima.
Musca,[9] egesegrima.
Masca, grima.
Marsopicus, fina.

Marruca, snegl.[10]
Magialis, bearug.[11]
Malistis, scyhend.
Mastice, hwiteweodu.[12]
5 *Marubium*, hune, odde beowyrt.
Matrix, quitha.[13]
Marsmar, tig.[14]
Mantega, tig.[15]
Marsius, logeþer.[16]
10 *Macilentus*, gefæsted.[17]
Macilia, eagflea.
Merula, drostle.
Megale, hearma.[18]
Mendacio conposito, gerenode.
15 *Metricus*, meterwyrhta.
Mesaulum, cafertun.
Miluus, glida.
Mimopara, deofscip.[19]
Milium, mil.
20 *Mitra*, hæt.[20]
Mitras, hættas.
Miniaci, hlifendre.[21]
Molles, fam, hwastas.
Morgit, milcet.[22]
25 *Mossiclum*, ragu.[23]
Molibus, ormetum.[24]
Morenula, æl.
Mora, heorutberge,[25]
Murica, gespan.
30 *Munila*, beah.[26]
Musiranus, screawa.[27]
Mugil, hacod, odde heardra.

[1] Read: wigrodes. R. W.
[2] *læla* means: scars, marks from beating; *mastigium* a whip, scourge. Cf. next line and pag. 441 l. 20. R. W.
[3] Read: *geometricam (artem)* or *geometriam*. R. W.
[4] The glossator translated *medicam (artem)*. R. W.
[5] Cf. pag. 31 l. 24. R. W.
[6] Read: *manutergium*. R. W.
[7] Cf. pag. 31 l. 36. R. W.
[8] So has the MS. R. W.
[9] Read: *masca*. Cf. pag. 29 l. 8. R. W.
[10] An error for *murana*? R. W.
[11] Read: *maialis*. Cf. pag. 271 l. 32. R. W.
[12] Cf. pag. 271 l. 18 and pag. 298 l. 29. R. W.
[13] Cf. pag. 159 l. 28. R. W.
[14] So has the MS. Read: *Mars, martis*. R. W.
[15] Cf. pag. 32 l. 17. R. W.
[16] Cf. Bosw. D. 42y. R. W.
[17] Cf. pag. 441 l. 4. R. W.
[18] Cf. pag. 32 l. 28. R. W.
[19] Cf. pag. 32 l. 37. R. W.
[20] Cf. pag. 442 l. 4. R. W.
[21] Cf. pag. 32 l. 38. R. W.
[22] Cf. pag. 33 l. 2. R. W.
[23] Cf. pag. 33 l. 3. R. W.
[24] Cf. pag. 33 l. 5. R. W.
[25] Cf. pag. 33 l. 12. R. W.
[26] Read: *monilia*. Cf. pag. 33 l. 18. R. W.
[27] Cf. pag. 33 l. 22. R. W.

Murus,[1] bremel.
Myrtus, wir, wirtreow.
Mystice, gerynelice.
Mine, healfsester.
Macies, hlænnes.
Munimentum, fæstnung.
Masculinum, wæpnedcyn.
Mutuo, borge, odde wrixle.
Mina, drif.
Musac,[2] bleostæning.
Malo ingenio, yfele ordance.
Masdi, magan.
Mutuare, wrixlan, hlænan.
Mutare, hrædlicre.
Molestus, unyþe.
Molestissimum, earfodlicost.
Murenulas, mynas.
Monstra, scinlac.
Mutilum, hnot.
Mutilatis, hnottum.
Mergulis, seealfor.
Mursopicius, fina.[3]
Musca, fleoge.
Murenula, æl.
Microchosmos, se læssa middangeard.
Mala, ceacan.
Maxilla, ceacan.
Mentem, cinn.
Mandibulas, cinban.
Manus, hand.
Mammille, tittas.
Medulla, mearh.
Meatis,[4] utgan.
Mel, hunig.
Moros, slan.
Mento, minte.
Mentastrum, eal mintan cyn.
Malua, hocleaf.
Malua, hoc, cottue.
Metallum, clympre.

Massa, clyno.
Misarius,[5] steda.
Mulus, mul.
Molosus, rodhund, rydda.
5 *Millefolium,* gearwe.
Mensa, beod.
Merum, hluttor win, odde swerum.
Mero, wine.
Manile, læfel.
10 *Maniterium,*[6] handlin.
Matile, seeat.[7]
Melle dulci, leoht beor.
Melopius, leodwyrhta.[8]
Mimum, gliw.
15 *Momentum,* seutel.[9]
Mustella, wesle.
Mus, mus.
Messor, riftre.
Muriceps, cat.
20 *Mollibus,* hnescum.
Manicabat, morgenwacode.
Metretas, gemetfatu.
Munificentiam, cyste.
Mergule, dopfugeles.
25 *Murice,* wurma, weoloc.
Melote, hredan.[10]
Murex, wurma.[11]
Musica, da dreamlican.
Malleoli, tyndercyn.
30 *Matrice,* ewidan.[12]
Mathematicorum, tunglera.
Merulenta, da ahlytredan.
Mancipium, þede.
Missarum, senduessa.
35 *Melancoliæ,* dæs sweartan galgan.[13]
Monaptalmis,[13] ænegum.
Marsorum, wyrmgalera.[14]
Manipulo, were.
Mala punica, da Affricanisean æppla.
40 *Melodiam,* sealmsang.

[1] Cf. pag. 33 l. 34. R. W.
[2] *Musaic, musiuus.* The Anglo-Saxon word is curious enough, artistically.
[3] Read: *marsopicus.* Cf. pag. 286 l. 8. R. W.
[4] Read: *meatus.* R. W.
[5] For *emissarius (equus).*
[6] For *manutergium.* (Cf. pag. 442 l. 25. R. W.)

[7] Read: *mantile.* R. W.
[8] Read. *melopains.* R. W.
[9] Cf. pag. 33 l. 4. R. W.
[10] Read: *melotes.* R. W.
[11] Cf. l. 25. R. W.
[12] Cf. pag. 443 l. 6. R. W.
[13] A very literal translation of the Latin word.
[14] Cf. pag. 441 l. 31. R. W.

Manipulares, cempan.
Matricularis, þearfum.
Modulare, singan.
Modulabor, singe.
Membrarum, filmena.[1]
Mirteta, wirgræfen.[2]
Maturesceret, weox.
Marmora glauca, þa hæwnan sæs.
Munia, þenunge, hæse.[3]
Maculam, **mal**.
Maculam pullam, þone sweartan speccan.
Madentia, þa þanan.
Molam, hweorfan.
Martem, gefeoht.
Misellis, earmum.
Macerare, mægeregan, gehlænian.
Malis, mæstum.
Mercimonium, ceping.
Mulceat, hnesce.
Myrtea, denu.[4]
Multate,[5] acwealde.
Marcida, þa gescruncenan and þa þynhlænan.
Morota, mageecte.[6]
Mascam, griming.
Miserescat, gemiltsige.
Melos, swinsunga.
Melodia, swinsang.
Mantilia, hacelan.
Malas, haguswind, odde þunwange.
Multans, witniende.
Meatus, **færeltu**.
Meat, færed.
Menstrua, ða monaðlecan.
Musica, þa gliwhleoðriendlican.
Murmure, grymetunge.
Metallis, cladum.
Metaplasmus, wlite.

Madescunt, daniað and wætigað.
Milleno, ðusendlicre.
Monoceros, anhyrne.
Materia, þæt oðer antimber.
5 *Mitia*, milde.
Mandit, eteð.
Mando, ic ete.
Madendum, lotendra.
Mandeo, ic bite.
10 *Maculabat*, þæt is sang on þæt wæter.
Murice, telge.
Mefariam,[7] manigfealde.
Mordax, bitende and slitende.
15 *Machina*, weorc.
Madidæ, þære druncnan.
Musis, mid sangum.
Madens, myltende.
Manes, deadas and deadgodas.
20 *Mechus*, gewemmend and forliegend.[8]
Minuta, lytle.
Morsum, bite.
Modis, wrencum.
Muttire, abyffan.
25 *Murotenus*, wið ðone weall.
Marcebat, lænede.
Minacibus, heum.
Meretricabitur, forligeð.
Manseres, *filii meretricum*.[9]
30 *Mutulat*, stommeteð.
Matrenas, godmodra.[10]
Marra, bill.
Mastellas, stanbill.
Muscus, treowes meos.
35 *Mula*, æl.[11]
Murenula, sææl.[12]
Mugilis, sleow.
Musculus, muscle.
Metallum, bloma.[13]

---

[1] Read: *membranarum*. R. W.
[2] Cf. pag. 444 l. 2. R. W.
[3] Read: *munera* R. W.
[4] Read: *myrteta*. R. W.
[5] Read: *mulctate*. Cf. l. 32. R. W.
[6] Cf. pag. 441 l. 23. R. W.
[7] For *multifariam*, arising probably from misreading a contraction.
[8] Cf. pag. 441 l. 32 and 33. R. W.

[9] Read *manzeres* (a word of Hebraic origin). R. W.
[10] Read: *matronas*. R. W.
[11] Cf. *mulus* pag. 180 l. 31. R. W.
[12] Cf. pag. 180 l. 30. R. W.
[13] The origin of our modern terms *bloom* and *bloomery*, in the making of iron. (Cf. pag. 141 note 1. R. W.)

Malleus, slecg, hamur.
Malleolus, handhamur.[1]
Molaricus, spediende.[2]
Mandibula, þæt wange wið þa ceocan ufan.
Medius, middelfinger.
Medicus, læcefinger.
Mentedra, muðadl on goman.[3]
Myrteus, bleoread, musfealu.[4]
Mentagricus, tanede.[5]
Minctio, miging.
Mordiculus, bitela.[6]
Morsus, snæd.
Macetum, mealt.
Mutinus, gadinca.
Molitura, grist.
Mula,[7] mylen.
Molendarius, myleweard.[8]
Munificentia, est.
Mellena, ðusendmæle.[9]
Multimodam, manigfealdne.
Marsi, galdergalend.[10]
Matronalis, ða wiflican.
Melancolia, gealla.[11]
Metropolis, ealdorburh.
Marginis, stæðum.
Manum, menigdu.
Medullata, gebatad.
Mortariola, mortere.
Mirstillago, cneowholen.[12]
Maura, elehtre.[13]

Metitur, **wende**.[14]
Medosa mandata, mid ligespelle.[15]
Machinis, wigeræftum.
Mussantes, þæs wregendan.
5 *Meoilus*,[16] ðohte.
Matura satus,[17] swide ripe.
Molita miram, dæt gemynte irre.
Munitum castrum, ða fæstan ceastre.
Mas, ceorl.
10 *Mars*, Tuu.[18]
Merx, med.
Mango, ic menge.
Minax, beotende.
Madeo, þæne.
15 *Medor*, lacnie.
Meatim, minlice.
Maiusculus, lytle.
Margo, mænge.
Madefactum, gehweted.
20 *Mares*, wæpnedman.
Mitigaret, gestilde.
Mantile, beodscyte, oððe beodsceat.
Malagma, quod sine igne maceretur, et conprehendetur; maceretur autem
25 gecneden bið *siue* gebered bið, *conprehendatur uero* in heap bið gesamnod.
Mandatum, handfæstnung.
Mancipatio, handselen.
30 *Mutuum*, mutung *siue* wrixlung.
Merces, cypeþing.

---

[1] This interpretation of *malleolus* is rather singular; the glossator evidently thought it was a mere diminutive of *malleus*, and in this sense the word was used in medieval Latin.
[2] Perhaps *swediende* in the MS. Cf. Bosw. D. 71x. R. W.
[3] Cf. pag. 158 l. 26. R. W.
[4] Cf. pag. 163 l. 23. R. W.
[5] Cf. pag. 161 l. 7 and 28. R. W.
[6] Cf. pag. 122 l. 8. R. W.
[7] For *mola*.
[8] Opposite this word, in the margin, we have the letters *reagl'*. Short abbreviations of words thus placed are found not unfrequently in the MS., which I have not printed because they seem to be mere private indications, perhaps, of a new book from which the glosses are taken, and they seem now to admit of no very intelligible interpretation.
[9] Read: *millena*. R. W.
[10] Cf. pag. 445 l. 37. R. W.
[11] Cf. pag. 445 l. 35. R. W.
[12] Cf. pag. 133 l. 27, pag. 269 l. 22, pag. 300 l. 12 and l. 21. R. W.
[13] Cf. Cock. III, pag. 324. R. W.
[14] An error for *mutatur*? R. W.
[15] Read: *mendosa*. R. W.
[16] Perhaps an error for *meditatus*? R. W.
[17] For *satis*.
[18] Or *Tiw*, the war-god of the Anglo-Saxon mythology, from whom we derive the name of Tuesday. He is here naturally enough identified with Mars. (Cf. pag. 32 l. 10. R. W.)

Mercatus, ceapunggemot.
Malum, wite.
Matutinum, uhttid, *siue* beforan dæge.
Mane, ærmergen.
Meridies, middægtid.
Morarius, begbeam, *unde* **merota** *dicta, morarius etiam celsa uocatur, mora, hæc, commune nomen est*, bergena.
Macula, mæscre.
Momentana, helur.[1]
Momentum, helerunge.[1]
Missa, mæsse.
Munera propriæ, medsceattas.
Mactatio, sniding.
Magi, scinlæcan.
Maides,[2] sææælfenne.
Miles ordinarius, anlang cempa, *uel* heanra cempa, *idem gregarius*.
Manipulis, twahund cempena.
Municipales, innihte beborene.
Manumissus, gefreod.
Manumissor, freotgifa.
Matrona, hæmedwif.
Mater, anes cildes modor.
Materfamilias, manigra cilda modur.
Menstrum, monaðblod.
Murenam, merenædre, *Grece myrina dicitur*.
Malleolus, sumerlida.[3]
Mioparo, hydscip.[4]
Modius, mæstcyst.[5]
Mataxa, wæde.
Maciones, scylfas.
Mastruga, hæden.
Martisa, gebeaten.
Melicratum, gemilscad win.

Mulsurum, gemilscad wæter.
Medus, winberge te hunige awylled.[6]
Mozicia, sealtleaf.[7]
Melinum, geolu.
5 *Mentrati*, fenminte.
Muscum, meose.
Malumterra, galloc.[8]
Manus færne, forreotes folm.[9]
Mula, elene.
10 *Mandragina*, þung.
Melleuna, meodowyrt.[10]
Merculialis, cedelc.[11]
Merculiaris, merce.[12]
Mentasri, feldminte.[13]
15
Nauiter, horslice, hwætlice.[14]
Naucleri, scipweredes.[15]
Nectareum, þone hunigtearlican.
Neuorum, wensprynga, læla.
20 *Non desistunt*, ne ablinnað, ne ateoriað.
Normam uite, regol.
Normam, regol.
Nondum, na ða git.
25 *Noualibus*, wyrðelandum.
Nimborum, wolcna.
Naptarum, heordena, æbreda, acumba.[16]
Nuptiales, þa giftelican.
30 *Nequiquam*, holenga.
Nutibus, beacnengum.
Nundinarum, wicdaga, oððe ceapstowa.
Negotium, scir.
35 *Notariorum*, notwritera.
Nausiam, wlatunge.[17]
Neofitus, niwancumen.

---

[1] Cf. Bosw. D. 35⁰ and 35q. R. W.
[2] A blunder of the glossator for *Naiades*.
[3] Read: sumerlida (= *malleoli*). R. W
[4] Read: *myoparo*. R. W.
[5] *Modius* denotes the hole in which the mast is fixed. R. W.
[6] Cf. pag. 128 l. 9. R. W.
[7] Cf. Bosw. D. 61⁰. R. W.
[8] Cf. pag. 133 l. 20. R. W.
[9] Cf. Cock. III 327. R. W.
[10] Cf. pag. 134 l. 27. R. W.

[11] Read: *mercurialis*. Cf. Cock. III 317. R. W.
[12] Cf. Cock. III 338. R. W.
[13] Read: *mentarium*. Cf. pag. 301 l. 30. R. W.
[14] The manuscript is so much defaced here that the correct reading of this word is very uncertain. (Cf. pag. 33 l. 38. R. W.)
[15] The glossator confounded *nauta* with *naucleri*. R. W.
[16] Cf. pag. 33 l. 40. R. W.
[17] Cf. pag. 33 l. 37. R. W.

Nititur, he higode, odde tilode.
Nepotum, sweostorbearna.
Nec lenonum, leassponunge.[1]
Notitiæ, cyþþe.
Natalibus, gebyrdum.
Nenias, leasspellunga.
Natiua, acennedlicum.
Natum, acennedne.
Nefandum, þæt god wræce.
Non mixta, se unmengeda.
Nitebar, ic girnde.
Notricauerit, ne geswiced.
Ni torpens, sio slawe.
Nitar, ic onginne.
Nastucium, tuncærse.[2]
Napta, blæcteru.[3]
Napis, næp.[4]
Napus, Englis næp.[4]
Nabulum, færæscæt.[5]
Neptam, tynder.[6]
Netila,[7] hearma.
Nepa, hæfern.[8]
Nitorium, spinl.[9]
Neo, ic spinne.
Ninguit, sniwed.
Netum est, aspunnen is.
Non subsciuum, unfæcne.[10]
Neent, spinnad.
Notæ, speccan.
Non neunt, ne spinnad.
Norma, rihtebred.
Nugigerelus, ærendwrecan unnytnesse.
Nux, hnutbeam, odde walhhnutu.
Nugacitas, unnytnes.

Nucli, cyrnlas.[11]
Nucleus, cyrnel.
Non placui, ic ne gecwemde.
Nisus, tilgende.
5 *Nauticos,* nedlingas.[12]
Nauta, nedling.[12]
Non adquieuit, ne gedafode.
Non abnui, ic ne wiþsoc.
Nouerca, steopmodur.
10 *Ne cuncteris,* ne lata þu.
Noctua, ule.
Nocticorax, nihthremn.[13]
Naris, nosu.
Nates, earsenda.
15 *Nigra spina,* slahdorn.[14]
Nasturcium, leaccærse,[15] *id est,* tuncærse.
Nicalalbum, milisc æppel.[16]
Non detracta, ne forsace ic.[17]
20 *Nauacula,* scyrseax.[18]
Nanus, werc.[19]
Ne uellitis, ne willad ge.
Non cognoscebat, ne grette.
Non peram, ne fætels.
25 *Nuruum,* snoru.[20]
Nequiores, wyrsan.
Nummularior, mynetera.[21]
Nuptias, giming.
Nanciscunt, begitad.
30 *Nardo,* elesealf.
Non ut passiuis, nales swa wide.
Neuorum, wlitewomma.
Nutabunda, wagiende.
Neutericis, þæm niwum.[22]
35 *Nemoribus,* bearwum.

---

[1] Cf. pag. 430 l. 21 and pag. 436 l. 12. R. W.
[2] Read: *nasturcium.* Cf. pag. 135 l. 36 and pag. 270 l. 32. R. W.
[3] Cf. pag. 451 l. 27. R. W.
[4] Cf. pag. 135 l. 12 and 30. R. W.
[5] Cf. pag. 34 l. 3. R. W.
[6] Read: *naphtam.* Cf. l. 16. R. W.
[7] An **error** for *mitella,* a sort of female headdress. (Cf. pag. 34 l. 6. R. W.)
[8] Cf. pag. 34 l. 7. R. W.
[9] Cf. pag. 34 l. 14. R. W
[10] So has the MS. R. W.
[11] Read: *nuclei.* Cf. next line. R. W.

[12] The meaning of nedling is: a *slave, servant.* R. W.
[13] Cf. pag. 132 l. 3. R. W.
[14] The black-thorn, the thorn which produces sloes.
[15] Cf. pag. 452 l. 15. R. W.
[16] Cf. pag. 269 l. 28. R. W.
[17] Read: *detracto.* R. W.
[18] Read: *novacula.* R. W.
[19] Read: dwere or dwerg. R. W.
[20] Read: *nurum.* R. W.
[21] Read: *numularius.* Cf. pag. 34 l. 29. R. W.
[22] **Read:** *neotericis.* R. W.

Nebulis, scinlæcan.
Non calcitres, ne spornette þu.
Nugaciter, unnytlice.
Nectunt, bundan.
Neophytus, se niwa.
Nodosi, ostihtum.
Nodus, ost.[1]
Nicolatis, palmæpla.
Naufragauerunt, gedurfan.
Non dissona, nalles ungerade.
Numina, gild.
Nardi pistici, þære getrywan elesealfe.
Nenias, bismerleod.
Nexibus, salum.
Non tricauerit, ne leted.
Natricis, nædrum.[2]
Natrix, nædre.
Nutu, meahte.
Nec balsamorum, ne crismena.
Non cunctante, ne tweoge.
Nanctus, begitende.
Ni forsan, nimde wen wære.
Nutum, willan.
Nec Bachus, ne wines god.[3]
Nilotica, sio Ægiptisce.
Nodatis, gecnyttum.
Non usquam, neowerno, nawern.[4]
Nodos, bende.
Nat, swam, swimd.
Nectantem, bindende.
Nantes, swimmende.
Nummismate, mynete.
Necessitudinum, neadsibba.
Notabiliter, tælwyrdlice.
Non refragabatur, no widdon.
Nyctilia, nihtgild.
Nymphas, gydena.

Non quibat, ne meahte.[5]
Natam, dohtor.
Non cunctante, no latiendum.
Nactus, begiotende.
5 *Nati*, suna.
Numen, sunu, odde meahte.[6]
Non cessit, no abeag.
Nitria, þæt is of leadre.[7]
Notetur, sio geleahtrad.
10 *Nec minus*, mete gemæres.
Nebulam, scingedwolan.
Nectar, win, þone swetan smæc.[8]
Nectare, wingedrince.
Nauta, sciprowend.
15 *Nauita*, scip.[9]
Nauigeros, þa sciplidendan.
Nimbis, stormum.
Naualia, scipropor.
Nectar, hunig, odde mildeaw.
20 *Neuis*, wommum.
Nefandas, da unascegendlican.
Noxax, leahtras.[10]
Non scando, ne **astige** ic.
Nunc, hwilum.
25 *Neunemo*, torrebrande.[2]
Niuibus, snawum.
Non uereor, no ic me onsitte.
Nilotica, þa Egiptisce.[11]
Nepa, crabba, odde hæfern.[12]
30 *No trano*, no ic fleoge.
Noxam, gylt.[13]
Non uergo, ne ga ic on setl.
Non errantes, rihtwise.
Necarent, cwealdon.
35 *Nimbo*, scure.
Nemphe, cudlice.[14]
Nitatur, tilige.
Non retur, ne demed he.

[1] The MS. has *nudus* or *nodus*. R. W
[2] So has the MS. R. W.
[3] The Anglo-Saxon mythology has not a god answering exactly to Bacchus.
[4] Cf. Bosw. 481 and 48w. R. W.
[5] Cf. Nr. XII, XLVIII. R. W.
[6] Cf. Nr. XII, XXXIX and LXIX. R. W.
[7] Cf. pag. 456 l. 14. R. W.
[8] Several different interpretations of the word *nectar* occur in these and following articles, and the compiler of these glosses was evidently very doubtful about its true character.
[9] Read: sciper, or sciptmon. R. W.
[10] Read: *noxias*. R. W.
[11] Cf. pag. 454 l. 26. R. W.
[12] Cf. pag. 34 l. 7. R. W.
[13] Cf. l. 22 and pag. 456 l. 7. R. W.
[14] Read: *nempe*. R. W.

Nigro colore, þa blacan betlas.[1]
Nisa, wreðed.
Nuda, nacod and ceald.
Non pigra, unlæt.
Non gratus, no liofwende.
Ne uioler, þæt ic ne sie besmiten.
Noxam, dare.
Nemoris, bearwes.
Nothus, suðan wind, oððe dooc, hornungsunu.[2]
Nodorum, rapa.
Non abortabit, no miscalfað.[3]
Ne inniaris, ne gilp ðu.
Nitrum, leaðor.
Nasus, nosu.
Nares, næsþyrel.
Natius, dunu.
Nectar, frummeoluc.[4]
Nanciscuntur, andfindende.
Normulis, gemetum.
Numquit,[5] ac þu cwiðst.
Natilicium, gecynda.
Nodaretur, gefæstnod.
Nubigenu, wolcenwyrcende.[6]
Nupte,[5] bryd.
Nauarcas, scipmen.[7]
Numine, leso.[8]
Numquam sunt sera, ne beoð æfre to late.
Nudapes, bærfisce.[9]
Nidore, stence.
Nex, cwealm.
Non dissimulamus, ne lætað we.
Nyctalmus,[10] nihteage.

Nuncupatio, *est* undyrne yrfebec.
Nerui, fotcopsas.
Nonœ, ceapdagas, *a nundinis; idus*, swæsenddagas, *ab edendo. Isemeria Greci æquinoctium uocant.*
Neuum, weargebræde.[11]
Nicromantia, þurh deades witgung.
Nymfœ, wæterælfenne.[12]
Naides, sæælfenne.[12]
Nodus, getrum.
Numerarii, gafeles andfendgend.[5]
Nepos, suna sunu, *neptis; pronepus*, þridda sunu, *proneptis.*
Nuculeus, siue nucleus, hæslhnute cyrnel.
Nam siluatica, smerowyrt.
Nepita, nepte.[13]
Nymphea, colloncrog.[14]
Obtutus, gesihð.
Oracula, gespreco.
Obsequia, ðenunga.
Olfactum, stenc, swæc.
Odoratus, swæc.
Opulentique, þære wistgifendan.
Obrizum, þæt smæte.[15]
Obliterantes, adiligiende, forgitende.
Oblectamenta, lustfulnes.
Obriza lammina, þa smæte gyldnan claðas.
Opinatur, wenð.
Ob indaganda, fore to aspyrianne.
Operculis, oferwrigelsum.
Operam, girnesse.

---

[1] *betlas* has no Latin equivalent. R. W.
[2] No doubt, in the original text in which this word stood, it was *notus*, the south wind, and was glossed as such, but in the debased orthography of medieval Latin, another glossator seems to have supposed it might be *nothus*, a bastard.
[3] In the text where this gloss was found, the word *abortare* was no doubt used in a restricted sense, as applied to a cow, and hence it is interpreted, *to miscalve*.
[4] Another guess at the meaning of the word nectar.
[5] So has the MS. R. W

[6] i. e. begotten of a cloud, applied to the Centaurs, as the offspring of Ixion and the cloud.
[7] Read: *nauarchos*. R. W.
[8] Cf. Sommer's Dict. R. W.
[9] Read: *bærfot*. R. W.
[10] Ducange supposes this to be a corruption of *nyctalops*, i. e. seeing by night.
[11] Cf. Bosw. pag. 88o. R. W.
[12] i. e. water-elves and sea-elves, a curious bit of illustration of our Anglo-Saxon popular mythology.
[13] Read: *nepeta*. R. W.
[14] Cf. Cock. III, pag. 319. R. W.
[15] Cf. pag. 34 l. 40. R. W.

Obolisci, stanrocces.[1]
Obscenitatis, fracodnesse.
Oraculum, spæc.
Oraculorum, spreca.
Obliqua, scytehealden.
Oromate, gastlicre gesihðe.[2]
Occa, furh, fylging, walh.
Opinatissimus, se hliseadgesta.
Oriundus, ypped.
Orthodoxis, rihtgeleaffullum.
Occasione, intingan.
Ob detectum, þære onwrigenan.
Obuncabat, oferfeng.
Obrutos, oferhrerede.
Olosericis, mid eall seoleenum.[3]
Oratores, þylæs.
Obstinatam, anwille.
Obsecundans, hierende.
Offenderet, abulge.
Ordiretur, wæs awefen.
Obeuntem, þa fordfarenan.
Ob potiorem, foræmeran.[4]
Obtemperare, hyrsumian.
Obstipuit, forhtode, ofercymen wæs.
Orbibus, hringum.
Obscæne, þære fulan.
Obscena, þa ladlecan.
Obsidione, fæstenne, and ofsetenesse.
Offam, snæd.
Obolitio, eþung.
Obreptione, creopunge.
Obomates, gesidas.
Obuncans, gecnyclede.

Obestrum, beost.
Obesca, beost.
Obunca, crump.
Obuix, widerstal.[5]
5 *Obligamentum*, lyb, lyfesn.[6]
Obiecte, ongensete.[7]
Obsedatu,[8] gisldu.
Obtinuit, ofercom.
Obiectionibus, gestalum.
10 *Obex*, ogengel.[9]
Obicula, geoesticca.[10]
Occupauit, onette.
Ocreis, banbeorgum.[11]
Occipui, hnecca.[12]
15 *Occabat*, egede.[13]
Occearium, style.[14]
Offendit, mette.
Officit, wyrde.[15]
Offirmans, clæmende.[16]
20 *Ogastrum*, æggemang.[17]
Oligia, nette.[18]
Olor, swon, ilfetu, swan.
Olastrum, stæf.
Omnimoda, æghwylce þinga.[19]
25 *Omentum*, massa.
Onocratulus, fealefor.[20]
Opere plumario, besiwed federge-
    weorc.[21]
Oppilate, besparrade.
30 *Oridanum*, elene.
Orcus, ore, þyrs, odde heldeofol.[22]
Oripilato, cylewearte.[23]
Oresta, dræs.[24]

[1] Read: *obelisci*. R. W.
[2] Read: *oramate* or *horamate*. R. W.
[3] Read: *holosericis*. R. W.
[4] So has the MS. R. W.
[5] Cf. pag. 35 l. 9. R. W.
[6] Cf. pag. 35 l. 10. R. W.
[7] Cf. pag. 35 l. 12. R. W.
[8] Cf. pag. 35 l. 15. R. W.
[9] Cf. pag. 35 l. 20. R. W.
[10] Cf. pag. 35 l. 21. R. W.
[11] Cf. pag. 35 l. 23. R. W.
[12] Read: *occiput*. Cf. pag. 35 l. 26. R. W.
[13] Cf. pag. 35 l. 27. R. W.
[14] Steel. *Occearium* is apparently a corruption of *aciarium*, explained as meaning *indurata ferri acies*.
[15] Cf. pag. 35 l. 31. R. W.
[16] Cf. pag. 35 note 4. R. W.
[17] Cf. pag. 35 l. 32. R. W.
[18] Cf. pag. 35 l. 34. R. W.
[19] Read: *omnimodo*. R. W.
[20] A fieldfare. The Latin is a corruption of *onocrotalus*, which, however, means a different bird from a fieldfare.
[21] Cf. pag. 36 l. 8. R. W.
[22] *Orcus* was a name for Pluto, the god of the infernal regions, hence we can easily understand the explanation of *heldeofol*. *Orc*, in Anglo-Saxon, like *thyrs*, means a spectre, or goblin.
[23] Cf. pag. 36 l. 14. R. W.
[24] Cf. pag. 36 l. 13. R. W.

Orbita, hwcoglrad.
Ortigomera, erschen.
Or, onginnende.
Oreæ, fræne.
Oscille, totridan.
Osma, swice.
Ostriger, brunbaso.[1]
Onustus, gehlæden.
Oram, læppan.
Occubuit, geerang.
Obrigesceret, astifode.
Obtuperabitis, gedemað, and tælað.
Oscitauit, sworette.
Obriguerunt, astifedan.[2]
Oppansum, aþened.
Ophiomachus, broc.
Obelus, scilling.[3]
Ossifragus, herefong.
Onocratarum,[4] raredumle.
Ostrea, ostre.
Oculus, cage.
Os, muð.
Oscedo, mudcoðu.
Oss,[5] ban.
Onentem, midhryþere.
Oliua, elebeam.
Oleaster, windeltreow.
Oleastri, eletwiges.
Ortus pomorum, apuldertun.
Ortus olerum,[6] leahtun.
Ostrum, wurma, read godweb.
Omganum,[7] wurmille.
Officina, smiðde.
Olatrum, scafa.
Ordeum, bere.[8]
Olla, greoua.
Omelias, spræce.[9]

Orthodoxus, wuldorlic.
Onix, blere.
Obstupum, feorstudu.[10]
Olimpiaci, þæs pleglican.[11]
5 *Orbes, orbibus,* hringa, hohhwyrfinge.
Ortagraphorum, rihtwriterum.[12]
Oppilatum, gedyrned.
Obliqua curuatura, sio scytchealde onbegnes.
10 *Obcognate,* þære sibban.
Oportunus, sio tidlice.
Obuncabat, ymbclypte.
Obsidem, gisl.
Obses, gisl.
15 *Operepretium,* ræd.[13]
Oculum, sprece.[14]
Ordine prepostero, onwendedre endebyrdnesse.
Olfactoriola, þe hiera elescalfa on-
20   wæran.
Ostro, telge, deage.[16]
Ostentationis, gylpes.
Obstacula, widsteallas.
Obstrusus, deagol.
25 *Opace,* deagle.
Oras, ofras.
Ora, andwlita.
Occellorum, egna.[17]
Oppetere, gecrang.
30 *Ordo,* hade.
Oramina, gebedo.[18]
Ocius, raðe.
Opacis, þæm diglum.
Obesus, fæt.
35 *Organa,* þeotan.
Orbes, heofinga.[19]
Olo, eall.[20]

[1] Cf. pag. 36 l. 28. R. W.
[2] Cf. l. 11. R. W.
[3] Read: *obolus.* R. W.
[4] For *onocrotalus,* a bittern. (Cf. pag. 260 l. 1. R. W.)
[5] So has the MS. R. W.
[6] A herb-garden. Of course, in this and the preceding article, *ortus* is a mere corruption of *hortus.*
[7] For *origanum.*
[8] Read: *hordeum.* R. W.
[9] Read: *homelias.* R. W.

[10] Read: *obstipum.* R. W.
[11] Cf. Nr. XII, I. R. W.
[12] Read: *orthographorum.* R. W.
[13] Cf. Nr. XII, XXX. R. W.
[14] Read *oraculum.* R. W.
[15] Cf. Nr. XII, XXXVI. R. W.
[16] Cf. Nr. XII, XLII. R. W.
[17] Read: *ocellorum.*
[18] Cf. Nr. XII, LXX. R. W.
[19] Cf. l. 5. R. W.
[20] Read: *olos* or *olon* (= *holos, holon*). R. W.

Obeuntem, sweltende.
Oppido, swiðe.
Oraret, wyrdade.
Oppeteret, swulte odde feolle.
Opimus, se strengese.[1]
Octena, eahta sidum.
Opimis, mid þæm genihtsumestan.
Olimpi, roderes.[2]
Octauam, strælas.[3]
Odas, leoð.
Opimum, þæt wiolie.[4]
Olidas, þa fulan.
Ocumbat, aswelte.
Obliquat, fyred.
Oceano, on garsecge.
Orco, deade.
Oppida, tunas.
Oppidani, burhsetan.
Ostriger, tælberend.[5]
Origo, frymd.
Occidat, aswelte.
Olim, iu, fyrn.
Obsequitur, folgað.
Obrasum, ascæfen.
Obulum, sceat.[6]
Oscitantes, ganiende.
Obtigit, gelamp.
Obtani,[1] geara gewunan odde gewunede.
Oraria, orelu
Orbita, sol.[1]
Ofella, spiceshis.[7]
Ornus, eow.
Ouicula, lytel sceap.
Oppilius, scephyrde.[8]
Ouile, sceapahus.
Omina, hwata.

Ortodoxiæ, þæs rihtgelyfdan geleafan.
Obrirum metallum, asoden weax.[9]
Olidarum, unsyfra.
Opriant, onscyniað.[10]
5 *Ob quam rem*, fore foleum.
Oppilauit, betynde, gegiscde.
Onocharois, ancorlie setl.[11]
Obruerunt, slogon.
Obstergunt, on wega dydan.
10 *Obstrictas*, forfyldan.
Occulit, gehydde.[12]
Obpositum,[1] widerbrecan.
Orbata, benumen.
Opis, meahte.
15 *Origanum*, wurmillæ.
Obtenuit, begeat.
Ordinatissimam, þa gesettan.
Obnixe, geornlice.
Obligamentum, lyb.
20 *Occas*, **fealga**.
Occiput, **hracca**.
Obpressus, ofercumen.
Obpressit, ofercom.
Olla aenea, cytel; sed ideo additus
25 *aenea quia est et olla fictilis, id est* crocca.
Olagraphum,[13] *testamentum est*, eall writene yrfebec.
Obuoluere, bewæfan.
30 *Omeliæ uerba*, folclare.
Ostiarii, duruweardas.
Oreades, wuduælfenne.
Origanum, feltwurma.[14]
Opratanum, wælisc.[15]
35 *Opiffera*, helpendrap.[16]
Ostriago, liðwyrt.[17]
Ortica, netele.[18]

---

[1] So has the MS. R. W.
[2] The Anglo-Saxon glossator of course took Olympus for heaven.
[3] The glossator did not translate *octauam*, *stræl* means *sagitta, telum*. R. W.
[4] *wiolie* = weolig. R. W.
[5] Cf. pag. 460 l. 7. R. W.
[6] Cf. pag. 460 l. 17. R. W.
[7] The meaning of *ofella* is a *bit, little bit*. R. W.
[8] Read: *opilio*. R. W.
[9] Read: *obryzum metallum*. The glossator did not understand the Latin text. R. W.
[10] Read: *operiant*. R. W.
[11] Read: *anachoresis*. R. W.
[12] Read: *occuluit*. R. W.
[13] Read: *olographum* or *holographum*. R. W.
[14] Cf. pag. 136 l. 30 and pag. 299 l. 19. R. W.
[15] Read: *abrotanum*. R. W.
[16] *Opifer* answers to helpend-bær. R. W.
[17] Cf. pag. 302 l. 3. R. W.
[18] Read: *urtica*. R. W.

GLOSSES, LATIN AND ANGLO-SAXON.

Oxylapatium, sio scearpe docce.[1]
Ocimum, mistel.[2]
Optalmon, magoþe.[3]
Offensa, forhælde.

Paucorum, feara.[4]
Passiuus, sio widgille.[5]
Proreta, foresteora.
Propinaret, fordscencte.
Prestulanti, onbidendum.
Per augustam, þurh þæt rume.
Propositi, ingehygdes.
Panuclis, weflum.
Punica, þa Affricaniscan.
Prestare, forestandan.
Perpes, swift.
Promontorio, foremunte.
Posteritatem, æfterweardnesse.
Propensius, geornlicor.
Peripsema, geswæpa.
Pelta, plegscylde.
Phalanx, firdwerod.
Prosapia, tuddor.
Per atauos, þurh ildran fæderas.
Parsimonia, gnednes.
Practicæ, þære dorlecan.
Prerogatiuam, sundorweordunge.
Plantaria, plantunga, seten.
Prostibuli, geligeres.
Preoccupetur, geonet odde geefest.
Prescius, forewis.
Prediti, gewelegode.
Prefecturæ, scire.
Paradigma, bispel, bysene.
Pululantes, upspryttende.
Penticotharcos,[6] ealdormen, *uel quinquagenarios*.
Promulgatur, fordypped.
Proceritatis, legen.[7]
Procumberet, gefeoll.
Portentorumque, foretacna.

Portendentes, beenende, taeniende.
Puberes, cnihtas, geonglingas.
Pulmentum, fosternod.[8]
Pronepotum, fornefena.
5 *Penitudinis*, hreowsunge.
Paranymphus, drihtguma.
Propalat, openiende.
Pastinantem, settende.
Precipuum, seo healice.
10 *Pubescens*, weaxende, fordframiende.
Pausantis, þa restendan.
Pubesceret, þah.
Per tenera, ðurh ða myrwan.
Petulantiam, galnesse.
15 *Prestrigias*,[9] wiccecræftas, scinhiw.
Politissimis, ðæs smicerestan, and þæs smeðestan.
Philosophiæ, wisdomes.
Philargiria, gifernesse.
20 *Penniger*, feþerberend.
Probrosas, onscuniendlican.
Presago, mid witedomes.[11]
Prouenerunt, gelumpen.
Palmitum, telgena.
25 *Periclitatur*, frecelsod.
Propinquitatis, nehsibbe.
Prerogatiua, sundorgife.
Probrosum, onscuniendlic.[10]
Preconia, mærnessa.
30 *Pollesceret*, dunge.
Probrosis, facenfullum.
Pallor, blæco.
Procaciter, awille.
Profugus, flima.
35 *Proficiscens*, ferende.
Potiretur, wæs brucende.
Profanare, gewidlian.
Pendiculo, segne.
Pedetemtim,[11] fægere, liþelice.
40 *Palestrarum*, gestrynga, plegstowa.
Preses, gerefa.

---

[1] Cf. pag. 136 l. 35. R. W.
[2] Cf. pag. 299 l. 28. R. W.
[3] Cf. pag. 300 l. 11. R. W.
[4] So written in the manuscript, but evidently an error for *feawa*.
[5] Cf. Nr. XII, XLIII. R. W.
[6] A corruption of *pentecontarchus* (πεν-
τηκόνταρχος), a commander of fifty men.
[7] An error for: lenge? R. W.
[8] Cf. Nr. XII, IIII. R. W.
[9] Sic, for *prastigias*. The word occurs again in the next column.
[10] Cf. l. 21. R. W.
[11] So has the MS. R. W.

Preside, healigerefan.
Patrocinium, mundbyrde.
Perfidorum, treowleasra.
Puplica,[1] openlecre.
Proscriptionem, forewritenesse.
Procaciter, bealdlice.
Promiscui, gehwæderes.
Præstigia, scincræfte.
Putamina, þa hnyglan.[2]
Pluma, feþere.
Parasitis, geneatum, geeoþum.
Putores, fulnesse.
Pignus, bearn.
Propugnaculum, breostgebeorh.
Perpetitur, ræfnde.
Phanaticæ,[1] godgildliere.[3]
Processere, fordeodan.
Patrimonium, fædergestreona.
Per tanta, þurh swa manigera.
Procul, longe.
Penitus, longe.
Prope modum, neah and efene.
Probauit, gecydde.
Predia, sundorland.
Pro foribus, beforan þæm durum.
Prepostero, æfterfylgendre.
Piacula, synna, scylda.
Plectro, sceeele odde slegele.
Plumemus, sceeen we.[4]
Pelices, cifesene.
Pellexerint, beswicon.
Procum, brydguma.[5]
Pateretur, lete.
Phantasmate, scinhiwes.
Prestantissimus, se betesta, and se fyrmesta.
Purpurescit, readode.
Pedisequis, þinennum.

Pedisequas, þinenna.
Parentelæ, fæderen, enosles.
Proserpinam, gydene.[6]
Peritiam, gleawnesse.
5 *Presbiteri*, recceras.
Parricida, mægmyrþra.
Puplicum, cynestræte.[7]
Properare, efstan.
Pertesum, swide lang.
10 *Portunalia*, þa hydlican.[8]
Possessuræ, gesittende.
Pittacia, ærendgewrito.[9]
Passim, welhwær.
Prepostero, oncirredre.
15 *Patronus*, mundbora.
Populose, þære folewelegan.
Plausu, dæm plegan.
Paruit, hirde.
Parentibus, hirsumiendum.
20 *Purulentus*, wurmsi.[10]
Parricidium, myrþrunge.[11]
Probabilis, hergendlic.[12]
Palmam, sigores.
Propago, tudor, odde cyn.
25 *Pompulenta*, sio glenglice.
Probrum, hosp, lehter.
Plasmatica, þære frumheowunge.
Peritorum, witena.
Periscelides, scanegegirelan.
30 *Pertinax*, anwille.
Plenilunio, fullum mone.
Presidio, mundbyrde, and fultome.
Presumpsimus, we gebristlæcton.
Protelaretur, wæs geeldod.[13]
35 *Progeniem*, forecynren.
Presidet, wylt.
Presagia, dihta, odde saga.
Prestantior, fromra.

---

[1] So has the MS. R. W.
[2] Cf. pag. 42 l. 14. R. W.
[3] Cf. pag. 236 l. 1—5. R. W.
[4] Cf. Nr. XII, XXVII. R. W.
[5] Cf. pag. 42 l. 5. R. W.
[6] It is hardly necessary to say that *gydene*, in Anglo-Saxon, means simply a goddess. The writer of these glosses appears not to have had a very clear notion of the classical mythology.
[7] i. e. a king's road.
[8] Read *portumnalia*. Cf. Bosw. 39b. R. W.
[9] *Pittacium*, in medieval Latin, was used to signify a tablet on which messages were written to be sent as letters.
[10] Cf. Nr. XII, XLIII. R. W.
[11] Cf. l. 6. R. W.
[12] This is the medieval meaning of the word *probabilis*.
[13] *Protelaretur* denotes; to defer, postpone. R. W.

Procax, fræuol,[1] odde litig.
Precordia, forebreost.
Portum, hyde.
Pratrauerat, þa durhteah.
Pretendere, geræcean.
Partim, sume dæle.
Palpitans, brodetende.
Parce, wyrde.[2]
Papilio, fiffalde.[3]
Papula, wearte.[4]
Papiluus, eolugsecg.[5]
Papila, wifel.[6]
Passos, gerostode.[7]
Palagra, æcelma.[8]
Pastinaca, wealmore.
Parula, mase.
Pariulus, sinfulle.[9]
Pastellus, hunigæppel.
Papauer, popig.
Pariter, gelice.
Palmula, steorroder.
Parruca, yce.[10]
Papulatores, horshyrdas.[11]
Perstrenue, framlice.
Per seudoterum, þurh ludget.[12]
Per uispellones, þurh byrgeras.[13]
Perpendiculum, colþræd.
Petigo, teter.
Pelta, scyld.
Perspicuus, heahþungen.
Pero, hemming i. ruh sco.

Pessum, clifhlyp.
Petra focaria, fyrstan, flint.
Pella, sadolfelg.[14]
Pendulus, ohylde.
5 *Phitecus*, apa.[15]
Piratici, wicingsceaþan, sæsceaþan, æsemen.
Pingit, fegd.
Pistrimum, cofa.[16]
10 *Pistrilla*, cofincel.
Pila, doþor.
Petuita, sped.
Pix, picia, pic.
Perplexitans, manifealdnes.[17]
15 *Plantago, uel septineruia*, wegbræde.[18]
Platissa, flooc.[19]
Plectra, awunden.
Plus minus, ymb þæt.
Populus, byrce.
20 *Polimita*, hringfag.[20]
Polimitarium, ceasterwyrhta.[21]
Porfyrio, fealfor.[22]
Porcopiscis, styria.[23]
Porcaster, foor.[24]
25 *Porcellus*, fearh.
Pons, bryc.
Promaritima, sægesetu.[25]
Pretextutus, gegirwed.[26]
Propera, freahræde.[27]
30 *Proscripsit*, forrædde.
Profligatis, forslægenum.

[1] So has the MS. R. W.
[2] The Latin word is intended for *Parcæ*, the Fates, represented by the Anglo-Saxon Wyrde. (Cf. pag. 37 l. 3. R. W.)
[3] Cf. pag. 37 l. 8. R. W.
[4] Read *papilla*. Cf. pag. 37 l. 9. R. W.
[5] Cf. Leo Gl. pag. 475 l. 55. R. W.
[6] Cf. pag. 37 l. 22. R. W.
[7] The glossator translated *assos*. Cf. pag. 37 l. 25. R. W.
[8] Cf. pag. 37 l. 24. R. W.
[9] Cf. pag. 37 l. 32. R. W.
[10] Cf. pag. 38 l. 2. R. W.
[11] Read *pabulatores*. R. W.
[12] Read *pseudothyrum*. R. W.
[13] Read *uespillones*. R. W.
[14] Cf. Bosw. 56ᵛ. R. W.

[15] Cf. pag. 39 l. 22. Read *pithecus*. R. W.
[16] Read *pistrinum*. R. W.
[17] Read *perplexitas*. R. W.
[18] Cf. pag. 134 l. 13 and pag. 322 l. 30. R. W.
[19] Read *platessa*. R. W.
[20] Read *polymitus*. R. W.
[21] This word and its gloss are added in a different hand in the manuscript. (Read *polymitarium*. R. W.)
[22] Cf pag. 259 l. 5. R. W.
[23] Cf. pag. 40 l. 19. R. W.
[24] Cf. pag. 40 l. 20. R. W.
[25] Cf. pag. 40 l. 38. R. W.
[26] Read *pratextatus*. Cf. pag. 41 l. 1. R. W.
[27] Cf. pag. 41 l. 2. R. W.

Preuectue, frodre.[1]
Prouecta, gefremed.
Pretersorim, waad.[2]
Pretersorim, waad.[2]
Prifeta, þrie wintre steor.[3]
Prurigo, gicenes.
Prouentus, sped.
Prunus, plyme.
Progna, swealwe.[4]
Prorostris, hehseldum, foreweard- scip.
Prodigus, strydere.
Pridie, dæge ær.
Pustula, angseta.
Pus, worms.
Puntus, brord.[5]
Prenotatur, foremearcod.[6]
Pentatheucum, fifbocum.[7]
Prouerbium, biwyrde.
Patruus, fædera.
Pertritus, getyrge.
Prerupti, widerstægre.
Preputia, scama, þa wæpenlican limo.
Peruie, ungefere.[8]
Precidit, forcearf.
Pauimus, we feddan.
Pithonis, helrun.
Porrectus, arœht.
Parui, ic hyrsumige.
Precipitas, widscyfs þu.
Piaculum, man.
Polymitarius, ceasterwyrhta.[9]
Postes, durustod.

Plectas, gewind.
Primitiua, þa frumcennedan.
Per turbinem, þurh gestun.
Psalter, salteras.
5 *Proditor,* læwend.
Pacatos, gesibsume.
Preceps, scyteheald.
Precipitate, scufad.
Peruagatus, swiciende.
10 *Phase,* eastran.[10]
Pauxillum, lytel.
Postumus, unlaf.
Palestricis, þæm wærstlicum.
Pando, geape.
15 *Propeta,* steora.[11]
Portisculo, hamere.
Per patentes, þurh þa ruman.
Per cola, þurh sticceo.[12]
Pariat, hereþ.[13]
20

Prenotatur, foremearcod.
Pentatheucum, fifbocum.
25 *Prouerbium,* biwyrde.
Patruus, fædera.
Pertritus, getyrged.
Prerupti, wiþerstægre.
Preputia, scama, þa wæpenlican limo.
30 *Peruie,* ungefere.
Precidit, forcearf.
Pauimus, we feddan.
Pithonis, helrun.[14]

[1] Cf. pag. 41 l. 13. R. W.
[2] Cf. pag. 41 l. 26 and Bosw. 85ₐ. R. W.
[3] Cf. pag. 41 l. 27. R. W.
[4] Read *progne.* R. W.
[5] Read *punctus.* R. W.
[6] Read *prenotatus.* R. W.
[7] Read *pentateuchum.* R. W.
[8] The glossator confounded *inuie* with *peruie.* R. W.
[9] Cf. pag. 469 l. 21. R. W.
[10] This word seems to be a corruption of *paschæ, pasche.* R. W.
[11] Read *proreta.* R. W.
[12] Cf. Nr. XII, 1. R. W.
[13] With this line our alphabetical glosses end abruptly, perhaps by the loss of the latter portion of the manuscript. It ends with the foot of the left-hand column of a page, the pages of this MS. consisting of two columns each, and the right-hand column had been left blank by the original writer, but another hand distinctly different, though still Anglo-Saxon, and of a rather later date, has filled it up by making a copy of fourteen consecutive words from the preceding page, with the addition of three new ones. Some further remarks on this subject will be found in the Introduction to the present volume. (These alphabetical glosses refer to Aldhelm's works. Cf. Nr. XII. R. W.)
[14] Read *Pythonis, Pythonissa.* R. W.

Pithonissa, helrynegu.
Porrectus, aræht.
Parui, ic hyrsumige.
Polimitarius, ceasterwyrhta.[1]

[1] Cf. pag. 470 l. 32. R. W.

Palatarum, proprium nomen arboris.
Palpitraret, clæppette, and sprangette.[2]

[2] Read *palpitaret.* R. W.

XII.

MISCELLANEOUS ANGLO-SAXON GLOSSES.

(Cf. Nr. VIII and Nr. XI.[1])

[1. *Miscellaneous Glosses.*]
Detracta, ic forsace.[2]
Non detracto, ne forsace ic.
Detrans,[3] egor.
Decrepito, tobigende.[4]
Dilibatus, gesmired.[5]
Diocessim, ...[6]
Echo, windumær.[7]
Exactoratus, gehened.[8]
Eologium, gedd.[9]
Effeta, berende biþ.[10]

Excubias, weardsetl.
Eucharitia, husl.[11]
Exagia, handmitta.[12]
Epithalamium, brydsang.
5 *Ergastulum*, hengen.[13]
Fofex, seer.[14]
Nauacula, scirseax.[15]
Tonsura, scaro.
Fucus, telg, deah.
10 *Flegma*, horh.[16]
Sputum, spatl.

[1] The foregoing Glosses are followed in the manuscript, MS. Cotton. Cleopatra, A III, by a Vocabulary of the ordinary kind (cf. Nr. VIII), which passes, almost imperceptibly (fol. 87 r°), into another series of miscellaneous Anglo-Saxon glosses, which are not, except partially at the beginning, in alphabetical order. It may be remarked, that the orthography of this collection is more corrupt even than that of the former.
[2] Read *detracto*. Cf. pag. 17 l. 15. R. W.
[3] A corruption of *dodrans*.
[4] Cf. pag. 17 l. 2 (dobgendi) and pag. 386 l. 30. R. W.
[5] Cf. pag. 17 l. 40. R. W.

[6] No Anglo-Saxon equivalent given, as is the case not unfrequently in this collection of glosses. (But cf. pag. 386 l. 32. R. W.)
[7] Perhaps for *wudu-mær*, the popular name for the echo.
[8] Read *exauctoratus*. Cf. pag. 20 l. 15. R. W.
[9] Read *eulogium*. Cf. pag. 19 l. 6. R. W.
[10] Cf. pag. 18 l. 42. R. W.
[11] Read *eucharistia*. R. W.
[12] Cf. pag. 20 l. 20. R. W.
[13] Cf. pag. 394 l. 29. R. W.
[14] Read *forfex*. R. W.
[15] Cf. pag. 142 l. 22. R. W.
[16] Cf. pag. 23 l. 28. R. W.

Frugus, forcuþ.
Ferinum, hold.[1]
Furca, wearhrod.
Fucatum, gedelgod.
Hostimen, leasung.[2]
Fascia, wræd.
Gramen, ...[3]
Gladiolum, sege.
Gannatura, ganung.[4]
Histrio, ...[5]
Hostimen, wundor.[6]
Iteramen, inilfe.[7]
Iurisperiti, rædboran.
Mimum, gliw.
Karus, leof.
Carissi,[8] gefo.
Kalende, begannes.
Kalamus, hreod.
Larbanum, segl.[9]
Lurco, sur.[10]
Larbula, grima.
Lunules, mene.[11]
Luscus, anege.
Lurdus, lemphealt.[12]
Lodix, loþa.
Lixa, leah.[13]
Legumen, bean.
Lenticula, pyse.
Latrena, genge.[14]
Lotium, hland.
Latex, burna.
Luxus, wyn.

Limax, snegl.
Lumbricus, regnwyrm.
Luscinus,[15] frox.[16]
Rana, yce.
5 *Lacertus*, efete.
Sanguisuga, læce.
Mancus, anhende.
Manica, glof.
Momentum, scutil.
10 *Malagma*, sealf.
Mastigia, swipe.
Manticum, handful.[17]
Massiranus, screawa.[18]
Mustella, wesle.
15 *Mus*, mus.
Sorex, scirfemus.[19]
Pelx, musfealle.[20]
Mulio, horshierde.
Messor, riftre.
20 *Muriceps*, catt.
Falcis,[21] rifter.
Falcastrum, siþe.
Nux, hnutbeam.
Napta, tero.[22]
25 *Nanus*, were.[23]
Neo, ic spinne.
Netum est, aspunnen is.
Inbibit, *degluttiuit*.
Discrepare, *non cordare*.
30 *Lectitat*, *frequenter legit*.
Falsariam, *mendacem*.
Interpres, *qui linquam*[21] *transfert*.

---

[1] The meaning of *ferinum* is: game, venison; *hold* denotes: a dead body, carcass, *rotted flesh*. R. W.
[2] Cf. pag. 417 l. 29. R. W.
[3] No Anglo-Saxon equivalent given; but cf. pag. 412 l. 1 and pag. 416 l. 12. R. W.
[4] Cf. pag. 23 l. 43. R. W.
[5] No translation given, but cf pag. 150 l. 17. R. W.
[6] Cf. l. 5. R. W.
[7] Cf. pag. 26 l. 25 and note 4. R. W.
[8] So has the MS. Read *charis*. R. W.
[9] Cf. pag. 430 l. 27. R. W.
[10] Cf. pag. 30 l. 39. R. W.
[11] Read *lunula* or *lunulæ*. R. W.
[12] Cf. pag. 433 l. 17. R. W.

[13] Read *lixiuia*. R. W.
[14] Read *latrina*. R. W.
[15] Read *luscinius*. R. W.
[16] *frox* is the translation of the next word: *rana*, frox, yce. R. W.
[17] Cf. pag. 442 l. 28. R. W.
[18] Read *musarancus*. Cf. pag. 443 l. 31. R. W.
[19] Cf. pag. 47 l. 27. R. W.
[20] A mousetrap. The compiler has here given a list of vermin, with the trap and the cat for taking them.
[21] So has the MS. R. W.
[22] Cf. pag. 451 l. 27. R. W.
[23] Read *dwerc* or *dwerg*. Cf. pag. 453 l. 21. R. W.

Ribula,[1]
Ex mineoo,[2] of bocreadc.
Discolorem,[1]
Uerbi gratia, worde cwedene.
Congeries, heap.
Proemium, profatio.[3]
Crura, sconcan.
Nemas,[4] lodrung.
[2. *Glosses referring to the Gospel of St. Matthew.*]
Sciscitabatur, interragabatus.[5]
In principibus, in ealdormannum.
Clam, oculte.
Percidentes, cadentes.
Secessit, gewat.
Delusus, afered, wæged.
A bimatu, abeate *duorum annorum*.[6]
Et infra, and beniopan pam.
In Rama, in eccelsum.[7]
De pilis, of hærum.
Locuste, stapan.
Mel siluestre.[8]
Ne uellitis,[9] ne willap ge.
Securis, æx.
Uentilabrum, windsobl.[10]
Sine modo, forlæt nu pus.[11]
Conplacui, gelicodo, gefag.
Pinnaculum,[12] *circuitus templi*.
Retro, under bæc.
Traditus esset, gesceald wæs.
Reficientes, conponentes.
Opinio, fama.
Lunaticos, bræcseoce.

Paraliticor, laman.[13]
Euanuerit, agætþ.[9]
Sub modio, undernmete.[14]
Donec transeat, oddæt þe gewiteþ.
5 *Iota una*.[15]
Apex, acumen litere.
Concilio, gemote.
Fatue, gemad.[16]
Reconciliare.[17]
10 *Quadrantem*.
Moechatus est, fornicatus est.
Scandalizat, offendit.
Erue,[1]
Repudii, utdrifan.[18]
15 *Non cognoscebat*, ne groette.
Prebe, da.
Angarizauerit,[19] beadætþ.[9]
Mutuare,[20] wrislan, hlenan.
Ethnice, æthna.
20 *Elioquin*,[21] elcor.
Exterminant, unrotlice doþ.
Simplex, purum.
Ad stauram, to wermete.[22]
Neent, spinnaþ.[23]
25 *Fistucam*,[24] *sanctum*,[25] strewu, eglan.
Tribulus,[26] *genus frutis*.
Inruunt, anhreosaþ.
Stridor, girstbitung.
Febricitantem, feferseoce.
30 *Fretum*, deop.
Modice fide, parue fidei.
Porro, eonu.
Seui, neþe.

[1] No Anglo-Saxon equivalent given. R. W.
[2] Read *ex minio*. R. W.
[3] Read *præfatio*. R. W.
[4] For *nenia*.
[5] Read *interrogabatur*. R. W.
[6] Cf. Matth. II, 17. R. W.
[7] Cf. Matth. II, 18. R. W.
[8] Cf. Matth. III, 4. R. W.
[9] So has the MS. R. W.
[10] For *wind-scobl*. (Cf. Matth. III, 12. R. W.)
[11] Cf. Matth. III, 15. R. W.
[12] Our compiler has made a strange mistake in his interpretation of this word.
[13] Read *paralyticos*. R. W.
[14] The Anglo-Saxon word denotes: a *breakfast*. Cf. Matth. V, 15. R. W.
[15] Read *unum*. R. W.
[16] Cf. Matth. V, 18. R. W.
[17] Read *reconciliari*. R. W.
[18] Cf. Matth. XIX, 7. R. W.
[19] Read *angariauerit*. R. W.
[20] Read *mutuari*. R. W.
[21] For *alioquin*.
[22] Read *staturam*. Cf. Matth. VI, 27. R. W.
[23] Read *nent*. R. W.
[24] Read *festucam*. Cf. Matth. VII, 3. R. W.
[25] Cf. Matth. VII, 6. R. W.
[26] Cf. Matth. VII, 16. R. W.

Impetu, wære.
Prepleceps,[1] oferclif.
Puplicani, awiscferinend.
Commissuram, gefog.
Tubicines, bemeras.
Tumultuantem, hlydende.
Comminatus, beotigende.
Diffamauerunt, gewidmærdan.
In Belzebul,[2] *in principe demonorum.*
In zonis, in gyrdelsum.
Non peram, ne fætels.
Castellum, castel.
Presides, gerefan.
Super *tecta,* on hrofum.
Asse *ueneunt,*[3]
Ueneunt, uenduntur.
Murum,[4] snore.
Socrum, sweger.
Mollibus, hnescum.
Inter natos, betuh bearnum.
Uim, neadhade.
Per sata, þurh æceras.
Uellere, hnoppiam.[2]
Accussor,[5] wregend.
Diriet,[6] gegripeþ.
Nequiores, wyrsan.
In parabolis, in prouerbis.[2]
Zizania, atan, odde lasor.[7]
Satis tribus, þrim myddum.[8]
Eructuabo, arecco.[9]
Dissere, gerece.[10]

Tetracha, quartam.[11]
Triclinio, yferan hyse.[12]
Pedestres, feþemen.
Coffinos,[13] manda.
5 *Fantasma,* uisio.
Ducatum, ladscipe.[14]
Bar Iona, filius columbe.[15]
Commutatio, gewrixle.
Transfiguratus, on oþrum hiwe.[16]
10 *Didragma, due dragma.*[17]
Hamum, angul.
Staterem, genus nummi.[18]
Scandalizauerit, offenderit.
Expedit ei, proderit ei.[19]
15 *Asinaria,* esul cweorn.[20]
Castrauerunt, eumicizauerit.[21]
Per foramen acus, þurh nædle þyrel.
Conducere, aheran.[22]
Conuentione, gemote.
20 *Percuratori,*[2] gerefan.
Betfage, nomen castelli.
Subiugalis, tam.[23]
Strauerunt, bættan.
Nummulariorum, munetera.
25 *Lactantium,* meolcsucgendra.
Reuerebuntur,[24]
Nuptias, gemung.
Altilia, fuglas.[25]
Ad exitus, to gelætum.[26]
30 *Ut caperent,* gæsoden.
Nomisma, denarius.[27]

[1] Read *præceps.* Cf. Matth. VIII, 32. R. W.
[2] So has the MS. R. W.
[3] Cf. Matth. X, 29. R. W.
[4] Of course this is a mere error of the collector of the glosses for *nurum.*
[5] Read *accusator.* R. W.
[6] Apparently for *diripiet.* Cf. Matth. XII, 29. R. W.
[7] Cf. Matth. XIII, 29 and 38. R. W.
[8] Cf. ibid. XIII, 33. R. W.
[9] Read *eructabo* XIII, 35. R. W.
[10] Cf. XIII, 36: *edissere.* R. W.
[11] Read *tetrarcha* XIV, 1. R. W.
[12] Read *huse.* Cf. Bosw. 97 1. R. W.
[13] Read *cophinos.* R. W.
[14] Cf. XV, 14. R. W.

[15] Cf. XVI, 17. R. W.
[16] Cf. XVII, 2. R. W.
[17] Read *didrachma.* Cf. XVII, 23. R. W.
[18] Cf. XVII, 26. R. W.
[19] Cf. XVIII, 6. R. W.
[20] Cf. XVIII, 6 *mola asinaria.* R. W.
[21] Read *eunuchizauerunt.* Cf. XIX, 12. R. W.
[22] Cf. XX, 1. R. W.
[23] Cf. XXI, 5. R. W.
[24] The Vulg. has *uerebuntur* XXI, 37. R. W.
[25] Cf. XXII, 4. R. W.
[26] The Vulg. has *ad exitus uiarum* XXII, 9. R. W.
[27] Read *numisma.* R. W.

Filacteria, lyfesna.[1]
Proselitum, aduenam.
[3. *Miscellaneous Glosses referring to the New Testament.*]
Cominatus est, beotode.
Conquirerunt, ætsamne sohton.
Uolo, mundare,[2]
Blasuemiat, tæleþ, yfelsaþ.[3]
Quidem facius dicere,[4]
Leui Alphei, Mathei Alphei.[5]
Adsumentum,[6]
In parabulis, in gelifnessum.[7]
Dispertitus est, todæled is.
Ultro, be selfwille.
Puppi, steorstefn.
Ceruicat, wangere, heafodp'.[8]
Legio, ui. milia.[9]
Non peram.[10]
Scandalis, soccus est, uel genus calciamentorum.[11]
Contuberniam, gadorwiste.[12]
Et adplicuerunt, gelidun.[13]
Urceorum, crucena.
Set, gestillid.[14]
Et spumat, and spætled.
Luscum, anigne.
Equor, sæ.
In bino, in twega wega gelæte.[15]
Numulariorum, munetera.
Uersutias, gesweopotnessa.
Sub obtentu, under intingan.

Decimatis, teoþingsceat.[16]
Mentam, mintan.[17]
Rutam, rutan.[18]
Edem, huss.[19]
5 *Ueneunt*, bebycgaþ.[20]
Depondio, duobus pondis.[21]
Non neunt, ne spinnaþ.[22]
Socrus, sweger.[23]
Norus, snoru.[24]
10 *Nimbis*, scur.
Minutum, paruum.
Non capiet, ne fętel.
Peram, fætel.
Hidripicus, wæterfull.[25]
15 *Baiulat*, bierd.
Saginatum, amæsted.
Simfonia, lignum concauum.
Chorum, strang heap.
Cados, anphora, i. amber.
20 *Cautionem*, gewrit.
Apicem, ord, cnol, heanes.[26]
Cahus,[27] dwolma.
Sicinorum, Sychemware.[28]
Ymnas, c. dragmas appendit.
25 *Sudorium*, swatlin.
Austerius, reþe.
Suspensus, ahangen, bidende.
Arescentibus, forweosnodon.
Manicabat, morgen wacode.
30 *Pacti sunt*, geþingodon.
Occidit Pascham, occidi[29] *agnum*.

[1] Read *phylacteria* Matth. XXIII, 5. R. W.
[2] Cf. Marc. I, 41. R. W.
[3] Read *blasphemat* Marc. II, 7. R. W.
[4] Read *quid est facilius*. Cf. Marc. II, 9. R. W.
[5] Cf. Marc. II, 14. R. W.
[6] Cf. Marc. II, 21. R. W.
[7] Read *in parabolis*, in gelicnessum. R.W.
[8] So has the MS. Cf. Marc. IV, 38. R. W.
[9] Cf. Marc. V, 9. R. W.
[10] Cf. Marc. VI, 8. R. W.
[11] Read *sandaliis*, cf. Marc. VI, 9. R. W.
[12] Read *contubernia* VI, 39. R. W.
[13] Cf. VI, 53. R. W.
[14] Read *sedatus*. R. W.
[15] Read *in biuio*. R. W.
[16] Read *decima*. R. W.
[17] Cf. pag. 134 l. 37. R. W.
[18] Cf. pag. 134 l. 2. R. W.

[19] Read *ædem*, hus. R. W.
[20] Cf. pag. 480 l. 16. R. W.
[21] Perhaps an error for *dispondeo, duobus ponderibus*? R. W.
[22] Cf. pag. 479 l. 24. R. W.
[23] Cf. pag. 480 l. 18. R. W.
[24] Cf. pag. 480 l. 17. R. W.
[25] It may be doubted if this were ever used as an Anglo-Saxon word for the disease, but it was an attempt by the glossator at a literal translation of the Latin, which is here written sufficiently corruptly. (Read *hydropicus*. R. W.)
[26] Cf. pag. 479 l. 6. R. W.
[27] For *chaos*. Cf. pag. 12 l. 43. R. W.
[28] The inhabitants of Sichem, or Shechem — the Shechemites. This gloss is probably taken from the Pentateuch.
[29] Read *occidit*. R. W.

Amphoram, amber.
Expetit, gesohte, gewilne.
Cribraret, sifte.
Auulsus, aweg abroden.
Imagonia, inelue.[1]
Inualescebant, strangadan, swidodon.
Decurio, qui officium carum egerit.
Parasceuem, preparatio.[2]
Metretas, gemetfatu.
Architriclino, principi triclino.
Piscina, fiscmere, *et quamuis piscem.*
In nataria, on fundmere.[3]
Scenophegia, tabernaculorum dedicatio.[4]
Liniuit, smirede.
Encenie, noue dedicationis.
In stitis, in swaþum.[5]
Loculos, scodas.
Hesitantes, tweogende.
Si quo minus, elcor.
Coors, þreat.[6]
Palmam, brade hand.
In preterium, in mæþelern.
Gazofilacium, welahord, feoh.[7]
Quadrans, quarta pars uncie.[8]
Azyma, andbida, beorma.[9]
Nardi pistici.[10]
Lagenam, watercrog.
In cateno, in disce.
Tedere, swa swa unrot.[11]
Anathematizare, frendian.[12]

Plectentis, flustriende, windende.
Conuiciebant, teon, ewidon.
Decurio, consiliarius.
Acurio, decurio dicitur.
5 *Pugillarem,* writbrec.[13]
Tetracha, feorþan dæles aldor.[14]
Lysania, nomen principis.
Abilina, nomen regionis.
Et ageliater,[15] *et ducebatur.*
10 *Supra pinnam,* ofer ymbgang.[16]
Prenoctans, þurh niht wæter.[17]
Si mutuum, gif wrixle.
Confertam, gecrumen.
Coagitatum, gehrysed.
15 *Loculum,* seodcist.
Cophinus, mand.[18]
Inprouitatem, gemagnesse.[19]
Suxisti, þu suge.
Simplex, anfeald, clæne, hluttor.[20]
20 [4. *Aldhelmi de Laudibus Virginitatis.*]
Dissertitudinem, g .. awnesse.[21] II.
Urbanitatis, burhspræce.[22]
Gimnosophistas, plegmen.
Palestricis, dæm wærstlicum.
25 *In gimnasio,* on leorninghuse.
Olimpiaci, dæs pleglican.
Agonis, gewinnes.
Nauiter, hrædlice.
Nanciscunt, begitaþ.[23]
30 *Strenua,* þa strangan, odde foremihtiglice.

---

[1] Read *intextina* or *interanea* R. W.
[2] Read *parasceue* Cf. Marc. XV, 42. R. W.
[3] So has the MS Read *sundmere*. R. W.
[4] Read *scenopegia* = feast of the *tabernacles*. R. W.
[5] An error for *in semitis*? R. W.
[6] Read *cohors*. Cf. pag. 14 l. 41. R. W.
[7] Read *gazophylacium*. Cf. Marc. XII, 41. R. W.
[8] Cf. Marc. XII, 42. R. W.
[9] Cf. Marc. XIV, 1. R. W.
[10] Read *nardi spicati*. Cf. Marc. XIV, 3. R. W.
[11] An error for *tædet me?* R. W.
[12] So has the MS. Cf. *fremdian*, Rosw. 27 f. R. W.
[13] Read *writ-brec*.
[14] Read *tetrarcha* Cf. pag. 481 l. 1 R. W.
[15] Read *agebatur*. R. W.
[16] Cf pag. 478 l. 28. R. W.
[17] Read *pernoctans*. The meaning of *pern.* is: þurh niht wæccend, waciend. R. W.
[18] Cf. pag. 481 l. 4. R. W.
[19] Read *inprobitatem*. R. W.
[20] After this line, in the manuscript, follow a column and two-thirds blank, and then, at the head of the first column of the next page, the glosses commence again, as though intended as a new collection.
[21] Damaged by the cutting of the leaf and uncertain in the manuscript (Read *gleawnesse*. Cf. pag. 386 l. 41. R. W.)
[22] Burh-spræc, courtly speech, such as was used in the town.
[23] Read *nanciscuntur*. R. W.

Anthletarum, cempena.¹
Cum emulo, mid widerweardum.
Flagrante, stincende.²
Sinuosis, ðæm fædmlice.
Scammatis, gewinstowe.
Nardo, elescalfe.
De obstrusis, of ðæm diglum.
Non ut passiuis, nu les swa wide.³
Pando, geap.
Strepente, swogende.
Stridende, brehtniende.⁴
In stadio, octaua pars mil.
Falerato, gehyrste.
Cornipede, equo.
Calcaribus, spurum.
Lupatis, cenepum.
Facetus, linguosus.
Orbes, orbibus, hringa, hohwerfinge.
Classicis, ðæm sciplicum.
Liburnam, nauem.
Lintrem, bat.
Proreta, steora.
Naucleri, princeps nauis.
Portisculo, hamere.
Spumosis, ðæm famegum.
Algosis, ðæm warihtum.
Tractibus, drohtum.
In propatulo, on æwiscnesse.   III.
Theatrales, ða pleglican.
Circentium, hringseta.⁵
Liquido, andgitlice.   IV.
Facessante, swedriende.
Per patentes, ðurh þa ruman.
Caltarum, clafrena.
Maluarum, geormanleafa.
Lento, þyton.⁶
Carene, cerenes.⁶
Receptacula, uiscera.

Coxarum, bana, þeona.
*Corimbas, uuas.*⁷
Tilie, linde.
Catalectico, dymetcunda.
5 *Brachia catalecto*,⁸
Generam et rorum,⁹
Allearii,¹⁰ hyfe.
Uestibulo, foredyre.
Enucleata, ascyled.
10 *Tropologiam*, beacnunge.
Anagogen, celsissimo intellectu.
Digesta, scripta.
Cronographorum,¹¹ tidwritera.
Grammaticorum, stæfwriterum.
15 *Ortograuorum*,¹² rihtwriterum.
Percola, þurhsticced.
Commata, membratim.
*Direptas, diuisas.*¹³
Sequestratim, gedæled edlice.
20 *Codicibus*, rindum.¹⁴   VI.
Ad incolatum, to eldeodignesse.
Pariat, hered.
Gurgustio, ceolan.
Nardi, elescalfe.
25 *Spirantis*, þære stincende.
Olfactum, odorem.
Ammodum,¹⁵ ualde.   VII.
Charismatum, diuinorum donorum.
Potissimum, ealra swiðost.
30 *Priuatam*, ða synderlican.
Munificentiam, cyste.
Sanctimonie, haligdomes.
Malagma, læcedom.
Gabuli, patibuli.
35 *Euentus*, wyrd.
Prestulanti, bidendum.¹⁶
*Septies uicena, et quaterna.*¹⁷
Uirginumilia, cxliiii milia.

¹ Read *athletarum*. R. W.
² Aldh. *fragrante*. R. W.
³ Aldh. *non ut passiuos*. R. W.
⁴ Read *stridente*. R. W.
⁵ Read *circensium*. R. W.
⁶ Aldh. *lento careni defruto*. R. W.
⁷ Aldh. *corymbos*. R. W.
⁸ Aldh. *brachycatalectico*. R. W.
⁹ So printed Wright. Read *genera metrorum*. R. W.

¹⁰ Aldh. *alvearii*. R. W.
¹¹ Read *chronographorum*. R. W.
¹² So has the MS. Read *orthographorum*. R. W.
¹³ Aldh. *direnptas*. R. W.
¹⁴ Aldh. *corticibus*. R. W.
¹⁵ Aldh. *admodum*. R. W.
¹⁶ Aldh. *præstolanti*. R. W.
¹⁷ Aldh *septies vicena et quater dena Virginum millia*. R. W.

In oromate, on gæstlicre gesihðe.[1]
Extaseos, diuinitatem.
Augustam, amplam.
Ardui, dæs heanhades.   VIII.
Scismaticorum, ereticorum.[2]
Stirpidus, owæstmum.[3]
De conca, of muscellan.[4]
Obrizum, smæte.[5]   IX.
Uenustas, fægernes.
Bombicinum, siolcen.
Cittis, filmenum.
Contecta, beþeaht.
Palmeti, palmbearwes.[6]
Dactulus, pomis.[7]
Nicolaum, alius nomen eius.
Commoditas, utilitas.
Baltheus, gyrdel.
Bullifer, æstæned.
Hauritoria, hlædhwiogl.
Arcuum, bigelsa.
Fornicibus, bogum.
Tubo, þeote.
Autumo, ic wene.
Uoracis, dæs gifran.
Merule,[8] dopfugeles.
Iacturam, æwyrdlan.
Crepundia, ornamenta.
Pulpa, lira.
Cauliculus, stela.
Questu, gestreonde.
Farus, beacanstan, *in promontoria rupis posita, i. fyrtor.*
Dehonestare, unweorðian.
Quisquiliarum, bensæala.   X.
Peripsema, geswepo.
Querulosis, sarseofunge.
Questibus, quidungum.
Supercilio, oferhigd.

Inter scillam, betweonan,
id nomen loci, þa freccnesse.
Ratibus, flietum.
Baratrum, pytte.
5 *Lintre*, bate.
Gestiunt, gernað.
Neuorum, wlite, womma.
Deformatos, geatelod.
Atromento, nigritudinis.[9]
10 *Cœrcilo*, scipe.[10]
Glomeratis, ymbheapod.[11]   XI.
Uertigo, wendend.
Ambronibus, dæm frecum.
Lurconibus, sigirgendum.
15 *In gastrimargie*, in gifernesse.[12]
Rumusculus, mærð.
Cenodoxie, uane glorie.
Tirunculis, militibus.
Genuinis, tuscum.[13]
20 *Malaribus*, cweorntodum.[14]
Lacertosis, dæm earmswidum.
Manipulatim, heapmælum.
Strophose, dæs fæcnan.[15]
Uenabulis, eoforspreotum.
25 *Umbonibus*, randbeagum.
Pugiles, sweordboran.
Macheram, gladium.
Inextricabilem, ða untolesende
Pelta, scuto.
30 *Leuiathan*, se draca.
Cerethei, eoredmen.[16]   XII.
Feletei, foreirnerum.[17]
Apparatu, gedrece.
Falarica, lancca.
35 *Indeptæ*, dære begitenan.
Successibus, spedum.
Natrix, genus serpentis.[18]
Elimatus, adrifen.

---

[1] Read *oramate*. Cf. pag. 458 l. 6   R. W.
[2] Read *schismaticorum, hereticorum*.   R. W.
[3] Read *stirpibus*.   R. W.
[4] Read *concha*.   R. W.
[5] Cf. pag. 457 l. 26.   R. W.
[6] Aldh. *palmetis*.   R. W.
[7] Read *dactylus*.   R. W.
[8] Read *merguli*. Cf. pag. 284 l. 8.   R. W.

[9] Read *atramento*.   R. W.
[10] Aldh. *circilo*.   R. W.
[11] Read *glomeratus*   R. W.
[12] Aldh. *in gastrimarçiæ voraginem*.   R. W.
[13] Read *gingivis*.   R. W.
[14] Read *molaribus*.   R. W.
[15] Aldh. *strophosæ fraudis*.   R. W.
[16] The glossator translated *coti*.   R. W.
[17] Cf. pag. 399 l. 27.   R. W.
[18] Cf. pag. 454 l. 17. 18.   R. W.

Orci duodecies, inferni,
twelf sidum, *quinquages,* fiftig þu-
senda.¹
Expeditionum, fyrda.
Flustris, sigendum.²
Obumbrando, figurando.
Internicionis, spildes.
*Decalogii,*³ *uerborum.*
Non refragabatur, non resistet.
Territorii, tunas.
Pronepotibus, bearna bearn.
Conspirati, coniurati. XIII.
Propugnacula, breostweal.
Calones, wuderas.
Clientes, ðegnhyssas.
Cum lixarum, mid wæterbererum.⁴
Emeritos, perfectos.
Funebre, heofendlice.
Epicedion, licleod,⁵
Et epitaphion, byrigleoð,
Utrumque est carmen super tumulum.
Collationes, ymbeahtas.
Massilliensis, Melselea.
Elimauit, interpretauit.
Disceptare, flitan.
Disputare, interpretare.
Conflictu, gefeohte. XV.
Residuo, altero.
Tendiculum, seada. XIII
*Sityriaca,*⁶ wyrtdrenc wið atre.
Facula, decele. XIV.
Theorice, contemplatiue.
In practice, in actuali.
*Edylio, esu.*⁷
Supplemento, stilnesse, gefylnesse.
Collegio, winescipe. XV.
Curtinarum, uelarum, wagryfta.⁸
Textura, weofung, gewef.

Panucla, wefla.⁹
Fucate, getelgade.
Plumario, ðy awundenan ryfte, feþer-
cræfte.¹⁰
5 *Textrinum,* þæt weblice.
*Thoracibus, imaginibus.*¹¹
Iacintho, hewen.¹²
Cocco, weolocread.
Uermiculo, wealhbaso.
10 *Bisso retorto,*¹³ hwite twine geþrawen.
Murice, wyrman.
Comminiscimur, resiat.¹⁴
Electri, eolhsandes.
Sucine, glæres.¹⁵
15 *Sauciant, uulnerant.*¹⁶ XVI.
Dracontia, gimrodor. XV.
Delicate, dære wrastlican. XVI.
Pedagogio, mægeðhade.
Repetante, eftsidgendum.¹⁷
20 *Extirpatus,* asuefecad.
Passionum, uncysta.
Inmunitas, orceasnes.
Solitare, anlaga.
Recapitulatio, eftspelling.
25 *Intercapidine,* firstmearces.¹⁸ XVII.
Lunulis, mynum, *uel argenteis.*
*Calomistro, ferro.*¹⁹
Cincinnorum, capillarum.
Stibio, herba.
30 *Mandibulas,* cinban.
Suatim, suarum more.
Indruticans, wræstende.²⁰
Arctissima, angustima. XVIII.
Factiosam, da fæcnan.
35 *Senticosis,* ðæm ðorhnihtum.
Separatim, gescadenlice. XIX.
Mediocritas, paruitas rerum.
Noualibus, wyrðelandum.

---

¹ Aldh. *phalanx duodecies quinquage-*
nis expeditionum milibus R. W
² Cf. Bosw. 63ᵇ. R. W.
³ Read *decalogi.* R. W.
⁴ Aldh. *cum lixarum coetibus* R. W.
⁵ Read *epithrenion.* R. W.
⁶ A blunder of the glossator. The Latin
words are: *etsi theriaca.* R. W.
⁷ Read *edulio.* R. W.
⁸ Read *cortinarum.* R. W.
⁹ Read *pannicula* R. W.

¹⁰ Cf. Aldh. *arte plumaria.* R. W.
¹¹ Cf. Aldh. *toraciclis.* R. W.
¹² *iacintho = hyacintho* R. W.
¹³ *bysso retorto.* R. W.
¹⁴ So has the MS. R. W.
¹⁵ Aldh. *succini.* R. W.
¹⁶ Cf. Aldh. *sauciatur.* R. W.
¹⁷ Aldh. *repedanti.* R. W.
¹⁸ Aldh. *intercapedinis.* R. W.
¹⁹ Aldh. *calamistro.* R. W.
²⁰ Aldh. *infruticans.* R. W.

Clumula, broudasiunetura.[1]
Contexere, plectere.
(I. *De Elia.*)
Uegitatione, uehementione.[2]   XX
Addicti, damnati.
Ineuitabile, ineffugabile.
Pendere, reddere.
ii. *De Eliseo.*
Quadrupes, cealf.
Bombose, dære thundendan.
Reboasse, ahlowan.
Melote, hredan.
In propatulo, in manifesto.
iii. *De Danielo, retinaculum.*[3]
Ob indaganda, to aspyrienne.   XXI.
Colludio, fraude, deceptione.
Texuisse, þæt he awrite.
Conlufio, contagione, immunditia.[4]
Fabrefactam, pulchre opere.
Sine uirili uola, butan weres geman.
Minutatim, sticcemælum.
Proceritas, celsitudo.
Coniectura, resong.
Cono, heanes.[5]
Perpeti, da hradan.[6]
Nutabunda, þa wagiende.
Luxoriante, fæstegeþuf.
Caraxatis, conscriptis.[7]
Potentatus, meahte.
Portendentes, figurantes.
Inminiculo, adiutorio.
Bibertitam,[8] *duplicem.*
iiii. *De iii. pueris.*
Auita, yldrafæder.
Externe, aliene.
Pulmentum, bilifen, andlifen.
Musica, da dreamlican.
Naptarum, fomitum, heordan.[9]
Refragabantur, widsocan.
Malleoli, tyndercyn, *id est* dyþhomer.

Crepitantes, ræscetende.
Ex amussim, diligenter.[10]   XXII.
Terimus, tredad.
Neutericis, dæm niwum.[11]
5 *Suppeditent, auxilient.*
Adfatim, ubertim.
Carptim, breuiter.
Obolisci, genus lapidis.
Glaucoma, eagsung.
10 *Subfundit,* orretted.
Scotomaticorum, cecorum.
Uictricia, da sigelican.
Concessum, gemote.
Librantis, heolorende.
15 *Labara,* segelgyrd.
Salebrosos, da unsmeþan.   XXIII
Anfractus, dwerfuru.
v. *De Iohanne.*
Lima, feol.
20 *Hymeneos,* hemedo.
Aporians, onscunigende.
Laturus, passurus.
Matrice, quidan.
Paranympus, drihtguman.
25 *De Iohanne.*
Stipis, ælmæssan.
Nemoribus, bearwum.
E frondosis, of dæm helmihtum.
Congeries, gesomnung.
30 *Sophiste,* dæs wordwisan.
Friabat, confregit.[12]
Sumptuosa, diliciosa.
Sequestra, byrgea.
Haustum, potum.
35 *Roboete,* yeean.[13]
Confectio, gereohnung.
vi. *De Paulo et Necromatia. Idem.*
Pithonissa, heahrun.   XXIV.
Manubia, wælreaf.[14]
40 *Quinquies quadragenas* cxcv.

[1] Aldh. *glumula.* R. W.
[2] Aldh. *vegetatione.* R. W.
[3] The copyist seems here to have placed the gloss by mistake over the title of the chapter of which he was copying the glosses.
[4] Cf. l. 25. R. W.
[5] Aldh. *sub cono sublimi verticis.*
                                R. W.
[6] Aldh. *præpeti.* R. W.
[7] Aldh *charazatis* R. W.
[8] For *bipartitam.*
[9] Aldh. *naptarum fomite.* R. W.
[10] Aldh. *ex amussi.* R. W.
[11] Aldh. *neotericis.* R. W.
[12] Aldh. *fricabat.* R. W.
[13] Aldh. *robetæ.* R. W.
[14] Aldh. *manubias.* R. W.

Rimatur, meditabat.
Siquipedas, ministri.[1]
Decretalibus, dæm rædendlicum.
   vii. *De Luca.*
Cauterio, hoce.
Cataplasma, medicina.
Purulentis, dæm wyrmsigum.
Incommoditas, infirmitas.
   viii. *De Clementi.*
Cernua, da mowelan.
Flebotomo, blodseax.
Baptisterio, fulwihtstowe.   XXV.
Taxauerat, figurabat.
Propaginibus, twigo settende.[2]
Elimauit, geriæahte.
   viiii. *De Siluestro.*
Auxoniæ, Italiæ.[3]
Alpium, montium.
Cautibus, stanum.
Speleo, spelunce.
Inextricabili, dy untolysendum.
Callario, saule.[4]
Eleuantuosa, dære unsmeðan.[5]
Sine tricarum, sine mora.[6]
Oppilatim, gedyrned.[7]
   x. *De Martino.*
Bigarum, cratwa.   XXVI.
Fatu, wyrde.
Parcarum, dearum.
Perniciter, hrædlice.
Reclinem, onhylded.
Obliqua, sio scythealde.
Curuatura, onbegnes.
Anatholi, dæs anatholes.[8]
Nebulis, scinlæcan.
Prestigiis, scin.[9]
A cimentario, wealwyrhtum.[10]

[1] Aldh. *sequipedas.* R. W.
[2] Aldh. *propagines.* R. W.
[3] Aldh. *Ausoniæ.* R. W.
[4] Aldh. *collario.* R. W.
[5] Aldh. *elephantinosa corporis incommoditas.* R. W.
[6] Aldh. *sine tricarum obstaculo.* R. W.
[7] Aldh. *oppilatum.* R. W.
[8] Aldh. *Anatolii nebulonis.* R. W.
[9] Aldh. *præstigias.* R. W.
[10] Aldh. *a cementario.* R. W.

Imbricibus, hroftigum.
   xi. *De Gregorio.*
Laturi, doonde.
Acathemice, dære udwitlican.[11]
                 XXVII.
Sophisma, scientia.
Cautum, scriptum.[12]
Scedarum, librorum.
Scissitationibus, domum.[13]
Gulio, gyddo.[14]
Contionatorum, gemotmanna.
   xii. *De Basilio.*
Usquequaque, lenge-swidor-awa.[15]
Pro rostris, in gemotstowum.
Fruniscantur, brucað.
Attonis, hlosnendum.[16]
Nutibus, potentatibus.
   xiii. *De Antonio.*
Stibarius, sulhhæbbere.[17]   XXVIII.
Occa, wealh, oþþe wyrðing.
Noualibus, wyrdelandum.
In atomo, in breahtme.
Aductabant, ham feredan.
Barritus, raringe.
   xiiii. *De Paulo.*
Bucellam, cicel.[18]
Bissenis, sexaginta.
Crustule, healstanes.
Hiulco rostro, gangende muþe.
   xv. *De Hilarion.*
Uulgo, welhwær.   XXIX.
Spinam, bodig.
Titionibus, brandum.
Inexperto, dy unandwisan.[19]
Consulatus, gerefscipes.
Contente, dæres gehealdnan.
   xvi. *De Iohanne.*

[11] Aldh. *Academiæ.* R. W.
[12] Read *cantum.* Cf. Aldh. R. W.
[13] Aldh. *scissitationibus.* R. W.
[14] Perhaps an error for *elogio?* Cf. Aldh. R. W.
[15] Cf. Bosw. 41e. R. W.
[16] Aldh. *attonitis.* R. W.
[17] The MS. has XII. *De Antonio.* Aldh. *stivarius.* R. W.
[18] Aldh. *buccellam.* R. W.
[19] Aldh. *in experto.* R. W.

Ciliarcho, tribuno.
From feowertienum oþ hundnigontig,[1] *quinquies bilustris.*
Consulta, rædas.
Liniamento, limgelecg.
Afflatus, eacen, *uel* gelicnes.
  xvii. *De Benedicto.*
Fortunatum, done gewilsæligan.
      XXX.
Eulogie, benedictionis.
Liberalitatis, rumheortnesse.
Mactus, mæced.
Per augustam, ðurh þæt rume.
Hesperie, Eotoles.
Cum aduocato, mid þingere.
Authentico, principali.
Classibus, heapum.
Diruta, gehriered.
Fato, gewife.
Fortune, wyrde.
Haut[2] frustra, non frustra.
Genesi, fatu.
Mathematicorum, tunglera.
Secundis, gesundelican.
Constellationem, steorrscewere.
Priuilegium, bonorem.[3]
Prouerunt,[4] gelumpon.
Falce, riftre.
Fiscillis, tænelum.[5]
Refertis, gefyldum.
Onustis, gehladenum.
Corbibus, caulum.
Exprimendos, to awringenne.
Merulenti, da ahlytredan.[6]
Idem et de peccati defruto.
Cærenes, apothecis.[7]
Recondenda, to gehealdenne.

Cauponibus, winbryttum.
Commendenda, to bebeodenne.[8]
Nundinarum, ceapstowa.
Exosas, afeonge.[9]   XXXI.
5 *Rapaci,* ðære risendan.
Sub pretextu, under mundbyre.
Inter biothonatas, betweonan sylfmyrde.[10]
Abolere, aiedan.
10 xviii. *De Hilarione.*[11]
Uulgo, late.   XXIX.
Exmergeret, surgeret.
Succumberet, getrunge.[12]
Familice, þa ungerlican.[13]
15 *Frugalitatis, abstinentie.*[13]
Non calcitres, ne spornette.
Epidaurum, ðære mægðe.[14]
Dalmatie, ðære burge.[14]
Municipium, burgscipe.
20 *Bouem,* oxan.
Peduces, owes.[15]
Armenta, hridero.
Bobulcos, oxena hierdas.
Subulcos, swanas.
25 *Superi,* upgodo.
Strue, fine.
Scindulis, scidum.
Crates, hyrdlas.
Assantibus, brædendum.
30 *Legislator, Moyses.*
Obtruncati, breuiati.
  xix. *De Malcho.*
Ob cognate, ðære gesibban.[16]   XXXI.
Instinctu, tihtnesse.[17]
35 *Strofose,* ðæs fæcnan.[18]
Liminio, wræcside.[19]
Mancipium, þeow.

---

[1] The glossator translates *usque nonagenariam (senectam)* cap. XXIX; not *quinquies bilustris* cap. XXIX. R. W.
[2] So has the MS. R W.
[3] Read *honorem.* R. W.
[4] Read *prouenerunt.* R. W.
[5] Aldh. *fiscellis.* R. W.
[6] Aldh. *merulenta.* R. W.
[7] Aldh. *merulenta defecati nectaris defruta apothecis cælestibus.* R. W.
[8] Aldh. *committenda.* R. W.
[9] Aldh. *exosus.* R. W.
[10] Aldh. *inter biothanatos.* R. W.

[11] Cf pag. 495 Nr. XV. R. W.
[12] Aldh. *succumbere.* R W.
[13] Aldh. *famelica frugalitatis parsimonia.* R. W.
[14] Aldh. *iuxta Epidaurum Dalmatiæ municipium.* R. W.
[15] Read *pecudes.* R. W.
[16] Aldh. *ob cognatæ propinquitatis curam.* R. W.
[17] Aldh. *instructu.* R W.
[18] Aldh. *strophosi.* R. W.
[19] Aldh. *postliminium.* R. W.

Glebulis, turfum.
Nugaciter, unnytlice.
In genetali, in ðære gecyndelice.[1]
Profanando, maculando.
Non feram, non sinam.
  xx. *De Narciso.*
Delitiscere, bemidan.
Anastasis, resurrectionis.
Fortuito, semnendlice.
Oportunus, sio tidlice.
Exorcizans, haligende.
Cicindilibus, weocum.
Aruna, rysele.[2]
Seuo, smerwe.
Madefactus, ofdæned.
Probrosum, edwid, fullic.
Chirographatur, scribebat.
Apologeticam, excussationem.
Concinnatas, cumulatas.
Presbiteros, senes.
Emulabantur, imitabantur.
Deuotabant, wyrgdon.
Domatis, huses.
Tigillo, tecti.
A triplici, from dæm.[3]
cerebre, þriefealdan brægene.[3]
Inprecabatur, bæd.
Rancidis, ðæm dreorum.[4]
Inauditum, ungefræge.
  xxi. *De Anastasio.*
Altor, fosterfæder.
Periodas, circuitus.[5]
Affabiliter, luflice.
Latrine, gengan.
Cuniculum, grep.
Carismatum, gifena.[6]
Indolis, geogoðe.
Gesticulatio, plega.
Missarum, sendnessa.
Conspicatur, sceawode.
Inuestes, absque barba.

XXXII.

Serio, georneste.
Expertus sit, oncunnende wæs.
Delatum, geferedne.
Commentis, searwum.
5 *Inletus*, getyhted.[7]
Inconsulte, unrædlice swa.
Scenam, sceadwe.
Flamen, biscop.
Attrite, gegnidenan.
10 *Uelantem sospitem*, halne.[8]
Prostituta, forliges.
Prostibuli, forliggange.
Insimulare, wregian.
Melancoliæ, ðæs sweartan galgan.
15 *Nausiam*, wlætan.[9]
De recessibus, of heolstrum.
Procax, hwal.
Obuncabat, ymbclypte.
Exulat, wracode.
20 *Potiretur*, utebatur.
Cote, hwetstane.
Insectiones, ehtnesse.[10]
Conspiratio, coniuratio.
Artus, liðo.
25 xxii. *De Babillo.*
Excubias, weardsetl.
Mandras, eowestras.
Arcebat, bewerede.
Palatias zetas, ða heallican seld.[11]
30 *Yppodromi*, þæs huses.[12]
Conflictibus, geflitum.
Perpendiculo, reht.
Uergeretur, wære onsigen.
Cleri, biscophirede.
35 *Boias*, beagas.
Nec tunc, bundan.[13]
Fallere, decipere.
Ictibus, slegum.
  xxiii. *De Cosma et Damiano.*
40 *Albo, nombred, in quo consulis nomen scripserant.*

XXXIII.

[1] Aldh. *in genitali.* R. W.
[2] Aldh. *aruina.* R. W.
[3] Aldh. *a triplicis summitate cerebri.* R. W.
[4] Read *raucidis.* Cf. Aldh. R. W.
[5] Aldh. *periodos.* R. W.
[6] Read *charismatum.* R. W.
[7] Aldh. *illectus.* R. W.
[8] Aldh. *ualentem sospitem.* R. W.
[9] Aldh. *nauseam.* R. W.
[10] Aldh. *insectationes.* R. W.
[11] Aldh. *palatinas zetas.* R. W.
[12] Read *ippodromi* or *hippodromi.* R. W.
[13] Read *nectunt.* Cf. Aldh. R. W.

Archiatros, heahlæcas.
Litterature, scripture.
Apostasie, fleamlastes.
Pedemtimi, softe.[1]
Monaptalmis, ænegum.[2]
Balbis, stamerum.
Blessis, wlipsum.[3]
Refocilando, hyrttende.
Fortune, gewife.
Cassibus, wyrdum.[4]
Ad superos, ad uiuentes.
Consternati, conterriti.
Effera, sio rede.
Eculei, cruci.
Agonizarunt, þreowedan.
xxii(i). *De Crissanti.*
Gymnosophistis, weoroldsnottrum.

XXXV.

Rethoribus, wodborum.[5]
Ualitudines, adle.[6]
Cataplasma, læcedomnessa.
Uisco, fugellime.
Glutinarum, gelimedne.[7]
Arihtmitica, rimcræft.[8]
Astronomia, tungelcræft wisan.
Astrologia, ratio siderum.
Mechanica, searocræft.[9]
Cathagorias, x. predicamenta.[10]
Commentis, scarwum.
Prestare, elicre wæs.[11]
Neophytus, se niwa.
Precipuus, se mæsta.
Proscriptionem, gestrod.
Infiscaretur, gegafelod.

XXXIV. *Libitos*, licongum.[12]
Elosericis, ealgodwebnum.[13]
Sagina, fodre.
Epithalami, brydleod.[14]
5 *Uestalis*, gydenlice.
Sed secus cessit, ac on odre wisan rynde.
Syllogismi conclusionibus.
Phitronieade.[15]
10 *Herculis*, hearge.[15]
Udis, wætum.
Nodosi, ostihtum.
Cibbo, copse.[16]
Pudentissimis, dæm fulæstum.[17]
15 *Lotio*, hlande.
Chaldeorum, tungelcræftum.
Hierophantorum, scincræfta.
Ariolorum, da þæt womfreht reniad.
Marsorum, wyrmgalera.
20 *Lustramenta*, lybsin.
Ambrosiam, suauem odorem.
In rosatum, on rosena.
Deglobere, behyldan.[18]
Byrse, hyde.[19]
25 *Supparum*, æcemban.[20]
Putamina, hniglan.
Lanterne, leohtfætes.
Singillatim, singulariter.
Cloacarum, flodena.
30 *Cuniculi*, grep.
Ingesserunt, onheapedon.
De clatris, of pearrocum.
Sugillaretur, osogen wære.
De congestu, be gesomnungum.[21]

[1] Aldh. *pedetentim*. R. W.
[2] Aldh. *monophtalmis*. R. W.
[3] Aldh. *blæsis*. R. W.
[4] Aldh. *casibus*. R. W.
[5] Read *rhetoribus*. R. W.
[6] Read *inualetudines*. R. W.
[7] Read *glutinatum*. R. W.
[8] Read *arithmetica*. R. W
[9] In the dictionaries, this word is wrongly explained as derived from *searo*, in the sense of deceit, and as meaning a deceitful art or stratagem. It is evidently derived from the word in the sense of a machine, or instrument.
[10] Aldh. *categorias, quæ prædicamento-rum generibus distinguuntur.* R. W.
[11] So has the MS. Aldh. *præstaret.* R. W.
[12] Aldh. *libitus.* R. W.
[13] Aldh. *olosericis.* R. W.
[14] Aldh. *epithalamii.* R. W.
[15] Aldh. *Amphitrioniadæ, id est, Herculis sacello.* hearge is a translation of *sacello.* R. W.
[16] Aldh. *cippi.* R. W.
[17] Aldh. *putentissimis.* R. W.
[18] Aldh. *deglubere.* R. W.
[19] Aldh. *birsæ.* R. W.
[20] Read *stuparum.* R. W.
[21] Aldh. *de congesta copia.* R. W.

MISCELLANEOUS GLOSSES.

Pignus, wed.   XXXVI.
   xx(v). *De Iuliano.*
Competem, getælne.[1]
Magnopere, swide.
Tedas, spelde.
Faces ardentes.
Bis quingentenum, tua fiftig
Effebo, ungebarde.[2]
Hircitallo, hysse.[3]
Theca, fodre.
Damnatorum, ræplinga.
Fasciarum, swepela.
Tragoediam, sarlicleoð.
Ter denis, þreotienum.
Cuparum, tunnena.
Bituminis, scipteran.
Farciuntur, acrummene wæron.
Pyrebele, id est, fyr.[4]
Obolisci, dæs stanes.[5]
Spere, æpples.[6]
In conum, on heahnisse.
De torrente, of ðam byrnendum.
Licis, hefeldþrædum.[7]
Pollices, þuman.
Alloces, þa miclan tan.
Filis, þrædum.
Lurcare, fretan.
Gurguliones, þrotan.
Oppilauit, behydde.
Callositas, unsmeðes.
Tabo, hune, *uel* adle.
Deturpans, onretteþ.
In sabanis, on sabanum, *id est* scete.
Boiolabantur, borene wæron.[8]
Uoti compos, wilfægen.
   [xxv]i. *De Ammon.*
Commercia, ceapunge.   XXXVII.
Inuisi, dæs laðan.

Ceni, wasan.
Pubescentem, weaxende.
Deprenderint, onfundon.[9]
Obstinatam, þa anwillan.
5 *Conibentia*, hæbbenga.[10]
Obsecundans, herende.
Anhelat, desiderat.
Acutum, son, sona.[11]
Direpta, þa genumenan.
10 *Depeculata*, þa ofdrifenan.
Abegerunt, fram adreofon.
Strictim, sceortlice.
Consummatim, scyndendlice.[12]
Doleum, wæterbyden.[13]
15 *Obeuntem, morientem.*[14]
Cyppum, hoferedne.[15]
Melote, hreðan.
Amiculis, gegerelican.
Lucum, hearga.
20 *In citeriorem*, in ðone firran.
Discifer, discberend.
Rudentum, bremmendra.[16]
Affatim, ubertim.
Manipulo, were.
25 *Cernuas*, neole.   XXXVIII.
   xxvii. *De Apollonio.*
Cleratis, clerochade.[17]
Anfractus, þwyrhfero.
Exorbitans, aswifende.
30 *Subterfugiens*, bifleonde.
Dilituisse, gediernan.[18]
Antipatris, pater Herodis.[19]
Thoraciclas, imaginibus.
Octenis temporum, lustris xl.[20]
35 *Interpellans*, gretende.
Curbo, gebegde.[21]
De stuppe stamineo, be cembum wearpe.[22]

[1] Aldh. *compotem*. R. W.
[2] Aldh. *ephebo*. R. W.
[3] Aldh. *hircitallo*. R. W.
[4] Aldh. *flammantis pyræ*. R. W.
[5] Read *obelisci*. R. W.
[6] Read *sphæræ*. R. W.
[7] Aldh. *licis*. R. W.
[8] Aldh. *baiulabantur*. R. W.
[9] Aldh. *deprehenderent*. R. W.
[10] Read *cohibentia*. R. W.
[11] So has the MS. Aldh. *actutum*. R. W.
[12] Aldh. *et summatim*. R. W.
[13] Aldh. *dolium* R. W.
[14] Aldh. *abeuntem*. R. W.
[15] Aldh. *gibbum*. R. W.
[16] Aldh. *rudentium*. R. W.
[17] Aldh. *clericatus*. R. W.
[18] Aldh. *delituisse*. R. W.
[19] Aldh. *Antipatri* R. W.
[20] Aldh. *octonis temporum lustris*. R.W.
[21] Aldh. *curuo*. R. W.
[22] Aldh. *de stuppæ stamine*. R. W.

Putamine, hniglan.
Ordiretur, wefen wæs.
Ex terite glomere, of sinuwealtum cliwen.[1]
Fuso, spinele.
Netum, aspunnem.
Radiis, hrislum.
Stridentibus, hristlendum.
Extricabatur, tolesed wæran.[2]
Parsimonia, fæstenbehæfednes.
Hortorum, wyrtuna.
Condito, gecocanade.
Culine, cycene.
In focularibus, on heordum.
Intempestiue, in swigean modrenæhte.[3]
Lautune, carcerne.[4]
Circumquaque, ymb þæt.
Sub diuo, under lyfte.
Aliorsum, elles hwyder.
Strictis, getogene.
Offendisset, inuenisset.
Simultatem, unsibbe.
Incentor, tyhtend.
Sequestra, byrgea.
Leto tenus, oð dead.
Clasma, mal.
Fors, wyrd.
Glomerarentur, gesomnedon.
Familicis, hungregum.[5]
Calcatur, teled is.
Iubeleus, annus.[6]
Remissionum, exenium, lac.[7]
Eulogie, benedictionis.
Parasitis, ministris.
Propostero, onwendedre.[8]
Mala Punica, þa Affracaniscan æppla.
Dactulus, ficæppel.[9]

Idem et palatas, and cariarum.[10]
Nicolaos, palmæppla.
Massas, clyno.
Antes, ordines.
5 *Racemis*, bergeum.
Mitescere, milesa.
Flauescentibus, falewende.
Calamitosa, dy earmlican.
Crustulis, halstanum.
10 *Tortellis*, ceaum (?)
Exibuit, gebryttade.[11]
Simila, melewes, smedma.
Polline, gryttes.
Crasso, dy fættan.
15 *Corbos*, caulas.[12]
Legythum, crog
Equiperat, widmeteþ.[13]
Nutabunto, dy wagigendan.[14]   XL.
Secundum, dy æfterlicum hade.[15]
20 *Gradatim*, softe.
Spatiantes, hweorfende.
Amminiculum, adiutorium.[16]
Expiauit, gefelsode.
Plecta, windonge.[17]
25 *Plumemus*, windan.[17]
Uestibula, foredyre.
Enucleare, ascilian.
    xxviii. *De Sancta Maria*.
Gerula, berend.
30 *Nurus*, snoro.
Germana, soror.
Pelices, cyfesa.[18]
Priuilegium, honorem.
Obsidem, gisl.
35 *Receptacula*, andfengnessa.
    xxix. *De Cecilia*.
Indulte, þæs alefdan.
Proci, bidderes.

---

[1] Aldh. *ex tereti filorum glomere*. R. W.
[2] Aldh. *extricabantur*. R. W.
[3] Read *midrenæhte*. Aldh. *intempestæ noctis*. R. W.
[4] Aldh. *lautumia*. R. W.
[5] Aldh *famelicis*. R. W.
[6] Aldh. *Iubileus*. R. W.
[7] Aldh. *xenium*. R. W.
[8] Aldh. *præpostero*. R. W.
[9] Aldh. *dactylis*. R. W.

[10] Aldh. *et palatas, id est, caricarum massas*. R. W.
[11] Aldh. *exhibuit*. R. W.
[12] Aldh. *corbes*. R. W.
[13] Aldh. *æquiparat*. R. W.
[14] Read *nutabundo*. R. W.
[15] Aldh *secundi sexus*. R. W.
[16] Aldh. *adminiculum*. R. W.
[17] Aldh. *plectro plumemus*. R. W.
[18] Aldh *pellices*. R. W.

Purgamenta, cwead.
Latrinarum, gengena.
Bis quinquagenis et ter quinis, i. centum quindecim.
Sirenarum, meremennena.
Inexpertus, unandwis.
Pellexerunt, beswican.[1]
Sub pretextu, under mundbyre.
Leuirum, tacor, þæt is brydguma brodor.
Distinatus, onsended.[2]
Serta, hringas.
Edicta, gebodo.   XLI.
    xxx. *De Agatha.*
Aguste, þære ruman.[3]
Trinacria, Sicilia.
Lictorum, þegna.
Sacrafragnum, þa scearwan gebr'.[4]
Siculus, se Sicilisca.
Adstipulantur, adfirmant.
Turris, wighuses.
Opere pretium, ræd.   XLII.
    [xx]xi. *De Lucia.*
In catalogo, in rime.
In tribuli, in ðæm gesibban.[5]
Siracusas, sio burg.[6]
Successibus, spedum.
Rerum, ceatta.
Distratio, bibycgong.
Marsupia, siodas.
Aeri, grimme, angere, sorge.
Lenonum, sponera.
Atras offulas, ðas sweartan snæda.[7]
Resine, scipteran.
Tabuerunt, dwinan.
Prædo, hloþere.
Archiparatta, heahsedeof.[8]

Saroastren, rex Bahtianorum gentis.[9]
                                    XLIII.
    xxxii. *De Iustina.*
Expedire, reccan.
Apicibus, stafum.
Scemmatizarunt, licetton.[10]
Disparuit, forswealt.
Aruspicum, hælsera.
Adibitis, todonum.[11]
Exterminans, aiedende.
Ineluctuabilis, þa unoferwinnene.[12]
Exorcismi, halgunge.[13]
Catacizatus, geeristnad.[13]
Bissemis, tuwahealfum.[14]
Bisternis sextum, drim binnan drim butan.[14]
Adsciceretur, togeladede.
Peruicax, gemah.
Refragatur, widwinnend.[15]
Roborabiliter, stranglice.[16]
Oculum, spræce.[17]
Ultro, hraþe.
Purpurescit, readode.
Sectas, þeawas.   XLIV.
    xxxiii. *De Eugenia.*
Argumenta, searwe.
Ob potiorem, fore meran.
Caccabatum, besciten, behrumod.
Atramentum, sweartnesse.
Basterne, scrides.
Uehiculo, fore.
Pedisequis, degnum.
Spadonibus, afyrdum.
Rassis, scorenum.[18]
Fortuis, semnendlice.[19]
Casibus, wyrdum.
Ademptam, genumene.

---

[1] Aldh. *pellexerint.* R. W.
[2] Aldh. *destinatus.* R. W.
[3] Read *augustæ.* R. W.
[4] Aldh. *nec aera testularum fragmina.* R. W.
[5] Aldh. *contribuli.* R. W.
[6] Aldh. *Syracusæ oppidum.* R. W.
[7] Aldh. *atræ picis offulas.* R. W.
[8] Aldh. *archipirata.* R. W.
[9] This no doubt means Zoroaster, though the title given to him is not easily explained, and must have arisen from the ignorance of the glossator. (Aldh. *Soroastrem.* R. W.)
[10] Aldh. *schematizarunt.* R. W.
[11] Aldh. *adhibitis.* R. W.
[12] Aldh. *in eluctabile.* R. W.
[13] Aldh. *exorcismo catechizatus.* R. W.
[14] Aldh. *bis seni uel bis terni.* R. W.
[15] Aldh. *refragator.* R. W.
[16] Aldh. *fauorabiliter.* R. W.
[17] Read *oraculum.* R. W.
[18] Read *rasis.* R. W.
[19] Read *fortuitis.* R. W.

Proserpinam, hiera deofla sum.
Minerua, dea artium.
Adplaudunt, gulpan.
Stolida consulta, þa dolan rædas.
Scrupulum, incan.
Municipium, burh.
Sub modio, under mittan.
De sceuo, of dæm sceolan.[1]
Infamis, orretscipe.
Clanculis, dæm diglum
Deliberaret, geþohte.
Traducta, georwyrded.
Inpingere, ætspornan.
Catapultas, speru, boltas.
Recorsit, eft ongenbigde.[2]
Antiquitus, gefyrn.
Calcor, spura.[3]
Dissona, ungerade.
Quadrare, gefegan.
Fotam, sealfode.
    xxxiiii. *De Agne.*
Celibes, hegstealdman.   XLV.
Emulatores, onhyrgendras.
Uernantibus, grenum.
Frontosa, sio balde.
Dedecus, unwlites.
Donatur, geweordad.
Adgrederetur, geeode.
Porcinus strepitus, þæt symlice gestun.[4]
Cumiterio, byrgenstowe.[5]
Caraxabimus, writat.
    [xxx]v. *De Tecla et Eulalie.*
Incommodum, unbehefe.   XLVI.
Duxit, tealde.[6]
Clatros, pearrocum.
Enixte, geornlice.[7]
Pyrarum, bæla.

    xxxvi. *De Scolastica ac Cristina, simulque, Dorohthea.*
Tiara, hæt.   XLVII.
Fulminauit, lixte.
5 *Inportune,* gemalice.[8]
Reluctaretur, widstod.
Eliciens, abeodende.
Minaci, oferlifiende.
Proceritate, heannesse.
10 *Porrectam,* aræredne.
Forti, fæstes.
Liture, liming.
Indegitamentum, þara boca.[9]
Sudibus, stengum.
15 *Uenusti,* þæs fegeran.
Obstipuit, ofercymen wæs.[10]
Carminibus, galdorledum.
Inritabant, gremedan.
Catastarum, witacyn.
20 *Adplicuit,* todyde.[11]
Naufragauerunt, gedurfan.[12]
Deprauandam, to mishwofenum.
Ordine prepostero, onwendedre endebyrdnesse.
25 *Pretorium,* domhus, domærn.
Cauillatione, geslitgliwe.
Prosperare, feran.[13]
Gannature, bysmires.[14]
Indolem, giogude.   XLVIII.
30   xxxvii. *De Constantine.*
Pretorum, ealdormanna.[15]
Subarrauit, geweddade.[16]
Apparatu, geþræce.
A circio, nordan.
35 *Traciarum,* traciana.[17]
Passim, wide.   XLIX.
    xxxviii. *De Eustochie.*
Scedulis, bocum.[18]

---

[1] Aldb. *dum sauo.* R. W.
[2] Aldh. *retorsit.* R. W.
[3] Read *calcar.* Cf. Aldb. R. W.
[4] Aldh. *porcinus paganorum strepitus.* R. W.
[5] Aldh. *cæmiterio.* R. W.
[6] Aldh. *duxi.* R. W.
[7] Read *enize.* Cf. Aldb. R. W.
[8] Aldh. *opportune.* R. W.
[9] Aldb. *indigamentorum.* R. W.

[10] Aldh. *obstupuit.* R. W.
[11] Aldh. *applicauit.* R. W.
[12] Aldh. *naufragauerant.* R. W.
[13] Aldh. *properare.* R. W.
[14] Aldh. *gannitura.* R. W.
[15] Aldh. *procerum.* R. W.
[16] Aldh. *subarraret.* R. W.
[17] Aldh. *Thraciarum.* R. W.
[18] Aldh *schedulis.* R. W.

Sexies terna, eahtatiene.
Interpres, wealhstod.
Pertessum, adrotsumis.[1]
Insigniter, mærlice.
Edidit, awrat.
Caracteribus, angelicnessum.[2]
Lepida, getinge.
Citro pontum, ofer sæ.[3]
Tenacissimis, þæm fæstestum.
Bilancee, twyfealdre heolra.[4]
Trutinabat, heolrode awæg.[5]
Ad stridule, to swege.[6]
Remugiet, blowed.
De Chione et Hierene et Agape.
Rusticis, cierliscum.
Arcersire, geladian.[7]
Exorbitantes, aswifende.
Carybdibus, swelgnessum.[8]
Non dissona, nales ungerade.
Cirris, loccum.
Consparsione, gecynde.
In luxum, in lust.
Labescit, aglad.
Suppellex, geloma.
Lebetes, hweres.
Bassiare, cyssan.
Instinctu, tyhtnesse.
Debachatus, wedende.
Ludificatus, weged.
Effeta, ealde.[9]
Habitudine, onsiene.
Artubus, liodum.
Inceptis, onginnissum.
Lupercia, æt ðam gilde.[10]
Competalia, æt þam wega gelætum wæran.[11]

Portunalia, oþþe æt ydum wæran gesette.[12]
Et suouetaurili,[13] odda þa þe æt þæm geldum þær wæs swin and scep.
5 *Numina*, gield.
Melodiam, sealmsang.
xl. *De Rufina et Secunda.*
Incanduisset, onhatode LI.
Manipulares, cempan.
10 *Laturi*, þrowigende.
Fumigabundis, þæs stincendan.
Nardi pistici, þære getreowan elesealfe.
Emersisse, þe hie uparisan.
L. 15 *Elisa*, asliden.
Sine murmura, butan hearmheortnesse.
xli. *De Anatholia et Uictoria.*
Decriminalia, heafodfretennesse.[14]
20 LII.
Perhiscelides, ornamenta crurum.[15]
Matricularis, þearfum.[16]
Prodiga, þæs stryndedan.
Liberalitatem, rumheortnesse.[17]
25 *Pitacia*, ærendbec.[18]
Lupercalibus, þæm gildendum. *Luperci uocantur illi sacerdotes qui ministrant deo qui uocatur Pan.*
Ad agapem, to ælmessum.
30 *Basilisci*, þære nædran.
Flara, blædas.[19]
Calamitosam, þæt earme.[20]
Orbitationibus, biastepnessum.[21]
Arceretur, bewered wære.
35 *Diane*, ricenne.[22]
Larbatos, hreofe.[23]

---

[1] Aldb. *pertæsum.* R. W.
[2] Aldb. *characteribus.* R. W.
[3] Aldb. *citra pontum.* R. W.
[4] Aldh. *bilance.* R. W.
[5] Aldh. *trutinabit.* R. W.
[6] Aldh. *ad stridulæ buccinæ sonum.* R. W.
[7] Aldh. *accersiri.* R. W.
[8] Aldh. *charybdibus.* R. W.
[9] Aldh. *effecta.* R. W.
[10] Aldh. *lupercalia.* R. W.
[11] Aldh. *compitalia.* R. W.
[12] Aldh. *portumnalia.* R. W.

[13] Aldh. *et suouetaurilia.* R. W.
[14] Aldh. *discriminalia.* R. W.
[15] Aldh. *periscelides.* R. W.
[16] Aldh. *matricularis.* R. W.
[17] Aldh. *liberalitate.* R. W.
[18] Aldh. *pittacia.* R. W.
[19] Aldh. *flabra.* R. W.
[20] Aldh. *calamitosum.* R. W.
[21] Aldh. *flebilibus orbitatis quæstibus.* R. W.
[22] Cf. pag. 387 l. 38. Cf. Kemble, the Saxons in England, Book I, chap. XII. R.W.
[23] Aldh. *laruatos.* R. W.

Camitiales, gebræcseoce.¹
Cantando, galdorgalende.
Spiris, hringum.
Capulo tenus, oð hielt.
Adacto, þurhwrecen.
   xlii. *De Iosep et Dauid et Samson et aliis plurimis.*
Exosa, scounga.   LIII.
Conspiratio, facengecwis.
Argutis, þæm swogendum.
Fidibus, strengum.
Mandibulas, cinban.
Rictus, ceaflas.
Frustatim, in sticce.
Crista, cambihte.
Cassidis, helme.
Thoraca, byrne.²
Falarica, spere.
Umbonis, randbeages.
Parma, scylde.
Singulariter, anwiglice.
Congrediens, feohtende.
Utpote, swa hit wæs.
In basileon, on cyninga bocum.
Percellitur, slægen.³
Pelicatus, cyfeshade.⁴
Eneruiter, waclice.
Flaminium, biscophade.   LIV.
Ratam þa gerisnan.⁵
Ostro, telgedeage.
Simultate, unsibbe.
Cum fratrueli, mid broðorsuna.
Meri, wines.
Nenias, bismerleod.
Elucubrate, þy ahlytrede.⁶
   xliii. *De uestimento uirginum.*
Delicatis, wræstlicum.   LV.
Legulam, hringan.⁷

Subripuit, forstæl.
Colerata, geælged.⁸
Probrum, edwit.   LVI.
Ostentationis, gylpes.
5 *Prostitutis*, forlegesum.
Sumptuosius, behydelice, wistfullice.
Inlicias, spones.
Setosa, ðy hrisehtan, þa hærihtam.
Conquilii, telges.⁹
10 *Bacciniorum*, bergena, oððe ofeta.
Per hironiam, þurh hucx.¹⁰
Crocea, þa geolwan.
Luto, wyrmaman.¹¹
Sandix, wyrt, oððe wad.
15 *Adinuentionibus*, aspyrgengum.¹²
Plastica, gewyrce.
Infectum, ungeffremed.
Refragatur, widsoc.
Iurisperitorum, ræfborena.
20 *Inproperasse*, þæt hie ætwite.
Cum infami eulogio, mid þy unæþelan gidde.¹³
Prouerbiorum, gydda.
Manicas, slyfan.
25 *Redimiculo*, eyre, widðan.¹⁴
Mitre, hættes.
Theristotedes,¹⁵oþþe wudewan gierela.
                         LVII.
Solario, cenaculo.
30 *Equitatum*, etrodum.¹⁶
Abra, þinnenne.
Conopio, nette, fleogryfte.¹⁷
Uecordem, gemædedne.
Elisisse, ascrencan.¹⁸
35 *Insolentiam*, þa forwenedan. LVIII.
Subucula, hacele.
Bysina, hwit.¹⁹
Iachinthina, hæwen.²⁰

---

[1] Aldh. *comitiales*. R. W.
[2] Aldh. *thorace*. R. W.
[3] Aldh. *percutitur*. R. W.
[4] Aldh. *pellicatus*. R. W.
[5] Aldh. *rata*. R. W.
[6] Aldh. *elucubratam*. R. W.
[7] Aldh. *ligulam*. R. W.
[8] Aldh. *colorata*. R. W.
[9] Aldh. *conchilii*. R. W.
[10] Aldh. *per ironiam*. R. W.
[11] Aldh. *croceo . . . luto*. Cf. pag. 436

l. 18. R. W.
[12] Aldh. *adinuentionum*. R. W.
[13] Aldh. *cum infami prouerbiorum elogio*. R. W.
[14] Aldh. *redimicula*. R. W.
[15] Aldh. *theristro*. R. W.
[16] Aldh. *equitatu*. R. W.
[17] Aldh. *conopæo*. R. W.
[18] Aldh. *elicisse*. R. W.
[19] Aldh. *bissina*. R. W.
[20] Read *hiacinthina*. R. W.

Capitum, healsed.
Manice, slyfan.
Ambitiuntur, ymbhumne.[1]
Antiæ, loccas.
Timponum, þunwongena.[2]
Pulla, þa blacan.
Mafortibus, scyfelum.
Cedunt, rumad, steppad.
Uittarum, nostlena.
Nexibus, salum.
Talo tenus, oðan cleow.
Falconum, wealhhafeca.
Cauannarum, ulena.
Obunca, þa crumban.
Fuscinula, awel.
Arpagine, sutunge.
Sorices, mys.
Puplicatam, þa geopenedan.[3]
Indisciplinatorum, undeawfulra.
Sugillatinis, telnesse.[4]
Malagma, læcesealfe.
Purulentis, gewyrms'.[5]
Experiamur, onfindeu.
Stipulatorem, trymmend.
Libida, þa wannan.
Uibex, læl.
Assentatrix, sio geþafigende.
Exacerbauit, gremede.
Passiua, sio wide.
Rethoricamur, we sprecaþ.[6]
Gratuita, sio uncype.
Subpeditat, fultumaþ.
Philosophare, þæt we sprecen.[7]
Yppone regensi, þære burge.[8]
Tectis, bedeahtum.
Suatim, hiora deawe.[9]
Infesta, þa teonfullan.
Antiquariis, writerum.
Tricabatur, geeylded.

Fenus, hiereborg.
Tricatio, ylding.
Rimosa barca, þæt cinene scip.
Quassata, gecnysed.
5 *Sero*, sið.
Adtigisset, gylaþ, gelamp.[10]
Carbasa, segelbosma.
Antemnarum, segelgyrda.
Sinuata, gebesmed.
10 *Sylocismi*, þære uncyste.[11]
Inter Scyllam, betwuh þa freenesse stowe.
Barbarismi, þa uncyste.
Indisruptis, untoslitenum.
15 *Rudentibus*, wæderapum.
Laudacismi, ðære uncyste.[12]
Antefatis, wærwordum.
Non obqerit,[13] ne swylteþ.
Non tricauerit, ne leteð.
20 *Imbricibus*, hroftiglum.
Lepida, þære getyngan.
Discrepent, scadað.
Sapa, ciern.[14]
E merulento, a from þam hlutrum.[15]
25 *Temeto*, wine.
Fucorum, telga.
Fabrefactis, gesmicerade.
Iconisma, gelicnes.
Stemmate, wlite.
30 *Uersor*, hwerfigo.
Uacillare, wine wealtigan.
Triste, þæt swære.
Deuote, holdlice.
Turificatur, onsægd sie.[16]
35 *Matertere*, modrigan.
Helior, id est, Ierusalem.
Auroresceret, lihte.
Extemplo, sona.
Quasi arx, swa wefæsten.

[1] Aldh. *ambiuntur*. R. W.
[2] Aldh. *temporum*. R. W.
[3] Read *publicatam*. R. W.
[4] Aldh. *sugillationis*. R. W.
[5] So has the MS. Cf. *geteyrmsi* pag. 467 l. 20. R. W.
[6] Read *rhetoricamur*. R. W.
[7] Aldh. *philosophari decreuimus*. R. W.
[8] Aldh. *Hipponensis*. R. W.
[9] hiora *i. e.* swina deawe. R. W.
[10] Aldh. *attigit*. R. W.
[11] Aldh. *soloecismi*. R. W.
[12] Aldh. *lautacismi*. R. W.
[13] Sic MS. R. W.
[14] Read *dulcisapa*. R. W.
[15] Aldh. *a merulento temeto*. R. W.
[16] Aldh. *thurificatur*. R. W.

Editissimae, þæt hiehste.¹
Ansatas, speru.
Tueri, scylded beon.
Subsistentia, aweosung.
Ualete, wesaþ hale.
Alumne, fosterbearn.²
Tirones, cempan.
Per sudum, þurh þa hlutran.
Confer, forgeaf.
Predo, sceaþa.
Pellax, fræcness oþþe se beswicenda.
Rabula, se risenda.
Raptor, strudend, oððe gripend.
Bis dicere, þæt he tuwa cweðe.
Pup pup, tæg tæg.
Bibramine, scilbronge.³
Fiant prosa.
  (x)liiii. *De metro incipit.*
Imbribus, scurum.
Demis, nimis.
Cynthia, luna.
Prepedibus, hradum.⁴
Rostris, ceaflum.
Pipant, pritigead.
Modulare, singan.⁵
Fati, gewrites.⁶
Ruricolas musas, landælfe.
Castalidas nymphas, dunælfa.
Elicona, swa hatte sio dun.⁷
Delo, swa hatte þæt ealand.⁸
*Latamina, mater solis.*⁸
Argutus, se gleawa.
Garrula, sio hlydende.
*Cola, idem membrum.*⁹
*Commata,⁹ pars membrim.*¹⁰
Bombosa, þære rarigendan.

Deuotaturus, wiergende.
Plectra, sceacelas.
Fidibus, strengum.
Follibus, bylgum.
5 *Capsis,* cystum.
Carbo, gled.
Calculus, cealcstan.
*Uualbas,*¹¹ dureras.¹⁰
Decies senes, id est lx.
10 *Depromsit,* ypte.
Garbas, manipulas, sceafas.
Stirpis, owæsmum.
Fana, heargas.
Ilia, inneþas.
15 *Extirpans,* awyrtwalad.
Peculantis, þæs scion.¹²
Obridzum, smæte gyldne.¹³
*Punicio,*¹⁴ ðy brunan oðde þy brunbasewan.
20 *Tinctura,* telgunge.
Murice, wyrman.
Concineasque, and þa weolocreade.¹⁵
Puluerulenta, ðy dystgan.
De cortice corni, of corntreowes rinde.
25 *Dactulus,* palmappel.¹⁶
Unio, searogemme.
De conca, of muscellan.¹⁷
Sablo, molde, sande.
Bratea fila, se gyldna ðræd.
30 *Bino uersu,* þy twyfealdan fere.¹⁰
Sena paradigmata, siexfealdre anlicnesse.
Palmite, wintwiges.
Antes, ordines.
35 *Ligustra,* hunigsuge.
Per dumos, þurh græfan.

---

¹ Aldh. *editissima.* R. W.
² The following words are taken from the poetical 'De Laudibus Uirginum, Prafatio ad Maximam Abbatissam.' R. W.
³ Aldh. *uibramine.* R. W.
⁴ Aldh. *præpetibus.* R. W.
⁵ Aldh. *modulari.* R. W.
⁶ Aldh. *fasti.* R. W.
⁷ Aldh. *Helicona.* R. W.
⁸ Aldh. *quem Delo peperit Latona.* R. W.
⁹ Aldh. *Colaque cum pedibus pergant et commata ternis.* R. W.

¹⁰ So has the MS. R. W
¹¹ Aldh. *ualuas.* R. W.
¹² Aldh. *petulantis.* R. W.
¹³ i. e. beaten gold. It meant the thin plate-gold which was much in use for ornamenting rich dresses, and other purposes, during the Frankish and Anglo-Saxon periods. (Aldh. *obrizum.* R. W.)
¹⁴ Aldh. *puniceo.* R. W.
¹⁵ Aldh. *coccineosque.* R. W.
¹⁶ Aldh. *dactylus.* R. W.
¹⁷ Read *concha.* R. W.

Circio, hringsete.¹
Fibula, sigel.
Bullis, bylum.
Petala, goldfyld fel.
Tergore, hyde.
Saliginis, sælenum.²
Membrarum, filmena.³
Ex centro, of midle.
Anthlia, hlædhweogl.⁴
Mergula, scealfor.
Alis, fiderum.
Grauculus, hroc.⁵
Leti, wyrðenna.
Occas, fealge.
Uersiculos, hweorfende.⁶
Teretes cycli, þæs sinewealtan hringes.
Fulua, sio fealwe.
Uenustas, fægernes.
Porro, fior.
Molimine, searwe.⁷
Strophosa, þy fæcnan.⁸
Rictu, ceafle.⁸
  xlv. *De Elia*.
Tenia, honore uel cyninggierela.⁹
Actus, gebæded.
Bigis, cratum.
Obstacula, widsteallas.
In Tempis, on scenfeldum.¹⁰
Cruda, dura.
Bustis, byrgelsum.
Antichristus, contrarius Christo.
Bucula, cealf.
  xlvi. *De Eliseo*.
Bombis, hlowengum.
Sacra, gield.
Ultro, ræde.
Lauta munia, þa clænan þenunga.
Carismata, gyfa.¹¹

¹ Aldh. *in circo*. R. W.
² Aldh. *salignis*. R. W.
³ Aldh. *membranarum*. R. W.
⁴ Read *antlia*. R. W.
⁵ Read *graculus*. R. W.
⁶ Aldh. *uersicolor*. R. W.
⁷ Aldh *molimina*. R. W.
⁸ Aldh. *strophoso rictu*. R. W.
⁹ Aldh. *tenuia*. R. W.
¹⁰ The glossator has here taken the classical beauties of Tempe as a name for all localities of extreme beauty, and has in-

Carpere, telan.
Plectit, witnað.
Scurrarum, sceawera.
Speculum, sunscin.
5 xlvii. *De Hieremia*.
Dignissimus, se weorþesta.
Hirsutus, ruh.
Mirteta, wirgræfen.
Flaminibus, episcopis.
10 *Sacelli*, hearges.
Belis, water.¹²
Massam, clyne.
Atram offam, þa sweartan snæd.
  xlviii. *De tribus pueris*.
15 *Fistula*, wistle.
Puberibus, onihtum.
Cultum, gield.
Nodarent, bundan.
Nequibat, non potuit.¹³
20 xlix. *De Danielo*.
Ignicomis, se fyrfeaxna.
Sedans, gestilde.
  l. *De Iohanne Baptista*.
Prodat, cyded.
25 *Adfatim, ubertim*.
Obstrusus, deagol.
Frugi, abstinentie.
Ocula, sprece.¹⁴
Adultus, geweaxen.
30 *Maturesceret*, weox.
Natrix, cwiþ.¹⁵
Potior, mara.
Marmora glauca, þa hæwnan sæs.
Tomant, hlynredan.¹⁶
35 *Conpellens*, gretende.¹⁷
Confertur, widermeten is.
Ringescens, abolgen.¹⁸
Stomachatur, iersað.

terpreted the word by a general term signifying 'bright fields.' (Aldh. *in templis paradisi*. R. W.)
¹¹ Read *charismata*. R. W.
¹² Aldh. *Belis delubra nefandi*. R. W.
¹³ Aldh. *non quibat*. R. W.
¹⁴ Read *oracula*. R. W.
¹⁵ Read *Matrix*. R. W.
¹⁶ Read *tonant*. R. W.
¹⁷ Aldh. *compellans*. R. W.
¹⁸ Aldh. *ringens*. R. W.

Consanguine, þære gesibban.[1]
Incestans, gewemde.
Lances, beodas.
Uectant, feredan.
Per natam, per filiam.
Scenica ludicra, þy pleglican plegan.
Uectifera ualue, þære forscytlican dura.[2]
Crustra, clusterlocu.[3]
 li. *De Iohanne Euangelista.*
Ingurgitat, wæted.
Salebroso, þwyresfura.
Armonia, swinsunge.[4]
Haustus, potus.
 lii. *De Paulo Apostolo.*
Paulus, pius, i. mirabilis.
Furuo, þy sweartan.
Ingeminans, twyfealde.
Expers, ordæle.
 liii *De Luca euangelista.*
Quadrupes, cealf.[5]
Quattuor decies cum uii. degeret annos, id est lxx, et quattuor annos.[6]
Procurans, læcnende.
Ulcera, poccas.
Fotu, sealfe.
Fidis, getreowum.
 liiii. *De Clementi.*
Equat, hine widermet.[7]
Uisere, uidere.
Censebat, scop.
 lv. *De Siluestro.*
Cartis, bocum[8]
Natricis, nædrum.
Sacelli, huses.

Conflictum, gefiit.
Certantes, flitende.
Certamine, on gefiite.
Molosos, rothundas.[9]
5 *Consternati,* ofercymene.
Ferit, sloh.
Exertis, onbundon.[10]
Armento, hrydero.
Culcita, bedde.
10 *Rugosa,* þære gehrumpnan.
In extasi, in modes heahnesse.
Deformem, atole.
Turpabat, orretted.
Antisitus, æryeldo.[11]
15 *Conglobatur,* somnode.[12]
Gymnica, þa upwitlican.
Grues, yeldo.[13]
Scobem, gilp.[14]
Infindens, gerawende.
20 *Turribus,* wighusum.[15]
Ductum, gedon.
 lvi. *De Ambrosio.*
Hesperie, on Eotole.
In cunis, in cildcladum.
25 *Bis terna, sex.*
Nutu, meahte.
Munia, degnunge.
 lvii. *De Martino.*
Nec balsamorum, ne crismena.
30 *Unctum,* smyrenesse.
Faminem, spræce.[16]
In ueribus, in snasum.[17]
Exta, iesendne, isend.
Fomentat, læcnode.
35 *Extat,* wæs.

[1] Aldh. *consanguinei.* R. W
[2] Aldh. *uectiferæ ualuæ.* R. W
[3] Aldh. *claustra.* R. W.
[4] Aldh. *harmoniam.* R. W.
[5] Aldh. *quadrupedis uituli.* R. W.
[6] Aldh. *quatuor et decies* etc. R. W.
[7] *i. e. æquat.* R. W.
[8] Read *chartis.* R. W.
[9] So has the MS. Cf. pag. 445 l. 4. R. W.
[10] Aldh. *exsertis.* The MS. *has* bundṅ. R.W.
[11] Aldh. *ante situm.* R. W.
[12] Aldh. *conglobat.* R. W.
[13] Miswritten for *caries.* Cf. pag. 374 l. 4. R. W.

[14] The glossator translates *scobem.* Aldh. has *scrobem.* R. W.
[15] The fortifications of the Anglo-Saxons in their earlier times consisted merely of an intrenchment, surrounded by an earthen bank or mould. Hence they had to express their notion of a tower by calling it a *wig-hus,* or war-house. We have further on the Latin *castrum* explained similarly by *here-wic.*
[16] Aldh. *diserto famine.* R. W.
[17] Aldh. *in ueribus.* R. W.

lviii. *De Gregorio.*
Sollers, gleaw.
Istuc, hidere.
Libelli, pundes.
  lix. *De Basilio.*
Librate, ahiolorod.
Sceui, sceolan.
Digessit, awrat.
Cuderet, smidode.
Inmunis, orceas.
Accola, buend.
  lx. *De Antonio*
Conquirens, begitende.
Diuexa, þa healdan.¹
Cararit, ielde.²
Gener, aþum.
  lxi. *De Paulo.*
Infidus, ungetreowe.
Gestu, gebæro.
Demebat, nom.
Facescunt, swederedan.³
Pro aprico, for dære wearman.
Aliger, fiðerberende.
Eximia, fremere.
  lxii. *De Hilarione.*
Simulare, giliccetton.
Perpendicula, waldræd, þæt is riht-
  nesse.
Cypsam, dracan.⁴
Turbida, drefende.⁵
Stricta lege, þære fæstan æ.
Oras, obras, ofras.
Marmora, sæ.⁶
  lxiii. *De Iohanne.*
Uirgineo claue, mid dam unwemlican
  cægan.
  lxiiii. *De Benedicto.*
Faustus, felix.
Capisterium, hridder.
Uictoria, þa sigelican.
Rimarum, filmena, oþþe cinena.

Germanas, getwisan.⁷
Chalibem, isern.
  lxv. *De Narciso.*
Annua uota, þa gerlican gehtte.
5 *Fontona,* willican.⁸
Edaces, þa eotendan.
Papirus, paper.
In centro, in midle.
Scrofe, suge.
10 *Aruina,* rysle.
Fantam famam, þone cadegan
  hlisan.⁹
Concinnant, heapedan.
Sugillent, tældon.
15 *Maculam,* mal.
Lacessant, wliten, oþþe gremeden.
Glaucoma, eagsiong.
Lippos oculos, þa surigan eagan.
Crudescentes, þa swiþfeormende.
20 *Frusta,* aidlad.¹⁰
Stellis, eagum.¹⁰
Ora, andwlita.
Occellorum, ætna.¹¹
Altor, fosterfæder.
25 lxvi. *De Anastasio.*
Ani, þæs earses.
Apicum, plegena.
Seria, heorneste.
Infamare, georrettan.
30 *Arceri,* gefetadne.
Porro, feorran.
Inertes, earge.
Contrita, ofermened.
Mecham, forlegisse.
35 *Obuncat,* ymbfeng.
Tecta et tigilli, hrofes.¹²
Lustris, fifum.
Uoluentibus, fealdendum.
Uetre, radores.¹³
40 *Lautos,* clæne.
Desistit, ablon.

¹ Aldh. *deuexa.* R. W.
² Cf. note 13, pag. 520. Aldh. has
curarit. R. W.
³ Aldh. *fatiscant.* R. W.
⁴ Aldh. *gipsum.* R. W.
⁵ Aldh. *turgida.* R. W.
⁶ Aldh. *marmora ponti.* R. W.
⁷ Aldh. *germano.* R. W.
⁸ Aldh. *fontana.* R. W.
⁹ Aldh. *faustam famam.* R. W.
¹⁰ Aldh. *frustrataque stellis.* R. W.
¹¹ Cf. pag. 461 l. 28. R. W.
¹² Aldh. *tecta tigilli.* R. W.
¹³ Read *othra.* Cf. Aldh. R. W.

lxvii. *De Babyllo.*
Cartula, boc.[1]
Excubias, wæccan.
Non cunctante, ne tweoge.
Stemmate, frætenisse.
Absidan, cleofan.[2]
Pullis, besmitenum.
Inflictis, onslægium.[3]
Inuestis, ungebyrd.[4]
Effebi, geongan.
Ouantes, gaudentes.
    lxviii. *De Cosmi et Damiano.*
Urbene, mid dam getingelinc.[5]
Groceos, þa geolwan.[6]
Gemellos, getwysan.
Curam, læcedom.
Luscos, ænige.
Pellantes, adrifende.[7]
Strabos, sceolige.
Marsupia, seodas.
Farsa gorgoneis, acrumne þam hellicum.[8]
Proto, þære ærestan.[9]
    (lxix.) *De Crissanti.*
Indolis, geogoðe.
Donatus, forgifen.
Puber, geong.
Nanctus, begytende.
Ultro, bewillan, selfwilles.
Excussit, framswengde.
Iaculatas, þa flanihtan.
Lentescunt, toadan, tedan.[10]
Uestalis, gydenlic.
Ueneris, lustes.
Numina, gield.
Ueste, gydene.
Neuum, wom.
Maculam pullam, þone sweartan speccan.

Excubias, reaf.[11]
Lodix, loda.
Ni forsan, nimðe wen wære.
Restes, rapas.
5 *Suras,* sconca.
Cipporum, cospa.
Turgida, þa toswolnau.
Findit, toslaf.
Lotia, hlond.
10 *Lictor,* þegn.
Putenti, þære fulan.
Buculam, stirc.
Byrse, hyde.[12]
Arta, mid þa nearwan.
15 *Inpiger,* unsleac.
Oppetere, gecrong.[13]
Dehiscit, tocinet.
Emersit, aras.[14]
Habenis, salum.
20 *Tomis,* bocum.
    lxx. *De Juliano.*
Stricto, getogene.
Dialectica, wordlocum.
Rethoricis, þæm getingelicum.[15]
25 *Diui,* godes.
Nutum, willan.
Lectum, bedde.[16]
Dote, weotoma.
Rigidus, anwille.
30 *Facessit,* fremede.
Direxit, onsende.
Cenabium, mynsterlif.[17]
Gurgustia, mynsterlif.
Discriminet, scadet.[10]
35 *Ordo,* hade.
Limen, duru.
Nodosa, þy ostihan.[18]
Monoptalmi, aneges.[19]
Forti, þy fæstan.

---

[1] Read *chartula.* R. W.
[2] Read *absidam.* R. W.
[3] The MS. has *onslægiũ.* R. W.
[4] Aldh. *in uestes.* R. W.
[5] Aldh. *urbanus.* R. W.
[6] Read *croceos.* R. W.
[7] Aldh. *pellentes.* R. W.
[8] In Aldhelm we do not meet with *farsa gorgoneis. gorgoneis* is used pag. 166 l. 11; *farsa* (*marsupia farsa*) p. 165 l. 35. (Aldh. ed. Giles). R. W.

[9] Aldh. *tempore proto.* R. W.
[10] So has the MS. R. W.
[11] Aldh. *exuuias.* R. W.
[12] Aldh. *birsa.* R. W.
[13] Aldh. *oppeteret.* R. W.
[14] Aldh. *emerserit.* R. W.
[15] Aldh. *rhetoricas.* R. W.
[16] Aldh. *lecto.* R. W.
[17] Read *coenobium.* R. W.
[18] Aldh. *nodoso.* R. W.
[19] Read *monophtalmi.* R. W.

Inspirans, onspecende.
Minerua, dea artium.
Nec Bachus, ne wines god.
Crustis, ornamentis.
Tesellum, tæslum.¹
Neptunus, deus aquarum.
Alcidis, Heleol.²
Centauri, þæs centaures.
Caci, cacuses.
Claue, stenge.³
Oramina, gebedo.
Catax, sio healte.⁴
Statis, wælfyl.⁵
Peruzotos, giond þa burh.⁶
Dagon, swa hatte se god.
Uulsum, abrogden.
Lutea, þam geolwum.
In diuos, in god.
Cassata, aidlad.
Ioppiter, þunor.⁷
In Latio, in Eatole.
Demptis, genumenum.
Pluton, deus inferni.
Falsato, þy leasan.
Arcadie, þære mægþe.
Glus, lim.
Pangit, fægde.
Calcis, limes.
Quadratur, gefegde feoþersceette.⁸
Fascia, sweoþolas.
Postumus, unlaf.⁹
Madentia, þa þanan.
Callosi, hreofe, odde wearrihtnm.¹⁰
lxxi. *De Amos*.
Nilotica, sio Ægiptisce.
Frondosis dumis, þæm gehilmdum græfum.

Procurans, begende.
Rotante, þrawende.
Molam, hweorfan.¹¹
Discifer, discberend.¹²
5 *Crusta*, hlaue.¹³
Amens, gemæd.
Luxerunt, weopan.
Fata, wyrde.
Consulta, rædas.
10 lxxii. *De Apollonio*.
Suppea, acumba.¹⁴
Signa, gelicnessa.
Conpeta clausa, þa belocenan yndanwega.¹⁵
15 *Friens*, brytende.¹⁶
Lis, gecid.
Bellona, wælcyrge.
Infecit, geblond.
Classica, swege.
20 *Martem*, gefeoht.
Incentor, tyhtend.
Pignora, wed.
Adsciscere, gelaþgan.
Misellis, earmum.
25 *Geruli*, berend.
Turtas, hlafas.¹⁷
Colobostrum, beost.¹⁸
Lenticule, croges, oþþe ampellan.
lxxiii. *De Hieronimo*.
30 *Clancula*, þa diglan.
Bargina, þa eldeodigan.¹⁹
Elicuit, gerehte.
Commentis, trahte.
Enumerans, arimende, *i. de inlustribus*.
35
Aprum, eofor.
Saltu, wudu.

¹ Aldh. *tessellis*. (Giles *lesellis*) *taslum* miswritten for *taflum*? R. W.
² Aldh. *Alcides*. R. W.
³ Aldh. *clauam*. R. W.
⁴ Giles has *cutax*. R. W.
⁵ Aldh. *stragis*. R. W.
⁶ Aldh. *per Azoton*. R. W.
⁷ Read *Iupiter*. R. W.
⁸ Cf. fiþerfot = four-footed, quadruped. R. W.
⁹ For *posthumus*, a posthumous child.
¹⁰ Aldh. *callaso*. R. W.
¹¹ Aldh. *molem*. R. W.
¹² The glossator translates *discifer*. Aldh. has *piscifer*. R. W.
¹³ Aldh. *crustula*. R. W.
¹⁴ Aldh. *stuppea ... uelamina*. R. W.
¹⁵ Aldh. *compita clausa*. R. W.
¹⁶ Read *fricans*. R. W.
¹⁷ Read *tortas*. R. W.
¹⁸ Read *colostrum*. R. W.
¹⁹ Read *peregrina* or *peregrinas*. R. W.

Carolios, unkere.[1]
Dilubra, gield.[2]
  lxxiiii. *De sancta Maria.*
Proco, brydguman.
Feta, eacene.
Salamonis, in Hierusalem.[3]
Puerperium, hysebeord.
Labe, womme.
  lxxv. *De Cicilia..*
Uiuacem, þæt lifigende.
Ludrica, plegan.[4]
Bassia, cossas.
Puerio, þy pueriscan.[5]
Inlexit, beswac.
Leuirum, tacor.
Luendi, þrowgende.
  lxxvi. *De Agapem.*
Effarier, asecgan.
Pipillis, papillis, breostum, þæt is, foreweardum.[6]
Torribus, brandum.
Trinacrie, Sicilie, id est Pachmus.
Peleros, Lybiis.
Cluris, æþelum.[7]
  lxxvii. *De Lucia.*
Patula, þa ruman.[8]
Altercaretur, cidde.
Lenonum, sponera.
Crepitat, ræscetted.[9]
Nodatis, gecnyttum.
Modulabor, singe.
  lxxviii. *De Justina.*
Astus, bred.
Nugaci, þy unnyttan.
Scemmatizans, liccettende.[10]
Expertur, onfindende.[11]
Usquam, ohwær.
  lxxix. *De Eugenia.*
Reboat, onhwiled.
Refellit, beswac.

Per deuia, þurh westen.
Creuere, gesion.
Curis, sorgum.
Casibus, gegongum.
5 *Euo*, yldo.
  lxxx. *De Agnen.*
Fasce, gegyrlan.
Togatus, gegyred.
Uisco, fugellime.
10 *Auceps*, fugelere.
Subarrauit, geweddade.
Ditis, helgodes.
Gestu, gebærnessum.
  lxxxi. *De Tecla.*
15 *U[U]lcanus*,[12] fyr, oþþe fyresgod, hellesmiþ.
Non usquam, neowerno, nawern.
Scammate locus, on gewinstowe.
  lxxxi(i). *De Eulalie.*
20 *Satagit*, gernde.
Maniplis, heapum.
  lxxxiii. *De Scolastica.*
Ex scola, of scole.
Uoto, gyrnesse.
25 *Conpellere*, þæt hio gebædde.[13]
  lxxxiii(i). *De Constantia.*
Peripsema, geswepa, gonswæpa.
Cursant, þocerodan.
Probo, gecorenum.
30 *Satrape*, gesidas.
Inertam, þa eargan.[14]
Ocius, rade
  lxxxv. *De Constantino.*
Exemplo, sona.[15]
35 *Pretor*, ealdorman.
Nodos, bende.
Tedasque, and biernende speld.
Compturum, gefrætwadne.
Erepta, þa ætgenumenan.
40 *Facessunt*, fremmaþ.

[1] I do not find this word in Aldhelm. R. W.
[2] Aldh. *delubra*. R. W.
[3] Aldh. *Solymis*. R. W.
[4] Read *ludicra*. R. W.
[5] Aldh. *Pierio*. R. W.
[6] Aldh. *papillis*. R. W.
[7] Here and pag. 3, l. 1. 29 read *claris*. Cf. Aldh. R. W.
[8] Aldh. *patulas*. R. W.
[9] Aldh. *crepitabant*. R. W.
[10] Aldh *schematizans*. R. W.
[11] Aldh. *expertus*. R. W.
[12] So has the MS. R. W.
[13] Aldh. *subnixis precibus gestit compellere uirgo*. R. W.
[14] Read *inertem*. R. W.
[15] Read *extemplo*. R. W.

Lacessat, sliteþ.[1]
Conpressit, þyde.
Dramate, þy brydelican gewrite,[2] *id est, mutatio personarum, ut est Cantica Canticorum.*
Digessit, gerehte.
Faminem, spræce.[3]
Argolicas, þa Creaciscan.
Opacis, þæm diglum.
Pelasgos, þa Creaciscan.
Pinguntur, awriten wæran.
Lectissima, þæt gecoreneste.
Propere, fræofestlice.
Comis, feaxum.
   lxxxvi. *De Triades.*
Titulis, wyrþmyndum.
Carperrabat, geniclede.
Segmentata, golde siowode.
Innuba, unhæmedo.
Buccis, muþum.
Gramate, gewrite.[4]
Eximiam, þæt fræmicle.
Commate, gewrite.[5]
Certa, gewis.
Acerra, stete, *uel* gledfæte.
   lxxxvii. *De Chione et Agape et Hierene.*
Bernas, þeowenna.[6]
Fellax, leas.
Misellis, earmum.
Calcabis, hwerum.[7]
Deluditur, wæged wæs.
Larbam, be colan, egesgriman.[8]
Fantasma, scin, *idem et nebulum.*
Fautor, fultumend.
Quirent, mehton.
Larbata, se unfægera.
Autumant, wendan.[9]

Ciclades, gegirelan.
   lxxxviii. *De Rufina et Secunda.*
Adgreditur, onginned.
Rugis, hrypellum.[10]
Calce, stige.[11]
Fimi, scearnes.
In thermas, on bæðe.
Fax, fæcele.
Scopuli, stanes.
Planca, weel.[12]
Nat, swam.
Chao, dimnesse gastas.[13]
   lxxxix. *De Anatholia.*
Latrat, beorced.
Depopulans, idende.
Ructabat, blew, odðe roccette.
Incultis, unbeganum.
Exulat, wræclastode.
Uibrabat, bliccette.
Lacerti, earmes.
Callosa, þa wearrihtan.[14]
Scatens, weallende.
Consulis, gearcyninges.
Artis, nearewum.
Butra, dysige.[15]
Marsum, wyrmgalere.
Toruam, þa unhieran.
Irritat, gremede.
In spira, in hringe.
Glomeravit, ymbhringde.
Cursum, hrædlice.[16]
Eliminate, adrifene.[17]
Fatescunt, geswederiað.[18]
Castra, herewic.
Classica, sweg.
Digessit, gerehtum.[19]
Salpix, byme.[20]
Martem, gefeoht.

---

[1] Aldh. *lacessit.* R. W.
[2] Aldh. *sponsali dramate.* R. W.
[3] Aldh. *famina.* R. W.
[4] Read *grammate.* R. W.
[5] Aldh. *scribit commate uitam.* R. W.
[6] Read *uernas.* R. W.
[7] Read *cacabis.* R. W.
[8] *cola*, *colla* denotes *a helmet.* R. W.
[9] Aldh. *autumat.* R. W.
[10] Read *hrympellum.* R. W.
[11] Read *calle.* R. W
[12] Aldh. *plana carina.* R. W.
[13] Aldh. *absque chao* R. W.
[14] Aldh. *callosa.* R. W.
[15] Read *bruta.* R. W.
[16] Read *cursim.* R. W.
[17] The next glosses are taken from Aldhelm's poem: *De Octo Principalibus Uitiis.* Read *eliminata.* R. W.
[18] Aldh. *fatiscunt.* R. W.
[19] Read *digestis.* R. W.
[20] Read *salpinx.* R. W.

Cassida, healm.
Thoracis, byrnan.
Achile, scyld.[1]
Duelli, gefeohtes.
Macheram, sweord.
Senspatium, þeohseax.[2]
Parmarum, scylda.
Testudine, scyldredan.
Contundunt, forstyntaþ.
Sparorum, spera.
Macerare, mægeregan, gehlænian.
Uibice, læle.
Capessit, nam, hæfde.
Grassantibus, hidendum.
Peruadens, þurhferende.
Ingluuiem, gifernesse.
Potestur, possum.
Falanx, feða.
Cetra, scyld.
Lurcatur, freted.
Gestit, gyrmed.
Extis, iesende.
Farcire, acrymman.
Prepinguibus, fræfættum.
Gulosa, þy frettan.
Ambro, gifre.
Aristis, elgum.
Eneruare, aslacige.
Pastinat, sette.
Uite, wintreow.
Ueretrum, scamescan lim.
Procaci, hwalle.
Probrum, edwit.
Deuotaret, wyrgde.[3]
Defruti, cerenes.
Dapsilis, rumheort.
Cenidos, atole.[4]
Auitum, yldranfæder.

Lentus, druncen, odde orsorg.
Cient, hrewad.
Celebrem, mærne.
Scarilitas, sceawendspræc.[5]
5 *Nectantem*, biddende.[6]
Philargiria, gitsunge.
Puplica,[7] þa cynelican.
Lita, atre gemæled.[8]
Periuria, manswara.
10 *Hymenis*, penninge.[9]
Clausam, þinge.[10]
Credita, þa bebodenan.
Compilat, strad.[11]
Lincxere, liccigan.
15 *Tabo*, heolfe.
Sistin, hearnes.[12]
Incursere, onslogan.[13]
Arcibus, hrofum, odde bigelsum.
Numismate, mynete.
20 *Paradigmate*, gelicnesse.
Furiarum, hægtessa.
Gorgoneo, þæm hellicum.
Contos, spreotas.
Tessa, flanas.[14]
25 *Ydris*, waternedrum.[15]
Allecto, wælcyrge.
Ad scandala, to geswicum.
Accidia, slecnes.[16]
Nouitatum, hereticorum.
30 *Tiro*, helme.[17]
Pila, flanas.
Typhus, wlanc.
Gliribus, eglum.
Protus, ealdorman.
35 *Farsit*, fylde.
Scabra, unsmeðe.
Uillicat, twiccad.[18]
Ruminet, edreced, ceoweþ.

[1] Read *ancile*. R. W.
[2] The glossator translated *semispata* (*semispatha*). Aldh. *se in spatium*. R. W.
[3] Read *deuoraret*. R. W.
[4] Aldh. *cinædos*. R. W.
[5] Aldh. *scurrilitas*. R. W.
[6] Aldh. *nectentem*. R. W.
[7] So has the MS. R. W.
[8] Aldh. *spicula lita ueneno*. R. W.
[9] Read *nummis* or *nummi*. R. W.
[10] Read *causam*. R. W.
[11] Read strad. R. W.
[12] So has the MS. hearnes (= *raucedo*) is a curious translation of *sistrum*. R. W.
[13] Read *incussere*. R. W.
[14] Read *tela*. R. W.
[15] Read *hydris*. R. W.
[16] Read *acedia* (= ἀκήδεια). R. W.
[17] So has the MS Cf. pag. 516 l. 7. R. W.
[18] Aldh. *uellicat*. R. W.

MISCELLANEOUS GLOSSES.

Cenosis, þæm adlihtum.
Uolutabro, sole.[1]
Rumen, edreced roc.
Porcaster, bearg.
Obesus, fæt.
Iuncis, rixum.
Filicumque, and fearnes.
Folliginis, bylgum.[2]
Organa, þeotan.
Ocius, citius.
Barbita bombis, organum.

Acescatur, asurige.[3]
Malis, mæstum.
Antemnas, segelgyrdas.[4]
Rudentum, wæterrap.
5 Barca, scip.
Racemos, bergean.
Capulus, holt.
Spinam, bodig.
Ocreos, banberge, scangebeorg.[5]
10 Natrix, nædre.
Ex herebo, of helle.[6]

[1] Aldh. uolutabri. R. W.
[2] Read folligenis. R. W.
[3] Aldh. ascescant. R. W.
[4] The scribe, or a scribe, has written in the margin, after this word: þa þe æfre coste.
[5] Read ocreas. R. W.
[6] So has the MS. R. W.

XIII.

SEMI-SAXON VOCABULARY.[1]

(OF THE TWELFTH CENTURY.)

Uertex, nol.
Cer[*uix*], necca.
Timpus, þunwænge.
Timpora, mo.[2]
Maxilla, leor.
Facies, onsene.
Palpebre, bre(awas).
Pupilla, seo.
Labium, weler.
Labia, mo.
Adeps, rusel.
Aruina, ungel.
Uiscus, ...
Uiscera, mo.
Exta, þermes.
Ulna, elbowe.
Femur, uel coxa, þih.

Clunis, hupe.
Pulpa, ...
Sura, sperlire.
Crus, sceonke.
5 *Tibia*, seine.
Talus, oncleou.
Planta, fotwelm.
Al(*lox*),toa.
Ungula, hof, *uel* clau.
10 *Diocesis, uel parochia*, biscopriche.
Heremita, westense(tla).
Coniunx, imæcca.
Coniuges, uel coniugales, isinheowen.
Coniugium, uel matrimonium,
15 sins(cipe).
Castus, clæne.
Formosus, wel iwlitegod.

[1] The vocabulary given above, which appears from the decadence of the grammatical forms, and from the orthography, to belong to about the middle of the twelfth century, is an abridgement of Nr. X. It was discovered, in the fragmentary form in which it is here printed, on some leaves of vellum used as the cover or binding of one of the old registers of Worcester Cathedral, by Sir Thomas Phillipps, who printed a few copies privately. It there followed a copy of Ælfric's Grammar, written in the same language, and is an extremely curious monument of this latter in its state of transition. It has been carefully corrected in the present edition.

[2] *Mo*, i. e. more, (*ma* in the purer Anglo-Saxon text,) is merely the mode of indicating the plural number.

SEMI-SAXON VOCABULARY.

Deformis, hcowleas.
Decorus, wliti.
Sobole[s, *uel*] *liberi*, bearn.
Uictricius, stepfeder.
Priuiuignus, stepsune.
Fileaster, stepd(oh)ter.
Nepos, neva.
Altor, uel nutritor, fosterfæder.
Altrix, uel nutrix, fostermoder.
Alumnus, fostercild.
Propinquus, mæi.
Affinis, uel consanguineus, sibling.
(*Proge*)*nies, uel tribus*, mæiþ.
Generatio, cunrun.
Gener, oþam.
Socer, sweor.
So(*crus*), sweger.
Nurus, snore.
Princeps, aldermon.
Dux, heretowa, *uel* lætteow.
Comes, aldermon, *uel* ireva.
Clito, æþeling.
Obses, gysel.
Primas, heavedmon.
Satrapa, þein.
Iudex, dema.
Miles, uel athleta . . . , kempe
Procinctus, furding.
Edictum, iban.
Uulgus, cheorlfolc.[1]
Congregatio, uel contio, igæderung.
Conuentus, uel conuentio, imeting.
Sinodus, sinoþ, *uel* imot.
Dominus, uel herus, loverd.
Materna, ... wif.[2]
Cliens, uel clientulus, inkniht.[3]

. . . . (wy)ln, *uel* þinen.
Cu(*stos*) . . . .
. . . . (unspreccn)de child.
Paterfamilias, hiredes loverd.

Consiliarius, rædbora.
Con[*cio*]*nator*, imotmon.
Operarius, wurhta.
Faber, uel cudo, smiþ.
5 *Officina*, smiþ(ðe).
Ærarius, mæstlingsmiþ.
Arator, urþling.
Artifex, cræftca.
Opus, were.
10 *Opi*[*fex*], cræftca.
Architectus, eldest wurhtena.
Amus, angel.
Uenator, hunta.
Uena(*bul*)*um*, borsper.
15 *Auceps*, fuwelare.
Trapezeta,uel nummularius,munctare.
Num[*i*]*sma*, munet.
Sollers, menituwe.
Iners, creftleas.
20 *Nanus*, dwæruh.
Fidis, (str)eng.
Tubicen, bemare.
Tibicen, pipare.
Musa, pipe, *uel* hwistle.
25 *Fidicen*, fiþela.
Fistula, hwistle.
Liticen, truþ.
Lituus, truþhorn.
Poeta, scop, *uel* leoþwurhtæ.
30 (*Mi*)*nus, uel scurra*, gleomon.
Mercator, uel negociator, mangare.
Classis, scip(her)e.
Remus, roþer.
Remex, uel nauta, reþra.
35 *Gubernator, uel nauclerus*, steor[mo]n.
Proreta, ankermon.
Prora, þer þe ankermon sit.
Puppis, steor(setl).
Antenna, scilgerd.
40 *Uelum*, seil, *uel* wahreft.
Clauus, steorscofle, *uel* næil.
(*Mala*)*gma*, cliwa.[4]
Sartor, seammære.

[1] Cf. pag. 309 l. 39. R. W.
[2] Cf. pag. 309 l. 44. R. W.
[3] The leaves of the MS. had been cut at the top and bottom, when they were used to form the cover of a book, which caused the lacunæ indicated by these breaks. The lesser deficiencies are the result of mutilations of the edges of the leaves.
[4] Read clida. Cf. pag. 312 l. 10. R. W.

Sartrix, heo [1]
Dispensator, dihtnare.
Di(uiso)r, delare.
Pincerna, birle.
Caupo, tæppare.
Diues, weli.
Locuples, lond(spe)di.
Inops, havenleas.
Pauper, þærfa.
Egenus, wædla.
Fur, þeof.
Latro, (sc)aþa.
Merx, waræ.
Concors, iþwære.
Profugus, flemæ.
Exul, utlawe.
Conten[tios]us, iflitful.
Iniuriosus, teonful.
Piger, slac.
Hebes, dwæs.
Parasitus, (leas)olæcere.
Augur, wielare.
Incantator, galere.
Ueneficus, unlibwurhta.
[*Ma*]*leficus*, ufeldede.
Magus, dri.
Phitonissa, wicche.
Centurio, hundredes (eald)or.
Persecutor, ehtere.
Dispendium, uel damnum, hinþ.
Iactura, lure.
Commodum, hinþ.
(*Ar*)*milla*, beah.
Diadema, kinehelm.
Capicium, hæt.
Monile, mune, *uel* sweorbeah.
(*Spi*)*nter*, dalc, *uel* preon.
Fibula, oferfeng.
Uitta, snod.
Inauris, earpreon.
Indigena, uel incola, inlendisc.
Aduena, utancumen.
Peregrinus, alþeodi.
Messor, riftere.
Messis, irip.
Aceruus, hreac, *uel* hupel.

Stimulus, gode.
Aculeus, sticels.
Circus, uel circulus, wiþþe.
Epistola, ærindiwrit.
5 *Quaternio*, cine.
Planta, spelt.
Diploma, bowa.
Scedla, uel scedula, ymele.
Pictor, metere.
10 *Pictura*, meting.
Minium, teapor.
Gluten, lim.
Sculptor, grafere.
Grafium, græf.
15 *Sculptura*, græf.
Agalma, onlicnesse.
Scalprum, uel scalpellum, græf[sex].

20
. . . *oleum*, w . . . .
(*Luscus*) *uel monoptalmus*, oneiqe(de).
. . . . ., sculeigede.
Lippus, sureigede.
25 *Mancus*, onhende.
Infirmus, untrum.
Eg(*er*), *uel languidus*, adliq.
Paraclitus, frofergost.
Paraliticus, bedreda.
30 *Leprosus*, licþroware.
Lunaticus, monaþsic.
Demoniacus, deofelsic.
Energuminus, ...
(*Mor*)*bus*, adl.
35 *Pestis*, cwuld.
Amens, uel demens, imundleas.
Rabidus, uel insanus, ...
. . . . , wodnesse.
Incolumis, isund.
40 *Frenetus*,[2] þe þet þuruh slopleaste
awet.
Letargicus, unilimpliche slapel.
Peruigil, þuruhwacol.
Pius, orfest.
45 . . . ., (ar)leas.
Famosus, hlisful.

---

[1] *heo* = *she*, i. e. a female seamer, woman tailor. R. W.

[2] Read *freneticus*. R. W.

Fama, hlisa.
Infamis, unhlisful.
Infamia, unhli(sa).
. . . . . , custi.
Tenax, festhafol.
Parcus, uncusti.
Frugi, vel parcus, sparhende
S(agax, uel gna)rus, gleaw.
Prudens, snoter
Imprudens, unsnoter.
Astutus, pæti.
Stultu(s), ...
(Ue)rax, soþfest.
Ueridicus, soþsawel.
Fallax, uel mendax, leas.
Falsidicus, un(soþsawel).
. . . . , iwita.
Testimonium, iwitnesse, *uel* icuþnesse.
Cursor, runel.
Superbus, modi.
. . . . , (mo)dinesse.
Humilis, edmod.
Humilitas, edmodnesse.
Aer, luft.
Auro, hwiþa.
N(imbus), scur.
Procella, storm.
Nubes, weolcne.
Ver, leinten.
Autumnus, herfest.
Uernum temp(us), ...
Uernalis dies, leintenlic dæi.
Cauma, sweoli.
Humor, wæte.
Sterilitas, un(wæstmbernes)se.
Fertilitas, wæstmbernesse.
Color, bleo.
Ruber, read.
Fuluus, uel flauus, ...
. . . . , fouh.
Discolor, mislices bleos.
Forma, heow.
Fantasma, idwimor.
Merul . . . . , meav.[1]
Turdus, ster.

[1] Read *mergulus.* R. W.

Coternix, ediscine.
Pullus, chiken, *uel* brid, *uel* folc.
Uespertilio, re(remus).
(Noctua), uel strix, uel bubo, ule.
5 *Graculus,* roc.
Parrax, wrænna.
Apis, beo.
Fucus, dro(n).
. . . . (hyr)nette.
10 *Scarabæus,* scearnbudoa, *uel* budda.
Cinomia, hundesfliæ.
Culex, stut.
Cetus, ...
. . . . . , mæreswin.
15 *Ysicius, uel salmo,* lex.
Taricus, uel illec, hæring.
Fannus, ro(che).
. . . . , crabbe.
Polipes, loppestre.
20 *Murena, uel murenula,* mereneddre.
. . . .
Belua, eislic nuten on sæ oþer on londe.
Concha, scel
25 *Fera,* wilde d(eor).
. . . . (imenge)d hund and wulf.
Unicornis, uel rinoceron, uel monoceron, onhurne deo(r).
(Me)lus, broc.
30 *Camelus,* olfend.
Onager, wilde assa.
Elefans, ylp.
Lutrius, ...
. . . . , beofer.
35 *Lubricus,* ongeltwæcche.
Capreolus, roadeor.
Caprea, roa.
. . . . . . , bucca.
Caprea, uel capella, got.
40 *Damma, uel dammula,* do.
Ceruus, heort.
C . . . . . , kælf.[2]
Hinnulus, hind.[2]
Hedus, ticchen.
45 *Scroffa,* suwa.

[2] Read *ceruss.* hind; *hinnulus* hindkalf. R. W.

Aper, uel uerres, b(or).
. . . , bæruth.[1]
Uacca, uel bucula, ku.
Iuuenencus,[2] steor.
Canis, hund.
Molo(sus),
(Ru)beta, tadde.
Lacerta, evete.
Stellio, slowurm.
Locusta, greshoppe.
Li(max), ...
(Testu)do, þe þe haveþ hus.
Eruca, mæslesceafe.
Cimex, maþe.
Tine(a), ...

. . . . wurt.
Abrotanum, suþerwude.
Malua, hoc.
Malua crispa, (symeringwu)rt.
Simitia, grundeswulie.
Anetum, dile.
Polipodium, rifnesfot.
. . . . , (d)eieseien.
Solsequium, ...
. . . . . . , rude.
Betonica, þeo lesse biscopwurt.
Ta(nacetum, hel)de.
Saxifragia, sundcorn.
Gitsana, fæarn.
Calamus, uel canna, uel (arundo, re)od.
Papauer, popi.
Absinthium, wermot.
Urtica, netle.
Archan(gelica, blin)denetle.
Plantago, weibreode.
Uinca, pervenke.
Marrubium, hor(hune).
. . . . . . , stræberiewise.
Modera, chicnemete.
Apium, merc.
Lappa, clote, *uel* clif . . . .
. . . . , horselne.
Sandix, wod.

Caula, uel magudaris, caul.
Cresco, carse.
. . . . e.
Artemisia, mugwurt.
5 *Felterræ, uel centaurea,* eorþgalla.
Ambrosia, ...
Hermodactula tidolosa, crowelec.
Pastinaca, walmore.
Uiola, ...
10 *(Agr)imonia,* gorclifu.
Rafanum, redic.
Filex, fearn.
Carex, seg.
Arbor, ...
15 *(Querc)us, uel ylex,* oc
Taxus, iw.
Fagus, boctreow.
Alnus, olr.
Malus, æp(eltre).
20 *(Uir)ga,* gerd.
Uirgultum, telgra.
Granum, kurnel.
Ulcia, holi.
Populus, ...
25 . . . . . palmtwig.
Genesta, brom.
Sentes, þornes.
Frutex, þifel.
Ramnus, ...
30 . . . , bremelas.
Apies, æps.
Morus, morbeam.
Uitis, wintreow.
Salix, wiþi.
35 . . . .
Lignum, iheawen treow.
Ligna, drige wude.
Truncus, stoc.
Stirps, ...
40 *(Nemus), uel saltus,* holt.
Desertum, uel heremus, westen.
Uia, wei.
Semita, peþ.
. . . . (buta)n weie.
45 *Iter,* siþfæt.
Patria, eþel.

[1] An error of the scribe for *baruh* = *bearh*? R. W.
[2] So has the MS. R. W.

Prouincia, uel pagus, scyr.
Mons, ...
. . . ., hul, *uel* beoruh.
Uallis, dene.
Fenum, hei, *uel* græs.
Ager, aker.
Se(ges, asowen)æker.
Campus, feld.
Uadum, ford.
Litus, sæstrond.
Alueus, stream.
. . . ., (burn)a.
Riuus, riþ.
Aqua, water.
Gutta, uel stilla, drope.
Stangnum, ...
(Amni)s, eaa.
Flumen, flod, *uel fluuius.*
Ripa, steþ.
Gurges, wæl.
Lacus, ...
. . . ., (br)oc, *uel* burna.
Unda, uþæ.
Domus, hus.
Eclesia, chirche, *uel* ilcafful(gader-
 ung).
. . . . *uel* ilaþung.
Pagina, tramet.
Archa, serin
Loculus, cheste, *uel* . . . .
(Cal)ix, calic.
Patena, huseldisc.
Crux, uel staurus, rod.
Cathedra, ...
Fundamentum, grundwal.
Pauimentum, uel solum, flor.
Tectum, þecen.
. . . . *uel fornix,* bigels.
Columna, sweor.
Clausura, loc.
Clauis, keie.
. . . . *uel sera,* hespe.
Chorus, chor.
Gradus, stæpe.
Indicatorium, ...
(Legul)a, sticke.

Regula, regolsticke.
Lampas, uel lucerna, uel later(na), . . .
. . . . **ab.**
Lichinus, blacern.
5 *Munctorium,* irene tonge.
Clo(cca), ...

(Cingu)lum, uel cinctorium, uel zona,
 gurdel.
10 *Caliga, uel ocrea,* hosa.
(Calciamen)tum, isco.
Suptalaris, swiftlere.
Tractorium, tigel.
Flagrum, uel flag(ellum), ...
15 *Dormitorium,* slepern.
Stramentum, bedding.
Stragula, wæls . . . .[1]
. . . ., hwitel.
Puluinar, pule.
20 *Sindo,* scete.
Fulcra, al bedreaf.
F(emoralia), . . .
Perizomata, uel campestria, wædbrec.
Fimbria, fnæd.
25 *Colobi(um),* . . . . . . suric.
Pedula, meo.
Commissura, clut.
Toral, roc.
Tela, uel pep(lum), ...
30 . . . ., cleowen.
Colus, distæf.
Fusus, spindle.
Textrinum opus, teowli(c were).
. . . . ., gong.
35 *Trabes,* beam.
Tignum, refter.
Laquear, first.
Cleta, hu(rdel).
(Refecto)rium, beoddern, *uel* ireord-
40 unghus.
Tapeta, setræigel.
Mensa, ...
Discifer, discþein.
Minister, þein.
45 *Lardum,* spic.
Puls, bri.[2]

[1] Cf. pag. 328 l. 1. R. W.
[2] Read *pullus* = brid. R. W.

A . . . .
(Me)do, meodu.
Idromellum, uel mulsum, beor.
Cicera, ilches cunnes iw(rinc buton) win one.[1]
Manuterium, uel mantele, scet.
Cultellus, sex.
Artauus, h . . . .[2]
. . . . ., drunccuppe.
Anaphus, nep.
Patera, bledu.
Andena, bron(disen).
. . . . ., brond.
Olla, crocke.
Cacabus, chetel.
Lebes, hwer.
Caro, flæsc.
. . . .
(Iu)tilis canis, broþhund.
Fuscinula, owul.[3]
Uncinus, hoc.
Comm(edia), ...
Daps, sonde.
Ferculum, bærdisc.
Ueru, spite.
Assura, bræd.
. . . . ., irene ponne.
Frixorium, hursting.
Coctio, isod.
Coctus, isod(en) . . . .
Frustum, stucche.
Offa, snode.
Uestiarium, ræilhus.
Sigillum, ...
(Cel)larium, heddern.
Celerarius, hordare.
Mola, cweornstan.
Ui(ctus, bigleo)ue.
Pecunia, feoh.
Marsupium, scod.
Pistrinum, bakern.
For(nax, uel cliba)nus, oven.
Pistor, bakestre.
Bracium, malt.

Acus, sifeþe.
Crib(ra) . . . ., sife.
Furfures, gruta.
Fex, drosne.
5 Anfora, sester.
Lagena, b(uk).
. . . . ., cuf.
Cupa, tunna.
Utensilia, andloman.
10 Suppellex, yddi(sce).
(Triclini)um, bur.
Solarium, upflor.
Cardo, heorre.
Strigil, uel strigilis, ...
15 Risus, leihter.
Tristis, unrot.
Mestus, dreori.
Abundantia, . . ., inihstumnesse.
Corpulentus, þiccol.
20 Inualidus, unstrong.
Solli(tus), ...
Amurca, i. fex olei, dersten.
Securus, orseoruh.
Tutus, siker.
25 C(au)sa, intinga.
Occasio, inca.
Excusator, beladiend.
Mento, feh.[4]

30 (Signife)r, tocnebora.
Lancea, uel talarica,[5] spere.
Uictor, sigefeit.[6]
Uictoria, ...
Capulum, hilta.
35 Mucro, swerdes ord, uel oþres wæpnes.
Sica, lutel(swerd, uel han)d sex.
Asta, uel quiris, scæft.
Telum, flo.
40 Fustis, sowel.
Ueetis, steng.
Faretra, ...
Clipeus, sceld.
Umbo, randbeah.

[1] Cf. pag. 329 l. 13. R. W.
[2] Read k(nlf). Cf. pag. 329 l. 17. R. W.
[3] Cf. pag 330 l. 1. R. W.
[4] Cf. pag. 332 l. 9. R. W.
[5] Read falarica. R. W.
[6] Cf. pag. 332 l. 29. R. W.

Atrium, cafertun, *uel* inburh.
(*F*)*undibalum*, stefliþere.
Ciuitas, chestre.
Cluis, cheasteriwara, *uel* (portmon).
(*Prec*)*o*, budel.
Oppidum, fæsten.
Castellum, wic, *uel* lutel port.
Urbs, bu(ruh).
. . . . . ., buruhwita.
Suburbanus, þe þe sit buton þære buri.
Car(*cer*), ...
Oppidanus, þe þe on fæstene sit.
Uillanus, tunmon.
Uillicus, ...
(*Or*)*tus*, orchard.
Ortolanus, orchardweard.
Pomerium, æpeltun.
. . . . . ., wurtun.
Predium, worþig.
Ferramentum, tol.
Securis, æx.
Ascia, ade(sa).
. . . . ., (na)vegar.
Terebro, ic bore.
Uanga, *uel fossorium*, spade.
Lico, becca.
. . . . (ston)æx.
Palus, pal.
Serra, snid.
Falx, sicol.
Falcastrum, ...
Acus, nelde.[1]
(*A*)*uricalcum*, goldmestling.
Æs, bres.
Electrum, smulting.
Metallum, (ilches cunnes w)eeg.
Massa, bloma, *uel* dah.
Lapis, *uel petra*, ston.
Fissura, hcone.[2]
Marmor, ...
Saxum, wereston.
Silex, flint.
Gipsum, spærston.
Gemma, gimston.

. . . ., (me)regrota.
Calcx,[1] chalcston.
Aries, rom.
Cimentum, andweore to walle.
5 *Cemen*(*tarius*, walwur)hta.
Rogus, od.
Iocus, pleiga.
Prophanus, monful.
Exosus, *uel perosus*, and(sete).
10 . . . . gleaw (geap?).[3]
Simulator, heoware.
Hipocrita, licettere.
Adulator, lufe(tere).
(*Adula*)*cio*, luffetung.
15 *Deceptor*, *uel seductor*, beweehend
Proditor, ...
(*H*)*omicida*, monsleia.
Patricida, *matricida*, *fratricida*, parracida.
20 (*C*)*icatrix*, dolhswaþe.
Truncus, heafedleas bodi
Corpus, lic.
Funis, ...
(*Cad*)*auer*, lic, *uel* hold.
25 *Feretrum*, bære.
Defunctus, forþfaren.
Longeuus, ...
(*Nobi*)*lis*, æþelboren.
Ignobilis, unæþelboren.
30 *Uilis*, woclic.
Carus, leof.
Limen, ofersleie, *uel* þreoxwold
Sciffus, læfel.
Urceus, ceac.
35 *Peluis*, ...
(*P*)*laustrum*, *uel carrum*, wein.
Currus, *uel basterna*, *uel heseda*, kert.
Stabu(*lum*, fold, *uel* hu)s bi weige.
Caula, loc
40 *Tugurium*, hulc.
Cella, cot.
Mausoleum, þruh . . .
Monumentum, *uel sepulcrum*, buriles.
Sargofagum, þruh.
45 *Donum*, *uel datum*, ...

[1] So has the MS. R. W.
[2] Read *keone*. R. W.

[3] Cf. pag. 334 l. 39. R. W.

Munus, loc.
Uter, butte.
Flasco, buttruc.
Tentorium, uel taberna(*culum*), ...

(*Nouacu*)*lum,* nœilsex.
Cos, hweston.[2]
Apricus locus, **leowstude.**
Apricitas, leowþ.
Edific(*ium*), itimbrung.
Palatium, kinelic botl.
Bassis, sulle.
Postis, post.
Compes, uel cippus, f(otcops).
Boia, ioc *uel* sweorcops.
Manica, hondcops.
Complex, igada.
Pœna, uel sup(*plicium*), **wite.**
Nebris, næst.[1]
Mercennarius, hurmon.
Horologium, dæimæl.
Goomon,[2] (dæimæ)les pil.[3]
Hospes, cuma.
Hospitium, gesthus.
Hostis, uel osor, feond.
Thesaurus, hor(d).

[1] Cf. pag. 337 l. 3. R. W.
[2] So has the MS. R. W.

(*Gaza*)*filacium,* madmhus.
Edax, uel gluto, oferetel.
Ambro, fræc.
Gulosus, gifre.
5 *P*(*rocax*) imouh.
Procacitas, imouhnesse.
Obstinatus, onwille.
Obstinantia, onwilln(is).
Uerecundus, sceomefest.
10 *Inpudens,* unsceomefest.
Pudicus, sideful.
Inpud(*icus*), unsideful.
Interpres, wealhstod.
Reus, sculdi.
15 *Damnatus, uel condemnatus,* for-
(demed).
Sceleratus, uel facinorosus, forscul-
degod.
Scelus, sculd.
20 *Facinus, uel culpa,* gi(lt).
Adulter, forliger, *uel* æwbræche.
Gibberosus, uel strumosus, hoferede.
Gibb(*us, uel*) *struma,* hofer.
Meretrix, uel scorta, multestre.
25 *Pelex,* cyfes, *et cetera.*

[1] Cf. pag. 337 l. 6. R. W.

XIV.

VOCABULARY OF THE NAMES OF PLANTS.[1]

(OF THE MIDDLE OF THE THIRTEENTH CENTURY.)

CHAUDES HERBES.

Artimesie, i. mugwrt, i. merherbarum.
Marubium, i. maruil, i. horehune.
Ruta, i. rue.
Apium, i. ache.
Buglosa, i. bugle, i. wudebrune.
Saniculum, i. sanicle, i. wudemerch.
Sinapium, i. seneuel, i. senci.
Zizania, i. neele, i. cockel.
Absinthium, i. aloigne, i. wermod.
Elna enula, i. ialne, i. gretwurt.
Bethonica, i. beteine.
Abrotanum, i. aueroine, i. suþewurt.

Pulegium, i. puliol, i. hulwurt.
Agrimonia, i. agremoine, i. garcline.
Consolida, i. consoude, i. daiseie.
Cumfiria, i. cumfirie, i. galloc.
5 *Mentastrum*, i. mentastre, i. horsminte.
Auencia, i. avence, i. harefot.
Porius, i. poret, i. lek.
Regina, i. reine, i. medwurt.
Millefolium, i. milfoil.
10 *Ebulum*, i. eble, i. walwurt.
Leuisticum, i. luuesche, i. luuestiche.
Cepa, i. oingnun, i. knelek.[2]
Saluia, i. sauge, i. fenuern.
Centauria, i. centoire, i. hurdreue.

[1] This vocabulary of names of plants, evidently intended for the use of a medical practitioner, is preserved in a manuscript in the British Museum (MS. Harl. No. 978, fol. 24, vo), which appears to have been written in the period intervening between the battles of Lewes and Evesham, that is, in 1264 or 1265. The explanations of the Latin names are given in Anglo-Norman and in English; and in a few instances either the Anglo-Norman or English is omitted, and even in one or two cases the Latin. It is given here as illustrating the lists of plants in the other vocabularies in the present volume. The history of the popular nomenclature of plants is a very curious and interesting subject; and the manuscripts of all periods are very rich in materials for it. There is another list of names of plants in the three languages, resembling the one here printed, but arranged in alphabetical order, and rather more full, in a manuscript of the fourteenth century in the British Museum, MS. Sloane, No. 5.

[2] Cf. pag. 131 l. 1y. R. W.

Arcangelica, i. mort ortie, i. blinde netle.
Pollipodium, i. poliol, i. reuenfot.
Felix arboratica, i. pollipode, i. eueruern.
Saluinca, i. gauntelee, i. foxesgloue.
Butunus, i. butuns, i. hoepe.
Nasturtium, i. kersuns, i. cressen.
Coliandrum, i. coriandre, i. chele priem.
Petrosillum, i. peresil, i. stoansuke.
Closera, i. alisaundre, i. wilde percil.
Fauida, i. fauede, i. leomeke.
Sandix, i. waisde, i. wod.
Gladiolum, i. flamine, i. gladene.
Febrefugia, i. fewerfue, i. adrelwurt.
Tanesetum, i. tanesie, i. helde.
Pilosella, i. peluselle, i. musere.
Uermiculum, i. warance, i. wrotte.
Raffarium, i. raiz, i. redich.
Silimbrium, i. balsamitis, i. brocminten.
Ambrosia, i. ambrose, i. hindehele.
Althea, i. ymalue, i. holihoe.
Saxifragium, i. saxifrage, i. waiwurt.
Bidella, i. samsuns, i. lechis.
Bursa pastoris, i. sanguinarie, i. blodwurt.
Feniculum, i. fanuil, i. fenecel.
Quinquefolium, i. quintfoil, i. fiflef.
Tapsus barbatus, i. moleine, i. softe.
Fabaria, i. fauerole.
Trifolium, i. trifoil, i. wite clouere.
Diptannum, i. ditaundere.
Cotula fetida, i. ameruche, i. miwe.
Persicaria, i. saucheneie, i. cronesanke.
Lanceolata, i. launceleie, i. ribbe.
Matersilua, i. cheuefoil,[2] i. wudebide.[1]
Sambucus, i. suew, i. ellarne.
Ueruena, i. uerueine, i. irenharde.
Arundo, i. rosel, i. reod.
Osmunda, i. osmunde, i. bonwurt.
Olibanus, i. encens, i. stor.
Fungus, i. wluesfist.

Cerfolium, i. cerfoil, i. villen.
Camomilla, i. camemille, i. maiwe.
Nepta, i. nepte, i. kattesminte.
Argentea, i. argentine, i. lilie.
Enula, i. alne, i. horselne.
Ysopus, i. ysope.
Spurgia, i. spurge, i. guweorn (guwcorn?).
Lauendula, i. lauendre.
Fion, i. camglata, i. foxesgloue.
Euscute, i. doder.
Satureia, i. satureie, i. timbre.
Borago, i. burage.
Tribulus marinus, i. calketrappe, seapistel.
Fumus terre, i. fumetere, i. cuntchoare.
Calamentum, i. calemente.
Ypis, i. herbe Johan, i. uelderude.
Organum, i. organe.
Origanum, i. puliol real, i. wde minte.[2]
Menta, i. mente, i. minten.
Anetum, i. anete, i. dile.
Elitropium, i. solsegle, i. gloden.
Eptaphilos, i. salerne, i. uarewurt.
Elleborum album, i. alebre blonc.
Eleborum, i. ellebre, i. lungwurt.
Pionia, i. pioine.
Ortica, i. ortie, i. nettle.
Ualeriane, i. stichwurt.
Celsi, i. murer, i. murberien.
Auellane, i. petite noiz, i. litel nute.
Frisgonem, i. fresgun, i. enehole.
Sponsa solis, i. grinnil.
Pinpernele, i. pinpre, i. briddestunge.
Lingua canis, i. chenlange, i. hundestunge.
Dormentille, i. ortie griesche, i. doc nettle.
Lappa, i. bardane, i. clote.
Burneta, i. sprungwurt.
Epitime, i. epithimum, i. fordboh.
Turmentine,[3] i nutehede.
Widebawme[3] i. haluewude.[4]

---

[1] So has the MS. Read *wudebinde*. F. W.
[2] So has the MS. R. W.
[3] No Latin equivalent is given. R. W.
[4] *idebawme* in *widebawme* is obliterated. R. W.

Malua cripia, i. screpemalue.
Consolida media, i. þundreclouere.
Herba benedicta, i. herbe beneit, *i.* hemelue.
Hedera nigra, i. iere, *i.* oerþiui.
Herba Roberti, i. herbe Robert, *i.* chareüille.
Hinnula campana, i. sperewurt.
Hastula regia, i. muge de bois, *i.* wuderoue.
Intiba, i. muruns, *i.* chienemete.
Iregerontis, i. cenesuns, *i.* grundeswilie.
Iuniperii, i. geneiure, *i.* gorst.
Ligustrum, i. triffoil, *i.* hunisucelcs. 15
Labrusca, i. hundesberien.
Alleum, i. ail, *i.* garlec.
Murum, i. blakeberie.
Genesta, i. genest, *i.* brom.
Omfacium, i. winberi stones.
Ostragnam, i. herbyue, *i.* liþewurt.
Plantago, i. planteine, *i.* weibrode.

FREIDES HERBES.

Morella, i. morele, *i.* atterloþe.
Ionis barba, i. iubarbe, *i.* singrene.
Lactuca, i. letue, *i.* slepwurt.
Fraga, i. fraser, *i.* streberilef.
Ramni, i. grosiler, *i.* þefeþorn.
Astula regia, i. popi. 30

Atriplex, i. arasches.
Mercurialis, i. euenlesten, *i.* mercurial.
Malua, i. malue, *i.* hoc.
Caulus, i. cholet, *i.* kaul.
5 *Andiuia, i.* letrun, *i.* þugeþistel.
Psilliun, i. lusesed.
Uirga pastoris, i. wilde tesel.
Ypoquistidos, i. hundesrose.
Iusquiamus, i. chenille, *i.* hennebone.
10 *Uiola, i.* uiole, *i.* appelleaf.
Alimonis, i. wilde popi.
Aizon, i. sinfulle.
Tucia, i. tutie.
Litargirum, i. escume de or.

INTER FRIGIDUM ET CALIDUM.

Lapis lazuli, i. pere.
Manna.

20 INTER FRIGIDUM ET CALIDUM TEMPERATUM.

Mirtus, i. gagel.
Bragagantum, i. dragagant.
Mirobolani, i. mirobolanam.
25 *Bedagrage, i. spina alba, i.* witþorn.
Bolum, i. bol.
Arnoglosa, i. plauntein.
Argentum uiuum, i. nif argent.
Berberis.

XV.

A LATIN AND ENGLISH VOCABULARY.

(OF THE FIFTEENTH CENTURY.[1])

Ab, *preposicio*, an^{ce} fro.
Abecula, *le* an^{ce} the bake of a knyf.
Abestis intestina hostiarum aspiciens, et an^{ce} a gyller of bestys.
Abhinc in antea, an^{ce} fro hen forth ward.
Abies . . . an^{ce} a fyrre.
Ablacto . i. a lacte remouere, an^{ce} to awenye.
Abrotanum . . . an^{ce} wodesoure.
Absconsa . . . an^{ce} a sconse.
Absinthium . . . an^{ce} wermod.
Ac eciam an^{ce} and also. *vel* and forsothe.

Acantus, [an^{ce} hoppyn.]
Acaluaster . . . an^{ce} ballyd byfore.
Acellarius . . . an^{ce} a spenser.
[Acorsus . . . an^{ce} Redmerche.]
Acopa . . . an^{ce} an obligacion or a tayl.
Acra . . . an^{ce} an aker of lond.
Acrementum . . . an^{ce} encres.
Acroceramen . . . an^{ce} a wawe of the see.
Actenus . . . an^{ce} tyl now.
[Acsi . . . an^{ce} as thowe.]
Acticola . . . an^{ce} Ramsyn.[2]
Acuarium, an^{ce} an agulere.

[1] This vocabulary is preserved in a manuscript in the Library of the Trinity College, Cambridge. The MS. is of the 15th century.

Our text is based on a copy made by Mr. W. Aldis Wright.
[2] In the margin.

Acumen, an^ce a popyn.
Acupictor, an^ce a broderer.
Acusile, an^ce a trenket.
Adagonista, an^ce a man of lawe.
Adicio, an^ce to cast to.
Adhereo, to drawe or to cleuy to.
Adiectivo, an^ce to cast to.
Adipatum, an^ce browes.
Adinvicem, an^ce to gedyr.
Ador, [*an^ce* flowr.]
Adsum, an^ce to be ny
Adtrica, an^ce the mase.
Aduenio, to come to.
Adultus, an^ce ygrowe.
Adunco, an^ce to drawe wyth an hooke.
Advoco, an^ce to clepy to.
Adustio, an^ce brennynge.
Affinis, an^ce bysybbe.
Affinitas, an^ce sybrede.
Agalancia, an^ce a plover.
Agelarius, an^ce an hayward.
[*Agerarius, an^ce* a curdogge.]
Agnus castus, an^ce toutsayne.
Agonia, an^ce anger.
Agrestis, an^ce wylde.
[*Agromellum, an^ce* Growt.]
Agulus, an^ce a shephoke.
Alabrum, [a reel.]
Alaris, an^ce a company of hors.
Alator, an^ce a wanelasour.
Alarica, an^ce a coronel.
Alauda, an^ce a lark.
Alba, an^ce an awbe.
Albor, an^ce whytnesse.
Albus, an^ce whyte.
[*Albus candidus, an^ce* mylke whyte.]
Alcedo, an^ce a colmose,* [a wodewale.]
Alcanna, an^ce alkenet.
Alcion, an^ce a Semewe.
[*Alchinum vel Alchimum, an^ce* Alkemyn.]
[*Algea,* ffletwort.]
Algenia, an^ce the coold ache.
Algorismus, an^ce augrym.
Alicitor, an^ce an hobeye *et hic Peregrinus idem est.*
Alietus, an^ce an hobey.

Aliquamdiu, an^ce somedellonge.
Aliquantus, [*an^ce* sumwhat.]
Allec , an^ce an heryng.
Alleluya, [*an^ce* wodesoure]
Allicio, an^re to drawe to.
Allium, an^ce garlyk.
Allumen, ang^ce alme.
Allux, an^ce the grete to.
[*Alo, an^ce* to reme.]
Alopitis, the braun.
Alnus, an^ce an eldertree.
Alphinus, an^ce an awfyn.
Alpinus, an^ce longend to hylle of alpys.
Altarium, an^ce a superaltarye.
Altea malua, [*an^ce* the holy hokke.]
Alterutrum, an^ce fro on tyl an othyr.
Altus, [*an^ce* hye.]
Aluta, cordewayne.
Alutarius, an^ce a cordewaner.
Alvus, an^ce a trowe.
Ama, he that muche loueth.
Amabo, an^ce a louely worde.
Amarusa, an^ce a mathge.
Amasius, Amasia, an^ce a leman.
Ametus, an^ce a merlyn.
Amethon, an^ce a slykston.
Amflo, an^ce to travayle.
Amfora, uel amphora, an^ce a tankard.
Amictum, an^ce an amyte.
Amictoria, an^ce a couerture.
[*Amica, an^ce* a paramour.]
Amminiculor, an^ce to helpe.
Amissis, an^ce a squyre.
Amphibulus, an^ce a sclauayn or faldyng.
Amphivia, an^ce Seles.
Amphistrum, an^ce a sterne, or an helme.
Anabatrum, [*an^ce* a style.]
Anabolandium, an^ce a rochet.
Anabulla, an^ce spurge.
Anadrogia, an^ce a deye.
[*Anagallus, an^ce* Pympernele.]
Anas, an^ce a doke.
Anacius, an^ce a tele.
Anatus, an^ce a mallard.
Anata, a doke.
Anatene, an^ce up cuttynge.

37

Anca, an^ce the knebon.
Ancha, an^ce a tache.
Ancer, an^ce a gander.
Ancerulus, an^ce a goslynge.
Andena, an^ce an Andyre.
Androchia, an^ce a deye.
Anelo, an^ce to panty & blowe.
Anetum, [dylle.]
Angivs, an^ce a shepardestaf.
Anhetum, an^ce Aneyse.
Annicito, an^ce to twynkele.
[*Annodoma, an^ce* feltwort.]
Anuncio, an^ce to shewe.
Anquiromagus, an^ce the sterne of the shypp.
[*Ansea, an^ce* a trusse.]
Anser, an^ce a gander.
Ansorium, a shavyngknyf, or a trenket.
Anterior, an^ce byfore.
Antesellum, an^ce for asyon of the sadell.
Antica, [*an^ce* an hache.]
Antipera, an^ce a screne.
Antiphora, an^ce evensonge.
Antiquitus, [*an^ce* yn olde tyme.]
Antrax, an^ce the felon.
Apago, an^ce a lether to bere ynne thynge.
[*Apastinata, an^ce* Chervylle.]
Appendium, an^ce a yernwynder, or a reel.
Aper, an^ce a boor.
Aperio, an^ce to opene.
Apertus, an^ce openyd.
Apium, an^ce Ache [*vel* Merche].
Aplustrum, [*an^ce* an hashe.]
Apoca, an^ce aquytaunce.
[*Apolinaris, an^ce* closwort.]
Aporima, ioys of gras.
Appareo, an^ce to seme or to apere.
Appendicium, an^ce a lady trayne *et an^ce* a pendaunt of a gyrdyll.
Applico, an^ce to ryve or to shypye.
Apposissio, an^ce puttyng to.
Apto, an^ce to shappe or to araye.
Aquaductile, an^ce a condyt.
Aquagium, an^ce a gutur or a condyt.

Aquarium, an^ce a gutur.
Aquenomio, an^ce a spute.
Aquebaiulus, an^ce an holy water clerk.
Aquillus, an^ce an Oxebowe.
5 *Aquitannia vel Aquitania, an^ce* Gascune.
[*Arallus,* a plow fote.]
Arano to flowe to reme as water & make fayre.
10 *Aratrum, an^ce* a plowe.
Arbia, an^ce a bosum.
Arbitus, an^ce a crabtree.
Arbitum, an^ce a crabbe.
Arcella, an^ce a fforser.
15 *Archangelica, an^ce* the blyndnetel.
Archimacherus, an^ce a mayster cooke.
Archonizo, an^ce to moweye.
Archonistus, an^ce a mowyer.
Arcista, an arcetere.
20 *Architenens, an^ce* an Archer.
Arconio, an^ce to stake.
Arcubilus, an^ce an Archer.
Arcuarius, a bowyer.
Arcubius, an^ce a wayte.
25 *Arculus, an^ce* the Arsyon of a sadelle.
[*Ardicomata, an^ce* a quayle.]
Arena, an^ce gravel.
Arenus, an^ce a pane of goold.
30 *Areola, an^ce* a lykbedde.
Argentifilum, sylver wyre.
Argentum, Quyksylver.
Argilla, [*an^ce* Cley.]
Arista, an^ce an eyle.
35 *Aristologia,* [*an^ce* Smerwort.]
Armamentum, an^ce takelyng.
Armariolum, an^ce an almarye.
Armelausa, an^ce a cloke.
Armilausa, A sclavayn.
40 *Ars metrica, an^ce* arsmetryke.
Artemesia, an^ce moderwort.
Artificialis, an^ce a craftiman.
Artocopus, an^ce a symynel.
Artocrea, an^ce a tart.
45 *Arthochasius, an^ce* a flawun.
Arvambulus, an^ce a londlepar.
Ascarida, [A Teke.]
[*Ascio, an^ce* to thwyte or schyrpe.]

Asculto, an^ce to lystny.
Aserra, an^ce a shyppe.
[*Asitabulum, an^ce* a sawser.]
Asina, [the pose.]
Aspa, an^ce an haspe.
Aspergo, an^ce a cormeraunt.
Aspersorium, an^ce an holy water stykke.
Assa, an^ce roost.
Assacula, an^ce an hastelet.
Assatus, an^ce yrosted.
Assedula, an^ce surdokke.
[*Assedella, an^ce* a table dormant.]
Asser, [*an^ce* a latche.]
Assidela, an^ce a table dormant.
Assilo, to stroke.
Asso, an^ce to rooste.
Astayda, an^ce a tyke.
Astrum, an^ce a sterre.
Astularegia, an^ce woderofe.
Asura, an^ce azure.
Athachiacio, an^ce athachyment or arestynge.
Athleta, an^ce a champyon.
Attractorium, an^ce a trayne, sed melius* a trays.
Atramentum, an^ce Bleche.
Atriplices, [*an^ce* Orage.]
Attat interiectio timentis ut expavescentis, an^ce for dowte.
Attenuo, to make thynne or feble.
Attollo, an^ce to lyft up, or to do a way.
[*Aucarius,* a gosherde.]
Auca, an^ce a goos.
Auccionor, an^ce to hukke.
Auccionator et Auccionatrix, an hukker & an hukkester.
Auccupacio, an^ce fowlynge.
Aucupator et Aucupatrix et Aucuparius idem sunt, an^ce fowlers.
Auccupacio, an^ce fowlynge.
Audacia, an^ce hardynesse.
Audio, an^ce to huyre.
Audiencia, an^ce an hurynge.
Auencia, an^ce avance.
Auicipula, an^ce a putfalle.
Auigerulus, an^ce a pulter.

Auleum, an^ce a doser.
Aumentum, an^ce an hagase.
Aurealis, an^ce an erewygge.
Aureatus, an^ce ygyld.
5 *Auricalcum, an^ce* latoun.
Auricula muris, an^ce mushere.
Auriflum, an^ce gooldwyre.
Aurifrisius, an^ce an hospray.
Aurifrigium, an^ce goldwyre.
10 *Auxilior, an^ce* to helpe.

Baburra, an^ce Sothede.
Bacis, an^ce a truel.
Bacillus, an^ce a warderere.
15 *Baco, an^ce* bacon.
Bacallarius, an^ce a bachyler.
Baffa, an^ce a flycche of bacon.
Bafer, an^ce gretwombed.
Balbutio, [*an^ce* to stamery.]
20 [*Balbio, an^ce* to blaty.]
Balducta, an^ce a crudde, Item dicitur, an^ce* poshet.
Balla, an^ce a bale.
Ballivus, an^ce a baylyf.
25 *Balneo, an^ce* to bathye.
Balo, an^ce to blete.
Balteus, [*an^ce* a baudrek.]
Balteo, an^ce a bancker.
[*Bancorium vel Bancarium, an^ce* a bankere.]
30
Bancia, an^ce pasnep or skyrwyt.
Barba jovis [*an^ce* syngrene.]
Barbillus, an^ce a ruget vel melius* a barbyle.
35 [*Bardana, an^ce* Clote.]
Barellus, an^ce a barell.
[*Barusia, an^ce* a barhyde.]
Basilisca, an^ce baldemonye.
Batillus, a belle clapere *vel* a swyngell.
Baucia, an^ce skyrwyt.
Batus, an^ce a bushell vel secundum alios trium modiorum an^ce* a pecke.
Beatus, an^ce yblessyd.
45 *Bedellus, an^ce* a bedull.
Belberici marini sunt similes vmbilicis vmbilicus ci an^ce navelwort.
Belua, an^ce an engyne.

Benedictus, [an*ce* yblessed.]
Beneficium, an*ce* a good dede.
Benevolentia, an*ce* good wyl.
Berberi sunt fructus cuiusdam arboris, an*ce* berberynes.
Berbica, an*ce* ewe.
Bernix, an*ce* vernysh.
Bernix cantabre veronice idem sunt vernyshe.
[*Berula*, an*ce* Bleddere.]
Betacius, an*ce* bete.
[*Betonica*, an*ce* Bytayne.]
Bethonica, an*ce* betayne.
Bever, an*ce* bever.
Bibera, an*ce* a beverache.
Bigata, an*ce* a kartlode.
Bilbus, an*ce* a welke.
Birrus vel Birrum, i. grossum vestimentum, an*ce* a dudde.
Biriscus [a feyldefare.]
Bisacuta, an*ce* a twybyl.
Bismalua (MS. *Bismabua*), an*ce* bysmalwe twymalwe.
Blodius, an*ce* Blewe.
[*Bodarius*, an*ce* heybrere.]
Boletus, an*ce* tender old cloth.
Bombacinum, an*ce* *secundum quosdam* Aketoun.
Bombicinum, an*ce* a lakke.
Bombinco, to crye as a bee.
Bondagium, an*ce* Bondage.
Bostio, an*ce* a Boye.
Bostare, an*ce* a Snyte.
Bovectus, an*ce* a stere.
Braciologia, an*ce* a shortspekynge.
Brachiale, an*ce* a wardebrace.
Brachium, an*ce* an arme.
Brancia, an*ce* a gyle.
Brandium, an*ce* Bokeram.
Brasicta, an*ce* lutes.
Brasio, an*ce* to brewe.
Brasium, an*ce* malt.
Brasiarium, an*ce* a brewehous.
Brasiarius, an*ce* a brewer.
Brasiaria, an*ce* a brewestere.
[*Bremetica*, a breme.]
Brevigerulus, [an*ce* a Brevytour.]
[*Brella*, an*ce* sterche.]

Breno, an*ce* bran.
[*Brionia*, an*ce* wyldenepe.]
[*Briscus*, an*ce* a feyldvare.]
Britages, an*ce* britage.
Britannia, an*ce* brytayne
Brodium, an*ce* broth.
Brucus, an*ce* a taddepol.
Brueris, an*ce* heth
Bubo, an*ce* an vle.
Bucco [an*ce* to blowe.]
Bucula, an*ce* a bucule.
Bufo, an*ce* a tode.
[*Bugla*, an*ce* Bugle.]
Bulgra, an*ce* bugres.
Bullio, an*ce* to buly.
Bullicio, an*ce* berme.
Burcida, an*ce* a purskyttere.
Burnetus, an*ce* burnet, *color quidam est.*
Burbilium, an*ce* nombles.
Burris, an*ce* the plowebeme.
[*Bursa pastoris*, an*ce* shepardespurse.]
Butus, an*ce* Shadde *sed melius Bustus*.
Buxus, an*ce* box.

Cachinnor, an*ce* to mowe.
Caculipes, an*ce* a page.
Calamandrum, an*ce* a voluperc.
Calatus, an*ce* a panyer.
Calcar, an*ce* a spore.
Calcatrepa, an*ce* a kalketrappe.
Calciamentum, an*ce* Chausure.
Calculus, an*ce* a cowntes.
[*Calea*, a lyndtre.]
Calefactorium, an*ce* a Chawfur
Calefurcum, an*ce* galwes.
[*Calendarium*, an*ce* a kalendere.]
Calibs, an*ce* Steel.
Calix, an*ce* a Chalys.
Calopodium, an*ce* a tapyn.
Calor, an*ce* hete.
Calvicies, an*ce* balledness*e*.
Cama, an*ce* a shortbedde.
Cambucca, an*ce* a busshoppys cros.
Cambuccarius, an*ce* a Croser.
Camamilla, an*ce* Camamylle.
[*Camedreos*, an*ce* Teterwose.]
Camelinus, an*ce* camelyn.

[*Camerarius, an^ce* a chamberlayne.]
Caminus, an^ce a chymeney.
Campanile, an^ce a styppyl.
Campester, an^ce a feyldefare.
Campio, an^ce a champion.
Camus, an^ce a barnacle.
Canabum, an^ce hempe.
Cancellus . . . ala palacij. i. parvum foramen parietis, an^ce a kernell.
Candeo, an^ce wylde madur.
Canevasium, an^ce Canevas.
Canendula, an^ce a Plover.
Canicies, an^ce hoorenesse.
Canistrum, an^ce a basket.
[*Canus, an^ce* Grenew or hore.]
Capa, a cope.
Capana, an^ce a kot.
Capana, an^ce a pynsour.
Capellus, an^ce an hatte.
Capellarius, an^ce an hattere.
Caper, an^ce a gotbukke.
Capra, a gootdoo.
Capicium, an^ce an hode.
Capisterium, an^ce a vanne [or a Seve.]
Capistrum, an^ce an haltre.
Capitanius, an^ce a captayn.
Capito, an^ce a cole.
Cappa, an^ce the cappe of a fleyle.
Cappilegium, an^ce a fleylbond.
Capra, a gotdo.
Caprifolium, an^ce wodebynde.
Capus, an^ce a musket.
Caracalla, an^ce a sclavayn or a cope.
Caracus, an^ce a carryk.
Caraxis, an^ce tokenynge.
Carbonella, [*an^ce* a colhoppe.]
Carchesia, [the saylyerd.]
Carcosium, an^ce a carkoys.
Cardinalis, an^ce a cardynal.
Cardo, an^ce a thystell, or a tesell.
Cardinarius, an^ce a teselere.
Carduelis, an^ce a goldfynche.
Carduus, an^ce a tesel.
Cardus, an^ce a corde.
Carectarius, an^ce a cartere.
Carentivillum, an^ce a kanvas.
Carex, an^ce Segge.

Carinis, an^ce a make.
Carnarium, [*an^ce* a charnel.]
Carniprivium, an^ce shrofday, *quia tunc privamur carnibus.*
5 *Carinis, an^ce* a mathe.
Carpa, [*an^ce* a toppe.]
Carporo, an^ce to wynde.
Carptare, an^ce to karde.
Carptarius, an^ce a kardemakere.
10 *Carrucarius,* a p[l]owman.
Carrucata, a plowelond.
Caruca, an^ce Suthernewode.
Cassa, an^ce a mowe.
Cassator, an^ce a moweare.
15 *Casilius, an^ce* myd amene.
Cassis, an^ce an helme.
Castrimargus, an^ce a wodecocke.
Catallum, an^ce catall.
Catantrum, an^ce a frendell.
20 [*Cathapia, an^ce* Spurge.]
Catapucia, lesse spurge.
Catasta, an^ce a cage.
Catello, to mewe or to tykele.
Catta, an^ce a hecatte.
25 *Cavatus, an^ce* ymade holwe.
Cauilla, an^ce a pyn.
[*Cavilla,* an ancle.]
Cavni, an^ce fayryes.
[*Cauterium ferrum ustum, an^ce* Synder.]
30
Cavus, an^ce holw.
Cavitas, an^ce holwnehse.
Cecula, an^ce a Slowerme.
Cecuta, an^ce hemlok.
35 *Cefalia, an^ce* the hede Ache.
Celarium, an^ce a celer.
Celatorium, an^ce a celour, or a coverlyt.
Celeps, an^ce a chesell to peynte
40 wyth.
Celerarius, an^ce a celerer.
Celectis, an^ce hevenlyche.
Celioforum, an^ce an alepot.
Cellens, an^ce Overcomynge.
45 *Celtica,* spikenard.
Cementum, an^ce morter.
Cenositas, an^ce felthede.
Cenovectorium, an^ce a berwe.

Cenovectorium rotatum, a whelberwe.
Ce[no]vectorium manuale, an handberwe.
Cenovectorium, an^ce a berwe.
Cepa, an^ce an oynon.
Cephalia, an^ce the hede Ache.
Cepiarium, an^ce Sewe.
Ceplatum, an^ce cyne.
Cepulatum, an^ce sew.
Cepum, an^ce talwe.
Cerasus, an^ce a Cherytree.
Cerifolium, [an^ce honysouke.]
Ceruida, an^ce a tapstaf.
Ceruisia, an^ce Ale.
Cervus, Cerva, an^ce hert and hynde.
Cesia, an^ce a pokke or frakene.
Cespes, an^ce a turf.
Cesso, an^ce to leue of.
Chamus, an^ce a bernake.
Cherub, a cherube.
Cherucus, an^ce a fane.
Chilindrus, an^ce a leucl *vel est instrumentum quo hore notantur* [an^ce a chylaundre.]
Chorea, an^ce a karole.
Choricista, [an^ce a crowdere.]
Chorinus, an^ce a dawneere.
Chorealus, an^ce a daunceleder.
Chorus, an^ce a crowde.
Chorusta, an^ce a querester.
Chrismale, an^ce a Crismere.
Cicada, an^ce a grashoppere.
Cicuta, an^ce an homeluk.
Cignus, an^ce a swan.
Cilix [*quidam piscis*, a loche.]
Cimbale, a cymbale.
Cimbus, an^ce a vat.
Cimicia, herba fetens, mathge.
Ciminum, an^ce Comyn.
Cinasus, an^ce a puddynge.
Cincinnus, an^ce a lok.
Cingulum, a gurse.
Cinomia, an^ce a fleys flye.
Cinopre, an^ce Cynopre.
Cinus, an^ce an haythorne & an hawe.
Cipharius, an^ce a cuppere, or a dysshere.
Circumspectus, an^ce Skylful.

Circulator, an^ce a tornur.
Circumcido, an^ce to kytte a boute.
Circumpres (so in MS.), an^ce a prayer of a worde.
Circumuolo, an^ce to fle a boute.
[*Ciromellum*, an^ce wort.]
Cirrus, *i. plicatura capillorum et* an^ce a cop.
Citator, an^ce a Sompnere.
Citacus, an^ce a popinjay.
Citharedo, an^ce to harpe.
Citheres, a name of an hylle.
Citator, an^ce a Sumnere.
Cito, an^ce to sompny.
Citola, an^ce a cytole.
Claretum, an^ce Clareye.
Classatorium, an^ce a clapere, or a styppyll.
Claudeo, an^ce to halte.
Claudus, an^ce halt, or lame.
Clavigarius, a lorymere.
Clavus, an^ce a nayle.
Clepsedra, an^ce a tappe.
Clericatus, an^ce Clergye.
Clerimonia, an^ce clergye.
[*Clibanicius*, a loof.]
Clinus, an^ce bedlyche.
Clipeola, *i. anulus quia fit ad modium clipei* ., an^ce a lytylbreche.
Clipsedra, an^ce a spyket.
Clitella, an^ce a cliket, or a forsere.
Clitorium, an^ce a clyket.
Cloca, an^ce a cloke.
Cloto, on of thre shapsisterys *vel* shappystrys [*vel* an^ce destynyes.]
Cnusticium, *i. quedam pars sotularis*, an^ce a Ryvette.
Coaccio, an^ce dystresse.
Coagulatorium, a mylkefessell, or a cherne.
Coagulum, an^ce rennynge.
Coagulum, an^ce a crudde.
Coagulo, an^ce to make a crudde.
Coaugeo, an^ce to eche to gedyr.
Coccinium, an^ce coton.
Cochlea . . . *Item est alta et rotunda turris* [a topcastel.]
Coctinus, an^ce a Quynstre.

*Codex, an^ce coode.
*Coliandrum herba est, an^ce colyandre.
[*Coliteralis,* a Costrel.]
*Colus, an^ce a dystaf.
*Collaphus, an^ce a buffet.
*Collarium, an^ce a colere.
*Collatinea, an^ce a thynned.
*Collistrigium, an^ce a pyllory.
*Collofium, an^ce a coffyn.
*Colatorium, an^ce a Colyndore.
*Colon, the endelez gutte.
*Colomelli, an^ce tuskes.
*Colostrum, an^ce rennet.
*Coluber, [an^ce a snake.]
*Colum, [an^ce a colyndore, or a tunnyng dysch.]
[*Columbare, an^ce a culverhous.]
*Comatulus, an^ce lytyl heryd.
*Commater, an^ce a godmodur.
*Comissarius, an^ce a commissarye.
*Commissio, an^ce a commyssion.
*Commissura, an^ce a mortays.
*Complutus, an^ce wet wyth rayne.
*Complustrum, an^ce a clowster of notys.
*Conca, an^ce a loppyster.
*Concedo, an^ce to graunte.
*Concavia, an^ce a maner mace.
*Concludo, an^ce to close, or to conclude.
*Condilus, an^ce a knokyl.
*Conditio, an^ce Saverynge.
*Conductum, an^ce a saf condyt.
*Conduum, an^ce a Quaryndoun.
*Conduus, an^ce a Quaryndon tre.
*Confectio, an^ce confyt.
*Confidencia, an^ce trust.
*Confido, an^ce to truste.
*Confinia, an^ce trypys.
*Confiria, an^ce confyrye.
*Confiria, an^ce confyrie.
*Confisco, an^ce to sese in the gyngyshonde.
*Conflatorium, an^ce an herth.
*Confortamen, an^ce confort.
*Conforto, an^ce to conforte & make myrthe.
[*Confusus, an^ce ashamed.]
*Conniveo, [an^ce to twynely.]
[*Congelima, an^ce prane.]
*Conophorum, an^ce a Costrell.
*Conqueror, an^ce plany.
[*Consida, an^ce Brovnwort.]
*Consobrini, an^ce systersones.
*Consolida, an^ce consowde
*Conspicamen, an^ce clene.
*Conspicacio, clenynge.
*Consternor, [an^ce to be astoned.]
*Contentor, an^ce to hold a payd.
*Contero, an^ce to breke or defoule.
*Contra, an^ce ayens.
*Contravaria, an^ce a luller.
*Contraversia, an^ce Debat.
*Contristor, an^ce to be made sory.
*Contus, an^ce a potstykke.
*Contutatus, an^ce yhyd.
*Contutator, an hydere.
*Conualesco, to rekevere.
*Cooperculum, an^ce a Covercule.
*Coopertorium, an^ce a coverlyt.
*Copula, an^ce a codde.
*Copularius, an^ce a cuple.
*Corgigatorium, an^ce a cherne.
*Corium, [an^ce an hyde.]
*Coriza, an^ce ryflynge of the nose.
*Coristerium, an^ce a barbyde.
*Corigia, an^ce a thwange.
*Cornale, an^ce a cornal.
*Cornicarius, an^ce an hornere.
*Corniculum, an^ce a cornet.
*Corniculatum, an^ce a blowyng wyth an horne.
*Cornix, an^ce a crowe.
Cornus, an hepetre.
*Cornubium, an^ce an hornpipe.
*Coronale, an^ce a cornal.
*Corporale, an^ce a corporas.
*Corptrix, an^ce a kardestere.
*Corrigiarius, a gyrdeler.
*Corrigiatus, an^ce Ithonged.
*Corrodium, an^ce a lyvereye.
*Corruca, an^ce a buntynge.
*Corulus, an^ce an haseltre.
*Costa, an^ce a ryb [et est instrumentum pistoris, a rybbere.]
*Costa pastalis, an^ce a doweryb.

Costus, [an^(ce) Costmarye.]
Cotagium, an^(ce) a cotage, or a cot.
Coutranus, slep to beth fet mete.
Crabo, an^(ce) a dore.
Cranium, an^(ce) the braynpanne.
Crapulo, [an^(ce) to surfet.]
Crariolum, an^(ce) a rake.
Cras, an^(ce) to morwe.
Crassipulum, Crassipularium, Crucibolum, an^(ce) a Cresset.
Crassula, an^(ce) orpyne.
Crassula minor, an^(ce) Crawsope.
Crates, an^(ce) an hyrdyl.
Craticulatum, an^(ce) a latyse.
Creagra, [an^(ce) an owel.]
[*Crepidium, an^(ce)* Clowtys.]
Crepita, a boote.
Crepundarius, an^(ce) a rokkere.
Crepundaria, an^(ce) a rokkestere.
Cresco, an^(ce) to wexe or growe.
Creta, an^(ce) chaalke.
[*Cressula, an^(ce)* Mader.]
Cretifico, an^(ce) to marly.
Certificatum (so MS.), *an^(ce)* marle.
Certificatio, an^(ce) marlynge.
Cribrum, an^(ce) a rydder *vel* a syve.
Criminor, an^(ce) to blame, or be blamed.
Crisma, an^(ce) creyme.
Crispus, [an^(ce) cryps.]
Crispatura vel Crispacium, quoddam genus cibi est, an^(ce) Crispes.
Croceus, an^(ce) yelwe.
Crosia, an^(ce) a swal ponde.
Crucibolum, an^(ce) a cresset.
Crucifixum, an^(ce) a Crucifix.
Cruma, an^(ce) a pouche.
Crurale, an^(ce) a Quysson.
Crusto, an^(ce) to tynky.
Crustator, an^(ce) a tynkere.
Crustellum, [an^(ce) a cruste.]
Cubile [an^(ce) a cuche.]
Cubitus, an^(ce) an Elbowe.
Cuculo, to crye as a Cokow.
Cucumer, *an^(ce)* a Goorde.
Culcitra, *an^(ce)* a Quylte.
Culex, an^(ce) a Gnat.
Cultellus, an^(ce) a knyfe.

Cultrus, [an^(ce) a Cultur.]
Cumularius, an^(ce) a muwyer.
Cunabulator et Cunabulatrix, a rokkere & a rokkestere.
Cunctitenens, an^(ce) almyghty.
Cuneus, [an^(ce) a wegge.]
Cuniculus, an^(ce) a Conynge.
Cunio, an^(ce) undermyne.
Cunus, [a wegge.]
Cupa, an^(ce) a cupe, or a Cowle.
[*Cupatorium,* a worpynfat.]
Cuparius, an^(ce) a cowpare.
[*Cuprum, an^(ce)* Copar.]
Currax, an^(ce) lyght to renne.
Curtina, an^(ce) a curtyn.
Cu[r]ruca, an^(ce) an heysugge.
Curvo, an^(ce) to croke.
Cuspis, an^(ce) a Soket.
Cuscute, an^(ce) Doder.
Custus, an^(ce) costys.
Cutum, an^(ce) Donge.
Cuva, an^(ce) a cuve or a vaat.

Dacia, an^(ce) Denmarke.
Dalmatica, an^(ce) a tunycle.
Dampnis, an^(ce) a loreytre.
Damus, an^(ce) a bukke.
Dama, an^(ce) a doo.
Dea, an^(ce) a goddesse.
Debacor, an^(ce) to wex wilde.
Decaudo, to kytte of the tayle.
Decet, an^(ce) hyt semyth.
Deciduus, an^(ce) lygtly fallen.
Decius, an^(ce) a des.
Decresco, an^(ce) to wanye.
Dedignacio, an^(ce) dysdeygne.
Defectus, an^(ce) a defawte.
Deforis, an^(ce) bethowte.
Degaudeo, an^(ce) to ioye by hynde.
Degelo, [an^(ce) to thawe.]
Degener, an^(ce) vnkynde.
Delibero, an^(ce) to delyuery or to a = vyse.
Delibutus, an^(ce) be bawdyd or vntyd.
Deliciositas, an^(ce) delyte.
Delicius, an^(ce) a Cokeney.
Delicium, an^(ce) Delyte.
Deluo, an^(ce) to wasty awey.

Deluvius, an^ce a floode.
Demullo, an^ce to drede.
Denariatus, an^ce a Penyworthe.
Denique, an^ce at laste, or forsothe.
Dentrix, an^ce a pyke.
Denuncio, an^ce to shewe.
Depastino, to do away grapys.
Depositor, an^ce a sewer.
Deprecor, an^ce to beseche, pray.
Depetro, to by hynde stonde.
Deprimo, an^ce to cast doun.
Deprope, an^ce fro ny.
Deputo, an^ce to ordeyne *vel an^ce* to trowe.
Derelinquo, an^ce to forsake.
Desperacio, an^ce wanhope.
Destruo, an^ce to destruye, or waste.
Deturpo, an^ce to defoule.
Devenio, an^ce to come fro.
Devolvo, an^ce to turne vpsodoun.
Deus, an^ce god.
Dextrarius, an^ce a stede.
Diafragmen, an^ce the mydryf.
[*Diametrus,* a duble metre.]
Diaphosia, sunuoys *vel melius* soun of voys.
Dictatura, an^ce dytynge.
Difficilimus, an^ce hardest.
Digitale, an^ce a themyl.
Dignosus, an^ce worthy.
Dinodium, an^ce a lytyl hulle.
Discrusus, curyng ouer.
Diplois, [*an^ce* a dublet.]
Diptania, an^ce dytayne.
[*Dironomon, an^ce* a kervare.]
Discinctus, an^ce ungyrd.
Discingo, an^ce to ungyrd.
Discredentia, an^ce mysbyleve.
Discretinus, an^ce skylful.
Discrimen, [*an^ce* þe shode of the hed.]
Discriminale, [*an^ce* an herstrenge.[1]]
[*Disco,* to make dyshys.]
[*Disgerbigator, an^ce* a Teddere.]
Dispensa, an^ce a spense, *vel an^ce* spendynge.

Displico, an^ce to displaye.
Displicatus, an^ce displayd.
Displiceo, an^ce to dysplese.
Dispondeo, an^ce to by hote or trowthe.
Dissimulo, an^ce to lykeny or feyne or myslykene.
Distillo, an^ce to stylle or droppe.
Distrigio, an^ce to stryde.
[*Ditanus, an^ce* dytayne.[2]]
[*Divinacio, an^ce* wychecraft.]
Docillus, an^ce a dussel.
Doctificus, an^ce makyng wys.
Dola, i. docillus, an^ce a dosel.
Doma, [*an^ce* the ryggynge.]
Domicilium, an^ce Ouese.
Domina, an^ce a lady.
Dominus, a lord.
Dominatus, an^ce a lordshyp.
Dominus legum, an^ce a man of lawe.
Donativum, [*an^ce* a waryson.]
Dormito, [*an^ce* to nappe.]
Dormitorium, an^ce a Doortur.
Dorsorium, an^ce a dorsere.
Draganti, an^ce vytryole, or coporose.
Dragetum, an^ce drageye.
Dromo, an^ce a dromond.
[*Dromus, an^ce* sharp wyn.]
Duca, an^ce a leste, or a molde.
Dulcia, an^ce Ducettus.
Dulcor, an^ce swetnesse.
Duricies, [*an^ce* hardnesse.]

Ebulus, an^ce walwort.
Eciam, an^ce forsothe.
E contra, [*an^ce* ayeward.]
Edentator, an^ce a tothdrawere.
Edepol, by the hous of edepol.
Edia, an^ce Ese.
Educamen, an^ce a teme of checonn.
Educamentum, an^ce brodynge.
Edulia, an^ce sowell.
Edus, an^ce a kyde.
Effodio, an^ce to dyke, or delve.
Effosso, an^ce to dygge up.
Egeator, an^ce a comander of a shyp.
Egestas, an^ce nede.

---

[1] This article is inserted in the margin. [2] In margin.

[Eleborus, an^ce byshyppeswort.]
[Eleborus niger, an^ce longwort.]
Electum, an^ce a lefe of goolde.
Elephantus, [an olyfaunt.]
Elixer, a mater of metall in alcomye.
Emiperus, an^ce a sprot.
Emolumentum, [an^ce tolle.]
Emula, an^ce a dokke.
Emungo, an^ce to quenche.
Emunctus, an^ce a queynte.
Encletico, to bowe.
Enula campana, an^ce horshelyn.
[Enula, an^ce scabwort.]
Enulus, an^ce a fawn.
Epatica, an^ce lyverwort.
Epaticum, an^ce a lyverpaddyng.
Epallio, to ordeyne.
Epefio, to hamb.
Ephimera, an^ce a sperlynge.
Epyfemur, an^ce breygyrdyl.
Epyglotum, an^ce the throtebolle.
Epyphanes, an^ce god schewynge.
Epyphium, an^ce an hamborwe.
Epyphio, an^ce to hamburwe.
Epitogium, an^ce a gowne.
Equicium, an^ce a rake [a level.] [et an^ce haras.]
Equiferus, [an^ec an hakeneyman.]
Equidromium, an^ce a rake.
Equilibrum, an^ce a lewel.
Equillus, an^ce an hakeney.
Equitibia, an^ce a kambrell.
Erarius, an^ce a brasyer.
Erifilum, an^ce Braswyre.
Eripio, an^ce to delyvere.
Erpica, an^ce an harwe.
[Eruus, an^ce quechyn.]
Eruca, an^ce whytpyper [vel skyrwyt.]
Erudero, an^ce to myne.
Erula, an^ce the core.
Escaria, an^ce Dresserbord.
Escarium, an^ce ees.
Estaurinus, an^ce a Gurnard.
Esursum, an^ce fro above.
Esustum, an^ce brende bras calce- monie.
Eticies, a voys to answere.
Euado, an^ce to a skapye.

Euaneo, an^ce to vanshe a wey.
Evaporo, an^ce to wexe hote.
Euersum iri, [an^ce go to be turnyd vpsedoun] [sic dicitur amatum iri go to be loued.]
Euersum, an^ce vpsodoun.
Euidens, an^ce cler opyn.
Eulogio, an^ce to prayse and alowe.
Eugenes, an^ce noble wytty.
Eupatorium, an^ce ambrosye, or wylde sauge.
Eupatica, an^ce lyuerwort.
Euiro, an^ce to gylle.
Euitaneus, an^ce wythoute ende.
Eupheamismos, an^ce good chaungynge.
Exactor, an^ce a puruyour.
Examitum, an^ce a myte, or an Amys.
Exancio, an^ce to vnbynde.
Exardeo, an^ce to brenne.
Exarmigio, to make faste.
Excerpno, an^ce to clense.
Excessus, an^ce excesse, passynge oute, or surmountynge.
Excludo, to shut oute.
Excoquo, an^ce to sethe brenne or purge.
Excudio, an^ce to squyngyl.
[Excudia, a swyngylstok.]
Excussorium, an^ce a swyngelstok.
Exestuo, an^ce to wexe hote, or byle.
Exhumo, to vnberye.
Exorrior, an^ce to be born, or sprynge.
Expello, an^ce to put oute.
Expericlus, an^ce a squyrel.
Expollio, an^ce to pulshe, or furby.
Expugno, an^ce to bete doun, overcome.
Exsacco, an^ce to vnsacke.
Exscaturizo, an^ce to scaldy.
Exsucco, an^ce to drawe out Iuse.
Exterius, an^ce wythoute.
Extinguo, an^ce to quenche.
Extollo, an^ce to bere up, or to hye.
Extraduco, an^ce to lede out.
[Extunc, an^ce fro thanne.]

Fabafresa, an^ce a spelked bene.
Fabrica, an^ce a forge.
Fabricatus, an^ce y forged.
Facimia, an^ce a forspeker or a tylystere.
Faculo, an^ce to make faget.
Facuminaria, an^ce a lullere.
Fagus, an^ce a beche.
Fala, an^ce Brytage.
Falco, an^ce to repe, or mowe.
Falerarius, an^ce a sompterhors.
Falerator, an^ce a sompterman.
Fanula, an^ce a fanon.
Farraga, an^ce forrage.
Farcimen, an^ce Farsure.
Faricapsa, an^ce a bynne.
Farina, an^ce mele.
Farna, an^ce a forme.
Farracio, an^ce Melwynge.
Farrago, an^ce forage.
Fascennina, i. femina que novit incantare; an^ce a tylyester.
Faselus, an^ce a galey.
Fatesco, an^ce to ffayle to feble to wexe weyry.
Favonius, [the west wynde.]
Febrimacio, an^ce sturrynge of londe.
Fecontria, an^ce a martret.
[*Fedorarius, an^ce* a fewtrer.]
Fel, an^ce galle.
Felicitas, an^ce selyhede.
[*Feltrum, an^ce* ffelt.]
Femorale, an^ce a strapul.
Fenestra, an^ce a wyndowe.
Fenestrale, an^ce a ffenestral.
Fenissa, an^ce an heymakere.
Feniseca, an^ce a mowere.
Fenicarius, an^ce a theseler.
Fenile, an^ce an heyrek.
Fere, an^ce almost.
Ferecia, an^ce a quylte.
[*Fersura, an^ce* fetherveye *sed melius* febrifuga.]
Ferina, an^ce venesoun.
Feritorium, an^ce a batyndore.
Ferme, an^ce almost.
Ferrarius, [*an^ce* a ferrour.]
Ferrifilum, an^ce wyre of yre.

Ferrus, an^ce an hors schoo.
Ferrarius, an^ce an yreworchere or an yremongere, or a ferrour.
Feruca, an^ce a throstylkock.
Festuca, an^ce the blaad of corn, or a strawe.
Festum, [*an^ce* the furst.]
Fetuntrus, an^ce a fulmere.
Fetontria, an^ce a martron.
Fibula, a tache or a laas [or a botun].
Ficedula, an^ce a rooke.
Fidelica, an^ce a cherne.
Fidicen, [*an^ce* a fydelere.]
Filatrix, an^ce a spynnester.
[*Filiandra,* gosesomere.]
Filica, an^ce a kote.
Fillis, an^ce a ffylbertre.
[*Fillum,* a ffylbert.]
Filix, an^ce fferon.
Filtrum, an^ce a quylte, or a materas.
Fimbria, an^ce an hem.
Financia, an^ce a ffynaunce.
Firmaculum, an^ce a clapse, or a broche.
Firmacularius, an^ce a brouche = makere.
Fiola, an^ce a ffyole or a cruet.
[*Firmatius,* a loof.]
Firmamenta, an^ce takelynge.
Fistulista, an^ce a Pypere.
Fixura, an^ce prykkynge or festenynge.
Flabellum, an^ce a swyvyer.
Flabrum, [a blast.]
Flagellator, an^ce a threschere.
Flagellum, an^ce a ffleyle, or a scorge.
Flagito, an^ce to axe or aske beseche wyth cry.
Flameum, an^ce kerchef.
[*Flaketta,* a flaket.]
[*Flammula, an^ce* sperwort.]
Flasca, an^ce fflagot.
Flato, an^ce a flavon.
Flecto, an^ce to wrynge mony.
Flexarius, an^ce a floccher.
Florenus, an^ce a ffloreyn.
Florencius, an^ce a goldfynche.
Fluctus, a flode.

Foca, an^ce a Porpays.
Focale, an^ce fewel.
Folliculus, an^ce a flexhoppe.
Fongia, an^ce stokfyshe.
Fontinella, an^ce the nekke putte.
Forago, an^ce a lyste, or a purrel.
Foramen, an^ce an hol.
Forarium, an^ce an hedelonde.
Foresta, an^ce a forest.
Forestarius, a forstere.
Forefactura, an^ce a forfet.
Formella, [an^ce a forme.]
Formipedium, an^ce a leste.
Formosus, an^ce Welshape.
Formula, an^ce a leste or a lytyl molde.
Formula, an^ce a fforme.
Forulus, an^ce a forel.
Fossa, an^ce a dyche.
Fosso, to dyche.
Fossorium, an^ce a moolde
Fovea, an^ce a dyche.
Fractillus, an^ce a rag, or a dag.
Fraculus, an^ce a Pyperquerne.
Fragilius, an^ce a grate.
Fragmen, an^ce brokemete.
Fragus, an^ce the wryste, or a knokyl.
Fragum, an^ce a strebery.
Fragus, an^ce a streberytre.
Francursina, an^ce Berefot.
Fraria, an^ce a brotherhede.
[*Fratruelus,* a broþer sone.]
[*Fratruela,* a broþer dowter.]
Fraxinus, an^ce asche.
Frequento, an^ce to haunte.
Fretum, i. feruor maris, an^ce a walke.
Frico, an^ce to frote.
Frigellus, an^ce a rudduk.
Frigeo, [to wexe colde.]
Frigilla, an^ce a rudduk.
Frigmareventus, an^ce Wynchelsee.
[*Fringulus,* a grundyl.]
Frigucio, an^ce [to Oyvery or quake.]
Frixa, an^ce a colhoppe, or a smachecok.
Frixum, an^ce a ffrytour.
Frixatura, an^ce fryynge *vel quod frigitur,* an^ce a ffroyse.

Frondator, an^ce an hekemose.
Frontale, an^ce a frontell.
Frugella, an^ce a rooke.
Frumentum, [an^ce whete.]
Frunito, an^ce to tanny
Frunitor, a Tanner.
Frunitorium, a tanhous
Frutex, [underwode.]
Fuga, an^ce a chas, or a fleynge.
[*Fugarius,* a dryvere or a drovare.]
Fugius, a drone & gret.
Fulgur, an^ce the leme that brennyth.
Fulica, an^ce a Semewe.
Fuligo, [an^ce soot.]
Fumus, [an^ce smoke.]
Fumus terre, an^ce fumytere.
Fundator, an^ce a ffounder or slynger.
Fundulus, **an^ce** a looche.
Fungia, an^ce Stokfysh.
Fungea, quidam panis [koket.] *Item, i. boletus. Item* an^ce a taddechese.
Fungus, a ffynch [*vel* an Estrich, *secundum quosdam.*]
Funifex, an^ce a ropere.
Furfura, an^ce the scales of the hede or berde.
Furniculus, an^ce a fferet.
Fuscus, an^ce broun.
Fuscamen, an^ce ffustayn or ffustyan.
Fustibulum, an^ce a stafslynge.
Fusus, an^ce a spyndel.
Fusura, an^ce spynnynge.

Gagas, an^ce Geet.
Galanga, an^ce Galyngale.
Gallacia, an^ce blancmanger.
Galla, an^ce a kokkescombe.
Gallus, an^ce a Cok.
[*Galliare,* an^ce a chapelet.]
[*Galus, li, hec. i. soror mariti sororis mee,* an^ce my systerys husbande syster.]
Gallitricum, an^ce clareye.
Galliprelium, an^ce kokkysfythynge.
Gamarus, an^ce a banstikyl.
[*Gannerius,* an^ce a bannynge.]
Garba, an^ce a Shefe.
Garcio, an^ce a grome.

*Gardicus, an*ᶜᵉ a wardeyn.
*Gariofilata, an*ᶜᵉ auens *vel* gilofre.
*Gariofilus, an*ᶜᵉ Cloves.
*Garus, an*ᶜᵉ greue.
*Garennia, an*ᶜᵉ wareyne.
*Garriofila, an*ᶜᵉ glowgelofre.
*Gavata, an*ᶜᵉ a bolle.
*Gaudeo, an*ᶜᵉ woode or madur.
*Gelicidium, an*ᶜᵉ thawe.
Gello, **an**ᶜᵉ **a** cherle.
[*Gelopto,* **an**ᶜᵉ to waloppe.]
Gemo, [*an*ᶜᵉ to wayle.]
Gentiana, [*an*ᶜᵉ stanmerche.]
Genesa, a bond of cloth.
*Genesta, an*ᶜᵉ brome.
*Genetaliacus, an*ᶜᵉ a tellere of kynde.
[*Geralogodion, an*ᶜᵉ Tryacle.]
*Gerio, an*ᶜᵉ to ordeyne.
[*Gerlinus, a, um, an*ᶜᵉ sherlokked *et dicitur de equo.*]
[*Gerolotista, an*ᶜᵉ a sompturman.]
*Gerra, an*ᶜᵉ a doggedraue.
*Gerusa, an*ᶜᵉ a goode, *vel an*ᵉᵉ a Gesarme.
Gibbus, [*an*ᶜᵉ kybe.]
*Giga, an*ᶜᵉ a gytterne.
*Gingium, an*ᶜᵉ Gyngebred.
*Gipsum, an*ᶜᵉ cley or morter.
*Giraculum, an*ᶜᵉ a trendel.
*Girgillus, an*ᶜᵉ a reel.
Girgillo, [*an*ᶜᵉ to rele.]
Glabella, [*an*ᶜᵉ the schulle.]
Glabra, **an**ᶜᵉ a scalle.
Glabrosus, scalled.
*Gladiatura, an*ᶜᵉ a swerdpleyynge, or bokeler pleyynge.
Glans, a slyngston.
*Glaucus, an*ᶜᵉ gelu.
Glimo, to be gyle.
Glis, [*an*ᶜᵉ a glonsers.]
*Glomus, an*ᶜᵉ a clewe.
*Glorior, an*ᶜᵉ to ioye.
*Glosa, an*ᶜᵉ a loche.
*Glustrum, an*ᶜᵉ Cowslyppe.
*Glutinum, an*ᶜᵉ glewe.
*Gobio, an*ᶜᵉ a gurnard *vel secundum alios* a goioun.
*Gomerus, an*ᶜᵉ a banstykyl.

*Gracilis, an*ᶜᵉ smal.
Gracillo, to cakele as an hen.
*Graculus, an*ᶜᵉ a Jaye.
[*Gracus,* a whytynge.]
*Gramen, an*ᶜᵉ gras.
Gran, **a wryt.**
*Grana paradisi, an*ᶜᵉ grayn de parys.
*Granomellum, an*ᶜᵉ growte, *vel* wort.
*Granum solis, an*ᶜᵉ Gromylle.
[*Grapa,* an hol to putte yn a barre.]
*Gratarium, an*ᶜᵉ a grate.
*Gratanter, an*ᶜᵉ gladly.
*Grato, an*ᶜᵉ to cracche.
*Gravitudo et Gravitas et Gravedo, an*ᶜᵉ hevynesse.
*Gravia, an*ᶜᵉ the hewe, or the webbe.
*Gregarius, an*ᶜᵉ a fflockere, *et est canis pastoris.*
Gregatim, **an**ᶜᵉ **to gedyr.**
Gressenus, **an**ᶜᵉ **a brokke.**
Griseus, **an**ᶜᵉ grey.
*Grossitas, an*ᶜᵉ Gretenesse.
*Grunnus, an*ᶜᵉ a gruyn, or a wrot.
*Grus, an*ᶜᵉ a Craan.
Gulio, [a gyle.]
*Gumma arabica, an*ᶜᵉ **Gumme arabyk.**
Gurtus, **an**ᶜᵉ a were.
*Guttatus, an*ᶜᵉ pomeled *ut equus.*
*Gutta, an*ᶜᵉ a drope.
*Guttorium, an*ᶜᵉ a guttur.
*Guttulus, an*ᶜᵉ Menuse.
*Gutturna, an*ᶜᵉ Quynsy.

*Habena, an*ᶜᵉ a rayne.
*Hac, an*ᶜᵉ hydur *vel* hydurward.
*Hactenus, an*ᶜᵉ hydur to *vel* in to thys tyme.
Hasta, [a shaft.]
*Hastule, an*ᶜᵉ Stykkes.
Hauritorium, [*an*ᶜᵉ a boket] *vel an*ᶜᵉ a ladell.
Hausorium, [*an*ᶜᵉ a boket.]
Hedera, [*an*ᶜᵉ yvy.]
*Henociani, an*ᶜᵉ stronge geantes.
*Herbagium, an*ᶜᵉ herbage.
[*Herba paralisis, an*ᶜᵉ Couslyppe.]
*Herbiseca, an*ᶜᵉ a mowere.
*Herbarius, an*ᶜᵉ a teddere.

Hereditas, an^ce herytage.
Herniosus, an^ce brokyn.
Hic, an^ce here.
Hyemo, an^ce to wyntry.
Hyematus, an^ce acumelyd.
Hymnare, [a hymnale.]
Hylle, an^ce trypys.
Hinc, an^ce hennys.
Hyo, [to galpe.]
Hornulus, an^ce sumdel orible.
Horreo, [to agryse.]
Hostio, an^ce to stryche.
Hostorium, a stryche.
Huc, an^ce hydur, *vel* hydyrward.
Humano, an^ce to clothe yn manhede.
Humecto, an^ce to moyste.
Humeralis, [*an^ce* a spanbelere.]
Humerus, an^ce a shuldur.
Humilio, to a bowe.
Humor, an^ce moystnesse.
Huscus, an^ce an holme.

Jacinctinus, an^ce ynde colour.
Jaculum, [*an^ce* a dart.]
[*Jam nunc, an^ce* rygth nov *vel* nov nov.]
Jam tunc, an^ce nowe thanne, *vel* nowe as thanne.
Jarus, an^ce Cokkupyntel *et an^ce* Calvysfote.
Icarpa, an^ce a wolletoppe.
Iconomia, an^ce husbondrye.
Ictericia, an^ce the Jawnes.
Ideo, an^ce therfore *vel* forthat.
Idio, an^ce a clynche of gres.
Jecur, an^ce the mawe.
Jejuno, an^ce to vaste.
Jesa, an^ce a gesarme.
[*Ignacia,* a chesekake.]
Ignitegium, an^ce keuerfve.
Ile, [*an^ce* the pythe of a penne.]
Ilex, an^ce a traytour.
Illicitus, an^ce vnbehouely *vel* vnlefful.
Illitus, an^ce bydavbyd.
Illorsum, an^ce thydyrward.
Illuc, an^ce thydur, *vel* thydyrward.
Illudo, an^ce to scorne, or deceyue.
Imber, an^ce a shure.

[*Imnale et Imnarium, an^ce* an ymnere.]
Impaciens, an^ce vnbuxum.
Impedio, an^ce to lette.
[*Impedia, an^ce* an ouerlether.]
Impeto, an^ce to asayle.
Impetus et Impes, an^ce a folhaste.
Impinguo, an^ce to fatty.
Impinguo, an^ce to do a way drye shabbe.
Implico, an^ce to emplye, to folde yn.
Imposterum, an^ce hereafterwarde.
Impotens, an^ce unmyghty.
Impotencia, an^ce feblenesse.
Impromptus, an^ce unredy.
Improprium, an^ce unpropre.
Imputo, an^ce to a twyte.
In ante [fro hennes forthward.]
Inarto, an^ce to yoke.
Incanto, an^ce to enchaunte.
Incaustorium, an^ce an ynkehorn.
Incommodo, to make wrake.
Incredulus, an^ce unlefable.
Incredulitas, an^ce unbylefe.
Incrudo, to make rawe.
Incurro, to ren yn.
Incussorium, an^ce a causer, *quidam malleolus est.*
Inde [therby.]
Indignor, an^ce to dysdeyne.
Indomitus, an^ce vntame, wylde.
[*Indela, an^ce* a gelet.]
Induro, an^ce to make harde.
Infernas, an^ce a vende of helle.
Infigo, an^ce to styke.
Infula, an^ce a chesyble.
Infundo, an^ce to gete in.
Inglorio, an^ce to unmerthe.
Inguen, an^ce the grynde.
Inicio, an^ce atamye.
Inicius, bygynnynge.
[*Inicius, cia, cium, an^ce* bygynnynge.]
Innaturalitas, an^ce vnkyndenesse.
Innodius, an^ce the nave of wheole.
Innumerus, an^ce wythoute numbre.
Insequor, an^ce to folwe.
Insero, an^ce to plante to gedyr, or brace to gedyr, or graffe.

Insidior, an^(ce) to traye, or aspye seytfully.
Insigne, an^(ce) a Cote armere.
Insitus, an^(ce) planted or graffed.
Inspiro, an^(ce) to enspyre.
Instita . . . . quedam vestis talaris, que dicitur stola, an^(ce) a roket.
Intellectus, an^(ce) vnderstondynge.
Inter, an^(ce) bytwene.
Interamentum, an^(ce) entraylys.
Interclausum, an^(ce) an enterclos.
Interclusorium, an^(ce) a pyndefolde.
Interdico, an^(ce) interdyte.
Interea, an^(ce) the mene whyle.
Interfinium, an^(ce) the grystell of the nose.
Interim, an^(ce) the menwhyle.
Internodium, an^(ce) the knepanne, or wherlebon.
Interrogo, an^(ce) to axe, or enquyre.
Interula, [an^(ce) a smok.]
Intestinum, [an^(ce) guttys.]
Intrepidus, an^(ce) bold.
Invenio, an^(ce) to fynde.
Invetero, an^(ce) to be olde.
Invicem, an^(ce) to geder, to hepe.
Inunco, an^(ce) to faste with an hoke.
Inuolutarium, an^(ce) a voluper.
Inurbanitas, an^(ce) vylonye.
Jocale, an^(ce) a jewel.
Iperica, an^(ce) seynt Johnys worte.
Ipoletum, an^(ce) a mawe.
Ipopirgium, an^(ce) andyre.
Iratus, an^(ce) wroth.
Irreveror, an^(ce) to unworshepy.
Iris, an^(ce) *dicitur* flourdelys *et Ireos,* an^(ce) gladyyn.
Irudo, an^(ce) a waterleche.
Irruo, an^(ce) to falle in.
Isophagus, an^(ce) the weysande.
Istac, an^(ce) herawey.
Juba, an^(ce) a mane.
Juliafera, an^(ce) a yong hynde.
Juncata, an^(ce) Juncade, *sive* a crudde ymade yn ryshes.
Junctura, an^(ce) a Juynt.
Jussellum, quidam cibus factus ex ovis et lacte, an^(ce) Jussell.
Jusquiamus, mi, qui et Insania dicitur, herba est, an^(ce) hennebane.
[*Justiciarius,* an^(ce) a Justyse.]
Justicius, an^(ce) ryghtful.
Justorium, an^(ce) a clappe of the mylle.
Jutto, an^(ce) to Jutteye.
Jutum, an^(ce) Jutus.
Knipulus, i. parvus cultellus, an^(ce) a knyvet.

Labina, [an^(ce) a myre.]
Labedo, an^(ce) a blotte.
Laciferis, an^(ce) a newe shappere.
Lacinia, [an^(ce) a gore.]
Lactis, an^(ce) a chesleb.
Lactes, an^(ce) roof of fyshe, or mylke of fyshe.
Lactissinium, an^(ce) whyt mete.
[*Lactis,* an^(ce) rennet, or rennynge.]
Lactitarium, an^(ce) charlet.
[*Lattrinum,* an^(ce) laton.]
Lacunar, an^(ce) a lase [or a louer.]
Laganum, an^(ce) a pancake.
Laero, -ronis, est quoddam animal pilosum ut Cuniculus [*secundum alios* a wylde cat.]
Laguncula, an^(ce) a potel.
Lama, a plate [*Item lama,* sleybrede.]
Lameres, an^(ce) Elmawes.
[*Lamina calibina,* an^(ce) a Gad of stele.]
[*Lanceolata,* an^(ce) Rybwort.]
Lanix, an^(ce) a sherde.
Lanugo, an^(ce) a loke of wulle.
Lappa, an^(ce) a clote.
Lapacia, [an^(ce) the rededokke.]
Lapicidium, an^(ce) a quarrey.
Lappates dicitur cibus ex oleribus factus, an^(ce) Jutes.
Laquearia, an^(ce) a lase.
Laqueus, an^(ce) a lace *vel* an^(ce) a grene.
Lardum, an^(ce) laard.
Lata, an^(ce) a lache.
[*Lazulum,* an^(ce) azure.]
Laterale, an^(ce) a Corset.
[*Latoma,* an^(ce) a stonax.]
Latus, an^(ce) a syde.

Latrocinium, an*ce* thefte.
Lauacrum, [an*ce* a lauer.]
Lauandria, an*ce* lauandre.
Laurus, an*ce* a loreytre.
Laxa, an*ce* a lees.
Lechitus, an*ce* an elevat.
Lectisternium, an*ce* bed clothes.
Lectiuncula, an*ce* a lessun.
Legatus, an*ce* a legat.
Legenda, an*ce* a legende.
Lena, an*ce* a bawde.
Lenochides, an*ce* mercury.
Lens, an*ce* a nyte.
Lenticula, [an*ce* a pokke.] *Item est vas oliarium ex auro et argento* [an*ce* a crismatorye, or an Elvat.]
Lentigo, i. lenticula, [frekun.]
Lentiscus, an*ce* a beeche.
Leporarius, [a grehunde.]
Lepido, to speke fayre.
Lepus, [an hare.]
Lepusculus, [an*ce* a leveret.]
Lesca, an*ce* a shefure of brede [or of fleys or fyshe or a leshe.]
[*Lesco*, to leshe.]
Leuia, an*ce* a spanne.
Libertinus, [an*ce* a frankelayn.]
Libertas, an*ce* ffredom.
Libum, an*ce* a wastell.
Lichinus, an*ce* the weke of a candele.
Lichinus, -na, -num, an*ce* gnast of candele.
Liciatorium, an*ce* a tredel.
[*Licisca*, a grebyche.]
Licium, [a throme.]
Lienteria, an*ce* the flux.
Ligeus, an*ce* lygeman.
Ligeancia, an*ce* lygeance.
[*Lignipedium*, an*ce* a stylte.]
Ligumen, an*ce* Grewell.
Ligustrum, an*ce* a primerose.
Lima, an*ce* a vyle.
Limaca et limax, an*ce* a snayl.
Limas, an*ce* a barmclothe.
Limatorium, an*ce* lytarge or lymayle.
Limax, i. limaca, an*ce* a snayle.
Limen, an*ce* a thresfolde.
Limes, the cop of an hylle.

Limo, an*ce* a rygwythe.
[*Linguagium*, an*ce* langage.]
[*Lingua avis*, an*ce* stychwort.]
[*Lingua bovis*, oxtunge.]
[*Lingua canis*, an*ce* hundystonge.]
[*Lingua cervi*, an*ce* hertystonge.]
Lingulo, an*ce* to slynge.
Linipes, an*ce* lynfet.
Linipulus, an*ce* a streche of flaxe.
Linodium, an*ce* a flexhoppe.
Linosina, an*ce* a curtyn.
Lintheamen, an*ce* a shete.
Linum, [flex.]
Lippo, an*ce* to watery with ye.
Liridus, i. diversi coloris, an*ce* Pykeled.
Liripipium, an*ce* a typet.
Lista, an*ce* Segge.
Litatorium, an*ce* a slykston.
Litor, an*ce* a dauber.
Lituus, an*ce* a lylkynghorn.
Locax, an*ce* a brace.
Locium, an*ce* lye, or pysse.
Locusta, an*ce* a honysouke.
Lodix, an*ce* a blanket.
Lodium, an*ce* a lover.
Loligo, [a codelynge.]
Lolium, [cokkul.]
Lolidodium, an*ce* a kartsadell.
Longanimitas, an*ce* longnesse of soule, or durynge.
Lorimarius, an*ce* a sporyare, or a lormener.
Lotrix, an*ce* a lauander.
[*Lubrica, -ce*, aruwbale.]
Lucanica, [frankemyl.]
Lucar, [an*ce* a park.]
Lucarius, an*ce* a fforstere, [or a parkare.]
Lucterinus, an*ce* an Otyr.
Lucetum, an*ce* Wareyne.
Lucibricunculum, an*ce* a fforborystok.
Luciferum, an*ce* the day sterre.
Lucinus, an*ce* a luce.
Lucillus, an*ce* a pyke.
Luctor, [an*ce* to wraxle.]
Luctuosus, an*ce* ful of mornynge.
Lucubrax, wonynge of monythe.

Ludus, an^{ce} a game or a pleye.
Lugeo, [an^{ce} to grone.]
Lumbricus, an^{ce} a maddock.
Lumbus, an^{ce} the lende.
Lupinus, [an^{ce} Tylles.]
Lupus, [an^{ce} a wolf] Item an^{ce} a pyke.
Lurcisca, an^{ce} a luyre.
[Lurcisco, an^{ce} to luyre.]
Luteus, an^{ce} skarlet.
Lutericius, [an Oter.]
Lutus, an^{ce} skarlet.
Luxiuium, an^{ce} lye.
Luxidromium, an^{ce} a broke.

Machera, an^{ce} a dressurenyf.
Macianus, a crabbetre.
Macianum, a crabbe.
Macula, an^{ce} a mayl.
Mafora, an^{ce} a voluper.
Maglis, an^{ce} a cavlstok.
Magnitudo, an^{ce} gretnesse.
Majus, an^{ce} more.
Malaxo, an^{ce} to cnede.
Male, an^{ce} wykkedly.
Malvia, an^{ce} the ebbe.
Malum macianum, an^{ce} a Crabbe.
Malum quiriacum, an^{ce} a Costard.
Malus, an^{ce} a maste.
Mamphora, an^{ce} a mokedore.
Mammonetus, an^{ce} a marmoset.
Mandarus, an^{ce} a wortstoke.
Mango, an^{ce} a cursure.
Manglisa, an^{ce} a choppechurche.
Mangonale, an^{ce} a mangnel, or a gunne.
Manerium, an^{ce} a manere.
Manica, [an^{ce} a manicle.]
Manicula, an^{ce} a Pynet [or Pyuet.]
Maniculo, [an^{ce} to manycle.]
Mancipium, an^{ce} a spayre.
Mansio, an^{ce} a dwellynge.
Mantus, an^{ce} a metayn.
Manubium, an^{ce} a spayre.
Manubrium, an^{ce} an hafte.
Manulia, an^{ce} a spayere.
[Manuus, an^{ce} an hakneyman.]
Manutercium, an^{ce} an handstaf. Item an^{ce} an handele.

Manceres, an^{ce} a sylkethrede.
Marascallus, an^{ce} a Marchal.
Margus, an^{ce} a plovere.
Marito, an^{ce} to marye.
5 Maritagum, an^{ce} wedloke.
Marsupium, an^{ce} a pautener.
Martirologium, an^{ce} the martylogye.
Martrix, an^{ce} a martron.
Mastixo, [an^{ce} to chowe.]
10 Mastromaticus, an^{ce} a sothseyer.
Mataxo, an^{ce} to hychele.
Mataxa, an hychele.
Mataxator, mataxatrix, an hycheler.
Mataxarius, an hychelmaker.
15 Materfamilias, an^{ce} an huswyf.
Materacium, an^{ce} a materas.
Matertera, an^{ce} a beldame.
Matria, an^{ce} the panetrie.
Matrix, an^{ce} mader.
20 Mauiscus, an^{ce} a thryshe.
Mediamna, an^{ce} a moot.
Medo, [an^{ce} meth.]
Medum, an^{ce} mede.
Megarus, an^{ce} a makerel.
25 Meger, an^{ce} wode sek.
Melanurus, a merlynge vel ut quibusdam videtur a makerel.
Melaturus, an^{ce} a breme de mere.
Melessa, an^{ce} medeswote.
30 Mellilotum, an^{ce} hertyluere.
[Mellissa, an^{ce} Medewort.]
Melota, [an^{ce} a sclavayn.]
[Mellotum, an^{ce} threleuedgras.]
Membranarius, a perchymyner.
35 Mempirium, an^{ce} a wyps.
Mendium, an^{ce} a dressyngbord.
Mensaculum, an^{ce} a bordenyf.
Mensacula, an^{ce} a dressyngenyf.
Mensifium, an^{ce} a cuppebord.
40 Mensuro, an^{ce} to mesure.
[Mentascum, an^{ce} horsmynte.]
Menticulosus, [an^{ce} Ballukod.]
Mentum, an^{ce} a chyn.
Mephas, an^{ce} the mose.
45 Menusa, an^{ce} menuse.
Mercimonium, an^{ce} Merchaundyse.
Mercurialis, an^{ce} Mercurye.
Meremium, an^{ce} tymber.

Mergus, an^ce a Cormeraunt.
Ventus meridialis, an^ce Southwynde.
Merlinus, an^ce a merlyn.
Merula, an^ce a throstel.
Mespila, a medeler.
Messuaginm, an^ce a mesplace.
Metellus, an^ce a reperefe.
Micatorium, an^ce a grate.
Millefolium, an^ce Myllefoyle *vel* Noseblede.
Mimilogium, [*an^ce* mynstrisye.]
Mineria, an^ce a myne *vel* Ore *vel minera secundum quosdam et an^ce* ore . . ., as **gold** ore, syluer ore etc.
Minilo, an^ce to gye, or gouerne.
Minium, an^ce vermylon.
Mintuosa, an^ce Smerwort.
Minutal, [a kantel.]
Mirra, an^ce Maser.
[*Misothonium,* a Spytylhous.]
Missile, an^ce a shafte & a shetel & a gauelot.
Mixtilio, an^ce Draggeye.
Mixtus, an^ce medled.
Mola piperis, an^ce pyperquerne.
Molendinum, an^ce a mylle.
Molendinarius, an^ce a mylnard.
Mollis, *an^ce* neshe.
Molosus, [a blod honde.]
Moluerum, [the mylle spyndelle.]
Monacha, an^ce a nunne.
Mongotorium, an^ce Mongcorn.
Monicio, an^ce an heste, or warnynge.
Monitum, an^ce a byddynge, or a warnynge.
Mono, an^ce a maner of bef.
Moracia, [*an^ce* a walnote.]
Morbillus, an^ce the meseles.
Morella, an^ce Morelle.
Moris, an^ce a roche.
[*Morsus galline, an^ce* Chykemete.]
Morus, an^ce a mulberytre. *Item morus est quidam piscis, an^ce* an haddock.
Moticium, an^ce colys.
Motorium, an^ce a Potstykke.
Motus, an^ce sterynge.

Motus terre, an^ce erthequave.
Mucidus, an^ce yvyned.
Mucido, an^ce to **vynye**.
Muco, an^ce to movle.
5 *Mugil,* a myluel.
Mulcitrum, an^ce a payle.
Multicolor, an^ce Medle.
Multipes, an^ce a lokecheste, or a shrympe.
10 *Multo, an^ce* a wether or a moton.
[*Munella, an^ce* a shakel.]
Musculus, [*an^ce* the sperlyner.]
Mussetum, an^ce musserouns.
*Mussum, **an^ce*** endelyshame.
15 *Mustilio, an^ce* Mestylyon.
*Muta, **an^ce*** a meet of hundys.
[*Mutilamen,* a meym.]
Mutilatus, [*an^ce* meymed.]

20 *Nappa, an^ce* a rybbe.
Napta, an^ce herdys.
Napus, an^ce Nep.
Naris, an^ce a nose, or a Nostrel.
Nasturcium, [*an^ce* walcarse.]
25 *Nativus, an^ce* bonde.
Navigator, an^ce a rower.
Nebula, an^ce a wafur.
Nec, an^ce nouqt.
Nefandus, an^ce a cursed.
30 *Negligencia, an^ce* slowthe.
Negocius, -cij, hic dicitur demon nocturnus qui illudit homines, vel qui ludit cum hominibus, an^ce the game gobelyn.
35 *Neriges, est spiritus malignus torquens homines de nocte, an^ce* the mare *i. Epialtes.*
Neutropogoldium, an^ce a lumpe of brede.
40 *Nimius, an^ce* Overmyche.
Ninerus, an^ce a Cokewolde.
Nisi, an^ce but.
Nisilla, an^ce a lytyl shynynge.
Niscus, an^ce shynynge.
45 *Niseo, an^ce* to shyne.
Nitrum, [fullers cley.]
Nodus, an^ce a Cnotte, or a botun.
[*Nodosa,* a nosul, *avis est.*]

Noster, an*ce* owre.
Notio, an*ce* knowyng.
Noxa, an*ce* a gnawynge.
Nucha, an*ce* the hole of the polle.
[*Nubula*, a wafur.]
Nucleum, an*ce* rede pyle.
[*Nucifragus*, an*ce* a notehach.]
Nucleus, an*ce* the kernell.
Nudius tercius, thys day thre days.
Nudius quartus, thys day foure days.
Nullatenus, an*ce* no manere.
Nullo, an*ce* anoynter.
Numacius, an*ce* a penitollere.
Numella, an*ce* a shakel.
Nuncubi, an*ce* Now where.

Obba, genus est calicis, an*ce* a Juyste.
Obduro, an*ce* to make harde.
Obelo, to shete and smyte wyth a bolte.
Oblacio, an*ce* offerynge.
Oblecto, to lycoruse delyte.
Oblector, an*ce* to helpe, or delyte.
Oblata, an*ce* an obeley.
Obligar, an*ce* a gartur.
Obolatus, an*ce* an halfpeny worth.
Obprobrium, an*ce* despyte.
Obrigeo, an*ce* to be a ferd.
Obsequium, an*ce* buxumnesse, or servyse.
Obsitus, an*ce* by set a bowte, or plantyd a bowte.
Obstupefacio, an*ce* to make a ferd, or a gast.
[*Obstupesco*, an*ce* to wexe aferd, or dulle, or an egghe, *ut dentes filiorum obstupescunt.*]
Obvadio, to legge wagere.
[*Ocellulus*, an*ce* an ylet.]
Ocra, an*ce* Oker.
Ocrea, an*ce* a boot.
Odorinsequus, [a brachet or a spaynel.]
Oestrum, [an*ce* a brese.]
[*Officialis*, an*ce* an Offycyal.]
[*Olementum*, an*ce* the element.]
Olosa, an*ce* a breme, or an Alose.
Omasus, an*ce* a grete puddynge.

Omembrana, an*ce* a ballue cod.
Omentum, an*ce* a pauncheclout [*vel* Myggerne.]
Omestra, an*ce* a myggerne.
[*Omiplata*, an*ce* the shulderblad.]
Omo, an*ce* of o manere.
Omoplata, an*ce* the shulderbon.
Onoforium, a costrel.
Operarius, a werkman.
Operarium, an*ce* a shoppe or a werkehous.
[*Opifium*, an*ce* an hamburwe.]
[*Opiridium*, þe raye.]
Opploma, a targett. *Opplamacus*, an*ce* a peeler.
Orca, an*ce* a tankard.
Ordinale, an*ce* an ordynal.
Orditura, an*ce* warpe.
Orexis, an*ce* drevel.
Orexo, [an*ce* to dryvele.]
Orgeo, seynge wyth mowth.
Origo, an*ce* a berthe, or a begynnynge.
Oristrum, an*ce* a roket.
[*Orare*, an*ce* to hemny.]
Orobus, an*ce* a vech.
Orpina, an*ce* orpyne *vel* hassewort.
Ortocopus, an*ce* a Symenel.
Ortogonium, an*ce* a squyre.
Ostorium, an*ce* a stryche.
Ovilactum, an*ce* Jussel.
Oxillo, an*ce* to wexe soure.

Pabulum, an*ce* voddur.
[*Pagania*, an*ce* hethnesse.]
Pala . . . *Item dicitur latum instrumentum ferreum ad opus ignis* [a pele.]
Palalia, an*ce* festys of palys.
Palatum, an*ce* the roof of the mowthe.
Palea, an*ce* chaf.
Paleare, an*ce* a dewlappe.
Palestris, an*ce* a morhen.
[*Palicium, -cij, est quedam clausura facta ex palis*, an*ce* a Palys.]
Palladium, an*ce* an ymage of palas.
Palliditas, [an*ce* palnesse.]
Pallidus, [an*ce* pale.]

Palmito, an^ce bargayne.
Palpebra, an^ce an yeled.
Palus, [*an^ce* myre.]
Palus, an^ce a stake, or a stode.
Pandoxina, an^ce a brewhous.
Panduca, an^ce a baggepype.
Panellus, an^ce a panell.
Panetarius, an^ce a pantere.
Panificina, an^ce a bakhous.
Panillus, an^ce a panell.
Panitor, an^ce a Panytere.
Pannagium, an^ce Pannage.
Pannator, an^ce a drapere.
Pannicipium, an^ce a presse.
Pannosus, **an^ce** thredbare.
Panus, *-ni, hic, virgula illa circa quam trama involvitur. Idem et canellus dicitur, an^ce* a Quele. *Item i. spola. Item est quidam piscis, an^ce* a lynge.
Paniceus, an^ce ragged.
Papatum, an^ce pap.
Papaver, an^ce Popy.
Papilio, an^ce a boturflye.
Papirus, an^ce a bulryshe.
Papirum, an^ce Papyre.
Papula, an^ce a whelke.
Paradella, an^ce the rede dokke.
Paragus, an^ce a bryd of yuel hap.
Parasivus, an^ce the heue of a knyf.
Parcimonia, an^ce sparynge.
Parella, an^ce dokke.
Parcus, an^ce a Park.
[*Paritonius, an^ce* the rownde of the erth.]
Parcior, an^ce to party.
Parura, an^ce a Parure.
Pascua, an^ce a ffedyngstede.
Passim, an^ce fro pas to pas.
Passio, an^ce a passyon, or a tholynge.
Pasta, an^ce Dowe.
Pastellus, *an^ce* a Pastey.
Patera, an^ce a bolle.
Paterfamilias, an^ce an housbondeman.
Patina, [*an^ce* a Peele.]
Sacerdotissa patrina, an^ce a wommangossyb.

Patroniso, **an^ce** to wowe, or to defende.
Paulo ante, a lytylbyfore.
Paxillus, an^ce a culture.
5 *Pecten, -tinis, hic, est instrumentum pectendi,* a combe, *et texendi* a sleye . . . *et quidam piscis, an^ce* a plays, *et dicitur, an^ce* a batyndore.
10 *Pectrix, an^ce* a kembestere.
Pecia, an^ce a pece, or lytyl part of a thyng.
Pecoides, an^ce a ffulmere, or a Pulkat.
Pedalis, [a laste.]
15 *Pedana, an^ce* a vampey.
Pedano, an^ce to vampeye.
Pedica, an^ce a panter.
Pedinus, an^ce a pawne.
Pedules . . . pars caligarum que pedem capit, an^ce a vampey.
Pedulus, [*an^ce* a pynson, or a sok.]
Pegma, baculus cum massa plumbi in summitate pendente et an^ce a babul.
25 *Pelegum, an^ce* Pylyole.
Pellicia, an^ce a pylche.
Pellicium, an^ce a pylche.
Pellicillum, an^ce a brushe.
Pellicula, an^ce a rybbyngskyn.
30 *Pelliparius,* [a Scynner.]
Pellura, an^ce Pellure.
Pelvis, a basyn.
Pendulum, an^ce a Pendaunt.
Pennarium, an^ce a Pennere.
35 *Pensaciones, an^ce* truage.
Penucella, parvum vexillum, an^ce a penselle.
Penulatus, an^ce yfurred.
Penularius, an^ce a parmenter [or a scynnere.]
40 [*Penus,* an horstayle.]
Pepillo, to crye as a pecock.
Peplum, an^ce a wynpul.
Pepo, [*an^ce* mortreuus.]
Pepulus, an^ce a bolastre.
45 *Peraptum, an^ce* Papelotes.
Perazitus, an^ce a gloton.
Perca, an^ce a perche.

Perdilla, an^{ce} a dokke.
Perdix, an^{ce} a Partryche.
Peregrinus, an^{ce} an hobeye.
Perendinator, a Surgyon.
Pergamenum, an^{ce} Perchemyn.
Pergulum, an^{ce} a Pyndfold.
[*Perjacio,* an^{ce} to perjette.]
Perimetrum, an^{ce} aboute mesure.
Pipsimo, -as, to pare a thynge.
Peritoria, an^{ce} Perytorye.
Perjuro, an^{ce} to forswerye.
Perma, an^{ce} a Bokelere.
Perna, an^{ce} a flycche.
Pero, -ronis, hic, quoddam calciamentum rusticorum amplium et altum, quod alio nomine dicitur Culponeus [an^{ce} Cokeres.]
Peronizo, an^{ce} to purchase.
Perpendiculum, [a plumet.]
Perseverancia, an^{ce} long lestynge.
Persicaria, culrage.
Persoleo, assidue discere vel an^{ce} to welwone.
Persuadeo, an^{ce} to egge or to tyse.
Pertica, an^{ce} a Perche.
Pervigil, an^{ce} a Wayte.
[*Pervinca,* an^{ce} Pervynke.]
Pescorvi, an^{ce} Crowfot.
Pessellum, an^{ce} a barre, or a laeche.
Petilius, an^{ce} a bolt.
Petulium, an^{ce}, a bolt.
Petulus, -la, -lum, an^{ce} whyt foted *et dicitur de equo.*
Phalanga, an^{ce} a coveltre.
[*Philosella,* an^{ce} lanworte, or Mushere.]
Phocus, an^{ce} a Purpays.
Pica, [a powch.]
[*Picarius, quidam ciphus,* an^{ce} a curskyn.]
Pictacio, -as, an^{ce} to puynte, or to clovte.
Pictaciarius, an^{ce} a Cobulare, or a Cloutere.
Picten, an^{ce} a tye.
[*Pigma,* a babul.]
Pigreo, an^{ce} to be slow.
Pilestros, wode.

Pindo, an^{ce} to cnede.
Pindo, an^{ce} a baker, or a kneder.
[*Pionia,* an^{ce} Pyonye.]
Piper longum, an^{ce} longpiper.
Piper album, whyt pyper.
Piperis mola, an^{ce} a Pyper querne.
Piponella, an^{ce} Pympernele.
Pipunculus, an^{ce} a ffavcoun.
Piramus, hegh shap oftreys.
Piracium, an^{ce} a Perehorde.
Piretum, an^{ce} Pereye.
Pisto, an^{ce} to knede or bake.
Pistrinum, an^{ce} a bachous.
Pistrio, an^{ce} to moolde or bake.
Pistrio, an^{ce} a moolder or a bakere.
Pituita, an^{ce} the Pyppe.
Placenta, [a symnel.]
Placito, an^{ce} to plede.
Placitum, an^{ce} plee.
Planatorium, an^{ce} a boture, *instrumentum ferrarij est.*
Planicies, an^{ce} Playn *et etiam in panno* an^{ce} *dicitur* Champe.
Plantaria, an^{ce} plontes.
Platanus, an^{ce} a plane.
Plebs, an^{ce} rascayl of folke.
Plectrum, an^{ce} a wreste.
Plostrum, an^{ce} a chare of ij whelys.
Plumacius, an^{ce} a plumere *avis est.*
Pluma, an^{ce} a ffether.
Plumbatum, an^{ce} a coope of leed.
Plumbum, an^{ce} leed.
Plumbarius, an^{ce} a plomer.
Plumbaria, an^{ce} a plomerye.
Plumbilamina, an^{ce} a plate of leed.
Pluscula, an^{ce} a bocule.
Plutum, an^{ce} rayn.
Podarius, an^{ce} a Croser.
Podex, an^{ce} the endeles gut.
Podiarius, an^{ce} a croser.
Podium, an^{ce} a croos.
Polenta, an^{ce} wort.
Polentriticum, an^{ce} a bultur.
Polentritico, an^{ce} to bulty.
Polceacus, an^{ce} longynge to berthe.
Polimitus, Ray or motle or medlee.
Polipus, a loppestere.
[*Politridium,* a bultyngcloth.]

[*Pollisium*, an^(ce) an ynche.]
Pollictor, an^(ce) a bornyshour.
Pollubrum, an^(ce) a broshe.
Polictorium, an^(ce) a broshe.
Pomacium, an^(ce) pomys.
Popliliga, an^(ce) a gartour.
Populatus, an^(ce) folk wonyynge.
Populus, an^(ce) a populertre.
Porca, a porpays.
Porcarium, an^(ce) a swynstye.
Porrigo, an^(ce) pokkes.
Porretarium, an^(ce) a lekbed.
Porrata, an^(ce) porrey.
Porretum, an^(ce) a porrete.
Porrum, an^(ce) **leeke.**
[*Portale*, an^(ce) a porche.]
Porticus, an^(ce) a porche.
Portisus, an^(ce) ful of hetys.
Portoforium, an^(ce) a Porthos.
Posse, an^(ce) a lytyl hauynge, or a lytyl myght.
Posterior, an^(ce) hyderour.
Postis, an^(ce) a post.
Postsellium, an^(ce) the **hyndur assyoun** of a sadyl.
[*Potella*, an^(ce) a potel.]
Potisso, [an^(ce) to syppy.]
Potus, [an^(ce) drynke.]
Prece, an^(ce) bedus.
Precinctus, an^(ce) ygurd.
Precox, an^(ce) sunnerysynge.
Prefero, an^(ce) to bere by fore.
Prefiguro, an^(ce) to tokyn byfore.
Prepositor, an^(ce) a setter of mes.
Prepositus, an^(ce) a reue.
Presellum, an^(ce) the assyon of a sadelle.
Presento, [an^(ce) to presenty.]
Presumptuo, an^(ce) to mystake.
Presumo, an^(ce) to take on honde, or awntur.
Pretendo, an^(ce) to go by fore.
Preteritus, an^(ce) ypassyd.
Preteritus, an^(ce) a passynge.
Prevaleo, an^(ce) to be myghty, or more worthe.
Prevenio, an^(ce) to come by fore.
Previdencia, a forsyghte.

Priaula, an^(ce) a perche.
Primulus, an^(ce) a lytylfurst.
Priorissa, an^(ce) a Pryorysse.
Privignus, a stypsone.
Privigna, a stypdowtur.
Prius, an^(ce) rather.
Procella, [a storme.]
Processionale, an^(ce) a processional.
Procor, an^(ce) to wowe.
Procus, an^(ce) a wowere.
Proditor, an^(ce) a traytour, or a turmentour.
Proditus, an^(ce) betrayed.
Prodicio, an^(ce) tresoun.
Produculus, madprud.
Prolego, to outlawe.
Promereor, an^(ce) to deserue.
Promico, to shewe, or shyne.
Promitto, an^(ce) to behote.
[*Promotorium*, an^(ce) a prychel.]
Pronuba, an^(ce) a bawdstrot.
Pronubus, an^(ce) a bawde.
Prope, an^(ce) ny.
Propono, }an^(ce) to purpose et
Propositum,} an^(ce) a purpos.
Propugnacula, an^(ce) kerneles.
Proreto, an^(ce) to sterne or to stere out.
Prosectum, an^(ce) a Jeblet of the goos.
Prosequor, an^(ce) to purchase.
Prostro, an^(ce) to caste dovn.
Prostro, an^(ce) to cast down.
Prossus, an^(ce) owterly, *sed melius prorsus*.
Provideo, an^(ce) to purveye, or to see byfore.
Provoco, an^(ce) to tourne & to calle out.
Proximo, an^(ce) to make next, or ny.
Prurio, [an^(ce) to ytche.]
Psalterium, an^(ce) a sawtrey.
Pudoro, an^(ce) to shame.
Pugil, [a champyon.]
Pula, an^(ce) medlyng of water and wyne.
Pulex, an^(ce) a flee.
Pulegium, [an^(ce) hullewort.]

Pullificio, to hacche chykyn, to make derke.
[*Pullegium, an^{ce}* hullewort.]
Pulliferus, an^{ce} a pultur.
Pultria, an^{ce} pultrie.
Pullificacio, an^{ce} hacchynge.
Pulmo, an^{ce} the longon.
Puls, an^{ce} Gruel.
Pulsatorium, an^{ce} a clapere.
Pulso, an^{ce} **to rynge.**
Puluinar, an^{ce} a bolster.
Pumex, an^{ce} pomys.
Pupilla, an^{ce} the appul of the ye.
Pusio, an^{ce} a sneuelard.
Pustula, an^{ce} pokkes.
Putacia, an^{ce} a skantulon.
Putacio, to poynte, or to cloute.
Putor, an^{ce} stenche.

Quactum, an^{ce} creyme.
Quadra, an^{ce} a cantel.
Quadratus, an^{ce} squared.
Qualia, an^{ce} a Quayle.
Quantum, an^{ce} how myche.
Quare, an^{ce} why.
Quarrura, an^{ce} **a quarre.**
Quaternus, an^{ce} a Quayer.
Quaxillum, an^{ce} **a tappehose.**
Querela, an^{ce} **a playnt.**
Querelor, an^{ce} to playne.
Querimonia, an^{ce} a playnt.
Queremonior, an^{ce} to playne.
Questor, an^{ce} a Pardonere.
Quia et quoniam, *an^{ce}* for why.
Quini, an^{ce} but.
Quinterno, an^{ce} a gytterne.
Quintus, an^{ce} the fyfihe.
[*Quiriacum,* a Costard.]
[*Quoversum, an^{ce}* vhodurward.]

Rabulum, i. organum, an^{ce} **glee.**
Radius, an^{ce} a spoke.
Ralus, an^{ce} a fleyng addur.
Rana, an^{ce} a frogge.
[*Raphanus, an^{ce}* Rapys.]
Rapax, an^{ce} a rauenere, or Rauaschynge.
Rastella, an^{ce} a thrusbe.

[*Rasta, an^{ce}* doder.]
Ratonicida, an^{ce} a ratoner.
Recano, to crye as a tygre.
Recedo, an^{ce} to go ayen.
5 *Recensitus, an^{ce}* newe rype.
Recepcio, an^{ce} a receyuynge.
[*Receptor, an^{ce}* a receyuor.]
Recinum vel Recinium, matronale operimentum sive quedam vestis vel
10 *pallium quod vulgo dicitur Movortem vel quoddam rete.*
Reclusorium, an^{ce} a Pyndfold.
Recreo, an^{ce} to fylle or aye make.
Recubitus, an^{ce} syttynge or lyynge.
15 *Recupero, an^{ce}* to rekeuery.
Recussorium, an^{ce} a hamour.
Reda, an^{ce} a thylle.
Refrigerium, an^{ce} helpe kepynge.
Regilla, an^{ce} a Quenyscloth.
20 *Regina prati, an^{ce}* medesewte.
Regimen, an^{ce} Gouernayle.
Regnum, an^{ce} a kyngdome.
Rella, pannus est an^{ce} Ray.
Relaxo, an^{ce} to relese.
25 *Remex, an^{ce}* a sterysman.
Renuncio, an^{ce} to forsake.
Repecio, an^{ce} to clute.
Repeciarius, an^{ce} a clutere.
Repente, an^{ce} Sodenly.
30 *Repentinus, an^{ce}* sodeyn.
Repeto, an^{ce} to aske ayen.
Repetundus, an^{ce} Sad ayen askyng.
Repofocilium, an^{ce} an hedbronde.
Repositorium, an^{ce} an almarye.
35 *Reprehendo, an^{ce}* to vndernyme.
Reprobo, an^{ce} to repreve.
Repulvero, an^{ce} to poudere ayen.
Requies, an^{ce} rest.
Requiesco, an^{ce} to bygynne to rest.
40 *Respublica, an^{ce}* **a comyn thynge.**
Resero, an^{ce} to vnluke, or to shewe.
Respondeo, an^{ce} to **answere.**
Resupinus, an^{ce} **wyde ope.**
Reticula, an^{ce} a calle.
45 *Reticulum,* a calle. *Item reticulum,* a rayle [*vel* a rayne.]
Retinaculum, an^{ce} a Rayne.
Retiolum, an^{ce} **a calle.**

Retrogradus, [an*ᶜᵉ* Restyfe.]
Retrorsum, an*ᶜᵉ* bakward.
Retroverto, to turne abak.
Retundo, an*ᶜᵉ* to smyte ayen.
Revolus, an*ᶜᵉ* a Pedeler.
Ricus, vndoynge of thowt.
Rimatorium, an*ᶜᵉ* a serchour.
Ringo, an*ᶜᵉ* to grenne [or rory.]
Risidus, an*ᶜᵉ* a slyngeston.
Ritmus, an*ᶜᵉ* ryme.
Roba, an*ᶜᵉ* a Robe.
Rochia, an*ᶜᵉ* a Roche.
Rocus, *homo scacci*, an*ᶜᵉ* a Roke.
Roga, an*ᶜᵉ* a Dole.
Rogitum, an*ᶜᵉ* a roket.
Rosa marina, [an*ᶜᵉ* Rosemaryne.]
Rostrum, [an*ᶜᵉ* a byle.]
Rostrum porcinum, an*ᶜᵉ* sowthystell.
Rotula, an*ᶜᵉ* a rolle.
Rotundus, an*ᶜᵉ* rond.
Rubella, an*ᶜᵉ* a ruget, *piscis est*.
Rubeta, an*ᶜᵉ* a tode.
[*Ruberca, quodam herba*, an*ᶜᵉ* Gladyne.]
Rubescens, an*ᶜᵉ* shamfast.
Rubedo, an*ᶜᵉ* rednesse.
Rubea, an*ᶜᵉ* mader.
Rubiaria, wyn of grapys.
Rubiginator, an*ᶜᵉ* a fforbour.
Rubus, an*ᶜᵉ* a bushe.
Ructo, an*ᶜᵉ* to balke.
Rudentes, an*ᶜᵉ* Cables.
Rudes, an*ᶜᵉ* a Cable.
Rugella, i. rubella, an*ᶜᵉ* a ruget.
Ruga, [an*ᶜᵉ* a wrynkyl, or a playt.]
Ruino, an*ᶜᵉ* to falle.
Rumbus, an*ᶜᵉ* a Sturgyon.
Rupa, an*ᶜᵉ* a braoke.
Ruscus, an*ᶜᵉ* a grost, or furses.
Russetus, an*ᶜᵉ* Russet.

Saber, an*ᶜᵉ* grauell.
Saccus, an*ᶜᵉ* a sakke.
Sacristerium, an*ᶜᵉ* the sextrye.
Saginum, an*ᶜᵉ* saym.
Salamandra, an*ᶜᵉ* Creket.
[*Salatrum*, Suredokke.]
Salgea, an*ᶜᵉ* sawge.
Salgearium, an*ᶜᵉ* a sawger.
Salpo, i. cornubium, an*ᶜᵉ* an hornpype.
Salsiamentum, an*ᶜᵉ* sauce.
Salsicix, an*ᶜᵉ* a sawsyge.
Salsarium, an*ᶜᵉ* a sawcere.
Saltulus, an*ᶜᵉ* a loppystere.
Salutaris, an*ᶜᵉ* helful or holsum.
Sambuca, an*ᶜᵉ* eldertre. *Item sambuca est quoddam genus simphonie musicum*, an*ᶜᵉ* a Gytterne.
[*Sanalam*, an*ᶜᵉ* Prymerole.]
Sandix, [an*ᶜᵉ* madur.]
Sanguinacium, an*ᶜᵉ* a blodpuddynge.
Sanguineus, an*ᶜᵉ* blody.
Sanguisecus, an*ᶜᵉ* a blodhonde.
Saponaria, an*ᶜᵉ* Crowsope.
Sarabarra, sunt fluxa et sinuosa vestimenta, vel capitum tegmina, vel an*ᶜᵉ* a sclauayn.
Sarabra, toches of maystre.
Sarculum, [an*ᶜᵉ* a wedehoke.]
Sardallus, a sparlynge.
Sarrio, an*ᶜᵉ* to clene, cutte or wede.
Sarissa, an*ᶜᵉ* a materas, *et quoddam genus armorum*, an*ᶜᵉ* a Jakke of defense.
Saticulum, an*ᶜᵉ* a sedlepe.
Satisfacio, an*ᶜᵉ* to do ynowe.
Satrape, an*ᶜᵉ* seriawntes.
[*Saturia*, an*ᶜᵉ* Ballokwort.]
Satureia, an*ᶜᵉ* sauereye.
[*Sauponaria*, an*ᶜᵉ* Crovsope.]
Savina, [an*ᶜᵉ* sauyne.]
Sauma, an*ᶜᵉ* a Sadylcharge.
Scabiosa, an*ᶜᵉ* scabiose.
Scrabo, -bonis, hic, i. vespe longiora crura habentes. Item invenitur Crabo, -bonis et scabo, an*ᶜᵉ* a dore.
Scaccarium, an*ᶜᵉ* a Chekere.
Scaccus, an*ᶜᵉ* the meny of the cheker.
Scale, an*ᶜᵉ* a laddere.
Scalpo, [an*ᶜᵉ* to cracche.]
Scalprum, an*ᶜᵉ* a grate, or a shaue.
Scansile, an*ᶜᵉ* a styrop *et* an*ᶜᵉ* a style.
Scannarium, an*ᶜᵉ* a bankere.
Scarabo, an*ᶜᵉ* a scharabot [*et* an*ᶜᵉ* a bytylle.]

*Scariaballum, an^ce a Cogge.
*Scarifacio, an^ce to grate.
*Scarifactor et Scarifactrix, an^ce a gratere.
*Scariola, an^ce the mylkthystel.
5 *Scarletum, an^ce Scarlet.
*Scarpsella, an^ce a scryppe.
*Scaurus, an^ce longe heles.
*Scedaculum, an^ce a scantulon.
*Scelero et sceleror, an^ce to do felanye.
[*Scia, an^ce the whyrlebon.]
*Scientum, an^ce a sparre.
*Scindula, an^ce a shyngul. Item an^ce a blad.
*Scindularius, a bladesmyth.
*Scipio, an^ce a maner of an hokedstaf.
*Scissorium, an^ce a trenchere.
*Scitor, an^ce a querour.
*Sclavina, est vestis peregrinorum, an^ce a Sclauayne.
*Scocia, an^ce Scotlond.
*Scon, interjectio, an^ce showe, ut dicitur gallina lirida scon, an^ce pykeled hen show.
*Scordion allia, [an^ce wyldgarlyk.]
25 *Scordiscus, an^ce a shave.
[*Scorioballum, an^ce a cogwhele.]
*Scorpio, quoddam animal venenosum. Item dicitur quidam piscis vel vermis, an^ce a stykelyng.
*Scrato, an^ce to cracche.
*Screa, [an^ce Spotel.]
*Screo, [an^ce to spete.]
*Scrinium, vas vel locus ubi libri vel thesauri servantur. Item an^ce a Serene.
*Scrophus, an^ce a lytyl grauel.
*Scruta, exta i. tripe, an^ce the felvelde.
*Sculpo, an^ce to graue.
*Scurulus, a squyrel.
*Scutella, an^ce a dyyshe.
*Scutica, an^ce a whippe.
*Scutiger, [an^ce a qeman.]
*Scutra, an^ce a chawfur.
*Scutum, [a bokeler.]
*Secretum, an^ce privyte.
*Securicula, [an hachet.]
*Sedemus, an^ce the syxtenethe.

*Sedile, [an^ce a banker.]
*Sedum, an^ce a worde space.
*Seforniculum, an^ce a porteolygs.
*Seysina, an^ce a sesyng.
5 *Seisino, an^ce to sese.
*Selabicalis, an^ce a kartladdere.
*Sello, an^ce to sadely.
*Semianimis, half coragyous.
*Semicinctorium, an^ce a synk or a lace.
*Semilio, an^ce a sedlepe.
*Seminus, an^ce lesse.
*Seminimus, half lesse.
*Semiorculus, an^ce an arche.
15 *Semiquarta, an^ce a pynte.
*Semoveo, an^ce to do a wey.
*Senecta, an^ce age.
*Senescallus, an^ce a steward.
*Senio, an^ce an hasard.
20 *Sensualitas, an^ce a scylle, reson.
*Septiformis, an^ce seuenfolde.
*Sepum, an^ce talwe.
*Sericum, an^ce selk.
*Serarius, an^ce a lokyere.
25 *Seromollum, an^ce wort.
*Seropelinus, an^ce thredbare.
[*Seropellina, an^ce a roket.]
*Serpedo, an^ce meseles.
*Serpigo, an^ce a tetyr.
30 *Serpillum, an^ce peletur [vel honysouke.]
*Servicium, an^ce servyse.
*Serula, an^ce a stapul.
*Serum, an^ce whey.
35 *Seta, an^ce an hoggeshere.
*Setosus, an^ce brystely.
*Shopa, an^ce a shoppe.
*Sibula, an^ce an ale.
*Sicca, quidam piscis est, an^ce a codel.
40 *Siccus, an^ce drye.
*Siccatus, an^ce dryed.
*Sigesterium, an^ce draaf.
*Signaculum, an^ce a clapse.
[*Silenius, a gogyn.]
45 *Siler, an^ce an Osyer.
*Scilicet, an^ce that is to sey [or to wyte.]
*Siligo, an^ce rye.

[Silion, soulond.]
Silvanus, an^ce a wodewose.
Silurus, an^ce a loche.
Simallus, an^ce a sperlynge.
[Simicosus, an^ce Nockestrange.]
Simio, to make Sfnattyd.
Simplicitas, an^ce Symplenesse.
[Simplo, an axebathere.]
Sinautem, an^ce or ellys.
Sinapium, an^ce Mustard.
[Sinamomum, an^ce Synamome.]
Sincopi, an^ce Swonynge.
Sindon, an^ce Sendel.
Singularis, an^ce a bor.
Singultio, [to snobbe, or syche.]
Singulatim, an^ce fro on to an other.
[Sinimone, an^ce Grundyswylye.
Sinoglostorium, an^ce a flodegate.
Siquidem, an^ce forsothe.
Siquominus, an^ce wythoute lesse.
Sirma, i. cauda vestis feminarum, an^ce a trayne.
[Sirentorium, a warrok.
Sirna, an haddok.]
[Siromellum, an^ce wort.]
Sistarca, [an^ce an Almarye.]
Sitractio, an^ce fallynge.
Smaragdus, an^ce an emerawde.
Smigmator, an^ce a sopere.
Solatrum i. morella, an^ce smalmorell.
Soldanus, a Sowdan.
Soldarius, an^ce a Sowdeour.
Soldatura, an^ce Sowdere.
Solea, an^ce a Sole.
[Solfo, an^ce to solfe.]
Solicitus, an^ce besy.
Solidatus, an^ce a shyllyngworth.
Sororitas, an^ce a systerhede.
Spadix, [an^ce bay.]
[Sparagus, an^ce Colverfot.]
Sparrus, an^ce a rowe.
Spasmus, an^ce the Crompe.
Spatula, an^ce a Cambrel, and a selyse.
Spectaculum, an^ce wordelys vanyte. Item est instrumentum iuvans visum, a spectacle.
Sperula, i. parva spera [et an^ce a bowle.]

Spica, [an^ce an Er.]
Spinter, an^ce a pyn.
Spinus, an^ce a Slotre, vel a thorn.
Spiramen, an^ce a blast.
Spissus, an^ce thykke.
Splen, an^ce the mylte.
Spola, an^ce a Quyl, or a Spole.
Sponda, an^ce a bolster [et an^ce a forme.]
Spondile, an^ce the ryggebon [vel the brest bone.]
Sporta, an^ce a lepe [or a basket.]
Spuma, an^ce berme.
[Spumatorium, a skemere.]
Squama, an^ce a scale or a mayle.
Squinancia, an^ce the Quynsy.
Stabes, an^ce a spotte.
Stalerum, an^ce a colrake.
Stamen, an^ce warpe.
Stannum, an^ce tyn.
[Stapulum, an^ce a Stapul.]
Statuncula, an^ce a tryst.
Staurus, an^ce stoore.
Stauro, an^ce to store.
[Sterea, an^ce the ysecrace.]
Sterlingus, an^ce a striylyng or a peyspeny.
Sternium, an^ce a bedstede.
Sternulo, [an^ce to fnese.]
Sterquilinium, an^ce a donghepe.
Stibio, to starche.
[Stilio, an^ce uely.]
Stinctum, i. satirion, [an^ce sanycle.]
Stipa, an^ce stode.
Stoica, an^ce a porche peyntyd.
Storilicitor, an^ce a Purvyour.
Storium, an^ce a matte, or a bed.
Storiator, a mattere.
Stragulum, an^ce ray.
Stratum, an^ce lytour.
Strena, Anselle.
Strengula, quidam piscis, an^ce a cheveyne.
Strido, [an^ce to grenne or grente with the theth.]
Strigilis, an horscombe.
[Stropa, a styrop.]
[Strophiarius, a Gyrdelere.]

Studia, an^{ce} a swyngelstok.
Stupa, an^{ce} herdes.
Stupo, an^{ce} to stoppe with herdes.
Sturnus, quedam avis, an^{ce} a staar.
Suador, an^{ce} monyshynge.
Subdivo, i. sine tecto vel sub celo, an^{ce} theroute.
Suber, [an^{ce} sape.]
Subjectus, an^{ce} vndurcast.
Subitus, an^{ce} sodeyne.
Sublapheum, an^{ce} a Shelvingstole.
Subligar, [an^{ce} a gartur.]
Sublimare, an^{ce} ouerslaye.
Subpedium, an^{ce} a tredel.
Subsellium, [a panel.]
[Subspicio, an^{ce} to loure.]
Subula, an^{ce} an ale.
Subverto, an^{ce} to destruye, to turne vpsedoun.
Succidium, an^{ce} Sovse.
Succingo, an^{ce} to gyrde vndur.
Succuticus, an^{ce} ful of juse.
Sucus, an^{ce} Juys.
Suctus, an^{ce} a tenche.
Sudarium, an^{ce} a mokedore.
Sudoro, [an^{ce} to swete.]
Suffarcino, an^{ce} to tukky.
Suffragina, an^{ce} a knokel.
Suffulcio, an^{ce} to putte vndur.
[Suillus, i. parva sus, a yelte.]
[Suistacium, a Swynysty.]
Supera, ... quedam vestis, an^{ce} a roket.
Supero, i. pannum rugare, an^{ce} to rydely.
Superaltare, an^{ce} a superaltarye.
Supercilium, an^{ce} a browe.
Superculum, an^{ce} a covercule.
[Superfilo, an^{ce} et gallice, to surfyle.]
Superliminare, [an^{ce} a lyntel.]
Superpellicium, an^{ce} surplys.
Supertunica, an^{ce} a Syrcote.
Supinus, an^{ce} wholnyd.
Supara, an^{ce} a roket.
Suppa, an^{ce} a Sope.
Suppo, an^{ce} to Supe.
Supplicio, an^{ce} fallyng under man.
Suppono, an^{ce} to undersette, or to suppose.

Surculus, [an^{ce} a Graffe.]
Suscito, an^{ce} to arere, or to areyse.
Suspendium, an^{ce} a tredel.
Suspirium, an^{ce} a syghynge.
Suspiro, [an^{ce} to syche.]
Sutura, an^{ce} a Sem.

Tabulatus, an^{ce} a kyrnelle of the walle.
Talpefodium, an^{ce} a wonthylle.
Talus, an^{ce} an hele.
Tam, an^{ce} aswell.
Tamen, an^{ce} neuertheles.
[Tansetum, Tansey.]
Tantillus, an^{ce} a dwrfe.
Tapetum, [a tapyt.]
Tapisterium, an^{ce} a Testour.
Taratantara, ... est instrumentum quo farina colatur. Et instrumentum cujus percussione granum defluit inter molas molendini, an^{ce} a clacke [et an^{ce} an hersystete] et est clangor tubarum.
Tardarius, an^{ce} a tarcel quoddam genus nisi.
Tardus, an^{ce} slowe.
Targia, an^{ce} a targat, or a pavys.
Tarinus, quidam vermis lardi, an^{ce} a mathe.
[Tarta, a tarte.]
Tassis, an^{ce} a mowe.
Taxus, an^{ce} a brok.
Taxus, an^{ce} an Eev.
Tegilectum, an^{ce} a coverlyth.
Temo, [a thylle.]
Temporatus, an^{ce} ytempored.
Tena vel Tenia, [an^{ce} a ffrenge vel a coyfe.]
Tenaculum, [an^{ce} a rynge of a dore.]
Tener, [an^{ce} tendere or neshe.]
Tenere, an^{ce} sherdes.
Tenia, an^{ce} an herstrynge.
Tengiagio, an^{ce} a tenche.
Tenorcula, an^{ce} a telor of an arblast.
Tensa, an^{ce} a vedme.
Tenta, an^{ce} a tente, or an harwe.
Tentigo, i. extensio vel arrectio virilis membri. Item dicitur an^{ce} a kyker.

Tentum, an^ce a tenon, *quod ponitur in commissura.*
Tenuale, an^ce a barbykan.
Tercellus, [a tercel.]
Terebellum i. Furfuraculum, [*et an^ce* a Persour.]
Terebrum, an^ce an augur, or a Persour.
Terga, an^ce a targe.
Terremotus, an^ce erthequake.
[*Terro, i. terram alicui supponere, an^ce* to tere or daube.]
Tersorium, an^ce a swepelles [a malkyn.]
Tersus, an^ce a turfh.
Testa, an^ce a shylle.
Testudo, an^ce a snayl.
Tetrarco, to rayne.
Textum i. semicinctorium, an^ce a scynt.
Theca, an^ce a cas.
Theoroticus, an^ce a dyuyn.
Thuribulus, an^ce a castere of cense.
Tibiarius, an^ce a Pypemaker.
Tigna, an^ce restoureg.
Tigrus, an^ce a tygur.
Tilia, an^ce lynde.
Timbia, an^ce a cherne.
Timetitas, an^ce a dampnyngge.
Timpanum, a taber, or a tymbre.
Tina, an^ce a Covelle.
Tinctor, an^ce a dyere.
Tinex, an^ce a mathe.
Tirocinium, an^ce a tornement.
Tispatum, an^ce umbles.
Titer, an^ce a belwether.
Titimallus, an^ce spurge.
Toga, an^ce a gowne.
Togella, an^ce a towayle.
Tolerancia, an^ce sufferaunce.
Tolus, an^ce a pomel.
Tomentum dicitur quia aut in filo aut in tela tumeat, nec subtilitatem habet, an^ce abbe.
Tonstrix, an^ce a Shyppestere.
Toral vel Torale, an^ce a keverlyt.
Torcio, an^ce a grevaunce.
Tornamentum, an^ce a tornament.
Tornatrix, an^ce a tumbelyster.
Torta, an^ce a kake.

Torta et Tortula, a tapur or a torche.
Torticius, an^ce a torche.
Tortillus, an^ce a shakyl.
Torrundo, an^ce a kake.
[*Tostum, an^ce* a toste.]
[*Totomalus, an^ce* ffeterwort.]
Tractorium, an^ce a trays.
Traha, hoc genus est vehiculi a trahendo dicta, quia rotas non habet, [*an^ce* a Dreye.]
Trahiculum, an^ce a trabys.
Trama . . . est filum inter stamen discurrens, an^ce abbe, *dicitur et quoddam instrumentum textricum quod inequale est. Item Trama, an^ce* an hem.
Tramellum, an^ce a traysus, *vel quoddam genus retis, an^ce* a tramayle.
[*Tramerium, an^ce* Traveys. *Ergasterium idem est.*]
Transfigo, an^ce to styke.
Tremulus, quedam arbor, an^ce an Apse.
[*Trenga, an^ce* a dreye.]
Trepica, i. ocrea, an^ce a boot.
Trevulgo, to shewe trewys or tretys.
Tribracca, an^ce a breeyghgyrdyll.
Tribula, an^ce a shovell.
[*Tricatura,* a warde of a lok.]
Triclinum, an^ce a bed.
Trimatria, hallys.
Tripa, an^ce a trype.
Tristellus, an^ce a Trestell.
Tritor, an^ce a defoulere.
Tritorium, [a pystel.]
Triturator, an^ce a thresshere.
Trochus, et Torpillus, an^ce a top.
Troparium, quidam liber, an^ce a tropere.
Trucio, to make fel.
Trudela, avis est, an^ce a tele.
Trufa, an^ce a trefele.
Trufo, an^ce to trefele.
Truga, quedam avis, an^ce a wewestrete.
Trulla, an^ce a trulle.
Trunculus, [*an^ce* a lytyl waste.]
Truncus, [the wast.]

Trussula, an^{ce} a trussell.
Truta, quidam piscis, an^{ce} a trwght.
Trutinator, an^{ce} a weyere.
Tubera, an^{ce} taddechese.
Tuitus, an^{ce} lokynge.
Tumentum, an^{ce} abbe.
Tuo, an^{ce} to thuy, *et dicitur a tu.*
Turba, an^{ce} a Turbut.
Turbacio, trobelynge, lettynge.
Turcus, an^{ce} a Turke.
Turdinus, an^{ce} a Quayle.
Turgesco, [an^{ce} to balky.]
Tussumulus, i. pulsatorium, an^{ce} the rynge of a dore.
Tussis, an^{ce} the koghwhe.
Tutibo, an^{ce} to tumble.
Tutibarum, vel Tutibarium, an^{ce} a tumbrell.

Vaccarium, an^{ce} a vacherye.
Vacceuallis, hic est locus in silva quadam, ubi sanctus kenelmus occubuit et sepeliebatur, an^{ce} Covbach.
Vaccinium, an^{ce} a coweslyppe.
Valatrum, an^{ce} a cherne.
Valectus, an^{ce} a yeman.
Vanga, an^{ce} a spade.
Varratum, i. novale, valwe.
Varracio, an^{ce} valwynge.
Varro, an^{ce} to valwe londe.
Vello, [an^{ce} to-wedy.]
Venaticus, an^{ce} a brache, *vel* a rache [or a spaynel.]
Venor, an^{ce} to hunty.
Venatus, huntynge.
Venilia, flowynge of the see.
Ventilabrum, pala ventilandi, instrumentum ventilandi [or a wynne shete.]
Ventilogium, an^{ce} wethercock.
Ventitricum, an^{ce} a wyndmylle.
Verbescor, an^{ce} to chyde.
Vermiculum, an^{ce} vermyloun.
Vermis, [an^{ce} a worme.]
Verruca, [an^{ce} a werte.]
Vertebrum, an^{ce} a wherve, or a reele.
Vertitor, an^{ce} a tornour.
Vertinellus, an^{ce} a twyste.

Verugirus, an^{ce} a turnebroche.
Vesicula, i. parva vesica. Item dicitur illa tenuis pellicula in gutture avis in qua cibaria congregantur, a croppe, or a case.
Vespa, an^{ce} a waps [*et est vespa major illa,* an^{ce} an hernet.]
Vester, an^{ce} gowre.
Vestibulum, [an^{ce} a vestrye.]
Vestiplicium, an^{ce} a presse.
Vestis, an^{ce} clothynge.
Vestitus, an^{ce} yclothed.
Vetulana, an^{ce} an old quene or an old wymman.
Vexus, an^{ce} a trussell.
Vibix, [a wale.]
[*Vibrilla,* a penywygtle.]
Viburnium, an^{ce} a brome.
Vicecomes, an^{ce} a shreve.
Vicia, [a wech.]
Vicemonitor, an^{ce} a submaystere.
Vidulo, to vydele crowthe & Sytole.
Vidularius, an^{ce} a vythulare.
Vidula, an^{ce} a vythule.
Vietum, an^{ce} wronge.
Villifico, an^{ce} to walle, or to bylle.
Vimen, [an^{ce} twygge.]
Vindemix, an^{ce} vendage.
Viniferum, an^{ce} a wynpot.
Vinitria, an^{ce} vyntrye.
[*Virga pastoris,* an^{ce} wylde tesel.]
Virgata, an^{ce} a yerdlond.
Viridarius, an^{ce} a hayward, or a Forster.
Viride grecum, an^{ce} verdegrece.
Viridissiccus, an^{ce} verinys.
Viridium, an^{ce} vernysh.
Virificum, an^{ce} vernysh.
Vita, an^{ce} a fylet.
Vitellicium, an^{ce} Cavdell.
Vitrum, an^{ce} glaas.
[*Vitro,* to glase.]
Vitrarius, a glasyare.]
Vitulo, an^{ce} to calue.
Vitula, an^{ce} a fythele.
Vlcus, [a buyle or a boch.]
Vlmus, an^{ce} an Elme.
Vlphus, i. Aleator, an^{ce} an hasardour.

Vmbilicus, an^ce Nauelworte.
Vmbrus, an^ce a maystyf, or a blode-
    hunde.
Vna, an^ce togedere.
Vnitas, [an^ce Onhede.]
Volemus, an^ce a Perwarduntre.
Volo, an^ce a whele.
Volta, an^ce a wont.
Volutus, an^ce bywrappyd, or bytra-
    nyd.
Vranuscopus, an^ce a Raye.
Vrba, an^ce a reuers.
Vrceolus, [an^ce a Posnet.]
Vrector, an^ce a brenner.
Vssim, i. ardenter, an^ce brennyngly.
Vstrina, an^ce a bakhous.
Vstrinatorium, an^ce a kylle.
Vsus, an^ce a holyntre.
Vter, an^ce whether.

Vtlagatus, an^ce vtlawyd.
Vtlagaria, an^ce vtlawrye.
Vtrum, an^ce whether.

5 [*Warena*, a wareyne.
Warenarius, a warner.
Waldum, an^ce wode.]
Vuapassa, an^ce resonn.
Wlturnus, [the north wynde.]
10
Xpianus, an^ce Crystene.
Xrismale, an^ce a Crysmere.
Xrismatorium, an^ce the Eluat.

15 *Zeduarium, quedam herba est*, an^ce
    zeduale.
Zitanus, i. taxus, an^ce a brook.
Zonico, an^ce to gyrde vp.

Additions.

The original MS. is in the Gale Collection in Trinity College Library and the Class mark is O. 5. 4. — The words in square brackets are in a later hand.

Page 560, 561. Add.:

Abdenago . . . interpretaten serviens tacens an^ce a stylle.

XVI.

METRICAL VOCABULARIES.[1]

(OF THE FIFTEENTH CENTURY.)

---

        stumlyth yn harneys   i. purpura i. superbus
   Cespitat in phaleris yppus, blattaque suppinus;
i. lingua   i. uino   i. sermo i. stulto
   Glossa uelud themato labat emus infatuato,
s. ille i. bonus i. in operacione   i. fidelis i. sermone
   Qui calus   in praxi   simul est, et pisticus emo,
      i. laus   i. loquitur uel predicat
   Illius[2] oda placet, hic recte   theologizat,
                     tresory   i. diuitis
   Qui cupide seruas ypogeum gazophilacis.
         i. celestis   i. altas sedes
   Cerdus ad vranici scandes algalmata regni.
falses[3] homines i. deuoratores qui stant in falsis causis i. depredantes
   Pseustes,   ambrones,   sicophantes,   uispiliones,
primus fluuius inferni 2us fluuius 3us fluuius 4us fluuius inferni i. circuibunt
     Stix   et Cochitus   Lethe   Flagitonque rotabunt.

---

[1] These curious vocabularies are printed from a manuscript of the fifteenth century (MS. Harl. 1002, fol. 113, r°), but the text is in all probability of an earlier date. The name of Spencer is subscribed to the end of it, but names signed in this way are those more usually of the copyist than of the author. From the occurrence in the interlinear gloss of several words, such as *sullow* and *bannut*, peculiar to the dialects of the West of England and the Welsh border, we may perhaps conclude that the MS. was written in that part of the island. The Latin contains a rather large number of words adopted from the Greek.

[2] A Latin commentator states in the margin that this word has „Media corrupta causa metri."

[3] Read *falsos*. R. W.

the hanches i. cerni   i. capre   i. quoquine
Targa[1]   laphi[2] dorceque latus delata popine,
       i. aqua cocta   rosste   a payge of the keschyn
An sint elixa, sint assaue, scit bene   lixa.
a stode[3]   i. generosi   everey i. sponsas
Bulla uelud proceres, stola[4] sic eburnea nuptas;
pro sicut i. lectum i. coopertorium i. ornat i. mensale bordeclothe
Vtque   cubile   thoral   decusat,   gausape   mensam,
a keruere   i. uacat a surgyon or a chamerleyne
Cironomon mensis, lectis assistit   aleptes.
         fowlere   a murtherer of men her derke hernys
Dumetis[5] auceps latet, et   sicarius   antris,
gracilis puer bysuevyllyd   colte   i. uillosus   i. hirsutus
Puseo   reumaticus, pullus lappatus et hirtus,
a foome   i. uobili
Hinnulis heredi nunquam spernantur herili.
              a byttore
Hinc elephas barrit,[6] onocrotulus hiccine bombit,
i. asinus siluestris   a lytulle frogge   crowkyt
Hin[7] onager rudit, ranunculus inde coaxat.
bowre-mayde   glasse   i. dominam
Abra   tenens speculum sese speculatur et heram;
pro sicut mayster coke i. domino
Vtque machirus   hero, sicque sibi preparat escas.
truncus arboris   a anudyre
Stipes   ut andena sustentus deperit ardens,[8]
                     i. falsi seruuli   lordlyche
Seruicio sic sepe spenduli res tabet herilis.
              hic dulus i. seruus
Qui multis duliam promittit heris placitura,[9]
Sphendulus alterius fiat et non assecla uerus.[9]
grauiter accentuans i. nomen   acuto accentu proferri
Baritonans   onoma cum debeat   oxitonari,
          i. rectus gramaticus   i. illiteratus
Non hic ortographus, sed agrammatus esse probatur.
         tauehere[11] i. estus aeris
Fecula non acinum[10] caupo   canina   repellit,
                   uermes, Anglice myntys[13]
Et bibulus[12] musti   bibiones   arcet amurca.
         i. sanctus   i. uana gloria
Non est hic agnus quem sinodoxia tangit,

---

[1] Read *terga*. R. W.
[2] Read *elaphi*. R. W.
[3] *i. nodus in cingulo*, Latin gloss.
[4] *i. uestis longa mulieris*, Latin gloss. R. W.
[5] *locus ubi multi dumi crescunt*, Latin gloss. R. W.
[6] In the margin here we read, 'Barri, -orum, sine singulari, sunt ludi, Anglice *bace*, sed hic harrne eliphas est.'
[7] Read *hinc*. R. W.
[8] A commentator adds. the gloss: Antipera anglice a strene. R. W.
[9] These two verses are added in the margin of the MS. R. W.
[10] The Latin glossator adds: et dicas acinum quod in vua cernis acutum. R. W.
[11] So has the MS. R. W.
[12] *est qui multum bibit*, Latin gloss. R. W.
[13] The word *mint*, in the signification of a mite, is still preserved in the dialects of the west of England.

METRICAL VOCABULARIES.

        i. granat malus mos   bonum opus orationis dicte
Quemque premit cathesis non potest   diasinaxis.
     i. homines cubitales   qui obliquo uidet
Inter   pigmeos   nanus regnat, strabo luscos,
Loripes extales, monotalmus quoque cecos.
        whey i. olla whey potte
Assit[1] plena cero mea   seria, theca leco,
 dispensator, botelere   bakere uel panttere
Promus   et   arthocopus   acerna popina ferinis.
broke-ballockyd   a wowere   i. immundus   pame of the honde[2]
Hernia   praua   proco spurcum genus, et uola cassa,
a loppyster or a crabbe[3]   nostrelle   i. macula in oculo
Polipus[4]   et rini   glauconia sit tibi talmi.[5]
        a botelere buschel   uas olearium
Fert anaphos pincerna bathos, abatis[6] quoque orcam,
      a costrelle   cofer
Et puer onophorum,[7] capsa, caper, armiger, arpen.[8]
waturpotte,   watur   barel
Ydria   dat latices, oleum cadus, anphora uinum;
   a narowcase[9]   bow
Et telum pharatra, corito conditur archus.
princeps omnium, pastor ecclesiæ   i. pius
Archimandrita sit celebs,[10] eusebiusque.

  horse   palfray   kolte   stede   mare
Equus, caballus, pullus, dextrarius, equina;
  bole   oxe   cowe   bulloke   calfe   hayfare
Taurus, bos, uacca, buculus, uitulusque, iuuenca;
   wether schepe lombe   lombe a ram
Est ueruex, ouis, agnellus, simul agnus, aries;
  goote   buk kede   goote idem est   doo   herte
Hircus, capriolus, caper, capra, damaque, ceruus;
  bore   pygge   swyne sow   gelte   sowpyg
Aper, porcellus, porcus, sus, scropha, suilla.
  hond   whelpe   greyhownd   blodehownde
Canis, caniculus, leporarius, atque molosus.
    catte   idem est chytte whesille rotte mowse
Murelegus, catus, catulus, mustela, rato, mus.
  kocke   henne   chekynge capone pokoc swanne
Gallus, gallina, pullus, capo, pauoque, signis.
  gandur   goslynge   mallard doke   gose
Ancer, et ancerulus, anas, anata, simul auca.

---

[1] serio i. ordinatim et est aduerbium, Latin gloss. R. W.

[2] A Latin commentator adds the words, *concauitas palme*.

[3] est piscis, Latin gloss. R. W.

[4] The Latin glossator adds, *sed hic est fetor naris*.

[5] talmon græce oculus latine inde hic talmus (read *ophtalmus*. R. W.) i. oculus.

[6] Hic est Abathis qui præbet auenam, anglice a avenere. R. W.

[7] hic onaphus i. ciphus (read scyphus) supernis (superne?) latens. R. W.

[8] hic arpeps gladius mercurii i. gladius curuatus ad modum falcis. R. W.

[9] hic carichus i. est techa facta de corio, anglice bowcase. R. W.

[10] quasi celestem uitam ducens et idem est quod castus. R. W.

                sparow   larke   pye   revyn   colvyr
        Passer, et alauda, pica, coruusque, columba;
        partbyryd   quayle   wodekoc   jay
        Perdix, coturnix, castrimargus, graculusque;
                    wodekoc   pynok[1] sparowhawke   wrenne
        Gallus siluester, lirifa, nisus, regulusque,
            kyte   chowge   snyte hayron   grype
        Miluus, monedula, sic ibis, ardea, uulter.
        crane   owle popynyay   swalow   nygttyngale
        Grus, bubo, psitagus, et irundo, sic philomena.
            flee   lowse   nete   mothe houdwerme   worme
        Pulex, pediculus, lens, tinea, curio, uermis;
            flye   gnatte   bee   dogflye   addurcop[2] drane
        Musca, culex, apis, ciniphex, aranea, fucus.
        toode   frogge   addure   snayle wateraddure foayle or a snayle
        Bufo, rana, serpens, testudo, uipera,   limax;
        wont[3]   ematte   reremowse   grashoppere butturflye
        Talpa, formica, uespertilioque, cicada, papilio.
        bawsyn[4]   conyng   hare   lyon   lebard
        Castor, cuniculus, lepus, leo, uel leopardus.
        stokfyche wale   eyster   lytul fiche   whelke
        Fungia, cete, uel ostria, pisciculus quoque, concha;
            fyche   neele   samoun lampray   heryng
        Piscis, et anguilla, salmo, murena, uel allec.
        barlyche beene pyse   rye   wheete   otyn
        Ordium, faba, pisa, siligo, frumentum, auena;
                malte   vache   dragge   medylde corne
        Et brasium, uicia, dragetum,[5] mixtilioque.
        Worte siromellum, sed *growte* dicas agromellum;
        sychere   ale   wyne drastys   methe
        Sisera, ceruisia, uinum, feces, ydromellum.
            botyr   whey dordus. curddys[6] chese   mylke
        Butirum, serum, coagulum, casius, et lac;
        crayme   sowre mylke   whey   pushoote[7]   boystryg[8]
        Quactum, exigalum, serum, balducta, colustrum.
        halle   howse   chamer   garner   grange   schepyn
        Aula, domus, camera, granarium, grandia, boscar;
            soler   spence or botrye   kychyn   idem est
        Solarium, promptuarium, coquina, popina;

---

[1] *Pinnock* was a name for the hedge-sparrow.
[2] Cf. pag. 120, note 6.
[3] *Want*, or *wont*, the old name for a mole, is still in use in some of the provincial dialects.
[4] *Bawson, bawsin*, or *baustone*, was a common name for the badger.
[5] This word seems misplaced here. A *dragé*, as representing the Latin word *dragetum*, was a sort of comfit; but in English the word *draggé* was given to a mixed corn, called by Tusser *dredge*, which is evidently the meaning of it in this place. The Promptorium Parvulorum gives „Draggé, menglyd corne, *mixtio*."
[6] This is perhaps the meaning of *dorde* in the old ballad of the Feest, —
Ther was castrell in cambys
And capuls in cullys,
With blandamets in dorde.
[7] A posset. The Prompt. Parv. has „Possot, *balducta*."
[8] I have not met with this English word elsewhere. *Colustrum* is explained in an old glossary quoted in the Dictionary of Ducange by „*novum lac*."

METRICAL VOCABULARIES.

  brewarne bakehouse stabulle stye, or a swyne holke
Pandoxatorium, pistrinum, stabulum, ara.
 tempulle chyrche idem est synagoge chapelle
Templum, ecclesia, basilica, sinagogaque, capella;
(a)nawter oratory chyrche-haye[1] beryels
Ara, oratorium, cimiteriumque, sepulcrum.
 bedde schete chalon[2] quylte bedde-strawe[3]
Lectus, linthiamen, tapetum, culcitra, stratum;
 bolstar coverlyte pelowe blancketh celynge
Seruical, toral, puluinar, lodexque, uelamen.
brasyn potte posnette cawdrune brondyre[4] fryyn-panne panne or potte
Vrceus, vrciolus, cacabus, tripos, lebes, olla;
 mortare pestelle gredyre broche nowle
Mortarium, pila, craticula, ueruque, creagra.
 dysche ladylle erokstyke dobeler plater
Discus, metorium, contus, scutella, parapsis.
 sawsesere spone coop pece[5] salte
Salsarium, coclear, ciphus, crater, simul sal.
 bordeclothe towelle trenchere clothe broche
Gausape, manitergium, scissoria, mappa, uerutum.
 spykkett[6] chesewate oylepott tankard barelle
Clepsidra, casiarium, lechitus, amphora, cadus,
 basyn lauere baucare spere schylde
Peluis, lauatorium, bancarium, lancia, scutum.
 perche checure tabelere dyce idem est
Pertica, scaccarium, alea, decius quoque, talus;
 kyng roche alphyn knyȝt quene pewne
Rex, rocus, alphinus, miles, regina, pedinus.
 hede top molde[7] nolle ere
Est capud et uertex, est cinceput, occeput, auris;
 templys schede lokke here idem est. here
Tempora, discrimen, coma, crinis, siue capillos.
 vesayge scolle brayne werte scrofe or scalle.
Est facies, cranium, cerabrum, papula quoque, glabra.
 yebrowe lede of þe eye space bytwene nostrelle
Est supercilium, cilium, sic palpebra naris.
white of þe face ye happulle ye, i. oculus
Albucies, facies, oculus, pupillaque, talmus;
 forehede nose nostrelle grystylle poose
Frons, nasus, rinus, cartulagoque, caturrus;
 mowthe lyppe berde cheke gummys rofe of the mowthe
Os, labrum, barba, faux, et iangiua, palatum;
 chekebone idem est chynne tonge idem est
Mandula, mandibula, mentum, dens, glossaque, lingua,
 schynyȝt thombe schewyt forefyngure
Pollet enim pollex, res uisas indicat index,

---

[1] *Church-haye*, or *church-hawe*, was not an uncommon name for a churchyard.
[2] „Chalun, bedde-clothe, *thorale, chalo.*" Prompt. Parv.
[3] Straw was the usual material of beds.
[4] A brandreth.
[5] A cup. The Catholicon has the word, „A pece of silver or metalle, *crater, cratera.*"
[6] A spigot.
[7] The suture of the skull.

        medylle fyngure   lechefyngure   acordyt
Stat   medius   medio, medicus iam conuenit egro,
               ere   lytil fyngure
Quas tua fert auris sordes trahit auricularis.
    brest   armepytt syde   tete   idem est   idem est
Pectus, et acella, latus, vber, mamma, mamilla;
    hele foote   too   hele   sole   hele
Calx, pes, articulus, calcanius, plantaque, talus.
  bone flesche yuncte   marowe
Os, caro, iunctura, medio fit in osse medulla;
  werelbone   vayne   zenew   skyn   idem est
Uertebra, cum uena, neruus, pellis, cutis atque.
  thye   hepe the tendurnesse of þe thye ham   grete too   kne
Crus, femur,   et famen   poples, alluxque, genu sit.
  body   hert gal mylt kedney myddereffe
Corpus sunt infra cor, fel, splen, ren, diafragma;
  bowellys   longys   mawe bladdure   ynwarde   throte
Uiscera, pulmo, iecur, uesica, precordia, guttur;
  lyndy   lyuere i. stroma flyxrop blode   idem est
Lumbus, epar, matrix, lien, cruor quoque, sanguis.
  rede blode, a gibelet   gotte
Exta   manent extra, sunt intestina sed intra.
  þe hoole of a prevay arswyspe   gong   idem est   hoole
Gumphus,   menpirium, latrinam, cloaca, foramen.
Dum paro menpirium, sub gumpho murmurat anus.
  ars wolde woman   qwynsys   rawe
Anus   anus   pedit, quia coctona cruda comedit.
       nappyt   hyssyt
Dum dormitat anus, uelud ancer sibulat anus.
  corne mylle mylston   bynne   kog
Far, mola, molaris, faricapsa, scariaballum;
    clakke[1] whele   flodeyate   spyndulle
Batillum, rota, sinoglostorium quoque, fusus.
  forge   fyre   tonge below   marchel   anfeld
Fabrica, pir, forceps, follis, marcollus, et incus;
  pynsors   nayle   cawser   horschoe
Pallatum, scalpum, clauus, incussoria, ferrus.
  schofylle   spade pycows   whelebarow   forke
Tribula, uanga, ligo, ceneuecthorium quoque, furca;
  cracche   idem est   myxon
Presepe, cum presepio, starquiliniumque,
  flexe   welle   hempe selkeworme hordy[2]   selke
Linum, lana, canapus, bumbax, stupa, ceriumque;
               wase   stoppe
Cum grossa stupa rimas edis bene stupa.
  dystafe   spyndylle warbe   threde   reele
Colus cum fuso, uertebrum, filum, alabrumque;

---

[1] The clapper of the mill.
[2] I have not before met with the word *hordy* in the sense of *stupa*. The next line is added in the margin of the manuscript.

METRICAL VOCABULARIES.   628

<small>garnewyne   clewe   warpe   offe¹</small>
Iurgillum, glomerus, subtegmen, sic quoque stamen;
<small>spole   webbe   clothe   idem est   darte</small>
Panus, cum tela, pannus, uestis quoque, telum.
<small>   webbe   dartys</small>
Nos uestit tela, gerimus ad prelia tela.
<small>brydyll   barnaculle²   cropyn³   paytrelle⁴</small>
Frenum, cum chamo, postela, uel antela sit.
<small>solowhanddul solowbeme   solow⁵ cultere chyppe   chare</small>
Stiua,   buris, aratrum, culter, dentale, uomerque.
<small>extre   spokys   cartenave   vely</small>
Est axis duplex, radii sunt, timpana, canti;
<small>solowborde   goke   bonde   wythe</small>
Barcha iugum iungas, hic demum uincula, retorta,
<small>bytylle   wegge</small>
Mallus, intersimonium, meditiliumque.
<small>thombe   harpe   schare   vorow</small>
Pollice tango liram, facio cum uomere liram,
<small>wayne   chare the perrepyllis   carte   thylle</small>
Plaustellum, currus, epredia, bigaque, reda;
<small>barnaculle   brydulle   reyne   idem est   halter</small>
Camus, cum freno, lorum, uel abena, capistrum.
<small>brode axe   persere   axe   hachet   sawe</small>
Est dolabrum, penitral, securis, ascia, cerra.
<small>swerde   idem est basselard⁶   daggar</small>
Ensis, sic gladius, seca, sic sit armicudium.
<small>cordedenare sowter   clowte of a schoo</small>
Est alutarius, sutor quoque, pictacium sit;
<small>clowtere or cobelere   tynkere   lethere brystylle</small>
Pictaciarius, incrustator, corria, seta.
<small>lest   overlether</small>
Formipedia, licinia, impedia sit.
<small>baryngsexe⁷   sole   nalle   corduane</small>
Sunt ausoria, solie, sibula, cordibanumque.
<small>blacchepot   blacche   blacke</small>
Attramentorium, sunt attromenta, sed atrum.
<small>clowtyst   corduane   lest of a boote</small>
Incrustas allutam, dic et quitibiale.

---

¹ „Oof, threde for webbynge, *trama, stamen*," *Prompt. Parv.*; an illustration of which Mr. Way quotes from the Wicliffite version of Leviticus xiii. 47,—" A wullun clooth, or lynnen, that hath a lepre in the *oof* (*in stamine*, Vulg.) or in the werpe, it shall be holdun a lepre."

² I have not before met with this word in the sense of a horse's bit (*camus*.)

³ *Cropon* occurs in the Promptorium Parvulorum as synonymous with crupper.

⁴ The strap across the horse's breast. In the early ballad of True Thomas (in the text of the Cambridge MS.), the caparison of the horse is described thus —

Hir paytrelle was of a rialle fyne
Hir cropur was of arate,
Hir bridulle was of golde fyne,
On every side honge bellis thre.

⁵ The Anglo-Saxon name of the plow, preserved only in the dialects of the West of England. See before, p. 105, note 2.

⁶ The baselard was a long dagger, usually worn suspended at the girdle.

⁷ The Anglo-Saxon *seax*.

METRICAL VOCABULARIES.

   taylere webstere dyere tannare idem est
Est scissor, textor, tinctor, serdoque, frunitor;
 smyth towkere[1] mason skynnere
Est faber, fullo, latamus, penularius atque
 carpyntere   dawbere leche
Carpentarius, est cementarius, aleptes;
 karvere lavendere glovere fowlere
Cironomon, lotrix, cerotecarius, auceps.
 appultre peeretre hasyl note bannenote-tre[2] fygge
Pomus, pirus, corulus, nux, auelanaque, ficus;
 plumtre vyne qwynstre bepetre thewe-thornys[3] ellarue
Prunus, uitis, coctanus, cornus, morusque, sambucus.
 wythy wardentre aspe chasteyn oke
Salix, uolemus, tremulus, castania, quercus;
 beche burche populere asche elme
Fagus, lentiscus, populus, six fraxinus, vlmus;
 ewe boxe vertre wythy mapulle
Taxus, sic buxus, abies, cilor, acer addes.
 busche idem est brere cherytre wyld vyne
Et rubus, dumus, tribulus, cerasus, oliaster;
 yvy pynetre jenupyrtre wylde vyne masere
Edera, pinus, iuniparus, labruscaque, mirra.
 baytre tre bowe more[4] or roote   levys
Laurus, lignum, ramus, radix sunt arbore, frondes,
 smokke brechys schyrt gowne a chymere
Est interula, bracce, camisia, toga, et iupa;
 a bond hoode braygurdylle taberde
Instita, capicium, perysomaque, collobiumque;
 keyfe cappe pyllyon hoose vampey
Thenaque, caleptra, pilius, caligaque, pedana.
 cloke sleve coote kyrtylle
Est armilansa,[5] manica, tinica, tinicella;
 kotyn or pakclothe dobelat   panchere
Est bumbicinium uestis, diploydis, epifemur,
 pope patryarke cardynalle buschope
Papa, patriarcha, cardinalis, presul, atque
 archebyschope prelatte or byschop suffrygane
Archipresul, antistes, suffraganius sit,
  chapyllayne prest idem est
Atque capellanus, sacerdos, presbiter addes,
 decone subdeacone benott idem est
Diaconus, subdiaconus, exorsista, benedictus.
 kyng emparowre pryuce duke a lord of thowsond knygtes
Rex, imperator, princeps, dux, et ciliarcha;

---

[1] A dyer.

[2] In the dialects of the West of England a walnut is universally called a *bannut*. This is by much the earliest example of the word I have met with.

[3] The Anglo-Saxon *thefe-thorn* is usually explained as meaning the wild-briar, or dog-rose, and *ramnus* is given as its Latin equivalent. Perhaps it is intended here for the blackberry.

[4] *More*, a root, is also a word peculiar to the West of England.

[5] Read *armilausa*. R. W.

<small>erle   baron knygth   juge   deacon</small>
Comes, et baro, miles, iudex, diaconusque.
<small>   reve   baylé   vplond-man   cherle</small>
Prepositus, balliuus, rusticus, et colobertus;
<small>towneman   gentylmen bondeman   gentylman</small>
Uillicus, et proceres, natiuus, et est generosus.

Explicit liber Equus caballus, quod Spencer R.

XVII.

NAMES OF THE PARTS OF THE HUMAN BODY.[1]

(OF THE SAME DATE AS THE PRECEDING.)

_{a mowthe   face   chyn   tothe   throte   tonge   rofe of þe mowthe}
Os,   facies,   mentum,   dens,   guttur,   lingua,   palatum;
_{berde   browe   brye² forehede tempelle   lyppe}
Barba,   supercilium,   cilium,   frons,   tempora,   labrum.
_{þe lede   sygt   ye whyte of þe ye   appulle of þe ye}
Palpebra sunt,   acies,   oculus,   albugo,   pupilla.
_{cop of þe nose   snevel of þe nose   the brygge of þe nose   nostrelle}
Purula,   pus nasi   sunt,   interfinia,   naris.
_{fore party of þe hede myddul party   nolle   the brayne}
Sinciput,   interciput,   occiput,   ac cerabrum,   pars
_{hede   scolle   foretop schade of þe here   ere}
Est capitis,   cranium,   uertex,   discrimen,   et auris.
_{cheke   gummes   here}
ffaux,   et iungiue,   cum frontinella,   capillis.
_{grystyl of þe nose   lap of þe ere   cheketothe}
Est cartilago,   sic legia,   sic genuinus.
_{pame of þe honde   iutys³   handus   cubyte   a feme}
Palme,   iuncture manibus sunt,   vlna,   lacertus;
_{nayle   fyngurys   schuldur   breste   nekke}
Vngues cum digitis,   humerus,   cum pectore,   collum.
_{armepytt   fyste   a cubyte   blodde   tete}
Acella,   pugnus,   cubitus,   cum sanguine,   mamma;

---

[1] This is printed from the same manuscript as the preceding more general vocabulary, which it follows immediately as a sort of supplement (MS. Harl. No. 1002, fol. 116, v°).

[2] The eyelashes.

[3] So has the MS. Read *iuntys*. R. W.

PARTS OF THE HUMAN BODY.

   wombe   bladdur   bakke   rybbebone   rybbe
Uenter, uesica, tergum, spondilia, costa.
     a navyle   syede   flesche skynne buttok
Est vmbilicus, latus, et caro, pelle, nates sunt.
  hert mylte   longes long gutte gal kydney mydrefe   mawe
Cor, splen, pulmo, lien, fel, ren, diafragma, iecurque.
 a narce thye   schare   bakke backebone arcehoole
Anus, crus, pubes, dorsum, sic spina, podexque.
smal-pypys[1] stomake   inwarde   lyver
Arterie,   stomacus, post intestina, sic epar.
 whyrleboue   kneys   kneepanne   zenew
Uertebra cum genibus, sunt internodia, neruus;
   hamme   schene modure   ancle
Poples, atque sura, matrix hiis additur, anca,
the sperlyver[2] vayne   legge   the mayster vayne
Musculus, et uena, sic tibia, sicque sophena.
   tooyn sole of þe foote   heele   marow   a pynne
Articuli,   planta,   cum calce, medulla, cauilla.
  part foote   hele   pathe idem est
Pars pedis est hic calx, sed dicitur semita callis.
          grete too thome   reder
Istis coniungas[3] allux, pollex quoque, lector.
a mane hys thyng idem est   a pyntyl   idem est   idem
Menticula,   testiculi, ueratrum, tentigo, priapus.
     thombe forefyngur medulle fyngur lechefyngur lityllefyngure
Est pollex, index,   medius,   medicus, auricularis.
        lemys   of a beste
Hec sunt menbra uiri, sed dic partes animalis.

---

[1] A rather curious name for the arteries.
[2] More usually *sperlire*, or *sparlire*, the Anglo-Saxon name for the calf of the leg.
[3] The MS. has *coniugas*. R. W.

XVIII.

ENGLISH VOCABULARY.[1]

(OF THE FIFTEENTH CENTURY.)

NOMINA MENBRORUM HOMINIS.

Hoc capud, A^c hede.
Hoc incipud, A^c frunte.
Hoc intercipud, est media pars.
Hoc occipud, A^c nodulle, capitis.
Hec cesaries, A^c fortoppe.
Hic crinis, A^c hare.
Hic pilus, A^c here.
Hic cicinnus, A^c lokkes.
Hec corona, A^c crowne.
Hic cirrus, A^c nodulle.
Hec ceruex, A^c hatrelle.[2]
Hec auris, A^c nere.
Hoc cilium, A^c here of the hee.
Hoc supercilium, A^c browe.
Hoc intercilium, i. spacium inter cilia.
Hic oculus, A^c hee.
Hec palpebra, A^c heelyde.
5 Hec albugo, A^c wyte of the hee.
Hec pupilla, A^c perylle.[3]
Hec acies, A^c syght.
Hic nasus, A^c nese.
Hoc interfinium, A^c bryg of the nese.
10 Hec naris, A^c nesestyrlle.
Hic purulus, A^c neschende.
Hoc labium, A^c lyppe.
Hoc labrum, idem est.
Hoc os, -ris, A^c mowthe.
15 Hoc momentum,[4] A^c chynne.
Hec menta, A^c chyne.

---

[1] This vocabulary of names of things, in Latin and English, is printed from a manuscript of, I think, early in the fifteenth century, in the old Royal Library in the British Museum, MS. Reg. 17, C. XVII., fol. 21, ro. The MS. contains other tracts of the same character.

[2] The crown of the head. The Latin should be vertex instead of cervex. Halliwell, Dict. of Archaic Words, gives the following illustrative lines from a MS. of the fifteenth century:

Also from the haterel of the croun
To the sole of the foot ther doun.

[3] Perle means an affection in the eye, apparently what we now call a sty.

[4] Read mentum. R. W

ENGLISH VOCABULARY.

Hec gena, A^e cheke.
Hec mala, idem est.
Hoc ffaus, idem est.
Hec maxilla, A^e chekebane.
Hoc genobodum, idem est.
Hoc tempus, A^e thonwangues.
Hec cartulago, A^e gro.
Hoc collum, A^e necke.
Hec barba, A^e berde.
Hoc cranium, A^e harnpanne.
Hoc cerebrum, A^e harnes.
Hic dens, A^e thothe.
Hic geminus, A^e wangtotht.
Hic molaris, idem est.
Hec lingua, A^e tong.
Hec glossa, idem est.
Hec gula, A^e troht.
Hoc guttur, idem est.
Hic ysofagus, A^e waysande.
Hoc frumen, A^e code.
Hic humerus, A^e schuldyre.
Hoc brachium, A^e arme.
Hic cubitus, A^e helbow.
Hic musculus, A^e brawne.
Hec sura, idem est.
Hec pulpa, idem est.
Hec manus, A^e hande.
Hec palma, bola, et ir, idem sunt.
Hic pollex, A^e thowme.
Hic digitus, A^e fynger.
Hoc corpus, A^e body.
Hoc dorsum, A^e bake.
Hic uenter, A^e wambe.
Hec caro, A^e flesche.
Hic pectus, A^e breste.
Hoc corium, A^e hyde.
Hec cutis, idem est.
Hic sanguis, A^e blode.
Hic humor, idem est.

Hoc os, ossis, A^e bone.
Hec medulla, A^e marow.
Hec febra, A^e wayne.
Hec uena, idem est.
5 Hoc palatum, A^e palate.
Hic orexis, est anelitus oris.
Hic polipus, A^e snotte.
Hec vlna est spatium inter manum et capud.
10 Hic nodus, A^e knokylle.
Hoc epilacium, A^e honde-mowle.[1]
Hec junctura, A^e joynte.
Hec vnguis, A^e nayle.
Hec vngula, idem est.
15 Hec mamma, A^e pappe.
Hec mamilla, idem est.
Hoc vber, idem est.[2]
Hic torax, A^e brestbone.
Hic vmbelicus, A^e nawelle.
20 Hic clunis, idem est.[3]
Hec nates, A^e thees.
Hic lumbus, idem est.
Hec piga, idem est.
Hec pinguedo, A^e grese.
25 Hic pirtomen, A^e arsholere.
Hec wlua, A^e cuntte.
Hoc oilinetum, A^e mygrayne.
Hec tentigo, A^e kykyre.
Hoc epar, A^e lywer.
30 Hoc splen, A^e mylte.
Hoc fel, A^e galle.
Hic pulmo, A^e lunggys.
Hic stomacus, A^e stomak.
Hoc gecur, A^e maw.
35 Hoc diafragma, A^e myddere.[4]
Hoc ren, A^e nere.[5]
Hoc uiscus, A^e bowelle.
Hoc perecordium, idem est.
Hoc ueretrum, A^e pyntylle.

---

[1] The honde-mowle appears to have been the palm of the hand. It is the gloss on copinole in Walter de Biblesworth.

[2] Another vocabulary in the same volume of MS. (MS. Reg. 17 C. XVII., fol. 38 v°.) gives „uber, -is, Anglice hyddere," the latter word no doubt representing the modern udder.

[3] The glossator has misinterpreted this word and the next. The Nominale in the same MS. (Reg. 17 C. XVII., fol. 39, ro) explains, „hec natis, Anglice luddockes."

[4] For mydderede, the midriff.

[5] An old name for the kidney, still preserved in the dialects of East Anglia, though it is more usually employed popularly to denote the fat of the kidneys.

Hic priapus, est finis ueretri.
Hic cirbus, A^e harstharme.
Hoc femur, A^e thee.
Hic poplex, A^e hamme.
Hoc genu, A^e knee.
Hec tubia, A^e schanke.
Hic pes, -dis, A^e fote.
Hic talus, A^e hele.
Hic artuculus, A^e tho.
Hec cauilla, A^e ankylle.
Hec anta, A^e knebone.
Hoc mandibulum, A^e chewylle.[1]
Hec fragus, A^e kneborde.
Hec matrix est in qua inuoluitur puer.
Hec homopleta, A^e schulderbane.
Hec allux, A^e grete to.
Hec acella, A^e harmole.
Hec uarex, -cis, est quedam uena tendens a uertice capitis vsque ad plantam, que si bedatur reddet hominem curuum.

NOMINA ANIMALIUM.

Hic et hec bos, A^e neete.
Hic trio, idem est.
Hic bouiculus, A^e bullok.
Hec uacca, A^e kowe.
Hec jumenta, A^e que.
Hec junix, idem est.
Hic taurus, A^e bulle.
Hic uitulus, A^e calfe.
Hic equs, A^e horse.
Hec equa, A^e mere.
Hic caballus, A^e carthors.
Hoc equicium, A^e harres.
Hic equiferus, A^e wyld hors.
Hic dextrarius, A^e stede.
Hic mannus, A^e rownse.[2]
Hic bladius, A^e hackenay.
Hic equilas, idem est.

Hic palifridus, A^e palfray.
Hic tradarius, idem est.
Hic emissarius, A^e stalon.
Hic pullus, A^e fole.
5 Hec porca, A^e sowe.
Hic porcus, A^e swyne.
Hic porcellus, A^e gryse.
Hoc aper, A^e bore.
Hic cingulus, idem.
10 Hic oderinsicus, A^e spanegeole.[3]
Hic leporarius, A^e grayhownd.
Hec licesta, A^e byche.
Hic canis, A^e dogge.
Hic molosus, A^e banddogge.
15 Hic ancer, A^e gandyr.
Hec auca, A^e gosse.
Hic ancerulus, A^e geslyng.
Hec aucula, idem.
Hic gallus, A^e cocke.
20 Hec gallina, A^e henne.
Hic pullus, A^e chekyn.
Hic capo, A^e capon.
Hoc astile, idem.
Hic spado, -inis, idem.
25 Hic catus, A^e catte.
Hic mureligus, A^e idem.
Hic pilax, idem.
Hic juba, A^e horsemane.
Hec caprona, idem.
30 Hic dromedarius, A^e drowmondere.
Hic rato, A^e raton.
Hic soriex, idem.
Hic mus, A^e mowse.
Hic ouis, A^e schepe.
35 Hic aries, A^e wedyr.
Hic gargia, A^e gymbure.[4]
Hic agnus, A^e lamme.
Hec ambigua, est ouis portans duos agnos.
40

---

[1] Chewylle, for chowl, or jowl, the jaw.
[2] Rounse. A rouncy is generally interpreted as meaning a common hackney horse. Thus, in the romance of Ipomydon (Weber, Met. R., vol. ii., p. 340), when the hero went to disguise himself as an half-witted and clownish fellow —
Armure he toke that was rusty,
And horsyd hym on an old rouncy.
[3] A spaniel.
[4] In Lincolnshire, they still call a female sheep which has been twice shorn a gimber; in the north of England it is called a gimmer.

NOMINA ANIMALIUM FERARUM.

Hic leo, Aᵉ lyon.
Hec liona, Aᵉ lyonys.
Hic lupus, Aᵉ wlfe.
Hic lepus, Aᵉ hare.
Hic wlpes, Aᵉ foxe.
Hec mustela, Aᵉ weysyl.
Hic fetonarus, Aᵉ fulmerde.
Hic erinacius, Aᵉ hurchon.
Hec melota, Aᵉ broke.[1]
Hic taxus, idem.
Hec talpa, Aᵉ molle.
Hic pardus, Aᵉ leparde.
Hec parda, est femella.
Hic pardus, est qui generat cum leona.
Hic ceruus, Aᵉ harte.
Hec cerua, Aᵉ hynde.
Hic hinulus, Aᵉ fawne.
Hec simea, Aᵉ nape.
Hic vrsus, Aᵉ bere.
Hic vrcus, Aᵉ buke.
Hoc elephas, -tis, Aᵉ elyfawnte.
Hec pantera, Aᵉ pantere, cum multis coloribus.
Hic et hec linx, est animal habens oculos acutos.
Hic scurellus, Aᵉ a squyrylle.
Hic sirogrillus, idem.
Hic Cuniculus, Aᵉ conninge.
Hic zenozephalus, Aᵉ maremusset.
Hic furestus, uel forestus, Aᵉ forest.[2]

NOMINA AUIUM.

Hic fornix, Aᵉ wodekok.
Hec orna, idem.
Hec philomena, Aᵉ nyghtyngale.
Hec lucar, i. lucia.
Hec nicticorax, Aᵉ nyghtcrake.[3]
Hec avia, idem.

Hec ardua, Aᵉ heyrune.
Hec columba, Aᵉ dowwe.
Hic palumbus, Aᵉ stokedowef.
Hic mauiscus, Aᵉ mawysse.
5 Hec fidedula, idem.
Hec merges, Aᵉ cote.
Hic sturnus, Aᵉ sterlyng.
Hic regulus, Aᵉ wrenne.
Hic sperrus, idem.
10 Hic carduelis, Aᵉ goldefynche.
Hic cabus, Aᵉ crawe.
Hec aquila, Aᵉ negglc.
Hec miluus, Aᵉ glede.[4]
Hic pascer, Aᵉ sparow.
15 Hec vpipa, Aᵉ wype.[5]
Hic tercellus, Aᵉ hawke.
Hic prepes, idem.
Hic nisus, Aᵉ sperhawke.
Hic ancipiter, Aᵉ goshawke.
20 Hic erodius, Aᵉ gerfawcune.
Hic graculus, Aᵉ jay.
Hic citacus, Aᵉ papinjay.
Hec alauda, Aᵉ larke.
Hic arundo, Aᵉ swalo.
25 Hec nodula, Aᵉ kae.[6]
Hec bubo, -is, Aᵉ nowle.
Hic coruus, Aᵉ rawyn.
Hic frondator, Aᵉ tytmase.
Hec olor, Aᵉ swane.
30 Hic signus, idem.
Hic grus, Aᵉ crane.
Hic cuculus, Aᵉ cucko.
Hec frigella, Aᵉ robynet, redbrest.[7]
Hec ciconia, Aᵉ storke.
35 Hec marula, est auis habens nigrum rostrum.
Hic pellicar, Aᵉ pellicane.
Hic rostellus, Aᵉ spynke.
Hec frugella, Aᵉ roke.
40 Hec agalauda, Aᵉ plowere.
Hic perdix, Aᵉ pertrycke.

---

[1] The broke was the badger.
[2] The ferret.
[3] The caprimulgus Europaus, still called in Yorkshire a night-crow. Its more usual name is night-jar.
[4] A kite. The Anglo-Saxon name. See p. 132 l. 16.
[5] The lapwing.
[6] A chough. The A.-S. ceo.
[7] i. e., „little Robin" redbreast. It is the earliest instance of the use of this popular name that I have met with. Robin was a common appellation of affectionate familiarity.

Hec *fuliga*, A*e* semawe.
Hic *campester*, A*e* feldfare.
Hic *merulus*, A*e* marlyon.
Hic *cornix*, A*e* crawe.
Hic *pauo*, A*e* pacok.
Hic *coturnix*, A*e* morehene.
Hic *vltur*, A*e* grype.[1]
Hic *fasianus*, A*e* fesant.
Hoc *rustrum*, A*e* nebbe.[2]
Hic *mergus*, A*e* cote.
Hec *qualia*, A*e* quayle.
Hic *pellicanus*, A*e* pellycane.
Hic *fenix*, A*e* fenys.
Hic **capus**, A*e* muskett.[3]

NOMINA PISCIUM.

Hoc *allec*, A*e* heryng.
Hic *salmo*, A*e* salmon.
Hoc *mugyl*, idem.
Hic *uronoscopus*, A*e* thornbak.
Hic *fundulus*, A*e* playsse.
Hic *pecten*, idem.
Hic *luceus*, A*e* pyke.
Hic *dentrix*, idem.
Hic *lucellus*, A*e* pyckerylle.
Hic *gamerus*, A*e* spyrlyng.
Hic *silurus*, A*e* loche.
Hic *scorpio*, A*e* stytlyng.[4]
Hec *muprena*, A*e* lamprune.
Hec *lampada*, A*e* lampray.
Hic *caput*, A*e* caboche.[5]
Hec *anguilla*, A*e* nele.
Hic *cancer*, A*e* crabbe.
Hec *balena*, A*e* qwalle.
Hic *cetus*, idem.
Hec *ceta*, idem.
Hoc *cete*, idem.
Hic *congruus*, A*e* conggyre.
Hic *epimora*, est piscis qui moritur eodem die quo nascitur.
Hoc *cochile*, est quilibet piscis obtecta.

[1] *Grype* was an old name for the vulture, and is not unfrequently found in that sense in the early metrical romances, though it is sometimes used to signify a griffin.
[2] A bird's neb or beak.
[3] The male of the sparrowhawk.

Hoc *ostrium*, A*e* ostyre.
Hic *megarus*, A*e* makyrelle.
Hic *ypotamus*, est marinus.
Hic *rochea*, A*e* roche.
5 Hic *brumillus*, A*e* brone.[6]
Hec *tortuga*, A*e* wylke.
Hic *rumbus*, A*e* storjon.
Hic *clanitus*, A*e* wytyng.
Hic *torpedo*, est piscis habens multos
10 pedes.
Hec *phoca*, A*e* porpas.
Hec *delphin*, A*e* sawmone.
Hec *merula*, A*e* lamprone.
Hec *rogaterea*, A*e* thornbacke.
15 Hic *textus*, A*e* tenche.
Hic *mullus*, A*e* codlyng.
Hic *codlingus*, idem.
Hec *perca*, A*e* perche.
Hec *gamorus*, A*e* hornekek.
20 Hic *gobio*, A*e* gojune.
Hoc *turtur*, A*e* turbote.
Hic *polupus*, A*e* lopstere.
Hec *conca*, A*e* cochilt.

25 ## NOMINA UERMIUM.

Hec *cerpigo*, -nis, A*e* regworme.
Hec *lacerta*, A*e* newte.
Hec *vria*, est pediculus porci.
Hec *lens*, -dis, A*e* nyte.
30 Hec *salamandra*, A*e* cryket.
Hic *grillius*, idem.
Hec *apes*, A*e* bee.
Hec *saguisuga*, i. irundo.
Hec *pala*, A*e* wode.
35 Hec *sicada*, A*e* gyrssoppe.
Hec *irania*, A*e* erane.[7]
Hec *amittena*, A*e* scheptyke.
Hec *culex*, A*e* knate.
Hic *fucus*, A*e* drane.
40 Hec *uaspa*, A*e* waspe.
Hic *papilio*, A*e* butterfle.

[4] The stickleback.
[5] The bulhead, or miller's-thumb, called in old French *chabot*.
[6] *Brone*, the bream.
[7] *Erane*, or *irane*, from the A.-N., was a common name for a spider.

Hec teredo, est uermis corodens ligna.
Hic cimex, A⁶ mawke.¹
Hec tinea, A⁶ moke.²
Hic cirus, A⁶ handworme.
Hic scarabeus, A⁶ wode.
Hec incedula, A⁶ glydeworme.³
Hec nocticula, A⁶ idem.
Hec noctuluca, idem.
Hec tanterida, est uermis terre.
Hic emigramus, est uermis capitis.
Hic lumbricus, est uermis uentri.
Hic tarus, est uermis lardi.
Hic bombex, A⁶ sylkworme.
Hic bufo, A⁶ tade.
Hic erinacius, A⁶ nurchon.
Hic glis, -ris, A⁶ dormowse.
Hec formica, A⁶ pysmyre.
Hec testugo, A⁶ snele.
Hic limax, -cis, idem.

NOMINA HERBARUM.

Hoc petrocillum, A⁶ percylle.
Hoc ciler, A⁶ mynte.
Hec menta, idem.
Hoc nausticium, A⁶ waterkyrs.
Hoc milifolium, A⁶ mylfoile.
Hec beta, A⁶ bete.
Hic ysopus, A⁶ ysoppe.
  Ysopus est harba, ysopo spergitur unda.
Hec altea, A⁶ wyld malle.
Hec saliunca, A⁶ wyne.
Hec uepres,
Hec vua, A⁶ grapys.
Hic calamus, A⁶ rede.
Hec rosa, A⁶ rose.
Hoc lilium, A⁶ lylle.

Hec minifera, A⁶ waterlylle.
Hec embroca, A⁶ maythe.⁴
Hic daucus, A⁶ clapwype.⁵
Hoc olus, -ris, A⁶ worte.
5 Hoc magudere, A⁶ calstok.
Hic caulus, A⁶ uwle (?) or thyme.
Hec cuna, A⁶ croppe.⁶
Hec saliua, A⁶ salwe.
Hec vrtica, A⁶ nettylle.
10 Hec pimpinella, A⁶ primerolle.
Hoc ligustrum, idem.
Hoc pringrius, idem.
Hec uiola, A⁶ wyolet.
Hoc uaccinium, A⁶ cowsokulle.⁷
15 Hec papauer, A⁶ chesbolle.⁸
Hoc omella, idem.
Hic felix, -cis, A⁶ brakyn.
Hoc solsequium, A⁶ sawsykylle.
Hoc ditaneum, A⁶ dytan.
20 Hoc columbina, A⁶ colybyn.
Hec lactuca, A⁶ letys.
Hic muscus, A⁶ muske.
Hic carduus, A⁶ thystylle.
Hoc gramen, A⁶ bent.⁹
25 Hec murica, A⁶ wermⁱne brome.
Hec edera, A⁶ iwyn.
Hec licoricia, A⁶ licorys.
Hoc alleum, A⁶ garle.
Hoc sinapium, A⁶ warkecok.
30 Hec sepula, A⁶ chesbolle.
Hec salgea, A⁶ sawge.
Hec selidonia, A⁶ solydyne.
Hoc feniculum, A⁶ fynkylle.
Hec malua, A⁶ malle.
35 Hoc apium, A⁶ the.
Hoc trifolium, A⁶ hartclauer.
Hic sicassis, idem.

---

¹ *Mawke*, a maggot, still in use in the northern dialects.
² A moth.
³ The glow-worm.
⁴ Camomile (the *anthemis cotula* of botanists), still called in some districts *may weed*; the A.-S. *mageda*. See the A.-S. Vocabularies.
⁵ *Clap-wype. Daucus* is understood to mean the parsnip.
⁶ Perhaps it should be *cima*, the crop, or top, of a plant. The Catholicon has „a croppe, *cima.*"
⁷ Apparently another name for the cowslip.
⁸ *Chesbolle* was an old name for the poppy.
⁹ The word *bent* was applied usually to the long coarse grass growing on the moors, but often in a more general sense to grass of all kinds.

Hoc *pentifolium*, A*ᶜ* filife.
Hoc *sirpillum*, A*ᶜ* petergrys.¹
Hoc *piper*, A*ᶜ* pepyre.
Hoc *siminum*, A*ᶜ* comyne.
Hoc *synamomum*, A*ᶜ* canelle.
Hoc *strigillum*, A*ᶜ* morelle.
Hoc *solatrum*, idem.
Hec *ueruena*, A*ᶜ* warwayn.
Hec *agremonia*, A*ᶜ* ogremoyne.
Hec *pimpernella*, A*ᶜ* pimpernolle.
Hec *sintecula*, A*ᶜ* synthon.
Hec *scandur*, A*ᶜ* madyr.
Hic *sendo*, idem.
Hec *pionia*, A*ᶜ* pyon.
Hic *tintimalius*, A*ᶜ* spowrge.
Hec *rapa*, A*ᶜ* rape.
Hoc *bacar*, A*ᶜ* nepe.
Hic *crocus*, A*ᶜ* safurroun.
Hic *plantago*, A*ᶜ* waybred.
Hoc *raparium*, A*ᶜ* raddyk.
Hic *tipus*, A*ᶜ* homelok.
Hec *secuta*, idem.
Hic *cardo*, A*ᶜ* cardoun.²
Hic *carduus*, A*ᶜ* tasylle.
Hic *arundo*, A*ᶜ* rede.
Hec *canna*, A*ᶜ* cane.
Hec *carix*, *-cis*, A*ᶜ* segge.
Hec *papirio*, A*ᶜ* reschebusk.
Hic *junctus*, A*ᶜ* resche.
Hic *sirpus*, idem.
Hic *papirius*, idem.
Hoc *borago*, A*ᶜ* borage.
Hoc *sepe*, A*ᶜ* hongon.
Hec *concilida*, A*ᶜ* consaude.
Hoc *absinthium*, A*ᶜ* wormode.
Hec *costus*, A*ᶜ* coste.
Hec *febrifuga*, A*ᶜ* fevyrfew.
Hec *gensta*, A*ᶜ* gromylle.³
Hec *lappa*, A*ᶜ* clete.⁴
Hec *endiua*, A*ᶜ* endywe.

NOMINA ARBORUM.

Regula est quod omnia nomina arborum sunt feminini generis exceptis quatuor,
5 *hic oliaster, et hic piaster, hic rubus, et hic dumus. Hic oliaster est vua sterilis.*

Hec *quarcus*, A*ᶜ* ake.
10 Hec *uolemus*, A*ᶜ* permayntre.
Hec *ibex*, *est juuenis quarcus*.
Hec *sambuca*, A*ᶜ* hyllortre.⁵
Hec *taxus*, A*ᶜ* hawtre, newtre.
Hec *corolus*, A*ᶜ* hesylletre.
15 Hec *auelana*, A*ᶜ* walnottre.
Hec *arbutus*, A*ᶜ* crabtre.
Hec *fraxinus*, A*ᶜ* heschetre.
Hec *pepulus*, A*ᶜ* popultre.
Hec *ascer*, *-ris*, A*ᶜ* mapulletre.
20 Hec *abies*, A*ᶜ* fyrretre.
Hec *prunus*, A*ᶜ* plumtre.
Hec *castania*, A*ᶜ* chestantre.⁶
Hec *ficus*, A*ᶜ* fyketre, *uel fructus*.

Nux, auelana, pirus, glans, et castania,
25 ficus,
Fructum cum ligno sub eodem nomine signo.

Hec *mesculus*, A*ᶜ* meletre.
Hec *sorbus*, A*ᶜ* opynharstre.⁷
30 Hec *sirasus*, A*ᶜ* cheritre.
Hec *oliua*, A*ᶜ* olyftre.
Hec *sentis*, *est spina*.
Hec *silex*, A*ᶜ* wyllotre.
Hec *lentiscus*, A*ᶜ* byrketre.
35 Hec *coccinus*, A*ᶜ* quoynetre.
Hec *tremulus*, A*ᶜ* hespetre.
Hec *malus*, A*ᶜ* apultre.
Hec *pomus*, idem.
Hec *tribulus*, A*ᶜ* brame.⁸
40 Hec *uepres*, idem.

---

¹ Serpillum is understood as meaning, in the older vocabularies, wild thyme.
² Cardon (Lat. *carduus*), the old French name for the thistle; in modern French, *chardon*.
³ *Gromylle*, the plant now called gromwell, the *lithospermum officinale* of botanists.
⁴ The clote, or yellow water-lilly.
⁵ *Hyllor*, the elder, still called in some parts of England a *hilder-tree*.
⁶ *Chestan-tre*, the chestnut. See before, the note 3 on p. 138.
⁷ See before, p. 137 l. 36.
⁸ i. e., a bramble.

Hec singinerperus, est quedam arbor cuius cyneres uolunt ignem seruare per annum.
Signiperus quod glens pir tibi dicitur arbor,
De gigno, -is, et pir, quod dicitur ignis,
Et cuius cyneres innolent ardere per annum.

Hoc uimen, A^e osere.
Hic uiburius, A^e idem.
Hec cornus, A^e pettre.
Hec morus, A^e mulberytre.
Hec tilia, A^e bastetre.
Hec vssis, A^e olyntre.
Hec damasenus, A^e damyssyntre.
Hec cedrus, A^e sydyretre, et est talis nature quod nunquam putrescet in aqua nec in terra.
Hec cipressus, est arbor odorissimus et tepida, et habet naturam et rubrum colorem, A^e cypyrtre.

NOMINA FRUCTUUM.

Hoc pomum, A^e apulle.
Hec nux, A^e notte.
Hic nuclius, A^e kyrnelle.
Hec auelena, A^e walnot.
Hoc pirum, A^e pere.
Hec glans, A^e acorne.
Hoc ciresum, A^e chery.
Hoc uolemum, A^e permayne.[1]
Hoc prunum, A^e plumme.
Hoc stragum, A^e strabery.
Hic ficus, A^e fyke.
Hec racemus, A^e rasyn.
Hec vuapassa, idem.
Hec rua, A^e grape.
Hoc sorbum, A^e hopynhars.
Hoc malum granatum, A^e pounkarnet.[2]
Hoc malum punicum, idem.
Hoc coccinum, A^e quoyne.[3]
Hoc masuclum, A^e orange.

Hoc cornum, A^e pete.

NOMINA PERTINENCIA ECCLESIE.

5 *Hoc delebrum, i. ecclesia.*
Hoc altare, i. ara.
Hic calix, A^e chalys.
Hec patena, A^e patent.
Hic sercophagus, i. petra.
10 *Hec tumba, idem.*
Hec libitina, A^e bere.
Hoc feretrum, idem.
Hoc tribulum, A^e sensours.
Hoc tus, A^e cense.
15 *Hec ascera, A^e a lytil chyp.*
Hec campana, A^e belle.
Hoc tintinabilum, A^e lytylle belle.
Hoc uentilogium, A^e wedercok.
Hec ymago, A^e ymage.
20 *Hoc semitorium, A^e kyrgarth.*[4]
Hoc marmor, A^e marbulle.
Hec candela, A^e candylle.
Hoc candelabrum, A^e candylstyk.
Hoc campanile, A^e stepulle.
25 *Hoc aspersorium, A^e strynkylle.*[5]
Hic ysopus, A^e idem est.
Hic ambo, -is, A^e letrune.[6]
Hoc campanare, A^e belhowse.
Hoc ablatum, A^e obley.
30 *Hoc antiphonarium, A^e anfenare.*
Hoc missale, A^e mesbok.
Hoc gradale, A^e grayel.
Hoc troperium, A^e tropure.
Hoc martilogium, A^e martilage.
35 *Hec bibleoteca, A^e bybulle.*
Hoc armariolum, A^e almery.
Hoc sacrarium, A^e sacrary.
Hoc orologium, A^e orlage.
Hoc uitrum, A^e glasse.
40 *Hoc sudarium, A^e sudary.*

---

[1] A sort of apple, of which Drayton speaks as being a modern importation into our island.
  The pearemaine, which to France long ere to us
      was knowne,
  Which careful frut'rers now have denizen'd our
      owne.
        Polyolb., Song xviii.

[2] The pomegranate.
[3] *Quoyne*, or *coyne*, the quince.
[4] The churchyard, still called a *kirkgarth* in the north.
[5] The holy-water sprinkler, or *aspersoir*.
[6] The lectern, or reading desk.

Hec cera, A^e wax.
Hec cancella, A^e chawnsylle.
Hic corus, idem est.
Tres sunt partes columne, talus, stilus, et epistilium; uasis est fundamentum, stilus est media pars, epistilium est superior pars.
Hoc superpelicium, A^e surplys.
Hec crisma, A^e creme.[1]
Hoc crismatorum, A^e crismator.
Hec alba, A^e haube.
Hec stola, A^e stole.
Hec crux, A^e crosse.
Hoc lauatorium, A^e lavatory.
Hec fons, A^e welle.[2]
Hic cereus, A^e serge.
Hic lampas, A^e lampe.
Hic absconsus, A^e sconse.[3]
Hec lucerna, A^e lantyrne.
Hoc pulpitum, A^e polepyt.
Hec fiola, A^e fiolle.
Hoc oleum, A^e oyle.
Hec pixis, A^e boyst.[4]
Hoc alabaustrum, A^e idem est.
Hec hostia, est corpus Christi.
Hoc uiaticum, idem est.
Hoc uestiarium, A^e rewystre.
Hoc clamparium, A^e clochere.[5]
Hec restis, est corda.
Hoc fedus, idem.
Hic laqueus, idem.
Hic funiculus, idem.
Hic batillus, A^e clapyre.
Hoc manutergium, A^e towelle.
Hec peruria, A^e perrore.
Hoc uelum, A^e wayle.
Hic amittus, A^e amytte.
Hic tiera, idem est.
Hec fanulla, A^e fanone.
Hic manipulus, A^e idem est.
Hec zona, A^e gyrdylle.
Hec poderis, A^e rochytt.

Hec infula, A^e chesibylle.[6]
Hoc ostrum, i. purpura.
Hoc ordinale, A^e ordinalle.
Hic ordinarius, idem est.

NOMINA ARTIFICIORUM.

Hic excubus, A^e wayte.
Hic liricen, qui canit in lira.
Hic secuticen, qui canit in scituta.
Hic tibicen, qui canit in tubia.
Hic monetarius, qui facit monetam.
Hic aurifaber, A^e goldesmythe.
Hic candidarius, A^e lawnder.
Hic, hec formicapola, uenditor vnguentorum.
Hic sementarius, A^e mason.
Hic littamus, idem est.
Hic mango, A^e horsemownger.
Hic mores, i. quod stultus.
Hic sissor, A^e taylegour.
Hic carpentarius, A^e kartwryght.
Hic molendinarius, A^e mylur.
Hic frunes, A^e barkare.[7]
Hic tannator, idem est.
Hic serdo, idem est.
Hic pandoxatrix, A^e bacstare.
Hic architector, A^e thekare.[8]
Hic cuparius, A^e cowpare.
Hic aliator, A^e hassardore.
Hic triculator, A^e tresorre.[9]
Hic tesaurarius, idem est.
Hic figulus, A^e potter.
Hic pistor, A^e backstare.
Hic carnifex, A^e bochere.
Hic seroticarius, A^e glowere.[10]
Hic pelliparius, A^e schynnere.
Hic scriba, A^e chaunsyllere.
Hic cancellarius, idem est.
Hic sinescallus, A^e stewerede.
Hic uicecomes, A^e scheryf.
Hic comes, A^e herrylle.
Hec comitissa, A^e cowntasse.

---

[1] The crism, or consecrated oil.
[2] More correctly the font.
[3] A sort of candlestick made to be attached to the wall. The word is still in use for such candlesticks in the north of England.
[4] The box for holding the oil, &c., a pyx.
[5] Read campanarium. R. W.
[6] The MS. has chesibylle or clesibylle. R. W.
[7] i. e., a tanner.
[8] Literally a thatcher.
[9] Tresorre, a treasurer.
[10] A glover. The Latin word should be cirotecarius, for chirothecarius.

Hic baro, A^e baron.
Hec baronissa, A^e baronys.
Hic abbas, A^e abott.
Hic prior, A^e pryor
Hic monacus, A^e monk.
Hic canonicus, A^e chanon.
Hic opilio, A^e scheperd.
Hic subulcus, A^e swynard.
Hic bubulcus, A^e hoxhard.
Hic ortolanus, A^e gardyner.
Hic nugator, A^e trifulere.
Hic pincerna, A^e botelere.
Hic, hec aduena, A^e comelyng.[1]
Hic temerarius, A^e folehardy.
Hic cocus, A^e coke.
Hic coquinarius, idem est.
Hic lixa, idem est quod lixo, A^e quystrone.
Hic barbitansor, A^e barbur.
Hic auceps, A^e fowlere.
Hic piscator, A^e fyschere.
Hec pectrix, A^e kemster.
Hic textor, A^e webstere.
Hic fullo, A^e fullare.
Hic faber, A^e smythe.
Hec fabrissa, A^e smytwyfe.
Hic uxcors, A^e cowharde.
Hic apotecarius, A^e spycere.
Hic ninarius,[2] A^e cokwalde.
Hic triumphus,[3] A^e constabulle.
Hic alutarius, A^e cordewenere.
Hic scellarius, A^e sadyllar.
Hic pustularius, A^e botullere.
Hic lorimarius, A^e gyrdylhare.
Hic capistrius, A^e helterere.[4]

Hic archarius, A^e bowere.
Hic pannarius, A^e drapure.
Hic cicarius, est ille qui facit cicas.[5]
Hic mercator, A^e marchand.
5 Hic institor, A^e idem est.
Hic fleobotomator, A^e blodelater.
Hic scarificator, A^e carsare.[6]
Hic tonsor, A^e cuttere.
Hic rasor, A^e shawere.
10 Hic sitator, A^e somundare.[7]
Hic edituus, est custos domus.
Hic sortilegus, A^e wyche.
Hec siren, A^e meremaydyn.
Hic eruginator, A^e forbushere.[8]
15 Hic armiger, A^e sqwyere.
Hic latro,[9] idem est.
Hic scutifer, idem est.
Hic sitharista, A^e harpure.
Hic sitharizo, idem est.
20 NOMINA FLUMINUM.
Hoc mare, A^e see.
Hoc pelagus, idem.
Hoc fretum, idem.
25 Hoc equor, idem.
Hoc altum, idem.
Hic fluuius, idem.
Hic cathaclismus, inundacio aque.
Hic fons, A^e welle.
30 Hic puteus, A^e pytt.
Hec limpha, A^e water.
Hec latex, idem.
Hic riuus, A^e syke.[10]
Hoc uiuarium, A^e wywere.
35 Hoc stagnum, A^e poynde.

[1] The common name for a stranger or guest.

[2] *Ninnarius.* This low-Latin word, sometimes spelt *minarius*, is usually employed to signify what we call a *wittol*, or contented cuckold.

[3] *Triumphus.* This word is not found in this sense in Ducange.

[4] *Helterer*, one who makes halters.

[5] *Sicarius* (incorrectly written *cicarius*) is here used for one who makes *sicas*, or daggers.

[6] *Carsare.* I have not met with this word before. The practice of scarification was extensively employed by the mediæval surgeons.

[7] *i. e.*, a somner.

[8] *Forbushere.* This was a business of considerable importance when armour and arms were in general use, and were in continual need of furbishing, or scrubbing. The name Frobisher is probably derived from it.

[9] This is a very extraordinary use of the word *latro*.

[10] *Syke* is still used in the dialects of the north of England to signify a small stream or gutter.

Hoc medianum, est spacium inter aquas.
*Hec piscina, A*ᵉ *pole.*
Hoc amnis, est aqua tantum precens.

NOMINA METALLORUM.

*Hoc aurum, A*ᵉ *golde.*
*Hoc argentum, A*ᵉ *sylwor*
*Hoc es, -ris, A*ᵉ *brasse.*
*Hoc plumbum, A*ᵉ *lede.*
*Hoc ferrum, A*ᵉ *yryn.*
*Hoc electrum, A*ᵉ *pewtyre.*
*Hec calibs, A*ᵉ *stele.*
*Hoc stagnum, A*ᵉ *tyne.*
*Hoc auricalcum, A*ᵉ *latone.*[1]
*Hoc cuprum, A*ᵉ *copurre.*

NOMINA ARMORUM.

*Hec spata, A*ᵉ *fawchon.*
*Hic pugis, A*ᵉ *myserecord.*[2]
Hec fustis, hic baculus, idem sunt.
Hec sudes, idem.
*Hec lorica, A*ᵉ *hawbyrgon.*
*Hec claua, A*ᵉ *mase.*
*Hec galea, A*ᵉ *helme.*
Hec cassis, idem.
*Hec ensis, A*ᵉ *swerde.*
Hic gladius, idem.
*Hec gesa, A*ᵉ *gysserne.*[3]
*Hoc telum, A*ᵉ *darte.*
Hoc jaculum, idem.
Hoc missele, idem.
Hoc pilum, idem est.
*Hec balista, A*ᵉ *awblast.*[4]
*Hoc petillum, A*ᵉ *bolte.*
Hec petulio, idem.

Hic tripolus, idem.
*Hic bipennis, A*ᵉ *twybyle.*
*Hic clipeus, A*ᵉ *schelde.*
Hoc scutum, idem.
5 *Hec lancea, A*ᵉ *spere.*
Hec hasta, idem.
*Hic cuspis, A*ᵉ *poynte.*
Hec catepulta, a bradharrow.[5]
*Hec feretra, A*ᵉ *qwywere.*
10 *Hec pelta, A*ᵉ *boculere.*
*Hec umbo, -nis, A*ᵉ *wose.*
*Hec antile, A*ᵉ *halnase.*
Hec cathena, idem.
*Hic arcus, A*ᵉ *bow.*
15 *Hic tropheus, A*ᵉ *bawdryk.*
*Hec cica, A*ᵉ *misericord.*
*Hec funda, A*ᵉ *slyng.*
*Hec lorax, A*ᵉ *haburione.*
*Hic mucro, A*ᵉ *swerd.*
20 *Hec securis, A*ᵉ *axe.*
*Hec securicula, A*ᵉ *hachytt.*
*Hoc braciolum, A*ᵉ *brasor.*[6]
Hoc brachiale, idem.
*Hec targea, A*ᵉ *targett.*

25 ## NOMINA ORNAMENTORUM.

*Hec camicia, A*ᵉ *sarke.*
*Hec inchila, A*ᵉ *rochett.*
*Hoc femorale, A*ᵉ *broke.*
30 *Hee bracce, -arum, idem.*
*Hec tunica, A*ᵉ *cote.*
*Hec supertunica, A*ᵉ *surkote.*
*Hec caliga, A*ᵉ *hose.*
*Hec pedana, A*ᵉ *wampe.*[7]
35 *Hec formula, A*ᵉ *last.*
Hoc formipedium, idem.

---

[1] The metal formerly called in English *laten*, or *latten*, from the French *laiton*, was a compound of copper, very much resembling brass, which was extensively used in the middle ages, but the exact composition of which seems not now to be known.

[2] Read *pugio. Myserecord.* This name was given to a thin bladed dagger worn by the warrior, and used to dispatch one who was dangerously wounded, intended, as it is said, to imply that this was an act of mercy. (Cf. pag. 654 l. 16. R. W.)

[3] The *gisarme*, or *giserne*, was the bill or battle-axe. It has been identified with the Latin *gesa* by an older authority, the commentator on John de Garlande.

[4] *Awblast*, the arbalest, or crossbow.

[5] A broad-arrow was distinguished by a large forked head.

[6] *Brasor*, the brasser, or armour for the arm.

[7] *Vampe*, or *vampy*, bottoms of hose covering the foot; or, perhaps here, the upper leather of a boot.

*Hoc perplicar, A*ᵉ gartere.
Hoc subligar, idem.
*Hoc lumbare, A*ᵉ brekgyrdylle.
Hoc perizoma, idem.
*Hec toga, A*ᵉ gowne.
*Hec linistema, A*ᵉ tarteryne.[1]
Hec lacuna, est extremitas uestis.
*Hoc gremium, A*ᵉ scyrtte.
*Hoc fimbrium, A*ᶜ hemme.
*Hec pera, A*ᵉ strype.
*Hoc presegmen, A*ᵉ serede.
*Hec armilausa, A*ᵉ cloke.
*Hec instita, A*ᶜ rokytte.[2]
*Hec tena, A*ᵉ howe.
*Hec tenea, A*ᵉ tappe.
*Hoc reticulum, A*ᵉ kelle.[3]
*Hoc sertum, A*ᵉ garland.
*Hoc capellum, A*ᵉ hatte.
*Hec mitra, A*ᵉ mytyre.
Hec galliare, idem.
Hec nata, idem.
*Hec laurea, A*ᵉ crowne.
Hoc dyadema, idem.
Hec corona, idem.
*Hec manica, A*ᵉ myttan.
*Hoc epitogium, A*ᵉ cowrteby.[4]
*Hoc limpidium, A*ᵉ idem.
*Hoc bombacilium, A*ᵉ idem.
*Hec capa, A*ᵉ cope.
*Hec clauus, A*ᵉ mantylle.
Hoc pallium, idem.
Hec lacerna, idem.
*Hec caretta, A*ᵉ lasse.[5]
*Hec caxacalla, A*ᵉ idem.
*Hoc stropheum, A*ᵉ gyrdylle.
Hic balteus, idem.
Hoc singulum, idem.
*Hec ligula, A*ᵉ garter.

*Hec corigia, A*ᵉ thowyng.[6]
*Hoc braccale, A*ᵉ brygyrdylle.
*Hic loculus, A*ᵉ purse.
Hoc marsupium, idem.
5 *Hic oeria, A*ᵉ bote.
*Hic sotularis, A*ᵉ scho.
*Hoc antepedale, A*ᵉ wampe.
Hoc pedium, idem.
*Hic pero, -ri, A*ᵉ wolyng.[7]
10 *Hec mantica, A*ᵉ male.
Hec zonata, idem.
Hoc redimentum, est ornamentum.
Hoc discriminale, est ornamentum capitis mulieris.
15 *Hec caracalla, A*ᵉ kelle.[8]
*Hoc peplum, A*ᵉ wympulle.
*Hoc tricatorium, A*ᵉ tressure.
*Hec uitta, A*ᵉ bend.
Hoc seruale, idem est quod sertum.
20 *Hec inauris, est annulus in aure.*
Hoc armillum, est ornamentum.

NOMINA INSTRUMENTORUM AULE.

25
*Hec aula, A*ᵉ halle.
*Hec mensa, A*ᵉ borde.
*Hic tristellus, A*ᵉ treste.
*Hoc bancarium, A*ᵉ banquere.
30 *Hoc dorsarium, A*ᵉ dosur.
*Hec buda, A*ᵉ natte.
Hoc scorium, idem.
*Hec cillaba, A*ᵉ tabulle dormawnd.[9]
*Hec peluis, A*ᵉ basyn.
35 *Hoc lauatorium, A*ᵉ laworre.
*Hic ignis, A*ᵉ fyr.
Hic focus, idem.
Hic pir, idem.

---

[1] Tarterine is described as a kind of silk stuff, said to have been so named because it was obtained from the Tartars.

[2] Cf. *Catholicon Anglicum* p. 310. R. W.

[3] *Kelle*, a covering of network for the head.

[4] A *courtby*, or *courtpy*, was a short cloak of coarse cloth.

[5] *Lasse*, a cassock.

[6] *Thowyng*, a thong.

[7] *Wolyng*, a leathern sack.

[8] *Kelle* signifies properly a smock, or petticoat; perhaps it is used here for what we call a smock-frock. (Cf. note 3.)

[9] *Table dormaunt* appears to have been the name for a permanent table in the hall, as distinguished from the board which was placed temporarily upon trestles. The Latin *cillaba* appears to have been applied to a round table.

Hoc focarium, A^e harthe.
Hec fax, -cis, A^e brande.
Hec torris, idem.
Hec teda, idem.
Hic tissio, idem.
Hoc ricrepofocilium, A^e golestok.[1]
Hic, hec ciner, A^e askys.
Hec andena, A^e awndyren.
Hoc sedile, A^e langsedylle.[2]
Hec cathedra, A^e chayere
Hec forceps, A^e tangges.
Hoc scannum, A^e bynke.[3]
Hoc stabellum, A^e stole.
Hoc fultrum, A^e cosyn.
Hoc focale, A^e wode to the fyre.
Hic culigna, A^e pare belows.
Hec antipera, A^e serene.

NOMINA PERTINENCIA AD PINCERNAM.

Panis fluentatus, A^e gurbred.
Panis furfurius, A^e branbred.
Panis ordiccius, A^e barlybred.
Panis triticius, A^e whetbred.
Panis similaginius, A^e paynmayn.[4]
Panis fabicius, A^e benebred.
Panis pisacius, A^e pesbred.
Panis auenacius, A^e hafyrbred.[5]
Panis siliginius, A^e tharfbred.[6]
Panis sigalinus, idem.
Panis muscidus, A^e mowldebred.
Hoc libum, A^e wastelle.[7]

[1] What is still called in the north a yule-clog, or yule-log.

[2] The long wooden seat with back and arms, which is still called a *settle*.

[3] *Bynke*, a bench — the usual seat in the hall.

[4] *Payn-mayn* was the name given to the bread of finer quality.

[5] *Hafyr-bred*, bread made of oats; oatcakes.

[6] This term is now used in the north for unleavened bread.

[7] *Wastelle*, a cake, the Fr. *gâteau*.

[8] *i. e.*, a shive, or slice.

Hic artocopus, A^e **symnelle.**[8]
Hic panis, A^e lof of bred.
Hic lesca, A^e scywe.[9]
Hic torcellus, A^e cake.
5 *Hoc minutal, A^e* cantelle.
Hic mucor,¹ A^e mowlde.
Hec briba, A^e lumpe.
Hoc frustrum, A^e mese, gobyt.
Hoc ferculum, idem.
10 Farcla sunt frustra, dicuntur fercula uasa.

Hec mica, A^e crowm.
Hec mappa, A^e bordeclathe.
Hoc gausape, A^e sanap.[9]
Hic morsus, A^e bytte.
15 *Hoc manutergium, A^e* towelle.
Hoc selarium, A^e celare.[10]
Hoc sal, A^e salte.
Hoc cocliar, A^e spone.
Hec sporticula, A^e relef.[11]
20 *Hoc dolium, A^e* townne.
Hic vter, A^e buffylle.[12]
Hic collator, A^e costylle.[13]
Hoc murra, A^e masere.
Hoc vinum, A^e wyne.
25 *Hoc merum, A^e* mede.
Hoc claretum, A^e clarett.
Hec seruicia, A^e ale.
Hec selia, idem est.
Hic ciphus, A^e coppe.
30 *Hoc cooperculum, A^e* cowerkylle.
Hec fex, A^e dregges.
Hoc nectar, A^e pyment.
Hoc armariolum, A^e almere.

[9] *Sanap*, a napkin. The romance of Sir Degrevant, l. 1387, speaks of —

> Towellus of Eylyssham,
> Whygth as the sees fame,
> Sanappus of the same,
> Thus servyd thei ware.

[10] *Celare*, a salt-sellar.

[11] *Relef*, a small basket.

[12] *Buffylle*, a leather bottle, for liquors, as would appear from the Latin equivalent.

[13] *Costylle*. A costrel was a bottle or vessel of wood, resembling that which the labourers still carry with them in harvest time.

Hoc sissorium, A^e trenchure.
Hic casius, A^e chese.
Hoc cepe, A^e hongon.¹
Casius et cepe ueniunt ad prandia sepe.
Hoc butirum, A^e buttyre.
Hic cadus, A^e barylle.
Hic ducellus, A^e dosylle.²
Hoc poculum, A^e drynk.
Hic potus, idem est.
Hic cophinus, A^e hampere.
Seruicia noua, A^e new ale.
Seruicia deficata, A^e stale ale.
Seruicia acerba, A^e sowre ale.
Hoc placentum, A^e wastelle.

Hec pustula, A^e bokylle.
Hoc speculum, A^e meror.
Hic fusus, A^e spyndyle.
Hec madula, A^e jurdan.
5 *Hic jurdanus, idem est.*
Hoc tapetum, A^e tapyt.
*Hoc **coopertorium**,* A^e coverhyde.
Hoc carentreuillum, A^e canwas.
Lectus plumalis, A^e fedyrbed.
10 *Hic lectus,* A^e bede.
Hoc stratum, A^e bedlytter.
Est lectus stratum, uia regia sit tibi strata.
Hoc epicaustorium, A^e chymne.
Hic caminus, idem est.
15

NOMINA PERTINENCIA AD CAMERAM.

Hoc pecten, A^e combe.
Hoc colobium, A^e tabarde.
Hec armilausa, A^e cloke.
Hic clauus, idem.
Hoc capicium, A^e hode.
Hec supertunica, A^e furdcote.
Hec tunica, A^e cote.
Hec toga, A^e gowne.
Hec manica, A^e slewe.
Hec glitella, A^e kostyre.³
Hec sista, A^e kyst.
Hec arca, A^e arke.
Hec teca, idem.
Hec capsa, idem est.
Hic nodulus, A^e boton.
Hoc calcar, A^e spore.
Hec stupa, A^e barre.
Hoc monile, A^e broche.
Hec aguaria, A^e nedylhows.

NOMINA PERTINENCIA AD COQUINAM.

Hic coqus, A^e coke.
20 *Hic, hec lixa,* A^e quystron.⁴
Hoc mortarium, A^e mortere.
Hic pilus, A^e pestylle.
Hoc micatorium, A^e myowre.⁵
Hoc mortorium, A^e postyk.
25 *Hec olla,* A^e potte.
Hec anca, A^e potere.
Hic vrceus, A^e posnett.
Hic vrciolus, A^e idem.
Hec ollula, A^e idem.
30 *Hec patella,* A^e panne.
Hec tripes, A^e burnderthe.⁶
Hec scapha, A^e bolle.
Hoc frixorium, A^e friyngpan.
Hic limas, A^e naprunc.
35 *Hoc succidium,* A^e sowsse.
Hoc ramentum, A^e ramayle.⁷
Hoc sepum, A^e tallo.

---

¹ *i. e.*, an onion. From the verse which follows we may perhaps conclude that it was usual to eat onions with cheese.

² *Dosylle*, the faucet of a barrel. Robert of Gloucester, describing the disturbances in Oxford in the thirteenth century, and the mischief the scholars did in the townsmen's houses, (ed. Hearne, p. 542), says —
Vor the mer was vioster, hii breke the vinfterie,
And alle othere in the toun, and that was lute
maistrie;
Hii caste awei the d o s l l e ; that win orn abrod so,
That it was pité gret of so much harm ido.

³ *Kostyr*, the hanging of the wall of the room — *aulæum.*

⁴ *Quystron*, the cook's assistant, or scullion.

⁵ *Myowr*, an implement for reducing bread into crumbs, in old French *esmicure.*

⁶ *Burnderthe*, a brandreth, or iron tripot, to place over a fire for supporting a pot or kettle.

⁷ *Ramayle*, scrapings.

Hoc *ueru*, A*e* spytt.
Hoc *uerutum*, A*e* spit with mete.
Hic *fumus*, A*e* reke.
Hec *flamma*, A*e* low.
Hec *fuligo*, A*e* sote.
Hoc *brodium*, A*e* brothe.
Hoc *ferculum*, A*e* mese.
Hoc *potagium*, A*e* potage.
Hoc *edulium*, A*e* sowle.[1]
Hoc *adipatum*, A*e* browys.
Hoc *lacticinium*, A*e* wyttemet.
Hoc *lac*, A*e* mylke.
Hoc *serum*, A*e* way.
Hoc *coagulum*, A*e* crodde.
Hoc *coactum*, A*e* reme.
Hec *perapsis*, A*e* doblere.
Hoc *sallarium*, A*e* sowser.
Hec *taleteca*, A*e* blawmunger.
Hoc *pepe*, A*e* mortrus.
Hic *garrus*, A*e* brewett.
Hoc *sepulatum*, A*e* sewe.
Hic *pastillus*, A*e* pastyth.
Hic *baco*, A*e* bacon.
Hec *perna*, A*e* flyk.
Hoc *lardum*, A*e* lardyre.
Hoc *fertum*, A*e* podynge.
Hec *salucia*, A*e* sauseyre.
Hoc *tuncetum*, A*e* hagase.[2]
Hec *olda*, A*e* hyspyn.
Hic *omasus*, A*e* trype.
Caro *recens*, fresche flesche.
Caro *salsa*, salt flesche.
Caro *bouina*, beyfflesche.[3]
Caro *porcina*, swyneflesche.
Caro *uitulina*, calfflesche.
Caro *mutulina*, chepeflesche.
Caro *aucina*, goseflesche.

Caro *spadonia*, capuneflesche.
Caro *caponina*, caponflesche.
Caro *gallinacia*, heneflesche.
Caro *grossa*, grete flesche.
5 Caro *assota*, rost flesche.
Caro in *brodio*, in broth.
Caro *cocta in pasta*, bakyn.
Hic *pugio*, A*e* pejon.
Hoc *caldarium*, A*e* caldron.
10 Hec *ferina*, A*e* wenyson.
Hoc *senapium*, A*e* mustarde.
Hoc *alleum*, A*e* garly.
Hoc *ius uiride*, A*e* warins.
Hec *emulaga*, A*e* batyre.
15 Hic *chalaphus*, A*e* pangere.
Caro *cruda*, A*e* ra flesche.
Caro *rancida*, A*e* rest flesche.
Hic *scamellus*, A*e* dressyn-knyfbord.
Hic *nidor, sapor coquine*.
20 Hic *afingea, pinguedo porci*.
Hoc *abdomen, idem est*.
Hec *nebula*, A*e* noble.
Hec *uafra*, A*e* wayfyre.
Hic *flato*, A*e* flaune.[4]
25 Hec *cratericula*, A*e* rostyryn.
Hec *artocria*, a pie *de pundio*.

NOMINA PERTINENCIA AD
BRASORIUM.

Hec *brasiatrix*, A*e* brewster.
Hec *cima*, A*e* kymnelle.[5]
Hec *tina*, A*e* sa.
Hic *fornax*, A*e* furnasse.
35 Hoc *alueum*, A*e* trogh.
Hoc *brasium*, A*e* malte.
Hec *barzisa*, A*e* wortte.

---

[1] *Sowle*, anything eaten with bread, like cheese, &c., still called in some of the English dialects *sool* or *sowl*. Thus, in the romance of Havelok, l. 767 —

Kam he nevere hom hand-bare,
That he ne brouete bred and s o w e l.

[2] *Hagase*. The *hagas* was the paunch, or stomach, of the animal, stuffed with minced-meat, &c., something in the manner of a sausage; the origin of the modern Scottish *haggis*.

[3] These interpretations would seem to show that the Anglo-Norman terms, beef, pork, &c., had not yet entirely superseded the names of meat of Anglo-Saxon derivation.

[4] *Wayfire . . . flaune*. Wafers were a very light kind of cakes; in old French *gauffres*; flauns were custards.

[5] *Kymnelle*, a tub for household purposes; a vat.

Hoc *dragium*, A*e* draf.
Hoc *calderium*, A*e* caldron.
Hic *cacabus*, idem.
Hoc *taratantarum*, A*e* temse.[1]
Hec *cuuella*, A*e* kuulioun*e* [2]
Hoc *cilicium*, A*e* hayre.
Hoc *ydromellum*, A*e* growte.
Hec *mola*, A*e* quernes.
Hec *pruera*, lingge.[3]
Merica, idem est.

NOMINA PERTINENCIA AD PISTRINUM.

Hic *pistor*, A*e* baestere.
Hec *ferina*, A*e* mele.
Hic *furfur*, A*e* bran.
Hic *flos*, A*e* flowre.
Hec *similago*, est purissimus flos.
Hec *pasta*, A*e* dagh.
Hoc *leuamentum*, A*e* lewan.[4]
Hoc *fermentum*, A*e* surdagh.[5]
Hoc *crebrum*, A*e* syfe.
Hoc *pellen*, A*e* floure.
Hoc *pollitridium*, A*e* bultclathe.
Hec *falanga*, A*e* satre.
Hec *pela*, A*e* pele.
Hec *uertebra*, A*e* cobarde.
Hoc *tresorium*, A*e* scomure.
Hic *furnus*, A*e* oven.
Poletriduare, to bulte.
Hoc *sinarium*, A*e* sotre.
Hec *casta*, A*e* rybbe.
Hic *cultellus*, A*e* knyfe.
Hec *sindula*, A*e* blade.
Hoc *manubrium*, A*e* hefte.
Hoc *penum*, A*e* egge.
Hic *perrasmus*, A*e* tonge.
Hec *cuspis*, A*e* poynte.
Hec *sperula*, A*e* werylle.

NOMINA PERTINENCIA AD ORRIUM.

Hec *garba*, A*e* chef.
5 Hic *manipulus*, A*e* repe.
Hec *corbex*, A*e* lepe.
Hoc *uentilabrum*, A*e* wyndylle.
Hic *modius*, A*e* buschelle.
Hic *corus*, A*e* mesure.
10 Hec *prebenda*, A*e* probend.
Hic *abbatis*, A*e* prowande.
Abbatis auenam dat equis abbatis auenam.
Hec *auena*, A*e* otys.
Hoc *ostorium*, A*e* stryke.[6]
15 Hec *ala*, A*e* wenge.
Hoc *flagellum*, A*e* flayle.
Hoc *rastrum*, A*e* rake.
Hoc *granum*, A*e* corne.
Hec *spica*, A*e* cornehere.
20 Hoc *frumentum*, A*e* wete.
Hoc *triticum*, A*e* whete.
Hec *pisa*, A*e* pese.
Hec *faba*, A*e* bene.
Hec *uicia*, A*e* feche.
25 Hec *lens*, A*e* lentylle.
Hoc *ordium*, A*e* barly.
Hec *siligo*, A*e* rye.
Hoc *sigalum*, idem.
Hec *curalis*, A*e* crappys.
30 Hoc *lollium*, A*e* popnle.
Hec *cratis*, A*e* fleke.
Hoc *tribulum*, A*e* schowulle.
Hec *solea*, A*e* sole.
Hec *pedana*, A*e* wampay.[7]
35 Hoc *intercucium*, A*e* weltte.
Hoc *pictacium*, A*e* clowte.

UERBA SOLI DEO PERTINENCIA.

40 *Pluit*, raynes, Deus meus.[8]

---

[1] *Temse*, a sieve. The word is still in use in the North of England.
[2] *Cuvella* signifies a small tub.
[3] *Pruera* is a corruption of *bruera*, and *merica* of *mirica*. Ling, the *calluna* of modern botanists, is introduced here because it was used largely for making brooms, and other domestic purposes.
[4] Leaven.
[5] *Sur-dagh*, i. sour dough.
[6] A strike, or bushel measure.
[7] Wampay. See before, p. 654 l. 34.
[8] *Deus meus* etc. is added in a different hand-writing. R. W.

Gelat, freses, *Deus tuus.*
Degelat, thowes, *Deus suus.*
Floctat, snawes, *Deus ilius.*
Ningit, snawes, *Deus ipsius.*
Tonat, thoneres, *Deus sanctus.*
Grandinat, hayles, *Deus omnipotens.*
Fulgurat, lewnes, *Deus creator.*
Fulminat, idem, Deus dat omnia.

NOMINA PERTINENCIA AD CARECTARIAM.

Hec beta, est secundus panis.
Hec gerusia, A^c gadde.
Hec mantica, A^c male.
Hec mastiga, A^c wyppe.
Hec reda, A^c chare.
Hic aculeus, A^c brode.[1]
Hoc plaustrum, A^c wayne.
Hec tema, A^c teme.
Hec torques, A^c wythe.[2]
Hic currus, A^c karte.
Hec bina, est currus habens duos equos.
Hec rota, A^c qwele.
Hic radius, A^c spake.
Hoc meditulium, A^c nawef.
Hic axis, A^c axyltre.
Hoc hunullum, A^c lynpyne.
Hic limo, A^c thyllys.
Hoc fricsorium, A^c pynne.
Hic uiredus, A^c thylhors.
Hoc dorsilollum, A^c cartsadylle.
Hec singula, A^c garthe.
Hec postela, A^c taylerape.
Hec antela, A^c paytrylle.
Hec trane, -arum, A^c trays.
Hoc capistrum, A^c heltyre.
Hoc scansile, A^c styroppe.
Hec stropa, idem.
Hec strigilis, A^c horscombe.
Hoc aratrum, A^c plogh.
Hoc iugum, A^c gokke.

NOMINA PERTINENCIA AD LACTITIUM.

Hoc multrum, A^c chesfat.[3]
Hoc lac, A^c mylk.
Hoc butirum, A^c buttyre.
Hic caseus, A^c chese.
Hoc coagulum, A^c crodes.
Hec bedulta, A^c possyt.
Hoc serum, A^c way.
Hic lacsugo, A^c way.
Hec antipera, A^c kyrne.
Hoc almariolum, A^c almary.
Hoc torcular, A^c prassur.
Hoc coactum, A^c reme.
Hec multra, A^c payle.
Hec lactis, -cis, A^c cheslypp.[4]

NOMINA LUDORUM.

Hoc hastiludium, A^c iustyng.
Hoc tirocinium, A^c turnament.
Hoc interludium, A^c entyrlute.
Hic trocus, A^c toppe.
Hec scutica, A^c scowrge.
Hec pila, A^c balle.
Hoc pedum, A^c cambok.[5]
Hic pirrus, A^c chekyr.
Hic scaccarius, idem.
Hic scaccus, A^c chesse.
Hic talus, A^c dyse.
Hec alea, idem.
Hec tabella, A^c tabulles.
Hec tuba, A^c trumpe.
Hec buccina, idem.
Hec fistula, A^c pype.
Hec idraulis, A^c waterpype.
Hec anduca, A^c belepype.
Hec cithera, A^c harpe.
Hec lira, A^c harpestring.
Hoc plectrum, A^c wrastt.
Hoc tympanum, A^c taburne.
Hic sambucus, A^c sytholle.

---

[1] *Brode,* a prick, or goad.
[2] A with, or twisted rod.
[3] *Ches-fat,* a milkpall.
[4] *Cheslyppe.* Perhaps runnet, which is still called *cheselop* in the north.
[5] *Cambok,* an old game at ball played with a crooked stick, mentioned under this name by Stowe.

Hec *uetella*, A*e* rybybe.
Hec *symphonia*, A*e* synphane.
Hec *palpita*, A*e* sawtre.
Hec *uiella*, A*e* fythylle.
Hoc *symbalum*, A*e* symbale.
Hoc *organum*, A*e* organs.

NOMINA PERTINENCIA DOMORUM.

Hoc *fundum*, A*e* growndwalle.[1]
Hec *bassis*, idem.
Hec *paries*, A*e* walle.
Hic *murus*, idem.
Hic *cardo*, A*e* thriswald.
Hoc *limen*, idem.
Hoc *sublimen*, idem.
Hec *postis*, A*e* post.
Hoc *laquear*, A*e* postband.
Hec *fania*, A*e* pautre.
Hec *trabes*, A*e* balk.
Hec *tegula*, A*e* teylle.
Hoc *later*, idem.
Hoc *laquear*, A*e* postband.
Hec *cauilla*, A*e* pynne.
Hic *cuneus*, A*e* wegge.
Hec *tingnus*, A*e* howschessyng.
Hoc *domicilium*, idem.
Hoc *edificium*, idem.
Hec *columna*, A*e* pelere.
Hec *uolta*, A*e* wowte.
Hoc *lodium*, A*e* lowere.[2]
Hoc *spelare*, A*e* wyndow.
Hec *fenestra*, idem.
Hoc *ostium*, A*e* dore.
Hec *sera*, A*e* lok.
Hec *uictinella*, A*e* stapulle.
Hec *clauis*, A*e* kay.
Hoc *repagulum*, A*e* dorebar.
Hoc *pessulum*, idem.

Hec *uectis*, idem.
Hic *clatrus*, idem.
Hic *obex*, idem.
Hoc *ostiolum*, A*e* hek.[3]
5 Hoc *superliminare*, A*e* ouverslay.
Hoc *superlimen*, idem est.
Hoc *tignum*, A*e* spere.
Hoc *tigillum*, A*e* idem.
Hoc *festum*, est lignum ad quod omnia
10 tigna conueniunt.
Hec *trapecula*, A*e* byndbalk.
Hoc *doma*, A*e* rofe.
Hic *hamus*, A*e* hoke.
Hec *sericula*, A*e* clykyt.
15

NOMINA AD NUTRIARIUM.[4]

Hec *obstatrix*, A*e* mydwyfe.
Fassiatus, A*e* swathild.
20 Hoc *cunabulum*, A*e* credylle.
Reperre, to crepe.
Salmare, to slawer.
Hec *salnacio*, A*e* slaveryng.
Hoc *salmarium*, A*e* slaveryngclout.
25 *Alutare*, to fyle.
Mutulare, to mamere.
Hec *mutulatio*, A*e* mameryng.
Uagire, i. clamare sicut infans.
Hec *ancilla*, A*e* maydyn.
30 Hec *puella*, idem.
Hec *trocus*, A*e* toppe.
Hec *mataxa*, A*e* hekylle.
Hic *limphus*, A*e* topflax.
Hec *fascia*, A*e* credylbande.
35 Hic *colus*, A*e* roke.
Hic *fusus*, A*e* spyndylle.
Hec *lacrima*, A*e* tere.
Surdus, -a, -um, deffe.
Surdaster, -a, -um, A*e* halfedeffe.
40

[1] *Ground-walle;* this is the old Anglo-Saxon term. See before, p. 326 l. 22.
[2] *Lowere*, a louver. The open turret, or lantern, on the roof of a building, especially on the old baronial halls, the original object of which was to carry off the smoke from the fire in the middle of the hall.
[3] *Hek* is perhaps used in the same signification which it still bears in the north, the lower half of the door, which remains shut while the other half opens.
[4] The MS. has *Nutriariam.* — The words follow each other in this chapter as though they had been taken from the „Treatise" of Walter de Biblesworth.

NOMINA PERTINENCIA AD BOUARIUM.

Hic bubulcus, A^e oxarde.
Hic, hec bos, A^e ox.
Hic taurus, A^e bulle.
Hec uacca, A^e cow.
Hic bouiculus, A^e styrk.
Hec juuenca, A^e quee.
Hic uitulus, A^e calfe.
Hoc presepe, A^e crybe.
Hoc bouerium, A^e oxstalle.
Hic palus, A^e stak.

NOMINA SERPENTUM.

Hic idrus, serpens antiqua.
Hec emfimenia, serpens cum duobus capitibus.
Hic cholendrus, serpens qui moritur in aquis.
Hic scps, serpens exiguus.
Hic dipsas, serpens magne malicie.
Hec saipia, serpens qui non uidetur.
Hic coluber, A^e snake.

NOMINA PERTINENCIA AD SUARIUM.

Hic porcarius, A^e swyneherde.
Hic aper, A^e bore.
Hic, hec sus, A^e sowe.
Hec porca, i. quod scrofa.
Hic frendis, A^e galt.[1]
Hic neufrendis, A^e gylt.
Hic porcellus, A^e gryse.

NOMINA PERTINENCIA DOMORUM.

Hoc monasterium, A^e mynstre.
Hec ecclesia, A^e kyrk.
Hic cancellus, A^e chawnsylle.
Hic chorus, idem est.
Hec capella, A^e chapylle.

Hoc oratorium, A^e oratory.
Hoc refectorium, A^e frature.
Hoc dormitorium, A^e dorture.
Hoc capitulum, A^e chapytur.
5 Hoc locutorium, A^e parloure.
Hoc claustrum, A^e clostyre.
Hec porticus, A^e porche.
Hec proaula, idem est.
Hec aula, A^e halle.
10 Hec camera, A^e chawmbur.
Hec talamus, idem est.
Hec latrina, A^e wardroppe.
Hec cloaca, idem est.
Hoc selarium, A^e selare.
15 Hec panteria, A^e pantre.
Hec botelaria, A^e botelary.
Hoc lardarium, A^e lardyrhouse.
Hec quoquina, A^e kechyn.
Hoc pistrinum, A^e bachouse.
20 Hoc brasorium, A^e brewhouse.
Hoc torale, A^e kylnhowse.
Hoc furnium, A^e ovenhouse.
Hoc orreum, A^e lathe.
Hoc granarium, idem est.
25 Hoc palare, A^e chafhouse.
Hoc boster, A^e schyppune.
Hoc stabulum, A^e stabulle.
Hoc columbare, A^e dowecote.
Hec barcaria, A^e schepehouse.
30 Hec porcaria, A^e swyncote.
Hoc suarium, idem est.
Hec ara, idem est.
Hoc ouile, A^e falde.
Hoc tigurrium, A^e cheperdhowse.
35 Hoc gallinarium, A^e henecote.
Hec salina, A^e saltecote.
Hoc repositorium, A^e hordehouse.
Hec garbana, idem est.
Hoc argastulum, A^e prisoun.
40 Hic bocardo, idem est.
Hoc prostipulum, est domus meretricis.
Hoc lupanar, idem est.
Hec quinquatria, est domus habens quinque porticus sub se.
45

---

[1] Galt, a boar-pig.

NOMINA CONSANGUINIORUM.

Hic pater, A*e* fadyre.
Hic genitor, idem est.
Hic, hec parens, est pater uel mater.
Hic uictricus, A*e* stepfadyre.
Hec uictrica, A*e* stepmodyre.
Hic filiaster, A*e* stepsone.
Hec preuigna, A*e* stepdoghter.
Hec filiaster, idem est.
Hic compater, A*e* godefader.
Hec commater, A*e* godemoder.
Hic filiolus, A*e* godeson.
Hec filiola, A*e* goddoghter.
Hic frater, A*e* brother.
Hic germanus, idem est.
Hec soror, A*e* syster.
Hec germana, idem est.
Hic sororius, A*e* syster hosband.
Hic socer, A*e*[1] pater in lege.
Hec socrus, A*e* mater in lege.
Hec nurus, A*e* filia in lege.
Hic gener, A*e* sone-in-law.
5 Hec amita, soror patris.
Hec matertera, soror matris.
Hic auus, A*e* eldfader.
Hec auia, A*e* eldmoder.
Hic proceser, pater patris in lege.
10 Hic nepos, est filius filii.
Hec neptis, est filia filii uel filie.
Hec glos, -ris, est soror in lege.
Hic leuir, est frater in lege.

15 NOMINA TEMPORA ANNI.

Hic yemps, A*e* wyntyre.
Hoc uer, -ris, vere.
Hec estas, A*e* summure.
20 Hic autumnus, A*e* harwest.

[1] So the MS. R. W.

XIX.

A NOMINALE.[1]

(OF THE FIFTEENTH CENTURY.)

Incipit nominale sub compendio compilatum tam de fixis quam de mobilibus.

DE VOCABULIS AD SINGULA
MEMBRA HUMANI CORPORIS
SPECTANTIBUS.

Hoc principium,
Hoc inicium,
Hoc exordium,   } A begynnyng.
Hoc primordium,
Hic origo,
Hoc caput, A^{ce} hede.
Hoc occiput, a nodyle.
Hoc cinciput, i. pars anterior.
Hoc interciput, i. media pars.
Hoc ffrontispicium, a fortope.
Hec vertex, A^c hatrelle.
5 Hoc discrimen, the schade of the hede.[2]
Hic crinis,
Hic capillus, } A^{ce} hare.
Hec coma,
10 Hic pilus,
Hoc cerebrum, a brayn.

[1] A common title for the vocabularies of the fifteenth century was that of *Nominale*, intimating that it was strictly a vocabulary of nouns, or names of things, classified under their different heads. The nominale here printed is taken from a very curious MS. of the fifteenth century, in the collection of Joseph Mayer, Esq., F.S.A., of Liverpool, which had no doubt belonged to the schoolmaster who taught with it, and remains in its original cover of vellum, contrived so as to roll up to make it more portable, with a string attached, to tie it when rolled. It is unfortunately not quite complete, a leaf having been lost; but to judge from the part which remains, that which is lost was probably the least important part of it, and may be supplied from the complete vocabularies of the fifteenth century, printed in the present volume.

[2] Schede, or shed, was the common name for the separation of the hair on the top of the head, from which it spread down on either side (= Germ. *scheitel*. R. W.).

Hoc crinium, a harnpane.
Hec ffacies, a face.
Hec ffaciecula, i. parva facies.
Hoc tempus, a tunwonge.[1]
Hec macula, a spote.
Hec papula, a blane.
Hec maxilla,
Hec mola, } A chekbone.
Hec jaux,
Hec frons, a forete.
Hoc cilium, a brow.
Hoc supercilium, a browbone.
Hoc intercilium, the space betwene the eyn.
Hic oculus, } *A*ᶜᶜ ne.[2]
Hic talmus,
Hec palpebra, the eelyde.
Hec pupilla, the appylle of the ee.
Hec albedo,
Hec albucies, } the whyte of the ee.
Hoc albumen,
Hec acies, the scharpnes of the ee.
Hic nasus, a nese.
Hec naris, a nesthyrylle.
Hoc interfinium, the bryg of the nese.
Hec purila, the poynt of the nese.
Hec cartilago, a grystylle.
Hoc rostrum, a bylle.
Hic cirrus, a topylle.[3]
Hic polipus, the fylth of the nese.
Hec saliva, a spyttynge.
Hec orexis, a spewynge.
Hec glabra, a scale.
Hoc mentum, a chyn.
Hec uteelaris, a wongtothe.[4]
Hoc os, -ris, a mowthe.
Hec gena, } cheke.
Hec bucca,

Hec lingua, } a tonge.
Hec glossa,
Hoc labium, } a lype.
Hoc labrum,
5 *Hic dens, -tis*, a tothe.
Hec jungiva, a gume.
Hec auris, a nere.
Hec auricula, i. parva auris.
Hec colera, the ersope.[5]
10 *Hec mandibula*, a chekebone.
Hic porrigo, a poke.
Hec veruka, a warte.
Hoc ulcus, a kylle.[6]
Hic gibbus, a byle behynde.
15 *Hic gibber*, a byle before.
Hec struma, idem est.
Hoc collum, a neke.
Hec gula, } a throte.
Hoc guttur,
20 *Hec frontinella*, the pyte in the neke.
Hoc frumen, i. summa pars gutturis.
Hec ructa, } *idem est*.
Hoc rumen,
Hic ysophagus, a wesande.
25 *Hoc epiglotum*, a thotegole.
Hic stomacus, a stomake.
Hoc brachium, a narme.
Hec acella, a narmehole.
Hic cubitus, a cubyte.
30 *Hic humerus*, a chwdyr.
Hic manus, a hande.
Hic digitus, a fyngyr.
Hec palma,
Hoc ir, irris, } the lone of the hande.
35 *Hec vola,*
Hic pollex, a thome.
Hic index, the secunde fynger.
Hic medius, the longe fynger.

---

[1] The Anglo-Saxon þunwang, a temple. See the A.-S. vocabularies in the present volume.

[2] *Ne*, an eye. This practice of prefixing the final *n* of the article to the noun, when the latter commences with a vowel, is of constant recurrence in these vocabularies of the fifteenth century.

[3] *Topple* was used by old writers to signify a tuft or crest.

[4] *Wong*, or *wang*, was the A.-S. word for a cheek; wang-tod meant a grinder. *Wangtooth* is, I believe, still used in this sense in the north.

[5] A Nominale in MS. Reg. 17, C. XVII, fol. 38, v⁰, gives, „colera, *Anglice* arwax."

[6] A kile, or ulcerated sore.

Hic mèdicus, the therde fynger.
Hic auricularis, the lytyle fynger.
Hic pugnus, a fyste.
Hec unguis,} a nayle.
Hec ungula,
Hec junctura, a joynt.
Hoc corpus, a body.
Hec cutis,} a skyne.
Hec pellis,
Hoc tergum,} a bake.
Hoc dorsum,
Hoc spondile, a bakebone.
Hic torax, a brestebone.
Hic venter,} a wame.
Hic alvuus,
Hic umbelicus, a navyle.
Hec natis, a bottoke.
Hec cawda,} a tayle.
Hec dica,
Hic lumbus, a hype.
Hoc uber,
Hec mamma,} a pape.
Hec mamilla,
Hoc pectus, a breste.
Hoc latus, a syde.
Hec costa, a rybe.
Hec pubes, gong hore.[1]
Hoc femur,} a the.
Hoc crus,
Hoc veretrum,} a pyntyle.
Hic priapus,
Hec vulva, a cunte.
Hic testiculus, a balloke.
Hic ramex, locus genitalium.
Hoc genitale, a balloke stone.
Hec piga, a balloke code.
Hic anus,} a ners.
Hic culus,
Hec poplex, a hame.
Hec matrix,
Hec stera,   } *pellis in qua conci-*
Hec secundina,   *pitur infans.*
Hec secunda,

Hoc viscus,
Hoc intestinum,} a bowyle.
Hoc extum,
Hoc scrutum, a trype.
5 *Hec diafragma,* a mydrede.
Hec pulpa, A^{ce} brawne.
Hoc epa, -tis, a lyver.
Hoc splen, a mylte.
Hoc cor, -dis, a herte.
10 *Hoc ren, -is,* a nere.[2]
Hic lien, -nis, a longegute.
Hic pulmo, the lownges.
Hoc jecor, a mawe.
Hoc cadaver, a caryoun.
15 *Hoc burburium,* owmlys.[3]
Hoc cepum, talow.
Hoc adumen,} *A*^{ce} gres betwen the
Hic pinguedo, skyn and the . . .
Hic adeps, idem est.
20 *Hic sanguis,*} *A*^{ce} blode.
Hic cruor,
Hec omomestra, a medryn.[4]
Hoc fel, -lis, a gale.
Hoc sperma, A^{ce} fry.
25 *Hoc stercus,*} a torde.
Hec merda,
Hoc cirbrum, a gute.
Hoc genu, a kne.
Hoc internodium, the knope of the
30   kne.
Hec tibia, a lege.
Hec sura, a chynbone.
Hic nervus, a synow.
Hec vena, a vayn.
35 *Hoc os, -sis,* a bone.
Hec medulla, margthe.[5]
Hoc crus, -ris, a the.
Hec cavilla, a nankyle.
Hic musculus, the calfe of the lege.
40 *Hic fragus,* a wyrste.[6]
Hic talus,} a hele.
Hic cals, -cis,
Hec duricies, hardnes of the hande.

---

[1] *i. e.,* young hair. The Nominale in MS. Reg. 17, C. XVII., fol. 38, v⁰, explains *pubes* and *picten (pecten)* by „Anglice rawne."
[2] Cf. p. 636 note 5.
[3] The umbles.
[4] The midriff.
[5] The marrow; A.-S. *mearh*, or *mearg*.
[6] The bend of the knee.

Hic pes, -dis, a fote.
Hec planta, the sole of the fote.
Hec apostema, a postym.
Hec vertebra, the wherlbone.
Hic sinus, a bosome.
Hoc grabatum, penultima corrupta, a skyrte.
Hoc gremium, a heme.
Hic allux, -cis, a grete too.
Hic articulus, a lytyle too.
Hoc vulnus, } a wonde.
Hec plaga, }
Recia, regna plage dicuntur, vulnera plage.
Hic sudor, -ris, A^{ce} swete.
Hec lacrima, a tere.
Hic porus, a sweteholle.
Hec scabia, a skale.
Hic corona, a crowne.
Hec vesica, a bledyr.
Hec urina, A^{ce} pysse.
Hec urinula, idem est.
Hoc bumbum, a ferte.
Hec lirida, a fyse.
Hic passus, a rayke.[1]
Hoc progressus, a goynge forthe.
Hic regressus, } a tornyng agayne.
Hec revercio, }
Hic adventus, } commyng to.
Hic accessus, }
Hic recessus, } a departynge.
Hec discessus, }
Hic gustus, a taystyng.
Hic olfactus, a smellyng.
Hic auditus, a heryng.
Hic visus, a syghte.
Hic tactus, a towchyng.
Hec anima, a salle.
Hic spiritus, a spret.
Hec mens, a mynde.
Hic sensus, a wyte.
Hoc factum, a dyde.
Hec vita, A^{ce} lyfe.
Hec conversacio, idem est.
Hec voluntas, a wyle.

Hoc carecter, } a nerre.[2]
Hoc cicatrix, }
Hec lenticula, a frakyn.[3]
Hec omoplata, a schuldyrbone.
Hoc pollicium, a nynche.

CAPITULUM 2ᴹ.
NOMINA DIGNITATUM CLERICORUM.

Hic papa, a pape.
Hic apostolus, A^{ce} apostyle.
Hic patriarcha, a patriarke.
Hic cardinalis, a cardynale.
Hic archyepiscopus, an ersbychope.
Hic episcopus, a byschope.
Hic archidiaconus, a narsdekyn.
Hic diaconus, a dekyn.
Hic decanus, a dene.
Hic legatus, a legate.
Hic propheta, a profete.
Hic officialis, an offycyale.
Hic poeta, a poyte.
Hic archisinagogus, i. princeps sinagogie.
Hic cancellarius, a chanceller.
Hic suffraganus, a suffrykayn.
Hic abbas, a abbote.
Hic prior, a pryor.
Hic subprior, a subprior.
Hic causidicus, a vokyte.
Hic philosofus, a fylysofer.
Hic monachus, a monke.
Hic canonicus, a chanoun.
Hic celerarius, a celerer.
Hic sacrista, a secristoun.
Hic comissarius, a comyssari.
Hic rector, a person.
Hic vicarius, a vyker.
Hic presbiter, } a preste.
Hic sacerdos, }
Hic doctor, a dotyr.
Hic legista, a legistery.
Hic bacularius, a bachyler.

[1] A step. This word is no doubt connected with the old English word *rayke*, or *rake*, to proceed, or go.

[2] *Nerre,* a scar, or pock-mark, still called an *ar* in the north.
[3] A spot, or freckle.

Hic sophista, a sovyster.
Hic preco, -nis,
Hic bidellus, } a bedylle.
Hic diaconus,
Hec levita, } a dekyn.
Hic subdiaconus, a subdekyn.
Hic acolitus, a colyte.
Hic exorcista, a benyte.
Hic magister,
Hic pedagogus, } a mastyr.
Hic ostiarius, a uscher.
Hic, hec scolarius, a scoler.
Hic clericus, a clarke.
Hic discipulus, a dyscyple.
Hic scriptor, a wryter.
Hic minister, a mynester.
Hic gubernator, a governer.
Hic instructor, a submastyr.
Hic frater, a frere.
Hic novellus,
Hic novicius, } a novys.
Hic succellerarius, a sowthselerer.
Hic templarius, a templer.
Hic, hec heremita, a ermyte.
Hic, hec anacorita, a ancoryse.
Hic gramaticus, a gramaryoun.
Hic citator,
Hic aparator, } a summunder.
Hic iudex, a domsman.
Hic notarius,
Hic arbiter, } a noterer.
Hic lector, a redere.
Hic cantator, a synger.
Hic musicus, a musyker.
Hic modulator,
Hic dictor, -ris, } a endyter.
Hic versificator, a versyfyer.

[1] A querister, or chorister. It is a very unusual form of the word.
[2] A quire of vellum or paper. See before, p. 314 l. 10.
[3] A tablet, or table-book. The common use of table-books in the middle ages has been alluded to more than once in the present volume. According to the Boke of Curtasye (p. 22), the steward of the baronial household set down his accounts in a table-book before they were entered in the regular books—

Hic ebdomidarius,
Hic ceroferarius, } a cergberare.
Hic chorista,
Hic paraphonista, } a qwalester.[1]
5 *Hic hospitelarius*, a hosteler.
Hic patronus, a patrone.
Hic sequestarius, a sequesterer.
Hic latinista, a Latynmaker.

10 **CAPITULUM 3ᴹ.**
NOMINA RERUM PERTINEN-
CIUM CLERICO.

Hic cornu, indeclinabile, a horne.
15 *Hoc pennare*, a pener.
Hoc incaustum, A^{cc} ynke.
Hic calamus, a stalke.
Hec penna, a pen.
Hoc acuperium, } a wheston.
20 *Hic cos, -tis,*
Hic artavus, a penknyfe.
Hec vagina, a schethe.
Hec bursa, a purs.
Hoc percaminum, perchement.
25 *Hic papirus*, paupere.
Hec sidula, a scrowle.
Hec zona,
Hoc tropheum, media corrupta, } a gyrdyle.
Hic pumex, A^{cc} pomege.
30 *Hic quaternus*, a quare.[2]
Hec diptica, a smale tabyle.[3]
Hic stilus,
Hic graphus, } a poyntyle.[4]
Hoc plumbum, A^{cc} lede.
35 *Hoc regulare*, a rewler.
Hec crota, A^{cc} calke.
Hoc punctorium, a prykker.

At countyng stuarde schalle ben,
Tylle alle be brevet of wax so grene
Wrytten into bokes, without let,
That before in tabuls hase ben sett.

For the wax, or other similar substance, a composition was substituted in the course of the fifteenth century, which eventually gave place to what is known as asses' skin.
[4] The Roman *stylus*, and Anglo-Saxon *graf*. See before, p 314, note 4.

Hoc rasorium, \
Hec novacula, } a rasure.
Hic pulver, -ris, powdyr.
Hoc fulgur, A^{cc} bornston.[1]
Hec rosina, A^{ce} rosyle.

CAPITULUM 4^M.
NOMINA DIGNITATUM LAICORUM.

Hic imperator, \
Hic induperator, } a emperowre.
Hic rex, -gis, \
Hic regulus, } a kynge.
Hic princeps, a prynce.
Hic dux, -cis, a duke.
Hic comes, A^{ce} nerle.
Hic dominus, \
Hic herus, } a lorde.
Hic baro, a barone.
Hic miles, -tis, \
Hic eques, } a knyght.
Hic tiro, -nis,
Hic neoptolemus, a gong knyght.
Hic principatus, a prinshode.
Hic vicecomes, a scheryfe.
Hic siniscallus, a stewerde.
Hic armiger, \
Hic scutifer, } a squyere.
Hic heres, an are.
Hic ballivus, a bayle.
Hic villicus, \
Hic prepositus, } a grafe.[2]
Hic maior, \
Hic prefectus, } a mayr.
Hic senior, \
Hic decrepitus, } a nald man.
Hic, hec homo, \
Hic mas, } a man.
Hic homunculus, a lytyl man.
Hic paterfamilias, \
Hic iconimus, } husbandman.

Hic, hec burgensis, a burgys.
Hec civis, a cyttenere.
Hic arculius, a wayte.
Hic constabularius, a constabyle.
5 *Hic lictor,* a sargent.
Hic camerarius, a chamerlane.
Hic aresponsis, i. qui respondit pro principe.
Hic clariger, a kayberere.
10 Clava ferit, clavis aperit, clavus duo jungit.
Clavis nos vel vas qui fert sit claviger;
Indue te clavo, rege clavo, percute clavo.
Hic centurio, qui habet centum milites.
Hic quaternio, qui habet iiij^{or} milites.
15 *Hic decurio, qui habet x. milites.*
Hic tetrarcha, princeps 4^{or} regionum.
Hic proditor, a traytore.
Hic assecretis, a cowncellere.
Hic archimentrita, i. princeps omnium.
20 *Hic panterius,* a pantrer.[3]
Hic pincerna, a botler.
Hic cokus, a kuke.
Hic, hec lixa, a kychyn page.[4]
Hic archemerus, a master cuke.
25 *Hic ianitor,* a porter.
Hic Romanus, a Romayn.
Hic Iudeus, a Jew.
Hic Saracenus, a Sarzyn.
Hic predo, \
30 *Hic vespilio,* } a robber.
Hic primiplus, qui habet primam berbam.
Hic primipilus, qui fert pila ad prelia.
Primipilus berbam primam designat ha
35 bentem,
Ast primipilus qui fert ad prelia pila.
Hic venator, a hunter.
Hic ephebus, a gung man.
Hic cimiflo, a naskkyste.[5]
40 *Hic mango,* a cosyr.
Hic stabularius, a stabyler.
Hic macercator, a pleter.

---

[1] *Bornston,* perhaps brimstone.
[2] The Anglo-Saxon *gerefa,* a reeve.
[3] The panter, pantrer, or pantner, was properly the officer of the household who had the care and distribution of the bread (*panis*); and the pantry was especially the bread department of the household.
[4] Or a quistron.
[5] Called more usually an *askfyse,* the servant who made and blew the fire.

Hic *exelerarius*, a byrler.[1]
Hic *tribunus*, a sawdyn.

CAPITULUM 5.
NOMINA ARTIFICIUM.

Hic *emptor*, a byer.
Hic *venditor*, a seller.
Hic *mercator*, a merchande.
Hic *mercinarius*, a mercer.
Hic *pannarius*, a draper.
Hic *figalus*, a potter.
Hic *membrarius*, a perchmenter.
Hic *campanarius*, a belmaker.
[Hic *apo*]*ticarius*, a spycer.
[Hec *a*]*poteca*, a spycer schope.
Hic *revelus*, a peder.[2]
Hic *faber*, a smythe.
Hic *aurifaber*, a goldsmyth.
Hic *carpentarius*, a wryghte.
Hic *tector*, a theker.
Hic *tegularius*, a tyller.
Hic *auceps*, a fowler.
Hic *sissor*, a taylqor.
Hic *piscator*, a fychere.
Hic *piscarius*, a fychmanger.
Piscator prendit quod piscarius bene vendit.
Hic *textor*, a webster.
Hic *versor*, a tornere.
Hic *berbetonsor*, a berbor.
Hic *reciarius*, a netmaker.
Hic *fleobotomator*, a blodletter.
Hic *monetarius*, a monymaker.
Hic *serdo*, } berkere.[3]
Hic *frunitor*,
Hic *sellarius*, a sadyler.

Hic *urigenator*, a frobycher.[4]
Hic *sarrator*, a sawer.
Hic *fullo*, a walker.
Hic *tinctor*, a lytster.[5]
5 Hic *plumbarius*, a plumber.
Hic *sutor*, } a sowter.[6]
Hic *aluterius*,
Hic *picticiarius*, a cobbeler.
Hic *funerius*, a ropere.
10 Hic *restio*, id.
Hic *cribrarius*, A^{cce} fysmaker.[7]
Hic *pelliparius*, A^{cce} skynner.
Hic *molendinarius*, a milner.
Hic *farrator*, a ferrur.
15 Hec *murida*, a ratunner.[8]
Hic *cuperius*, a cowper.
Hic *victillarius*, a hukster.
Hic *capillarius*, a bokylmaker.
Hic *scutarius*, a scheldmaker.
20 Hic *corrigiarius*, A^{cce} gyrdilmaker.
Hic *lorinarius*, a loryner.[9]
Hic *cipharius*, a copmaker.
Hic *sirotecarius*, A^{cce} gloyfer.
Hic *firmacularius*, a brochmaker.
25 Hic *nauta*, A^{cce} schypman.
Hic *medicus*, a leche.
Hic *carnifex*, a bocher.
Hic *circulator*, *qui amputat vites*.
Hic *tibiarius*, A^{cce} legmaker.
30 Hic *carbonerius*, a colqer.[10]
Hic *pectinarius*, a comemaker.
Hic *cordex*, a stryngmaker.
Hic *plummarius*, a plumstere.
Hic *salinarius*, a salter.
35 Hic *anularius*, a ryngmaker.
Hic *corbio*, a pangermaker.
Hic *citaciarius*, a relmaker.

[1] The attendant who served the wine. The verb *birle*, (A.-S. *birlian*) to draw or pour out wine, is not an uncommon word in the old writers. In the metrical romance of *The Avowynge of King Arther* (Robson's Metr. Rom., p. 80), we are told that there was at a great feast —
— rialle servys and fyne,
In bollus birlutte thay the wyne.
[2] *Pedder* was the old name for a pedlar.
[3] *i. e.*, a tanner.
[4] See before, p. 652, note 8.
[5] *Lytster*, a dyer.
[6] *Sowter*, a shoemaker; the Latin *sutor*. It is preserved in the Scottish dialect.
[7] From the Latin word, this would seem to mean a maker of sieves. Perhaps it should be *syfmaker*.
[8] A rat-catcher.
[9] A maker of horses' bits.
[10] *i. e.*, a collier.

A NOMINALE.

Hic circumforarius, a mycher.[1]
Hic vascularius, a turner.
Hic ursarius, a berwarde.
Hic fossarius, a dyker.
Hic plantator, a **nymper**.[2]
Hic ortilanus, a **gardyner**.
Hic avigerulus, a **pulter**.
Hic tolonarius, a **toller**.
Hic rusticus, a **fyldman**.
Hic villicus, a townman.
Hic messor, a scherer.
Hic fulcator, a mawer.
Hic fugator, a dryfer.
Hic stinarius, a halder.[3]
Hic arator, a tyller.
Hic harpicator, a haroer.
Hic bigarius, a cartter.
Hic pastor, a hyrdman.
Hic vaccarius, a cowherd.
Hic equinarius, a horsharde.
Hic mulundinarius, a mulharde.
Hic asinarius, a nashard.
Hic bubulcus, a swynherde.
Hic aucarius, a gosherd.
Hic pictor, a panter.
Hic sculptor, a grafer.
Hic smigmator, a sopseler.[4]
Hic pugillus, a schampyon.
Hic latamus, a **mason**.
Hic simentarius, *idem est*.
Hec latomega, a mason ax.
Hic petro, -nis, a mason schype.
Hec regula, a mason rewlle.
Hoc perpendiculum, *idem*.
Hec amussis, a mason lyne.
Hec troclea, a wyndas.
Hic hostiarius, a nostyller.
Hic architenens, a narcher.

Hic pugnator, a fyghter.
Hic vestigator, a trufer.
Hic gemellus, a twynlynge.
Hic tortor, a turmenter.
5 *Hic lictor*, *idem est*.
Hic disculus, a trowean.
Hic trutannus, *idem*.
Hic cancellator,⎫
Hic alumnator, ⎭
10 *Hic ligator*, a bynder.
Hic baiulator, a berer.
Hic cultellarius, a cuteler.
Hic balistarius, *qui facit balistas*.
Hic murator, A^{cce} waller.
15 *Hic rotarius*, A^{cce} whelmaker.
Hic cassarius, a casmaker.
Hic ceparius, A^{cce} ungonseller.[5]
Hic pomilio, A^{cce} apulseler.
Hic tabernarius, A^{cce} taberner.
20 *Hic caupo*, *idem est*.
Hic candelarius, a candeller.
Hic cerarius, A^{cce} whaxmaker.
Hic archonista, a bower.
Hic metellus, A^{cce} reve.
25 *Hic inclusor*, a pynder.
Hic mendicus, A^{cce} beggere.
Hic ruscator, a tylkyllere.
Hic naucherus,[6] *qui regit navym*.
Hic polentradinator, A^{cce} a bulter.
30 *Hic pistor*, A^{cce} a baxter.
Hic pandoxator, A^{cce} brewster.
Hic focarius, a fewyller.
Hic ignarius, *idem est.*
Hic fauconerius, a faweoner.
35 *Hic prebitor*, *qui dat prebenda*.
Hic prebendarius, *cuius sunt prebenda*.
Hic dapifer, A^{cce} mettes gyffer.
Hic depositor, a serofer in halle.

---

[1] A *micher* means one who goes sneaking about for improper purposes, as to steal on the sly, to act as a messenger in illicit amours, &c. In the latter sense, the verb *to mich* was in common use among the Elizabethan writers.

[2] Properly one who grafts, or who plants settings of trees. From the A.-S. *impian*, to graft, or plant.

[3] The man who held the plow.

[4] A dealer in soap. *Smigma* is usually taken for an unguent for perfuming, or pomatum.

[5] *i. e.*, a seller of onions.

[6] Read *nauclerus*.

Hic depositarius, ille qui commedit.
Hec familia, a menge.¹
Hic peregrinus, A^cce a pylgrym.
Hic alienigena, A^cce a cumlynge.
Hic, hec comes, A^cce a felow.
Hic, hec sodalis, idem est.
Hic infans,
Hic pucio,   } A^cce a chylde.
Hic puer,
Hic adolescens, est puer xiiij^cem annorum.
Hic decrepitus, ille qui vadit cum baculo.
Hic tantillus, a dwarf.
Hic verbius, -ui, qui est beatus vel qui habet uxorem.
Hic perhendinator, A^cce a sogorner.
Hic liber, A^cce freman.
Hic libertinus, A^cce ille qui fit liber.
Hic gigas, a gyawnte.
Hic, hec pifundabalista, A^cce a slynger
Hic texillaris, a spy in batylle.
Hic bestiarius, a pescryere.
Hic solenciarius, idem est.
Hic apprenticius, a prentys.
Hic cathecuminus, noviter conversus et non baptizatus.

CAPITULUM 6.
NOMINA CONSANGUINITATIS ET AFFINITATIS.

Hic triavus, the thyrde fadyre.
Hec triava, the thyrd fro the modyre.
Hic attavus, the thyrde fadyre.
Hec attava, the thyrd modyre.
Hic abavus, the secund fro thy fadyr.
Hec abava, the secunde fro the modyr.
Hic proavus, the forne fadyre.
Hec proava, the forne modyre.
Hic avus, A^cce a neld fadyre.
Hec ava, a nold modyre.
Hic pater, a fadyr.

Hec mater, a modyre.
Hic compater, a godfadyre.
Hic paternus, idem.
Hec commater, a godmodyre.
Hec materna, idem est.
Hic filius,   }
Hic natus,   } a sune.
Hec filia,   }
Hec nata,   } A^cce a dowghter.
Hic filiolus, a godsune.
Hec filiola, A^cce a goddowghter.
Hic frater, a brodyr.
Hic germanus, A^cce a halfebrodyre.
Hec soror, a syster.
Hec germana, a halfesyster.
Hec fraternitas, a brotherode.
Hic fratruelis, filius patris.
Hec fraterna, filia fratris.
Hic sorarius, i. filius sororis.
Hec sororia, i. filia sororis.
Hic cognatus, a cosyne.
Hec cognata, a nese.
Hec neptis, idem est.
Hic affinis, a sybmane.
Hic consanguinius, idem.
Hec consanguinia, a sybwomane.
Hic avunculus, }
Hic patruus,   } a neme.
Hec ameta,   }
Hec matertera, } a nawntt.
Hec abamita, soror avi.
Hic rictricus, stepfadyr.
Hic patriarchus, idem.
Hic prevignus, a stepsune.
Hec filiaster, }
Hec previgna,   } a stepdowghter.
Hic gemellus, a twynlynge of men.
Hec gemella, a twynlynge of women.
Hic pupillus, a modyrles chylde.
Hic orphanus, a fadyrles chylde.
Hic orbus, qui privatur prole.
Hic abortivus, i. non suo tempore ortus.
Hic postimus, he that is born aftyr the deth of hys fadyre.

¹ More properly written *maisnie* (from the Anglo-Norman), the household; the whole attendance upon the personal establishment of the feudal lord. It has no connection whatever with the word *many* (the Anglo-Saxon *manig*).

Hic proculius, est filius natus patre existente procul.
Hec pupilla, que caret purentibus.[1]
Hec orba, que privatur prole.
Hec procuclia, est nata patre existente procul.
Hic sponsus, } *Hic coniunx,* } a husband.
Hec sponsa, } *Hec coniunx,* } a wyfe.
Hec domiduca, a bryde.
Hoc coniugium, } *Hoc sponsale,* } a maryage.
Hec affinis, a lyans.
Hic socer, a neldfadyre.
Hic socrus, a noldmodyre.
Hic gener, a dowghter husband.
Hec nurus, i. uxor filii.
Hic sorarius, sponsus uxoris.
Hec glos, } *Hec fratrissa,* } *i. uxor fratris.*
Hic levex, i. frater mariti uxoris.
Hec noverca, a stepmodyr.

CAPITULUM 7.

NOMINA DIGNITATUM MULIERUM.

Hec imperatrix, a e[m]prys.
Hec induperatrix, idem.
Hec regina, qwen.
Hec ducissa, a duches.
Hec regula, idem.
Hec comitissa, a comytiss.
Hec baronissa, a baronyss.
Hec domina, } *Hec hera,* } a lady.
Hec abra, } *Hec ancilla,* } a burwoman.[2]
Hec puella, } *Hec ampha,* } a madyn.
*Hec adolescentula, puella xiiij*ᶜᵉᵐ [*annorum*].

Hec materfa[*mi*]*lias,* huswyf.
Hec nutrix, Aᶜᶜᵉ norysch.
Hec vidua, a wydo.
Hec equitrissa, que equitat.
5 *Hec anus,* a nold wyff.
Hec claviger, que portat c[*laves*].
Hec ignaria, que facit i[*gnem*].
Hec ostiaria, a ostyllo[re].
[*Hec fem*]*ina,* a woman.
10 [*Hec f*]*abrissa,* Aᶜᶜᵉ a smyth wyfe.
Hec rustica, Aᶜᶜᵉ a feldman wyfe.
Hec obstetrix, a mydwyfe.
Hec abatissa, Aᶜᶜᵉ a abatyse.
Hec monialis, a nune.
15 *Hec patronissa, idem est*
Hec sacerdotissa est femina dans sacra.
Hic, hec sinobita, qui vel que manet in sinobio.
20 *Hec anacorita,* a ankrys.

NOMINA ARTIFICIUM MULIERUM.

25 *Hec pectrix,* a kempster.
Hec textrix, a webster.
Hec scutrix, a sewster.
Hec tontrix, a barbor.
Hec pistrix, a baxter.
30 *Hec pandoxatrix,* a brewster.
Hec filatrix, Aᶜᶜᵉ a spynner.
Hec carpetrix, a carder.
Hec lotrix, a lawnder.
Hec siccatrix, a dryster.
35 *Hec reciaria,* Aᶜᶜᵉ a kelmaker.
Hec palmaria, a brawdster.
Hec salinaria, a salster.
Hec avigerula, que vendit aves.
Hec sereatrix, a sylkmaker.
40 *Hec androchia,* a dayre.
Hec apoticaria, Aᶜᶜᵉ a spyser **wyfe**.
Hec auxiatrix, a hukster.

---

[1] Read *parentibus*.

[2] i. e., a chambermaid.

NOMINA IUGULATARUM MULIERUM.[1]

Hec citharista, a herper.
Hec lericina, idem est.
Hec tubicina, A^cce a trumper.
Hec fistilatrix, a piper wyfe.
Hec iugulatrix, a iugoler.
Hec saltatrix, a tumbler.
Hec secutissina, que canit in secuta.
Hec tripudiatrix, a dawnser.
Hec timpanizatrix, A^cce a tymburnar.

NOMINA REPREHENSIBILIUM UIRORUM.

Hic gulo, a gluton.
Hic ego, -nis, idem.
Hic leno, -nis, baustrott.[2]
Hic adulter, a spowsbreker.
Hic mecus A^cce lechowr.
Hic fornicator, idem est.
Hic fenerator, } a usurer.
Hic usurator,
Hic et hec scurra, a rebalde.

Hic et hec fur, a theffe.
Hic, hec latro, idem.
Hic ereticus,   } a herytik.
Hic sismaticus,
5 Hic spoliator, A^cce a robber.
Hic explorator, a spyer.
Hic muricidus, a losynge.[3]
Hic bilinguis, qui habet binas linguas.
Hic pelinguis, a horcoppe.[4]
10 Hic murmurator, a grocher.
Hic garcio, a knave.
Hic sacerdotulus, i. filius sacerdotis.
Hic spirius, a basterde.
Hic nothus, contrarius spirio.
15 Hic, hec homicida, a mansleer.
Hec, hic patricida, A^cce que vel qui occidit patrem.
Hec, hic matricida, que vel qui occidit matrem.
20 Hec, hic parenticida, qui vel que occidit parentes.
Hic duributus, a dasyberd.[5]
Hic aliator, a baserder.
Hic sarberus,[6] i. ianitor inferni.
25 Hic aquariolus,
Hic, hec exul, a nowtlay.

---

[1] A Nominale in MS. Reg. 17, C. XVII., fol. 43, v⁰, gives the following rather curious list relating to minstrelsy and games:
Hic castrator, Anglice lybbere.
Hic prestigiator, Anglice mynstralle.
Hec cithera, Anglice harpe.
Hec lira, Anglice harpestryng.
Hoc plectrum, Anglice warstr.
Hic citheredus, } Anglice harpure.
Hec cithereda,
Hic tubicen,   } Anglice troumpe.
Hec tuba,
Hic fidis, Anglice fydellere.
Hec viella, Anglice fedylle.
Hic arculus, Anglice fydylstyk.
Hic gigator, Anglice getyrnere.
Hec giga, Anglice getyrne.
Hic simbolisator, Anglice crowde.
Hoc simbolum, Anglice scotnyng.
Simbolisare, to crowde or scotnyg.
Hic simphonia, Anglice mynstrylsy.
Hic corallus, Anglice crowdere.
Hec coralla, Anglice crowde.
Hoc psalterium, Anglice sawter.

Hoc organum, Anglice orguns.
Hoc simpharium, Anglice synfan.
Hic joculator, } Anglice jogulour.
Hic mimus,
Hic tripidiator, Anglice dawnsere.
Hoc tripudium, Anglice dawnse.
Hec corea, Anglice carolle.
Hec fascia, Anglice credilsaug.
Hic fistulator, Anglice pypere.
Hec fistula, Anglice pype.
Hic excubius,   } Anglice wayte.
Hic expolator,
Hec colomaula, Anglice waytepype.
Hoc expiridium, Anglice rede.
Hec saltatrix, Anglice tumbullere.
Hic gestiarius, Anglice gester.
Hic scurra, Anglice harlot.
Hic nugator, Anglice iaper.
Hec nuga, Anglice iape.
Hic nugigerulus, Anglice trifulere.

[2] Baustrott, a bawd.
[3] Losynge, a worthless fellow.
[4] i. e., a bastard.
[5] Dasyberd, a simpleton, or fool.
[6] i. e., cerberus.

Hic tortor, a turmentur.
Hic et hec armifraudita, a skratt.[1]
Hic, hec apostita, qui bene incipit et statim recedit.
Hic antechristus, ancryst.
Hic zelotopus, a kukwald.
Hic nerenus, idem est.
Hunc dico zelotopum cui non sua sufficit uxor.

NOMINA REPREHENSIBILIUM MULIERUM.

Hec meritrix, } a strumpytt.
Hec tabernaria,
Hec saga, a weeh.[2]
Hec fornicatrix, a sinner.
Hec pronuba, a bawdstrott.[3]
Hec sacerdotula, i. filia sacerdotis.
Hec adulteria, a spowsbrekere.
Hec elena, A^cce a strumpytt.
Est meretrix elena, virgo vocatur Elena.
Hec caupana, A^cce a taverner wyffe.
Hec taberna, idem est.
Hec caricia, i. fallax ancilla.
Hec concubina, a leman.

NOMINA RERUM PERTINENCIUM UXORI.

Hic colus, a roke.
Hic fusus, a spyndylle.
Hoc alabrum, a relle.
Hec mataxa, a hekylle.
Hoc nirgilium, a par garnwyndilblades.
Hoc canabum, a hemp.
Hoc linum, A^cce lyn.

Hoc filum, A^cce threde.
Hoc glomus, a clewe.
Hoc lapsum, a top of lin.
Hic folliculus, a betylle.[4]
Hoc linerium, A^cce lynsed.
Hec rupa, a brake.
Hoc exculidium, A^cce a swyndylstoc.
Hoc excudium, a swyndilland.
Hec stupa, a hardes.
Hoc vertubrum, a whelle.
Hec rota, idem est.
Hic linipolus, a stric of lyne.[5]
Hec troilia, a trindylle.[6]
Hoc multrum, a kytt.[7]
Hec lamia, slay.[8]
Hoc pecten, idem.
Hoc multrale, A^cce a mylksele.
Hoc lacinatorium, a slekstone.[9]
Hoc laciatorium, A^cce a webbeme.
Hoc stamen, a warpe.
Hec trama, A^cce a wefte.[10]
Hec forigo, a lystynge.[11]
Hoc ventilabrum, a wyndyllynge.
Hic saccus, a seke.

NOMINA JUGULATORUM.

Hic jugulator, A^cce a jogoler.
Hic citharista, A^cce a herper.
Hic tubicen, A^cce a trumper.
Hic fistilator, A^cce a piper.
Hic vidulator, a fydeler.
Hic secuticen, qui canit in secuta.
Hic cornuten, qui canit a cornu.
Hic saltator, a tumbler.
Hic timpanizator, a taberner.
Hic gladiator, a swerdplaer.
Hic choricista, qui canit in choro.

---

[1] *Skratt*, a hermaphrodite. The word is still in use in the dialects of the north of England. It is the pure Anglo-Saxon word.
[2] *i. e.*, a witch.
[3] *Bawdstrott*. The meaning of the word is here identical with that in which it is used in a preceding chapter.
[4] *Betylle*, the instrument with which the flax was beaten.
[5] *Stric*, perhaps *strike*, a measure.

[6] The wheel. It is still in use in the dialect of Derbyshire.
[7] A pail.
[8] The name for a part of the weaver's loom.
[9] Perhaps for *flekstone*. The Latin *liciatorium* is interpreted in later vocabularies as the *yarnbeam*.
[10] The woof.
[11] The list of cloth.

Hic barbatissa, qui canit in barbita.
Hic simphonista, A^cce a simphoner.
Hic tripudiator, a dawnser.
Hic et hec lerecen, a herper.
Hic, hec coraula, qui vel que ducit coria in aula.
Hic organista, qui ludit ad organa.
Hic buccinator, a trumper.
Hic simphonizator, a simphoner.
Hic citolator, a cytolerer.

NOMINA OPERARIORUM.

Hic cultor, a tylman.
Hic, hec agricola, idem est.
Hic rusticus, a churle.
Hic frondator, a wodfeller.
Hic vector, A^cce a berer.
Hic triturator, A^cce a tasker.[1]
Hic vinitor, a wynmaker.
Hic septor, a hegmaker.
Hic litor, A^cce a dowker.
Hic aqueductor, a waterleder.
Hic aquebajulus, a holiwater-clerke.
Hic runcator,
Hic circulator, } lowker.[2]
Hic colibertus, A^cce a carle.[3]
Hic operarius, A^cce a werkman.

NOMINA ANIMALIUM DOMESTICORUM.

Hic equus, a hors.
Hec equa, a mer.
Hoc jumentum, quoddam animal adjuvans.
Hic dextrarius, A^cce a stede.
Hic succussarius, a trotter.
Hic gradarius, a hawmbler.
Hic emissarius, a stalan.
Hic caballus, A^cce a cabylle.[4]

Hic spado, -nis, a haknay.
Hic veredus, A^cce a cartthors.
Hic admissarius, equus qui portat arma.
5 Hic pullus, a folle.
Hic equiferus, a wyld hors.
Hec equifera, a wyld mer.
Hoc equicium, a hares.
Hic, hec bos, -vis, a nox.
10 Hic taurus, a bulle.
Hec vacca, a kowe.
Hic buculus, a stott.
Hec juvenca, a qwye.[5]
Hic vitulus, a calfe.
15 Hec vitula, qwye calffe.
Hoc armentum, a drowe.
Hec ovis, a schepe.
Hec ovicula, idem est.
Que male fetet ovis non est melior tribus ....
20 Hec adacia, i. ovis vitula.
Hec apica, a scabbyd ewe.
Hic titerus, A^cce a belwether.
Hec bidua, a gymbyre.
Hic agnus, a lame.
25 Hec agna, a new lame.
Hec cenaria, A^cce a cad.[6]
Hec aries,
Hec berbex, } A^cce weder.
Hic vervex, A^cce a tuppe.
30 Hic grex, a floke.
Hic singulus,
Hic aper, } A^cce a bore.
Hic nefrendus, a galtte.
Hec sus, suis, a sowe.
35 Hec scropha, idem est.
Hic porcus, A^cce a hoge.
Hic porcellus, idem est.
Hic ircus, a gat.
Hec capra, idem est.
40 Hec caprella, a sche gatt.
Hic capriolus, a lytil gatt.

---

[1] Tasker, i. e., a thrasher. The word is now used in some dialects for a reaper; perhaps so named as working by task, or piece.

[2] A weeder.

[3] The sense here given to the word carle, as synonymous with colibertus, generally taken to signify a freedman, is curious.

[4] i. e., a capul, or horse of burthen.

[5] Quye, a female calf.

[6] Cad. This word is at present used in the dialect of the eastern counties to signify a very small pig.

Hic asinus, A^cce a nas.
Hec asina, uxor ejus.
Hic burdo, i. genitum inter equum et asinam.
Hic mulus, A^cce a mule.
Hec mula, a mule.
Hic camelus, a camylle.
Hec camela, uxor ejus.
Hic dromedarius, a dromedary.
Hic dromedus, a dromund.
Hic, hec canis, a hunde.
Hic catellus, a whelpe.
Hec canicula, a byche.
Hic adorrinsicus, a spangelle.
Hic leporarius, a grayhund.
Hic molosus, a banddoge.
Hic aggregarius, a scheperd dog.
Hic luciscus, est canis genitus inter canem et vulpem.
Hec lucisca, est canicula similiter nata.
Hic caniculus, a kenet.[1]
Hic mureligus, a catt.
Hic catus, idem est.
Hic catulus, a kytylyng.[2]
Hic catellus, idem.
Hec polea, est colleccio vel pluralitas quorumcunque bestarum.

NOMINA FERARUM.

Hic leo, A^cce a lyon.
Hec lea, } A^cce a lyonys.
Hec leena,}
Hic leopardus, A^cce a leberde.
Hec leoparda, uxor ejus.
Hic, hec elephas, -antis, a elephawnt.
Hic unicornus, A^cce a unycorne.
Hec simia, A^cce a nappe.
Hic cervus, a hertt.
Hec cerva, A^cce a hynde.

Hec capra,} A^cce a rabuke.
Hec dacas,}
Hec dama, A^cce a doo.
Hic emulus, A^cce a fawne.
5 Hic lupus, A^cce a wolffe.
Hec lupa, uxor ejus.
Hic vulpes, A^cce a fox.
Hic ursus, A^cce a bere.
Hec ursa, uxor ejus.
10 Hic urunacius, A^cce a urchen.
Hic castor, A^cce a bever.
Hic canisponticus, idem.
Hic cirogrillus, a sqwerylle.
Hic taxus, A^cce a broke.
15 Hec melota, idem est.
Hic lutricius, a notyre.
Hec mustela, wesylle.
Hic sorex, A^cce a raton.
Hic mus, -ris, A^cce a mows.
20 Hic glis, } A^cce a dormows.
Hic sorex,}
Hic nex, -cis, media producta, animal simile capre.
Hic ferutus, A^cce a forytt.
25 Hic sinozephalus, a mancowe.[3]
Hic fetoutrus, A^cce a fulmard.[4]
Hic tigris, -ris vel -dis, velox animal.
Hic linx, animal penetrans parietes visu oculorum suorum.
30 Hic panter, animal diversi coloris.
Hic gamelion, animal varii coloris et sola aere vivit, a buttyrfle.
Hic onager, A^cce a wyld has.
Hic tragelaphus,} parte cervus parte
35 Hic hircocervus,} ircus.
Hic effimatus, animal inpungnans serpentes.
Hic cocadrillus, A^cce a cocadrylle.
Hec talpa, A^cce a molle.
40 Hic spinx, vermis lucens in noctibus.
Hic lepus, A^cce a hare.
Hic cuniculus, A^cce a conynge.

[1] A small species of hunting dog, mentioned often in the old writers on the chase, and not uncommonly in the metrical romances, and supposed by some to be equivalent with our harrier. The word, however, seems to be often used as the simple equivalent of a hound.
[2] A kitten.
[3] Mancowe, a baboon.
[4] A polecat. The word is still in use in the northern dialects.

NOMINA VOLATILIUM DOMESTICORUM.

Hic *gallus*, a coke.
Hec *gallina*, A^(cce) a henne.
Hic *capo*, A^(cce) a capon.
Hic *pullus*, A^(cce) a chekyn.
Hic, hec *natis, -tis*, A^(cce) a malerde.
Hec *anas, -tis*, A^(cce) a duke.
Hic *ancer*, A^(cce) a gander.
Hec *auca*, A^(cce) a gose.
Hic *ancerulus*, a geslynge.
Hec *columba*, a dowfe.
Hic *pavo*, A^(cce) a pecoke.
Hic *signus*,⎫
Hic *olor*,⎭ A^(cce) a swanne.

NOMINA VOLATILIUM INCOMESTILIUM.

Hec *ales*, A^(cce) a byrde.
Hec *volucris*, idem est.
Hec *aquila*, A^(cce) a negylle.
Hic *grifes*, a grefyne.
Hic *falco*, a fawkon.
Hic *erodius*, A^(cce) a jarfawkon.
Hic *ancipiter*, A^(cce) a goshawke.
Hic *tercellus*, a tercelle.
Hic *nisus*, a sperhawk.
Hic *capus*, A^(cce) a muskytt.
Hic *milvus*, a glede.
Hic *condulus*, A^(cce) a busherde.
Hic *corvus*, a rawyn.
Hic *cornix*, A^(cce) a crawe.
Hic *nicticorax*, a nyghtcraw.
Hic *struccio*, a nostryche.
Hic *bubo*, A^(cce) a nowlle.
Hic *castrimergus*, a wodkoke.
Hic *ibis, -dis*,⎫
Hic *ibex, -cis*,⎭ a snype.
Hic *onocrotalus*, a butturre.[1]
Hic *pelicanus*, A^(cce) a pelican.

Hec *upipa*, A^(cce) a wype.[2]
Hec *vespertilio*, a bake.[3]
Hec *monedula*, a kowe.
Hic *picus*,⎫
5 Hec *pica*,⎭ a pye.
Hic *graculus*, A^(cce) a jaye.
Hic *irundo*, a swalo.
Crescit harundo, sugit hirudo, canit hirundo
Hec *toda*, a wagsterd.[4]
10 Hic *regulus*, a wrenne.
Regulus est serpens, avis, et rex parvulus omnis.
Hec *frigella*, a roberd.[5]
Hic *psitacus*, A^(cce) a papynjay.
15 Hic *cuculus*, A^(cce) a cauko.
Hec *philomena*, a nyghtynggale.
Hic *phenix, media producta*, a phenes.
Hec *arpipia, i. rapax*.
Hec *alcedo*, a wodwale.
20 Hec *lucinia*,⎫
Hic *carduelis*,⎭ a goldfynche.
Hic *turtur*, A^(cce) a turtyldowff.
Hec *alauda*, A^(cce) a larke.
Hic *palustris*, a redesparowe.[6]
25 Hec *calendula*, a plovere.
Hic *conturnix*, a qwaylle.
Hic *fecianus*, a fesantt.
Hic *maviscus*, a thyrstylle.
Hic *sturnus*, a sterlynge.
30 Hic *frondator*, a sterkyng.
Hic *perdix*, a partryke.
Hic *ficedula*, a nuthage.[7]
Hec *ardia*, a haron.
Hic *palumbus*, a cowscott.
35 Hec *fulceca*, a semawe.[8]
Hic *passer*, a sparowe.
Hec *merges*, a cott.
Hic *ruruscus*, a feldfare.
Hic *garulus*, a thrus.
40 Hic *pratellus*, a buntyle.[9]
Hic *virudiarius*, a ruddoke.[10]
Hec *sarra*, a wyld drake.

---

[1] The bittern.
[2] *Wype*, the lapwing.
[3] *Bake* was the old form of bat.
[4] *Wagsterd*, probably the water-wagtail.
[5] The chaffinch.
[6] The reedsparrow.
[7] *Nuthage*, the nuthatch.
[8] *Semawe*, probably the sea-mew.
[9] *Buntyle*, the bunting, or woodlark.
[10] The robin. See, on the popular name of this familiar bird, a former note, p. 640.

Hic, hec grus, a crane.
Hic conturnix, a kyrlewe.
Hec campestrer, a feldfare.
Hic viscus, a byrdlyme.
Hoc viscerium, a lymepott.
Hec vitubila, a pyttfalle.
Hec discipula, a swyke.[1]
Hoc falconerium, a faweonere moe.
Hoc aucipium, a hawkynge.

PARTES ANIMALIUM BRUTORUM.

Hoc stirillum, a gaytt berde.
Hec juba, a hors mane.
Hec cornu, indeclinabile, a horne.
Cornu gerit cornus, pecudum sunt cornua ...
Militis est quando properat sua bella gerendo.
Hoc rostrum, a bylle.
Hec ceta, a brystille.
Hec crista, est crinis vel quod eminet super galeam et super capita quorundam animalium, the cokcome.
Hec galla, idem est.
Hic pugio, -nis, a tange.[2]
Hec ungula, a clee.
Hec calcar, a spure.
Hoc paliare, a dewlappe.
Hec cauda, a taylle.
Hec ala, a wenge.
Hec pinna, a fynne.
Hec pluma, a fedyre.
Hec penna, a penne.
Hoc ilum, the pyf of the penne.
Hec lana, wolle.
Hoc vellus, a fleys.
Hic villus, a lok of wolle.
Hec brunda, a harte horne.
Hec suama, a scalle.
Hec brancia, } a gylle.
Hec senecia,
Hec lactis, a cheslepe.[3]

[1] *Swyke*, a trap, or snare, for birds.
[2] *Tange*, a sting, still used in the north of England.

Hoc cepum, talowe.
Hic armus, a spawde.
Hec vicecolla, a gragge.
Hec membrana, est pellis ale vespertilionis.
Hoc jecor, a mawe.
Hoc reticulum, pinguedo circa jecur.
Hoc pectusculum, a bruskette.

NOMINA PISCIUM.

Hic piscis, a fyche.
Hic editur piscis, hec servat aromata pixis.
Hec belua, i. animal magnum m[a]ris.
Hic cetus, a whalle.
Est hominum coetus, set vivit in equore cetus.
Hec balena, a balene.
Hic salmo, -nis, a sawmun.
Hec amphinia,
Hic delfinis, } a porpas.
Hec foca,
Hoc allec, a herynge.
Hic congruus, a cungyre.
Hic megarus, a macrelle.
Hec lampreda, a lampray.
Hec murenula, a lamprun.
Hec anguilla, a nele.
Hic polanus, } a place.
Hic pecten,
Hic molanurus, piscis qui magnam caudam [habet].
Hic dentrix, a pyke.
Hic lucius, a lewse.
Hic luticulus, a pyke.
Hic turbo, -nis, a turbott.
Hic uronoscopus, a thornbake.
Hec ragadia, raye.
Hec epimera, a sprott.
Hec truta, a trowte.
Hic capito, a bulhede.
Hic morus, a haddoke.
Hic gulio, -nis, a goryone.
Hic solimicus, a menawe.

[3] Rennet is still called *cheeselope* in the north.

Hec alosa, a loch.
Hic gamerus, a styklynge.
Hec tenia, a tenche.
Hic brimellus, a breme.
Hic pelanius, a flewke.
Hic ipotamus, i. equus marinus.
Hic suamatus, a hundfych.
Hec squilla, piscis delecatus.
Hec sirena, a mermaydyn.
Hoc ostrium,} a nostyre.
Hec ostria, }
Hic musculus, a muscul.
Hic cancer, a crabbe.
Hic polipus,} a lopster.
Hec gorra, }
Hec cepia, est piscis de quo fit caustum.
Hic sperlyngus,} a sperlynge.
Hic thimalus, }
Hic rumbus, a sturyon.
Hec fungia, stokfyche.
Hic mulus, a mulett.
Hec folea, a folfyche.
Hic glaucus, a whytynge.
Hec balbena, a balbene.
Hic norus, a mellewelle.
Hoc conchile, -lis, alle manner schelfyche.

NOMINA VERMIUM ET MUSCARUM.

Hic vermis, a worme.
Hic drago, a dragone.
Hic serpens, a nedyre.
Hic basiliscus, rex serpencium.
Hic idrus, a watyrnedyre.
Hic natrix, -cis, violator aquarum.
Hic hispis, -dis, quoddam genus serpentis.
Hic ibis, -dis,} a neddyre.
Hic coluber, }
Hic ferastrix, a hornyde eddyre.

Hoc amphibim, est serpens cum tribus capitibus.
Hic jaculus,} a flyande eddyre.
Hic biceps, }
5 *Hec arena,* } a nerane.
Hec aranea, }
Hic bufo, a tode.
Hec rana, a frosche.
Hec lacerta, a newtt.
10 *Hic scorpio*, a scorpyone.
Hic pulex, a flye.
Hic lens, -dis, a nyte.
Lens, -dis, capiti, lens, -tis, convenitur ori.
15 *Hic multipes*, a welbode.[1]
Hec cencipita, idem est.
Hec scutula, a blyndworme.
Hoc tumultum, est vermis in cornubus arietum.
20 *Hec tinia*, a moke.
Hec terudo, -nis, a treworme.
Hic trunos, idem est.
Hic ciro, -nis, a handeworme.
Hic limax, a snyle.
25 *Hec eruca*, a coleworm.
Hec sanguissuga, a horsleche.
Hic pediculus, a lows.
Hic pedicus, idem est.
Hec ascarida, a scheplows.
30 *Hic tramus*, a mowght.
Hec lendex, -cis, idem.
Hic serastes, i. serpens cornutus.
Hic dipsas, -dis, i. quidam serpens.
Hec musca, a flye.
35 *In plurali numero hee screne sunt serpentes rolantes*.
Hec musio, -nis, a grett flye.
Hec apes, -is, a bee.
Hic fucus, a drane.
40 *Hoc examen*, a swarme.
Hec juxura, a hyfe.
Hec vaspa, a waspe.
Hic rambricus, a paddoke.[2]

---

[1] *Welbode*, a woodlouse.
[2] *Paddoke*. Possibly the Latin should be *lumbricus*, which is explained in the next glossary as signifying a tadpole. There appears to have been always some little diversity in the use of the word *paddok*. In some of the modern English dialects it is applied to a frog. We might naturally suppose it to be a diminutive of *pade*, which was also a name for a toad;

Hoc orameum, i. collectio apum.
Hic papilio, a buttyrflye.
Hec polemita, a somerboyde.[1]
Hec sicoma, a myge.[2]
Hic culex, a gnaytt.
Hic brucus, a breas.[3]
Hec cicada, a grysope.
Hec salamandra, a crekytt.
Hic crabius,[4] a cercole.
Hic bumbio, a hundflye.
Hic ariax, a hert horne.
Hec formica, a pysmyre.
Hec apaphsibena, a nedyr with ij. hedes.
Hec urma, a egesworme.
Hic papheas, serpens cum grosso capite.
Hec bredraca, serpens habens faciem hominis.

NOMINA MORBORUM ET INFIRMORUM VIRORUM.

Hec **lepra,** a mesylery.
Hec serpedo, a mesylle.
Hic cancer, the cankere.
Hec porigo, a poke.
Hec papula, a redspott.
Hoc glandulum, a waxkyrnylle.[5]
Hec pustula, a blane.
Hec scabies, a scabbe.
Hec glabra, a scalle.
Hec podegra,} a mowlle.
Hic perneo,
Hec sinnancia, a swynacye.
Hic gibbus, a boche in bake.
Hic figus, the fyge.
Hec struma, a boch in the brestes.

Hec siragra, i. nodositas manuum.
Hec tussis, -sis, the host.
Hic caterrus, the pose.
Hec spasma, the cramppe.
5 *Hec tisis,* the tyssyke.
Hec ypomanes, the fransey.
Hic bubo, -nis, i. morbus sub ano.
Hic frebris, the fevere.
Hic fluxus, the flux.
10 *Hoc ulcus, -ris,* a kyle.
Hec apostema, a postem.
Hoc vulnus,} a wonde.
Hec plaga,
Hec cicatrix, a festyre.
15 *Hic, hec intereus, est morbus inter carnem et cutem.*
Hec muliebria,
In plurali hec menstrua, sunt infirmitates mulierum.
20 *Hec idropis, -dis vel -pis,* dropsye.
Hic pruritus,} a gekynge.
Hec prurigo,
Hec extisis, -is, a swoynyng.
Hic litergus,} *i. infirmitas.*
25 *Hec litergia,*
Hec surditas, a defnes.
Hic tumor, -ris, bolnynge.
Hec cecitas, -tis, a blyndnes.
Hec dissentaria, est divicio vel ulce-
30 *ratio intestinorum.*
Hec lippitudo, est infirmitas occulorum.
Hec paralisis, pallsay.
Hec lentigo, } a frakkyne.[6]
Hec lenticula,
35 *Hec gutta,* a gutt.
Hec impetico, sicca scabies.
Hec sinax, -cis, pursenes, *vel quoddam festum.*

---

and a passage in the Coventry Mysteries, p. 164, evidently makes a distinction between the two words —
I seal prune that p a d d o k, and prevyn hym as a pad.
An English gloss of the latter part of the fourteenth century (Reliq. Ant., vol. I., p. 8), explains the Latin *rana* by a *paddoke,* which agrees with the English provincial use of the word just alluded to.

[1] The same Latin word is explained in the next glossary by a *bude* — apparently a species of beetle.
[2] A midge, or gnat.
[3] The breeze, or gadfly.
[4] Perhaps for *crabro,* a hornet.
[5] *Waxkyrnylle.* Palsgrave has the word *waxenkernel,* which is explained as meaning an enlarged gland in the neck.
[6] A freckle.

Hec gutturna, the qwynse, et inde gut.
Turnosus, -a, -um, full off that ewelle.
Hec commissialis, i. morbus caducus.
Hec glaucoma, a the gowyl sowght.
Hec ictaricia, the jandis.

NOMINA INFIRMORUM.

Hic infirmus, a sek mane.
Infirmus, -a, -um, seke.
Morbosus, -a, -um, full of ewylle.
Languidus, -a, -um, sorounde.
Leprosus, -a, -um, leperus.
Limatygus, -a, -um, lymatyke.
Limphaticus, -a, -um, hafande the fransey.
Hic erecticius, qui vexatur multis demonibus.
Surdus, -a, -um, defe.
Mutus, -a, -um, dowme.
Hec stroba, a woman glyande.[1]
Mutulatus, -a, -um, handles.
Cardiacus, -a, -um, purse.
Idropicus, -a, -um, hafand the dropsy.
Cecus, -a, -um, blynd.
Claudus, -a, -um,
Hic et hec loripes, qui habet pedem ligneum.
Extalus, media producta,} i. obliviosus.
Litergitus, -a, -um,
Hic strabo, -nis, a glyere.
Luscus, -a, -um, he that is sandblynde.[2]
Lippus, -a, -um, blereyed.
Hic monoculus, a oneeyd man.
Hic lanaculus, qui fert lanam ad oculos tergendos.
Paraliticus,- -a, -um, hafand the pallsy.
Harniosus, -a, -um, burstyn.
Calculosus, -a, -um, hafand the stone.

Gutturnosus, -a, -um, hafand the qwynsy.
Semicecus, -a, -um, halfblynd.
Gibbosus, -a, -um, bochy.

NOMINA ARBORUM ARABILIUM ET FLORUM.

Hec arba, a herbe.
Hec arbula, idem.
Hec salgia, a sawge.
Hec minta, mynt.
Hoc petrocillum, persylle.
Hic ditamnus, detane.
Hoc feniculum, fynkylle.
Hic isopus, -pi, ysope.
Hoc cerbellum, pellatur.
Hoc olus, -ris, cole.
Hec maguderis, a calstok.[3]
Hec beta, idem est.
Hec borago, -nis, borage.
Hoc porrum, a leke.
Hic bilbus, a lekes hed.
Hoc porrulum, a portte.
Hoc sepe, a nongone.[4]
Hec sepa, a chesbolle.[5]
Hec hinnula, a scalyone.
Hec fantula, idem est.
Fantulus est filius, sed fantula crescit in ortis.
Hec ascolonia, a holleke.
Hec allia, garleke.
Hoc allium, idem est.
Hec columbina, a columbyne.
Hic crocus, sapherone.
Hec ruta, rewe.
Hoc caliandrum, a caliawndyre.
Hoc cinamonum, canylle.
Hoc piper, pepyre.
Hoc seminum, comyne.
Hec eruta, whytte pepyre.
Hec lactuca, letys.

---

[1] Glyande, squinting.
[2] Sandblind, i. e. dimsighted.
[3] Calstok, called in the Prompt. Parv. a calkestoke, is explained by Palsgrave pie de chou, and is supposed to mean the stalk of the cale, or colewort.
[4] An onion.
[5] The word can hardly mean here a poppy.

Hoc lens, -tis, quoddam genus liguminis.
Hic sinollus, a chesbolle.
Hec rapa, a neppe.
Hoc rapum, idem.
Hec napus, genus liguminis.
Hec sinapis, herba ferens sinapia.
Hoc sinapi, indeclinabile, semen sinapis.
Hec camamella, camamelle.
Hec sandax, -cis maddyre.
Hoc sinicium, a tasylle.
Hec pionia, a pione.
Hoc lilium, a lylye.
Hoc apium, smalege.[1]
Hoc melo, -nis, genus liguminis.
Hic cucumur, vel -mis, a palmernutte.[2]
Hoc cucumerium, locus ubi crescunt.
Hec betonia, betony.
Hic flos, -ris, a flowre.
Hoc floretum, locus ubi crescunt.
Hec verveta, a verveyn.
Hec egromonia, egromonyn.
Hoc absinthium, wormwod.
Hec artemesia, mugwortt.
Hoc millefolium, A^cce garow.
Hic costus, rybbe.
Hec plantago, -nis, waybrede.
Hec paradilla, a doke.
Hec urtica, a netylle.
Hoc urticetum, a netylbuske.
Hec arundo, -nis, a red.
Hec buglossa, oxiunge.[3]
Hec secuta, a humloke.
Hec anacia, anas.
Hec genciana, a gencyan.
Hoc polipodicum, a pollypod.
Hoc folium, est herba natans sine radice.

Hec felix, -cis, media corrupta, brakyne.
Hoc felicetum, }
Hoc filacerium, } a brakynbuske.
5 Hec viola, a vyolytte.
Hic cardo, -nis, media corrupta, thystylle.
Hic cirpus, hic junceis, a rysche.
Hic papirus, a sene.[4]
10 Hic papirio, locus ubi crescunt.
Hec carex, -icis, a flege.
Hoc carecetum, locus ubi crescunt.
Hic scabius, ii, scabryge.
Hec malva, a maloo.
15 Hec celidonia, celydoun.
Hec filago, quedam herba.
Hoc vastucium, welcresse.
Hoc ligustrum, a primerose.
Hec elena campana, horshalle.[5]
20 Hec uticella, haryffe.[6]
Hic fragus, a streberewyse.
Hoc fragum, a strebere.
Hec cimnicia, hundfynkylle.
Hic ebolus, walwortte.
25 Hoc albatorium, sothernwode.
Hec amarusa, donfinkylle.[7]
Hoc consolidum, a daysey.
Hec hastula, wodruffe.
Hec lavendula, lavandyre.
30 Hec ipia, chekynmette.
Hec loriala, loryalle.
Hec scurea, saveray.
Hoc tansetum, tansaye.
Hoc epitimeum, tyme.
35 Hec vermicularis, stoncroppe.
Hec valmaria, penegrysse.
Hoc glustrum, flowrd of feld. Unde invenitur metrice de beata virgine:

---

[1] Smallage, or wild celery (the *apium graveolens* of botanists).

[2] *Palmer-nutte.* The next vocabulary explains *cucumer* by *a flage.*

[3] Bugloss, the *lycopsis arvensis* of botanists.

[4] The wild nasturtium.

[5] Called elsewhere *horsehelin.*

[6] *Haryffe.* In Gloucestershire the name hairiff is given to the plant called more usually cleavers, or goose-grass (*apium aparine*); in the north it is applied to catchweed.

[7] Perhaps *amarusa* is a corruption of *amaracus,* which is explained differently as meaning sweet marjoram (*origanum vulgare*), or feverfew (*pyrethrum parthenium*).

O mater, glustri decor, candorque ligustri,
Labe cadens lustri, necnon et sorde palustri,
Nato prelustri me jungas more colustri,
Ne regar amplustri Satane per lirida lustri.

Hec *spurgia,* a sporge.
Hec *tormentilla,* tormentyne.
Hec *alcia, est magna silvestris.*
Hec *caperis, i. herba frutex spinosus.*
Hec *bursa pastaris,* harebelle.
Hec *centaria,* centarye.
Hoc *ligustrum,* a cowslowpe.
Hoc *porarium,* a lekbed.
Hoc *subterrarium,* a debylle.
Papaver, *A*e a chespolle.[1]

DE NOMINIBUS SPECIERUM.

Hic *apoticarius,* a spyere.
Hec *species, -ei,* spyce.
Est species logicus, est altera grammaticorum,
Estque genus species, species et forma virorum,
Est eciam species gratum quod prestat odorem;
Totque modus species viriatur quot monitorem.

Hoc *piper, -ris,* peper.
Hic *crocus,* saferon.
Hoc *amigdalum,* a almunde.
Hoc *amigdalatum,* almund-mylk.[2]
Hec *ficus,* a fyke, or a fikes.
   Hic ficus morbus, hec ficus fructus et arbor.
Hoc *ciminium,* comyn.
Hoc *zinzibrum,* gyngyre.
Hec *liquirisia,* lycorys.
Hoc *amomum,* canylle.
Hec *galanga,* galyngaye.

Hic *gariofilus,* a cloyfe.[3]
Hec *masia,* a mace.
Hoc *quiperium,* a quybybe.
Hec *zucurca,* zugure.
Hoc *anisium,* anys.
Hoc *feniculum,* fynkylsede.
Hic *racemus,* a rasyn.
Hoc *risi, indeclinabile,* ryse.
Hoc *alexandrum,* alysandyre.
Hoc *granellum,* granes.
Hoc *zeduarium,* zeduarye.
Hoc *electuarium,* letwerye.
Hoc *balsamum,* bawme.
Hoc *ponderale,* haburdepays.
Hic *census,* rychenes.
Hoc *unium,* vyneloun.[4]
Hec *asura,* asyre.
Hoc *gummi, indeclinabile,* gume.
Hoc *dragetum,* drage.
Hic *pulver, vel -ris,* powdyre.
Hoc *pinetum,* a pyoun.
Hec *uncia,* a nowns.
Hec *semiuncia,* half a nouns.
Hoc *pondus,* a wehgt.
Hec *statera, idem est.*
Hic *bilanx, -cis,* belans.
Hoc *stateris, idem.*
Hoc *examen, lingua bilancis.*
   Est examen apum colleccio, lingua bilancis.
Hec *dragma, est octava pars uncie.*
Hec *rosina,* rosyn.
Hoc *butumen,* terre.
Hec *pix, -cis,* pyk.
Hoc *ponde,* a fowdrelle.
   Res sit vera staterem portate statera.
Hic *bipondus, i. genus ponderis ex duabus assibus appositum.*

---

[1] A poppy. See p. 710 l. 27.

[2] Almond-milk, or almond-cream, appears to have been a favourite article in the pastry and dessert department during the middle ages. The Forme of Cury (p. 17) gives the following receipt for making a „cawdel of almand-mylk": „Take almandes blanched, and drawe hem up with wyne; do thereto powdor of gynger, and sugar, and color it with saffron; boile it and serve it forthe." It seems to have continued in fashion until at least the end of the seventeenth century, as would appear from the following extract from one of the popular dramatists of that age:
„The devil take me, I love you so, that I could be content to abjure wine for ever, and drink nothing but a l m o n d - m i l k for your sake."— S h a d w e l l, E p s o m - W e l l s, 1673.

[3] *Cloyfe,* a clove.

[4] *Vyneloun,* a sort of spice.

Hec uvapassa, a raysyn.
Hec massa polatarum, a frayle ful of fyks.
[Hic dactilis, A^ce an almonde].[1]

NOMINA ARBORUM ET EARUM FRUCTUUM.

Hec arbor, vel -bos, a tre.
Hec pirus, a pertre.
Hoc pirum, a pere.
Hoc piretum, est locus ubi crescunt.
Hec pomus, a nappyltre.
Hoc pomum, a nappylle.
Hoc pometum, locus ubi crescunt.
Hec taxus, ew.
Hec serasus, a cheretre.
Hoc serasum, a chere.
Hec prunus, a plumtre.
Hoc prunum, a plum.
Hec pepulus, a bolystre.
Hoc pepulum, a bolysse.[2]
Hec corulus, a hesyltre.
Hoc coruletum, ubi habundant.
Hec nux, -cis, a nutte.
Hec avelana, a walnutte and the nutte.
Hec ficus, -ci vel -cus, a figtre or a fig.
Hec cariga, a fig.
Hec castania, a cheston, or the tre.
Hec cornus, -ni vel -nus, a slotre.
Hoc cornum, a slo.
Hoc cornetum, ubi habundant.
Hec ramnus, -ni, a thethorntre.[3]
Hoc ramnum, -ni, fructus ejus.
Hec ema, i. alba spina.
Hec arbitus, wodcrabtre.
Hoc arbitum, a crabe.
Hec amigdalus, a almund.
Hec morus, a fylberdtre.
Hoc morum, fructus ejus.
Hic cicomonis, a cycomyrtre.

Hoc cicomonium, fructus ejus.
Hec vitis, a vyntre.
Hec uva, a grape.
Hec pinus, -ni vel -nus.
5 Hoc pinum, fructus ejus.
Hoc pinetum, locus ubi crescunt.
Hec quercus, -ci vel -cus, a nak.
Hec glans, -dis, a nacorun.
Hec galla, a nake-appylle.
10 Hec ibex, -cis, a sapplynge.
Hec laurus, -ri vel -rus, a loryltre.
Hec fraccinus, a neschtre.
Hoc fraccinum, a kay of a nesche.
Hoc fraccinetum, locus ubi habundant.
15 Hic oliaster, i. oliva silvestris.
Hec abies, etis, a fyrre.
Hec acer, -ris, a mapultre.
Hec cedrus, a cedyrtre.
Hec salix, -icis, a welogh.
20 Hec tremulus, a nespe.
Hec ulnus, a nellyrtre.
Hec buxus, A^cce a boxtre.
Hec sambucus, a burtre.
Hec ussus, a holyntre.
25 Hec lentiscus, a byrktre.
Hoc bidellium, i. arbor dans bonum o[dorem].
Hec spina, a thorn.
Hoc spinetum, locus ubi crescunt.
30 Hec plantacius, a plantre.
Hec fagus, -gi, a bechtre.
Hec cilia, a lynde.
Hec cocianus, a coventre.[4]
Hoc socianum, fructus ejus.
35 Hec percitus, arbor quedam.
Hoc malagranatum, fructus . . . . .
Hec mespulus, a meltre.[5]
Hoc mespulum, fructus ejus.
Hec esculus, fructus ejus.
40 Hec populus, a popyltre.
Hec cipressus, a cypyrtre.
Hec malus punicus, quedam arbor.
Hoc malum punicum, fructus ejus.

---

[1] This line is written in a rather later hand than the rest of the manuscript.
[2] i. e., a bullace (prunus insititia).
[3] Generally interpreted as the dog rose, or wild briar, called þefe-þorn by the Anglo-Saxons. See before the Anglo-Saxon Vocabularies.
[4] The coigne-tree, or quince.
[5] The medlar, mespilus germanica.

Hec juniperus, parva arbor spinosa.
Hec sanguinus, arbor coloris sanguinii.
Hoc sanguinetum, locus ubi crescunt.
Hec nucliarius, est quelibet arbor ferens nuces.
Hoc nucliarium, locus ubi crescunt.
Hec silva, } a woyd.
Hec indago, }
Hec subuscus, undyrwod.
Hic titrus, arbor que cito surgit.
Hec volemus, a warduntre.[1]
Hoc volemum, fructus ejus.
Hec merica, media producta, a brome.
Hoc succetum, ubi crescunt frutices.
Hic rubus, -i, a buske.
Hoc rubietum, ubi crescunt vel rubiant.
Hic dumus, a thornbuske.
Hic tribulus,   }
Hec vepres,   } a brere.
Hec veprecula,   }
Hoc virgultum, a halte.[2]
Hec virga, a wand.
Hec viprex, -icis, a schyd.[3]
Hoc vimen, -nis, qwykyr.
Hoc vimitum, locus ubi crescunt.
Hec saliunca, -ce, a whyn.
Hec aborigo,   }
Hec abories,   } *sunt superflue faucies.*
Hec stipes, -tis, i. arbor.
Hec radix, a rot.
Hic truncus, a stok.
Hic vel hec cortex, -cis, bark.
Hic liber, interior pars corticis.
Hoc suber, intima pars corticis.
Hoc abdomen, grundsope.[4]

Hic frons, -dis, a gren bught.
Hoc folium, a lefe.
Hic ramus,   } a braunche.
Hic ramusculus,   }
Hoc ramale, a dry brawnche.
Hec palmes, -tis, a brawnch of vyne.
Hic pampinus, folium vitis.
Hic botrus, -i, flos vitis.
Hic racemus, a brawnch of grapys.
Hec acinus, est granellum uva.
Hec labrusca, est agrestis vitis, vel botrus amarus.
Hoc germen,   } a burjonyng.
Hec pululacio,   }
Hec astula, -e,   } a chype.
Hec quisquilie,   }
Hic saltus, a lawnd.
Hic rogus,   } a bronde.
Hic fax, -cis,   }
Hec ticio, -nis, a colpytte.
Hec fala, a fagot.
Hic faciculus, a kynch.[5]
Hec cima, the crop of a tre.
   Cima caput virge, verborum gloria sema
Hic fullus, a fylberdtre.[6]
Hec condimus, a warduntre.
Hoc condimum, a wardun.

   Arborium nomen femininum dic fore semper,
   Ni rubus, dumus, oliaster, sive plaster,
   Adda viburnum predictis, addito vimen.

HEE SUNT PARTES FRUCTUUM.

Hoc nauci, indeclinabile, defe.

---

[1] The warden was a large coarse pear used for baking.
[2] A bolt, or copse.
[3] *Schyd* means usually a billet of wood.
[4] *Grund-sope.* This appears to be a different meaning of the word to that which it usually bears. The Prompt. Parv. gives, „Growndesope of any lycoure, *fex, sedimen.*"
[5] *Kynch* must here mean a small bundle.
[6] The Latin should be *fillis.* „Filberdetree, *phillis,*" Prompt. Parv. Gower, Conf. Amant. vol. ii., p. 30 (ed. Pauli), has misrepresented the story of Phillis and Demophoon, in Ovid, in order to give a derivation of this word —

   And Demephon was so reproved,
   That of the Goddes providence
   Was shape suche an evidence
   Ever afterward ayein the slowe,
   That Phillis in the same throwe
   Was shape into a nutte-tre,
   That alle men it mighte se,
   And after Phillis philliberde
   This tre was cleped in the yerd.

Hic nuclius, a kyrnyl.
Hec moraria, a cobyng nut.
Hec perima, } a paryng.
Hec peripsima,
Hec pulpa, the mett.
Hec arula, the crok.
Hec pertica, the sterte[1] of a napulle.
Hec testa, a schelle, *vel cortex nucis*.

NOMINA DOMORUM ET RERUM ECCLESIASTICARUM.

Hoc monasterium, a mynster.
Hec cenobium, a nabbay.
Hec abathia, idem est.
Hoc hospitale, a nospytalle.
Hoc sinodogium, } *i. diversorium.*
Hoc diverticulum,
Hec ecclesia,
Hoc templum,
Hoc delubrum, } a kyrk.
Hoc fanum,
Hec basilica,
Hic cancellus, } a chawnsylle.
Hic chorus,
Hoc vestibulum, a revestre.
Hic porticus, a porche.
Hoc pulpitum, a pollepyt.
Hoc campanile, a stepulle.
Hoc oratorium, a oratory.
Hoc portiferium, a portas.
Hoc gradale, a grale.
Hoc missale, a myssalle.
Hic troporius, a tropery.
Hic calendarius, a calendar.
Hic ymnerius, a ymner.
Hoc ymnare, idem est.
Hic antiphonerius, a antyphonere.
Hec letania, letony.
Hoc alphabetum, a nabse.[2]
Hec gracia, a grace.
Hoc premorium, a primer.
Hoc psalterium, a sawtyr.
Hoc brevarium, a brevyar.

[1] The stalk.
[2] *i. e.*, an abc.
[3] The *nef*, a vessel in the form of a ship, used in the church from an early

Hoc processionale, a processyonar.
Hoc martilogium, a mertilloge.
Hec biblioteca, a bybulle.
Biblioteca mea servat meam bibliotecam.
5 *Hoc manuale*, a manuelle.
Hic passionerius, a passyonar.
Hoc regestrum, a regyster.
Hoc ordinale, a ordynalle.
Hic crucifixus, a crucyfixe.
10 *Hec crux, -cis*, a cros.
Hec ymago, } a ymage.
Hec statua,
Hec eucaristia, hostia sacrata.
Hoc altare, a nawtyr.
15 *Hoc superaltare*, a hye awtyr.
Hic fons, -tis, a font.
Hoc carisma, -tis, creme.
Hoc oleum, oylle.
Hic baptismus, a batym.
20 *Hec extremaunccio*, a nontment.
Hec confirmacio, confyrmynge.
Baptismum proprie fertur mundacio mentis,
Exterior querit per aquam, baptisma vocatur.
Hec vox baptismus signat utrumque simul.
25 *Hic catecuminus, est ille qui est conversus ad fidem et non est baptizatus.*
Hoc vexillum, a banere.
Hic calix, -cis, a chalys.
30 Vas cleris viniqne calix est et nomen
luertis.
Hoc corperarium, a corperax.
Hec fiola, a crewyt.
Hec pixis, -dis, a box.
35 Hic editur pissis, hic servat aromata pixis.
Hoc ostiarium, a obley, or a box.
Hoc ostia, a cyst.
Hoc thus, -ris, }
40 *Hoc thimiama,* } encens.
Hoc incensum, }
Hoc aspersorium, a strynkylle.
Hoc turibulum, a sensyr.
Hec acerra, a schyp for censse.[3]

period to hold the incense, as well as other articles. A similar vessel was used at the baronial table to hold wine, &c.

Hoc *sacrarium*, a sacrear.
Hoc *lectrinum*, a letyrn.
Hoc *vitrum*, glasse.
Hoc *feretrum*, ⎫
Hic *loculus*, ⎬ a ber.
Hec *libitina*, ⎭
Hoc *facitergium*, a towylle.
Hoc *manutergium*, a sanope.
Hoc *velum*, a vayle.
Hoc *crismale*, a crisome.
Hec *lucerna*, a lantron.[1]
Hec *absconsa*, a scons.[2]
Hec *lampas*, -*dis*, lawmpe.
Hoc *lurthium*, a nawtyrcloth.
Hoc *organum*, a organ.
Hec *decima*, tythe.
Hec *oblacio*, a offeryng.
Hec *alba*, a nawbe.
Hic *amictus*, a namyt.
Hec *fanula*, a fanune.[3]
Hec *casula*, ⎫
Hec *poderis*, ⎬ a chesapulle.
Hoc *spectaculum*, a spectakylle.
Hoc *pedum*, a clappe.[4]
Hec *capa*, a cape.
Hec *dalmatica*, a canturcope.[5]
Hec *zona*, a belt.
Hec *tunicula*, tunakyl.
Hec *mitra*, a mytyre.
Hec *patura*, a parur.
Hec *stola*, a stolle.
Hoc *superpellicium*, a surplys.
Hoc *orilegium*, a norlyge.
Hic *oronoscopus*, a orlegge.
Hoc *aurifigium*, a goldfre.
Hoc *superfemorale*, . . .
Hec *caleptra*, a coppe.
Hoc *pedum*, a crowche.
Hic *cerius*, a serge.
Hic *torticus*, ⎫
Hec *teda*, -*e*, ⎬ a sergberger.
Hec *candela*, a candyle.
Hic *lichinus*, a weke.

[1] A lantern.
[2] See before, p. 649 l. 18.
[3] The priest's maniple.
[4] *Pedum* occurs again below, where it is explained as a *crowche*, or pastoral staff.

Hoc *candelabrum*, a candylstyk.
Hec *secula*, a rysch.[6]
Hic *stilus*, a peller.
Est stilus unde scribit puer, stilus esto
    columna,
Dictandique modus ducitur esse stilus.
Hoc *circinatorium*, a circynatory.
Hoc *claustrum*, a clostyr.
Hoc *valitudinarium*, a fermery.
Hoc *ventilogium*, ⎫
Hec *cheruca*, ⎬ a wedyrcoke.
Hoc *semitorium*, ⎫
Hoc *atrium*, ⎬ a kyrkgerd.
Atria dic aulas, eadem semitoria dicas.
Hoc *sudarium*, a sudary.
Hic *gradus*, a degre.
Hic *certofagus*, ⎫
Hoc *mauseolum*, ⎪
Hic *tumulus*, ⎬ a grave.
Hec *tumba*, ⎪
Hoc *poliandrum*, ⎪
Hoc *bustum*, ⎭
Hoc *glossum*, a schryn.
    l. opilio   l. ovem l. lupi
Manda vetat maudrum licos lutrare
    dyssatt
    meandrum
Clausit Alexandrum magnum parvum
    poliandrum.

Hee *reliquie*, -*arum*, relyks.
Hic *bostarius*, a grafmakere.
Hec *capsa*, ⎫
Hec *capsulla*, ⎬ a kyst.
Hec *capcella*, ⎪
Hec *cista*, ⎭
Hec *crupta*, a hol in the erthe.
Per quem fit crupta, non fluut carmina
    scripta.
Hoc *consistorium*, a constre.
In plurali hec sacerdotorum dicuntur
loco inferiora, ad que omnis erit
a . . . . nus sacerdotibus.
Hoc *dormitorium*, a dortore.
Hec *cella*, a celle.

[5] We must conclude, from the Latin equivalent, that this word signifies a maniple.
[6] *Rysch*, a rushlight.

Hoc capitulum, a chapyture.
Hoc centorium, } a tabernakylle.
Hoc tabernaculum, }
Hec regia, est domus regis.
Hoc castellum, a castylle.
Hoc palacium, a palas.
Hoc atrium, a hawlle.
Hec aula, idem est.
Hic turrus, } a towre.
Hec arax, }
Hec phalca, turris lignea.
Hic citus, est passio vel mari domus.
Hec mancio, -nis, a dwellynge plas.
Hoc messuagium, a messe.[1]
Hoc contagium, a cotage.
Hoc opidum, a caystelle.
Hoc penetrale, a chawmbyre.
Hoc Syon, indeclinabile, Syon.
  Montem dic Syon, dic ecclesiam fore Syon.
Tres sunt partes columne, s. basis, stilus, et epistilium; basis est fundamentum, stilus est media pars, et epistilium est supprema pars.
Hec heremus, A^{cce} armytegke.
Hoc heremum, scitum illius loci.

NOMINA DOMO PERTINENCIA.

Hoc scamnum, a bynk.
Hec mensa, a tabylle.
Hec fultra, a cuschoun.
Hec cathedra, a chare.
Hic tristellus, a trestylle.
Hec pelvis, a basyn.
Hoc lavatorium, a lavyre.
Hoc mantile, a towylle.
Hoc sedile, a longsetylle.
Hec forceps, tange.[2]
Hec tripos, a brandrythe.
Hoc manutergium, a sanope.

Hoc selarium, a selere.
Hic sal, -lis, salt.
Hec cambuca, a cambok.[3]
Hoc coclier, a spon.
5 Hic calathus, a baskyt.
Hic corbes, } a tune.
Hoc dolium, }
Hoc uter, -ris, a busche.
Hic colateralis, a costrille.
10 Hec clipsidra, a spygotte.
Hic ciphus, a cope.
Hec servicia, ale.
Hoc vinum, } wyn.
Hoc merum, }
15 Hec fex, -cic, dregges.
Hoc claretum, a clarete.
Hoc nectar, -ris, pyment.
  Fex vini tibi sit, olei dicatur amurca.
Hoc scabellum, a stolle.
20 Hoc monile, a broche.
Hoc acuare, a nedylhows.
Hec pluscula, a bokylle.
Hoc speculum, a myrrore.
Hoc scissorium, a trencher.
25 Hic bino, a cartstaffe.
Hec traha, a sled.
Hec buris, a plughbeme.
Hec formepedia, a last.
Hoc senvectorium, a barow.
30 Hoc serculum, a wedhoc.
Hec mensacula, a bordknyf.[4]
Hec olla, a potte.
Hec idria, a watyrpotte.
Hic contus, } a postyke.[5]
35 Hec pila, }
Hic ursiolus, a posnet.[6]
Hec ampulla, est olla cum duabus auribus.
Hic discus, a dische.
40 Hic perapsis, -dis, a dobler.[7]

---

[1] A mansion, or manor.
[2] Tongs.
[3] Cambuck, and the medieval Latin words cambuca, or cambuta, were used in the sense of a bent or crooked staff or beam, and here perhaps means some implement for supporting or suspending articles, like those by which butchers hang up carcases of slaughtered animals.
[4] i. e., a carving-knife.
[5] A pestle.
[6] A skillet, or small pot.
[7] A dobler. The same Latin word is explained in the next vocabulary a platter.

A NOMINALE.

Hec *pila*, a pestylle.
Hic *fornax*, a fornes.
Et pila pes pontis, pila ludus, pila taberna;
Pila terit pultes, sed pila jeruntur in hostes.
Hoc *veru*, a spytt.
5 Hoc *pepe*, moteryls.
Hoc *striaballum*, a cog of a welle.
Hic *assicus*, a mylnerpyt.
Hoc *emolimentum*, a meltyre.
Hec *ferricapsa*, a hopyr.
10 Hoc *sinoglossotorium*, a flodgat.
Hoc *terratorium*, a clape.
Hic *alvus*, a trowght.
Hec *pala*, a pele.
Hec *vertybra*, a colrak.[1]
15 Hic *pastellus*, a pastethe.
Hec *mebula*, a mekylle.
Hec *vafra*, a wafron.
Hoc *placentum*, a wastylle.
Hic *artocopus*, a symnylle.
20 Hoc *fermentum*, surdowght.
Hoc *furfur*, branne.
Hec *costa*, a rybe.
Hec *mola*, a qwernston.
Hoc *cilicium*, a hare.
25 Hoc *idromellum*, growtt.[2]
Hoc *ciromellum*, wort.
Hoc *sigisterium*, draf.
Hec *cuva*, }
Hec *uva*, } a fat.
Hec *congelima*, a scowk.
Hic *arcomus*, a haystak.
Hec *arista*, a nawn.
Hec *spica*, a ner.
Hec *febula*, a bencodde.
Hec *tina*, a soe.
Hoc *tinarium*, a so-tre.
Hic *corbis*, }
Hec *sporta*, } a lepe.
Hec *garba*, }
Hec *merges*, } a schaffe.

Hic *manipulus*, a repe.
Hic *modius*, a buschylle.
Hic *corus*, a mesur.
Hoc *osorium*, a strikylle.[3]
5 Hic *vannus*, a fanne.
Hec *ala*, a weng.
Hoc *ventilabrum*, a scotylle.[4]
Hoc *flagellum*, a flaylle.
Hoc *rastrum*, a rak.
10 Hoc *granum*, corn.
Hoc *frumentum*, whet.
Hoc *ordium*, barly.
Hec *pise*, a pese.
Hec *faba*, a ben.
15 Hec *vicia*, a fech.
Hec *cruralis*, craps.
Hoc *exaticum*, byge.[5]
Hec *mixtilio*, -nis, idem est.
Hec *avena*, hafyr.
20 Hec *siligo*, ry.
Hoc *lolium*, a popylle.
Hec *cratis*, a flek.
Hoc *tugurrium*, a hollek.
Hoc *ovile*, a fald.
25 Hic *vomer*, vel hec, -mis, a seke.
Hoc *cultrum*, a cultyr.
Hoc *jugum*, a gok.
Hec *harpica*, a harowe.
Hoc *bidens*, a mattok.
30 Hec *liga*, vel mera, a pyk.
Hec *vanga*, a spathe.
Hec *furca*, a fork.
Hoc *tribulum*, a scownle.
Hoc *dolubrum*, a brodax.
35 Hec *securis*, a nax.
Hec *serucula*, a hachyt.
Hec *acia*, a thyxylle.
Hoc *terubrum*, }
Hoc *penetrale* } a wymbylle.
40 Hoc *sumen*, tharne.
Hoc *armoriolum*, a nalmry.[6]

---

[1] A coal-rake, or implement for raking the ashes of a fire.

[2] *Growtt*, a sort of ale. In the old play of Tom Tyler and his Wif, this liquor is mentioned in the two verses of a song —

   This jolly g r o u t is jolly and stout,
   I pray you stout it still-a.

[3] A strickle, or piece of wood for levelling the corn in the measure.

[4] *Scotylle*, a winnowing-fan.

[5] A kind of barley.

[6] An aumbry, or cupboard, formed from the Low Latin word *almariolum*.

Hoc *orium*, a lath.
Hoc *bostare*, a noxhows.
Hoc *stabulum*, a stabylle.
Hec *arena*, gravylle.
Hec *mantica*, a malle.
Hic *mergus*, } a bokytt.
Hec *situla*, }
Hec *postica*, a posturne.
Hoc *perforale*, a persure.
Hec *lima*, a fylle.
Hic *circinus*, a compas.
Hic *folus*, a bolle.
Hoc *clavarium, i. repositorium clavorum*.
Hec *revictica*, a grawyngern.
Hec *sarra*, a sawe.
Hoc *repagulum*, a barre.
Hec *gerula*, a gad.
Hec *mastica*, whypcord.
Hic *aculius*, a brad.
Hoc *plaustrum*, a wayn.
Hec *quadriga*, a chargott.
Hec *biga*, a cart.
Hic *currus, idem est*.
Hec *rota*, whele.
Hec *axis*, a naxyltre.
Hic *radius*, a spak.
Hoc *meditollium*, a nar.
Hic *cantus*, a felowe.
Hec *cavilla*, a nayle or a pyn.
Hic *temo*, a teme.
Hec *torques*, a wythe.
Hic *limo*, a thylle.
Hic *limarillum*, a thylpyn.
Hic *viredus*, a thylhors.
Hoc *dorsolallium*, a cartsadylle.
Hec *singula*, a horsgarthe.
Scingula scingit equum, singula sunt hominum.

Hoc *postela*, a croper.
Hec *trahicie*, trays.
Hec *antela*, a pettrylle.
Hec *opisie, -arum*, harnes.
Hoc *capistrum*, a heltyr.
Hoc *scansile*, a styroppe.
Hoc *calamistrum*, a horskame.

Hoc *ligatorium*, a tedyre.[1]
Hic *cacabus*, a cawdrun.
Hic *urcius*, a bras pott.
Hec *sterago*, a fryngpanne.
5 Hec *creagra*, a fleschok.
Hec *sertago*, a fryngpanne.
Hec *cratis*, a rostgern.
Hoc *ipopirgium*, a nawndyrn.
Hoc *spumatorium*, a scomur.
10 Hoc *ireposimum*, a horshamer.
Hic *arquelus*, a noxbowe.
Hec *lanea*, a slaye.
Hoc *hausorium*, a ladylle.
Hoc *scorium*, a natt.
15 Hec *navecula*, schetylle.
Hoc *jubar*, a neppe.
Hoc *licium*, a throm.
Hic *cathinus*, a gret doblere.
Hoc *micatorium*, a myere.
20 Hoc *trajecterium*, a potlyd.
Hoc *omentum*, a strengerd.
Hoc *bolideum*, a plum of lede.
Hec *conspica*, a glen.
Hec *iberna, i. tempestas maris*.
25 Hic *palus*, a stak.
Hoc *abditorium*, a cofyr.
Hec *clitella*, a pak.
Hec *cupa*, a stope.
Hec *trolla*, a trowylle.
30 Hic *rogus*, a fyre.
Hic *ignis, idem*.
Hec *roga*, almus.
Hic rogus est ignis, elemosina sit roga dicta.

35 Hoc *cunabilum*, a credylle.
Hec *rubigo*, a rust.
Hoc *torcular*, a pressur.
Hoc *falcastrum*, a bylle.
Hic *faux*, a chek.
40 Hec *falx*, a sykyl, or a seth.
Hec *scopa*, a besum.
Hec *paries*, a walle.
Hec *scala*, a leddyr.
Hoc *foramen*, a hole.
45 Hic *later, -ris*, a tylle.
Hic *marmor, -ris*, a marbylle.

[1] *Tedyre*, a cord to tie an animal to a stake, still called in Kent a *tether*.

Hoc gipsum, morter.
Hoc cementum, cyment.
Hic simentarius, a waller.
Hic asser, a latt.
Hec latta, idem.
Hec cratis, . . .
Hec escaria, a mettabylle.
Hic escarinus, a metdysch.
Hoc lorum, a brydille.
Hec abena, a rayn.

JAM DE EDIFICIIS DOMORUM.

Hoc edificium, a bygyng.[1]
Hec domus, a hows.
Hec casa, a lytille hows.
Hec talamus, \
Hec camera,   \
Hic conclavis, } a chambyre.
Hec zeta,   /
Hoc tristegum, i. *domus tricamerata*.
Hoc pretorium, a moythalle.
Hoc celarium, a spens.[2]
Hoc dispensorium, idem est.
Hoc lardarium, a lardyrhows.
Hec coquina, a kychyn.
Hoc pistrinum, a bakhows.
Hoc molendinum, myln.
Hec forica, a prevy.
Hec pennates, -*cium*, idem est.
Hoc stabulum, a stabulle.
Hoc boster, a bose.[3]
Noster erit, nomen proprium, stabulum quoque boster;
Bostaris facit hec gero, bostaris ille.
Hec amissis, a swyer.[4]
Hec fabrica, a forge.
Hec carcer, a presun.
Hoc argastulum, a denjon.
Hec taberna, a tabyrn.
Hec teges, *parva domus*.

Hec fornix, -*icis*, a bordylhows.[5]
Hoc scortorium, idem est.
Hoc opella, a schope.
Hec scopa, idem.
5 *Hoc oranum*, a tressurry.
Hoc gazaflacium, a hordhows.[6]
Hec prosenica, est domus mendicorum.
Hoc vinarium, est locus ubi vinum reponitur.
10 *Hec lapidisina*, est domus latamorum, vel est ubi lapides ceduntur.
Hoc toloneum, a tolboythe.
Qui mausoleum producit, aut canopeum,
Seu toloneum, non reor esse reum.
15 *Hoc asilum*, est domus refugii.
Hoc refectorium, a fermory.
Hoc brasinium, a malthows.
Hoc oratorium, est domus orationis.
Hoc triclinium, est domus trina sessione f[acta].
20
Hoc cellarium, a seller.
Hic papilio, -*nis*, i. tectorium.
Hoc fanuficium, a pantry.
Hec paraula, locus ante aulam.
25 *Hoc apendicium*, a pentys.[7]
Hoc repositorium, est locus ubi aliquid repo[nitur].
Hec apoteca, a spycerschope.
Hoc macellum, bochery.
30 *Hoc armentorium*, locus ubi fiunt arm[a].
Hec caula, schepcot.
Hoc mirrepolium, est domus unguenta . . .
35 *Hec mirreteca*, est repositorum ung . . . .
Hoc armamentorium, est repositorium.
Hoc columbare, dowfhows.
Hec menia, -*orum*, sunt muri civitatis.
40
Hoc genitorium, a buhows.

---

[1] *Byggng*, a building; from the A.-S. *bicgan*, to build.
[2] The spense, or buttery.
[3] A stable for cattle.
[4] The Latin word *amussis* means a carpenter's rule.

[5] A brothel; from the Anglo-Norman; the modern French *bordel*.
[6] A treasury; the Anglo-Saxon word.
[7] A pentise, or shed over a door.

Hoc argasterium, ubi aliquid opus fit.
Hec antica, a hek.¹
Hec postica, a postyrn.
Hoc posticum idem est.
Hec postis,   }
Hec postellus,   } a post.
Hec fultura, idem est.
Hec litura, a mortare.
Hic fundus, a grund.
Hic murus, a walle.
Hoc antemurale, a harchcame.
Hoc promurale, defencio ante murum.
Hoc signaculum, a bretys.²
Hoc saxum,   }
Hec petrilla,   } a stone.
Hec petra,   }
Hec calx, -cis, lyme.
Pars pedis est hic calx, lapis ustus dicitur hec calx.

Hoc plastrum, a plastyr.
Hec arena, sand or gravylle.
Hic palus, a palys.
Hec basisassis est future columpne.
Hoc periperium, est superficies parietis.
Hec archus, a vowt.
Hoc laquiare, a postband.
Hec trabia, a balk.
Hec trabicula, idem est.
Hec stipes, a stok.

Hic tignuus, vel hoc tegimen, a sparre.
Hec capula, a cuppylle.
Hec doma, a howsrof.
Hoc tectum, idem est.
5 Hec grunda, a eskyng.³
Hoc sugrunda, a bemfellyng.
Hoc lodium, a lovyre.
Hoc lucaner, -ris, idem est.
Hic caminus, a chymney.
10 Hoc epicausterium, idem est.
Dic epicausterium scriptoris esse cathedra.
Est epicausterium fornax ubi dequoquis ollas.
Ast illud longum que fumus ab ede recedit.
15 Hoc pinnaculum, a pinnakyl.
Hic cunius, a weg.
Hec pinna, est summitas cujuslibet rei.
Sit tibi montis apex, dicas pinna quoque templi.
20 Hoc pavimentum, a pament.
Hoc guttatorium, a guttar.
Hoc stillicidium, a drope.
Hec tectura, thak.
Hoc tegimen, idem.
25 Hoc tabellatum, a burdwogh.⁴
Hec calx,   } anterior pars do-
Hoc frontispicium, } mus.
Hoc hostium, a dore.
Hec fenestra, a wyndoe.
30

---

¹ *Hek.* A *heck-door*, in the north, is a door of which the lower part only is panelled, and the upper latticed. The word, which is not very common in this sense in old writers, occurs in the Townley Mysteries, which were written in the North (p. 106) —

Good wyff, open the h e k, seys thou not what
                                                I bryng.

It is explained in the glossary as „the inner door between the entry or lobby, and the house or kitchen."
² A bretasche.
³ *Eskyng.* A pentise is called an esking in Lincolnshire.
⁴ *Burd-wogh*, a wall, or partition, of boards — a wainscot. We meet with the Anglo-Saxon *bord-weall*, used in much the same way. It may be here remarked that the distinction between *wall* and *wogh*, in English, was the same as between the original words in Anglo-Saxon, namely, the latter was applied peculiarly to the walls of a house, and the former to a wall of enclosure, or separation, in general. Thus, in the following lines, Gower, telling the story of Pyramus and Thisbe, informs us that they lived so close together, that the walls of their houses, and those of their court or yard, adjoined to each other —

Amonge the whiche, two there were
Aboven all other noble and great,
Dwelleden tho within a strete
So nigh to-gider, as it was sene,
That there was nothing hem betwene,
But wowe to wowe and walle to walle,

Gower, Conf. Amantis, vol. i., p. 324, ed. Pauli.

Hoc *fenestrale*, a fenestralle.[1]
Hec *porta*,
Hec *janua*,
Hee *bifores*, -*rium*,
Hee *fores*,   } a gatt.
Hec *valva*, a wekyt.
Hec *valve*, -*arum*, faldyngates.
Hoc *limen*, -*nis*, thryswold.
Hic *cardo*, -*nis*, *penultima corrupta*, a har of a dore.[2]
Hec *vertibra*, *idem*.
Hec *cera*,
Hec *serula*,   } a lok.
Hic *clatrus*, a barre.
Cardo sus est foribus si cardonis sit generalis,
Et si cardonis est herba nociva colonis,
Cardonis est herba multum fullonibus apta.
Hec *clavis*,
Hec *clavicula*, } a key.
Hec *clava*, a mese.
Hic *clavus*, a naylle.
Clava ferit, clavis aperit, clavus duo jungit.
Hoc *pessulum*, a snek.[3]
Hec *mastiga*, a snekbank.
Hic *gumfus*, a dorbande.
Hec *haspa*, a hespe.
Hic *vectis*, a slott.[4]
Hec *grapa*, *est foramen in quo quiescit vectis*.
Hic *clitorium*, a clekyt.[5]
Hic *huncus*, a crok.
Hic *cava*, a guttyr in the herthe.
Hec *fistula*, *est instrumentum in quo aqua currit*.
Arbor aqueductus est fistula, musica, morbus.
Hoc *aquaductum*,
Hoc *guttarium*,   } a guttur.
Hoc *aqueductile*,
Hic *aqueductus*, a cundyth undyr the erthe.

Hec *barcaria*, *i. ovile*, a schepcott.

NOMINA VESTIMENTORUM.

5 Hec *vestis*, a clethyng.
Hoc *indumentum*, *idem est*.
Hoc *mutarium*, a chaungyngcloth.
Hoc *stragulum*, ray.
Hic *pannus*, clothe.
10 Hec *lanugo*, -*nis*, walkyng.
Hec *camisia*, a sark.
Hec *interula*, *idem est*.
Hec *bracce*, -*arum*, brek.
Hec *tunica*, a cot.
15 Hec *supertunica*, a furd cott.
Hec *dupliteca*, a doplyt.
Hec *toga*, a gown.
Hec *clamis*, a mantylle.
Hec *acupicta*, a jak of fens.
20 Hec *instita*, a rochyt.
Hic *superus*, *idem est*.
Hec *armiclausa*, a clok.
Hec *tribrica*, the strapuls of a pare brek.
25 Hoc *lumbare*, a brekbelt.
Hoc *braccale*, *idem est*.
Hoc *colobium*, a taberd.
Hoc *colobium*, *i. vestis collobia parvula dena*.
30 Hoc *colarium*, a colar.
Hec *manica*, a slefe.
Hec *lucina*, a gore.[6]
Hoc *mancupium*, a spare.
Hec *fibula*, a lase.
35 Hoc *pannideusium*, a boton.
Hoc *armiclausum*, a clespe.
Hoc *mominium*, a naglott.
Hec *consuetura*, a seme.
Hec *fimbria*, a heme.
40 Hic *lumbus*, a burdyre.

---

[1] A fenestral was a window formed of a frame of paper and cloth, instead of glass.

[2] *Har*, a hinge. In the dialect of Durham, a *har* is the hole in a stone in which the spindle of a gate rests.

[3] *Snek*, a latch of a door.

[4] *Slot*, the bolt of a door.

[5] *Clekyt*, a cliket, or latch-key.

[6] *Gore*, a hem, or gusset. In Walter de Biblesworth, it is given as the interpretation of the Anglo-Norman or French *geroun*.

Hoc stropheum, } a gyrdylle.
Hec zona, }
Zona die stropheum, palmam die esse tropheum.
Hoc cimicinctum, a saynt of sylk.
Hoc textum, est idem.
Hoc plusculum, a bokylle.
Hec lingula, a tung.
Hec stipa, a stoythe.
Hoc pendulum, a pendand.
Hec mardacula, a sparbelt.
Hoc mercipium, a pawtnere.[1]
Hic cultellus, a knyff.
Hoc acumen, } a neg.
Hec acies, }
Hec sindula, a blayd.
Hoc manubrium, a heft.
Hec spirula, a vyrille.[2]
Hoc tenaculum, } a tang.
Hic spirasmus, }
Hec vagina, a schethe.
Hoc capicium, a hod.
Hoc teripipium, a typitte.
Hec tena, a coyfe.
Hic pilius, a cape.
Hoc flameolum, } curchyfe.
Hoc multiplicium, }
Hoc sudarium, a sudary.
Hec tricatura, a trussure.
Hoc peplum, a wympulle.
Hoc craticulum, a kelle.
* * * * [3]
Hic affricus, the sowth-est wynd.
Hic circius, est ventus borialis sub aquilonem versus occidentem.
Hic aquilo, septentris, ventus boralis, idem est; ventus aquilonaris est sibi conjunctus versus orientem; ventus collateralis est intermedius inter bariam et subsolanum.
Hec nubes, a clowd.
Hic fulgur, leyfnyng.

Hic tonitrus, a thonderyng.
Hec nix, snawe.
Hec glacies, -ei, yse.
Hec grando, halle.
5 *Hoc gelu, indeclinabile,* frost.
Hec pruina, a rymfrost.
Hic ros, -ris, a dewe.
Hec pluvia, a rayne.
Hoc confragum, a plays where the
10   whyrwynd metes.
Hoc bivium, a gaytschadyls.[4]
Hec aqua, watyre.
Hec tectis, idem est.
Hec limpha etiam idem est.
15 Est aqua doctrina, populus, dolor, ac elementum.

Hoc mare, } the see.
Hic pelagus, }
Hoc fretum, a whalle.
20 *Hoc flumen,* } a flod.
Hic fluvius, }
Hic fons, -tis, a welle.
Hic rivus, a revyre.
Hic rivulus, a bek.[5]
25 *Hic virarium,* a vever.
Hec gurges, -tis, a strem.
Hec fovea, } a dyke.
Hec fossa, }
Hoc stangnum, a dame.
30 *Hoc filandrum,* a gossomyre.
Hic vel hec dies, a day.
Hec nox, -tis, a nyght.
Hic quadragesima, a lentyn.
Hoc natale, gole.
35 *Hoc pascha,* pase.
Hoc carnibrevium, . . .
Hoc ipopanti, candylmesse.
Hec pentetoste, -tes, whysunday.
Hec estas, somyre.
40 *Hic yems,* wyntyre.
Hoc ver, groyngtyme.
Hic bisextus, lepgere.

[1] *Pawtnere,* a purse.
[2] *Vyrille,* a gimlet, or wimble.
[3] Unfortunately a leaf of the original MS. has been torn out here, making a rather extensive lacuna, as the manuscript is written in three columns.

[4] Cross-roads; the word signifies literally, a separation or divergence of roads; „gateschadylle, *compitum,*" Prompt. Parv.
[5] A small brook; still in use in the north.

Hec terra, } erthe.
Hic humus,
Hoc saxifragium, a qwaryle.[1]
Hoc vallis, a daylle.
Hic mons, -tis, a hylle.
Hic collis, the top of a hylle.
Hoc pratum, a medowe.
Hec via, a way.
Hic vicus, a strett.
Hec ripa, a bank.
Hec insula, a nylle.
Hec gleba, a clott.
Hec rupes, a roche.
Hoc inclusorium, a pynfold.
Hic campus, } a feld.
Hic rus,
Hoc firmamentum, a fyrmament.
Hec aëra, a nakyre.
Hec boraga, a noxgang.
Hic selio, -nis, a butt.
Hec virgata, a rodlande.
Hec puppis, a schyppe.
Hec navis, idem est.
Hic lumbus, a bott.
Hic malus, a mast.
Hoc velum, a saylle.
Hic rudens, a cabylle.
Hic funis, a cord.
Hic funiculus, idem.
Hic remus, a nore.
Hee antenne, -arum, gret cabyls.
Hoc columber, a archole.[2]
Hec ancora, a naukyre.
Hoc troclea, a wyndas.
Hoc rete, } a nett.
Hec plaga,
Hic hamus, a hok.

NOMINA LUDORUM.

Hic ludus, a play.
Hoc hastiludium, a justyng.
Hic armilustras, a turnament.
Hec acies, a scheltrone.[3]

[1] A quarry.
[2] i. e., an air-hole — a small unglazed window.

Hec pila, a balle.
Hoc pedum, a clubbe.
Hoc pirrum, the chekyre.
Hec pirga, the poynt of the chekyre.
5 *Hoc scaccarium, idem est.*
Hic talus, a dyse.
Hec decies, idem est.
Hec alea, the menge.
Hec tuba, a trumpe.
10 *Hec fistula,* a pype.
Hec buccina, a beme.
Hic idraicus, a wadyrpype.
Hec cithera, } a harpe.
Hec lira,
15 *Hec fides,* a harpstryng.
Hoc plectrum, a wrast.
Hoc timpanum, a tymbyre.
Hic psalmatus, the sytalle.
Hec vitula, a rybybe.
20 *Hec simphonia,* a symphony.
Hec paupita, a sawtre.
Hoc psalterium, idem est.
Salterium dicitur organicum fore librum.

25
DE VITE ET MATERIIS IPSIUS.

Hec vitis, a vyne.
Hec vitula, idem est.
Hoc vitulamen est planta vite inf ...
30 Et vitis radix, sunt fructus viu ...
Pampinus est folium, botrus flos vin ..
Hec vinea, est locus ubique usitatus.
Hec renosa, idem est.
Hec labrusca, est vitis silvestris.
35 *Hic palmes,* a brawnch of vyne.
Hoc sincetum, est ramus pretentus a vite.
Hic botrus, flos vitis.
Hic racemus, a raysyn.
40 *Hic bubastus, est vitis vel uva in agro.*
Hic spado, i. circulus vitis.
Hec uva, } a grape.
Hec uvula,
Hec uvapassa.

[3] The sheltron was a square, or division of soldiers — a squadron.

Dant uvapassa elibano simeraria plebe,
Uva precerra, vel precox tibi primatura,
                      ubi preco
Quo quando vel precox tibi prematura sunt
                      uva.

Hec precocia, idem est.
Hec corda, est uva serotina.
Cordus, -a, -um, i. serotinus, -a, um.

DE CIBIS GENERALIBUS.

Hic cibus, } mete.
Hec esca, }
Hic dapis, -pem, -pe, idem est.
Nobilitas viles frons generosa dapes.
Hoc manna, awngyls fode.
Hoc jantaculum, a dynere.
Hoc auncinium, }
Hec imranda, } a myddyner
Hoc merarium, } undermete.[1]
Hec cena, a sopere.[2]
Hec musta, idem est.
Die mustam cenam, mustumque latens
                      odorem.

Hoc obsonium, a reresopere.
Hoc convivium, a fest.
Hec dieta, est cibus moderatus, etc.
Estque dieta cibus moderatus, iter quuque
                      diei.

Hoc corrodium, leverayc.

DE PANIBUS ET PARTIBUS EORUM.

Hic panis, brede.
Hic lifus, a lofe.
Hoc colifium, hardbred.
Hec placenta, wastylle.
Hic artocapus, a symnylle.

[1] A meal between the dinner and supper.
[2] A second supper, taken late in the evening.
[3] A small round loaf, as it is explained in the verse.
[4] Schyfe, or shive, a slice.
[5] Dor-cake. The collyrida was a sort of cracknell, or crisp cake, somewhat resembling biscuit.
[6] Pottage.

Hec torta, a cak.
Hec nebula, oblys.[3]
Est nubis nebula tenuis panisque rotundus.
Hec lesca, a schyfe.[4]
Hec colirida, a dorcake.[5]
Hoc crustrum, a crust.
Hoc frustrum, a lumpe.
Hoc minutal, a cantylle.
Hec mica, a crwme.
Hec pasta, doght.
Hec pasmacta, i. parvus panis.
Hec buccella, a morsylle.
Hic morcellus, idem est.

DE SPECIEBUS LIGUMINIS.

Hoc ligumen, potage.
Hoc olus, -ris, wortes.
Hec porreta, porray.
Hec vita, } sew.[6]
Hoc sepulatum, }
Hec sorbuncula, idem est.
Hoc pulmentum, browys.[7]
Hoc adipatum, idem est.
Hoc amigdalatum, almundmylke.[8]
Hoc risi, indeclinabile, ryse.
Hoc puls, }
Hec aplauda, } a mese.
Hoc ferculum, }
Fercula nos saciant, prelatos fercula portant.
Hec polenta, grewylle.
Hoc brodium, brewe.
Hoc pomarium, appuljuse.
Hoc jurcellum, jursylle.[9]
Hoc sarabracium, sarabrase.
Hoc lattum, lorray.[10]
Hoc mel, hony.
Hic garus, a fyscbrowe.[11]
Hoc oleum, oyle.

[7] Broth.
[8] See before, p. 713, note 3.
[9] Jussell was a favourite dish, composed of eggs and grated bread, boiled in broth, and seasoned with sage and saffron.
[10] Lorray, or lorré, was a dish, in ancient cookery, for which receipts are found in most of the cookery books.
[11] Literally, broth of fish.

Hoc omlaccinium, charlyt.[1]
Hoc morticum, a culys.

DE CIBIS GENERALIBUS.

Hec assa,
Hec assatura, } rost.
Hec carbonella, a colope.
Hec frixa, idem.
Hoc crimium, crowkoun.[2]
Hec frixura, fryd met.
Hoc frixum, idem est.
Frixa nocent, elixa juvant, assata cohercent.
Hec artocrea, a pye.
Hic pastellus, a pasthethe.
Hic artocasius, cibus factus ex pane et casio.
Hec tarta, a tartt.
Hec flata, a flawn.
Hoc opacum, idem est.
Hoc fertum, a podyng.
Hoc omasum, idem.
Hoc laganum, same cake.
Hec salsucia, a sawstyre.
Hec hilla, idem est.
Hee delicie,
Hec lauticia, } dantyths.
Hee galanticie,
Hoc frixum, a froys.[3]
Hoc strutum,
Hec tripa, } a tripe.
Hec perra, a flyk.
Hic petaso, -nis, idem est.
Hec petasiculus, half a flyk.
Hoc succidium, sowse.
Hoc tucetum, hagas.
Hec carnes bovine, beffe.
Hee carnes porcine, pork.
Hee carnes ovine, moton.

Hee carnes vitule, veylle.
Hec caro, -nis, man's flesche.
Carnes carnifices, carnem vendunt meretrices.
5 *Hec vipa,* a wynsope.
Hic ipa, a watyrsope.
Hec offa, a alesope.
Est crateris vipa, scutelle dicitur offa,
Sed limphe proprie dicitur ipa fore.
10

DE LECTIS ET ORNAMENTIS EORUM.

Hec torena, est lectus regis.
15 *Hoc plumale,* a fedyrbed.
Hoc cooportorium, a coverlyd.
Hoc toral, -lis, idem est.
Hec lodex, -icis, a blankytt.
Hoc linthiamen, a schett.
20 *Hic carentivellus,* canvas.
Hoc linthium, a tapytt.
Hec tapeta, idem est.
Hec culcitra, a matrys.
Hoc cervical, a peloware.
25 *Hec curtina,* a curtyn.
Hic lectus, a bed.
Hoc stratum, idem est.
Hoc grabatum, media producta, idem est.
30 Est lectus stratum, fertur via regia strata;
Mobile fit stratus ad quod depressus habetur.
Hic lectulus, i. parvus lectus.
Hic thorus, idem est.
Dicas esse thoros, pallaria, brachia, lectos.
35 *Hoc lectiferum, est lectus stratum vel locus ubi lectuli sternuntur, vel stramenta lectorum.*
Hec bojenila, i. lectus.
Hoc concubile, est lectus concubinarum.

---

[1] Charlet was a dish, in medieval cookery, of which the principal ingredient was minced pork.

[2] *Perhaps* the dish called in the early treatises on cookery *crayton,* or *criton* — a preparation of chickens.

[3] A froise was a sort of pancake. The word is still used in the dialect of the eastern countries. It appears to have been a favourite dish with the monks; for Gower (Conf. Amant., vol. ii., p. 92), describing the troubled sleep of Sompnolence, says —

> Whan he is falle in suche a dreme,
> Right as a ship ayein the streme
> He routeth with a slopy noise,
> And brustleth as a monkes froise,
> Whan it is throwe into the panne.

Hoc concubiculum, idem est.
Hic genialis, est lectus qui in nup-
  ciis sternitur.
Hec sponda, est exterior pars lecti.
Hoc fultrum, est pes lecti.
Lectus servorum, discumbentium gra-
  batum.

Cum soleas In eas caput Inclinari gravatum,
Disce graba signare caput, venit inde gra-
    batum.

Hec lectica, est lectus vel thorus, vel
  currus quod dicitur lectus, vel est
  curtina circa lectum.
Hee spinge, -arum, sunt lectuli in
  [quibus] sunt posite efigie.
Hoc torrium, est quidam lectus.
Hoc stramentum, letyr.
Hoc stratorium, idem.
Hoc stabum, idem est.
Hic punicanus, est lectus circumclu-
  sus tapicoleribus rubeis.
Hoc punicanum, idem est.
Hoc crepodium, a credyle.

Hec bamba, est lectus.

Sit cooportorium lecto lecturaque crinis,
Sit tectorem domibus regimen cat sic verge,
Armaque craterras quoque simul capulas.

5 *Hec amphicapa*, est tapeta ex utra-
  que parte villosa.
Hec sipha, idem est.

Amphicapam dicas gemma de parte villosa,
Sicut bistoriis simplex est sipha trapeta.

10 *Hoc subsiterium*, est tapetum sub pe-
  ditali.
Hec curtina, a curtyn.

Dicas curtinas quasi rerum corda tenentes;

Hoc conopeum, est curtina adinst...
15 ...repium recium texta ad ar-
  dendos culices et muscas.
Hoc auriale, a cord or a pelowe.
Hoc cervical, idem est.
Hoc pulviner, }
20 *Hoc cervicarium*, } a coschyn.
Hic pulvinus, }
Hoc limphum, } est po... ex line
Hoc limpheolum, } et lana contextus.

XX.

A PICTORIAL VOCABULARY.[1]

(OF THE FIFTEENTH CENTURY.)

NOMINA PERTINENCIA
HUMANO CORPORI.

Hoc caput, An^{ce} a hede.
Hoc occiput, An^{ce} the last parte of
the hede.
Hoc interciput, An^{ce} the myd parte
of the hede.
Hoc cinciput, An^{ce} the forme part.
Cinciput anterior capitis pars dicitur esse;
Occiput et partem designat posteriorem;
Ast mediam partem dicas interciput esse.
Hoc frontisipium, An^{ce} a forhed.
Hic vertex, An^{ce} a natrelle.[2]
Hoc discrimen, An^{ce} the seed of the
hede.
Sit tibi discrimen divisio, glabra, periclum.
Hic crinis,
Hic pilus,
Hic capillus, } idem sunt, An^{ce} a
Hec coma,   here.
Hec sesaries,

Sesaries hominum, sed crines sunt mulie-
rum;
Hujus vel illius bene dicitur esse capillus.
Hoc cranium, An^{ce} a hernpane.
5 Hoc cerebrum, An^{ce} a brayne.
Hec ffacies, An^{ce} a face.
Hec maxilla,
Hec mala,   } idem sunt, a scheke.
Hec gena,
10 Hic ffrons, -tis, An^{ce} a forhed.
Hic ffrons, -dis, An^{ce} brawnche.
Frons, -dis, ramus, frons, -tis, pars capi-
talis.
Hoc cilium, An^{ce} a here of the hie.
15 Hec bucca, } An^{ce} a scheke.
Hec ffaux,
Ad navem malus spectat, malus est viciosus,
Faux est mala, malum vicium, malum quo-
que pomum.
20 Hoc supercilium, An^{ce} a bro ....
Hoc intercilium, An^{ce} betwyn the
browes.

[1] This very curious vocabulary is preserved in a manuscript in the possession
of Lord Londesborough, which I think is
of the latter part of the fifteenth century.
The illustrative sketches, which occupy the
margins and what would have been otherwise blank places in the manuscript, are
here given, with the inscriptions attached,
of the same size, and as nearly as possible
facsimilies, of the original.

[2] The hatrelle.

A PICTORIAL VOCABULARY.

Hic oculus, An^{ce} a nye.
Hec palpebra, An^{ce} a nyelede.
Hec pupilla, An^{ce} the balle of the ye.
Hec abbcies, } *An^{ce} the qwyt of the ye.*
Hec abbedo,
Hic nasus, An^{ce} a nase.
Hic naris, An^{ce} the nesethyr . . . .
Hoc interficium, An^{ce} the bryd of the ne.
Hec piruela, An^{ce} the cop of the no . . .
Hec cartilago, An^{ce} a grystyl.
Hoc tempus, An^{ce} a tempylle.
Hic cirrus, A^{ce} the cop of the hede.
Hoc pus, snot.
Hic polipus, idem.
Polupus est naris fetor, et in equore piscis.
Hec mustilago, A^{ce} a mulere . . .
Hic mentum, A^{ce} a schyne.
Hec barba, } a berd.
Hoc genorbidum,
Hoc os, ossis, A^{ce} a bone.
Hoc os, -ris, A^{ce} a mowth.
Os, oris, loquitur, corio vestitur os, ossis.
Hec lingua, A^{ce} a tung.
Hec glossa, idem est.
Est membrum lingua, designat et hec igonis.
Hoc labium, A^{ce} a lyp super os.
Hoc labrum, An^{ce} a lyp.
Hec gingiva, A^{ce} a gome.
Hoc omestrum, A^{ce} a mygerne.

Hec auris, } a ere.
Hec auricula,
Hoc tolera,[1] *A^{ce} a eresop.*
Hec febra, A^{ce} a weyne.
5 *Hec mandebula,* a schekeboue.
Hic dens, -tis, A^{ce} a thothe.
Hoc maxillare, a walthothe.
Hic molaris, idem est.
Ventes molares, lapides dic esse molares.
10 *Hec veruca, A^{ce} a wrothe.*[2]
Hic gelbus, An^{ce} a wen.
Hoc collum, An^{ce} a nek.
Hec gula, } a throthe.
Hoc guttur,
15 *Hic jugulus,*
Est gula pars colli, vicium gula restat edendi.
Hec fontinella, A^{ce} the nekhole.
Hic isiofagus, A^{ce} a wesawnt.
20 *Hoc pupillum,* the blak of the ye.
Hoc bachium, }
Hic lacertus, } a harmehole.
Hec ulna,
Brachia dic ulnas, panni mensura sit ulna.
25 *Hic vultus, -tus, -ui, A^{ce} a schere.*[3]
Hec spina, } a rygbone.
Hoc spondile,
Hec spina, A^{ce} a thorne.
Me pungit spina, pars est in corpore spina.
30 *Hec acella, A^{ce} a harmhole.*
Hic subricus, idem est.

[1] *Colera.* See before, p. 676 l. 9.
[2] *Wrothe.* A wart is still called a *wrut* in some of the northern dialects.
[3] The word *schere,* in the sense of countenance or mien, is not a very common word, but it occurs more than once in the romances of Gawayne, edited for the Roxburgh Club by Sir Frederick Madden.

A PICTORIAL VOCABULARY.

Hic ricus, -ci, A^ce a kodlomb.
Hic ricus, -cus, -ui, A^ce the nest of the ye.
Hic ricus per -ci peculas fera dicimus esse.
Hic ricus dans -ui pars ultima constat ocelli.

Hic cubitus, A^ce a helbowe.
Hic umerus, A^ce a schuldere.
Hec arteria, A^ce the hole of the throt.
Hec uva, A^ce the knot of the nek.
Opptulio os uvam, fert vitis fertilis uvam.

Hic armus, A^ce a schuldyr.
Hic humerus, } idem sunt.
Hec scapula, }
Hoc platum, A^ce a schuldyrbone.
Hic stomacus, A^ce stomake.
Hec jecur, A^ce a maw.
Hec manus, -nus, -ui, A^ce a hand.
Hec palma, }
Hoc ir,   } the palme of the hand.
Hec vola,   }
Palma manus, palma arbor, victoria palma.

Hic digitus, A^ce a fyngyr.
Hic articulus, A^ce a too.
Est manuum digitus, articulusque pedum.

Hic junctura, A^ce junctur.
Hoc fren, A^ce the sckyn of the brayne.
Hec pellis, A^ce the sckyn of a best.
In capitis cerebro fren est tenussima pellis;
Pellitur a carne pellis, carnis cutis heret.

Hoc corium, A^ce ledyr.
Hic pollex, A^ce a thumb.
Hic allux, A^ce a grete too.
Est manuum polles, sed dicatur pedis allux.

Hec unguis, A^ce a nayle of a man.
Hec ungula, A^ce a claw of a best.
Unguis non brutis datur, sed ungula brutis.

Hoc tergum, A^ce a bak of a man.

Hoc tergus, } a bak of a best.
Hoc dorsum' }
Hic venter, }
Hoc uterus, } a wombe.
Hic alvus, }
Hic umbelicus, A^ce a nawylle.
Hec nates, A^ce a botok.
Hic lumbus, A^ce a hepe.
Hoc femur, idem est.
Hic vel hec clunis, A^ce a hepebone.
Hic torax, A^ce a brestbone.
Hoc pectus, A^ce a brest.
Hec mamilla, A^ce a lytyl pap.
Hec mamma, A^ce a pap of a woman.
Hoc uber, A^ce a pap of a best.
Nos hominum proprie mamillas dicimus esse,
Ubera et pecudum, sed mamme et mulierum;
Cuius mamillas dixisti, dicque patillas.

Hoc latus, A^ce a syde.
Hec costa, A^ce a rybe.
Hec costa, A^ce a baksterys slomb.
Pars lateris costa, res pistoris quoque costa.

Hec pubes,   }
Hic lanugo, } An^ce schere.
Hoc pecten, }
Hoc femur,   } a they.
Hoc crus,   }
Hic penis,   } idem sunt.
Hic priapus, }
Hic testiculus, a balokstone.
Hic piga, A^ce a balokcod.
Hec vulva, A^ce a cunt.
Hic cunnus, idem est.
Hic tentigo, A^ce a kykyr.
Hec caturda,[1] A^ce a bobrelle.

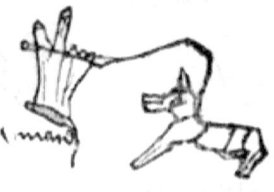

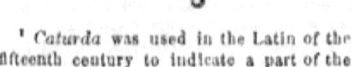

[1] Caturda was used in the Latin of the fifteenth century to indicate a part of the female sexual organs, either the labia pudendi, or the nymphæ.

A PICTORIAL VOCABULARY.

Hec munda,
Hec matrix, } a schyn that a schyld ys consevyd in.
Hec steria,
Hec cavilla, A^ce a hankyl.
Hoc extum A^ce a gret paugh.
Hoc viscus, A^ce a bowelle.
Hoc nytunum, A^ce a bowelle.
Hoc trutum, A^ce a tharme.
Hec struta, A^ce a startere of nete.
Hoc intestinum
Hic colus, } a nestarme.
Hec diafragma, A^ce a mydred.
Hoc cordis, A^ce a hert.
Hic splen, A^ce the mylt.
Hic ren, -nis, A^ce the nerys.
Hoc epar, -ris, A^ce the lywer.
Cor sapit, et pulmo loquitur, fel colligit iram,
Splen ridere facit, cogit amare jecur.

Hic pulmo, A^ce a long.
Hoc burbulum, A^ce a umblye.
Hec elia, A^ce flank.
Hoc cepum, A^ce talow.
Hec pinguedo, A^ce fatnes.
Erba sit hec fragus, hoc fragrum sit tibi fructus,
Hic fragrus, -gi, pomplex cernatur haberi.

Hic fragus, A^ce a hame.
Hec fragrus, A^ce a streberywyse.
Hoc fragrum, A^ce a strebery.
Hic talus, A^ce a hele.
Hic talus, A^ce a dyse.
Ludo cum talis, terram tango quoque talis.

Hic sanguis,
Hic cruor, } *An^ce* blode.
Sanguis alit corpus, cruor est a corpore sumptus;

Extractus venis cruor est, in corpore sanguis.
Hoc fel, A^ce the galle.
Hoc sperma, -tis, A^ce mankynd.
5 Semen quod seritur, set progenies quoque sperma.
Hoc alatum, A^ce a rofom.[1]
Hic condulus, A^ce a knokylle.
Hoc stercus,
10 *Hec meda,* } a torde.
Hoc genu, A^ce a kne.
Hic poplex, A^ce a hame.
Hoc internodium,
Hoc vertebrum, } a knebone.
15 *Hec tibea, A^ce* a leg.
Hec tibea, A^ce a trompe.
Tibia dat sonitum, me portat tibia totum.
Hec sura, A^ce a schynbone.
Hic nervus, A^ce a senow.
20 *Hic pes, -dis, A^ce* a fothe.
Hic poder, A^ce the fylthe of the fothe.
Hic callus, } *An^ce* the harde of the
Hec planta, } fothe.
Signat callus plantam collumque bovinum.
25 *Hic sudor, A^ce* swete.
Hec arcacis, A^ce slepe of the fothe.
Pes patitur artare, *An^ce* my fothe ys a slepe.
Hoc apostema, -tis, A^ce a postemet.[2]
30 *Hec glaucoma, A^ce* a gome.
Hic articulus, A^ce a too.
Hec vola, A^ce the holle of the fothe.
Est vola pars palme, pars ale, pars pedis una.
35 *Hic pollex, A^ce* a thombe.
Hic index, A^ce a lykpot.[3]

 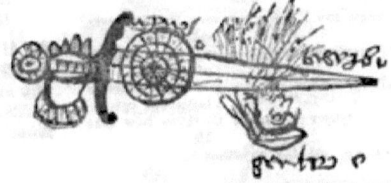

[1] *Rofom.* In the Devonshire dialect the waist is called *rofoam.*
[2] An aposteme, or abscess.
[3] The second cut at the bottom of this page, representing a hand, sword, and head, are drawn upside-down in the original, as here shown.

Hic medius, A*ᶜᶜ* the longman.
Hic medius, A*ᶜᶜ* the leche.
Hic auricularis, A*ᶜᶜ* the lythylman.[1]
Pollex, index, medius, medicus, auricularis.
Hec vesica, An*ᶜᶜ* a bleder.
Hic musculus, A*ᶜᶜ* a muskylle.
Hic musculus, A*ᶜᶜ* a lytyl mus.
Est musculus piscis, parvus mus, pars tibiales.

Hec solia, A*ᶜᶜ* the sole of the fote.
Hoc solium, A*ᶜᶜ* a kynges sete.
Sub pede sit solia, solium quoque regia sedes.

NOMINA ECCLESIE
NESSESSARIA.

Hoc altare, } a hawtere.
Hec ara,

Hoc superaltare, A*ᶜᶜ* ᵃ superaltori.
Hec crux, A*ᶜᶜ* a crosse.
Hec imago, A*ᶜᶜ* a ymage.
Hic lichitus, for a eylepott.
Hoc vixillum, A*ᶜᶜ* a banyre.
Hic calix, A*ᶜᶜ* a schalys.

Hec paterna, A*ᶜᶜ* a patyn.
Hoc corporarium, } A*ᶜᶜ* coperas.
Hoc corporale,
Hec fiola, } a cruet.
5 *Hic urcius*,
Hec osta, } a nobely.[2]
Hic panis,
Hoc sacramentum, A*nᶜᶜ* the sacrament.
10 *Hoc sacrium*, } sacrifyce.
Hoc sacrificium,
Hoc turibulum, A*ᶜᶜ* a sensere.
Hec aserra, a schyp that zychel ere in.
15 *Hoc thus*, } A*nᶜᶜ* ensence.
Hoc incesum,
Hec candela, A*ᶜᶜ* a candelle.
Hic almoriolum, A*ᶜᶜ* almery.
Hic lampas, A*ᶜᶜ* a lawmp.
20 *Hic lichinus*, A*ᶜᶜ* meche.
Hic mergulus, A*ᶜᶜ* herne in the lamp.
Hoc olium, A*ᶜᶜ* oylle.
Hic cerreus, A*ᶜᶜ* a torche.
Hic cerulus, a lytyl torche.
25 *Hoc candelebrum*, } a candyllestyk.
Hoc candelarium,
Hoc crisma, -tis, A*ᶜᶜ* a crem.
Hoc crismatorium, A*ᶜᶜ* a crismatory.
Hoc vestiarium, } a vestri.
30 *Hoc vestibulum*,

---

[1] These popular names of the fingers seem to be of considerable antiquity. The following curious lines are quoted by Mr. Halliwell (Dict. of Arch. Words) from a MS. of the fifteenth century in the University Library, Cambridge (Ff. v 48, fol. 83):

like a fyngir has a name, als men thaire fyngers calle,
The lest fyngir hat l i t y l - m a n, for hit is lest of alle;
The next fynger hat l e c h o - m a n, for quen a leche dos ogt,
With that fynger he tastes all thyng how that hit is wrogt;
L o n g - m a n hat the mydilmast, for longest fynger hit is;
The ferthe men calls t o w c h o r, therwith men touches i-wis;
The fifte fynger is the t h o w m b e, and hit has most mygt,
And fastest haldes of alle the tother, forthi men calles hit rigt.

A Nominale in MS. Reg 17, C. XVII., fol. 39, 1⁰, gives the following list, very similar to that in our text:

Hic pollex, A*ᶜ* thowme.
Hic index, A*ᶜ* lic-pote.
Hic medius, A*ᶜ* lang-fynger.
Hic medicus, A*ᶜ* leche
Hic auricularis, A*ᶜ* lytyl-fynger.

Mr. Halliwell has printed a modern nursery rhyme, (Nursery Rhymes of England, fifth edition, p. 155), in which names very similar to these are still used, namely, *thumbkin, foreman, longman, ringman*, and *littleman*. In Norfolk the fingers are called popularly, *Tom - thumbkin, Willwilkin, Long-gracious, Betty bodkin, Littletit.*

[2] *i. e.*, the oblay, or offering.

Hoc missale, A^ce a myssale.
Hoc gradale, A^ce a grayelle.
Hoc troparium, A^ce tropere.
Hoc callendarium, A^ce a calendere.
Hoc ymnare, A^ce a ymnere.
Hec leges,
Hec legenda, } a legend.
Hic legendus,
Hec letenia, } a letenyboke.
Hec laturia,
Hoc psalterium, A^ce a sawtereboke.
Hoc antifonarium, a amphanere.
Hoc primarium, A^ce a premere.
Hoc mertilogium, A^ce a mertelage.
Hoc manuale, a crystynningboke.
Hoc passionari[*um*], *A^ce* a passionari.
Hoc regestrum, A^ce a regestyr.
Hoc ordinale, A^ce a ordynal.
Hoc portiforum, A^ce a portes.
Hoc touale, A^ce a toual.
Hoc temperalium, A^ce a temperal.
Hec casula, A^ce a chesypyl.
Hec alba, A^ce a hawbe.
Hic amictus, A^ce a amyte.
Hec zona,
Hoc tropheum, } a gyrdylle.
Hic phano, -is, A^ce phanun.[1]
Hec capa, A^ce a cope.
Hoc superpelicium, a syrples.
Hec dalmatica, a tonykyl.
Hic ffons, -tis, A^ce a funte.
Hic gradus, -dus, -ui, A^ce a grese.[2]
Hic baptismus, A^ce crystyndome.
Hoc pixis,
Hoc alabastrum, } *A^ce* a box.
Hec campana,
Hec campanicula, } a belle.
Hoc campanile, A^ce a stepyl.
Hoc camparium, idem est.
Hoc tintinabulum, a lytyl belle.
Hic batillus, A^ce a clapyr.

[1] A standard; the gonfanon.
[2] A step. In the directions in the will of Henry VI., for the building of the colleges at Eton and Cambridge, we read, „Item, the height fro the streete to the enhancing of the ground of the cemetery, 7 feete dl., and the same walle in height

Hoc ventilogium, a wedercok.
Hoc calasisorium, A^ce a hers.
Hoc fferetrum,
Hoc sandapulum,
Hec libetina, } *An^ce* a bere.
Hic loculus,
Est loculus bursa, parvus locus, et lubitina.
Hec sera, A^ce wax.
Hoc vitrum,
Hoc ilum, } *An^ce* glas.
Hoc orologium, A^ce a horologe.
Hoc oritimum, A^ce a cloke.
Hoc organum, A^ce a orgon.
Hoc osculatorium, A^ce a paxbrede.
Hoc manutergium, } a hand-clothe.
Hic towalus,
Hic certofagus,
Hoc sepulcrum, } *An^ce* a grafe.
Hoc bustum,
Hoc tumba,
Hoc monumentum, } *An^ce* a tumb.
Hoc poliandrum, A^ce a byryelston.[3]
Hic ysopus, A^ce a sprenkylle.
Hoc aspersorium, idem est.
Hic stallus, A^ce a stalle.
Hoc mausolium, } *An^ce* a grafe.
Hic tumulus,
Hoc pulpetorium, A^ce a pulpyt.

Hec corda, } a rope.
Hec funis,
Hec lanterna, } a lanterne.
Hec lucerna,

above that, 5 feete dl., with greeces out of the way into the same pane, as many as shalle be convenient." — „And from the provostes stalle unto the greeces called Gradus Chori, 90 feete," &c.

[3] *Byriel*, or *byriels*, was the old name for a tomb.

Hoc lectrinium,
Hic ambo, } a leyterne.
Hic discus,
Hic obstratis, A^{ce} a pannyng.
Hoc velum, A^{ce} a veyle.
Hoc simutorium, } a schererd.
Hoc atrium,

NOMINA ANIMALIUM DOMESTICARUM.

Hic dextrarius, A^{ce} a stede.
Hic emissarius, a corsowyr.
Hic sucarius, A^{ce} a trotore.[1]
Hic palafridus, a palfrey.
Hic gradarius, A^{ce} a hawmlore.[2]
Hic mannus, A^{ce} a hakeney.
Hic cabo, A^{ce} a stalon.
Hic caballus, A^{ce} a capulle.
Hic viridus, A^{ce} a thylhors.
Hic spado, A^{ce} a gelt hors.
Hic equus, A^{ce} alle maner hors.
Hec equa, A^{ce} a mare.
Hic pullus, A^{ce} a schekyn.
Hic pullus, A^{ce} a fole.
Pullus, -a, -um, A^{ce} blak.
Pullus equs, pullus galline, pullus et ater.
Hic asinus, } a has.
Hec asina,
Hic saginarius, A^{ce} a palhors.[3]
Hic taurus, A^{ce} a bole.
Hic mulus, A^{ce} a mule.
Hic et hec bos, A^{ce} a hox.
Hec vacca, } a cow.
Hec vacula,

Hic bucculus, } a bullok.
Hic juvencus,
Hec buccula, } a hekfere.
Hec juvenca,
5 Hic vitulus, A^{ce} a calfe.
Hic vervex, A^{ce} a ram.
Hic aries, A^{ce} a wedyr.
Hec ovis, alle manner a chepe.
Hec verbica, A^{ce} a hew.
10 Hec adasia, A^{ce} pyllyd hew.
Hec erna, A^{ce} a hewlambe.
Hic agnus, A^{ce} a wedyrlombe.
Hic agnellus, a lytyl lambe.
Hic titirus, A^{ce} a belwedyr.
15 Hic equiferus, A^{ce} a wyld hors.
Hic aper, A^{ce} a wyld bore.
Hic verres, tam bore.
Hic porcus, } a hoge.
Hec nefrenda,
20 Hec porca,
Hic et hec sus, } a sow.
Hec scrofa,
Hec porcula, } a geldyd sow.
Hec nefrenda,
25 Hic porcellus, A^{ce} a pyg.
Hic caper, a get buk.
Hec capra, A^{ce} a gothe.
Hic edus,
Hic capriolus, } a kyd lomb.
30 Hic edulus,
Hic leporarius, a frefownd.[4]
Hic odorincicus, a stanyel.
Hic caniculus, a qwelpe.
Hic catulus, idem est.
35 Hec catula, a byche qwelpe.
Hec lacesca, A^{ce} a byche.
Hic molossus, A^{ce} a bonddoge.
Hic catus,
Hic mureligus, } a catt.
40 Hic pilax,
Hic catellus, A^{ce} a cytlyng.[5]
Hic bubalus, A^{ce} a bogelle.[6]

---

[1] *Trotore*, a trotter.
[2] *Hawmlore*, i. e. an ambler.
[3] *Pal-horse*, evidently a packhorse.
[4] i. e., a greyhound. The use of the letter *f* in this word is rather singular, and reminds us of the words *fynger*, for hunger, and *fyrst*, for thirst, which were forms of the dialects of the Welsh border in the fourteenth century.
[5] A kitten.
[6] *Bogelle*, a beagle.

NOMINA ANIMALIUM FERORUM.

Hic leo, An^{ce} a lywn.
Hec leena, } a leo-
Hec leonissa, } nys.
Hic cervus, A^{ce} a hert.
Hic servus, A^{ce} a serwant.
Hic cervus per c. scriptum sit bestia silve;
S. si scribatur servus, famulus vocitatur.

Hec cerva, A^{ce} a hynde.
Hic cervulus, A^{ce} a hertes calfe.
Hic damus, A^{ce} a dobuk.
Hic vel hec dama, A^{ce} a doo.
Hic hinnilus, A^{ce} a fowne.
Hec fferina, -ne, A^{ce} venisyn.
Hic lupus, A^{ce} a wulfe.
Hec lupa, A^{ce} a femel wulfe.
Hic ursus, A^{ce} a bere.
Hec ursa, idem est.
Hic leopardus, A^{ce} a lebard.
Hec leoparda, idem est.
Hic vulpes, A^{ce} a ffox.
Hec simia, A^{ce} a hape.
Hic cuniculus, A^{ce} a conyng.
Hec cunicula, idem est
Hic furo, -is, A^{ce} a foret.
Hic olefans, a olefawnt.
Hic sirogrillus, } a scurelle.
Hic scurellus, }
Hec mustela, a wesylle.
Hic lepus, A^{ce} a hare.
Hic rato, A^{ce} a ratun.
Hic sorex, idem est.
Hic mus, A^{ce} mowse.
Hic vel hec talpa, A^{ce} a molle.
Hic castor, }
Hec melota, } a brok.
Hic taxus, }
Hec taxus, a hewtre.[1]
Hic arbor taxus, hinc taxum dico melotam
Hic fetrunctus, } a sulmard.
Hic pecoides, }

Hic ericius, } a hurchyn.
Hic irmacius, }
Hic dromidarius, A^{ce} a dromedarye.
Hec ffera, A^{ce} a wyld best.
5 Hic camelus, A^{ce} a schamelle.
Hic lepusculus, A^{ce} a leveret.
Hic ffeber, } a otere.
Hic lutrissius, }
Hic grillus, A^{ce} a pryket.[2]
10 Hic unicornus, a unicorne.
Hic gurrex, A^{ce} a watermowse.
Hic roonideus, A^{ce} a redmowse.
Hic cornu, indeclinabile, A^{ce} a horne.
Hec ungula, A^{ce} a claw.
15 Hoc palare, A^{ce} a dewlap.
Hec crista. } a mane.
Hec juba, }
Hic Jubar rex fuerat, jubar hoc lux, hec juba crista.
20 Hec cauda, } A^{ce} a tayle.
Hic dica, }
Hic colimellus, A^{ce} thoyse.[3]
Hec ceta, A^{ce} a brystylle.

25

NOMINA AVIUM DOMESTICARUM.

30   Hic gallus, A^{ce} a cok.
Hec gallina, A^{ce} a hene.
Hic pullus, A^{ce} a cheke.
Hic ancer, A^{ce} a gander.
Hec auca, A^{ce} a gose.
35 Hic ancerulus, A^{ce} a guslyng.
Hic capo, -is, } a capun.
Hic altile, }
Hic pavo, A^{ce} a pocokk.
Hic anas, for drake.
40 Hec anota, a heynd.
Hic columbus, } a dowe.
Hec columba, }
Hic pipio, A^{ce} dowbyrd.

---

[1] A yew-tree.
[2] A pricket is, properly, a buck in his second year. The Prompt. Parv. has, "Pryket, beest, *capriolus*." But in our text it must be either an error for *cryket*, which is the equivalent of the Latin *grillus*, or a form of this word peculiar to one of the provincial dialects.
[3] *Thoyse*, the tusk of a boar.

Hic palumbus, }
Hec palumba,   } a stokdowe
Hic ancipiter, a goshawke.
Hic erodius, a gerfawkyn.
Hic nisus, A^{ce} a sperhawke.
Hic capus, A^{ce} a muskyte.
Hic acensorius, A^{ce} a hoby.
Hic aluctor, A^{ce} a merlone.
Hic aluctus, A^{ce} a stamel.
Hic basterdus, A^{ce} a laner.
Hic signus, }
Hic olor,   } a swane.

NOMINA AVIUM FFERORUM.

Hic regulus, A^{ce} a wrene.
Hic vultur, A^{ce} a grype.
Hic pascer, A^{ce} a sparow.
Hic carduelis, A^{ce} a goldfynche.
Hec alauda,   }
Hec antelucana,   } a larke.
Hec serris,   }
Hec filomena, A^{ce} a nytynggal.
Hec alcedo, A^{ce} a colmow.[1]
Hic sturnus, A^{ce} a sterlyng.
Hic irundo, A^{ce} a swalow.
Hic vespertilio, }
Hec lucifuga,   } a bake.
Hic corvus, A^{ce} a crow.
Hic cornix, A^{ce} a rewyn.
Hic niticorax, A^{ce} a nyterawyn.
Hec monedula, }
Hic nodus,   } a roke.
Hec ffrigella, A^{ce} a rodok.
Hec lonefa, A^{ce} a donek.[2]
Hic bubo, A^{ce} a howylle.
Hec aquila, A^{ce} a egyle.
Hec ulula, A^{ce} a semow.

Hic onux, A^{ce} a nothak.
Hic castrimergus, a wodcok.
Hic conturnix, A^{ce} a curlowyr.
Hec qualena, A^{ce} a quayle.
5 Hic milvus, A^{ce} a potok.[3]
Hec pica, A^{ce} a pye.
Hic citacus, a popynjay.
Hic garulus,   }
Hic gratulus, } a jay.
10 Hec ipipa, A^{ce} a wype.
Hic calendula, a plover.
Hic mariscus, }
Hic sturdus, } a mawys.[4]
Hic campestris, a feldfare.
15 Hic pelicanus, A^{ce} a pelycan.
Hec ardea, A^{ce} a herne.
Hec Ardea, the name of a towyn.
Ardea nomen avis, et nomen dicitur urbis.
Hec sigonia, A^{ce} a storke.
20 Hec ibis, A^{ce} a snyte.
Hic populus, a schevelard.[5]
Hic aspergo, a cormerawnt.
Hic pitus, -ti, A^{ce} a sethe.
Hic onocratulus, A^{ce} a betore.
25 Hec talendiola, A^{ce} a holste.
Hic filicus, A^{ce} a telle cok.
Hec filica, A^{ce} a telle hen.
Hic perdix, A^{ce} a partryk.
Hic utericius, a morcok.
30 Hic mergus, A^{ce} a cote.
Hic mergulus, A^{ce} a dokare.[6]
Hec agredula, a tetmose.
Hic cuculus, A^{ce} a cocow.
Hic turtur, A^{ce} a turtylle.
35 Hic merulus, A^{ce} a thyrstyllecok.
Hic merula, idem est.
Hic ornix.   }
Hic ffesanus, } a fesant.
Hic unnis, A^{ce} a scheldrak.
40 Hic frigella, A^{ce} a roke.
Hic selido, a kynges fychere.

---

[1] More usually written colmose, the A.-S. colmase, the sea-mew.

[2] Donek, or dunnock, the hedge-sparrow. A hedge-sparrow is still called a dunnock in the north of England, and a doney in Northamptonshire.

[3] A puttock, or kite.

[4] This is still preserved as the name for the singing thrush in the eastern counties.

[5] A water-fowl, the anas clypeata of naturalists.

[6] Docare, the diver, or didapper.

Hic icter, A^ce a wodake.[1]
Hic tradus, a wagstyrt.
Hic strix, -cis, A^ce a schryche.
Hoc grus, A^nce a crane.
Hoc rostum, A^ce a bylle.
Hec ala, A^ce a whynge.
Hec vola, pars quedam ale.
Hec vola, a parte of the harmehole.
Hec vola, the lowest parte of the fote.
Est vola pars palme, pars ale, pars pedis 10 ima.

Hec pluma, A^ce a fedyr.
Hec penna, A^ce a pen.
Hic calamus, A^ce a cane.
Hoc ilum, i. medulla penne. 15

NOMINA PISCIUM AQUA-
RUM RECENCIUM.

Hic crocodolus, A^ce a codlyng.[2]
Hec murena, A^ce a lamprey.
Hic salmo, A^ce a samwn.
Hic lucius, A^ce a lus.[3]
Hic dentrix, A^ce a pyke.
Hic lupis, idem est.
Hic lunculus, a pykrelle.[4]
Hic alosa, A^ce a leche.
Hic ganerius, A^ce a stekelyng.
Hic mullus, A^ce a bulhyd.
Hic fundulus, A^ce a flexpeng.[5]
Hee spunere, -arum, A^ce a spyrlyng.
Hec menusa, }
Hic serullus, } a menys.
Hic morus, A^ce a haddok.
Hic capito, A^ce a dar.[6]
Hic turtur, A^ce a gurnard.
Hic gobio, A^ce a gobon.[7]
Hec anguilla, A^ce a helle.
Hec truca, A^ce a tryotht.
Hec rocia, A^ce a roche.

[1] Wodake, the woodhock, or woodpecker.
[2] The Prompt. Parv. has, "Codlynge, fysche, morus."
[3] A luce, or pike.
[4] A young pike.
[5] Flex-peng. The Latin word fundulus is generally interpreted a gudgeon.

Hec poca, A^ce a pyche.
Hic echinus, }
Hic ectinus, } a tenche.
Hec frisgula, A^ce a chevender.[8]
Hic murex, A^ce a breme. 5
Hec murenula, A^ce a lampren.
Hec perca, A^ce a perche.
Hic guttulus, A^ce a gojon.
Hec sepia, A^ce a troyte.

NOMINA PISCIUM
MARINORUM.

Hec aurata, A^ce a sedow.[9]
Hec setus, }
Hoc setearum, } whalle.
Hec epimera, -e, }
Hic tumalus, } a sperlyng. 20
Hic sardellus, A^ce a swerdfyche.
Hec ostria, A^ce a hoystyr.
Hec ostra, A^ce a hoysterchelle.
Ostra notat testam, clausum notat ostria piscem. 25

Hic ausculus, A^ce a muskylle.
Hee telie, -arum, idem est.
Hec conca, A^ce a cokylle.
Hic bulbus, A^ce a wylke.
Hic cancer, A^ce a crabe. 30
Hic polupus, A^ce a lobstar.
Hic conchilus, A^ce a astsyche.
Hic saltilus, A^ce a hobstere.
Hic meganus, A^ce a makrel.
Hoc allec, } 35
Hec gerra, } a heryng.
Hec ragadia, A^ce a ray.
Hic uronoscopus, a thornbak.
Hic garus, A^ce a schate.[10]
Hic morus, A^ce a haddok. 40
Hic merlinggus, A^ce a merlyng.

[6] Dar, the dare, or, as it is now more usually called, the dace.
[7] Gobon, the whiting.
[8] Chevender, the cheven, or chub.
[9] Sedow, the fish called a gilthead (sparus).
[10] The skate.

Hic mugilus, A^ce a mowel.[1]
Hec rosina, A^ce a sehors.
Hic sepio, A^ce a leenge.[2]
Hic panus, } A^ce a hake.
Hic squylla, }
Hic congruus, A^ce a cungur.
Hoc pecten, A^ce a playse.
Hec ffoca, A^ce a floke.[3]
Hic molanus, A^ce a melet.
Hic turbo, -is, A^ce a but.[4]
Hec rubella, A^ce a rochet.[5]
Hec rugella, } a hornkeke.[6]
Hoc rustiforum, }
Hec solia, A^ce a sole.
Hic canis, a dokefyche.[7]
Hec ffingia, A^ce a stokfyche.
Hoc rasorium, A^ce a rasowyr.
Hic dolfinus, A^ce a dolfyn.
Hec balena, A^ce a porpeyse.
Hic rumbus, A^ce a sturgyn.
Hic branchia, A^ce a gylle.
Hec sqama, a scalyd fyche.
Hic puma, A^ce a ffyn.
Hoc zabulum, A^ce sond
Hoc laquamen, An^ce rownd.
Hec lactis, An^ce mylkere.[8]
Hec testa, An^ce a schylle·
Hec siren, An^ce a mermayd.

NOMINA VERMIUM.

Hic draco, a dragon.

Hic vermis, a worme.
Hec rana, A^ce a frog.
Hic bufo, A^ce a tode.
Hic scorpio, A^ce a scarpyn.
5 Hic serpens, alle maner naderes.
Hic agguis, A^ce a wateradder.
Hic coluber, A^ce a snake.
Hec vispera, A^ce a berard.
Hic idrus, }
10 Hec idra, } a blyndwurme.
Hec matrix, }
Hec cresta, A^ce a angyl.
Hic biceps, } a flyyn nedere.
Hic jaculus, }
15 Hic calus, a slowurme.
Hec septipedia, a gagrylle.
Hic cacadillus, } a cocatryse.
Hic basilicus }
Hec nocticula, a glouberd.
20 Hic lumbricus, A^ce a tadpolle.
Hec salomandra, A^ce a cryket.
Hec lacerta, A^ce a newte.
Hec formica, } a pysmere.
Hec murunca, }
25 Hic bibio, A^ce a hoxbame.
Hec aranea, a nedyrcopp.
Hic auriglus, A^ce a sylverwurme.
Hic multipes, A^ce a tuentifot-wurme.
Hec sanguifica, } a leche.
30 Hec irudo, }
Hec limax } a snayle.
Hec testudo, }
Hic pulex, A^ce a floo.

↳ draco

---

[1] The mullet, *mugil cephalus* of Cuvier.
[2] Ling, the *gadus molva* of Linnæus.
[3] *Floke*, or *flewke* (the A.-S. *floc*), the flounder.
[4] *Turbo* means properly a whelk.
[5] Perhaps the rouget, or piper-fish.
[6] *Horn-keck* appears in Palsgrave as the name of a fish, which is said to be called also a *greenback*.
[7] i. e., the dog-fish.
[8] *Mylkere*, the milt or soft roe of the male fish.

Hic pedicus, } lowse.
Hic pediculus, }
Hic lens -dis, A^(cc) a nyte.
Hec ascarida, a teke.
Hic tarinus } a maked.[1]
Hic simax, }
Hec impetigo, a ryngworme.
Hec mica, A^(cc) a mynte.[2]
Hec musca, A^(cc) a fflye, alle maner.
Hic carembes, -tis, A^(cc) a betylle.
Hoc eruga, A^(cc) a wurtwurme.

NOMINA MUSCA-RUM.

Hic apes, -pis, A^(cc) a bee.
Hic asilus, A^(cc) a drane.
Hec vespa, A^(cc) a waspe.
Hic tabanus, A^(cc) a humbylbee.
Hec sicada, A^(cc) a grashoppyr.
Hec sinomea, A^(cc) a hondflye.
Hic siniflex, An^(cc) a red fflye.
Hoc crestrum, A^(cc) a brese.
Hic culex, a knat.
Hoc gamalion, A^(cc) a myght.
Hec polumita, A^(cc) a bude.[3]
Hic stabo, A^(cc) a searbude.[4]
Hic papilio, A^(cc) a butterfflye.

NOMINA ME-TALLORUM.

Hoc aurum, ffor gold.
Hoc argentum, A^(cc) sylver.
Hoc es, eris, idem est.
Hoc es, -ris, A^(cc) brasse.
Hoc electrum, A^(cc) pewtyr.
Hoc cuprum, A^(cc) copyr.

Hoc plumbum, A^(cc) lede.
Hoc auricalcum, A^(cc) latun.
Hoc stagnum, A^(cc) tynne.
Hoc stangnum, A^(cc) a pond.
5 Est aqua stans arte stagnum, stannuum dic esse metallum.

Hec caleps, A^(cc) stele.
Hoc fferum, A^(cc) yryn.
Hoc metallum, A^(cc) metalle.
10

NOMINA LAPI-DUM.

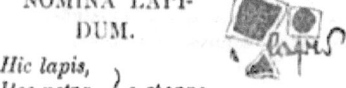

15 *Hic lapis,* }
Hec petra, } a stonne.
Hoc saxum, }
Hic mermur, A^(cc) a marbylstone.
Hic et hec silex, A^(cc) a flyntstone.
20 *Hic scripulus,* A^(cc) a lytyl stone.
Hec margarita, A^(cc) a perylle.
Hec Margareta, a maydyn.
   Margarita lapis, sed Margareta puella.
Hoc mola, A^(cc) a mylstonne.
25 *Hec acates,* A^(cc) a grynstone.
Hoc cos, -tis, A^(cc) a watstone.
Hic terebentus, A^(cc) a thone.
Hec gemma, A^(cc) a precius stone.
Hic jaspes, A^(cc) precioustone.
30 *Hic berellus,* A^(cc) a berelleston.
Hic saphirus, A^(cc) a safyr.
Hic stupelus, A^(cc) a precius stonne.
Hic cautes, A^(cc) a saltstone.
Hic rupes, A^(cc) a roche of stone.
35 *Hec pumes,* A^(cc) a nedyrstonne.[5]
Hec pama, A^(cc) a grapond.
Hic jacinctus, A^(cc) a precius stone.
Hic rudus, A^(cc) a cobylstone.
Hoc tapacior, A^(cc) a stone.
40 *Hic gagates,* } a ruby.
Hec smaragdus, }
Hec timeria, A^(cc) a frestone.

---

[1] *Maked,* a maggot.
[2] A mite. See before, p. 623, note 13.
[3] *Bude,* the weevil, a small insect of the beetle tribe which is destructive to grain. Tusser, as quoted by Halliwell, speaks of „bowd-eaten malt;" and the word is still preserved in the dialect of the eastern counties.
[4] *Scarbude,* or *scarnbude,* a kind of beetle.
[5] The adder-stone.

Hec magdalena, a balwyn.[1]
Hoc egipsum, A^ce a egypstone.[2]
Hic calculus, a ston in a mannys bleder.
Hic saxus, A^ce a bolokstone.
Hec tegula, A^ce a tilstone.
Hec cals, -cis, A^ce a calkestone.
Hic cals, A^ce a parte of the fote.
Pars pedis est hic cals, lapis ustus dicitur hec cals.

Hoc armum, A^ce grawelle.
Hec gloria, A^ce a schesellestone.
Hic carboculus, a carbokylstone.
Hic petro, a chyp of a stone.

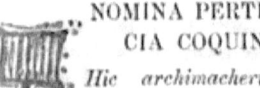

NOMINA PERTINENCIA COQUINE.

Hic archimacherus, a mastercoke.
Hic cocus, alle maner a cokys.
Hic lixa, a swyllere.[3]
Hic dapifer, a berere of mete.
Hic tripes, a brenlede.[4]
Hic cacabus,
Hic lebes, } a cawdurne.
Hoc caduum,
Hec machera, a dressyngburd.
Hec mensacula, a dressyngknyfe.
Hic urcius, A^ce a bras pot.
Hic urciolus, A^ce a posnet.
Hec sartago,
Hoc fricsorium, } a fryyngpan.
Hic discus, a dyche.
Hic cratus,
Hec craticula, } a rostyngyryn.
Hoc veru, indeclinabile, a spete.

Hic veruvertor, a speteturnere.
Hec andena, a handyryn.
Hoc ipegurgium, a gobard.
Hoc micatorium, a myure.
5 *Hec eriagra,*
Hec tridex, } a flechehoke.
Hec limas, a haprune.
Hoc spumatorium, a schomore.[5]
Hoc austorium, a ladyl.
10 *Hoc motarium*, a potstyk.
Hec laxis,
Hec aspiculna, } a selys.[6]
Hoc calafactorium, a schasure.[7]
Hec capana, a pothoke.
15 *Hoc morterium*, A^ce a mortere.
Hoc tribulum,
Hec pila, } a pestelle.
Hoc fractillum, a pepyrquerne.
Hic fractillus, a rage.[8]
a 20 *Hec patella*, a pane.
Hec scutella, a scotylle.
Hec parapcis, -idis, a plater.
Hoc assitabulum, a sauser.

25

30

NOMINA PERTINENCIA BOTULARIE.

35 *Hic botularius*, a botelere.
Hoc dolium, A^ce a tune.
Hic cadus, a barelle.

---

[1] Perhaps the baleis, a sort of ruby. It seems to be the same word as *balayn* in the following passage from the metrical romance of Richard Coer-de-Lion, l. 2979.

Her baner whyt, withouten fable,
With thre Sarezynes hedes off sable,
That wer schapen noble and large
Off b a l a y n, both scheeld and targe.

[2] Probably gypsum.

[3] A scullion, one who swills the disbes.
[4] The brandlet, or brandreth. Cf. p. 660 l. 31.
[5] i. e., a skummer.
[6] *Selys*, a slice, or implement for turning meat in the frying-pan.
[7] *Sekasure*, or *shasor*, a wine-cooler.
[8] In Somersetshire, a broken pan is still called a *rage*.

A PICTORIAL VOCABULARY.

Hoc mustum, A^{ce} moste.
Hoc idromellum, A^{ce} wurte.

Hoc onafrum, ⎫
Hic uter, -ris, ⎬ a flaget.[1]
Hec olla, ⎭
Hec lura, a mowth of a flaget.
Hec lura, a nek of a flaget.
Lura sit os utris, et collum luridus inde.

Hic cifus, alle manyr copys.
Hic crater, ⎫
Hec cateria, ⎬ An^{ce} a pese.[2]
Hec urna, a cowpe.
Hec murra, a masowyr.
Hoc coopertorium, a . . .
Hec clepsidra, a speget.
Hec urnula, a not.[3]
Hec orca, A^{ce} a cane.
Hic canterus, a colok.[4]
Hec amphora, a tancard.
Hec idria, a watyrpot.
Hec fidelia, idem est.
Hec justa, A^{ce} a gyste.
Hoc vinum, alle maner wyne.
Hoc tementum, A^{ce} strong wyne.
Hoc villum, A^{ce} febylle wyne.
Hoc ffalarnum, A^{ce} gode wyne.
Hoc tenulentum, A^{ce} thyn wyne.
Hoc merum, A^{ce} cler wyne.
Hec sapa, A^{ce} qeketh wyne.
Hoc amuennum, A^{ce} wyte wyne.

Hoc ciromellum, A^{ce} growte.[5]
Hoc claretum, a clerote wyne.
Hoc nectar, A^{ce} piment.[6]
Hec amurca, a lyf of wyn.
Hec servisia, alle maner ale.
Hec selea, A^{ce} stale ale.
Hec ffexs, A^{ce} dregys.
Hec spuma, A^{ce} berme.

NOMINA PERTINENCIA PANATRIE.

Hic panatrius, a pantre.
Hic panis, A^{ce} a lofe.
Hec quadra, a cantel of brede.
Hec lesca, ⎫
Hec colirida, ⎬ a schefe of brede.
Hoc peripsima, A^{ce} a paryng.
Hec mica, A^{ce} a crume.
Hic bolus, ⎫
Hic murcellus, ⎬ a musselle.[8]
Hec buccella, ⎭
Est buccella cibus quantum semel accipis ore.
Hoc salinum, ⎫
Hoc assitabulum, ⎬ a salere.
Hoc ffrustrum, A^{ce} a lumpe.

---

[1] A flask, a leathern bottle.
[2] Pece, or pese, was a common name for a drinking-cup.
[3] Not, or nut, a sort of small vase.
[4] Collock is the name given in the northern dialects to a large pail.

[5] See before, p. 725 l. 27.
[6] See before.
[7] The little figure at the head of this article is curious, as showing the usual form of the loaf of bread at this period.
[8] i. e., a morsel.

Hic sal, saltis, A^ce salt.
Hoc coclear, A^ce a spone.
Hoc candelebrum, A^ce a candylsteyke.
Hoc gausape, ⎫
Hoc toral,   ⎬ a burdclothe. 5
Hec mappa,   ⎭
Hoc sissorium, A^ce a trenchore.
Hoc manitergium, a hand- 10 clothe.
Hec culingna, A^ce a lineshark.[1]

NOMINA VESTIMEN- 15 TORUM.

Hec vestis
Hoc vestimentum, ⎫
Hoc indumentum, ⎬ *A^ce* clothe. 20
Hoc superum, An^ce a pryn.[2]
Hoc pelicium, A^ce a pylchen.[3]
Hoc scapilorium, A^ce a scaplorey.
Hec capa, A^ce a cope. 25
Hec sarabarda, A^ce a sclavene.
Hoc mantile,   ⎫
Hoc mantellum,   ⎬ a mantelle.
Hec seclas, -cis, idem est. 30
Hoc capellum, A^ce a hat.
Hic capellus, idem est.
Hic pilius, A^ce a cape.
Hec tena, A^ce a hewd.[4]
Hoc capucium, A^ce a hode. 35
Hec armilansa, a cloke.
Hoc colobium, a tabare.
Hec toga,   ⎫
Hoc epitogium, ⎬ a gowyn.
Hec supertunica, a syrcote. 40
Hec roba, A^ce a robe.

---

[1] *Lineshark. Culigna,* in good Latin, signified a drinking bowl.
[2] *Pryn,* a woman's smock.
[3] A furred outer-coat.
[4] *Hewd,* the extremity of the riband hanging from the bishop's mitre.

Hec tunica, A*ce* a cote.
Hoc ventrale, a corsete.
Hec camisia, } a scherte.
Hec subuncula,
Hec supera, } a rokete or a lyste.
Hec instita,
Hec lombesina, A*nce* a paltoke.[1]
He bracce, *-arum*, }
Hoc ffemorale, } A*nce* a breke.
Hoc perizoma, }
Hic fforulus, A*ce* a huwyng.
Hoc lumbare, A*ce* a bregyrdyle.
Hec legula, A*ce* a lanyr.
Hoc subligar, A*ce* a styltbonde.

Subligar est legula caligas quas sublygans alte.

Hoc tibiale, a strapylle.
Hec caliga, A*ce* a hose.
Hic mancus, A*ce* a meteyne.
Hec ffirotica, A*ce* a glofe.[2]
Hic sotularis, A*ce* a scho.
Hic pedulus, A*ce* a soke.
Hic ffractillus, A*ce* a dag of a gowyn.[3]

NOMINA PERTINENCIA CAMERE.

5 *Hic camrius*, } A*nce* a scham-
Hic et hec sinista, } berleyne.
Hoc lectum, alle maner off beddys.
Hoc grabatum, a seke mannys beddys.
Hoc torum, A*ce* a husbondes bedde
10 *Hec toreuma*, A*ce* a kynges bedde.
Hoc supralectum, } a selowyr.[4]
Hec tectora, }
Hoc capisterium, A*ce* a redcle.[5]
Hoc pallium, A*ce* a palle.
15 *Hoc tapetum*, A*ce* a schalun.[6]
Hoc coopertorium, a cowyrlythe.
Hoc torall, idem est.
Est toral mappa, tegmen lectoque vocatur.
Hic lodex, A*ce* a blanket.
20 *Hoc linthiamen*, A*ce* a schete.
Hoc carentivillum, a canvas.
Hoc ffultrum, A*ce* a matras.
Hec sponda, A*ce* a ffedyrbedde.
Hoc servical, A*ce* a pelow.
25 *Hec coma*, } a combe.
Hoc pecten, }
Hoc caliandrum, a wulpere.[7]

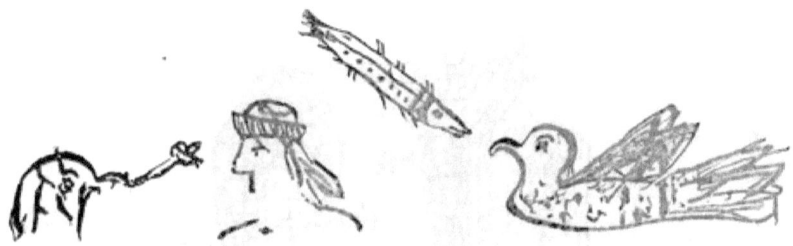

[1] A paltock was a doublet or cloak descending to the middle of the thigh. It is a word which has recently been brought into use again.

[2] For *cirotica*, *i. e. chirotheca*. It is another example of the curious use of the *f*, remarked in a former note.

[3] The dagging, jagging, or foliating, the edges of garments, came into fashion apparently in the reign of Edward III., and prevailed more or less till the latter part of the fifteenth century.

[4] The *celure*, or roof, of the bed.
[5] The *ridel*, or bed-curtain.
[6] See before, p. 626, note 2.
[7] *Wulpere*. The Latin word *caliandrum* signifies false hair — a periwig. A *wulpere* was perhaps a head-dress composed of false hair; probably the same word as *volupere*.

A PICTORIAL VOCABULARY.

Hoc anabatum, A*cc* a docer *addorsum*.
Hoc calatrale, A*cc* a sydedocer.
Hec fforma, }
Hoc schabellum, } a forme.
Hoc scannum, A*cc* a benche.
Hec antipera, A*cc* a screne.
Hoc scopum, a matte.
Hoc utensule, howseho.[1]
Hoc stramentum, lyttere.[2]
Hic stratus, -tus, -ui, }
Hoc stratum, -ti, -to, } a bed.
Stratus vel -tum confinguntur tibi lectum.

Hoc epicausterium, a thuelle.[3]
Hic caminus, a grete fyre.
Hic caminus, a chymny.
Emittens fumum tibi sit locus ipse caminus,
Maximus atque rogus tibi dicitur esse caminus.

Hec fagota, a fagat.
Hoc focale, fuelle.
Hic fax, -cis, An*cc* a chyde.

PARTES DOMUS.

Hec paries, -tis, }
Hic murus, } a walle.
Hoc doma, -tis, a roffe.
Hoc festum, a roffetre.

Hoc festum, a holyday.
Pars festum tecti et dicitur esse solenne.
Hoc tingnum, a spere.
Hec trabecula, a wynbeme.
5 *Hec trabes*, a refter.
Hic postis, -tis, a poste.
Hoc laquiare, A*cc* a postbondde.
Hoc sigillum, a barer of a rofetre.
Hec ffenestra, A*cc* a wyndow.
10 *Hoc lucanar*, a day of a wyndow.[4]
Hoc superuminare, A*cc* a lenterne.[5]
Hec antica, A*cc* a porche.
Hoc ostium, An*cc* a dore.
Hoc osticulum, A*cc* a hatche.
15 *Hoc limen, -nis*, . . .
Hec grunda, a hespe.
Hoc domicilium, . . .
Hoc institucium, . . .
Hec cavilla, A*cc* a pyn.
20 *Hoc manutentum* An*cc* a haginday.[6]
Hoc findolum, a lache.
Hec sera, A*cc* a loke.
Hec serula, A*cc* a clyket.
Hoc pesulum, A*cc* a hespe.
25 *Hec ventifica*, a screne.
Hec assia, -e, A*cc* a burde.
Hec pertica, A*cc* a pherche.
Hoc repagulum, a barre.

[1] *Househo*. Perhaps this singular word signifies a chamber-pot.
[2] Litter, the straw with which the bed was formerly made.
[3] The pipe of the chimney.

[4] Otherwise called a bay of a window, the space between the mullions.
[5] The lantern, or light from above.
[6] A sort of wooden latch for a door is still called a *haggeday* in Yorkshire.

Hic clatravus, A^ce a lache.
Hic obex, An^ce a hoke.
Hic gumser, An^ce a hengylle.[1]
Hec vectes, An^ce a hoke.
Hec area, An^ce a florthe.[2]
Hec capedo, dicitur spacium inter parietes.
Hoc scannum, A^ce a benche.
Hoc focarium, A^ce a hartstone.
Hic ffocus, idem est.
Hic focus, An^ce a hautere.
Hic ffocus, An^ce a fyir.
Est altare focus, locus et focus ignis.
Hoc reposilium, A^ce a fyirbelowys.
Hec basys, the growndpelyr.
Hic stilus, A^ce a smal of a pelyr.
Hic stilus, A^ce a poyntelle.
Hic stilus, alle maner speche.

Est stilus unde puer scribit modus atque loquendi;
Atque stilus media pars dicitur esse columna;
Dico basi portare domum stilumque victis ab ipsa,
Portat epistilium quibus est erecta columba.

Hec cobluma, An^ce a pylere.
Hec ffornix, } An^ce a . . .
Hic arcus,
Hec vouta, A^ce a wout.
Hec cardo, An^ce a durherre.

NOMINA ECCLESIASTICORUM.

Hic papa, A^ce a pape.[3]
Hic patriarca, A^ce a patriark.
Hic cardinalis, A^ce a cardinalle.
Hic archiepiscopus, A^ce a arsbyschop.
Hic episcopus, An^ce a byschop.
Hic legatus, An^ce a legat.
Hic suffraganeus, a suffrigan.
Hic decanus, An^ce a dene.
Hic canselarius, } a scawnceler.
Hic scriba,

[1] A hengle, or hinge.
[2] i. e., a floor.
[3] This word had been nearly erased in the MS., no doubt after the Reformation.

Hic archidiaconus, A^ce a arsdekyn.
Hic officialis, A^ce a offysere.
Hic comissarius, A^ce a comissere.
Hic rector, An^ce a persun.
5 Hic vicarius, An^ce a vecory.
Hic presbeter, }
Hic et hec sacerdos, } a pryst.
Hic capellanus, }
Sacris dicatus vel sacris deditus atque
10 Sacra dans, vel dux sacer esto sacerdos.

Hic diaconus, } a dekyn.
Hic levita, }
Hic subdiaconus, a subdekyn.
Hic acoletus, An^ce a colet.
15 Hic exorcista, An^ce a benet.
Hic et hec secrista, a sekyrsteyn.
Hic aquarius, a halywater-clerke.
Hic aquebachelus, idem est.
Hic abbas, An^ce a abotte.
20 Hic prior, -ris, A^ce a prier.
Hic supprior, An^ce a supprier.
Hic sellerarius, a selerer.
Hic subselarius, a subselerer.
Hic canonicus, a chanon.
25 Hic monacus, a mongke.
Hic ffrater, a frere.
Hic eremita, a heremyte.
Hic doctor, ⎫
Hic instructor, ⎪
30 Hic monitor, ⎪
Hic petegogus, ⎬ a mayster.
Hic auctor, ⎪
Hic imbutor, ⎪
Hic papas, ⎪
35 Hic didasculus, ⎪
Hic magister, -ri, -ro, ⎭
Doctor et instructor, monitor, petegogus, et auctor,
Imbutor, papas, didasculus, atque magister.
40 Hic legista, a legister.
Hic grammaticus, a grammaryon.
Hic dioleticus, } a arcister.
Hic arcista, }
Hic sophista, a sophister.

It is a curious example of the extent to which the order for erasing the pope's name from public documents was carried out.

A PICTORIAL VOCABULARY.

Hic bacularius, a bacler.
Hic clericus, a clerke.

Hic scolaris, a scoler.
Hic teologus, a mayster of divinite.
Hic sitarius, a sumner.
Hic apparitor, } idem sunt.
Hic sitator,

NOMINA DOMINORUM TEMPORALIUM.

Hic imperator, a nemperour.
Hoc diadema, lapis preciosus.
Hic rex, a kyng.
Hec laurea, corona regis.
Hoc certum, a garlant.
Hec corona, s. cleri.

Legis est certum clerique corona poete,
Aurea rex gestat diadema vel Induperator.

Hoc septrum, regis dignitas.
Hoc solium, a kynges sete.
Hoc fiscale, a kynges porse.
Hoc sistale, a kynges tax
5 Hoc gazophilacium, a tresure.
Hic dux, -cis, a duke.
Hic baro, -nis, a baron.
Hic barunculus, a baronet.[1]
Hic miles -tis, a knygte.
10 Hic armiger, a squyer.
Hic generosus, e gentylman.
Hic tiro, a yoing knygte.
Hic dominus, al maner lordes.
Hoc dominium, a lordechyppe.
15 Hoc donativum, a waresun.
Hoc corrodium, } a levery.
Hec armilla,
Hec nima, a sylver rodde.

20

NOMINA ARMORUM.

25 Hec arma, } a we-
Hec arma- } pyn.
tura,
Hic conus, a crest.

30 Hec galea, media producta, a galle.
Hec galea, media corrupta, a helme.
Induo me galea, galeatus duco galeam.

Hec bombecina, a acton.[2]
Hec tassis, a palett.
35 Hic tassis, a nett.

[1] i. e., a lesser or minor baron. Our modern title of baronet of course came in at a much later period.

[2] The ackctoun, or acton, was a sort of tunic worn under the coat of mail.

Hec tassis galea, hic tassis rethia monstrat.
Hec *lorica*, a habirjun.
Hec *suamata*, a plate.
Hec *brachialia*, A^{ce} a brasere.
Hec *larva*, A^{ce} a visere.
Hec *larva*, A^{ce} a dewylle.[1]
Hec *larva*, A^{ce} a selerelle.[2]
Larva fugit volucres, faciem tegit, est quoque demon.

Hic *torax*, A^{ce} a brystbone.
Hic *torax*, A^{ce} a brystplate.
Hec *femoralia*, A^{ce} a quischens.[3]
Hec *tibialia*, A^{ce} a legarnes.
Hic *gladius*, A^{ce} a swerd.
Hic *anceps*, A^{ce} a towhand swerd.
Hec *gesa*, A^{ce} a gysyryne.[4]
Non amat ille Jhesum qui fert ad prelia gesam.

Hec *spata*, A^{ce} a pleyend swerd.
Hec *sica*, A^{ce} a baselard.
Hec *soliferia*, A^{ce} a fauschune.
Hec *clava*, A^{ce} a mase.
Clava ferit, clavis aperit, clavus duo jungit.

Hic *armiturium*, A^{ce} a dagar.
Hic *dagardus, idem est*.
Hec *pugio, -onis, idem est*.
Hec *funda*, A^{ce} a sclyng.
Hoc *fustibulum*, a handsclyng.
Hec *babrilla*, A^{ce} a dongbabylle.
Hic *arcus, -cus, -i*, A^{ce} a bow.
Hec *sagista*, A^{ce} a arow.
Hec *catapulta*, a brodo arow.
Hec *petulium*, A^{ce} a bolte.
Hec *ceculicula*, a sparke.
Hec *ffudes*,[5] a pikestafe.
Fustes fetate poterint sudes bene dici.

Hec *ffustis*, A^{ce} a batte.
Hic *baculus*, A^{ce} alle maner stavis.
Hec *lancea*, An^{ce} a spere.
Hec *asta*, An^{ce} a schafte.
Hoc *scutum*,
Hoc *cliphium*, } a buceler.

Hec *daca*, An^{ce} a pollex.
Hec *petrima*, An^{ce} a gune.[6]
Hoc *telum*,
Hoc *pilum*, } a darte.
5 Hec *tela, -e*, An^{ce} a webe.
Nos vestit tela, volitant per prelia tela.
Hec *balista*, A^{ce} a arowblaste.
Hoc *mustile*,
Hoc *jaculum*, } a darte.
10 Hec *sestus*, A^{ce} a pavis.[7]
Hec *parma*, An^{ce} a bokeler.
Hec *umbo*, An^{ce} a bosbokelere.
Hoc *mangnalium*, An^{ce} a gyn.
Hec *brida*, A^{ce} a trappe.
15 Hoc *tribucetum*, An^{ce} a pytfalle.
Hec *ffalaa*, A^{ce} a lumpe of a walle.
Hoc *propinaculum*, A^{ce} a bretayge.[8]
Hoc *superfossorium*, a drawtebryge.
Hec *listia*, a castylledyche.
20

NOMINA BLADO-
25 RUM ET ARBO-
RUM.

Hec *seges*,
Hoc *satum*,
Hoc *bladum*,
30 Hoc *granum*, } corne.
Hoc *fruges*,
Hic *messis*,

Dum seritur seges, sata dum radisibus herent,
35 Blada virore virent, granaria grana reservant;
Fruges dum fruimur, sunt messes quando metuntur.

Hoc *frumentum*, A^{ce} whete.
40 Hoc *triticum, idem est*.
Hoc *essaticum*, An^{ce} bere.[9]
Hoc *ordium*, An^{ce} barly.

---

[1] i. e., a devil, or demon; a hobgoblin.
[2] This means apparently a scarecrow.
[3] More usually called *cuisses*, the pieces of armour which protected the thighs.
[4] See before, p. 653 l. 29.
[5] Sic, for *sudes*.
[6] This is the first occurrence of the gun among weapons in these vocabularies.
[7] The *pavis* was a large shield.
[8] The *bretasche*, or parapet.
[9] *Bere*, a kind of barley.

Hec siligo, } *An^{ce}* rye.
Hoc ergalum,
Hec avena, An^{ce} hotys.
Hec faba, A^{ce} a bene.
Hec pisa, A^{ce} a pese.
Hec viscia, A^{ce} a feche.[1]
Hoc viscium, A^{ce} a wyse.

Si comedes visclam non est visclum tibi magnum;
A viscio -as horum discendet utrumque.

Hec mixtilio, A^{ce} moge.
Hec avicula, A^{ce} wyld hote.

Radix, festuca, conculnio, nodus, arista,
Granum cum palia fer sufficit sit quoque scripta,
Sunt partes messis firma tellure manentes.

Hec seliqua, A^{ce} a pescodde.
Hec filupra, An^{ce} a bencodde.
Hic manipulus, a handfulle.
Hic arcomus, An^{ce} a stathele.
Hoc ffenum, An^{ce} hey.
Hoc ffenile, A^{ce} a heystakke.
Hec garba,
Hec merges, } *A^{ce}* a schefe.
Hec gelima,
Hec congelima, An^{ce} a schokke.[2]
Hoc pabulum, An^{ce} fodyr.
Hoc olus, -ris, An^{ce} wurtes.
Hec betana, An^{ce} betany.
Hec betate, -tes, A^{ce} bettes.
Hec borago, -nis, A^{ce} o broges.[3]
Hoc porrum, A^{ce} a leke.
Hoc sepe, indeclinabile, a hunyn.
Porri vel sepe fertur bulbus capud esse.
Hoc allium, An^{ce} garleke.

Hic sinolus, } a schybbolle.[4]
Hec sipula,
Hoc petrocillum, An^{ce} persely.
Hec salgea, An^{ce} sawge.
5 *Hoc lilium, An^{ce}* a lylly.
Hec columbina, An^{ce} a columbyn.
Hec violeta, An^{ce} a violet.
Hoc vaxinium, An^{ce} idem est.
Hic isopus, An^{ce} isopp.
10 *Hec ditanus, A^{ce}* detany.
Hec seladonia, a seladony.
Hec igromonia, a ygromony.
Hec urtica, An^{ce} a netylle.
Hic anagalidos, An^{ce} netyllesede.
15 *Hec paradilla, An^{ce}* a doke.
Hec secuta, An^{ce} a humlok.
Hec morella, An^{ce} morelle.
Hoc solsequium, An^{ce} a rode.
Hec perrica, An^{ce} a perwynke.
20 *Hec malvia, An^{ce}* a hok.[5]
Hec lancea, An^{ce} a robworte.[6]
Hec buglossa, A^{ce} lange-de-befe.
Hec ebula, A^{ce} a wallewurte.[7]
Hoc bigustrum, A^{ce} a prymrose.
25 *Hoc ligustrum, A^{ce}* a cowyslepe.
Hec rosa, A^{ce} a rose.
Hoc ffragrum, A^{ce} a strawbery.
Hec mentica, A^{ce} a mynte.
Hic papillus, A^{ce} a heyoffe.[8]
30 *Hec eruca, A^{ce}* a schynlok.[9]
Hec eruca, An^{ce} a carlok.
Hec ruta, A^{ce} rew.
Hec ffallax, A^{ce} madyr.
Hoc venenum, A^{ce} a wede.
35 *Hec plantago, A^{ce}* weybrede.
Hec maguderis, a calstok.
Hoc olusculum, a wurtplant.
Hic cirpus, An^{ce} a roysche.
Hic cucumer, A^{ce} a flage.
40 *Hec papirus, An^{ce}* a bolroysche.
Hoc feneculum, An^{ce} a ffenelle.
Hic crocus, An^{ce} safryn.

[1] i. e., a vetch.
[2] A shock, at the present day in the north, is twelve sheaves of corn.
[3] *Broges,* i. e. borage.
[4] A *chibbal,* or small onion.
[5] The holyhock.
[6] Perhaps the plant adders tongue, called in Latin *lancea Christi.*
[7] Wall-wort.
[8] Hayhofe, or ground-ivy.
[9] Rocket, the *reseda* of botanists.

Hec zizania, An^ce a drawke.[1]
Hec artimatia, An^ce wodrofe.
Hec seniglossa, An^ce hertestunge.
Hec mandracora, An^ce a maudrak.
Hoc aspium, An^ce a gresse.
Hec salmea, An^ce a pepyrgresse.
Hoc anisum, An^ce a culrayge.
Hec dragansia, An^ce a dragauns.
Hoc meretrum, An^ce ffenyllesede.
Hec camamilla, An^ce a camamy.
Hoc papaver, -ris, An^ce a papy.
Hec samina, An^ce a saveryn.[2]
Hic jusquianus, An^ce a hennebane.
Hoc jurbarium, An^ce a silfgrene.[3]
Hec letusa, An^ce letuse.
Hic cardo, -is, An^ce a nettille.
Hec avencia, An^ce a avans.
Hec vervene, An^ce vermyne.
Hec menoloca, An^ce a bothun.[4]
Hic suctus, An^ce a juse.
Hec locusta, An^ce a sokylblome.[5]
Hec arundo, -nis, } a redde.
Hec canna,
Hec carex, An^ce a sege.
Hec rapa, An^ce a neppe.[6]
Hoc colitropium, a paratory.
Hec conseria, An^ce a wyld fr ...
Hoc morsuspoli, a schykynw ...[7]
Hec lentige, a nedmet.[8]
Hec eufrasia, An^ce a heufrasy ...[9]
Hoc lollium, } An^ce kokylle.
Hoc git, indeclinabile,
Hoc pulmentum, benys and pese.
Hoc cirpillum, An^ce a pellek.[10]
Hec silago, An^ce wyld rye.

NOMINA ESSCARUM.

Hoc prandium, } An^ce mete.
Hoc epulum,
Hic cibus,
Hec esca, } An^ce mete.
Hec daps,
Hoc jantaculum, An^ce a dynere.
Hec cena, An^ce a soper.
Hoc obsenium, An^ce a rryresoper.
Hoc alleum, An^ce garleke.
Hic victus, -tus, -tui, } An^ce lyfefode.
Hoc victuale,
Hoc pulmentorium, An^ce a pulment.
Est cibus et semen pulmentum dicitur
                                    esse,
At cibus quidem sunt pulmentaria dicta.
Hoc edulium, An^ce sowylle.[11]
Hic repastus, -tus, -tui, An^ce mele.
Hic panis, An^ce brede.
Hic artocopus, An^ce a symnelle.
Hec placencia, An^ce a payman.[12]
Hoc labum, } a wa-
Hoc libellum, } stelle.
Hec ffrugia, An^ce fres-brede.
Hic panis subverucius, a meleres cake.[13]

---

[1] This word is still preserved in the dialects of the Eastern counties, where it is applied to a plant resembling darnell.
[2] Perhaps the savin-tree (Juniperus sabina).
[3] The houseleek.
[4] A button, or bud?
[5] Sokyl-blome, perhaps the honey-suckle.
[6] Catmint, or nep (nepeta cataria).
[7] i. e., chicken-wort.
[8] Nedmete, perhaps the lentil, a small kind of pulse.
[9] Eyebright (euphrasia officinalis).
[10] Pellek, a name for wild-thyme, or, as it is popularly called in some parts, ladies' bedstraw.
[11] See before, p. 661 l. 9.
[12] i. e., painmain. See before, p. 657 l. 26.
[13] A miller's cake. Perhaps this name alludes to the common report that the miller always stole the flour from his customers to make his cakes, which were baked on the sly. See The Reve's Tale in Chaucer.

Hec nebula, } a wafrun.
Hec gafra,
Hoc calenum, An^ce a ffyrmele.[1]
Hoc vitalium, An^ce charlett.[2]
Hic artocacius, An^ce a flawne.
Hec artocria, An^ce a tartelat.
Hic artocrius, An^ce a pye.
Hoc legumen, } An^ce potage.
Hoc puls,
Hoc polenta, An^ce grewelle.
Hoc laganum, An^ce a pancake.
Hec aplauda, An^ce a cawdelle.
Hoc adopatum, An^ce brues.
Hec carbonella, An^ce a colepe.[3]
Hec pepissa, An^ce fat fleyche.
Hoc consisum, An^ce alle maner sew.
Hoc sepelatum, An^ce a sew.
Hec pereta, An^ce leke-potage.
Hoc omentum, An^ce a womclotte.[4]
Hoc extum, } An^ce a trype.
Hoc esmum,
Hoc brodium, An^ce a brothe.
Hoc fferculum, An^ce a mese.
Hoc fferculum, a salt stole.
Fercula nos faciant, prelatos fercula portant.

Hoc fertum, }
Hoc omasum, } An^ce a podyng.
Hoc tucetum, }
Hec ulla, An^ce a sawsyrlyng.[5]
Hoc obsoniofgrus, a jusselle.
Hec assa, An^ce a rost mete.
Hoc lactatum, } An^ce a poset.
Hoc balductum,
Hec perna, An^ce a flyk of bacun.
Hec promulada, An^ce grovy.
Hoc ovum, An^ce a hey.
Hoc albumen, An^ce the whyte of the hey.
Hic vitellus, An^ce a gelke.
Tres partes ovi, albumen, testa, vitellus.
Hec pulpa, An^ce the brawn of a bore.

Hoc pomum, An^ce a nappelle.
Hoc pirum, An^ce a pere.
Hoc volemum, An^ce a wardyn.
Hoc perapsima, An^ce a paryng.
Hec pulpa, An^ce a meyte.
Hec arula, An^ce a croke.[6]
Tolle peripsima, post pete pulpam, dispernis arulam.
Hoc sinapium, An^ce mustarde.
Salgia, sirpillum, piper, alia, sal, petrocillum,
Ex hiis sit salsa, non est sentencia falsa.
Hic nuclius, a not.
Hic nucleus, An^ce kyrnelle.

NOMINA INFIRMITATUM.

Hec puscula, An^ce a whele.
Hoc ulcus, -ceris, An^ce a byle.
Hec scabies, -ei, An^ce a scabbe.
Hec impetigo, An^ce a tesyng.[7]
Hec veruca, An^ce a werte.
Hec glabra, An^ce a scalle.
Hec macula, An^ce a spote.
Hec lentecula, An^ce a frekyn.
Hec lepra, An^ce a mesellerye.
Hec ffebris, An^ce a fewer.
Hec ulorica, An^ce the chawndyse.
Hic spasmus, An^ce the crampe.
Hic tussis, An^ce the cowe.[8]
Hec extecis, -ce, An^ce a scunnyng.[9]

---

[1] *Fyrmele*, perhaps frumity, or furmity.
[2] A dish made of minced pork.
[3] A collop, or slice of meat, or rasher of bacon, broiled.
[4] The wombclout was properly the caul which envelopes the intestines.
[5] A sansage.

[6] *Arula* is explained in the Anglo-Saxon vocabularies as meaning a fire-pan, or vessel for holding lighted charcoal.
[7] An old name for a ring-worm.
[8] *Cowe*, a cough. This shows the old way of pronouncing the word.
[9] A disease of the heart.

Hic catarus, An^(ce) a pore.[1]
Hec reuma, An^(ce) a chynge.
Hec gutta, An^(ce) the gowte.
Hec leantaria, An^(ce) the flyx.
Nominativo clunucus, -ca, -cum, A^(ce) berede.[2]
Hic gibbus, An^(ce) a wenne.
Hec cardia, An^(ce) a cardiakylle.
Hec squacia, An^(ce) a queynose.[3]
Hic cancer, An^(ce) a cankyr.
Hec idrepia, An^(ce) the dropsy.
Hec antrax, An^(ce) a felun bleyn.[4]
Hec porigo, An^(ce) pokkys.
Hec serpedo, An^(ce) a tetere.
Hec paucitas, An^(ce) a cattes here.[5]
Hic morbus caducus, the fallyn evylle.
Hic paraliticus, A^(ce) the palsey.
Hic mutulatus, An^(ce) a mayn.[6]
Hoc vulnus, } a wonde.
Hec plaga, }
Hic sicatrix, An^(ce) a old wownde.
Hec peruda, An^(ce) a keybe hele.
Hec vibex, An^(ce) a strype.[7]
Hec anggrena, An^(ce) dede fleyche.
Hec insanies, An^(ce) a whele.
Hoc epilema, -tis, An^(ce) a playster.

NOMINA MULIERUM CUM SUIS INSTRUMENTIS.

Hec imperatrix, An^(ce) a hempryse.
Hec regina, An^(ce) a quene.
Hec duxissa, An^(ce) a dukes.
5 *Hec cometissa*, An^(ce) a cometas.
Hec baronissa, An^(ce) a baronys.
Hec domina, An^(ce) alle maner lady.
10 *Hec psraannia*, An^(ce) a barowwoman.
Hec damicella, An^(ce) a damselle.
Hec fflammia, } a cherchow.[8]
Hoc flamiolum, }
Hoc reticulum, An^(ce) a calle.
15 *Hoc splimter*, An^(ce) a pynne.
Hec vitta, An^(ce) a felet.
Hoc crinale, An^(ce) a herebond.
Hec tricatura, An^(ce) a tresewyr.[9]
Hoc monile, An^(ce) a broche.
20 *Hic limbus*, An^(ce) a rebant.
Hoc peplum, An^(ce) a wympylle.
Hoc teare, -ris, An^(ce) a bonet.
Hic anulus, An^(ce) a ryng.
Hoc certum, An^(ce) a garlond.
25 *Hec ffebula*, An^(ce) a lase.
Hoc calamustrum, a quiver.
Hec abatissa, An^(ce) a abeyse.
Hec priorissa, An^(ce) a pryoryse.
Hec monialis, An^(ce) a none.
30 *Hec presbeterissa*, } a prystes wyfe.
Hec sacerdotissa, }
Hic sacerdotulus, An^(ce) a prestes sun.
Hec sacerdotula, An^(ce) a prestes dowtyr.
35 *Hec uxor*, } a wyfe.
Hec sponsa, }
Hec femina, } a woman.
Hec mulier, }
Hec ustrinatrix, a kylme wyfe.
40 *Hec deciccatrix, idem est.*
Hoc ustrinum, An^(ce) a kylme.

---

[1] A pose, or cold in the head.
[2] *Berede*, perhaps bed-rid.
[3] The quinsy.
[4] A whitlow.
[5] Huloet has, "Cattes-heere, otherwyse called a felon, *furunculus.*"
[6] *i. e.*, a maim.
[7] *Strype.* The Nomenclator, a vocabulary printed in 1585, explains *vibex* by „the marke of a blowe or stripe remaining in the fleshe blacke and blewe."
[8] A kerchief.
[9] The tressure, or arrangement of the hair.

A PICTORIAL VOCABULARY.

Hoc ffulicium, An^ce a hayyr.
Hec androchia, An^ce a deyry.
Ilic casius, An^ce schese.
Hic tirus, An^ce nyw schese.
Hoc butirum, An^ce botyr.
Hoc mulsum, An^ce the wyte of botyr.
Hoc serum, An^ce tho whey of chese.
Sit liquor bos serum, defundat casins ipsum.
Hoc tolustrum, An^ce besning.[2]
Hec balducta, } a crud or a posset.
Hoc coagulum, }
Hoc occigalum, An^ce a sowyr mylke.
Ilic quactus, An^ce creme.
Hoc lacticium, An^ce wyte mete.
Hec sissma, An^ce a schesfatte.
Hoc valatorium, An^ce a scharne.[3]
Hoc coagulatorium, a scharnstafe.
Hoc multrum, An^ce a mylkepayle.
Hoc multrale, An^ce the tyn of the mylke.[4]
Hic mulsor, An^ce a mylker.
Hoc lac, An^ce mylke.
Hoc androchiatorium, An^ce a deyry.
Hec aucionatrix, An^ce a hoxter.
Hec virago, a sturdy qwene.
Hec armifodrita, An^ce a scrate.[5]
Hec mater, } a modyr.
Hec genetrix, }
Hec nutrix, An^ce a norys.
Hec cunia, } credylle.
Hoc cunabilum, }

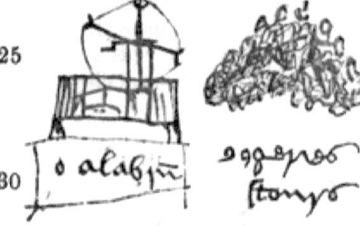

Hec ffassia, An^ce credylbond.
Hec mammus, }
Hec mamillo, } An^ce pappe.
Hoc uber, -ris, }
5 Hic panniculis, An^ce a clowte.
Hec virgo, An^ce vergyn.
Hec puella, An^ce maydyn.
Hec meretrix, An^ce hore.
Hec materffemilias, a hoswyf.
10 Hec vedua, An^ce a wedow.
Hec rustica, a fyldwyfe.
Hec pandoxatrix, a browstere.
Hec filatrix, An^ce a spynnere.
Hec colus, An^ce a dysestafe.
15 Ilic fusus, An^ce a spyndylle.
Hec pellicula, An^ce a rybschyn.
Hec nebryda, idem est.
Hoc vertebrum, An^ce a aworowylle.[6]
Hoc girgillum, An^ce a bladys.
20 Hoc alabrum, } An^ce a rele.
Hoc traale, -is, }

Hic virgillus, a yerwyndylleblad.
Ilic globus, An^ce a clew.
35 Hic glomicellus, idem est.
Hec glomeracio, a hep of threde.
Hec congeries, An^ce a hep of stonys.
Congeries lapidum tibi sit, glomeracio fili.
Hoc ffilum, An^ce threde.
40 Hec lotrex, An^ce a lavundare.
Hoc locium, An^ce ley and nettyng.
Hoc smigma, -tis, An^ce a soppe.[7]

---

[1] The inscription to this diagram is written at the edge of the paper and partly lost, but it was evidently casius, i. e., cheese.
[2] Besning, the first milk, now called the beastings. The Latin word should be colustrum.
[3] A churn.
[4] i. e., a milk-can.
[5] A hermaphrodite. See before, p. 695 l. 2.
[6] A whirle, or round piece of wood put on the spindle of the spinning-wheel.
[7] i. e., soap.

Hoc stigma, An^(ce) the dere yn a mannys hede.[1]

Smigma capud mundat, stigma dolore gravat.

Hoc sulfur, An^(ce) brynston.
Hec feratorium, } a batylledore.
Hoc pecten,
Hec textrix, An^(ce) a webster.
Hec matatrix, An^(ce) a hokylster.
Hec mataxa, An^(ce) a hekylle.
Hec excudia, An^(ce) a sungyllestok.[2]
Hec excudiatorium, An^(ce) a sungyllehand.
Hec stupa, An^(ce) herdys.
Hec narpa, An^(ce) schewys.
Hoc rupeste, a repyllestok.[3]
Hoc asperum, An^(ce) a top of lyne.
Hic limphus, a stryke of lyne.
Hec costa, An^(ce) a rybbe.
Hoc linum, An^(ce) fflax.
Hec sutrix, An^(ce) a sewer.
Hec brasiatrix, a brewster.
Hec contrix, a barbowres wyfe.
Hec pronuba, a bawstrop.[4]
Hec obstetrix, a mydwyfe.
Hec pectrix, -cis, a cemster.[5]
Hec carminatrix, idem est.

NOMINA TERRARUM.

Hec terra, -e,
Hec ruus, -i,   } An^(ce) the fyld.
Hoc arvum, -i,
Hoc campum, -i,

Arvum, campus, ager, rus, sic diversificatur;
Dum seritur sit ager, et semen conditur illo;
Campus dicatur dum fructibus expoliatur;
Messibus est arvum tectum flore vel erbis,
5 Incultum rus est, veluti sunt pascua silve.

Hec carucata, An^(ce) plowlode.
Hec bovata, a hoxgangyn lond.
Hec acra, An^(ce) a akyr lond.
Hec virgata, An^(ce) a eryd lond.
10 *Hic selis, -is,* An^(ce) a ryggyd lond.
Hic sulcus, } a fforow.
Hec lira,
Hec sulcacio, An^(ce) a balkyng.
Hec fforeta, An^(ce) a hedlond.
15 *Hec amsages,* An^(ce) a but of lond.
Hoc pratum, An^(ce) a medow.
Hoc marescum, An^(ce) a merche.
Hoc archifenium, } a crofe.
Hoc croftum,
20 *Hic ortus, -ti,* An^(ce) a gerd.
Hic ortus, -tus, -ui, a spryngyng.
Ortus, -ta, -tum, An^(ce) spryngyng.

Ortus origo datur, per quartam dum variatur;
25 Quo crescunt herbe locus est ortusque secunde;
Post ortum periit infantulus ortus in orto.

Hoc erbarium, An^(ce) a herbar.
Hoc virgultum, An^(ce) a holt.
30 *Hic mons, -tis,* An^(ce) a hylle.
Hec collis, An^(ce) a lytylle hylle.
Hic agger, idem est.

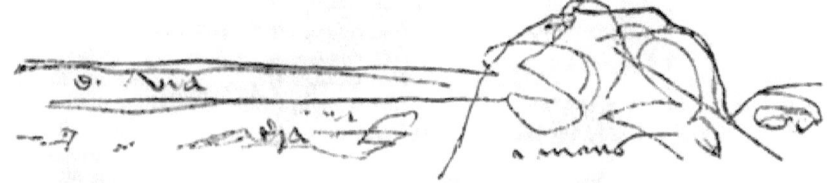

---

[1] A mark of disgrace, by burning, &c. on the head.

[2] A swingle-stock, a wooden implement for beating flax or hemp, to separate the outer coating from the fibre. *Swingle-hand* is another name for the same implement.

[3] *Repylle-stok,* an implement for cleaning flax.

[4] See before, p. 695 l. 18.

[5] A female who combs, a kembster.

Hoc montanum,
Hic alpes, } a grete hylle.

Distant montana sic, alpes, collis, et agger;
Designant magnum cumulum terre duo
    prima,
Alteria bina notant parvum cumulum quo-
    que terre.

Hec vallis, An^{ce} a wale.
Hec palis, An^{ce} a more.
Hec labina, An^{ce} a fenne.
Hec via, An^{ce} a wey.
Hec platea, a hye wey.
Hic vicus, An^{ce} a strete.
Hec trama,
Hec orbita, } *An^{ce}* a paytt.
Hec semita,

Trama parva via tibi sit tranversa per
    arvum.

Hec venella, An^{ce} a lane.
Hec specula, a totyngbylle.[1]
Hic fumus, An^{ce} smoke.

Hoc fimarium,
Hoc sterculinium, } a muckelle.[2]
Hoc sabulum, An^{ce} sonde.
Hec arema, An^{ce} gravelle.
Hoc argillum,
Hec argilla, } *An^{ce}* clay.
Hic linus, An^{ce} a sclott.[3]
Hoc fossatum, a sedyke.

---

[1] To *tote* was to spy, or watch. A *toting-hill* would be a mound, or hill, in a prominent position, raised or occupied for watching.

[2] A muck-hill, or dunghill.

[3] *Sclott.* Sticky clay is still called *slot* in Lincolnshire.

Hec rypa, An^{ce} a banke.
Hic et hec mergo, idem est.

Fontis mergo, maris litus, sic ripa fluentis.

Hoc senum, An^{ce} a modyngstrete.
Hec gleba, An^{ce} a clote.
Hoc cosidium, An^{ce} a torsy.[4]
Hec solitudo, a wyldernys.
Hec meta, An^{ce} a butte.
Hec lapifodina,
Hoc saccifragium, } a stonquarelle.
Hec aurifodina, a goldquarelle.
Hec argentifodina, a sylverquarelle.
Hec sertis, An^{ce} a sandbedde.
Hec insula, An^{ce} a hylyn of the see.
Hec ceclas, idem est.
Hec mediamnis, a frechewater-dyk.
Hec cateracta, An^{ce} a wey of hewyn.
Hec cateracta, An^{ce} a wyndowe.

Est cateracta via dicitur celique fenistra.

Hic traco, An^{ce} a hollewey.
Hic bivius,
Hic trivius, } a gateschedelle.
Hic quatrivius
He spelunca,
Hec caverna, } a denne.
Hec cripa,
Hoc volutabrum, An^{ce} a selot.[5]
Hic et hec et hoc specus, An^{ce} a wel-
  bryng.[6]
Hic scrobs, An^{ce} a swynwrotyng.

NOMINA AQUARUM.

Hoc mare,
Hoc pelagus, } *An^{ce}* the see.
Hoc equor,
Hoc salum, An^{ce} saltwater.
Hec aqua,
Hec latex,
Hec limpha, } *An^{ce}* water.
Hec unda,

---

[4] *Torsy.* Perhaps this is a blunder for *corsy,* and means a causeway.

[5] *Volutabrum* is explained in the Nomenclator, „A wallowing place for cattell, bores, and swine." A wide ditch is still called a *slot* in Devonshire.

[6] *Welbryng.* This word, to judge by the Latin equivalent, must mean a cave.

A PICTORIAL VOCABULARY.

Hec cloaca, An^{ce} a prevy.

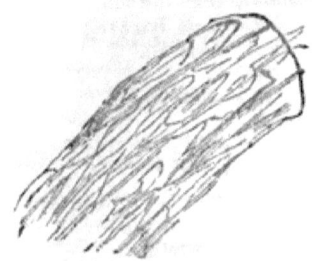

Hec aqua, An^{ce} sorow.
Hec aqua, An^{ce} lernyng.
Hec aqua, An^{ce} folke.
Est aqua qua fruimur doctrina, dolor, populusque.
Hec ammis, An^{ce} frechewater.
Hec pluvia, An^{ce} reyn.
Hec nix, An^{ce} snow.
Hoc gelu, An^{ce} a forst.
Hec pruina, An^{ce} a horeforst.
Hic ros, -ris, An^{ce} a dew.
Hec glacies, -ei, An^{ce} hyse.
Hec grando, -is, An^{ce} a hayle.
Hec fossa,
Hec fovia,
Hec cavea, } *An^{ce} a dyke.*
Hec antra,
Hic fons, -tis, An^{ce} a welle.
Hec scatebra,
Hec scatarigo, } a sprynge.
Hoc tolumen, An^{ce} a tumrelle.
Hoc stagnum, An^{ce} a ponde.
Hec lacuna, An^{ce} a playche of water.
Hoc vadum, An^{ce} a wadth.[1]
Hic rivus, An^{ce} a revyr.
Hic rivulus, An^{ce} a lake.
Hic gurges, -tis,
Hoc rudor, } a gotyr.
Hec rudor,

[1] i. e., a place you can wade through, a ford.

Hec catacumba, idem est.
Hec pissina, An^{ce} a wayir.
Hoc meandrum, An^{ce} a stynkyng pytt.
Hec stilla,
Hec gutta, } a drope.
Hoc stellocidium, An^{ce} a howsegoter.
Hoc stillicidium, An^{ce} a spowte.
Hic austrus, -us, -ui, An^{ce} a drawte.
Hec sorbicio, An^{ce} a spyung.
Hec catadurpa, An^{ce} a cundythe.
Hec ledonis, An^{ce} a sulse.[2]
Hec malma, a growndheve.
Hic cataclismus, An^{ce} Noys flode.
Hic portus, -tus, -tui, An^{ce} a hawyn.
Hic cataclismus, An^{ce} helle, ut patet per versus.
Designant tibi delivium, baratrique profundum.

NOMINA PLANETORUM.

Hoc celum,
Hic polus, } *An^{ce} hewyn.*
Hic paradisus, An^{ce} paradyse.
Hic sol,
Hic phebus, } *An^{ce} the sunne.*
Hic clipsis, the clyppes of the sunne.
Hec luna,
Hec phebe, } *An^{ce} the mone.*
Hoc plenilunium, An^{ce} fulmone.
Hec neomenia, An^{ce} a newmone.

[2] Sulse, the flow of the sea-tide.

A PICTORIAL VOCABULARY.

Hic aier,
Hec aera,
Hic ether,   } the wethyr.
Hec ethera,
Hic ventus, } the wynde.
Hec aura,
Hec nubes,
Hoc nubulum, } a clowde.
Hec nubula,
Hec stella,
Hoc astrum, } An^{ce} alle maner
Hoc sidus,   sterres.
Hic canis,
Hic esperes, An^{ce} hewynsterre.
Hic jubiter, a daysterre.

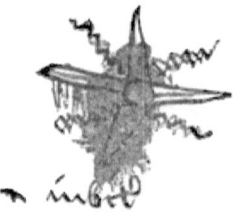

Hic diaspiter, } idem sunt.
Hic lucifer,
Hic saturnus, a pestlens planyt.
Hic unus, An^{ce} a lodsman.
Hic annus, An^{ce} a gere.
Hic mensis, An^{ce} a monythe.
Hec quindena, An^{ce} a fortenyte.
Hec septimana, } An^{ce} a weke.
Hec ebdomeda,
Hic vel hec dies, -ei, An^{ce} a day.
Hoc diliculum, An^{ce} a mornyng.
Hic meredies, An^{ce} a mydday.
Hec nox, -tis, An^{ce} a nythe.
Equinoxium, An^{ce} mydnythe.
Hoc crepusculum, } a hewyntyde.
Hoc vesper, -eris,
Hoc vesperum, An^{ce} a hewynsongtyde.
Hoc ignitegium, An^{ce} curfew.
Hoc intempestum, An^{ce} mydnythe.
Hic bisextus, a lepegere.

Hic tonitrus, An^{ce} thwndur.
Hoc fulmen, An^{ce} lytenyng.
Hoc fulgur, idem est.
Hic rogus,
Hic ignis,   } An^{ce} fyre.
Hic focus,
Hic iems,   } An^{ce} wynter.
Hec bruma,
Hec quadragesima, An^{ce} lenten.
Hec iris, An^{ce} a reynbowe.
Hec ira, An^{ce} wrethe.
Iris res mira, sed non est Iris in ira.
Hic ecto, -is, vox in aera respondens.
Hec ver, -ris, the tyme gruyng.
Hec esta, An^{ce} somer.
Hec filandra, a gossummer.
Solsticium estivale, An^{ce} mydsomer.
Hic autumnus, An^{ce} hervyst.
Hic infernus, -i,
Hic tartarus, -i,
Hic orcus, -i,   } An^{ce} helle.
Hec jehenna, -e,
Hec avernus, -i,
Hic antepos, } An^{ce} ffayery.
Hec lamea,

NOMINA DOMORUM.

Hoc monasterium, An^{ce} a mynster.
Hec eclesia,
Hoc templum, } An^{ce} a kyrke.
Hec baselica,

Hec capella, An^{ce} a schapelle.
Hoc vestiarium, } An^{ce} a vestry.
Hoc vestibulum, }
Hoc campanile, An^{ce} a bellehowse.
Hoc atrium, } An^{ce} a halle.
Hec aula, }
Hoc atrium, a kyrkegerde.
Atria die aulas, eadem sumitoria dicas.
Hec camera,
Hec simina,
Hic talamus, } An^{ce} a schambyr.
Hec conclavis,
Hec conclave,
Hoc solarium, An^{ce} a solere.
Hoc penu, indeclinabile, An^{ce} a seler.
Hoc cubile, An^{ce} a cowche.
Hec cubicila, An^{ce} a kenelle.
Hec domus, } An^{ce} alle maner of howse.
Hec edes, }
Hec casa, } An^{ce} a cote.
Hec casula, }
Hec casula, An^{ce} a schesepylle.
Dico domum parvam casulam tibi diminutivum,
Ac indumentum dicatur presbeterale.
Hoc dormitorium, An^{ce} a dorter.
Hoc larduarium, An^{ce} a lardyr.
Hec cansella, } a schanselle.
Hoc cansellum, }
Hec panatria, An^{ce} a pantyr.
Hec botolaria, An^{ce} a botry.
Hoc penus, } a spenyse.
Hoc dispensorium, }
Hec epoteca,
Hec coquina, } a kychon.
Hec pompina, }
Hec affina, An^{ce} a werkhowse.
Hec tabarna,
Hec caupona, } An^{ce} a taverne.
Hec pila,
Hoc granatorium, } a garnyr.
Hoc granarium, }
Hoc orium, An^{ce} a beyrne.
Hoc porcatorium, An^{ce} a hogstye.

Hoc galinarium, a hencote.
Hoc tigurium, An^{ce} a hoywl.[1]
Hoc magale, An^{ce} a lodge.
Hoc stabulum, An^{ce} a stabylle.
Hoc bostar, -aris, An^{ce} a sebepyn.
Hic carcer, An^{ce} a presunhowse.
Hoc pretorium, An^{ce} a motehalle.
Hoc toloneum, An^{ce} a tolbothe.
Hoc lupaner,
Hec fornix, } a horehowse.
Hoc prostibulum,
Hoc lanifisium, a wulhowse.
Hoc tabernaculum, a tabernakyl.
Hec foruca, } a prewy.
Hec laterrina, }
Hoc temtorium, An^{ce} a . . .
Hoc pandocsatorium, a brywhowse.
Hoc pistrinum, An^{ce} a bakehowse.
Hoc ustrinum, } a kylinhowse.
Hoc torale, }
Hec scola, } An^{ce} a scole.
Hoc studium, }
Hec sella, An^{ce} a selle.
Hoc predium, An^{ce} a maner.
Hec salina, An^{ce} a saltcote.
Hoc diversorium, } An^{ce} a hyn.
Hoc hospicium, }
Hec opella, An^{ce} a schoppe.
Hoc gazafilacium, a treserhouse.

NOMINA ARTIFICIUM CUM SUIS INSTRUMENTIS.

Hic cultor, } a londtyllere.
Hic et hec agricola, }
Hic nauta, } a shypman.
Hic navita, }
Hic proreta, An^{ce} a stereman.
Hic naucherus, a pursberer.
Hec prora, An^{ce} a forstanyg.
Hec puppis, An^{ce} the in parti.[2]
Hec ratis, An^{ce} the schyppes syde.
Hec carina, An^{ce} a holle.

---

[1] A hovel.
[2] The reading of these words is somewhat doubtful in the manuscript, and I am not sure that I have read them quite correctly.

Prora prior navis pars dicitur, ultima puppis,
Sic latus esse ratem, ventrem dicitur esse
carinam.

Hoc *naulum*, An^ce a schyppes tolle.
Hec *antemnis*, a hedrope.
Hic *parastes*, An^ce a cabylle.
Hic *rudens, -tis*, An^ce a seyllerope.
Hec *supera, -eris*, An^ce a seyllebonde.
Hoc *velum*, An^ce a scylle.
Hic *cherucus*, An^ce a fanne.
Hoc *cachesium*, An^ce a seylgerde.
Hec *ancora*, An^ce a ankyr.
Hoc *podrum*, An^ce a helme.
Hic *remex*, An^ce a rodyr.
Hoc *amplustrum*, idem est.
Hic *porticulus*, An^ce a maylat.
Hic *abbestus*, An^ce a fyirstone.
Hoc *pericudium*, An^ce a fyrhyrg ...
Hic *lacus, -cus, -cui*, An^ce a nedylle.
Hic *jaclus*, a thred in a nedyl ...
Hec *troclia*, An^ce a wynddas.
Hec *coclia*, An^ce a wyndylle.
Hec *navicula*, } a bote.
Hec *lembus*, }
Nos vestit limbus, nos vertat per mare
lembus.

Hec *facelus*, An^ce a sogbote.[1]
Hic *remus*, An^ce a hore.
Hec *palmula*, the brede of the hore.
Hoc *columbar*, An^ce the holle of the schyp.

Hoc *armamentum*, a hal takylle.[2]
Hec *saburra*, An^ce a lastage.
Hic *malus*, An^ce a mast.
Hic *paterfamilias*, } a husbond.
Hic *maritus*, }
Hic *tantellus*, An^ce a congyn.
Hic *vir*, } a man.
Hic *vel hec homo*, }
Hic *omunculus*, An^ce a duorow.[3]
Hic *membrarius*, a parchmeare.
Hic *servus*, }
Hic *famulus*, }
Hic *verna*, } a servante.
Hic *satrapa*, }
Hoc *mancipium*, }
Hic *garcio*, An^ce a knafe.
Hic *vel hec scurra*, An^ce a harlat.
Hic *vel hec alocropa*, idem est.
Hic *nugator*, An^ce chaper.[4]
Hec *nuga*, An^ce a chape.
Hic *nugigerulus*, An^ce a trifelle.
Hic *sponsus*, a wedman.
Hic *puer*, An^ce a schyle.
Hic *et hec latro*, a day-thefe.
Hic *fur*, An^ce a nyte thefe.
Tempore nocturno fur aufert, latro diurno

Hic *suffarcinator*, An^ce a bryber.
Hic *ursarius*, a berward.
Hic *victor*, a cummer.[5]

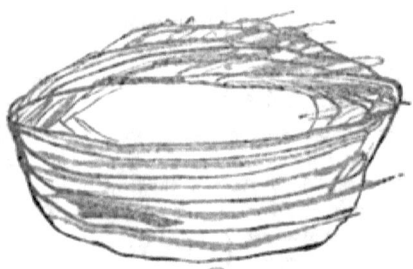

[1] *Sog-bote.* In the Nomenclator, *phaselus* is interpreted as signifying a pinnace.
[2] *Haltakylle*, I suppose, the whole tackle or furniture of the ship — *armamenta naris*.
[3] A dwarf.
[4] i. e., a japer, a jester or mocker.
[5] *Cummer*, probably a gossip, *Scottice*.

CUPERUS CUM SUIS INSTRU-
MENTIS.

Hic carpentarius, a carpenter.
Hic cuperus, a cowper.
Hoc dolebrum, a brodehax.
Hec securis, An^ce a hax.
Hec seculicula, a hachet.
Hec acia, a tyxhyl.[1]
Hoc aquiscium, a quyver.
Hoc perpendiculum, a plomet.
Hec regula, An^ce a rewylle.
Hoc terebrum, An^ce a wymbylle.
Hoc teribellum, An^ce a persowyr.
Hic bipennus, } a stybylle.
Hic bidens, -tis, }
Hec leviga, An^ce a plane.
Hec seltis, An^ce a scheselle.
Hec strofina, a gropyngyryn.
Hec sarra, An^ce a saw.
Hec vibra, An^ce a brake.
Hic circulus, An^ce a hope.
Hic aser, -ris, An^ce a borde.
Hic cunius, An^ce a sceselle.

PANDUCSATOR CUM SUIS
INSTRUMENTIS.

5 *Hic panducsator*, a brever.
Hoc brasium, An^ce malt.
Hoc plumbum, An^ce a lede.
Hec fornax, -cis, An^ce a fornys.
Hec cura, An^ce a fatte.
10 *Hec cupa*, a colle.[2]
Hec tina, idem est.
Hoc idromellum, An^ce wurte.
Hoc ciromellum, An^ce growte.
Hec falanga, An^ce a try.[3]
15 *Hec spuma*, An^ce barme.
Hoc multrale, a payle.
Hoc colum, }
Hoc infusorium, } An^ce tunnyng.
Hoc colatorium, a clenyngsefe.
20 *Hoc cinofegium*, } An^ce drafe.
Hoc sagisterium, }
Hec anurca, drowsyn.
Hec scafe, An^ce a bolle.
Hec scoba, An^ce a besum.
25

PISTOR CUM SUIS INSTRU-
MENTIS.

Hic pistor, An^ce a baker.
30 *Hic clibanus*, An^ce a rele.[4]
Hoc tersorium, An^ce a malkyn.
Hec pala, An^ce a forkyn.
Hoc furnorium, } An^ce pyle.[5]
Hec pila, }
35 *Hoc pollentridium*, a bultpele.
Polenduare, An^ce a bult.

[1] *Tyxhyl*, apparently a sort of axe.
[2] *Colle*, a hogshead, or large barrel.
[3] *Try*, a corn-screen.

[4] *Rele. Clibanus* means properly the oven.
[5] The baker's peel, or implement for putting the bread into the oven.

53

Hoc taratanterum, An^ce a tense.
Taratantarisare, An^ce to bult.
Hic taratantarizator, An^ce a censare.
Hec pasta, An^ce dowe.
Hec farina, An^ce mele.
Hoc furfur, An^ce bryn
Hoc polen,
Hoc polentum, } *An^ce flowyr.*
Hec simila,
Hoc ador, indeclinabile,
Hic panificator, An^ce a mouldere.[1]
Panificare, An^ce moulde.
Hoc jocabulum, An^ce a colrake.
Hec costa, } a rybe.
Hoc scalprum,
Hec vibra, An^ce a brake.[2]
Hec massa, An^ce a gobet of dow.
Hoc fermentum, An^ce sowyrdow.

Hic fossor, An^ce a dyker.
Hic murinator, a waller.
Hec merra, a mattoke.
Hec vanga, a spade.
Hec stribula, a schowle.
Hoc sinovectorium, a barow.
Hec furca, a forke.
Hec merga, idem.

Hic pomelio, gardyner.
Hic olitor, } *idem sunt.*
Hic ortolanus,
Hic plantator, a plantor.

Hic pomelio, venditor pomorum.
Hic pomelio, custos pomorum. Versus.
Pomelio custos, vector, vel venditor extat.

5 *Hoc pomerium, a norchard.*
Hoc pomerium, a whorde.
Hoc pomelium, idem.
Hec fals, scarpe.[3]
Hoc maxillium, a jyppe.
10 *Hec labrusca, the bark of the vyne.*
Hoc vitulamen, a branche.
Hoc sarmentum, the cuttyng.
Hec antes, a siron.[4]
Hec progago, a rote.
15 *Hic pamplus, a vyneleffe.*
Hec uva, a grape.
Hic acinus, a stongrape.
Hic botrus, a closter.

Pampulus est folium, botrus flos, vinea
20   totum.

Hic tector, An^ce a thaser.[5]
Hic contraitus, An^ce a crepylle.
Hec contraita, idem est.
25 *Hoc sustentaculum,* } a croche.
Hoc podium,

Hic auceps, An^ce a fowlere.
Hoc viscum, An^ce byrdlyme.
30 *Hic laquius, An^ce a snare.*
Hoc volatorium, An^ce a schafnet.
Hic avigerulus, An^ce a pulter.

[1] The person who makes the dough into loaves.
[2] One meaning of the word *brake* is a baker's kneading-trough. It occurs before, p. 807 l. 31, with the same Latin, but evidently in a different sense.
[3] *Scarpe*, an instrument for pruning vines. See the verse in the next column.
[4] *Antes*, a sprout.
[5] A thatcher.

Hic messor, An^{ce} a scherer.[1]
Hec fals, An^{ce} a sekylle.
Hic falcator, An^{ce} a mower.
Hec fals, An^{ce} a sythe.
Falso puto vineta, meto sata, tondeo prata.

Hic auriga,
Hic vereda, } a cartar.
Hic carectarius,
Hec carecta, An^{ce} a carte.
Hic capsis, An^{ce} a carte.
Hec biga, } a wayne.
Hoc plaustrum,
Hic currus, An^{ce} a carte.
Hoc carpentum, An^{ce} a schare.[2]
Hoc veredum, An^{ce} a thylle.
Hic veredus, An^{ce} a thylhorse.
Hec rota, An^{ce} a quele.
Hic cantus, -ti, -to, An^{ce} a felow.
Hic cantus, -tus, -tui, An^{ce} a song.
Cantus, -ti, bige, cantus cantantis in ore.

Hic radius, An^{ce} a spoke.
Hic radius, An^{ce} a sunbeme.
  Est radius rote, solis, tele, geometrie.
Hec axis, An^{ce} a exylletre.
Hoc meditulium, An^{ce} a nafe.
Hoc epuscium, An^{ce} a cartclowte.
Hoc retinaculum, An^{ce} a trayse.
Hoc traale, idem est.
Hec epicia, -orum, An^{ce} a berhom.[3]
Hec scutica, An^{ce} a quippe.
Hic funis, An^{ce} a rope.
Hec merga, An^{ce} a forke.
Hoc capistrum, An^{ce} a halter.
Hic inclusarius, An^{ce} a hayward.
Hic lucarius,
Hic viridarius, } An^{ce} a forster.
Hic forestarius,

Hic nemus, -ris,
Hic lucus, } a forest.
Hec feresta,
Hoc lucar, -ris, An^{ce} a forestax.
Hic parcarius, An^{ce} a parcar.
Hec indago, An^{ce} a parke.
Hoc vallum, An^{ce} a parke palys.
Vallo, -as, -i, vallum facere.
Hoc tribucetum, An^{ce} a sawtre.

Hic architenens, } a harchere.
Hic sagittarius,
Hic arcus, An^{ce} a bowe.
Hec arcitula, An^{ce} a bowstryng.
Hec catapulta, An^{ce} a brode arw.
Hec sagitta, An^{ce} a harow.
Hoc petulium, An^{ce} a bolt.
Hoc amentum, An^{ce} a nok.
Hec cuspis, An^{ce} a bolthed.
Hec faretra, An^{ce} a quiver.
Hic corintheus, a bowehowse.
Hec veltria, a lese of grehowndes.
Hic nullus, a grehownd colere.

---

[1] A reaper. Reaping is still called *shearing* in Scotland.
[2] i. e., a car.
[3] A barholm, or collar for a horse to draw by.

Hoc cornu, indeclinabile, An^(ce) a horne.
Hoc defensorium, } An^(ce) a braser.
Hoc brachitectum,
Hec fusticula, An^(ce) a lytyl pype.
Hic agamus, a sengyl man.

Hic archimendritas,
Hic opelio, } a schepard.
Hic pastor,
Hic grex, } a flok.
Hic villus,
Hic vellus, An^(ce) a slefe.
Hoc ovile, } a fold.
Hec caula,

Hec caulamaula, a scheperdes pype.
Hoc pedum, An^(ce) a scheperdes stafe.
Hic padus, An^(ce) a scheperdes croke.
Hic palus, } a foldstake.
5 *Hic paxillus,*
Hec cratis, An^(ce) a herdylle.
Hic pixus, An^(ce) a box.
Hoc butumen, An^(ce) a tere.
Hoc unguentum, An^(ce) grese.
10 *Hic vaccarius*, a cowhard.
Hoc armentum, An^(ce) a dryfte.
Hic equiarius, An^(ce) a horsheyrd.
Hic capriarius, An^(ce) a gateheyrd.
Hic edrius, i⁰ for a precher.

www.ingramcontent.com/pod-product-compliance
Lightning Source LLC
Chambersburg PA
CBHW022147300426
44115CB00006B/380